Exam Number	MCSE Course Title	Course Number	MCSE Study Series Title	Required or Elective?
70-59	Internetworking with Microsoft TCP/IP on Windows NT 4.0	688	TCP/IP MCSE Study Guide Bulette, 0-7645-3112-3	E
70-14	Supporting Microsoft System Management Server 1.2	732	SMS 1.2 MCSE Study Guide Bulette, 0-7645-3163-8	E
70-87	Implementing and Supporting Microsoft Internet Information Server 4.0	936	IIS 4.0 MCSE Study Guide Dillon, Linthicum, 0-7645-3118-2	E
70-81	Implementing and Supporting Microsoft Exchange Server 5.5	771	Exchange Server 5.5 MCSE Study Guide Robichaux and Glenn 0-7645-3111-5	E
70-28	System Administration for Microsoft SQL Server 7.0	832	SQL Server 7 MCSE Study Guide	E

WINDOWS NT® SERVER 4.0 MCSE STUDY GUIDE

WINDOWS NT® SERVER 4.0
MCSE STUDY GUIDE

Alan R. Carter

IDG Books Worldwide, Inc
An International Data Group Company
Foster City, CA • Chicago, IL • Indianapolis, IN • New York, NY

Windows NT® Server 4.0 MCSE Study Guide

Published by

IDG Books Worldwide, Inc.

An International Data Group Company

919 E. Hillsdale Blvd., Suite 400

Foster City, CA 94404

www.idgbooks.com (IDG Books Worldwide Web site)

Library of Congress Catalog Card No.: 98-72541

ISBN: 0-7645-3250-2

Printed in the United States of America

10 9 8 7 6 5 4 3 2 1

1P/RY/QZ/ZY/FC

Distributed in the United States by IDG Books Worldwide, Inc.

Distributed by Macmillan Canada for Canada; by Transworld Publishers Limited in the United Kingdom; by IDG Norge Books for Norway; by IDG Sweden Books for Sweden; by Woodslane Pty. Ltd. for Australia; by Woodslane (NZ) Ltd. for New Zealand; by Addison Wesley Longman Singapore Pte Ltd. for Singapore, Malaysia, Thailand, Indonesia, and Korea; by Norma Comunicaciones S.A. for Colombia; by Intersoft for South Africa; by International Thomson Publishing for Germany, Austria, and Switzerland; by Toppan Company Ltd. for Japan; by Distribuidora Cuspide for Argentina; by Livraria Cultura for Brazil; by Ediciencia S.A. for Ecuador; by Ediciones ZETA S.C.R. Ltda. for Peru; by WS Computer Publishing Corporation, Inc., for the Philippines; by Unalis Corporation for Taiwan; by Contemporanea de Ediciones for Venezuela; by Computer Book & Magazine Store for Puerto Rico; by Express Computer Distributors for the Caribbean and West Indies. Authorized Sales Agent: Anthony Rudkin Associates for the Middle East and North Africa.

For general information on IDG Books Worldwide's books in the U.S., please call our Consumer Customer Service department at 800-762-2974. For reseller information, including discounts and premium sales, please call our Reseller Customer Service department at 800-434-3422.

For information on where to purchase IDG Books Worldwide's books outside the U.S., please contact our International Sales department at 650-655-3172 or fax 650-655-3297.

For information on foreign language translations, please contact our Foreign & Subsidiary Rights department at 650-655-3021 or fax 650-655-3281.

For sales inquiries and special prices for bulk quantities, please contact our Sales department at 650-655-3200 or write to the address above.

For information on using IDG Books Worldwide's books in the classroom or for ordering examination copies, please contact our Educational Sales department at 800-434-2086 or 317-596-5499.

For press review copies, author interviews, or other publicity information, please contact our Public Relations department at 650-655-3000 or fax 650-655-3299.

For authorization to photocopy items for corporate, personal, or educational use, please contact Copyright Clearance Center, 222 Rosewood Drive, Danvers, MA 01923, or fax 978-750-4470.

™ is a trademark under exclusive license to IDG Books Worldwide, Inc., from International Data Group, Inc.

IDG BOOKS WORLDWIDE

ABOUT IDG BOOKS WORLDWIDE

Welcome to the world of IDG Books Worldwide.

IDG Books Worldwide, Inc., is a subsidiary of International Data Group, the world's largest publisher of computer-related information and the leading global provider of information services on information technology. IDG was founded more than 25 years ago and now employs more than 8,500 people worldwide. IDG publishes more than 275 computer publications in over 75 countries (see listing below). More than 90 million people read one or more IDG publications each month.

Launched in 1990, IDG Books Worldwide is today the #1 publisher of best-selling computer books in the United States. We are proud to have received eight awards from the Computer Press Association in recognition of editorial excellence and three from *Computer Currents'* First Annual Readers' Choice Awards. Our best-selling ...*For Dummies*® series has more than 50 million copies in print with translations in 38 languages. IDG Books Worldwide, through a joint venture with IDG's Hi-Tech Beijing, became the first U.S. publisher to publish a computer book in the People's Republic of China. In record time, IDG Books Worldwide has become the first choice for millions of readers around the world who want to learn how to better manage their businesses.

Our mission is simple: Every one of our books is designed to bring extra value and skill-building instructions to the reader. Our books are written by experts who understand and care about our readers. The knowledge base of our editorial staff comes from years of experience in publishing, education, and journalism — experience we use to produce books for the '90s. In short, we care about books, so we attract the best people. We devote special attention to details such as audience, interior design, use of icons, and illustrations. And because we use an efficient process of authoring, editing, and desktop publishing our books electronically, we can spend more time ensuring superior content and spend less time on the technicalities of making books.

You can count on our commitment to deliver high-quality books at competitive prices on topics you want to read about. At IDG Books Worldwide, we continue in the IDG tradition of delivering quality for more than 25 years. You'll find no better book on a subject than one from IDG Books Worldwide.

John Kilcullen
CEO
IDG Books Worldwide, Inc.

Steven Berkowitz
President and Publisher
IDG Books Worldwide, Inc.

WINNER

*Eighth Annual
Computer Press
Awards ≥1992*

WINNER

*Ninth Annual
Computer Press
Awards ≥1993*

WINNER

*Tenth Annual
Computer Press
Awards ≥1994*

WINNER

*Eleventh Annual
Computer Press
Awards ≥1995*

IDG Books Worldwide, Inc., is a subsidiary of International Data Group, the world's largest publisher of computer-related information and the leading global provider of information services on information technology. International Data Group publishes over 275 computer publications in over 75 countries. More than 90 million people read one or more International Data Group publications each month. International Data Group's publications include: **ARGENTINA:** Buyer's Guide, Computerworld Argentina, PC World Argentina; **AUSTRALIA:** Australian Macworld, Australian PC World, Australian Reseller News, Computerworld, IT Casebook, Network World, Publish, Webmaster; **AUSTRIA:** Computerwelt Osterreich, Networks Austria, PC Tip Austria; **BANGLADESH:** PC World Bangladesh; **BELARUS:** PC World Belarus; **BELGIUM:** Data News; **BRAZIL:** Annuário de Informática, Computerworld, Connections, Macworld, PC Player, PC World, Publish, Reseller News, Supergamepower; **BULGARIA:** Computerworld Bulgaria, Network World Bulgaria, PC & MacWorld Bulgaria; **CANADA:** CIO Canada, Client/Server World, ComputerWorld Canada, InfoWorld Canada, NetworkWorld Canada, WebWorld; **CHILE:** Computerworld Chile, PC World Chile; **COLOMBIA:** Computerworld Colombia, PC World Colombia; **COSTA RICA:** PC World Centro America; **THE CZECH AND SLOVAK REPUBLICS:** Computerworld Czechoslovakia, Macworld Czech Republic, PC World Czechoslovakia; **DENMARK:** Communications World Danmark, Computerworld Danmark, Macworld Danmark, PC World Danmark, Techworld Denmark; **DOMINICAN REPUBLIC:** PC World Republica Dominicana; **ECUADOR:** PC World Ecuador; **EGYPT:** Computerworld Middle East, PC World Middle East; **EL SALVADOR:** PC World Centro America; **FINLAND:** MikroPC, Tietoverkko, Tietoviikko; **FRANCE:** Distributique, Hebdo, Info PC, Le Monde Informatique, Macworld, Reseaux & Telecoms, WebMaster France; **GERMANY:** Computer Partner, Computerwoche, Computerwoche Extra, Computerwoche FOCUS, Global Online, Macwelt, PC Welt; **GREECE:** Amiga Computing, GamePro Greece, Multimedia World; **GUATEMALA:** PC World Centro America; **HONDURAS:** PC World Centro America; **HONG KONG:** Computerworld Hong Kong, PC World Hong Kong, Publish in Asia; **HUNGARY:** ABCD CD-ROM, Computerworld Szamitastechnika, Internetto online Magazine, PC World Hungary, PC-X Magazin Hungary; **ICELAND:** Tolvuheimur PC World Island; **INDIA:** Information Communications World, Information Systems Computerworld, PC World India, Publish in Asia; **INDONESIA:** InfoKomputer PC World, Komputek Computerworld, Publish in Asia; **IRELAND:** ComputerScope, PC Live!; **ISRAEL:** Macworld Israel, People & Computers/Computerworld; **ITALY:** Computerworld Italia, Macworld Italia, Networking Italia, PC World Italia; **JAPAN:** DTP World, Macworld Japan, Nikkei Personal Computing, OS/2 World Japan, SunWorld Japan, Windows NT World, Windows World Japan; **KENYA:** PC World East African; **KOREA:** Hi-Tech Information, Macworld Korea, PC World Korea; **MACEDONIA:** PC World Macedonia; **MALAYSIA:** Computerworld Malaysia, PC World Malaysia, Publish in Asia; **MALTA:** PC World Malta; **MEXICO:** Computerworld Mexico, PC World Mexico; **MYANMAR:** PC World Myanmar; **NETHERLANDS:** Computer! Totaal, LAN Internetworking Magazine, LAN World Buyers Guide, Macworld Netherlands, Net, WebWereld; **NEW ZEALAND:** Absolute Beginners Guide and Plain & Simple Series, Computer Buyer, Computer Industry Directory, Computerworld New Zealand, MTB, Network World, PC World New Zealand; **NICARAGUA:** PC World Centro America; **NORWAY:** Computerworld Norge, CW Rapport, Datamagasinet, Financial Rapport, Kursguide Norge, Macworld Norge, Multimediaworld Norge, PC World Ekspress Norge, PC World Nettverk, PC World Norge, PC World ProduktGuide Norge; **PAKISTAN:** Computerworld Pakistan; **PANAMA:** PC World Panama; **PEOPLE'S REPUBLIC OF CHINA:** China Computer Users, China Computerworld, China InfoWorld, China Telecom World Weekly, Computer & Communication, Electronic Design China, Electronics Today, Electronics Weekly, Game Software, PC World China, Popular Computer Week, Software Weekly, Software World, Telecom World; **PERU:** Computerworld Peru, PC World Profesional Peru, PC World SoHo Peru; **PHILIPPINES:** Click!, Computerworld Philippines, PC World Philippines, Publish in Asia; **POLAND:** Computerworld Poland, Computerworld Special Report Poland, Cyber, Macworld Poland, Networld Poland, PC World Komputer; **PORTUGAL:** Cerebro/PC World, Computerworld/Correio Informático, Dealer World Portugal, Mac*In/PC*In Portugal, Multimedia World; **PUERTO RICO:** PC World Puerto Rico; **ROMANIA:** Computerworld Romania, PC World Romania, Telecom Romania; **RUSSIA:** Computerworld Russia, Mir PK, Publish, Seti; **SINGAPORE:** Computerworld Singapore, PC World Singapore, Publish in Asia; **SLOVENIA:** Monitor; **SOUTH AFRICA:** Computing SA, Network World SA, Software World SA; **SPAIN:** Communicaciones World España, Computerworld España, Dealer World España, Macworld España, PC World España; **SRI LANKA:** Infolink PC World; **SWEDEN:** CAP&Design, Computer Sweden, Corporate Computing Sweden, Internetworld Sweden, it branschen, Macworld Sweden, MaxiData Sweden, MikroDatorn, Nätverk & Kommunikation, PC World Sweden, PCaktiv, Windows World Sweden; **SWITZERLAND:** Computerworld Schweiz, Macworld Schweiz, PCtip; **TAIWAN:** Computerworld Taiwan, Macworld Taiwan, NEW ViSION/Publish, PC World Taiwan, Windows World Taiwan; **THAILAND:** Publish in Asia, Thai Computerworld; **TURKEY:** Computerworld Turkiye, Macworld Turkiye, Network World Turkiye, PC World Turkiye; **UKRAINE:** Computerworld Kiev, Multimedia World Ukraine, PC World Ukraine; **UNITED KINGDOM:** Acorn User UK, Amiga Action UK, Amiga Computing UK, Apple Talk UK, Computing, Macworld, Parents and Computers UK, PC Advisor, PC Home, PSX Pro, The WEB; **UNITED STATES:** Cable in the Classroom, CIO Magazine, Computerworld, DOS World, Federal Computer Week, GamePro Magazine, InfoWorld, I-Way, Macworld, Network World, PC Games, PC World, Publish, Video Event, THE WEB Magazine, and WebMaster; online webzines: JavaWorld, NetscapeWorld, and SunWorld Online; **URUGUAY:** InfoWorld Uruguay; **VENEZUELA:** Computerworld Venezuela, PC World Venezuela; and **VIETNAM:** PC World Vietnam. 5/7/98

FOREWORD TO THE MCSE SERIES

Certifications are an effective way of "selling your skills" to prospective employers, as they represent a consistent measurement of knowledge about specific software or hardware products. Because of their expansive product line and tremendous marketing efforts, Microsoft certifications have become the gold standard in the exploding certification industry. As a Microsoft Certified Professional, you are recognized as a "Subject Matter Expert" as defined by objective standards. As a training organization, we recognize the value of offering certification-level training; in fact, approximately 55 percent of students in our Microsoft classes are working toward certification. I expect that number to continue to rise.

Studies have shown increased productivity among Microsoft Certified Solutions Developers versus noncertified programmers. Additionally, compensation for Microsoft Certified Systems Engineers and Microsoft Certified Solutions Developers averages higher than for those without certification. For individuals looking for a career in these areas, there is no better metric of legitimacy that can be placed on a resume than Microsoft certification credentials.

Information Systems/Information Technology (IS/IT) decision makers for ExecuTrain clients worldwide increasingly require certifications for their IS employees. Often, individuals are required to be certified or find that certification was their competitive edge in landing the job. Conventional wisdom and every study you read indicates these trends will continue as technologies become more a part of daily business in corporations.

Microsoft recently certified the 100,000th Microsoft Certified Professional. I expect this number to balloon as corporations make certification part of IS staff job descriptions. I predict certified candidates can expect better-paying jobs and positions with more technical responsibility to match their hard-won certification. Although the number of MCPs rises daily, that population is eclipsed by the more than 200,000 open IT positions reported today. Microsoft tracks these open positions and would like to fill each of them with MCPs. My bet is that if anyone can make the math work, they can.

Kevin Brice
Vice President/General Manager
Technical Training
ExecuTrain Corporation

CREDITS

Acquisitions Editor
Tracy Thomsic

Development Editor
Jennifer Rowe

Technical Editor
G. Chris Gradwohl, MCT,
MCSE + Internet, CNA

Copy Editor
Nicole Fountain

Project Coordinator
Susan Parini

Book Designer
Kurt Krames

Graphics and Production Specialists
Jude Levinson
Linda Marousek
Hector Mendoza

Quality Control Specialists
Mick Arellano
Mark Schumann

Illustrator
David Puckett

Proofreader
Christine Sabooni

Indexer
Richard Shrout

ABOUT THE AUTHOR

Alan R. Carter is an MCSE + Internet (Microsoft Certified Systems Engineer + Internet) and a Microsoft Certified Trainer. He teaches Microsoft Official Curriculum and custom courses throughout the United States. He also participates in the development of new courses and other educational materials. In addition to his Microsoft certifications, Alan is a Certified Network Professional, a Novell Master CNE, and a Certified Novell Instructor. He lives in Kirkland, Washington. He welcomes comments from his readers and can be contacted via the Internet at alan_carter@usa.net.

To Pat

FOREWORD

It is a privilege to inform you of the vast amount of knowledge and skill you will gain through the use of this book. Alan Carter's clear, concise expression will help you learn the complexities of Windows NT and develop the practical skills you need to pass the Microsoft Certified Professional Windows NT Server exam.

I came to know Alan three years ago when he was providing instructor-led training at Infotec. As a trainer, Alan became aware of a need for a resource that would provide the student with a deeper level of understanding than can be achieved in a week's time in the classroom. This book — which is the result of a year's research, writing, and classroom testing — is that resource.

I cannot speak to Alan's teaching skills from personal experience, but I can provide hundreds of enthusiastic testimonials from students and fellow trainers who attest to his depth of knowledge, professionalism, and ability to impart information to others. A seasoned professional, Alan has hundreds of hours of system-integration experience. This real-world experience shines through in Alan's teaching and writing, and not only helps students prepare for an exam, but also provides valuable skills they can use on the job.

And speaking of "on the job," it didn't take me long to realize that this book is an excellent on-the-job reference, because it includes numerous step-by-step, detailed instructions for performing various Windows NT configuration and management tasks. For example, you are carefully guided through the steps involved in creating, connecting to, sharing, and securing printers. This step-by-step format enables readers to perform complex tasks with confidence, both while preparing for an exam and later, on the job.

If you want to pass the Windows NT Server exam, or simply improve your Windows NT job skills, this book will take you where you want to go. This comprehensive accumulation of instructional material will give you the knowledge and skills you need to perform as a Microsoft Certified Professional, not just become one.

M. Tamara Taylor
Vice President NWD
Infotec Commercial Systems

PREFACE

Welcome to the MCSE Certification Series! This book is designed to help you acquire the knowledge, skills, and abilities you need to pass Microsoft Certified Professional Exam No. 70-067: Implementing and Supporting Microsoft Windows NT Server 4.0.

If you're *not* planning to take the NT Server exam, but you want to develop a comprehensive working knowledge of Microsoft Windows NT Server, then this book is also for you.

This book is designed to be the only book or course you need to prepare for and pass the NT Server exam; however, the goal of this book is *not* to make you into an NT guru. I cover Windows NT Server to the depth of the exam objectives, but don't go substantially beyond that point.

HOW THIS BOOK IS ORGANIZED

This book is organized into six major parts, followed by a Resources section that contains appendixes and supplemental materials, plus a compact disc. These major parts closely parallel the objectives for the Implementing and Supporting Microsoft Windows NT Server 4.0 exam.

Within these major parts, each chapter begins with an overview of the topics that will be covered in that chapter. Pertinent information on each topic is then presented. A Key Point Summary follows, summarizing the chapter highlights and reviewing important material. At the end of each chapter are Instant Assessment questions to make sure you understand and can apply what you've read. Additionally, at the end of many chapters there are Critical Thinking Labs and Hands-on Labs so you can master the specific tasks and skills tested by the Server exam.

Part I: Overview

The Overview discusses the basics of Windows NT Server, including a section on the architecture of Windows NT.

Part II: Installation and Configuration

This part covers, in detail, installing and configuring Windows NT Server, including chapters on using Control Panel, browsing, and the Computer Browser service, configuring disks, managing printing, and configuring Windows NT Server for client computers.

Part III: Managing Resources

This part explains how to use the features, services, and tools that come with Windows NT Server. It explains user and group accounts, account policy, user rights, auditing, user profiles, and system policy. This part also covers administering servers from client computers. Lastly, it teaches the reader how to share and secure file systems, and how to back up and restore data.

Part IV: Connectivity

Connectivity is all about how Windows NT Server functions in a network setting. Protocols, particularly TCP/IP, are examined. This section discusses the coexistence of Windows NT with Novell NetWare, including migrating from a NetWare environment to a Windows NT environment. Finally, you will learn how to install and configure Remote Access Service (RAS).

Part V: Monitoring and Optimization

This part explores how to monitor and optimize the performance of a specific Windows NT Server computer or an entire network. You will learn how to use Performance Monitor to gather and view data. This part includes a chapter on performance optimization, which features tips for identifying and resolving bottlenecks.

Part VI: Troubleshooting

From basic to advanced troubleshooting, this part covers it. You'll learn how to approach a troubleshooting situation, as well as which resources to consult when you're stumped by a problem.

Resources

The supplemental materials at the back of the book contain a wealth of information. In addition to a detailed glossary and thorough index, you'll find the following information in the appendixes: a complete listing of objectives for the Implementing and Supporting Microsoft Windows NT Server 4.0 exam (including a detailed cross-reference chart for study purposes); a listing of Critical Thinking Labs and Hands-on Labs in this book; answers to end-of-chapter Instant Assessment questions, Critical Thinking Labs, and Hands-on Labs; exam preparation tips; Windows NT planning forms; and a description of the compact disc contents.

CD-ROM

The CD-ROM included with this book contains the following materials: an electronic version of this book in PDF format, Adobe Acrobat Reader, Microsoft Internet Explorer version 4.0, Transcender test assessment software (demo versions), Micro House Technical Library (evaluation copy), and Diskeeper Lite (evaluation copy).

HOW TO USE THIS BOOK

This book can be used by individuals working independently or by groups in a formal classroom setting.

For best results (and we both know that the only acceptable result is a passing score on the Server exam), I recommend the following plan of attack as you use this book. First, read the chapter and the Key Point Summary at the end. Use this summary to see if you've really got the key concepts under your belt. If you don't, go back and reread the section(s) you're not clear on. Then do *all* of the Instant Assessment section questions and Critical Thinking Labs at the end of the chapter. Finally, do the Hands-on Labs. Remember, the important thing is to master the tasks that will be tested on the exam. There's really no way to master tasks without seeing the various NT Server screens over and over again.

note ▽ **When you do the Hands-on Labs and are asked to type something, the text you are instructed to type will be printed in bold, like this: password.**

Throughout this book, important words and concepts appear in italics, and all file names, folder names, directories, Uniform Resource Locators (URLs), and code appear as monospaced font, like this: `Winnt.exe`

The chapters are designed to be studied sequentially. In other words, it would be best if you complete Chapter 1 before you proceed to Chapter 2. A few chapters could probably stand alone, but all in all, I recommend a sequential approach. The Hands-on Labs have also been designed to be completed in a sequential order and often depend on successful completion of previous labs.

After you've completed your study of the chapters, reviewed the Instant Assessment questions, and done the Critical Thinking Labs and Hands-on Labs in the book, take the practice tests included on the compact disc. The practice tests will help you assess how much you've learned from your study and will also familiarize you with the types of questions you'll face when you take the real exam. Once you identify a weak area, you can restudy the corresponding chapters (including the Instant Assessment questions and labs) to improve your knowledge and skills in that area. Use the exam objectives cross-reference chart in Appendix A to help you determine the chapter(s) on which you need to redouble your efforts.

Prerequisites

Although this book is a comprehensive study and exam preparation guide, it does not start at ground zero. I do assume you have the following knowledge and skills at the outset:

1. Basic terminology and basic skills to use a Microsoft Windows product. (This could be Windows 95, Windows for Workgroups, or a Windows NT product.)

2. Basic mouse skills: being able to left-click, right-click, use the pointer, and so on.

3. Networking knowledge or experience equal to the scope required to pass the Microsoft Certified Professional Networking Essentials Exam (Exam No. 70-58).

If you meet these prerequisites, you're ready to begin this book.

If you don't have the basic Windows experience or mouse skills, I recommend you either take a one-day Windows application course or work through a self-study book, such as *Windows 95 for Dummies* (IDG Books Worldwide, 1995), to acquire these skills *before* you begin this book.

If you don't have the networking knowledge or experience, I recommend you use a tool such as the *Networking Essentials MCSE Study Guide* by Jason Nash (IDG Books Worldwide, 1998), to obtain this knowledge, and pass the Networking Essentials exam *before* you begin this book.

HARDWARE AND SOFTWARE YOU'LL NEED

You need access to various hardware and software to be able to do the Hands-on Labs in this book. It is extremely important that you do these labs to acquire the skills that are tested by the Server exam.

If you have the minimum hardware and software listed below, you will be able to complete almost all of the Hands-on Labs in this book, and certainly all of the critical ones. To be able to perform *all* of the Hands-on Labs, however, you will need the additional hardware and software, as well.

Minimum hardware requirements

- Intel-based computer with 486/33 processor, 16MB RAM, and 500MB – 1GB available hard disk space
- CD-ROM drive
- Mouse
- VGA monitor and graphics card

 tip **I strongly recommend that you use only hardware found on the Microsoft Windows NT Server Hardware Compatibility List, which is shipped with the NT Server product, or can be accessed via Microsoft's World Wide Web site at** `http://www.microsoft.com/hwtest/hcl/`.

Optional additional hardware

- Tape drive

- Printer

- Modem and Internet connection (so you can access online resources)

 Warning! Some of the Hands-on Labs in this book have the potential to erase or corrupt data on existing hard disk drives. Make sure you back up all important data and programs *before* you attempt to perform any of the labs. Or, do the labs on a computer that does not contain any vital data or programs.

Minimum software requirements

- Microsoft Windows NT Server 4.0

Optional additional software

- Microsoft Windows NT Workstation 4.0

ICONS USED IN THIS BOOK

Several different icons are used throughout this book to draw your attention to matters that deserve a closer look:

 This icon points you to another place in this book (or to another resource) for more coverage on a given topic. It may point you back to a previous chapter where important material has already been covered, or it may point you ahead to let you know that a concept will be covered in more detail later on.

 Be careful here! This icon points out information that can save you a lot of grief. It's often easier to prevent tragedy than to fix it afterwards.

 This icon identifies important advice for those studying to pass the Implementing and Supporting Microsoft Windows NT Server 4.0 exam.

I know this may be hard for you to believe, but sometimes things work differently in the real world than books — or software documentation — say they do. This icon draws your attention to the author's real world experiences, which will hopefully help you on the job, if not on the Server exam.

 This icon points out an interesting or helpful fact, or some other comment that deserves emphasis.

 This icon indicates an online resource that you can access to obtain products, utilities, and other worthwhile information.

 Here's a little piece of friendly advice, or a shortcut, or a bit of personal experience that might be of use to you.

I guess that about wraps up the general comments. From here you can get started on the nuts and bolts of learning about Windows NT Server and get ready to pass the Server exam. I wish you great success!

ACKNOWLEDGMENTS

In the book-writing business the author gets all the glory, but the truth of the matter is that a whole lot of people work on the project. For that reason, I'd like to take this opportunity to publicly acknowledge and thank the many people who had a part in the creation of this book.

First of all, thanks to everyone at IDG Books Worldwide, including: Tracy Thomsic, Acquisitions Editor; Jennifer Rowe, Development Editor; Nicole Fountain, Lead Copy Editor; Larisa North and Brian MacDonald, Copy Editors; and the entire graphics and production staff. Many thanks also to Steve Sayre, Associate Publisher, and to Brenda McLaughlin, Senior Vice President and Group Publisher of the Computer Publishing Group.

Thanks also to my family and friends for their support during this project. Last, but not least, special thanks to my wife, Pat, for your love, prayers, and countless hours of editorial work. You truly are the wind beneath my wings.

CONTENTS AT A GLANCE

Contents

Overview

Welcome to the wonderful world of NT! Chapter 1 introduces you to Windows NT Server 4.0. First, basic information about this operating system is presented. Then, foundational NT concepts, such as workgroups and domains, and the basic Windows NT 4.0 architecture, are explained. Finally, an overview of the Windows NT Server 4.0 user interface wraps up this part.

The key facts and concepts presented in Part I will help you to build a framework that will support you as you read the rest of this book. Mastering these basics will form the foundation of successful preparation for the Implementing and Supporting Microsoft Windows NT Server 4.0 exam.

Overview of Windows NT Server

About Chapter 1

This chapter explores the basics of the Windows NT Server 4.0 operating system. After a brief description of this Microsoft operating system, the chapter explains workgroups and domains, and how they are used.

Next, this chapter discusses the architecture of Windows NT. Several key NT concepts, such as modular architecture and the virtual memory model, are introduced. Even if you don't aspire to be an NT guru, a basic understanding of this terminology and how Windows NT is structured will serve you well.

Finally, a tour of the Windows NT Server 4.0 user interface is presented. All of you Windows 95 users will be happy to know that the Windows NT Server 4.0 interface looks and feels just like the Windows 95 interface.

THE MICROSOFT WINDOWS NT SERVER OPERATING SYSTEM

Windows NT Server 4.0 is a powerful 32-bit operating system that is optimized as a network file, print, or application server.

The minimum hardware required to run Windows NT Server consists of an Intel-based computer with a 486/33 processor, 16MB of RAM, 124MB of free hard disk space, and a VGA graphics card. Windows NT Server does not support Plug and Play.

Windows NT Server supports most MS-DOS-based applications, most 16-bit and 32-bit Windows-based applications, POSIX 1.*x* applications, and most OS/2 1.*x* applications. It does not support applications that require direct hardware access because this could compromise Windows NT Server's security. It also does not support software applications that require a *terminate-and-stay-resident* (TSR) program or a virtual device driver. Windows NT Server is the operating system of choice for the Microsoft BackOffice products, including SQL Server, Exchange Server, and SNA Server.

A Windows NT Server computer can support several processors to provide powerful multiprocessing capability.

Windows NT Server is a high-security capable operating system. User logon and authentication are required in order to use the Windows NT Server operating system and in order to access local or network resources. Security is controlled and administered via a domain directory database.

WORKGROUPS VERSUS DOMAINS

Before this overview of Microsoft Windows NT Server (from here on often referred to as simply Windows NT or NT) can progress much further, it's important that you get good and comfortable with two key concepts: workgroups and domains.

Workgroups and domains are two prevalent methods of grouping networked computers for common purposes. Computers and their users may be grouped based on common usage requirements or on departmental or geographical traits. For example, all the members of an accounting department or all the computers on the third floor of a building may be grouped together.

Workgroups

A *workgroup* is a logical grouping of networked computers in which one or more of the computers has one or more shared resources, such as a shared folder or a shared printer.

 note **The terms *folder* and *directory* are synonymous in the wonderful world of Windows NT. The NT user interface does not use these terms consistently. Sometimes the interface refers to a folder, and sometimes it calls the same (or similar) item a directory.**

In a workgroup environment, the security and user accounts are all maintained individually at each separate computer. Resources and administration are distributed throughout the computers that make up the workgroup. In a workgroup configuration there is no centrally maintained user accounts database, nor any centralized security. Figure 1-1 illustrates how security is distributed throughout a workgroup environment. Notice that security is maintained individually at each separate computer in the workgroup.

Although typically computers in a workgroup run desktop operating systems, such as Windows 95 or Windows NT Workstation, workgroup computers can be configured to run Windows NT Server.

FIGURE 1-1 **Security in a workgroup environment**

Domains

A *domain* is a logical grouping of networked computers in which one or more of the computers has one or more shared resources, such as a shared folder or a shared printer, *and* in which all of the computers share a common central domain directory database that contains user account and security information.

One distinct advantage of using a domain (or *domain model*, as it is sometimes called), particularly on a large network, is that administration and security for the entire network can be managed from a centralized location. Figure 1-2 illustrates how security is centralized in a domain environment. Note that all user account security is maintained at the domain controller.

In a Windows NT domain, at least one of the networked computers is a server computer that runs Windows NT Server. The server computer is configured as a *primary domain controller* (PDC), which maintains the domain directory database. Typically, there is at least one additional server computer that also runs Windows NT Server. This additional computer is usually configured as a *backup domain controller* (BDC). The other computers on the network normally run Windows NT Workstation or Windows 95 (although they may utilize Windows NT Server or other operating systems).

FIGURE 1-2   Security in a domain environment

Choosing Between the Workgroup and Domain Models

Choosing the appropriate model of grouping computers and managing shared network resources depends upon the size and security needs of the network.

Often, small- to medium-sized networks (two to twenty computers) can be managed fairly easily by using the workgroup model, with the user of each computer controlling the security to the specific resources that are shared by that user's computer.

In a larger network environment, administration and security become harder to manage; thus, the domain model, which provides centralized account administration and greater security, is usually the preferred choice.

ARCHITECTURE OF WINDOWS NT

An overview of Windows NT Server wouldn't be complete without discussing its architecture. If you develop a basic understanding of the operating system's architecture now, you'll have a framework on which to "hang" all of the concepts and facts you learn throughout the rest of this book.

 If you're already familiar with Windows NT Workstation, you'll notice that the architecture for Windows NT Server is identical. That's because even though there are differences between Windows NT Workstation and Windows NT Server, the two products are fundamentally the same operating system.

Windows NT uses a modular architecture. This means each component (or module) within the architecture has sole responsibility for the function it is designed to provide. In addition, no other module repeats the functions performed by another. Figure 1-3 illustrates the modular architecture of Microsoft Windows NT 4.0. Notice that the operating system has two pieces, or modes: user mode and kernel mode.

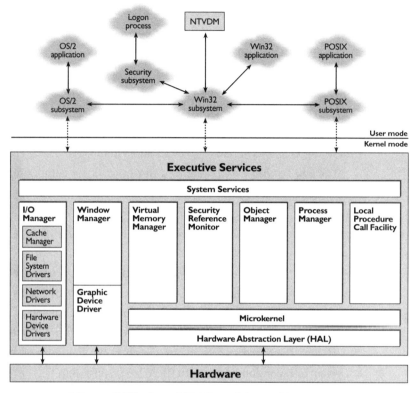

FIGURE 1-3   Microsoft Windows NT 4.0 modular architecture

User Mode

Applications and their subsystems run in *user mode*. This mode is referred to as a less privileged processor mode because it does not have direct access to hardware. User mode applications are limited to assigned memory address spaces and can't directly access other memory address spaces. User mode uses specific *application programming interfaces* (APIs) to request system services from a kernel mode component.

The purpose of separating the applications in user mode from the hardware, of restricting the memory address spaces that applications can access, and of forcing the applications to run all requests for system services through the kernel mode is to protect against the possibility of an application crashing the system. This also protects against unauthorized user access.

Examine Figure 1-3 again, and notice that there are several subsystems within user mode. You're now set to explore these subsystems.

User mode subsystems

There are four main subsystems in user mode: the Win32 Subsystem, the OS/2 Subsystem, the POSIX Subsystem, and the Security Subsystem.

The *Win32 Subsystem* is the primary application subsystem. All 32-bit Windows applications run in the Win32 Subsystem.

The *OS/2 Subsystem* is required to run OS/2 1.*x* compatible applications. The OS/2 Subsystem obtains its user interface and its screen functions from the Win32 Subsystem and requests Executive Services in kernel mode to perform all other functions for it. (Executive Services are covered in the next section of this chapter.)

The *POSIX Subsystem* is designed to run POSIX 1.*x* compatible applications. It functions very much like the OS/2 Subsystem. The POSIX Subsystem uses the Win32 Subsystem to provide all of its screen and graphical displays, and it requests Executive Services in kernel mode to perform all other functions for it.

Finally, the *Security Subsystem* supports the logon process. The Security Subsystem also communicates with the Win32 Subsystem.

In addition to the four formal subsystems, an *NT Virtual DOS Machine* (NTVDM) is a feature of user mode. Its function is to run MS-DOS-based and Windows 3.*x*-based (all 16-bit) applications.

Kernel Mode

Kernel mode refers to a highly privileged mode of operation. It is called "highly privileged" because all code that runs in kernel mode can access the hardware directly, and can also access all memory. A process running in kernel mode is not restricted to its own specific address space as is an application running in user mode.

The entire set of services that comprise kernel mode is called Executive Services (or sometimes the Windows NT Executive). Executive Services provide kernel mode services as requested by applications in user mode.

Notice how Figure 1-3 graphically presents the pieces of kernel mode. Observe how they fit together and interact with the hardware and user mode components. Allow me to now introduce you to the components of kernel mode.

Kernel mode components

Kernel mode is made up of numerous components integral to the Windows NT major operating system functions.

The *System Services* component functions as an interface between user mode and kernel mode. Its purpose is to pass information between user mode subsystems and kernel mode components.

The *I/O Manager* is responsible for all input and output to disk storage subsystems. As it manages input and output, the I/O Manager also serves as a manager and supporter of communication between the various drivers. The I/O Manager can communicate directly with system hardware if it has the appropriate hardware device drivers. Subcomponents of the I/O Manager include a *Cache Manager*, various *file system drivers*, and *network drivers*. Another subcomponent of the I/O Manager is the *hardware device drivers* that perform direct hardware access.

Window Manager is responsible for providing all of the graphical user interface. Window Manager communicates directly with the *graphics device drivers*, which in turn communicate directly with the hardware. In Windows NT 3.51, Window Manager and the graphics device drivers were a part of user mode. The developers of Windows NT 4.0 moved this component from user mode to kernel mode. This change enabled faster access to the graphics device drivers and eliminated the need for user applications to switch back and forth between kernel mode and user mode for calls for graphics services.

There are five other kernel mode subsystems: the *Virtual Memory Manager*, the *Security Reference Monitor*, the *Object Manager*, the *Process Manager*, and the *Local Procedure Call Facility*. Each one of these subsystems communicates directly with the Microkernel. The *Microkernel* is the very heart of the NT operating system. It handles interrupts, schedules threads, and synchronizes processing activity. The Microkernel, in turn, communicates with the *Hardware Abstraction*

Layer (HAL). The HAL is designed to hide the varying characteristics of hardware so that all hardware platforms appear the same to the Microkernel. As a result, only the HAL, and not the entire Microkernel, needs to address each and every hardware platform. The HAL can communicate directly with the computer's hardware.

Now that you've been introduced to user mode and kernel mode, you're ready to move on to the last major architecture topic: the NT memory model.

NT Memory Model

Windows NT uses a virtual memory model. *Virtual memory* is the physical space on a hard disk that NT treats as though it were RAM. Virtual memory can also be thought of as an extension of RAM, or "fake" RAM.

The virtual memory model used by NT is a demand-paged system based on a flat, linear, 32-bit address space. Through the use of virtual memory, each application is given access to what *appears* to be 4GB of memory address space. 2GB of the 4GB are reserved for application data, and the remaining 2GB are reserved for NT operating system data.

By using this scheme, the operating system is able to allocate more memory to applications than is actually contained in the computer. The advantage of this is that users can run more applications at one time than the computer's RAM would otherwise physically permit.

The Virtual Memory Manager manages memory in the Windows NT environment by using demand paging. (You may recall that the Virtual Memory Manager is a kernel mode component. It is included in Figure 1-3.) Here's how the Virtual Memory Manager (and demand paging) works: When the Virtual Memory Manager receives a request from an application to retrieve specific pages of memory, it redirects this request to the actual physical location where those pages are stored. This location could be in RAM, or it could be in virtual memory stored in a paging file on the hard disk. If it is in a paging file on the hard disk, the Virtual Memory Manager will move some pages of memory that have not recently been used from RAM to a paging file on the hard disk. It will then recover the pages that were requested by the application from the paging file on the hard disk and move them back into RAM, where the application can access them.

The 32-bit flat addressing scheme used by the NT memory model makes NT compatible with many popular processors, including the MIPS R4000, the PowerPC, the Intel, and the DEC Alpha AXP.

WINDOWS NT SERVER 4.0 INTERFACE

If you're familiar with the Windows 95 user interface, you can probably skip this section. The Windows NT Server 4.0 interface looks and feels like the Windows 95 interface.

Likewise, if you know the Windows NT Workstation 4.0 user interface, you'll find that the Windows NT Server 4.0 Interface is the same, except for the handful of features found on only NT Workstation or on only NT Server.

If this is your first exposure to Windows NT 4.0, Figure 1-4 shows how the desktop interface looks.

FIGURE 1-4 The Windows NT Server 4.0 desktop

The following is a brief explanation of the Windows NT Server 4.0 user interface, including the desktop and Windows NT Explorer.

The Windows NT Server 4.0 Desktop

After your computer boots Windows NT Server 4.0, it displays a screen called the desktop. The desktop replaces the Program Manager interface from earlier versions of Windows and Windows NT.

You can create shortcuts to programs you use frequently and place them on the desktop. You can also configure the display properties, such as icon size, background color, screen saver, display resolution, and so on, by right-clicking anywhere on the desktop and then clicking Properties.

There are several icons on the desktop, as well as a taskbar and a Start button. Each of these are discussed in the following sections.

My Computer

Double-clicking the My Computer icon displays the My Computer dialog box. This dialog box graphically represents every drive on the computer (including network drives, if any), as well as the Control Panel and the Printers folders. If you double-click any icon in the My Computer dialog box, another dialog box is displayed showing the contents of the drive or folder you clicked.

Network Neighborhood

The Network Neighborhood icon is only displayed if you are using a network. If you double-click the Network Neighborhood icon, a dialog box is displayed that contains an icon for your computer and an icon for the entire network. You can expand the icons in this dialog box to show all computers, shared folders, and shared printers on your network.

Internet Explorer

When you double-click the Internet Explorer icon, Microsoft Internet Explorer starts. You can use this application to browse Web pages on the Internet.

Recycle Bin

The Recycle Bin icon is a politically correct '90s version of the Macintosh trash can icon. When you delete files, the files are moved from their original location into the Recycle Bin folder. When you delete items in the Recycle Bin, the items are removed permanently from your computer. Remember to periodically empty your Recycle Bin.

My Briefcase

My Briefcase is a special type of folder that enables you to keep files synchronized between two computers, such as your laptop and your desktop computer.

Start button

The Start button is located on the left side of the taskbar. Clicking the Start button opens a menu that enables you to access programs quickly, recently used documents, settings (such as the Control Panel and Printers folders), and Help. The menu also enables you to run applications from a command line, find a document, and shut down your computer.

Taskbar

The taskbar at the bottom of the desktop contains the Start button, a button for each program that is currently running, and a clock. You can quickly switch between applications by clicking the button that represents the application you want to access. You can configure taskbar properties by right-clicking anywhere on the taskbar, and then selecting Properties. You can easily set the time and date by double-clicking the clock in the taskbar.

Close, minimize, and maximize buttons

At the upper right-hand corner of every window is a button, marked with an X. This button is called the close button and is used to close the window and exit the application.

Many windows have two additional buttons located adjacent to the close button: the minimize and maximize buttons. The minimize button looks like an underscore on a button. Clicking this button will minimize the application to its icon on the taskbar. The maximize button looks like either a single box with a dark line across the top, or like two overlapping boxes, each with a dark line across the top. Clicking the maximize button switches between a small view of the window and a full screen view of the window.

Windows NT Explorer

You can access any file, folder, printer, or application on your computer or on the network in Windows NT Explorer. Windows NT Explorer replaces File Manager from earlier versions of Windows and Windows NT. Windows NT Explorer is a useful tool for copying, moving, and deleting files.

To access Windows NT Explorer, select Start ⇒ Programs ⇒ Windows NT Explorer.

KEY POINT SUMMARY

This chapter covered the basics of the Windows NT Server 4.0 operating system. Chapter 1 also covered workgroups versus domains, several key components of the Windows NT architecture, and the Windows NT Server 4.0 user interface.

o Windows NT Server 4.0 is a powerful, 32-bit operating system that is optimized for server performance.

o A *workgroup* is a collection of networked computers in which administration of user accounts and security of resources are maintained individually, on each separate computer. A *domain* is a group of networked computers in which administration and user account security for the entire network is managed from a centrally located domain directory database that contains user account and security information.

o The architecture of Windows NT is separated into two modes: *user mode* and *kernel mode*. Applications run in user mode. User mode applications are only able to access their assigned address spaces, and cannot access hardware at all. Code running in kernel mode, in contrast, has direct access to all of memory and direct access to hardware. The NT memory model features a virtual memory system that utilizes demand paging. The Virtual Memory Manager is the kernel mode component that is actually responsible for performing demand paging.

- The *Windows NT Server 4.0 user interface* looks and feels like the Windows 95 interface, and is nearly identical to the Windows NT Workstation user interface. Several icons appear on the desktop: My Computer, Network Neighborhood, Internet Explorer, Recycle Bin, and My Briefcase. There is also a taskbar at the bottom of the desktop that contains the Start button, a button for each program that is currently running, and a clock. In Windows NT Server 4.0, Windows NT Explorer replaces File Manager from earlier versions of Windows and Windows NT.

exam preparation pointer **The Key Point Summaries in this book are excellent exam preparation tools. After you read each one, ask yourself if you have a sound working knowledge of the topics covered. If you don't, go back and reread the section(s) on the topics that are unclear to you. Then proceed to the questions in the Instant Assessment section.**

APPLYING WHAT YOU'VE LEARNED

Now it's time to regroup, review, and apply what you've learned in this chapter. The questions in the following Instant Assessment section bring to mind key facts and concepts. In addition, some of the questions also give you a chance to analyze situations and apply your knowledge of Windows NT to that particular situation.

exam preparation pointer **Take time to answer the questions in the Instant Assessment section at the end of each chapter. These questions give you an opportunity to apply the concepts you've just learned. Keep in mind that your investment of time and effort now will pay off later when you take the exam!**

Instant Assessment

1. What is the minimum hardware required to run Windows NT Server 4.0?

2. For what type of performance is Windows NT Server 4.0 optimized?

3. You are planning a small network (four computers) for your company. You want the administration and security of the network to be distributed equally among the users of the four computers. Which method of logically grouping computers should you use?

4. Which method of logically grouping computers should you use when you need centralized administration of the network's security?

5. Which mode of the Windows NT Server operating system has direct access to hardware, user mode, or kernel mode?

6. What type of memory model does Windows NT use?

7. Figure 1-5 is a partially filled-in model of the Windows NT 4.0 modular architecture. Fill in the missing titles in the chart to solidify your understanding of the Windows NT 4.0 architecture.

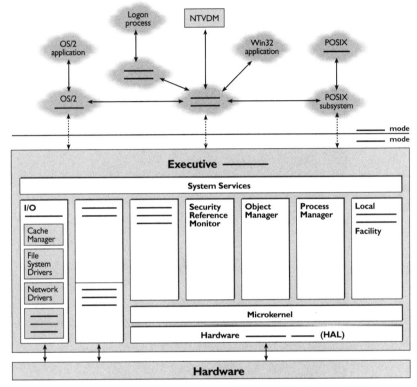

FIGURE 1-5   Microsoft Windows NT 4.0 modular architecture activity

   concept link   **For answers to the Instant Assessment questions see Appendix B.**

Installation and Configuration

This part kicks your exam preparation into high gear. Chapter 2 starts it off with complete information on how to install Windows NT Server 4.0. We also discuss how to troubleshoot common installation problems.

After installing NT, Chapter 3 explores all of the mini-applications in Control Panel. You may be surprised by what some of these applets can do!

Next, Chapter 4 explains browsing and the Computer Browser service. Common naming conventions are introduced here.

Then, Chapter 5 explores configuring a computer's hard disk(s). The various file systems are presented, and disk partitioning is explained.

At this point, Chapter 6 delves into the hefty topic of managing printing. Printing issues from A to Z are covered in this chapter.

Finally, Chapter 7 explains how to configure Windows NT Server for client computers. The topic of server-based deployment is presented, along with details on how to use Network Client Administrator.

This part maps to the Installation and Configuration exam objectives for the Implementing and Supporting Microsoft Windows NT Server 4.0 exam. You'll want to take advantage of the numerous Hands-on Labs in Part II that will give you an opportunity to practice important skills tested by the Server exam.

Installing Windows NT Server

About Chapter 2

This chapter spells out everything you need to know to install Windows NT Server, including the hardware requirements. It also includes a very practical preinstallation checklist for gathering all the information you'll need to perform the installation.

Chapter 2 explains how to start an NT installation locally from a CD-ROM drive and over the network using `Winnt.exe` or `Winnt32.exe`. Then it takes you through the entire installation process, step-by-step and phase-by-phase.

Finally, this chapter explores troubleshooting solutions to common NT installation problems.

This chapter includes two labs—a Critical Thinking Lab that prepares you to troubleshoot common Windows NT installation problems, and a Hands-on Lab that walks you through the process of installing Windows NT Server on your own computer.

The information in this chapter maps directly to several objectives in the Installation and Configuration and Troubleshooting sections in the Microsoft Windows NT Server exam objectives.

HARDWARE REQUIREMENTS FOR INSTALLATION

Before you can install NT, you need to make sure you have the appropriate hardware. To avoid problems, only use hardware that appears on the Windows NT *Hardware Compatibility List* (HCL). The HCL, which is updated periodically, ships with Microsoft NT products.

 web links **You can also access the latest HCL via Microsoft's Web site at** `http://www.microsoft.com/hwtest/hcl/.`

If you have hardware that is *not* listed on the HCL, contact the manufacturer of your equipment to see if the correct Windows NT 4.0 drivers for that device can be obtained.

Table 2-1 shows the minimum hardware required for installing Windows NT Server. The requirements listed apply only to Intel-based platforms. Windows NT can also be installed on DEC Alpha AXP, PowerPC, and MIPS R4000 platforms, but additional hardware may be necessary, depending on the type of processor you plan to use.

TABLE 2-1 MINIMUM HARDWARE REQUIRED FOR INSTALLATION OF WINDOWS NT SERVER 4.0	
HARDWARE COMPONENT	MINIMUM REQUIREMENT
Processor	486/33
Memory	16MB of RAM
Hard disk space	124MB
Display	VGA or better
Floppy disk drive	3.5-inch high-density
CD-ROM drive	Required (If your computer does not have a CD-ROM drive, you can still install NT Server by using an over-the-network installation.)
Network adapter	Optional (Required for over-the-network installation)
Mouse	Optional

in the real world

Table 2-1 shows the *minimum* hardware required for installation purposes only. More hard disk space is needed for applications and data files. Additional memory is required for some applications, and to speed up operations while running applications.

Do you know exactly what hardware you have in your computer? You can use the *NT Hardware Qualifier* (NTHQ) utility that comes with Windows NT to examine and identify your hardware configuration. NTHQ helps you determine if Windows NT can detect your hardware, and it identifies the hardware settings used for each adapter. To use NTHQ, you must create an NTHQ diskette, which you then use to boot your computer. (You can create an NTHQ diskette with a blank, formatted 3.5-inch floppy diskette by running `Makedisk.bat` from the `\support\hqtool` directory on the Windows NT Server compact disc.) NTHQ makes a text file you can print to help you complete the preinstallation checklist in the next section of this chapter.

INFORMATION REQUIRED TO INSTALL WINDOWS NT SERVER

A substantial amount of user input is required during the Windows NT installation process. To make the installation go smoother and to avoid the possibility of having to redo it, you should gather all the information you will need *before* doing the installation. This will enable you to give the appropriate responses as you are prompted by the Windows NT installation program.

Preinstallation Checklist

To assist you in gathering information about your computer and network environment so you can successfully complete the installation, I have designed a multipart preinstallation checklist for you. A detailed explanation accompanies each checklist item.

 tip **The preinstallation checklist is reproduced *without* the detailed explanations of each item in Appendix D. I encourage you to copy and use this checklist as well as the other planning forms.**

Mass storage devices: SCSI, IDE, and CD-ROM adapter information

You need to know the manufacturer's name, adapter name and model, and hardware settings for each SCSI, IDE, and CD-ROM adapter in your computer. Windows NT automatically detects ESDI and some older IDE controllers and might display a message during installation stating that there are no adapters present. If you see such a message during installation, it simply means NT didn't detect any adapters that could have a CD-ROM drive attached. Standard IDE adapters are not displayed, but are used by Windows NT. IDE dual-channel PCI adapters are displayed. If your hard disk controller is not displayed, continue with the installation. Your hard disk(s) should appear in the partitioning stage. You can choose to specify manually which adapters you have and skip the automatic detection process.

SCSI/IDE/CD-ROM Adapter	IRQ	I/O Port	DMA Channel
_____	___	_____	_____
_____	___	_____	_____
_____	___	_____	_____
_____	___	_____	_____

tip **Use the NTHQ utility described in the previous section, "Hardware Requirements for Installation," to examine and identify your hardware configuration, and to print out a text file that will help you complete the preinstallation checklist.**

Hardware and software components

o Computer type: _____

This refers to the type of architecture your PC uses, such as MPS Multiprocessor, IBM PS/2, Standard PC, and so on.

o Display: _____

This refers to the video display adapter in your computer. This component setting defaults to Auto Detect. If your display adapter is not on the HCL and you have the NT 4.0 drivers provided by the manufacturer of your display adapter, you can change this setting at the end of Phase 3 of the installation process.

o Keyboard: _____

This component's default is a single setting that includes XT, AT, or Enhanced Keyboard (83–104 keys). You can change this setting if you have a different keyboard and the appropriate drivers for it.

o Keyboard layout: _____

This setting defaults to U.S. Change this setting if necessary to support your keyboard layout correctly.

o Pointing device: _____

Setup should automatically detect your mouse or other pointing device. You can change the setting by selecting another pointing device from the list, or you can supply your own driver from a diskette.

Upgrade

Upgrade previous version of Windows? Yes_____ No_____

If the Windows NT Setup program detects a previous installation of Windows or Windows NT on your computer, it will ask if you want to upgrade that version of Windows or Windows NT to Windows NT 4.0.

Windows 3.*x* and previous versions of Windows NT can be upgraded in this manner. When you install Windows NT 4.0 in the *same* directory as the previous Windows installation to perform an upgrade, all application and user preference settings will be upgraded. You should install Windows NT 4.0 in a *different* directory than the previous Windows installation if you are upgrading from a previous version of Windows NT and you want to continue to use the previously installed version. When you install Windows NT 4.0 in a different directory than your previously installed Windows operating system, you must reinstall all applications that will be used with Windows NT and reconfigure all user preferences within those applications, such as screen colors, desktop settings, and so on.

note **When you install Windows NT 4.0 in a different directory than the original operating system, Windows NT automatically configures itself to *dual boot* between Windows NT 4.0 and the previously installed operating system. In addition, Windows NT 4.0 configures itself to dual boot between Windows NT 4.0 and Windows 3.*x* when you upgrade from Windows 3.*x* by installing Windows NT 4.0 in the same directory as Windows 3.*x*.**

Windows 95 and OS/2 cannot be upgraded to Windows NT 4.0 in this manner. You must install Windows NT 4.0 in a different directory than Windows 95 or OS/2 if you have previously installed either of these operating systems.

If you previously installed Windows 95 and you install Windows NT 4.0 in a different directory, you must reinstall all applications that will be used with Windows NT, and reconfigure all user preferences within those applications. If you previously installed MS-DOS or OS/2 1.*x* and you install Windows NT 4.0 in a different directory, you do not need to reinstall the applications that will be used with Windows NT, nor do you need to reconfigure the user application preferences.

Hard disk partition information

The space on hard disks is divided into areas called *partitions*. The Windows NT Setup program requires you to choose which partition you will use for the NT installation. Refer to Table 2-1 to make sure the partition you choose has enough available disk space.

Disk Partition Number	Type of Partition	Available Disk Space
1	_____	_____
2	_____	_____
3	_____	_____

Partition # to be used for installation of Windows NT: _____

Within the Windows NT operating system there are two important, required types of partitions: a *system partition* and a *boot partition*. These two terms are Windows NT jargon for primary and extended partitions that contain specific files and perform specific functions in Windows NT.

- System Partition: The *system partition* is located on the active primary partition of the first hard disk in the computer. (This is usually the C: drive.) The system partition contains several files that are required to boot Windows NT, including: `ntldr`, `Ntdetect.com`, `Boot.ini`, and sometimes `Bootsect.dos`, and `Ntbootdd.sys`, depending on the installation type and hardware configuration.
- Boot Partition: The *boot partition* can be located on either a primary or extended partition. The boot partition contains the Windows NT installation directory (usually the `Winnt` directory). This partition also contains all of the Windows NT operating system files.

 tip

The names of these two partitions often confuse people. Because of the types of files the partitions contain, many people think the boot partition should be called the system partition, and vice versa. You might find it helpful to make a mental note that these two partitions are named the opposite of what you intuitively think they should be!

In many cases, the system partition and the boot partition are physically located on the same partition of the hard drive. For example, suppose your computer's hard drive contains two partitions: an 800MB primary partition and a 200MB extended partition. If you install Windows NT on the 800MB partition, both the system partition and the boot partition will be physically located on the 800MB partition.

File system used for installation (choose one)
FAT _____   NTFS _____

Windows NT supports two file system types: FAT and NTFS.

- FAT: The *file allocation table* (FAT) file system is supported by Windows NT and many other operating systems, including MS-DOS, OS/2, Windows 3.*x*, and Windows 95. Normally, if you want your computer to dual boot between Windows NT and one of these other operating systems (and both operating systems are located on the same hard disk partition), choose the FAT file system. The FAT file system supports neither extended attributes nor file-level security.

- NTFS: The *Windows NT file system* (NTFS) is supported only by Windows NT. In general, choose NTFS if you do not want your computer to dual boot between Windows NT and another operating system and you want the added advantages provided by NTFS, including extended attributes and file-level security.

You can select FAT as the file system to be used during installation of Windows NT, and then later choose to convert the file system to NTFS; however, if you choose NTFS as the file system to be used during installation of Windows NT and then later want to convert to FAT, the process isn't so easy. To convert from NTFS to FAT, you need to back up all files, repartition and format the drive, reinstall Windows NT, and restore all the files from backup.

 tip **To avoid these time-consuming processes, plan ahead as much as possible when deciding which file system you will use.**

Windows NT 4.0 does not support the *high performance file system* (HPFS) used by OS/2. If you want to install Windows NT 4.0 on a computer that uses HPFS, you must back up all data, repartition and format the computer's drive with FAT or NTFS, and then restore all the files from backup before you can install Windows NT 4.0.

 concept link   **For a more in-depth discussion of file systems, see Chapter 5.**

Installation directory

Installation directory for new installation: _____

In this step you choose in which directory Windows NT 4.0 files will be installed. You may either accept the default directory displayed during setup (usually `c:\winnt`), or type the name of another directory. Be sure the directory you choose has enough free space for the Windows NT 4.0 files.

Registration

10 Digit CD Key #: _____-_____

You need to enter the ten-digit CD key number (located on the back of the Windows NT Server compact disc case) during the Windows NT installation. This entry is required.

Licensing mode

Choose one of the following licensing modes, and determine the number of client access licenses you have purchased.

Per server _____   Per seat _____

Number of client access licenses: _____

At this point during the installation, a licensing mode must be chosen, and its terms agreed to, in order to continue the installation. Windows NT Server has two licensing modes: *per server* and *per seat*.

- Per server: In the per server licensing mode, you must have one client access license for each concurrent connection to the server. For example, if you have 150 client computers (workstations), but only 100 of them would be logged on to the Windows NT Server computer at any one time, then you would need 100 client access licenses. You should enter the number of client access licenses you have purchased for this server in the box next to concurrent connections in the Choose Licensing Mode dialog box.

o **Per seat:** In the per seat licensing mode, you must have one client access license for each client computer that will ever connect to a Windows NT Server computer.

 The advantage to using the per seat licensing mode becomes apparent when you have multiple servers on a network. In such a situation, you only have to buy one client access license for each client computer, even if a client computer accesses multiple servers at the same time.

For example, suppose you have 500 client computers and 6 Windows NT Server computers on a network, and the client computers access several servers at a time. If you choose the per seat licensing mode, you only need to purchase 500 client access licenses, whereas if you choose the per server licensing mode, you probably need to have more than one client access license per client computer.

Computer name

Computer name: _____

During installation you need to enter the name your computer will use on the network. The *computer name* is also called a *NetBIOS name*, and can be up to fifteen characters long. All computers on the network must use different NetBIOS names. Uniqueness is the key here. If you have a small network, you can probably get by with naming the computers after the characters in your favorite movie, television series, or comic strip. If you have a large network, however, you will probably want to use some type of systematic naming scheme to ensure that each computer has a unique NetBIOS name.

Server type

You need to choose the role this server will play on the network. Planning is very important here, because once a server is installed as either a *primary domain controller* (PDC) or a *backup domain controller* (BDC), it can't become a stand-alone server or a member server.

Choose one of the following server types:

> caution ▽ **Careful here! Once a computer is installed as a domain controller in a domain, the domain controller cannot migrate to another domain without a complete reinstall of Windows NT Server.**

○ Primary Domain Controller

Domain name: _____

Choose primary domain controller (PDC) if you want the server to participate in a domain instead of a workgroup, and if you have not already installed any servers in this domain. If you are installing the only server to be used for a small network, you should choose this option.

○ **Backup Domain Controller**

Domain name: _____

Administrator's account name: _____

Administrator's password: _____

Choose backup domain controller (BDC) if you want the server to participate in a domain instead of a workgroup, and if you have already installed a server in this domain. Additionally, you need to enter the administrator's user account name and password to complete the installation of a BDC.

○ **Member Server**

Domain name: _____

Administrator's account name: _____

Administrator's password: _____

Choose member server if you want the server to join a domain but do not want the server to have to expend its resources authenticating user logon requests in the domain. Or, choose member server if you plan to move this server from one domain to another. If you want the server to be a member server in a domain, you will also need to enter the administrator's user account name and password to complete the installation.

o Stand-Alone Server

Workgroup name: _____

Choose stand-alone server if you want the server to participate in a work-group instead of a domain.

 If a stand-alone server later joins a domain, it becomes a member server at that point (and is no longer a stand-alone server). If, at some point after that, this member server no longer participates in a domain (unjoins a domain), it reverts to stand-alone server status.

Administrator password

Although you may not want to write down the password on this worksheet, you need to enter an administrator password during the installation process.

Emergency Repair Disk

Will an Emergency Repair Disk be created during installation? Yes___ No___

Here you choose whether to make an Emergency Repair Disk during the installation process. The Emergency Repair Disk is used to repair Windows NT when its configuration files have been damaged or corrupted. Always make an Emergency Repair Disk. A blank 3.5-inch high-density floppy disk is required during installation to make this disk.

 You can update your Emergency Repair Disk by using the `Rdisk.exe` utility. You should do this every time you change or update your computer's hardware configuration. (You'll get a chance to do this in Lab 5.10.)

Select components

This list represents a myriad of optional software components that can be added during the Windows NT installation/setup process. Choose the components you want to install. I've provided explanation for some of the components — others are self-explanatory.

o Accessibility options Yes___ No___

This component includes options to change the keyboard, sound, video display, and mouse attributes for people with mobility, hearing, or visual impairments. This option is either selected or not selected — it has no discrete components.

- **Accessories**

  Calculator ___   Character Map ___

  Clipboard Viewer ___   Clock ___

  Desktop Wallpaper ___   Document Templates ___

  Imaging ___   Mouse Pointers ___

  Object Packager ___   Paint ___

  Quick View ___   Screen Savers ___

  Wordpad ___

- **Communications**

  Chat ___   HyperTerminal ___

  Phone Dialer ___

- **Games**

  Freecell ___   Minesweeper ___

  Pinball ___   Solitaire ___

- **Multimedia**

  CD Player ___

  Jungle Sound Scheme ___   Media Player ___

  Musica Sound Scheme ___   Robotz Sound Scheme ___

  Sample Sounds ___   Sound Recorder ___

  Utopia Sound Scheme ___   Volume Control ___

- **Windows Messaging**

  Internet Mail ___   Microsoft Mail ___

  Windows Messaging ___

Type of network access

Select one of the following:

◉ Wired to the network: ___

Wired to the network means your computer has a direct physical connection to the network and uses either a network adapter or an ISDN adapter.

◉ Remote access to the network: ___

Remote access to the network means your computer uses a modem to connect remotely to the network by using Dial-Up Networking to connect to a *Remote Access Service* (RAS) server.

Microsoft Internet Information Server

Install Microsoft Internet Information Server? Yes___ No___

Here you choose whether or not to install *Microsoft Internet Information Server* (IIS). IIS can be used as a *World Wide Web* (WWW) server, a *File Transfer Protocol* (FTP) server, and as a *Gopher* server.

 Windows NT Server 4.0 does *not* include a separate FTP server. You must install IIS to get FTP server functionality.

Network adapter

Network adapter manufacturer (if applicable): _____

Network adapter name (if applicable): _____

Interrupt: _____ I/O Port: _____

You have two choices at this point of the installation: You can enable NT to detect your network adapter (if you have one) automatically, or you can select your network adapter manually from a list displayed by the Windows NT Setup program. Select your network adapter manually by choosing Select from list. If you use this option you have the opportunity to install drivers from a disk supplied by the manufacturer of the network adapter. If you want to install networking but do not have a network adapter, choose *MS Loopback Adapter* from the list. This adapter doesn't have any hardware associated with it — it is a fake adapter that will enable you to install networking services without having a network adapter.

You need to obtain the hardware settings (interrupt and I/O port) for your network adapter, because the Windows NT Setup program may prompt you for them later. (Some drivers automatically detect the network adapter configuration and will not prompt you for input.)

Network protocols

Each of the protocols below has strengths and weaknesses. Evaluate the needs of your network, and then choose all the protocols you need. NT Server 4.0 ships with support for TCP/IP, NWLink IPX/SPX Compatible Transport, and NetBEUI.

o TCP/IP: Yes ____ No ____

(If Yes, then Windows NT Setup offers you an opportunity to configure TCP/IP by using DHCP.)

o DHCP: Yes ____   No ____ (If No, fill in information below)

IP address: _____

Subnet mask: _____

Default gateway: _____

DNS server #1: _____

DNS server #2: _____

WINS server #1: _____

WINS server #2: _____

The *TCP/IP* protocol provides the most capability of the three protocols. It is routable, fast, and has powerful network-wide name resolution capabilities. It can be used on much larger networks than either of the other protocols. TCP/IP is the most commonly supported protocol. It is supported on many operating systems, including Windows NT, Windows 95, UNIX, MS-DOS, Macintosh, and IBM Mainframes. TCP/IP is the protocol used on the Internet.

The main drawback to using TCP/IP is that it requires substantial planning and configuration to implement.

concept link

For more information on TCP/IP and its configuration properties, see Chapter 14.

- NWLink IPX/SPX Compatible Transport: Yes___ No___

    (If Yes) Frame Type: _____

    NWLink IPX/SPX Compatible Transport is a protocol originally developed by Novell. It was designed for use on Novell NetWare servers. NWLink IPX/SPX is a routable protocol, but has some limitations when used on large NetBIOS-based networks such as Windows NT. It has no name resolution capabilities, so all broadcasts are forwarded across routers.

    NWLink IPX/SPX is very easy to configure and is a good choice for a small, routed network. NWLink IPX/SPX should be used on any network that has NetWare servers on it if Windows NT computers on the network need to access the NetWare servers.

    You should choose autodetect for the frame type selection, unless you know which frame types you want to support.

concept link

For more information on NWLink IPX/SPX Compatible Transport, coexistence with NetWare, and frame types, see Chapter 15.

- NetBEUI: Yes___ No___

    The NetBEUI protocol is designed for small, nonrouted networks. It does not require any configuration, and has minimal overhead. NetBEUI is included primarily to provide backward compatibility with earlier networking software that uses NetBEUI as its only protocol.

Network services

Network services to add: _____

At this point in the installation, several network services are preselected by default, and you cannot deselect them. You can also add additional services by clicking the Select from list command button.

concept link

Network services are examined in detail later in this book. Some of the services are covered in Chapter 3, and others are mentioned throughout the chapters in Part IV.

Network bindings

Network bindings to disable: _____

You have an option to disable and enable bindings of various services to protocols, and bindings of protocols to various network adapters. A *binding* is an association. For example, you might want to associate one protocol with one network adapter, and another protocol with a second network adapter. By default, all services are bound to all protocols that support that service, and all protocols are bound to all network adapters.

 note **This is an advanced feature. You should accept the default setting unless you have a specific reason to change it.**

Make this computer a member of

This section applies only when Windows NT Server is installed as a stand-alone server.

You *must* choose to participate in either a workgroup or a domain. (See the "Workgroups Versus Domains" section in Chapter 1 for more information on this topic.) Only Windows NT Server computers that are configured as stand-alone servers have this option.

o Workgroup: Yes_____ No_____

(If Yes) Workgroup name: _____

If you elect to be a member of a workgroup, only users that have user accounts physically located in this computer's directory database will be able to log on to this computer locally or to access it over the network. You need to supply a workgroup name during installation.

o Domain: Yes_____ No_____

(If Yes) Domain name: _____

Create a computer account in the domain? Yes ___ No ___

Administrator's account name: _____

Administrator's password: _____

If you decide to join a domain, two kinds of users will be able to log on to this computer locally or to access it over the network: users that have accounts in this computer's directory database, and users that have accounts in the domain directory database.

You also need to create a computer account in the domain. An administrator can do this before the Windows NT installation using Server Manager on another NT computer in the domain, or, you can create the computer account in the domain during the NT installation process. If you choose to create a computer account in the domain during installation, you need to supply an administrator's user account name and password.

Internet Information Server

Select the publishing directories you want to install:

World Wide Web publishing directory _____

FTP publishing directory _____

Gopher publishing directory _____

If you elected to install IIS earlier in the Windows NT installation process, you are now asked to choose publishing directories for it. The default directories are acceptable for most installations.

concept link   **For more information on IIS, see Chapter 14 or the *Microsoft Windows NT Server Internet Guide*, which is included in the *Microsoft Windows NT Server Resource Kit for version 4.0* (Microsoft Press, 1996).**

Time zone

Time zone: _____

Select the time zone for your location, and choose whether to adjust for daylight saving time.

Video adapter display settings

Video adapter type: _____

Display settings desired: _____

You need to know what type of video adapter is installed in your computer and how you want your display to appear. Appearance settings include Color Palette, Desktop Area (640 by 480, 800 by 600, and so on), Font Size, and Refresh Frequency. Windows NT will preselect some of these settings for you, but you can modify them during or after installation using Control Panel.

THE INSTALLATION PROCESS

Now that you know the minimum hardware required to install Windows NT Server and have all the information required to perform the installation, you're ready to move on to the actual installation process.

 My intent in this section is to explain the basic Windows NT Server installation process. The steps *you* take to perform your installation may be different than the steps listed here, depending on your hardware configuration, any previously installed operating systems on your computer, and so on. This description is only a basic guide — modify it to meet your needs. See Lab 2.2 at the end of this chapter for detailed installation instructions.

Starting Setup

Windows NT uses a program called *Setup* to accomplish the installation. There are three ways to start the installation process: from a CD-ROM drive, by using Winnt.exe, and by using Winnt32.exe. Installation can be done locally, from a CD-ROM drive; or over the network.

Starting from a CD-ROM drive

To start Setup from a CD-ROM drive, your computer must be configured with a local CD-ROM drive that is on the HCL. Place the Windows NT Server compact disc in the CD-ROM drive. Then boot the computer from the Windows NT Setup Boot Disk.

Using Winnt.exe

You can use `Winnt.exe` to start Setup from an unsupported CD-ROM drive (a CD-ROM drive that is not listed on the HCL), or to start an over-the-network installation. First boot the computer to MS-DOS, and then load either the CD-ROM drivers or network drivers (depending on the type of installation you're doing). Then use `Winnt.exe` to start Setup.

`Winnt.exe` has several command-line switches that enable customization of the setup process. Table 2-2 lists these switches and describes their functions.

TABLE 2-2 WINNT.EXE COMMAND–LINE SWITCHES

SWITCH	WHAT THE SWITCH DOES
`/S[:]sourcepath`	Specifies the source location of NT files. You must specify a full path, in the form `x:\[path]` or `\\server\share[\path]`. Default sourcepath is the current directory.
`/T[:]tempdrive`	Specifies the drive that contains NT's temporary setup files during installation. If not specified, Setup uses the first drive it finds (that it thinks has enough free space) for the tempdrive.
`/I[:]inffile`	Specifies the filename (no path) of the file containing setup information. Default inffile is `DOSNET.INF`.
`/OX`	Instructs Setup to create the Setup Boot Disk set.
`/X`	Instructs Setup *not* to create the Setup Boot Disk set.
`/F`	Instructs Setup not to verify files as they are copied to the Setup Boot Disk set (during the creation of the Setup Boot Disk set).
`/C`	Instructs Setup to skip the free-space check during the creation of the Setup Boot Disk set.
`/B`	Enables you to install NT without using the Setup Boot Disk set. Requires you to specify the sourcepath by using the `/S` switch.
`/U`	Allows you to perform an unattended NT installation and use an optional script file. Requires you to specify the sourcepath by using the `/S` switch.

continued

TABLE 2-2 *(continued)*	
SWITCH	**WHAT THE SWITCH DOES**
/R	Specifies an optional directory to be installed during installation.
/RX	Specifies an optional directory to be copied to the local hard drive during installation.
/E	Specifies a command to be executed at the end of the installation/setup process.
/UDF	Specifies that a Uniqueness Database File is used during an unattended NT installation.

 tip **These switches are not case-sensitive. You may type them in either upper- or lowercase.**

The syntax for the `Winnt.exe` command is

```
WINNT [/S[:]sourcepath] [/T[:]tempdrive] [/I[:]inffile
[/OX] [/X | [/F] [/C]] [/B] [/U[:scriptfile]]
[/RX]:directory] [/E:command]
```

To illustrate how the switches are used, suppose that you want to install Windows NT Server from a network drive (named drive K:) without using the Setup Boot Disk set. (This is often referred to as a floppyless installation.) To accomplish this, use the following command:

```
K:\I386\Winnt /B /S:K:\I386
```

Notice the /B switch is used to permit you to perform a floppyless installation, and the /S switch is used to specify that the sourcepath (the location of the NT files that will be installed on your computer) is a network drive named K:.

 concept link **For more information on unattended installation, see Chapter 7.**

Using Winnt32.exe

`Winnt32.exe` functions in the same way as `Winnt.exe`, except that `Winnt.exe` is designed to run on an MS-DOS-based computer, and `Winnt32.exe` is designed to be used on a Windows NT 3.*x* computer. All `Winnt32.exe` command-line options are the same as `Winnt.exe`, with the exception of `/F` and `/C`, which are not supported by `Winnt32.exe`.

Setup Flow

The installation of Windows NT Server takes place in four or five phases, depending on whether you install from a CD-ROM or use `Winnt.exe`. These phases are the Pre-Copy Phase, Phase 0, and Phases 1–3. During each phase, you perform specific tasks and enter requested information. The Windows NT installation program (Setup) causes the computer to reboot after the Pre-Copy Phase, and again after Phase 0.

Here's a detailed description of what takes place during each phase of the Windows NT installation.

Pre-Copy Phase (Winnt.exe and Winnt32.exe only)

The Pre-Copy Phase is the initial phase of the installation process. This phase applies only when the `Winnt.exe` or `Winnt32.exe` installation option is used. The Windows NT Setup program performs the following tasks:

1. Setup creates a set of three floppy disks to use during the installation process. These diskettes are similar to the diskettes used to perform an installation from a CD-ROM drive, except that they point to the directory that has a copy of the installation files instead of to a CD-ROM drive. The floppy disks are not created if the `/B` or `/U` switches are used.

2. Setup creates a `$Win_NT$.~ls` folder on the first local drive with enough free space, and then copies the installation files from the source directory to this folder. (The installation program deletes this folder after the installation is complete.)

3. Setup prompts you to restart the computer with the Setup Boot Disk.

Phase 0

Phase 0 begins when you boot the computer with the Setup Boot Disk, or when you reboot the computer after starting Winnt.exe using either the /B or /U switch. Setup prompts you to take the following steps during this phase:

1. Confirm all SCSI and CD-ROM adapters, and add drivers for adapters by using driver disks supplied by the manufacturer.

2. Agree to the terms of the Windows NT Licensing Agreement.

3. Choose the installation directory. Choose whether to upgrade previously installed versions of Windows 3.x or Windows NT, or to install Windows NT in a different directory to create a dual boot system, which can boot to more than one operating system.

4. Verify the hardware and software components in the computer.

5. Choose the disk partition on which to install Windows NT, and choose the type of file system to use on this partition.

Setup will then examine your computer's hard disk for corruption, and then cause the computer to reboot. Before the computer reboots, Setup prompts you to remove the floppy disk from drive A: if one is there.

Phase 1

In Phase 1, the NT Setup Wizard starts. Setup gathers more information from you about your computer and specific installation details. You are prompted to make the following choices and perform the following tasks during this phase:

1. Enter your name and the name of your organization.

2. Enter your CD key number.

3. Choose a Licensing mode.

4. Enter your computer name.

5. Choose a server type.

6. Enter and confirm a password for the Administrator account.

7. Choose whether to create an Emergency Repair Disk. (The Emergency Repair Disk is made at the end of the installation, but you must choose whether or not to make one at this point.)

8. Choose the optional components to install.

Phase 2

In Phase 2, Setup installs and configures networking components. To accomplish this, you provide more information and make the following additional choices:

1. Specify how (or if) the computer connects to the network.

2. Choose whether to install Microsoft Internet Information Server (IIS).

3. Indicate which network adapters are installed in your computer.

4. Choose the network protocol(s) you want to use, and enter related information requested depending on the protocol(s) chosen.

5. Choose additional network services to install.

6. Verify network adapter settings.

7. Configure network bindings for network services, protocols, and adapters.

8. (When Windows NT Server is installed as a stand-alone server only) Choose whether to make your computer part of either a workgroup or a domain. Enter your workgroup or domain name. If you join a domain, create a computer account in the domain and supply the domain administrator's user account name and password.

Phase 3

In Phase 3, Setup completes the installation. It is very short. You are prompted to do the following:

1. If you elected to install IIS in an earlier step, you must enter specific IIS setup and publishing directory information now.

2. Configure the date, time, and time zone information.

3. Configure and test the computer's video adapter settings.

tip **You *must* test the display configuration before the Setup Wizard will let you continue the installation process.**

4. Make an Emergency Repair Disk. Then remove this disk from Drive A:.

5. (Installation from CD-ROM only) Remove the Windows NT compact disc from the CD-ROM drive.

6. Restart the computer.

The Windows NT installation is complete.

TROUBLESHOOTING COMMON INSTALLATION PROBLEMS

There are many common problems that can cause your installation of Windows NT Server to fail. Most of these problems occur because of hardware incompatibilities. Most of the time your first troubleshooting step should be to ensure that all of your hardware is on the HCL or is supported by the manufacturer. Table 2-3 lists some common Windows NT installation problems and their possible causes and solutions.

TABLE 2-3 TROUBLESHOOTING COMMON INSTALLATION PROBLEMS

PROBLEM	POSSIBLE CAUSE/SOLUTION
You have the recommended amount of free disk space, but still run out of disk space during installation.	The recommended amount of disk space is based on the expectation that you are using 16K sectors on your hard disk. If you have a very large partition, you could be using 32K or 64K sectors. You would then need significantly more free disk space to complete your installation.
A blue screen or STOP message is displayed during installation or after a reboot.	This can be caused by several things. Some of the most common causes are a *corrupt boot sector* or a *boot sector virus*, which you can usually repair by using `Fdisk /mbr` from MS-DOS (many virus scanners can

PROBLEM	POSSIBLE CAUSE/SOLUTION
	also repair this error); and *hardware conflicts*, which you can check for by using NTHQ to examine all of your hardware settings. Look for two pieces of hardware with the same I/O port, interrupt, or DMA address. Reconfigure hardware so that there are no hardware conflicts.
You can't install from your CD-ROM drive.	This could be caused by an unsupported CD-ROM drive or by an unsupported SCSI adapter. Some SCSI adapters, such as PC card SCSI adapters, are not supported during installation, but you can install the drivers for them after the installation is complete. Try installing using `Winnt.exe`.
You can't join a domain during installation	Make sure that all network settings, both hardware and software, are correct. Confirm that you have correctly typed in the domain name and the administrator's user account name and password. (All passwords in Windows NT are case-sensitive.) Check the network cable and connections and verify that the PDC is up and accessible on the network.
Network services don't start correctly.	Verify that all network adapter and network protocol settings are correct, including interrupt, I/O port, and transceiver type. Confirm that the newly assigned computer name is unique—that it does not match any other computer, domain, or workgroup name used on the network. If you are installing a PDC, ensure that the new domain name is unique—that it does not match any other computer or domain name used on the network.

KEY POINT SUMMARY

Chapter 2 covered all of the important topics surrounding the installation and configuration of Windows NT Server, including the hardware requirements for installation, the information required to perform an installation, the installation process, and troubleshooting common Windows NT installation problems.

- It's important that you are thoroughly familiar with the hardware requirements for installing Windows NT. Only hardware on the Windows NT *Hardware Compatibility List* (HCL) should be used. You can use the *NTHQ* utility to examine and identify your hardware configuration and to get a printout of information needed to perform the installation.

- You need a substantial amount of detailed information to install Windows NT. It's a good idea to complete the Preinstallation Checklist to make sure you have all of the information you need *before* you start the installation.

- There are three ways to begin the Windows NT installation process: from a CD-ROM drive, by using `Winnt.exe`, and by using `Winnt32.exe`. Installation can be done locally from a CD-ROM drive or over the network. The installation process takes place in phases:

  - The *Pre-Copy Phase* applies only when the `Winnt.exe` or `Winnt32.exe` installation options are used. In this phase, Setup creates a set of floppy disks to use during the installation process and copies installation files from the source directory to a folder on your computer's hard disk.

  - In *Phase 0*, Setup identifies your computer's hardware, introduces the Windows NT Licensing Agreement, prompts you to choose an installation directory, and prompts you to choose a disk partition and corresponding file system.

  - In *Phase 1*, the NT Setup Wizard starts. You enter more information about your computer and specific installation details. You enter your name, your organization's name, and your CD key number. You choose a licensing mode and a server type. You choose whether to create an Emergency Repair Disk. Finally, you select optional software components for installation.

  - In *Phase 2*, Setup installs and configures networking components. You select a network connection type. Then you select and configure network adapters, protocols, services, and bindings. You choose whether to make this computer a part of a workgroup or a domain.

- In *Phase 3*, you configure date, time, and time zone information, then configure and test your computer's video display. Setup creates the Emergency Repair Disk. Then the installation is complete.

- Several common problems can arise during installation that require troubleshooting. Many installation problems occur because of hardware incompatibilities. Most of the time your first troubleshooting step should be to ensure that all of your hardware is on the HCL. Table 2-3 illustrates several common installation problems and their possible causes and solutions.

APPLYING WHAT YOU'VE LEARNED

Now it's time to regroup, review, and apply what you've learned in this chapter.

The questions in the Instant Assessment section that follows bring to mind key facts and concepts. Next, the Critical Thinking Lab tests your ability to solve common Windows NT installation problems. Finally, the Hands-on Lab will really reinforce what you've learned and allow you to practice installing Windows NT Server on your own computer.

 note

Critical Thinking Labs challenge your ability to apply your understanding of key concepts to a hypothetical problem or situation. These labs are scenario-based and typically require you to troubleshoot a problem or plan an implementation. You don't need to be at a computer to work through these labs.

Hands-on Labs are computer based. These labs provide you with opportunities to practice using Windows NT to perform many of the installation, configuration, resource management, connectivity, monitoring and optimization, and troubleshooting tasks tested by the Microsoft Windows NT Server exam.

Instant Assessment

1. What is the HCL?

2. What is the minimum processor, amount of RAM, and hard disk space required to install Windows NT Server on an Intel-based computer?

3. What is NTHQ and what can it do?

4. When you install Windows NT 4.0 in a different directory than a previously installed operating system, what will Windows NT automatically configure itself to do?

5. Which partition is the active partition that contains the files required to load and boot Windows NT?

6. Which partition contains the Windows NT installation directory (usually Winnt) and all of the Windows NT operating system files?

7. What are the two file system types that Windows NT supports?

8. What is the only operating system that supports NTFS?

9. You want to install Windows NT on an MS-DOS-based computer that does *not* have a local CD-ROM drive. Which of the three methods of starting Setup should you use?

 concept link **For answers to the Instant Assessment questions see Appendix B.**

Critical Thinking Lab

The following lab tests your ability to troubleshoot common Windows NT Server installation problems.

Lab 2.1 *Troubleshooting Windows NT installation problems*

For each of the following problems, consider the given facts and determine what you think are the possible causes of the problem, and also what course of action you might take to resolve the problem.

Problem 1   You are attempting to install Windows NT Server. During the installation, the process stops and you see a blue screen containing error information on your display.

Problem 2   You are installing Windows NT Server. You try to join a domain, and an error message is displayed stating the domain controller for this domain cannot be located.

 concept link   **For answers to the Critical Thinking Lab see Appendix B.**

Hands-on Lab

Now it's time to apply all of this head knowledge by doing a Hands-on Lab.

 exam preparation pointer   **The Hands-on Labs in this book are extremely important for your exam preparation. Don't even think about skipping them! There's no substitute for using Windows NT to master the skills tested by the Microsoft Windows NT Server exam.**

 concept link   **Refer to the "Hardware and Software You'll Need" section in the Preface if you're not sure you have the necessary equipment to do the Hands-on Labs.**

 caution   **Warning! Some of the Hands-on Labs in this book have the potential to erase or corrupt data on existing hard disk drives. Make sure you back up all important data and programs *before* you attempt to perform any of the Hands-on Labs. Or, better yet, do the labs on a computer that does not contain any vital data or programs.**

Lab 2.2 *Installing Windows NT Server*

The objective of this lab is for you to experience the process of installing Microsoft Windows NT Server and to develop the skills used to perform this task.

note ☞ **For you to complete some of the remaining labs in this book, you will need at least a 10MB partition on your hard disk that will be formatted in a later lab with NTFS. (If you don't partition your hard disk in this manner, you will not be able to do the labs on NTFS security and auditing.) You may create an extended MS-DOS partition for this use. This task should be done *before* MS-DOS is installed, and before you proceed with the rest of this lab. I recommend that you partition your hard drive into two partitions. The first partition should contain *all but* 10MB of the disk's capacity. The extended (second) partition should consist of the remaining 10MB of disk space.**

I assume, in all of the labs in this book, that drive C: is the large partition, and that drive D: is the 10MB partition. Your actual drive letters may vary from this configuration. If your drives are lettered differently, substitute your drive letters for the ones I use.

To perform this lab, first install MS-DOS on your computer's hard drive, and load the drivers for your CD-ROM drive. Make sure the Windows NT Server compact disc is in your CD-ROM drive. You will need one blank, 3.5-inch high-density floppy disk for this lab exercise.

Follow the steps below carefully to perform the installation:

PRE-COPY PHASE

1. Change the default drive to your CD-ROM drive by typing in the CD-ROM drive letter followed by a colon (for example, **D:**). Then press Enter.
2. Type **cd I386**, and then press Enter.
3. Type **winnt /b**, and then press Enter. (This command performs the installation without creating the Setup Boot Disk set.)
4. When Windows NT Setup asks you to enter the path where NT files are located, press Enter.
5. Setup copies files to your hard disk. (This process takes a few minutes. How about a stretch break or a fresh cup of coffee?)
6. When Setup displays the Windows NT Server Setup screen, press Enter to restart your computer and continue Windows NT Setup.

PHASE 0

1. After a minute or two, when the Windows NT Server Setup screen appears, press Enter to set up Windows NT now.

2. Setup displays a screen showing any mass storage devices, such as SCSI adapters, CD-ROM drives, and so on. Some older IDE controllers are not displayed here, but will still function and be recognized by NT. Specify additional devices by making changes on this screen if you need to. When you have completed all necessary changes, press Enter to continue.

3. The Windows NT Licensing Agreement screen appears. Read the licensing agreement, pressing PgDn to view additional screens. When you reach the bottom of the agreement, press F8 to continue setup.

4. Windows NT Server Setup displays a screen listing your computer's hardware and software components. Make any changes necessary. When you are finished, highlight "The above list matches my computer," and press Enter.

5. If you have a previous version of Microsoft Windows installed on your computer, Setup displays a screen stating that it detected a previous version. If this screen appears, press N to install Windows NT Server in a different directory.

6. Windows NT Server Setup displays a screen showing your computer's hard disk partitions. Highlight the partition on which you want to install Windows NT Server, and then press Enter. (Make sure the partition you choose has at least 124MB free.)

7. Windows NT Server Setup asks you to select the type of file system you want on this partition. Highlight "Leave the current file system intact <no changes>," and press Enter.

8. Windows NT Server Setup displays the location where it will install the NT Server files. In the highlighted area, edit the text so that it reads **\WINNTSRV**. (Don't type the period at the end.) Then press Enter.

9. Windows NT Server Setup offers to examine your hard disk for corruption. Press Enter to allow this. (This takes a few minutes.)

10. Windows NT Server Setup displays a screen that indicates this portion of Setup is complete. If you have a floppy disk inserted in drive A:, remove it now. Then press Enter to restart your computer and to continue with setup.

PHASE 1

1. After your computer reboots and the Windows NT Server Setup dialog box finally appears, click Next to continue.

2. Type in your name, press Tab, and then type the name of your organization. Click Next to continue.

3. When prompted, type in the 10-digit CD key number from the back of your Windows NT Server compact disc case (press Tab after you enter the first three digits). Click Next to continue.

4. Select a Licensing mode for the server. Select "Per Server for:" and enter the number of client licenses you purchased. Click Next to continue.

5. When prompted to type in a name for your computer, type **PDCLAB**. Click Next to continue.

6. Select Primary Domain Controller in the Server Type window. Click Next to continue.

7. Type **password** when prompted to enter an administrator password. Press Tab. Confirm the password by retyping it. Click Next to continue.

8. Windows NT Server Setup asks if you want to create an Emergency Repair Disk. Accept the Yes default. Click Next to continue.

9. Windows NT Server Setup displays a screen prompting you to Select Components. Add any components that you want to install, but do *not* deselect any components that are selected by default. Click Next to continue.

PHASE 2

1. Windows NT Server Setup displays a window indicating that Phase 2, Installing Windows NT Networking, is about to begin. Click Next to continue.

2. Accept the default check in the box next to "Wired to the network." (It's OK to select this option even if you don't have a network adapter in your computer.) Click Next to continue.

3. Accept the default check in the box next to "Install Microsoft Internet Information Server." Click Next to continue.

4. Windows NT Server Setup displays the Network Adapters box. If you have a network adapter, click Start Search. Your network adapter should then appear in the Network Adapters box. If your network adapter did not appear, or if you do not have one in your computer, click Select From List. If your network adapter is shown in the list, highlight it and click OK. If your network adapter is not on the list, and you have a driver disk from its manufacturer, highlight any network adapter and click Have Disk. Setup then prompts you to insert this disk. Insert the disk and click OK. Highlight your network adapter from the list and click OK. If you do not have a network adapter, highlight MS Loopback Adapter and click OK. You should now have either the MS Loopback Adapter or your network adapter displayed in the Network Adapters box. Click Next to continue.

5. Windows NT Server Setup displays the Network Protocols list box. Deselect NWLink IPX/SPX Compatible Transport. Ensure that the TCP/IP Protocol is the only protocol selected (it will have a gray check in the check box). Click Next to continue.

6. Windows NT Server Setup displays the Network Services list box. Accept all of the defaults selected in this window. Click Next to continue.

7. Click Next to have Setup install the selected components.

8. Setup prompts you to enter your network adapter card settings. (This screen may not appear for some network adapters.) Verify that the settings shown match the ones you used when you installed and configured your network adapter. Make changes only as needed. Click Continue.

9. A TCP/IP Setup warning screen appears. If you are on a network that has a DHCP server, click Yes. Otherwise, click No.

10. The Microsoft TCP/IP Properties dialog box appears if you clicked No in the previous step. If you are on a network that uses TCP/IP, or if you are connected to the Internet, obtain an IP address, subnet mask, and default gateway from your network administrator. Otherwise, type an IP address of **192.168.59.5** and a subnet mask of **255.255.255.0**.

 Do *not* use this IP address if you are on a network that uses TCP/IP, or if you are connected to the Internet.

11. Leave the Default Gateway blank. Click OK to continue.

12. Windows NT Server Setup displays a screen showing network binding information. Click Next to continue.

13. Click Next to start the network.

14. Instead of accepting the default domain name, edit the Domain text box so that it reads **LAB** and then click Next to continue.

PHASE 3

1. Click Finish to continue the setup process.

2. Accept the defaults selected in the Microsoft Internet Information Server 2.0 Setup dialog box. Click OK to continue.

3. Click Yes to create the directory.

4. Accept the default directories in the Publishing Directories dialog box by clicking OK.

5. Click Yes to create the directories.

6. Click OK in the Microsoft Internet Information Server 2.0 Setup dialog box. (You won't be configuring the Gopher functionality in this course.)

7. Click SQL Server in the Install Drivers dialog box to highlight it. Click OK to continue.

8. In the drop-down list box under the Time Zone tab, click your time zone to highlight it. Optionally, click the Date & Time tab and set the correct date and time. When you are finished, click Close to continue.

9. Setup displays a screen indicating that it has found your video display adapter. Click OK in the Detected Display dialog box to continue.

10. Adjust the display settings to suit your preferences. Click Test. The Testing Mode dialog box appears. Click OK to test. When the Testing Mode dialog box reappears, click Yes if you saw the test bitmap. When the Display Settings dialog box appears, click OK to continue. Click OK in the Display Properties dialog box to complete the installation. (This takes a few minutes.)

11. When prompted, label and insert a blank 3.5-inch floppy disk into drive A:. Setup formats and makes this disk into your Emergency Repair Disk. Click OK to continue. (This takes a couple of minutes.)

12. Windows NT Setup displays a window indicating that Windows NT 4.0 is successfully installed. Remove your newly created Emergency Repair Disk from drive A: (and save it for future use). Also remove the compact disc from your CD-ROM drive. Then click Restart Computer to reboot and start Windows NT Server. The setup is complete. Windows NT Server is now installed on your computer.

Using Control Panel

About Chapter 3

Thischapter explores Windows NT Control Panel—a collection of mini-applications that are automatically installed during the installation of Windows NT. After a brief overview, Chapter 3 discusses many of the Control Panel applications that are used to install or configure options, hardware, and hardware drivers.

Next, in-depth coverage of the Network application is presented. A comprehensive list of protocols and services is included in this section. Installing and configuring protocols and services is also covered.

The Server application is explained, with emphasis on configuring directory replication. Then the System application, which is used to configure virtual memory, among other things, is discussed. The chapter then describes briefly the remaining Control Panel applications, and concludes by providing tips for troubleshooting common configuration problems.

This chapter also includes two Hands-on Labs. In the first lab, you create a logon script and configure directory replication. In the second, you explore and use several Control Panel applications.

The information in this chapter maps to various protocol, services, network adapters, peripherals, and devices objectives listed in the Planning, Installation and Configuration, and Troubleshooting sections in the Preparation Guide for the Windows NT Server exam.

MANAGING PERIPHERALS AND DEVICES

This section examines the Control Panel applications that are used to install and/or configure options, hardware, and hardware drivers.

OVERVIEW OF CONTROL PANEL

Windows NT Control Panel is a collection of mini-applications, sometimes called applets. These applications, which are automatically installed during installation of Windows NT Server, are used to install and/or configure various options, hardware, protocols, and services.

Each Control Panel application is used for a different task. Some software packages and some installable services include their own Control Panel icon, which is displayed in the Control Panel dialog box after the new application or service is installed.

You can access Control Panel in several ways:

o Select Start ⇒ Settings ⇒ Control Panel

o Select Control Panel in Windows NT Explorer

o Open the My Computer dialog box and double-click Control Panel

Figure 3-1 shows a screen shot of Control Panel. Notice that there are twenty-seven icons displayed.

FIGURE 3-1   Windows NT Server Control Panel

You may have additional icons in Control Panel depending on the services or options you chose to install during installation and setup of Windows NT.

This chapter covers all of the common Control Panel applications, and organizes the applications into sections based on each application's functionality. The basic application functions include: managing peripherals and devices, licensing, networking, managing services, managing the server, managing the system, and miscellaneous other functions. The first function is all about the applications you can use to manage peripherals and hardware devices, and is the topic of the next section.

Accessibility Options

 The *Accessibility Options* application is used to configure the keyboard, sound, and mouse options on a computer to accommodate users that are physically challenged, including persons who have difficulty striking multiple keys simultaneously on a keyboard, persons with hearing disabilities, or persons who have difficulty holding or clicking a mouse.

The Accessibility Options application is available unless you deselected it during the installation of Windows NT, or you performed a compact installation. (Accessibility Options is normally installed by default, but if it's not installed on your computer, you can use the Add/Remove Programs application, discussed later in this chapter, to install it.)

 Another Control Panel application, Display, can be used to configure the display so that the visibility of some screen elements is enhanced. See the "Display" section later in this chapter.

Devices

 The *Devices* application is used to start and stop device drivers, to configure the startup behavior of device drivers, to view the status of a device driver, and to enable or disable a device driver within a hardware profile.

The startup behaviors (or types) available in this application include *boot*, *system*, *automatic*, *manual*, and *disabled*. If you choose boot, system, or automatic, Windows NT starts the device driver automatically every time the computer is booted. If you choose manual, a user (or another device driver) must start the device driver. If you select disabled, the device driver can't be started by a user.

 Use extreme caution when using the Devices application. Changing the startup type or disabling a device driver, such as Atdisk, can leave your computer in an unbootable state.

Display

The *Display* application is used to configure a computer's desktop background, screen saver options, desktop appearance, Microsoft Plus! options, and display adapter settings. You can also configure the display to use large fonts, large icons, and a high-contrast color scheme to accommodate a visually challenged person. The Display application can also be accessed by right-clicking the desktop and selecting Properties from the menu that appears.

Use the Settings tab to configure your computer's display adapter settings. Figure 3-2 shows the Settings tab of the Display Properties dialog box. Notice the various display options that you can configure, including: Color Palette, Font Size, Desktop Area, and Refresh Frequency.

FIGURE 3-2   The Settings tab

If you make any changes on the Settings tab, you must test the changes before you can apply them or save them.

Keyboard

The *Keyboard* application is used to configure specific keyboard features, including speed of character repeat and cursor blink rate, input locale (including keyboard layout), and keyboard type.

    The default input locale is English/United States. You can select other languages (localized for use in other countries) by clicking the Add command button on the Input Locales tab, and then scrolling through the drop-down list box.

    A list of keyboard layout options is displayed when you click the Properties command button on the Input Locales tab, and then scroll through the drop-down list box. Figure 3-3 illustrates the different U.S. keyboard layouts that can be selected.

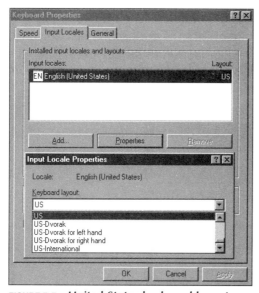

FIGURE 3-3   United States keyboard layouts

Modems

The *Modems* application is used to install and configure modems and to configure dialing properties.

When you install a modem, you can instruct Windows NT to detect your modem automatically, or you can select your modem manually from a list. If you choose to select your modem manually and your modem does not appear on the list, you can choose from the list of standard modem types.

 in the real world

When you troubleshoot modem connection problems, consider configuring Windows NT to record a log file of your modem connection activity.

To configure Windows NT to record a modem log file follow these steps:

1. **Double-click Modems in Control Panel.**

2. **Highlight your modem in the Modems Properties dialog box, and then click the Properties command button.**

3. **A specific Modem Properties dialog box is displayed for your particular modem. Click the Connection tab. Then click the Advanced command button to display the Advanced Connection Settings dialog box shown in Figure 3-4.**

FIGURE 3-4 Configuring the Modems application to record a log file

4. At the bottom left corner of the Advanced Connection Settings dialog box, check the check box next to Record a log file. Then click OK and exit the Modems application.

This log file will contain a detailed record of all commands sent to and from your modem starting from the time that you enable this feature. Windows NT saves this log file in your Windows NT installation directory as `ModemLog_your modem name.txt`. You can use any text editor to view this file.

You can use the Modems application to configure dialing properties, including the area code you are calling from, the country you are in, special instructions on how to access an outside line, whether to dial using a calling card, instructions on how to disable call waiting, and to specify tone or pulse dialing. To access the Dialing Properties dialog box, double-click Modems in Control Panel, and then click the Dialing Properties command button in the Modems Properties dialog box.

Mouse

The *Mouse* application is used to install and configure a mouse or other pointing device. You can choose the mouse button configuration, select a different pointer (this is the arrow on your screen that moves as you move your mouse), and configure pointer speed and double-click speed.

Multimedia

The *Multimedia* application is used to install and configure audio/visual devices. You can specify audio record and playback devices, MIDI output configuration, and how a video is shown on your computer's display. The types of devices you can install with this application include sound cards, MIDI devices and instruments, joysticks, video capture devices, and so on.

PC Card (PCMCIA)

The *PC Card (PCMCIA)* application is used to install, configure, and manage PC card drivers. However, often PC card drivers are installed and configured by other applications, such as the Modem application (for modem cards), and Network (for network adapters). The PC Card application is a convenient, one-stop application you can use to check the operational status of and resources used by your PC cards.

Always shut down and turn off your computer before inserting or removing PC cards. Hot swapping (removing or inserting PC cards while the computer is powered on) is *not* supported by Windows NT.

Figure 3-5 shows a list of the PC cards that are installed in my laptop computer. Note that in the PC Card (PCMCIA) Devices dialog box, the application detects two PC cards: a Megahertz modem card and a 3Com network adapter. After I click the Properties button, the MEGAHERTZ CC3288 Properties dialog box is displayed, which shows the device status and other information about the modem card.

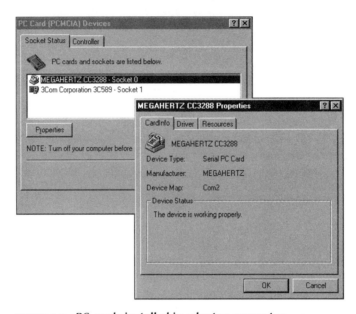

FIGURE 3-5   PC cards installed in a laptop computer

Ports

 The *Ports* application is used to add, configure, and manage the serial communication ports (COM ports) in a computer. You can use the Ports application to configure settings for your serial ports, including baud rate, data bits, I/O port address, and interrupt.

Printers

 The *Printers* application is used to install, configure, manage, and remove print-ers. It will be covered extensively in Chapter 6.

SCSI Adapters

 The *SCSI Adapters* application is used to install, configure, and manage SCSI adapters. The SCSI Adapters application looks, feels, and functions much the same as the PC Card (PCMCIA) application (discussed earlier in this chapter). SCSI adapter drivers are usually installed and configured during the installation of Windows NT. The SCSI Adapters application, however, is a convenient tool to add additional SCSI adapters after installation, and to view the operational status, con-figuration, and resources used by your SCSI adapters.

Figure 3-6 shows the two SCSI adapters installed in my desktop computer (a dual channel IDE controller and an Adaptec SCSI adapter), and the devices con-nected to each adapter. (Note: Windows NT treats dual channel IDE controllers as SCSI adapters.) After I click the Properties button in the SCSI Adapters dialog box, the IDE CD-ROM dialog box is displayed, which shows the driver status and other information about the IDE controller.

Tape Devices

 The *Tape Devices* application is used to install drivers for tape backup devices and to view the status of tape backup devices connected to your computer. This appli-cation functions much like the PC Card (PCMCIA) and SCSI Adapters applications.

You must install a driver for your tape backup device before you can access it in the Windows NT Backup application.

concept link **Using the Windows NT Backup application is discussed in more detail in Chapter 13.**

FIGURE 3-6   SCSI adapters installed in a computer

UPS

 The *UPS* application is used to install, configure, and manage an uninterruptible power supply.

 The UPS application is a basic UPS management tool. Most commercial quality UPS devices include application software that is much more sophisticated than the UPS application that ships with Windows NT. I recommend you use the application software that the manufacturer supplies with your UPS.

The Windows NT UPS application is adequate for managing an inexpensive UPS that does not include Windows NT-compatible UPS application software.

Figure 3-7 shows the configuration options available in the Windows NT UPS application. Note that you can configure the UPS interface voltages, expected battery life, the name of an executable program to run thirty seconds before shutdown, and other settings.

FIGURE 3-7   Configuring a UPS

 I strongly recommend you use a UPS on any Windows NT Server computer and on any computer that is critical to your operations. A UPS permits an orderly shutdown of your computer to avoid data loss during a power outage.

 Also remember that UPS batteries don't last forever. Follow the manufacturer's recommendations for battery replacement and maintenance. There's nothing so dissatisfying as finding out that your UPS battery is dead after the power fails. I know. I once spent an entire day during a big Seattle windstorm responding to customer calls concerning damaged hardware and lost data problems that were the result of failed UPS batteries.

LICENSING

 The *Licensing* application is used to manage licensing on your Windows NT Server computer. Normally, a licensing mode (Per Server or Per Seat) is chosen and the number of client access licenses is configured during the installation of Windows NT Server. However, if you purchase additional client licenses, or decide after installation to change your licensing mode, you can use the Licensing application to accomplish this.

concept link

The Licensing structure of Windows NT is discussed in detail in the "Licensing Mode" section of the Preinstallation Checklist in Chapter 2.

In addition, you can use the Licensing application to replicate licensing information to a centrally located (enterprise) server on your network.

NETWORKING

The *Network* application is used to control all aspects of networking services on the Windows NT computer, including changing the computer/domain/workgroup name, installing and configuring protocols and services, configuring bindings and network access order, and configuring network adapters. The Network application can also be accessed by right-clicking the Network Neighborhood icon and selecting Properties from the menu that appears.

Changing the Computer/Domain Name of a Domain Controller

Normally you will not change the computer or domain name of a Windows NT Server computer that is configured as a domain controller. However, you may need to change one or both of these names to conform to a naming convention standard that is developed or changed *after* the server is installed. If you want to change a computer or domain name of a domain controller, you can use the Network application to accomplish this.

When you start the Network application on a Windows NT Server that is configured as a domain controller, the Network dialog box is displayed, as shown in Figure 3-8.

Note that the Network dialog box has five tabs: Identification, Services, Protocols, Adapters, and Bindings. The Identification tab is on top initially. If you click the Change command button, the Identification Changes dialog box is displayed, as shown in Figure 3-9.

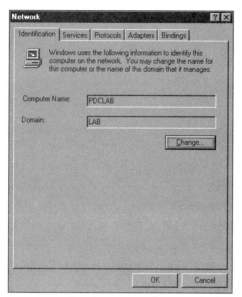

FIGURE 3-8   Starting Network on a Windows
                 NT Server domain controller

FIGURE 3-9   Making identification changes
                 on a Windows NT Server
                 domain controller

Notice that in the Identification Changes dialog box you can change the computer name or change the name of the domain.

note ⬗ **If you change the domain name of one domain controller in a domain, you *must* change the domain name of all other domain controllers, member servers, and Windows NT Workstation computers in that domain to match the new domain name you assign.**

You *cannot* change a domain controller's domain membership by changing its domain name. For example, if you have two domains on your network named EAST and WEST, you can't move a domain controller from the EAST domain to the WEST domain simply by changing the EAST domain controller's name to WEST. You have to reinstall Windows NT Server to move this domain controller from the EAST domain to the WEST domain. However, if you just want to change the name of the EAST domain to the FAR_EAST domain, you can do this by changing the domain name of all of the domain controllers, member servers, and Windows NT Workstation computers in the EAST domain to FAR_EAST.

Changing the Computer/Domain/Workgroup Name of a Stand-alone or Member Server

Occasionally you may want to change the computer, domain, or workgroup name, or change the domain membership status of a stand-alone or member server. For example, you might need to change the computer name of a stand-alone server that is assigned to a new employee to match the new user's name, instead of the name of the previous employee who used that computer.

When you start the Network application on a stand-alone server, the Network dialog box is displayed, as shown in Figure 3-10.

Note that the Network dialog box contains five tabs: Identification, Services, Protocols, Adapters, and Bindings. The Identification tab is on top initially. If you click the Change command button, the Identification Changes dialog box is displayed, as shown in Figure 3-11.

Notice that in the Identification Changes dialog box you can change the computer name or change the domain or workgroup the computer belongs to. A Windows NT computer must belong to either a workgroup or a domain.

FIGURE 3-10   Starting Network on a
stand–alone server

FIGURE 3-11   Making identification
changes on a stand–
alone server

If you select the Workgroup option button you can accept the workgroup name that is displayed, or, if no name is displayed, you must type in a workgroup name. A Windows NT computer can be a member of any existing workgroup, or it can be the only computer in a new workgroup.

Joining a domain

If you select the Domain option button, you must either accept the domain name that is displayed or type the name of any existing domain on the network. To be a member of a domain, a Windows NT computer must have a computer account in that domain. If a computer account does not exist in the domain for the computer you are configuring, you must check the Create a Computer Account in the Domain check box, and you must supply the administrator's user account name and password (or any other user account that has the right to add computer accounts to the domain). This entire process is called *joining a domain*.

Once a Windows NT computer has joined a domain, a user can log on to this computer interactively (locally) by using a user account in the domain directory database via a process known as *pass-through authentication*.

concept link

See the section "Workgroups Versus Domains" in Chapter 1 for more information on how to determine whether a computer should be a member of a workgroup or a member of a domain.

Protocols and Services

Windows NT supports a variety of protocols and services. This section identifies each protocol and service that ships with Windows NT Server and briefly describes the functionality of each.

concept link

Many of these protocols and services are covered in more depth in the chapters that make up Part IV.

Table 3-1 lists and describes the protocols that ship with Windows NT Server, and Table 3-2 lists and describes the services that ship with Windows NT Server.

TABLE 3-1 WINDOWS NT SERVER PROTOCOLS

PROTOCOL	*DESCRIPTION*
DLC Protocol	This protocol is a datalink protocol. In an NT environment, DLC is primarily used by Windows NT computers to communicate with Hewlett-Packard printers and IBM mainframe computers.
NetBEUI Protocol	This protocol is designed for small, nonrouted networks. It doesn't require any configuration and has minimal overhead. NetBEUI is included with NT 4.0 primarily to provide backward compatibility with earlier networking software that uses NetBEUI as its only protocol.
NWLink IPX/SPX Compatible Transport	This protocol is a routable protocol usually associated with NetWare networks. NWLink is fully supported for Windows NT networking.
Point-to-Point Tunneling Protocol	This protocol is used to provide a secure network communications path between computers over the Internet.
Streams Environment	Some applications require Streams for correct network functionality. I recommend you install Streams Environment only if it is required by an application or service you want to use.
TCP/IP Protocol	Of the protocols listed here, TCP/IP provides the most robust capabilities for Windows NT networking. It is a fast, routable enterprise protocol. TCP/IP is the protocol used on the Internet. TCP/IP is supported by many other operating systems, including Windows 95, Macintosh, UNIX, MS-DOS, and IBM mainframes. Its only drawback is the extensive configuration required to implement it.

TABLE 3-2 WINDOWS NT SERVER SERVICES

SERVICE	*DESCRIPTION*
DHCP Relay Agent	This service enables a Windows NT Server computer that is functioning as a TCP/IP router to forward DHCP packets to a DHCP server.

continued

TABLE 3-2 *(continued)*

SERVICE	DESCRIPTION
Gateway (and Client) Services for NetWare	This service enables a Windows NT Server computer to access files and printers on a NetWare server, and enables the NT Server to share NetWare printers and files with its non-NetWare client computers.
Microsoft DHCP Server	This service enables a Windows NT Server computer to provide TCP/IP addresses and other TCP/IP configuration information to DHCP-enabled client computers.
Microsoft DNS Server	This service is a TCP/IP-based name resolution service. It is used to resolve a host name to its associated IP address.
Microsoft Internet Information Server	This service enables a Windows NT Server computer to function as a WWW, FTP, and a Gopher server. It supports unlimited connections.
Microsoft TCP/IP Printing	This service enables Windows NT to connect to TCP/IP-based printers that use the *line printer daemon* (LPD). It also enables Windows NT to function as an LPD print server.
NetBIOS Interface	This service is installed by default and is an integral part of Windows NT networking.
Network Monitor Agent	This service enables Performance Monitor to obtain statistics about the network segment. In addition, computers that run the Network Monitor program from Systems Management Server can remotely access computers that use the Network Monitor Agent in order to capture packets from the segment and gather network statistics.
Network Monitor Tools and Agent	The Network Monitor that ships with NT Server is a limited version of the Network Monitor that ships with Systems Management Server. The NT version can't connect to remote agents. Also, the NT version uses a non-promiscuous network driver. (This means that Network Monitor captures only packets that are addressed to the computer that is running Network Monitor.)
Remote Access Service (RAS)	This service enables Windows NT to use serial ports and modems as network adapters, for both dial-in and dial-out networking. Windows NT Server supports 256 simultaneous connections.

SERVICE	DESCRIPTION
Remote Boot Service	This service enables client computers that do not have hard drives to load their operating systems across the network from a Windows NT Server computer that is running the Remote Boot Service.
RIP for Internet Protocol	This service enables a Windows NT Server computer that is functioning as a TCP/IP router to update its routing tables dynamically based on information from adjacent routers that also run RIP.
RIP for NWLink IPX/SPX Compatible Transport	This service enables a Windows NT Server computer to function as an IPX router.
RPC Configuration	This service is installed by default. It enables a program running on a Windows NT computer to contact a program that is running on another Windows NT computer directly. RPC stands for *Remote Procedure Call*.
RPC Support for Banyan	This service is required to support RPC communications on a Banyan Vines network.
SAP Agent	This service is used to advertise services on an IPX-based network. You should install the SAP Agent when you want to connect a Windows NT computer that runs SQL Server or SNA Server to a NetWare network.
Server	This service is installed by default. It enables a Windows NT computer to share its files and printers with other computers on the network.
Services for Macintosh	This service enables a Windows NT Server computer to share its files and printers with Macintosh client computers. When Services for Macintosh is installed, the AppleTalk protocol is automatically installed at the same time. Although the AppleTalk protocol never appears in the list of protocols on the Protocols tab, its functionality is present.
Simple TCP/IP Services	This service includes client programs such as Character Generator, Daytime, Echo, and Quote of the Day, for simple network protocols.
SNMP Service	This service enables a Windows NT computer to send trap messages to (and be managed by) an SNMP management station. In addition, this service enables Performance Monitor to obtain TCP/IP statistics. (This service used to be called SNMP Agent.)

continued

TABLE 3-2 *(continued)*	
SERVICE	DESCRIPTION
Windows Internet Name Service (WINS)	This service enables a Windows NT Server computer to function as a TCP/IP-based NetBIOS name server. It enables client computers to resolve NetBIOS names to IP addresses.
Workstation	This service enables Windows NT computers to access files and printers located on other computers across the network. This service is essentially the Windows NT client redirector software.

Planning for protocols and services

When planning and implementing a Windows NT installation, you should include all of the protocols and services needed to support every type of client computer that is likely to access the server. Sometimes you may want to limit the number of protocols and services used on the network to reduce network traffic. TCP/IP is often the protocol of choice for use in a large, heterogeneous network environment.

Installing and Configuring Protocols and Services

Once you have determined which protocols and services you want to install, you're ready to begin the installation process. Installing and configuring protocols and services on Windows NT computers are fairly straightforward procedures.

TO INSTALL A PROTOCOL OR SERVICE, FOLLOW THESE STEPS:

1. Select Start ⇒ Settings ⇒ Control Panel. Double-click Network. Choose either the Protocols or Services tab (depending on which you want to install).

2. Click the Add command button. The Select Network Protocol (or Select Network Service) dialog box appears.

3. Highlight the protocol or service you want to install. Click OK. (If the protocol or service you want to install is not listed, and you have the third-party software you need to install it, click Have Disk and follow the instructions displayed.) The Windows NT Setup dialog box appears.

4. Enter the path to the Windows NT installation source files (typically this is the path to the I386 folder on your Windows NT Server compact disc), and click Continue. Windows NT copies the files needed to install the protocol or service you selected. The Network dialog box reappears to give you the opportunity to add or configure additional protocols or services. At this point the protocol or service is added, but not yet configured.

5. Click Close. Windows NT examines the newly installed files, and then prompts you to perform any necessary configurations to the protocol or service.

6. Windows NT then prompts you to reboot your computer so that the new settings can take effect.

Occasionally you may need to reconfigure a protocol or service that was previously installed.

**TO CONFIGURE A PROTOCOL OR SERVICE
AFTER INSTALLATION, FOLLOW THESE STEPS:**

1. Select Start ⇒ Settings ⇒ Control Panel. Double-click Network. Choose either the Protocols or Services tab (depending on which you want to configure).

2. Highlight the protocol or service you want to configure. Click the Properties command button. A properties dialog box is displayed for the protocol or service you are configuring. Follow the instructions and provide the information requested in this dialog box.

 The name and content of this dialog box varies, depending on the specific protocol or service you are configuring. The dialog box may contain several tabs which may each need to be configured.

3. Click OK when you are finished. The Network dialog box reappears.

4. Click OK to complete the configuration. For some configurations, Windows NT will prompt you to reboot your computer so that the configurations can become effective.

Configuring Bindings and Network Access Order

Bindings and *network access order* specify which protocol or service Windows NT will use first when it attempts to connect to another computer.

Bindings and network access order don't have much effect on the speed of performance of the Server service on Windows NT. (The Server service is normally installed by default.) The Server service's performance is not affected because the Server service replies to the client computer that contacted it by using the same protocol the client computer used. For example, if a client computer uses NetBEUI to contact a server, the server will reply by using NetBEUI, even if TCP/IP is the server's first bound protocol.

Bindings and network access order can be very important to the performance of the Workstation service on Windows NT. (The Workstation service is also normally installed by default.) The Workstation service's performance can be affected because the Workstation service will try each of the protocols installed, in the order they are bound, when attempting to connect to another computer. For this reason, *if a Windows NT computer is primarily used as a client computer, you should configure the protocols and services that are used most often to be at the top of the bindings and network access order lists*.

Figure 3-12 illustrates the network bindings order on a computer. Notice that the WINS Client (TCP/IP) is the first protocol listed for the Workstation service, and that NWLink NetBIOS is listed second.

Assume that most of the servers you want to connect to from this computer use NWLink NetBIOS. If this is the case, you should move NWLink NetBIOS to the top of the Workstation bindings list. To do this, start the Network application in Control Panel. Select the Bindings tab in the Network dialog box, and then highlight the NWLink NetBIOS Workstation binding, and click the Move Up command button. Click OK to complete the configuration. Windows NT will prompt you to reboot your computer.

The result of this configuration change is shown in Figure 3-13. Notice that NWLink NetBIOS is now the first protocol listed for the Workstation service. Making this configuration change will improve the performance of the Workstation service on this client computer.

FIGURE 3-12 Bindings order on a
Windows NT computer

FIGURE 3-13 Modified Workstation bindings
order on a Windows NT computer

Occasionally you may want to disable network services on one or more network adapters in your server. For example, if you have a server that has two network adapters, one of which is connected to your local network, and the other is connected to the Internet, you might want to disable the Server service on the network adapter that is connected to the Internet so that users on the Internet can't connect network drives to your server. To disable a network binding, start the Network application in Control Panel, select the Bindings tab, highlight the protocol or service on which you want to disable the bindings, and click the Disable command button.

When configuring bindings, the primary emphasis is on ordering protocols. When configuring network access order, the primary emphasis is on ordering network service providers, such as Microsoft Windows Network, or NetWare or Compatible Network. Figure 3-14 shows the network access order on a computer. Notice that Microsoft Windows Network is the first provider listed in the Network Providers list, and that NetWare or Compatible Network is listed second.

FIGURE 3-14   Network access order on a Windows NT computer

Assume that you use the computer that has the network access order shown in Figure 3-14 primarily to connect to NetWare servers. If this is the case, you should move NetWare or Compatible Network to the top of the Network Providers list. Making this configuration change will improve the performance of the Workstation service on this computer.

To configure network access order, start the Network application in Control Panel. Select the Services tab in the Network dialog box, and then click the Network Access Order command button. Configure the order of Network or Print Providers by highlighting a provider and clicking the Move Up or Move Down command buttons. Click OK. The Services tab in the Network dialog box reappears. Click OK to complete the configuration. Windows NT will prompt you to reboot your computer.

 note **The Network Access Order command button appears on the Services tab in the Network dialog box *only* if you have installed more than one network provider, such as Microsoft Windows Network, or NetWare or Compatible Network.**

Configuring Network Adapters

Occasionally you may need to configure a network adapter. For example, assume that you install an additional card (of any kind) in your computer. You might have to change the settings on your network adapter to resolve an interrupt or an I/O port address conflict between the existing network adapter and the newly installed card.

Configuring a network adapter in Windows NT is usually a two-step process. First, you must configure manually the hardware settings of the network adapter. This can include setting jumpers or switches, or using a manufacturer-supplied configuration program. Second, you must configure the network adapter driver settings used in Windows NT by using the Network application in the Control Panel.

note **Some PC card network adapters are configurable in a single-step process by using the Network application in Control Panel. It would be great if the two steps required to configure most other network adapters were combined into a single step in a future release of Windows NT that fully supports Plug and Play.**

To configure the driver settings for a network adapter, start the Network application in Control Panel. Select the Adapters tab in the Network dialog box. Highlight the adapter you want to configure, and click the Properties command button. An adapter setup dialog box appears. Figure 3-15 shows a setup dialog box for a 3Com Etherlink III network adapter. Notice that you can modify the I/O port address, interrupt, and transceiver type.

FIGURE 3-15 Configuring a network adapter

Make any necessary modifications to the settings in the dialog box. Click OK when you are finished. The Adapters tab in the Network dialog box reappears. Click OK to complete the configuration. Windows NT will prompt you to reboot the computer.

 The options in the adapter setup dialog box vary depending on the specific adapter you select. Some adapters are not configurable at all. For example, to configure the 3Com 3C590 PCI Ethernet adapter, you must boot to DOS and run 3Com's configuration program. There are no configuration options in Windows NT for this adapter.

MANAGING SERVICES

 The *Services* application is used to start and stop services, to configure the startup type of services, to view the status of a service, and to enable or disable a service within a hardware profile.

The startup types available in this application include automatic, manual, and disabled. If you choose automatic, Windows NT starts the service automati-

cally every time the computer is booted. If you choose manual, a user must start the service. If you select disabled, the service can't be started by a user.

 Use extreme caution when using the Services application. Changing the startup type or disabling a service, such as Server or Workstation, can render your computer unable to access (or provide) network resources.

 Lab 3.4, at the end of this chapter, includes step-by-step instructions for configuring the startup behavior of the Directory Replicator service.

MANAGING THE SERVER

 The *Server* application is used to view user sessions (including the resources that users are accessing), disconnect users from the computer, view the status of shared resources, configure directory replication, and configure administrative alerts.

Most of the functions within the Server application are fairly intuitive and straightforward, but directory replication deserves an in-depth discussion.

Configuring Directory Replication

Directory replication was designed to copy logon scripts from a central location (usually the primary domain controller [PDC]) to all domain controllers, thus enabling all users to execute their own logon scripts no matter which domain controller validates their logon. Directory replication is also used extensively by Microsoft Systems Management Server.

 Directory replication can also be used to replicate system policy. System policy is covered in depth in Chapter 10.

Replication involves copying all subfolders and their files from the source folder on the source server to the destination folder on all Windows NT computers on the network that are configured as replication destinations.

The source replication folder, by default, is `<winntroot>\system32\repl\export`, where `<winntroot>` is the Windows NT installation folder, which by default is `c:\winnt`. During installation, Windows NT creates a folder named `scripts` in the `export` folder. The `scripts` folder is the default source location for logon scripts.

 note **Logon scripts are batch files. All MS-DOS 5.0 (and earlier versions) batch commands can be used in logon scripts. Logon scripts are covered in more detail in Chapter 10.**

Only subfolders and their files in the `export` folder are replicated. Individual files within the `export` folder are *not* replicated. The `export` folder is shared as the administrative share `REPL$`. This share is not visible in a network browse list.

 concept link **More information on shares is available in Chapter 12.**

The destination replication folder, by default, is `<winntroot>\system32\repl\import`. The `<winntroot>\system32\repl\import\scripts` folder is shared as `NETLOGON`. All client computers look to the `NETLOGON` share on the domain controller that validates their logon for their logon scripts. The `NET LOGON` share is visible in a network browse list.

Replication is configured between source and destination computers. Because of its central location, the primary domain controller (PDC) is usually configured as the source export server, even though any Windows NT Server computer can be configured as the source export server. It seems obvious that the PDC is configured as the export server and that all backup domain controllers (BDCs) are configured as import servers. What is not so obvious is that the PDC should also be configured to import from its *own* `export` folder. In other words, the PDC should be configured to replicate to itself. If the PDC is not configured this way, users that are validated by the PDC won't be able to access their logon scripts.

exam preparation pointer **Configuring directory replication is a fairly complicated task. The key points you should memorize are listed below. After reading the following steps, I recommend you immediately complete Lab 3.4 at the end of this chapter. (Lab 3.4 contains detailed, step-by-step instructions for configuring directory replication.) Then, come back to this section and review these key points.**

**TO CONFIGURE THE DIRECTORY REPLICATOR SERVICE,
FOLLOW THESE STEPS:**

1. Create and configure a user account for the Directory Replicator service by using User Manager for Domains. This user account must be a member of the Backup Operators group and the Replicator group. In addition, this user account must be granted the "Log on as a service" user right, and must be configured so that its password never expires. Figure 3-16 shows the replication user account being configured in User Manager for Domains. Notice that the user account (Repluser) is a member of the Backup Operators and Replicator groups, as well as the Domain Users group.

 note Windows NT Server 4.0 has a fairly significant bug that requires that the user account used by the Directory Replicator service be a member of the Administrators group (in addition to the Backup Operators and Replicator groups) when configuring directory replication between servers. This is not required when configuring directory replication on a single server from its own `export` folder to its own `import` folder.

FIGURE 3-16   Configuring the replication user account

2. Configure the startup type of the Directory Replicator service as Automatic, and configure the Directory Replicator service to log on using the user account created in Step 1. (Use the Services application in Control Panel to accomplish this.) Figure 3-17 shows the configuration of the

Directory Replicator service on a PDC. Note that the startup type is configured as Automatic, and that the Directory Replicator service is configured to log on as the Repluser account.

FIGURE 3-17   Configuring the Directory Replicator service

3. Configure replication by using the Server application in Control Panel. Figure 3-18 shows a PDC configured for replication. Notice that the PDC (named PDCLAB) is configured to export to all computers in the LAB domain, and that the PDC is configured to import from its own `export` folder.

FIGURE 3-18   Configuring replication on a PDC

4. Stop and restart the Directory Replicator service by using the Services application in Control Panel.

MANAGING THE SYSTEM

 The *System* application is used to configure foreground application performance, virtual memory, system and user environment variables, startup and shutdown behavior, hardware profiles, and user profiles. Each of these topics is discussed in the following sections.

Application Performance and Virtual Memory

You can use the System application to set the performance boost for the foreground application and to configure your virtual memory paging file(s).

Application performance

Foreground application performance involves giving a higher priority to the application running in the foreground than to other applications. The purpose of assigning a higher priority is to make the foreground application more responsive to the user.

To configure the foreground application priority, double-click the System icon in the Control Panel, and select the Performance tab. Adjust the slide bar for the amount of performance boost you want.

Virtual memory

Virtual memory is implemented in Windows NT by the use of paging files.

concept link
Virtual memory and paging files are discussed in detail, as you may recall, in the "NT Memory Model" section of Chapter 1.

You should consider both performance and recoverability when configuring virtual memory paging files.

If you want to configure your system for maximum paging file performance, you should put a small paging file on each physical disk, except on the disk that contains the Windows NT boot partition. This will provide the highest performance for virtual memory.

If you want to configure your system for optimum system recovery, you must put a paging file on the Windows NT boot partition that is at least as large as the amount of RAM in your computer. This paging file is used by Windows NT as a normal paging file, and, additionally, this paging file is required to enable Windows NT to write a `memory.dmp` file when the operating system crashes.

It's up to you to consider the tradeoffs between performance and recoverability, and then to determine the best configuration for your paging files.

You can configure virtual memory paging files by using the System application. On the Performance tab, click the Change command button in the Virtual Memory section. Then configure paging files on each drive as desired.

Environment Variables

You can use the System application to configure *system* and *user environment variables*. System environment variables apply to all users and to the operating system. User environment variables apply only to a specific user.

To modify a system environment variable, you must be logged on as a user that is a member of the Administrators local group. To modify a user environment variable, you must be logged on as the user whose variable you want to modify.

To configure system and user environment variables, start the System application from the Control Panel, and then select the Environment tab. Highlight the variable you want to modify in the appropriate list box (System or User), edit the value of this variable in the Value text box near the bottom of the dialog box, and then click the Set command button.

To add a new system or user environment variable, highlight any variable in the appropriate list box (System or User), and then type in a new variable name and value in the Variable and Value text boxes near the bottom of the dialog box. Then click the Set command button to create the new variable.

Figure 3-19 shows the layout of the Environment tab within the System application. Notice that the Variable and Value text boxes are located near the bottom of the dialog box.

Startup/Shutdown

You can use the System application to configure startup and shutdown behavior of Windows NT. Figure 3-20 illustrates the Startup/Shutdown tab within the System application. Notice the System Startup and Recovery options that can be configured.

FIGURE 3-19   Configuring system and user
environment variables

FIGURE 3-20   Configuring system startup
and recovery

In the System Startup section of the Startup/Shutdown tab you can configure which operating system will boot by default if no other selection is made from the boot loader menu. You can also configure the length of time the boot loader menu is displayed.

In the Recovery section of the Startup/Shutdown tab you can configure the actions Windows NT takes when a STOP error occurs. A STOP error is an error from which Windows NT cannot recover (in other words, a system crash).

The two most important options you can configure in the Recovery section are the "Write debugging information to" check box and the "Automatically reboot" check box.

The "Write debugging information to" option specifies a file that Windows NT writes the contents of RAM to in the event of a system crash. Remember that Windows NT requires a paging file that is at least as large as the amount of physical RAM on its boot partition in order to create the memory.dmp file.

in the real world

In the unlikely event you experience recurrent system crashes, the memory.dmp **file will be needed when you contact Microsoft Technical Support. Microsoft Technical Support personnel can use a debugger on your** memory.dmp **file to identify and resolve the cause of your system crashes.**

The "Automatically reboot" option, when selected, causes Windows NT to reboot the computer in the event of a system crash. If you select the "Automatically reboot" option, you should also select the "Write an event to the system log" option, so that you will be able to tell, when you view the system log, that the system has crashed and rebooted.

Hardware Profiles

You can use the System application to create and configure *hardware profiles*. Windows NT creates an initial hardware profile during installation.

The primary reason for creating hardware profiles is to manage the different hardware configurations of laptop computers. (A laptop computer that is used at the office in a docking station has a different hardware configuration than the same laptop computer when it is used at home or on the road without a docking station.) Hardware profiles make it possible to create custom configurations for the same laptop computer that is used both with and without a docking station.

Figure 3-21 shows the Hardware Profiles tab within the System application. Note that you can use the arrows on the right hand side to move profiles up or down in the Available Hardware Profiles list box. Windows NT uses the first profile in this list when no other selection is made during the boot process.

FIGURE 3-21 **Managing hardware profiles**

To create a new hardware profile, start the System application from Control Panel, and select the Hardware Profiles tab. Highlight any profile in the Available Hardware Profiles list box, and click the Copy command button. A Copy Profile dialog appears, permitting you to type in a name for your new hardware profile. The new hardware profile now has the same properties as the profile you highlighted and copied. You can configure this new profile as necessary.

To configure a new or existing hardware profile, highlight the profile in the Available Hardware Profiles list box and click the Properties command button. Then select the docking status for this hardware profile, and specify whether this is a network disabled profile. (A network disabled profile prevents any network services from starting on a computer.)

You can also use the Services and Devices applications to enable and disable services and device drivers within each hardware profile.

Once you have created multiple profiles, Windows NT displays the Hardware Profile/Configuration Recovery menu after the boot loader menu when your computer boots to Windows NT. This menu permits you to select the hardware profile you want Windows NT to use. You can configure the length of time this menu is displayed in the Multiple Hardware Profiles section on the Hardware Profiles tab.

User Profiles

You can use the User Profiles tab within the System application to copy, delete, and change the type of user profiles. The System application is the only application in Windows NT that can copy user profiles. You can't copy user profiles by using Windows NT Explorer.

 concept link   **User profiles are covered in depth in Chapter 10.**

OTHER CONTROL PANEL APPLICATIONS

Control Panel has several other applications. These applications are all fairly straightforward to use. Each application is briefly discussed in the following sections.

Add/Remove Programs

 The *Add/Remove Programs* application is used to install and remove third-party software and to add and remove Windows NT optional components.

Console

 The *Console* application is used to configure how MS-DOS windows appear in Windows NT. You can customize the cursor size, display options (such as window and full screen), font size and type, number of columns and rows, and colors used in each MS-DOS window.

Date/Time

 The *Date/Time* application is used to configure the date, time, time zone, and optional adjustment for daylight saving time.

You can also access the Date/Time application by double-clicking the clock in the right-hand corner of the taskbar on your desktop.

Fonts

 The *Fonts* application is used to install, delete, and manage fonts.

Internet

 The *Internet* application is used to configure whether a proxy server (such as Microsoft Proxy Server) is used when you use applications (such as Microsoft Internet Explorer, FTP.exe, and so on) to access the Internet.

ODBC

 The *ODBC* application is used to install and remove ODBC drivers. In addition, this application enables you to configure ODBC data sources.

ODBC-enabled applications (such as Microsoft Excel) can use the installed ODBC drivers to connect to data sources (such as Microsoft SQL Server and Microsoft Access).

Regional Settings

 The *Regional Settings* application is used to configure how certain objects, such as numbers, currency, date, and time are displayed in applications.

You can also use this application to configure your keyboard layout.

Sounds

 The *Sounds* application is used to assign sounds to system events. Some of the Windows NT system events that sounds can be assigned to are exit Windows, new mail notification, empty recycle bin, and many more.

Windows NT supports various sound schemes, including Jungle, Musica, Robotz, and Utopia. You can record new sounds and assign them to the system event you desire. You can also use the Sounds application to select the No Sounds sound scheme if you don't want sounds.

Telephony

The *Telephony* application is used to configure dialing properties for your computer, such as the area code you are calling from, the country you are in, special instructions on how to access an outside line, whether or not to dial using a calling card, instructions on how to disable call waiting, and to specify tone or pulse dialing. In addition, you can use this application to install, configure, and remove telephony drivers.

TROUBLESHOOTING COMMON CONFIGURATION PROBLEMS

Configuration problems are common and usually arise in three major areas: hardware, directory replication, and protocols. Troubleshooting configuration problems can be difficult, because it's easy to overlook a simple configuration issue, and to look instead for some complicated (and usually nonexistent) cause.

Some of the most common hardware configuration problems occur when two cards installed in the same computer are configured to use the same interrupt, I/O port address, or DMA address. To resolve this type of problem, you must reconfigure one of the cards to use a nonconflicting setting.

Another common hardware configuration problem occurs when a card is physically configured in one way (via switches or jumpers), and the software driver for that card is configured with different settings. To resolve this type of problem, you must either change the hardware settings or the software driver settings so that both use the same settings.

in the real world

Most of the troubleshooting problems I have seen were caused by omitting a step in a configuration process or setting configuration options incorrectly. The successful troubleshooter looks first to make sure that all steps in a configuration process have been completed and to verify that all configuration options are set correctly.

Directory replication is fairly straightforward to troubleshoot. Verify that each step necessary to configure replication has been properly completed. Ensure that the replication user account is a member of the Backup Operators and Replicator groups, has the "Log on as a service" user right, and is configured so that its password never expires. Make sure the Directory Replicator service is configured to start automatically, and that it is configured to log on by using the replication user account. Verify the password for the replication user account, and ensure that this password is being used by the Directory Replicator service. Verify that the source and destination servers are configured for replication. Finally, make sure to stop and restart the Directory Replicator service on all replication servers.

Troubleshooting protocols can be a detailed, painstaking task.

TCP/IP, for example, is easy to configure improperly. Several settings must be typed on each computer that uses this protocol, including IP address, subnet mask, and default gateway. The best way to prevent configuration problems in a TCP/IP environment is to use a DHCP server to configure TCP/IP automatically on each computer on the network. If you don't use DHCP, you should manually verify that the settings are correctly entered on each computer that experiences a network communications problem.

NWLink IPX/SPX Compatible Transport also has several configuration settings, and thus is prone to human error during protocol configuration. Verify that all of the settings for this (and every) protocol are correctly entered on each computer that experiences a network communications problem.

KEY POINT SUMMARY

This chapter introduced Control Panel and its numerous applications.

- Many Control Panel applications are used when managing peripherals and devices, including Accessibility Options, Devices, Display, Keyboard, Modems, Mouse, Multimedia, PC Card (PCMCIA), Ports, Printers, SCSI Adapters, Tape Devices, and UPS.

- The *Licensing* application permits you to change your Windows NT Server licensing mode or to reflect a change in the number of client licenses you have purchased.

- The *Network* application is used to change a computer/domain/workgroup name, to join a domain, to install and configure protocols and services, to configure bindings and network access order, and to configure network adapters. Remember that you can't change a domain controller's domain membership just by changing its domain name.

- The *protocols* and *services* that ship with Windows NT Server are identified and described. Of all the protocols listed, TCP/IP is often the protocol of choice for use in a large, heterogeneous network environment because of its routability, speed, and support by numerous operating systems. When planning a Windows NT installation, you should include all of the protocols and services needed to support every type of client computer that is likely to access the server, keeping in mind that you may need to limit the number of protocols and services used to reduce network traffic.

- To improve the performance of the Workstation service, *bindings* and *network access order* should be configured so that the protocol and service that are used most often are listed at the top of their respective lists.

- The *Services* application is used to start and stop services, to configure the startup type of services, to view the status of a service, and to enable or disable a service within a hardware profile.

- The *Server* application is used to view user sessions, disconnect users from the computer, view the status of shared resources, configure directory replication, and configure administrative alerts.

- *Directory replication*, which was designed to copy logon scripts from a central location to all domain controllers, involves copying folders and their files from a source folder on a source server to a destination folder on all Windows NT computers on the network that are configured as replication destinations. Follow these steps to configure the *Directory Replicator service*:

1. Create and configure a user account for the Directory Replicator service using User Manager for Domains. This account must be a member of the Backup Operators group and the Replicator group. This user account must also be granted the "Log on as a service" user right, and must be configured so that its password never expires.

2. Configure the startup type of the Directory Replicator service as Automatic (using the Services application). Configure the Directory Replicator service to log on using the user account created in Step 1.

3. Configure replication by using the Server application. Remember that the PDC should be configured to replicate to itself.

4. Stop and restart the Directory Replicator service by using the

Services application.

- The *System* application is used to configure foreground application performance, virtual memory (paging files), system and user environment variables, startup and shutdown behavior, hardware profiles, and user profiles.
  - Consider both performance and recoverability when configuring paging files.
  - When configuring startup/shutdown behavior, consider selecting the "Write debugging to" and "Automatically reboot" options, so that Windows NT will write the contents of RAM to a `memory.dmp` file (as long as it has a paging file that is at least as large as the amount of RAM on its boot partition) and so that NT will automatically reboot in the event of a system crash.
  - The primary reason for creating hardware profiles is to manage the different hardware configurations of laptop computers.
  - The System application is the only application in Windows NT that can copy user profiles.
- Other applications in Control Panel are briefly described, including *Add/Remove Programs, Console, Date/Time, Fonts, Internet, ODBC, Regional Settings, Sounds*, and *Telephony*.
- Some tips on troubleshooting common configuration problems are presented. Configuration problems normally arise in three major areas: hardware, directory replication, and protocols. When you troubleshoot, make sure that all steps in a configuration process have been completed and verify that all configuration options are set correctly. Also, verify that hardware devices do not have conflicting interrupt, I/O port addresses, or DMA addresses.

APPLYING WHAT YOU'VE LEARNED

Now it's time to regroup, review, and apply what you've learned in this chapter.

The questions in the following Instant Assessment section bring to mind key facts and concepts. In addition, the Critical Thinking Lab tests your knowledge of specific Control Panel applications. Finally, the Hands-on Labs reinforce what you've learned and provide you with an opportunity to practice several of the tasks tested by the Windows NT Server exam.

Instant Assessment

1. What three ways can you access Control Panel?

2. What is the Accessibility Options application used for?

3. Which Control Panel application is used to configure a computer's desktop background, screen saver options, desktop appearance, and Microsoft Plus! options?

4. If you change the domain name of one domain controller in a domain, what else must you do?

5. Which of the protocols that ship with Windows NT Server is a routable protocol usually associated with NetWare networks?

6. Which protocol is automatically installed when Services for Macintosh is installed on a Windows NT Server computer?

7. Which of the protocols that ship with Windows NT Server is a fast, routable enterprise protocol that is used on the Internet and is supported by many operating systems, including Windows NT, Windows 95, Macintosh, UNIX, MS-DOS, and IBM mainframes?

8. When configuring bindings and network access order, where should the protocol and service that are used most often be placed (ordered) on their respective lists to achieve the best Workstation service performance?

9. What are the four tasks that must be accomplished to configure the Directory Replicator service?

10. If you want to configure your Windows NT computer for optimum system recovery, how large must the paging file on your Windows NT boot partition be?

11. What is the only Windows NT application that you can use to copy user profiles?

12. You are troubleshooting what you believe is a configuration problem. What actions should you take?

T/F

13. You can't change a domain controller's domain membership by changing its name. _____

concept link **For answers to the Instant Assessment questions see Appendix B.**

Critical Thinking Lab

The following lab tests your knowledge of when to use specific Control Panel applications.

Lab 3.3 *Control Panel application matching exercise*

Do you know which Control Panel application you should use to perform various tasks? Match the letter of the Control Panel application from the list on the left that you should use to perform each task listed on the right. Applications may be used more than once.

Control Panel Application

A. Accessibility Options

B. Add/Remove Programs

C. Console

D. Date/Time

E. Devices

F. Display

G. Fonts

H. Internet

I. Keyboard

J. Licensing

K. Modems

L. Mouse

M. Multimedia

N. Network

O. ODBC

P. PC Card (PCMCIA)

Task

1. _____ You want to install the Windows NT games on your Windows NT computer.

2. _____ You want to change the screen saver settings on your Windows NT computer.

3. _____ You want to change your Windows NT Server licensing mode.

4. _____ You want to change your keyboard layout to a US-Dvorak layout.

5. _____ You want to change the computer name of a domain controller.

6. _____ You want to install the TCP/IP Protocol on your Windows NT computer.

7. _____ You want to configure bindings and network access order on your Windows NT computer.

Control Panel Application	Task
Q. Ports	8. _____ You want to stop and start the Directory Replicator service.
R. Printers	
S. Regional Settings	9. _____ You want to configure the replication import and export options on your Windows NT computer.
T. SCSI Adapters	
U. Server	
V. Services	10. _____ You want to copy a user profile.
W. Sounds	11. _____ You want to create a new hardware profile on your Windows NT computer.
X. System	
Y. Tape Devices	
Z. Telephony	12. _____ You want to configure a paging file on your Windows NT computer.
Z. UPS	

 concept link   **For answers to the Critical Thinking Lab see Appendix B.**

Hands-on Labs

The following Hands-on Labs provide excellent opportunities to explore and use the Control Panel applications you've learned about in this chapter.

Lab 3.4 *Configuring directory replication*

The purpose of this lab is to provide you with hands-on experience and the skills needed to configure and use the Directory Replicator service.

There are seven parts to this lab:

Part 1: Creating a logon script

Part 2: Creating a directory replication user account

Part 3: Configuring the startup type of the Directory Replicator service

Part 4: Configuring replication

Part 5: Stopping and restarting the Directory Replicator service

Part 6: Viewing the replication of the logon script

Part 7: Testing your logon script

Follow the ensuing steps carefully.

Part 1: Creating a logon script

1. Boot your computer to Windows NT Server. Log on Administrator. (Remember the password? It's *password*.) If the Welcome to NT dialog box appears, close it.

2. Select Start ⇒ Programs ⇒ Accessories ⇒ Notepad.

3. In the Untitled — Notepad dialog box, type the following:

@echo This is the logon script I created in Lab 3.4.

@echo

@echo

@pause

(Note: Make sure to type the text *exactly* as it is presented above.)

4. Select File ⇒ Save As. Edit the "File name" text box to read as follows:

c:\winntsrv\system32\repl\export\scripts\logonscript.bat

5. Click Save.

6. Exit Notepad.

Part 2: Creating a directory replication user account

1. Select Start ⇒ Programs ⇒ Administrative Tools (Common) ⇒ User Manager for Domains.

2. Select User ⇒ New User in the User Manager dialog box.

3. In the New User dialog box, type in the username **Repluser**. Type in a password of **password** (remember that passwords are case-sensitive in Windows NT). Confirm the password by retyping it in the Confirm Password box. Deselect the check box next to User Must Change Password at Next Logon. Select the check box next to Password Never Expires. Click the Groups command button at the lower left-hand corner of the dialog box.

4. The Group Memberships dialog box appears. In the "Not member of" text box, highlight Backup Operators and click the Add command button. In the "Not member of" text box, highlight Replicator and click the Add command button. There should be three groups listed in the "Member of" text box: Backup Operators, Domain Users, and Replicator. Click OK.

5. The New User dialog box reappears. Click Add. Then click Close.

6. The User Manager dialog box reappears. Exit User Manager.

Part 3: Configuring the startup type of the Directory Replicator service

1. Select Start ⇒ Settings ⇒ Control Panel.

2. Double-click Services.

3. The Services dialog box appears. Highlight Directory Replicator. Click Startup.

4. The Service dialog box appears. In the Startup Type section, select the Automatic option button. In the Log On As section, select the This Account option button. Click the . . . command button at the end of the This Account text box.

5. The Add User dialog box appears. In the Names list box, highlight Repluser, and click Add. Click OK.

6. The Service dialog box reappears. Highlight the asterisks in the Password text box and type **password**. In the Confirm Password text box, highlight the asterisks and type **password**. Click OK.

7. A Services dialog box appears indicating that the account LAB\Repluser has been granted the Log On As A Service right. Click OK.

8. The Services dialog box reappears. Click Close. The Control Panel dialog box reappears.

Part 4: Configuring replication

1. In Control Panel, double-click Server.

2. In the Server dialog box, click Replication.

3. The Directory Replication dialog box appears. Click the Export Directories option button. Click the Add command button at the bottom of the Export Directories section.

4. The Select Domain dialog box appears. In the Select Domain list box, click LAB. LAB should now appear in the Domain text box. Click OK.

5. The Directory Replication dialog box reappears. LAB should appear in the To List box. Click the Import Directories option button. Click the Add command button at the bottom of the Import Directories section.

6. The Select Domain dialog box appears. In the Select Domain list box, double-click LAB. Click PDCLAB. \\PDCLAB should now appear in the Domain text box. Click OK.

7. The Directory Replication dialog box reappears. PDCLAB should appear in the From list box. Click OK to save the directory replication configuration and automatically start the Directory Replicator service.

8. In the Server dialog box, click OK. The Control Panel dialog box reappears.

Part 5: Stopping and restarting the Directory Replicator service

1. In Control Panel, double-click Services.

2. The Services dialog box appears. In the Service list box, highlight Directory Replicator. Click Stop. A warning message appears, asking if you want to stop the Directory Replicator service. Click Yes.

3. A Service Control dialog box appears, indicating that NT is attempting to stop the Directory Replicator service.

4. The Services dialog box reappears. Note that the Status column no longer shows "Started" for the Directory Replicator service. Click Start.

5. A Service Control dialog box appears, indicating that NT is attempting to start the Directory Replicator service.

6. The Services dialog box reappears. Note that the Status column now shows "Started" for the Directory Replicator service. Click Close.

7. The Control Panel dialog box reappears. Exit Control Panel.

Part 6: Viewing the replication of the logon script

1. Select Start ⇒ Programs ⇒ Windows NT Explorer.

2. Maximize the Exploring dialog box. In the All Folders column on the left, click the + sign next to the `Winntsrv` folder. Then click the + sign next to the `system32` folder. Click the + sign next to the `Repl` folder. Click the + sign next to the `Export` folder. Click the `Scripts` folder. Notice that the `logonscript.bat` file you created in the first part of this lab appears in the Contents of 'Scripts' list box. (Remember that you saved this file in the `c:\winntsrv\system32\repl\export\scripts` folder in the first part of this lab.)

3. Click the + sign next to the `Import` folder (in the All Folders column on the left). Click the `Scripts` folder beneath the `Import` folder. After a few moments, notice, in the Contents of 'Scripts' list box, that the `logonscript.bat` file has been replicated from the `Export\Scripts` folder to the `Import\Scripts` folder. The Directory Replicator service is now fully functional. Exit Windows NT Explorer.

note Normally, directory replication occurs almost immediately. Occasionally, however, it may take up to several hours before directory replication occurs, even though your configuration of directory replication is correct.

Part 7: Testing your logon script

1. Select Start ⇒ Programs ⇒ Administrative Tools (Common) ⇒ User Manager for Domains.

2. In the User Manager dialog box, select User ⇒ Properties.

3. The User Properties dialog box appears. Click the Profile command button.

4. The User Environment Profile dialog box appears. In the Logon Script Name text box, type **logonscript.bat**. (Don't type the period at the end.) Click OK.

5. The User Properties dialog box reappears. Click OK.

6. Close User Manager.

7. Select Start ⇒ Shut Down. The Shut Down Windows dialog box appears. Click the "Close all programs and log on as a different user" option button. Then click Yes.

8. In the Begin Logon dialog box, press Ctrl + Alt + Delete to log on.

9. The Logon Information dialog box appears. Log on as Administrator. Click OK.

10. A command prompt window should appear. The logon script you created in Part 1 of this lab has run and appears like the following:

```
This is the logon script I created in Lab 3.4.

    ECHO is on.
    ECHO is on.
```

Press any key to continue . . .

11. Click anywhere inside the command prompt window. Press the spacebar to complete this lab.

 tip This logon script will appear every time you log on from this point. If you'd like to remove it, start User Manager for Domains, and then double-click the Administrator user. Click Profile. Highlight `logon-script.bat` in the User Environment Profile dialog box, and press Delete. Click OK. In the User Properties dialog box, click OK. Exit User Manager for Domains.

Lab 3.5 *Exploring Control Panel*

The purpose of this lab is to provide you with the skills required to use Control Panel applications.

This lab is divided into three parts. You'll use the following Control Panel applications in the following three sections:

Part 1: Using Add/Remove Programs

Part 2: Using System

Part 3: Becoming familiar with Display, Keyboard, Modems, Mouse, Ports, SCSI Adapters, Tape Devices, and UPS

Begin this lab by booting your computer to Windows NT Server. Log on as Administrator.

If the Welcome to NT dialog box appears, close it. (Hint: if you never want to see this dialog box again, before you close the dialog box, select the check box that will instruct Windows NT to *not* display this dialog box in the future.)

Part 1: Using Add/Remove Programs

In this part you use Add/Remove Programs to install an optional Windows NT component.

TO INSTALL MAIL, FOLLOW THESE STEPS:

1. Select Start ⇒ Settings ⇒ Control Panel.

2. Double-click Add/Remove Programs.

3. In the Add/Remove Programs Properties dialog box, click the Windows NT Setup tab. Scroll to the bottom of the Components list box. Click in the check box next to Windows Messaging. Click the Details command button. Ensure that the Internet Mail, Microsoft Mail, and Windows Messaging check boxes are all selected. Click OK.

4. In the Windows NT Setup tab in the Add/Remove Programs Properties dialog box, click OK.

5. NT copies files to your hard disk. If prompted, supply the path to your Windows NT installation source files (usually on your Windows NT compact disc). This process takes a few minutes.

6. The Control Panel dialog box reappears. Windows Messaging (Mail) is now installed. Exit Control Panel.

7. Optional: If you want, you can install games on your computer using the same steps, except click the check box next to Games (instead of Windows Messaging) in the Windows NT Setup tab. (Try Pinball if you have a sound card — it's really fun!)

Part 2: Using System

In this part you use System to create an additional paging file and create a hardware profile.

TO CREATE AN ADDITIONAL PAGING FILE, FOLLOW THESE STEPS:

1. Select Start ⇒ Settings ⇒ Control Panel.

2. Double-click System.

3. Click the Performance tab in the System Properties dialog box. In the Virtual Memory section, click Change.

4. The Virtual Memory dialog box appears. Click D: in the Drive list box. In the Paging File Size for Selected Drive section, type **5** in the Initial Size (MB) text box, and type **5** in the Maximum Size (MB) text box. Click Set. Notice that Drive D: now shows a Paging File Size of 5-5 in the list box at the top of the screen. Click OK.

5. On the Performance tab click Close.

6. Click Yes to restart your computer so the new settings can take effect.

TO CREATE A HARDWARE PROFILE, FOLLOW THESE STEPS:

Hardware profiles were originally designed to handle the unique needs of laptop computers. In this lab you create two hardware profiles: docked (connected to the network) and undocked (not connected to the network) to simulate the use of a laptop computer at work and at home.

1. When your computer reboots, log on as Administrator.

2. The Control Panel dialog box appears. Double-click System.

3. Click the Hardware Profiles tab. Highlight Original Configuration (Current) in the Available Hardware Profiles list box. Click the Rename command button.

4. In the Rename Profile dialog box, edit the To: text box to read as follows: **Docked**. (Don't type the period at the end.) Click OK.

5. The Hardware Profiles tab reappears. Highlight Docked (Current) in the Available Hardware Profiles list box. Click Copy.

6. In the Copy Profile dialog box, edit the To: text box to read as follows: **UnDocked**. (Don't type the period at the end.) Click OK.

7. The Hardware Profiles tab reappears. Notice that two profiles now appear in the Available Hardware Profiles list box: Docked (Current) and UnDocked. Highlight UnDocked and click the Properties command button.

8. In the UnDocked Properties dialog box, click the Network tab. Click the check box next to Network-disabled hardware profile. Click OK.

9. The Hardware Profiles tab reappears. Click OK. Exit Control Panel.

10. Select Start ⇒ Shut Down. Click the "Restart the computer" option button in the Shut Down Windows dialog box. Click Yes.

11. After you select Windows NT Server 4.0 from the boot loader menu, press the spacebar when the "Press spacebar now to invoke the Hardware Profile/Last Known Good menu" appears.

12. A Hardware Profile/Configuration Recovery Menu is displayed. You can select a Docked or UnDocked hardware profile at this point. (Select Docked if you are connected to a network; select UnDocked if you are not connected to a network.) Press Enter to continue booting Windows NT Server. Log on as Administrator.

Part 3: Becoming familiar with Display, Keyboard, Modems, Mouse, Ports, SCSI Adapters, Tape Devices, and UPS

In this part you explore several Control Panel applications. (You may even use a few of these applications to install devices that you have but which may not yet be installed.)

DISPLAY

1. Select Start ⇒ Settings ⇒ Control Panel.

2. Double-click Display.

3. In the Display Properties dialog box, click the Screen Saver tab.

4. In the Screen Saver drop-down list box, select 3D Pipes (OpenGL). Click the Settings command button.

5. In the 3D Pipes Setup dialog box, click the Textured option button in the Surface Style section. Click the Choose Texture command button.

6. In the Choose Texture File dialog box, double-click `lanmannt.bmp`.

7. The 3D Pipes Setup dialog box reappears. Click OK.

8. The Screen Saver tab reappears. Click Apply. (Your screen saver now consists of 3D Pipes that say "Windows NT Server" on them.)

9. Click the Settings tab. In the Desktop Area section, click and hold the slide bar and move it to the right until the display reads "800 by 600 pixels." (Note: If your computer does not support a display setting larger than "640 by 480 pixels", you can click the slide bar, but it won't move.) Continue to Step 10.

10. Click the Test command button. Click OK in the Testing Mode dialog box.

11. A test screen appears for about five seconds. When the Testing Mode dialog box appears, click Yes if you saw the test bitmap.

12. The Settings tab reappears. Click OK to apply your new display settings.

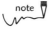 note

If you do not like the appearance of an 800 by 600 display, or your computer can't accommodate this setting, you can change your display settings to any resolution you desire. Follow Steps 9 through 12 to change your display settings.

KEYBOARD

1. The Control Panel dialog box reappears.

2. Double-click Keyboard.

3. In the Keyboard Properties dialog box, click the Input Locales tab. Click the Properties command button. Click the drop-down arrow in the Keyboard layout drop-down list box to view the optional keyboard layouts. Notice that US, several Dvorak options, and US-International are listed. Click US, and then click OK.

4. In the Input Locales tab in the Keyboard Properties dialog box, click Cancel.

MODEMS

You don't have to have a modem to complete this section. If you have already installed a modem in your computer using the Modems application in Control Panel, skip this section.

1. The Control Panel dialog box reappears.

2. Double-click Modems.

3. The Install New Modem dialog box appears. Select the check box next to "Don't detect my modem; I will select it from a list." Click the Next command button.

4. The Install Modem dialog box appears. Select your modem's manufacturer from the Manufacturers list box. If your manufacturer is not listed, or if you don't have a modem, highlight (Standard Modem Types). Select your modem speed or model in the Models list box, or select Dial-Up Networking Serial Cable between 2 PCs if you don't have a modem. Then click Next.

5. The Install New Modem dialog box appears. Click the "Selected ports" option button.

6. Highlight the COM port to which your modem is connected, or any available COM port (to which your mouse or another device isn't connected) if you don't have a modem. Click Next. Windows NT installs your modem.

7. A dialog box may appear at this point requesting the area code you are in and other information. If this box appears, enter the requested information and continue. If a dialog box does not appear, skip to Step 8.

8. Click the Finish command button.

9. In the Modems Properties dialog box, click the Dialing Properties command button.

10. In the Dialing Properties dialog box, configure the dialing properties for your location. Then click OK.

11. In the Modems Properties dialog box, click Close.

MOUSE

1. The Control Panel dialog box reappears.

2. Double-click Mouse.

3. In the Mouse Properties dialog box, click each tab and view the configuration options available. Customize your mouse to suit your personal preferences. Click OK to return to Control Panel.

PORTS

1. The Control Panel dialog box reappears.

2. Double-click Ports.

3. In the Ports dialog box, highlight a COM port, and click Settings.

4. In the Settings dialog box, notice the settings that you can configure for your COM port. Customize your COM port settings as desired. Click Advanced.

5. In the Advanced Settings dialog box, notice the settings that you can configure. Click OK.

6. In the Settings dialog box, click OK.

7. In the Ports dialog box, click Close.

SCSI ADAPTERS

1. The Control Panel dialog box reappears.

2. Double-click SCSI Adapters.

3. View the configuration options available on both the Devices tab and the Drivers tab by clicking each of the tabs. If you have a SCSI adapter but have not yet installed drivers for it, you may want to do so now. You can do this by clicking the Add command button on the Drivers tab and then selecting the appropriate manufacturer and SCSI adapter from the lists displayed. Click OK.

TAPE DEVICES

1. The Control Panel dialog box reappears.

2. Double-click Tape Devices.

3. View the configuration options available on both the Devices tab and the Drivers tab by clicking each of the tabs. If you have a tape drive but have not yet installed drivers for it, you may want to do so now. You can do this by clicking the Add command button on the Drivers tab and then selecting the appropriate manufacturer and tape device from the lists displayed. Click OK.

UPS

1. The Control Panel dialog box reappears.

2. Double-click UPS.

3. In the UPS dialog box, view the configuration options available. Click Help.

4. Read through the UPS help topics. Exit Windows NT Help.

5. If you do not have a UPS, skip to Step 6 now. If you have a UPS but have not yet configured it, you may want to do so now. Configure the settings in the UPS dialog box to match your UPS. Click OK. Stop here if you have a UPS (don't do Step 6).

6. Click Cancel in the UPS dialog box. Exit Control Panel.

Browsing and the Computer Browser Service

About Chapter 4

Chapter 4 focuses on how to find and access available network resources.

First, this chapter takes an in-depth look at browsing. The various browser roles played by different computers on the network are explained, including domain master browser, master browser, backup browser, potential browser, and non-browser. Then the browsing process is outlined, including browser elections.

Next, Chapter 4 explains how to configure the Computer Browser service, the Windows NT service that manages browsing. Then, the chapter examines how browsing functions on various transport protocols, including NetBEUI, NWLink IPX/SPX Compatible Transport, and TCP/IP.

Finally, this chapter details how to connect to shared network resources using Windows NT Explorer and how to connect from the command line. Using UNC and FQDN naming conventions is explained.

This chapter includes a Hands-on Lab in which you configure the Windows NT Computer Browser service.

The information presented in this chapter maps to the "Configure Windows NT Server core services" objective in the Installation and Configuration section of the Preparation Guide for the Server exam.

Browsing

Browsing enables users to find out what shared resources are available on the network (including resources in other workgroups and other domains), and facilitates connecting to those resources.

Browsing is managed by the Computer Browser service. The Computer Browser service is installed automatically during the installation of Windows NT. The service is configured, by default, to start every time Windows NT is booted.

The Computer Browser service is responsible for the process of building a list of available network servers — a *browse list* — and for sharing that list with other computers. (Throughout this chapter, the term *network servers* includes all computers that either have shared resources or are capable of sharing their resources.) The Computer Browser service is designed so that not all computers on the network have to maintain a browse list. Certain computers are designated to maintain a browse list and to provide that list to other computers on the network when they request it. A browse list is displayed when a user attempts to connect a network drive, or views the Network Neighborhood in Windows NT Explorer.

The following sections discuss the roles that various computers play in the browsing process, the actual process of browsing for available network servers, configuring the Computer Browser service, and how browsing works on different transport protocols.

Browser Roles

To avoid overloading any one computer on the network, the task of maintaining a browse list is distributed among many computers. A hierarchy of browser computers has been established, and each computer plays a different role in this process. The *browser roles* that computers can perform are domain master browser, master browser, backup browser, potential browser, and non-browser.

Each Windows computer on the network can be designated to perform any of these roles, with the exception of the domain master browser, which is always a function of the *primary domain controller* (PDC) for a domain.

Because each computer on the network does not have to maintain a browse list, processor overhead and network traffic are reduced.

The role each computer performs in the browsing process is determined, in part, by how the computer is configured and, in part, by an election process. (Both configuring computers for browsing and the election process are covered later in this chapter.)

Here's a more in-depth look at the various browser roles.

Domain master browser

The *domain master browser* performs different functions, depending on whether the network consists of a single subnet or multiple subnets.

If the network has only one subnet, the domain master browser and master browser functions are combined and are performed by a single computer — the PDC. The PDC compiles the browse list of available network servers and makes this list available to the backup browsers.

If the network consists of multiple subnets, the domain master browser maintains a list of available network servers located on *all* subnets in the domain. The domain master browser acquires this information from the master browser on each subnet. The domain master browser makes this list available to the master browser on each subnet, which, in turn, makes the list available to the backup browsers.

There can be only *one* domain master browser in a domain, and it is always the PDC. If the PDC is down, no other computer can assume the role of the domain master browser. If there is no domain master browser, users are only able to browse network resources located on their local subnet.

Master browser

The *master browser* builds the browse list — the list of available network servers — on its own subnet. Then the master browser passes this list on to the domain master browser, and to the backup browsers on its own subnet.

If a domain spans several subnets, there is a master browser for each subnet.

If multiple workgroups or domains exist on the same subnet, each workgroup or domain has its own master browser for that subnet. (Workgroup browsing is limited to browsing on a single subnet — the master browser for a workgroup can't pass browse list information across a router.) Each workgroup or domain is limited to having only *one* master browser on a subnet.

Any Windows NT Server, Windows NT Workstation, Windows 95, or Windows for Workgroups computer can perform the role of the master browser. However, because the role of master browser requires additional overhead (including CPU time and memory usage), you might consider configuring a more powerful computer to serve as a master browser.

Backup browser

The *backup browser* receives the browse list from the master browser and then makes the browse list available to any computer that requests it.

All computers on the network, when they request a copy of the browse list, do so from a backup browser. There can be more than one backup browser on each subnet.

Any Windows NT Server, Windows NT Workstation, Windows 95, or Windows for Workgroups computer can perform the role of the backup browser.

Potential browser

A computer that does not currently maintain or distribute a browse list, but is capable of doing so, is called a *potential browser*. By default, all Windows NT Server, Windows NT Workstation, Windows 95, and Windows for Workgroups computers are potential browsers.

It is the job of the master browser on a subnet to promote a potential browser to a backup browser should the need arise. Additionally, if the master browser becomes unavailable, a potential browser can be elected to fill the role of the master browser.

Non-browser

A *non-browser* is a computer that is not capable of maintaining and distributing a browse list. This is either because the computer has been configured to not function as a browser, or the computer's network software does not provide the capability to maintain a browse list.

All MS-DOS and Windows 3.1 client computers are non-browsers. These computers can request a browse list, but can't maintain or distribute such a list.

Any Windows NT Server, Windows NT Workstation, Windows 95, or Windows for Workgroups computer can be configured to be a non-browser. (Configuring Windows NT computers for browsing is discussed later in this chapter.)

The Browsing Process

The Computer Browser service is responsible for managing the browsing process. Browsing can be thought of as two distinct activities: building and maintaining the browse list, and distributing the browse list to computers that request it. This section discusses what happens during each of these functions.

How a browse list is built and maintained

1. When a master browser first comes on line, its browse list is empty. To initially build its browse list, the master browser sends a broadcast to all computers on the subnet requesting that all network servers announce their presence. (Remember, for the purpose of discussing browsing in this chapter, network servers include all computers that either have shared resources or are capable of sharing their resources.)

2. All available network servers respond to this request by announcing their presence within 30 seconds. The master browser incorporates this information into its initial browse list. The master browser then distributes this browse list to the domain master browser and to the backup browsers.

3. After initial creation of the browse list, when a Windows computer that functions as a network server is first booted, it broadcasts its presence to the network. The master browser receives this announcement and places the information in its browse list.

4. During normal operations, a Windows computer that functions as a network server continues to announce its presence to the network every 12 minutes. If the master browser does *not* receive a broadcast from a network server after three consecutive 12-minute time periods, it removes the computer from its browse list.

   (This is how the master browser maintains its browse list — it assumes that all network servers in its initial browse list are available until it fails to receive a broadcast announcement from a computer for three consecutive 12-minute periods, at which time it updates its browse list by removing this computer from its list. Therefore, it is possible for a network server to remain on the browse list for some time after it is no longer available to network users.)

5. During normal operations, backup browsers request an updated browse list from the master browser every 12 minutes. If the master browser does not respond to an update request from the backup browser, the backup browser initiates the master browser election process (covered in more detail later in this chapter).

6. During normal operations, the master browser sends an updated browse list to the domain master browser every 12 minutes. The domain master browser, in response, sends an updated domain browse list to the master browser. Additionally, every 15 minutes, the master browser announces its presence to master browsers of other workgroups and domains located on the same subnet.

What happens when a user browses the network

1. When a user of a Windows NT computer attempts to access browse information by double-clicking Network Neighborhood or by selecting Tools ⇒ Map Network Drive in Windows NT Explorer, the user's computer contacts the master browser and retrieves a list of available backup browsers.

   (This step occurs only the first time a user accesses browse information — the Computer Browser service on the local computer then retains the list of available backup browsers until the computer is rebooted or until the backup browsers on the list are no longer available.)

2. The user's computer then contacts a backup browser to request a list of available network servers. The backup browser processes this request and returns a list of available network servers in the requesting computer's workgroup or domain, plus a list of available workgroups and domains. The user's computer then displays this information for the user.

3. If the user selects an available network server, the user's computer contacts the selected server and requests a list of shared network resources. The selected server then sends a list of shared resources to the requesting computer, which is then displayed for the user.

If the user selects an available workgroup or domain, the user's computer contacts the master browser for the selected workgroup or domain and requests a list of backup browsers. The master browser sends a list of backup browsers for the workgroup or domain to the requesting computer. Then the user's computer contacts a backup browser in the selected workgroup or domain for a list of available network servers, which is then sent by the backup browser to the requesting computer and displayed for the user. The user then selects an available network server, and the user's computer contacts the selected server and requests a list of shared network resources. The selected server then sends a list of shared resources to the requesting computer, which is displayed for the user.

4. The user selects the specific shared resource he or she wants to access from the list that is displayed.

Browser elections are an integral part of building and maintaining browse lists. The browser election process is discussed in the next section.

Browser elections

A *browser election*, which determines which computer will function as the master browser, takes place when

- The PDC is booted

- A backup browser is unable to obtain an updated browse list from the master browser

- A computer is unable to obtain a list of backup browsers from the master browser

When one of these events occurs, the computer experiencing the event initiates the browser election process by broadcasting an election packet.

An election packet contains the computer's election criteria value. A computer's election criteria value is based on the computer's operating system, version, and on the computer's current browser role (for example, master browser or backup browser). The more powerful the operating system, the higher its election criteria value. The election criteria value ranking of operating systems, from highest to lowest, is Windows NT Server, Windows NT Workstation, Windows 95, and Windows for Workgroups. Additionally, newer versions of an operating system have a higher election criteria value than older versions.

For example, Windows NT Server has a higher election criteria value than Windows NT Workstation, which has a higher election criteria value than Windows 95, which has a higher election criteria value than Windows for Workgroups.

Also, Windows NT Server version 4.0 has a higher election criteria value than Windows NT Server version 3.51, which has a higher election criteria value than Windows NT Server version 3.5.

The result of the browser election process is that the computer with the *highest* election criteria value "wins" the election and becomes the master browser.

When a computer initiates the election process by broadcasting an election packet, each browser computer on the subnet (that is, every computer except non-browsers) examines the packet and compares the election criteria value contained in the packet to its own election criteria value. If the computer that receives the packet has an *equal or lower* criteria value than the packet it receives, it takes no action. If the computer that receives the packet has a *higher* criteria value than the packet it receives, it broadcasts its own election packet. This process continues until no further election packets are broadcast. The last computer to send an election packet (the computer with the highest election criteria value) then declares itself as the new master browser.

 note **Only the master browser is elected. The domain master browser is always the PDC. If the PDC is unavailable, there is *no* domain master browser.**

Configuring the Computer Browser Service

By default, all Windows 95 and Windows for Workgroups computers are configured as potential browsers. All Windows NT Server and Windows NT Workstation computers that are *not* domain controllers are also configured as potential browsers by default. Additionally, by default, all Windows NT Server domain controllers are configured to maintain a browse list and to function as a backup or master browser. You can change the default setting for the Computer Browser service on a Windows NT computer, and thereby change the computer's default browser role.

The Computer Browser service on a Windows NT computer is controlled by the following Registry entries in `\HKEY_LOCAL_MACHINE\SYSTEM\Current ControlSet\Services\Browser\Parameters`:

\MaintainServerList

\IsDomainMaster

The MaintainServerList Registry entry, which specifies whether a computer will maintain a browse list, can be configured with one of the following values:

o No — When this configuration is used, the computer functions as a non-browser.

o Yes — When this configuration is used, the computer maintains a browse list and will function either as a backup browser or a master browser. This is the default setting for all Windows NT Server domain controllers.

o Auto — When this configuration is used, the computer functions as a potential browser, a backup browser, or a master browser (depending on the outcome of a browser election). This is the default setting for all Windows NT computers that are nondomain controllers.

The IsDomainMaster Registry entry, which specifies whether a computer will initiate an election at startup and gives a computer a higher election criteria value than other computers of equivalent configuration, can be configured with one of the following values:

o True — When this configuration is used, the computer, at startup, initiates a browser election. In addition, the computer is assigned a higher election criteria value than it would normally be assigned, given its operating system, version, and current server role. This higher election criteria value gives the computer an advantage in a browser election, and causes it to become the master browser if all other factors are equal. For example, when this configuration is assigned to a *backup domain controller* (BDC), this BDC will have a higher election criteria value than all other BDCs (assuming that all BDCs use the same version of Windows NT Server); only the PDC would have a higher election criteria value. Either *True* or *Yes* can be used for this setting.

o False — When this configuration is used, the computer does *not* initiate a browser election at startup, and is *not* assigned a higher election criteria value than other computers with equivalent configurations. Either *False* or *No* can be used for this setting. This is the default setting for all Windows NT computers.

TO CONFIGURE THE COMPUTER BROWSER SERVICE'S REGISTRY SETTINGS, FOLLOW THESE STEPS:

1. Select Start ⇒ Run.

2. In the Run dialog box, type **Regedt32** in the Open drop-down list box. Click OK.

3. In the Registry Editor dialog box, select Window ⇒ HKEY_LOCAL_MACHINE on Local Machine.

4. Maximize the HKEY_LOCAL_MACHINE on Local Machine window.

5. Double-click the SYSTEM folder. Under the SYSTEM folder, double-click the CurrentControlSet folder. Double-click the Services folder. Scroll down and double-click the Browser folder. Click the Parameters folder. Figure 4-1 shows the contents of the Parameters folder in the Registry Editor dialog box. Notice the default settings for MaintainServerList and IsDomainMaster on a PDC.

FIGURE 4-1   Registry settings for the Computer Browser service

6. In the right-hand window, double-click either the MaintainServerList or the IsDomainMaster value (depending on the value you want to modify).

7. Edit the String Editor dialog box so that it contains the desired value. Click OK.

8. Exit Registry Editor. The changes will be effective the next time the computer is booted.

concept link

For information on configuring the Computer Browser service on Windows 95 or Windows for Workgroups computers, consult the *Microsoft Windows 95 Resource Kit* (Microsoft Press, 1995) or the *Microsoft Windows for Workgroups Resource Kit* (Microsoft Press, 1992).

Browsing on Transport Protocols

Browsing functions differently based on the transport protocol in use on the network. The following sections discuss how browsing is implemented on NetBEUI, NWLink IPX/SPX Compatible Transport, and TCP/IP.

Browsing on NetBEUI

NetBEUI is a nonroutable protocol. Because of the nonroutable nature of this protocol, browsing is always limited to a single subnet. Browsing traffic, and in fact, all network traffic in a NetBEUI environment, cannot be forwarded across a router.

Browsing on NWLink IPX/SPX Compatible Transport

NWLink IPX/SPX Compatible Transport (commonly associated with NetWare networks) is a routable protocol. All browsing communications on networks that use this protocol consist of NetBIOS broadcasts.

By default, NetWare routers are configured to forward NetBIOS broadcast traffic across up to eight routers. This means that browsing information is automatically forwarded to other subnets.

Third-party routers are usually configured, by default, to *not* forward NetBIOS broadcast traffic (type 20 packets). You must manually configure third-party routers to support the forwarding of NetBIOS broadcast traffic if you want browsing information to be forwarded to other subnets.

If you use Windows NT with routing enabled, *and* use the NWLink IPX/SPX Compatible Transport protocol, you must enable NetBIOS Broadcast Propagation (broadcast of type 20 packets) in order for browsing information to be forwarded across routers to other subnets.

Forwarding NetBIOS broadcasts across routers to other subnets can enable up to eight subnets to function as a single subnet for the purposes of browsing. Forwarding NetBIOS broadcasts can also create a serious increase in the amount of network traffic on all subnets, and should be carefully considered before being implemented.

Browsing on TCP/IP

TCP/IP is a routable protocol. By default, browsing communications on networks that use TCP/IP consist of NetBIOS broadcasts. Because TCP/IP is not normally configured to forward NetBIOS broadcasts, browsing information on networks that use TCP/IP is *not* typically forwarded to other subnets.

However, there are two methods you can use on TCP/IP networks to overcome this limitation and enable browsing information to be forwarded to other subnets. You can use LMHOSTS files, or you can use a WINS server to enable network-wide browsing on TCP/IP networks. Using LMHOSTS files or a WINS server enables the master browser to send and receive browsing information *directly* to and from the domain master browser (on another subnet) — but it does *not* enable forwarding of NetBIOS broadcasts across routers.

Because browsing on a TCP/IP network that uses LMHOSTS files or a WINS server does *not* involve forwarding broadcast traffic, browsing on TCP/IP networks is much more efficient than browsing on networks that use the NWLink IPX/SPX Compatible Transport protocol.

 concept link

For more information on NWLink IPX/SPX Compatible Transport, see Chapter 15. For more information on TCP/IP, see Chapter 14.

Browsing provides the user with a list of available shared network resources. Once the user knows what resources are available, the user can select a resource, and then connect to the shared folder in order to access the resource.

CONNECTING TO SHARED FOLDERS

Users must connect to shared folders before they can access the resources they contain.

The following sections discuss how to connect to shared folders, including how to use common naming conventions, Windows NT Explorer, and the command line to connect to shared network resources.

Naming Conventions

A *naming convention* is an accepted method of identifying individual computers and their resources on the network.

The two common naming conventions used in Windows NT are *universal naming convention* (UNC) and *fully qualified domain name* (FQDN).

A UNC name consists of a server name and a shared resource name in the following format: \\`Server_name`\`Share_name`. `Server_name` represents the name of the server that the shared folder is located on. `Share_name` represents the name of the shared folder. A UNC name in this format can be used to connect to a network share. For example, a shared folder named `Public` located on a server named Server1 would have the following UNC name: \\`Server1\Public`.

A UNC name can also specify the name of a subfolder and/or file within the share, using the following format: \\`Server_name`\`Share_name`\`Subfolder_name`\`File_name`. A UNC name in this format can be used to access a specific folder or file, such as a data file on a remote server. For example, a data file named `Salaries.doc` in the `Payroll` folder located in a share named `HR` on a server named CORP would have the following UNC name: \\`Corp\HR\Payroll\Salaries.doc`.

An FQDN is a fancy term for the way computers are named and referenced on the Internet. FQDNs are often used on networks that use TCP/IP and DNS servers. The format for an FQDN is `Server_name.Domain_name.Root_domain_name`. For example, the FQDN of a server named `Wolf` in a domain named `AlanCarter` in the `com` root domain would be `wolf.alancarter.com`.

If your network uses TCP/IP and DNS servers, you can replace the *Server_name* in a UNC with an FQDN. For example, to specify a share named Books on a server with an FQDN of wolf.alancarter.com, you could use \\wolf.alancarter.com\Books.

Both UNC names and FQDNs can be used to connect to shared network resources in Windows NT Explorer and from the command line.

Using Windows NT Explorer

Assuming that you have the appropriate permissions, you can connect to any shared network resource by using Windows NT Explorer.

TO CONNECT TO A SHARED NETWORK RESOURCE BY USING WINDOWS NT EXPLORER, FOLLOW THESE STEPS:

1. Select Start ⇒ Programs ⇒ Windows NT Explorer.

2. In the Exploring dialog box, right-click Network Neighborhood. Select Map Network Drive from the menu that appears.

3. The Map Network Drive dialog box appears, as shown in Figure 4-2. Notice the browsing information available in the Shared Directories list box. In this dialog box, you can use one of two methods to select the network resource to which you want to connect:

FIGURE 4-2 Using Windows NT Explorer to browse the network

- You can type in the UNC name of the resource you want to connect to in the Path text box.

- You can double-click any domain or server shown in the Shared Directories list box to browse the network. If you double-click a domain, a browse list of available network servers in that domain is displayed. If you double-click a server, a browse list of shared folders on that server is displayed. Highlight the shared folder you want to connect to. The UNC name of the shared resource then appears in the Path text box. Click OK.

4. The resource you select should appear with a drive letter under My Computer in the All Folders section of the Exploring dialog box, indicating that you have successfully connected a network drive to the resource.

5. Exit Windows NT Explorer.

Once you have connected a drive letter to a shared network resource, the new drive letter appears in Windows NT Explorer, My Computer, and the Open dialog box in standard Windows applications. You can then access the files and folders within the share in the same manner that you access files and folders on your local computer.

Connecting from the Command Line

You can use the Net.exe utility to browse the network and, assuming that you have the appropriate permissions, to connect to a shared network resource from the command line.

TO BROWSE THE NETWORK FROM THE COMMAND LINE, FOLLOW THESE STEPS:

1. Select Start ⇒ Programs ⇒ Command Prompt.

2. To obtain a list of available servers in your domain or workgroup, at the C:\> command prompt, type **net view** and press Enter.

3. To obtain a list of all domains on the network, type **net view /domain** and press Enter.

4. To obtain a list of available servers in another domain, type **net view /domain:***Domain_name* and press Enter. (For example, to obtain a list of available servers in the LAB domain, type **net view /domain:lab** and press Enter.)

5. To obtain a list of available shares on a network server, type **net view ***Server_name* and press Enter. (For example, to obtain a list of available shares on a server named PDCLAB, type **net view \\pdclab** and press Enter.) To exit the Command Prompt dialog box at any time, type **exit** at the command prompt and press Enter.

TO CONNECT TO A SHARED NETWORK RESOURCE FROM THE COMMAND LINE, FOLLOW THESE STEPS:

1. Select Start ⇒ Programs ⇒ Command Prompt.

2. In the Command Prompt dialog box at the C:\> command prompt, type **net use** *Drive_letter*: *****Server_name******Share_name* and press Enter. For example, to connect a drive letter, such as X:, to a share named `Data` on a server named Pdclab, type **net use x: \\pdclab\data** and press Enter.

3. A message appears indicating that the command completed successfully.

4. Exit the Command Prompt dialog box by typing **exit** at the command prompt and pressing Enter.

Once you have connected a drive letter to a shared network resource, the new drive letter appears in Windows NT Explorer, My Computer, and the Open dialog box in standard Windows applications. You can then access the files and folders within the share in the same manner that you access files and folders on your local computer.

KEY POINT SUMMARY

Chapter 4 covered browsing, which permits users to find out what shared resources are available on the network, and facilitates connecting to those resources. Browsing is managed by the Computer Browser service, which is responsible for the process of building a list of available network servers (a browse list), and for sharing that list with other computers. (For the purposes of this chapter, network servers include all computers that either have shared resources or are capable of sharing their resources.) Not every computer on the network has to maintain a browse list, and because of this fact, processor overhead and network traffic are reduced.

- The task of maintaining a browse list is distributed among many computers. The *browser roles* that computers can perform are domain master browser, master browser, backup browser, potential browser, and non-browser.

  - If a network has a single subnet, the *domain master browser* and master browser functions are combined and are performed by a single computer — the PDC. The PDC compiles the browse list and makes this list available to the backup browsers.

  - If a network has multiple subnets, the domain master browser maintains a list of available network servers located on all subnets in the domain and makes this information available to the master browser on each subnet, which, in turn, makes the information available to the backup browsers.

  - The *master browser* builds the browse list for its own subnet, and distributes this list to the domain master browser and to the backup browsers on its own subnet. Each workgroup or domain is limited to having only one master browser on a subnet.

  - The *backup browser* receives the browse list from the master browser, and then distributes the information to any computer that requests it.

  - A computer that does not currently maintain or distribute a browse list, but is capable of doing so, is called a *potential browser*. By default, all Windows NT Server, Windows NT Workstation, Windows 95, and Windows for Workgroups computers are potential browsers.

  - A *non-browser* is a computer that is not capable of maintaining and distributing a browse list, either because it has been configured to not function as a browser, or because the computer's network software does not provide the capability to maintain a browse list.

- The browsing process consists of two distinct activities: building and maintaining the browse list, and distributing the browse list to computers that request it. There are several steps involved in both of these activities.

- Because the master browser does not remove a network server from its browse list until *after* it has failed to receive a broadcast announcement from the network server for three consecutive twelve-minute periods, it is possible for a network server to remain on the browse list for some time after it is no longer actually available to network users.

- A *browser election*, which determines which computer will function as the master browser, takes place when the PDC is booted, when a backup browser is unable to obtain an updated browse list from the master browser, and when a computer is unable to obtain a list of backup browsers from the master browser.

    - The computer that initiates the browser election process broadcasts an election packet, which contains the computer's election criteria value. A computer's election criteria value is based on the computer's operating system, version, and on the computer's current browser role. The election criteria value ranking of operating systems, from highest to lowest, is: Windows NT Server, Windows NT Workstation, Windows 95, and Windows for Workgroups. Newer versions of an operating system have a higher election criteria value than older versions. The computer with the *highest* election criteria value, in a browser election, "wins" the election and becomes the master browser. Only the master browser is elected. The domain master browser is always the PDC. If the PDC is unavailable, there is no domain master browser.

- The Computer Browser service on a Windows NT computer is controlled by the MaintainServerList and IsDomainMaster Registry entries that are located in `\HKEY_LOCAL_MACHINE\SYSTEM\CurrentControlSet\Services\Browser\Parameters`. The default settings for these entries can be changed by editing the Registry if you want to change a Windows NT computer's default browser role.

    - The MaintainServerList entry, which specifies whether a computer will maintain a browse list, can be configured with a value of No, Yes, or Auto. Yes is the default setting for all Windows NT Server domain controllers. Auto is the default setting for all Windows NT computers that are non-domain controllers.

- The IsDomainMaster entry, which specifies whether a computer will initiate an election at startup, and also gives a computer a higher election criteria value than other computers of equivalent configuration, can be configured with a value of True or False. False is the default setting for all Windows NT computers.

- Because of the nonroutable nature of NetBEUI, browsing on a network that uses NetBEUI is limited to a single subnet.

- On networks that use the NWLink IPX/SPX Compatible Transport protocol (a routable protocol), all browsing communications consist of NetBIOS broadcasts. By default, NetWare routers are configured to forward NetBIOS broadcast traffic across up to eight routers, which can enable up to eight subnets to function as a single subnet for the purposes of browsing. However, this can create a serious increase in the amount of network traffic on all subnets.

- On networks that use TCP/IP (a routable protocol), browsing communication, by default, consists of NetBIOS broadcasts. However, because TCP/IP is not normally configured to forward NetBIOS broadcasts, browsing information is typically *not* forwarded to other subnets. This limitation can be overcome by using LMHOSTS files or a WINS server, which enables the master browser to send and receive browsing information *directly* to and from the domain master browser (on another subnet), but this is *not* accomplished in the form of a NetBIOS broadcast. When LMHOSTS files or a WINS server is used, browsing on a TCP/IP network is much more efficient than browsing on a NWLink IPX/SPX Compatible Transport network, because there is no forwarding of browsing broadcast traffic on the TCP/IP network.

- A naming convention is an accepted method of identifying computers and their resources on the network. The two common naming conventions used in Windows NT are: the universal naming convention (UNC) and fully qualified domain name (FQDN).

  - A UNC name consists of a server name and a shared resource name in the following format: *Server_name**Share_name*. A UNC name can also specify the name of a subfolder and/or file within the share, using the following format:
  *Server_name**Share_name**Subfolder_name**File_name*.

- An FQDN is a fancy term for the way computers are named and referenced on the Internet. The format for an FQDN is *Server_name.Domain_name.Root_domain_name*. If your network uses TCP/IP and DNS servers, you can replace the *Server_name* in a UNC with an FQDN. Both UNC names and FQDNs can be used to connect to shared network resources in Windows NT Explorer and from the command line.

APPLYING WHAT YOU'VE LEARNED

Now it's time to regroup, review, and apply what you've learned in this chapter.

The following Instant Assessment questions bring to mind key facts and concepts. Then, the Hands-on Lab reinforces what you've learned and allows you to practice some of the tasks tested by the Server exam.

Instant Assessment

1. What service manages browsing on Windows NT computers?

2. What is a list of available network servers called?

3. List the five different roles that computers can play in the browsing process.

4. Which computer is always the domain master browser?

5. How many master browsers can each domain have on a subnet?

6. Why are some computers non-browsers?

7. Briefly describe how a browse list is built and maintained.

8. Describe the process that takes place when a user browses the network.

9. You browse the network and are unable to connect to a server that is listed as available on your browse list. What timing issue inherent to the browsing process could account for this problem?

10. Which kind of browser is determined by a browser election?

11. What is contained in an election packet?

12. Which Registry entry specifies whether a given NT computer will be a browser?

13. Which Registry entry specifies whether a given NT computer will initiate a browser election at startup?

14. What type of network traffic does browsing communications consist of on an NWLink IPX/SPX Compatible Transport network?

15. What can you use on a TCP/IP network to enable the master browser to send browsing information *directly* to and from the domain master browser (on another subnet)?

16. Specify the format of a UNC name.

17. Specify the format of an FQDN.

18. If your network uses TCP/IP and DNS servers, what can you replace in a UNC name with an FQDN?

T/F

19. Because NetBEUI is a nonroutable protocol, browsing on a NetBEUI network is limited to a single subnet.   ____

concept link   **For answers to the Instant Assessment questions see Appendix B.**

Hands-on Lab

The following Hands-on Lab provides you with an opportunity to configure the Computer Browser service.

Lab 4.6 *Configuring the computer browser service*

The purpose of this lab is to give you hands-on experience in configuring the Windows NT Computer Browser service. You will edit the Registry to configure your Windows NT Server computer to force an election when it is booted, in an attempt to become the master browser for its subnet.

Begin this lab by booting your computer to Windows NT Server. Log on as Administrator.

FOLLOW THESE STEPS CAREFULLY:

1. Select Start ⇒ Run.

2. In the Run dialog box, type **Regedt32** in the Open drop-down list box. Click OK.

3. In the Registry Editor dialog box, select Window ⇒ HKEY_LOCAL_MACHINE on Local Machine.

4. Maximize the HKEY_LOCAL_MACHINE on Local Machine window.

5. Double-click the SYSTEM folder. Under the SYSTEM folder, double-click the CurrentControlSet folder. Double-click the Services folder. Scroll down and double-click the Browser folder. Click the Parameters folder.

6. In the right-hand window, double-click the IsDomainMaster value.

7. Edit the String Editor dialog box to read **TRUE**. Click OK. (This step configures the computer to force an election on startup and to attempt to become the master browser for its subnet.)

8. Notice in the right-hand window that the IsDomainMaster value is changed to TRUE.

9. The MaintainServerList value should be Yes. (If it isn't, double-click MaintainServerList and change the value to **Yes** in the String Editor dialog box.)

10. Exit Registry Editor. These changes will become effective the next time you boot the computer.

Configuring Disks

About Chapter 5

This chapter explores the basics of configuring a computer's hard disk(s) in a Windows NT environment.

It begins with a discussion of the various file systems that Windows NT supports, namely, FAT and NTFS. The strengths, limitations, and special features of these two file systems are explained. Converting from FAT to NTFS is also covered.

Chapter 5 then presents an in-depth explanation of working with partitions. Disk Administrator, a Windows NT tool used to create and format partitions, is introduced. Then various disk partitioning schemes are explored and compared, including disk mirroring, stripe sets, stripe sets with parity, and volume sets.

Finally, Chapter 5 provides valuable information on how to recover from a single or multiple disk failure. Updating the Emergency Repair Disk is also covered.

In addition to two Critical Thinking Labs, this chapter includes two Hands-on Labs. In the first Hands-on Lab you use Disk Administrator to manage partitions on your computer's hard disk. In the second, you get an opportunity to update your Emergency Repair Disk.

The material presented in this chapter maps to the various hard disk and fault tolerance objectives listed in the preparation guide for the Server exam.

FILE SYSTEMS

Before you attempt to configure disks in a Windows NT environment, you should have a clear understanding of the different file systems that NT supports. Windows NT Server 4.0 supports three file systems: the *file allocation table* (FAT) *file system*, the *Windows NT file system* (NTFS), and the *Compact Disc Filing System* (CDFS). Windows NT 4.0 does *not* support the *high performance file system* (HPFS), although earlier versions of NT did. (If you are upgrading from an earlier version of Windows NT that used HPFS, you must convert to NTFS before performing the upgrade.) Table 5-1 shows which file systems are supported by various operating systems.

TABLE 5-1 FILE SYSTEM SUPPORT BY OPERATING SYSTEM	
OPERATING SYSTEM	*FILE SYSTEMS SUPPORTED*
Windows NT 4.0	FAT, NTFS, CDFS
Windows NT 3.51 (and earlier versions)	FAT, NTFS, CDFS, HPFS
Windows 95	FAT, CDFS
Windows 3*x* and 3.1*x*	FAT, CDFS
OS/2	FAT, CDFS, HPFS
MS-DOS	FAT, CDFS

FAT

The *file allocation table* (FAT) *file system* used on Windows NT is a modified version of the FAT file system used by MS-DOS. FAT is the only hard disk file system supported by Windows 3.*x*,Windows 3.1*x*, Windows 95, and MS-DOS. So, if you want to configure a Windows NT computer to dual boot between Windows NT and Windows 3.1*x*, Windows 95, or MS-DOS, your computer's first partition must use the FAT file system.

Don't confuse the FAT file system with the FAT32 file system. Windows NT does not support the FAT32 file system (an enhanced rendition of FAT) that is supported on the original equipment manufacturer (OEM) version of Windows 95 that includes Service Pack 2.

 note **Service Pack 2 for Windows 95 is only available on the OEM version of Windows 95, not on the retail version.**

Now it's time to familiarize yourself with the characteristics and features of the FAT file system, including security, naming conventions, speed of access to files, and partition size.

Security

The FAT file system does *not* support file and folder security in Windows NT. Because file and folder security is not supported on a FAT partition, any user who is logged on locally to a computer has full control of all of the files and folders located in the FAT partition(s) on that computer. This applies only to local access.

However, you can use share permissions to control users' access to shared folders over the network. Share permissions affect only the access of files and folders over the network, not when someone is logged on locally. So, if you need local file and folder security, you should use an NTFS partition instead of a FAT partition.

Naming conventions

The FAT file system, as used by Windows NT, supports the use of long filenames. This file system permits the full path to a file (including the filename) to be up to 255 characters long.

Filenames can contain any character *except* \ / : * ? " < > | and should begin with an alphanumeric character. Filenames can contain spaces and multiple periods, and the characters after the last period are considered the filename extension.

The FAT file system preserves upper- and lowercase in filenames, but filenames are not case-sensitive. Because of this, I can request the file ALAN.DOC by typing **Alan.doc**, **ALAN.DOC**, or **alan.doc**, and Windows NT always retrieves ALAN.DOC.

Speed of access to files

Access speed to files on a FAT partition is dependent on many factors, including file type, file size, partition size, number of files in a folder, and fragmentation.

Windows NT accesses files on FAT partitions smaller than 500MB faster than it accesses files on other similar-sized file system partitions discussed here. Additionally, NT accesses certain types of files on FAT partitions more efficiently than on partitions formatted with other file systems.

On very large partitions, however, or when there is a large number of files in a folder, Windows NT accesses files on NTFS partitions much faster than it accesses files on a FAT partition of similar size.

Windows NT usually accesses files on a highly fragmented FAT partition slower than it accesses files on an NTFS partition of similar size.

Partition size

The maximum size of a FAT partition is 4GB. The maximum size of a file in a FAT partition is 4GB.

The FAT file system does *not* support file compression.

NTFS

The *Windows NT file system* (NTFS) is the most powerful file system supported by Windows NT. Only Windows NT supports NTFS — no other operating systems currently support this file system.

When it comes to security, naming conventions, speed of access to files, and partition size, NTFS has its own unique characteristics. Additionally, NTFS has some features not supported by the FAT file system.

Security

NTFS provides file and folder security for both local and remote users on a network. NTFS is the only file system discussed here that permits the assigning of permissions to individual files and folders.

So how does NTFS security actually work? NTFS security controls access to files on an NTFS partition by utilizing the user's *security identifier* (SID) to determine which files that user can access. (Each file and folder on an NTFS partition has an *access control list* (ACL) associated with it. The ACL is a list that contains user and group SIDs, with the associated privileges of each user and group.)

 concept link **NTFS and share security are covered in depth in Chapter 12.**

 note **In addition to the security provided by NTFS, remember that because Windows NT requires a user to log on before accessing files, NT's security is greater than operating systems that don't require the user to log on.**

Naming conventions

Like the FAT file system, NTFS supports the use of long filenames. Names of files and folders (including extensions) can be up to 255 characters long.

You can use most characters in NTFS file and folder names. However, the characters ? " / \ < > * | : can't be used.

NTFS preserves upper- and lowercase in filenames. Filenames are not case-sensitive (except when used by a POSIX application). For example, a Win32 application does not distinguish between Money.DOC, MONEY.DOC, and money.doc — it treats all three names as though they were the same file.

The POSIX subsystem, however, is case-sensitive with respect to filenames, because it does not translate a request for a file into all uppercase letters as the Win32 and other subsystems do. A POSIX application treats the filenames in the previous paragraph as though they were three separate files: `Money.DOC`, `MONEY.DOC`, and `money.doc`. You must use a POSIX application if you want to access these three different files — if you attempt to access `Money.DOC` with a Win32 application (no matter how you type the filename) you will normally always retrieve the `MONEY.DOC` file because the Win32 Subsystem translates file requests into all uppercase letters.

Speed of access to files

NTFS usually provides faster access to files stored on a large partition that contains many files than the FAT file system. NTFS is able to access files in this situation faster than the FAT file system because NTFS uses an enhanced binary tree to locate files. A binary tree search is a faster mechanism for searching through a large number of filenames than the sequential read mechanism used on FAT partitions.

Partition size

The maximum theoretical size of an NTFS partition is 16 exabytes (an *exabyte* is one billion billion bytes, or a giga-gigabyte). However, when you actually implement NTFS on current standard industry hardware, there is a functional limitation of 2 terabytes.

Additional features not supported by the FAT file system

NTFS has several other unique attributes and features that are not found in, nor supported by, the FAT file system.

- NTFS supports a compression attribute for each file. You can choose which files to compress and which ones to leave uncompressed. The compression algorithm NTFS uses is similar to the one used by Drivespace in MS-DOS. Using compression provides an approximately 40 to 50 percent increase in hard disk space.

 note **Compression can cause some performance degradation on partitions with substantial write activity. Additionally, accessing uncompressed files is faster than accessing compressed files.**

- NTFS is a highly reliable, recoverable file system. It is not necessary to periodically run Chkdsk.exe on an NTFS partition.

- Using NTFS greatly reduces fragmentation on partitions. However, files can still become fragmented when their size is increased. Windows NT does not include an NTFS defragmentation utility, but there are several third-party utilities available.

- NTFS maintains a recycle bin for each user.

A couple of final facts on NTFS: You can't use NTFS to format floppy disks, and NTFS does not permit you to change media in a removable media drive (such as a Zip drive) without rebooting. (The FAT file system does support changing media without rebooting.)

CDFS

The *Compact Disc Filing System* (CDFS) supports access to compact discs. It is only used on CD-ROM devices that read and/or write compact discs.

Converting from FAT to NTFS

In Windows NT you can format a new partition with either FAT or NTFS. But what do you do when you want to change the file system on an existing partition?

You can change an existing FAT partition, and retain the data on it, into an NTFS partition by using Convert.exe. This is a fairly simple procedure.

However, it is a one-way process — there is no way to convert an NTFS partition into a FAT partition without first backing up, reformatting the disk, and restoring the data.

To convert a FAT partition into an NTFS partition, use the following syntax:

CONVERT *drive*: /FS:NTFS [/V]

The following is an explanation of syntax:

- *Drive*: This specifies the letter of the drive to convert to NTFS.

- /FS:NTFS: This indicates that the file system should be converted to NTFS. This is an outdated switch, because NTFS is the only file system that you can use Convert.exe to switch to in Windows NT 4.0; but its use, in terms of command syntax, is still required.

- /V: This specifies that Convert.exe will run in verbose mode.

For example, to convert drive D: from FAT to NTFS, use the following command line: CONVERT D: /FS:NTFS

 To successfully use the Convert.exe **command,** Convert.exe **must be the** *only* **application that accesses the drive you want to change during the conversion process. If Windows NT Explorer accesses the drive you are trying to convert, if you are trying to convert the boot partition, or if your active command prompt has the drive you are trying to convert as its current drive, Windows NT will display an error message stating that** Convert.exe **can't gain exclusive access to the drive.**

If you can't gain exclusive access to a drive, run Convert.exe **as shown in the example. The file system conversion will occur when you restart your computer.**

WORKING WITH PARTITIONS

Before you can format a hard disk with a file system such as FAT or NTFS, you must mark the disk to identify which parts of it will contain a file system (or systems). This is called *partitioning*. A hard disk can be separated into a maximum of four partitions, or one partition can occupy all of the space on a disk.

You may recall that back in Chapter 2, when you installed Windows NT Server 4.0, you were presented with the option to create a partition on your computer's hard disk. Once Windows NT is installed, the primary tool for creating, formatting, and managing various types of partitions is Disk Administrator. The latter part of this chapter covers how to use Disk Administrator to perform specific tasks on partitions. But first, it's important that you understand the basic types of partitions.

Partition Types

Windows NT supports two types of partitions: primary and extended. Both types of partitions can coexist on the same hard disk. A disk can have more than one primary partition, but it can have only one extended partition.

Primary partitions

A *primary partition* can occupy all of the space on a disk, or any portion of it. A hard disk can have up to four partitions, and all four can be primary partitions. A primary partition can be formatted as a single logical drive (but not as multiple logical drives).

Any primary partition on the first hard disk in the computer can be designated as the active partition. The active partition is significant because when the computer boots, it attempts to load the operating system from the active primary partition on the first hard disk in the computer.

The Windows NT 4.0 system partition must be located on the active primary partition on the first hard disk in a computer.

 concept link

Remember the system partition and the boot partition? If your memory needs refreshing, take another look at the "Hard disk partition information" section of the Preinstallation Checklist in Chapter 2.

Extended partitions

There can be only one *extended partition* on a disk. An extended partition can't be marked active, and it can't be used for the system partition of a computer. The Windows NT boot partition, however, can be located on an extended partition.

An extended partition can be formatted as one or more logical drives, where each partition is assigned a different drive letter. Logical drives can be formatted with either FAT or NTFS. You can have one logical drive formatted with FAT, and another logical drive in the same extended partition formatted with NTFS.

Extended partitions are convenient for breaking up a physical disk into more than four logical drives.

Using Disk Administrator

Windows NT includes a useful tool to manage disks after NT has been installed: Disk Administrator. Disk Administrator can help you create, format, and otherwise manage various types of partitions.

caution It's good practice to use Disk Administrator only during times when no one else is accessing the server. Some of Disk Administrator's functions take a significant amount of time to complete, and some require the server to be rebooted. This means that service to clients during these times can be seriously slowed or interrupted. Plan to perform disk management tasks during nonbusiness hours whenever possible, just as you would other administration tasks that require the server to be down.

Figure 5-1 shows a screen shot of the main dialog box of Disk Administrator.

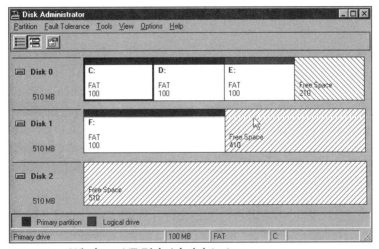

FIGURE 5-1 Windows NT Disk Administrator

The next several sections explain how you can use Disk Administrator to create partitions, format partitions, and establish various disk partitioning schemes, including disk mirroring, stripe sets, stripe sets with parity, and volume sets.

Creating partitions

You can use Disk Administrator to create partitions on your computer's hard disk.

I've always wished that some text or course would have given me more precise information and detailed instructions on working with Disk Administrator. It's for this reason that I've presented the instructions to perform several disk and partition management tasks in the rest of this chapter in a step-by-step format.

But this doesn't mean I want you to sit down at your computer and create some partitions right now. Even though the descriptions of how to perform these tasks are presented in a step-by-step format, they're meant to be informational — not actual lab exercises. (You can sink your teeth into Lab 5.9: "Managing partitions" at the end of this chapter soon enough.) What I really have in mind is for you to read through these steps and refer to them when you have a need to do these various disk management procedures.

Here's a look at the basic steps to create and format a primary partition, and the steps to create an extended partition.

Creating and formatting a primary partition   In order to create a primary partition on a hard disk, you must have an area of free space on the hard disk.

caution

The steps in the various how-to sections in the rest of this chapter are meant to be informational, not a lab exercise. (Lab 5.9: "Managing partitions" is found at the end of this chapter.) If you decide to create a partition on your computer, don't delete or reformat any partition that contains data you don't want to lose. And remember, back up all important data and programs *before* you make any changes to your computer's disk configuration.

in the
real world

The steps I've listed to create a primary partition and an extended partition should work as shown about 90 percent of the time. Don't be disconcerted, though, if an extra dialog box or two is displayed. Any number of hardware or system configuration differences can cause a minor deviation from the steps listed. If a different or extra dialog box is displayed, just provide the appropriate response and continue.

TO CREATE A PARTITION, FOLLOW THESE STEPS:

1. Start Disk Administrator. (Select Start ⇒ Programs ⇒ Administrative Tools (Common) ⇒ Disk Administrator.)

2. If this is the first time you have run Disk Administrator since installing NT, a dialog box appears. If this box appears, click OK to update the system configuration.

3. Click a diagonally striped area of the Disk Administrator dialog box marked Free Space.

4. Select Partition ⇒ Create.

5. Depending on the partitions that already exist on your computer's hard disk, a Confirm dialog box may appear stating that "This operation will result in a disk whose partition scheme may not be compatible with MS-DOS." Click Yes if you want to continue.

6. The Create Primary Partition dialog box appears. In the "Create partition of size" text box, enter the size, in MB, that you want the new partition to be. Click OK. The Disk Administrator main dialog box reappears, and the new partition is displayed in a boxed area with the next available drive letter. (If you have several network drives connected, the drive letter might be H:, even though the next local drive letter would be D:. Don't worry, you can fix this later.) The lettering in the box representing the new partition is gray rather than black like all the other partitions shown.

7. To complete the partition creation process, select Partition ⇒ Commit Changes Now.

8. Click Yes in the Confirm dialog box to save the changes to your disk.

9. Click OK in the Disk Administrator dialog box. This causes the Disk Administrator main dialog box to reappear, and your newly created partition appears in full color with black lettering.

After you've created a partition, you'll usually want to format it.

TO FORMAT THE PARTITION YOU JUST CREATED, FOLLOW THESE STEPS:

1. Start Disk Administrator (if the Disk Administrator main dialog box is not already displayed).

2. Click in the boxed area representing the new partition, and then select Tools ⇒ Format.

3. The Format dialog box (displayed in Figure 5-2) appears. Configure the characteristics you want this partition to have, including the file system type and volume label. (See the detailed discussion following these steps on the various options that are configured in this dialog box.)

4. When you are finished, click the Start button. A warning message appears, reminding you that formatting will erase all data on your disk. Only click OK if you want to continue.

5. Click OK in the Formatting dialog box that appears after the formatting is complete. Click Close when the Format dialog box reappears.

6. The Disk Administrator main dialog box reappears. A file system type (for example FAT, NTFS, and the like) now appears in the boxed area representing your newly created and formatted partition, directly beneath the drive letter of the new partition.

When you format a partition, you have the option to specify several of its characteristics. Figure 5-2 shows a screen shot of the Format dialog box within Disk Administrator.

FIGURE 5-2   Formatting a partition

As Figure 5-2 shows, there are several options in the Format dialog box to be configured:

- **Capacity:** This option displays "Unknown capacity" when you format a new partition. (When you format an existing partition, it displays the size of the partition.) This is an informational item only—no configuration is allowed.

- **File System:** The file system choices available are FAT or NTFS.

- **Allocation Unit Size:** Allocation Unit Size refers to the sector size Disk Administrator uses when it formats a partition. If you chose NTFS as the file system type, you can select the sector size to be used during formatting. Sector sizes in this menu vary from 512B to 4,096B.

If you want to use a sector size larger than 4,096B, you must format the partition from the command line using the Format.exe **command. The** Format.exe **command supports sector sizes up to 64KB for NTFS partitions. You can type format /? at the command prompt for a complete list of the switches that can be used with the** Format.exe **command. File compression is not supported when using sector sizes larger than 4,096B.**

If you choose FAT as the file system type, you can't set the Allocation Unit Size. You must accept the default Allocation Unit Size, which varies depending on the size of the partition being formatted.

For additional information on Allocation Unit Size, as well as detailed file system information, see Chapter 17 of the *Microsoft Windows NT Workstation Resource Kit for version 4.0*, published by Microsoft Press.

- **Volume Label:** This option permits you to give your partition a name. Type in the text you want to use for the volume label. Configuring this item is optional—an entry is not required in this box.

- **Format Options:**
  - Selecting the *Quick Format* option instructs NT to write only the necessary data to the disk to support a volume, and not to check for bad sectors during formatting.

○ The *Enable Compression* option is only available if you choose NTFS as the file system. (If you choose FAT as the file system, this check box is grayed out.) Selecting this option causes all files and folders placed in this partition to be compressed by default. You can also set this attribute later by using Windows NT Explorer.

Creating an extended partition   This section discusses how you can use Disk Administrator to create an extended partition.

TO USE DISK ADMINISTRATOR TO CREATE AN EXTENDED PARTITION, FOLLOW THESE STEPS:

1. Start Disk Administrator.

2. Click a diagonally striped, boxed area of the Disk Administrator dialog box marked Free Space.

3. Select Partition ⇒ Create Extended.

4. The Create Extended Partition dialog box appears. In the "Create partition of size" text box, enter the size, in MB, that you want the extended partition to be. Click OK.

5. Disk Administrator's main dialog box reappears. Notice that the area of free space is still marked Free Space, but the diagonal lines now run from top left to bottom right, which indicate an extended partition. (Free space that is not an extended partition is indicated by diagonal lines that run from top right to bottom left.) Select Partition ⇒ Commit Changes Now.

6. In the Confirm dialog box, click Yes to save the changes to disk. Then click OK to acknowledge that the disks were updated successfully. The Disk Administrator main dialog box reappears.

7. To create a logical drive(s) for this extended partition, select Partition ⇒ Create.

8. When the Create Logical Drive dialog box appears, enter the size you want the drive to be, in MB, in the "Create logical drive of size" text box. Click OK.

9. The Disk Administrator main dialog box reappears. Notice that a logical drive box is displayed at the bottom of this dialog box. Select Partition ⇒ Commit Changes Now.

10. Click Yes in the Confirm dialog box to save the changes to disk. A dialog box appears indicating that the disks were updated successfully, and reminding you to update your Emergency Repair Disk. Click OK. The Disk Administrator main dialog box reappears. The procedure is complete.

Disk Mirroring

Disk mirroring is a fault tolerance method that enables operations to continue when one hard disk fails. (Later in this chapter you'll learn how to recover from a single disk failure.)

The term disk mirroring is somewhat of a misnomer. It should be called partition mirroring. Any partition can be mirrored, including the system partition and the boot partition. In disk mirroring, Disk Administrator makes an exact replica of the partition being mirrored on a *separate* hard disk. You can't make a replica of a partition on the same physical disk—the mirror image must be produced on a different hard disk.

Disk mirroring is fairly expensive, as fault tolerance methods go, because twice the normal amount of disk space is required. However, you get a high level of fault tolerance for your money. Disk mirroring is used in situations where the integrity of data is more important than minimizing costs. For example, a financial institution might decide that disk mirroring is cost-effective for their company because the extra safety provided by disk mirroring outweighs the cost of additional disk space.

Disk mirroring does not provide fault tolerance in the event of multiple disk failure, and it does not guarantee continued operations if a server goes down. Disk mirroring is also known as RAID level 1. (RAID stands for *Redundant Array of Inexpensive Disks*.)

TO CREATE A MIRROR SET, FOLLOW THESE STEPS:

1. Start Disk Administrator, and then select (click) the partition you want to mirror. If you don't have any partitions on your hard disk, or you want to create a new partition to mirror, follow the instructions in the "Creating and formatting a primary partition" section earlier in this chapter to create and format a partition. Then do the steps listed here.

2. Press and hold Ctrl while you click an area of free space on a different hard disk that is at least as large as the partition you want to mirror.

3. Select Fault Tolerance ⇒ Establish Mirror. Figure 5-3 displays the Fault Tolerance menu of the Disk Administrator dialog box. Note that Establish Mirror has been selected and highlighted.

4. Disk activity occurs and may continue for quite a while, depending on the size of the partition to be mirrored and the amount of data on that partition. Finally, as Figure 5-4 shows, Disk Administrator displays its main dialog box. Notice that there are now two drives of the same size with the same drive letter, located on different hard disks. The mirrored partitions are highlighted in the color that corresponds to the mirror set box at the bottom of the dialog box. A mirror set has been established.

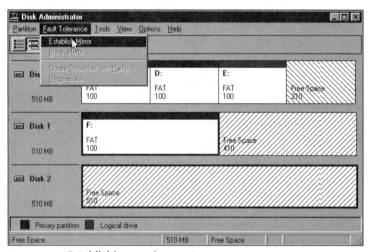

FIGURE 5-3   **Establishing a mirror set**

Now that a mirror set is established, a fault tolerance boot disk should be created in case the original disk in the mirror set (the disk that was mirrored) fails.

Creating a fault tolerance boot disk

A *fault tolerance* boot disk is a floppy disk that enables you to boot your computer in the event that one of the disks in your computer's mirror set fails. The fault tolerance boot disk should be created *before* the disk failure occurs.

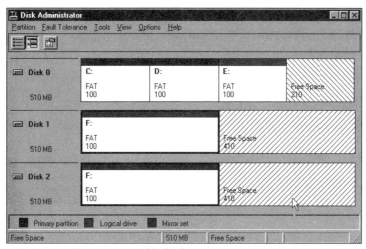

FIGURE 5-4   **Mirror set established**

If the original disk in a mirror set fails, and if that disk contains the original boot partition, you will not be able to reboot your computer because the Boot.ini file will be pointing at the failed hard disk and partition.

When this happens, you need to use a fault tolerance boot disk that points at the mirrored disk and partition that are still functional to boot your computer.

TO CREATE A FAULT TOLERANCE BOOT DISK, FOLLOW THESE STEPS:

1. Format a 3.5-inch floppy disk by using the Format menu from Windows NT Explorer. This *must* be done in Windows NT, not in Windows 95.

2. Copy the ntldr, Ntdetect.com, and Boot.ini files to the floppy disk. Also copy Bootsect.dos to the floppy disk if your computer is configured to dual boot, and copy Ntbootdd.sys to the floppy disk if this file exists in the root of your computer's system partition. (An Ntbootdd.sys file will exist in your system partition only if you have entries in your Boot.ini file that begin with scsi.)

3. Edit the Boot.ini file on the floppy disk (not the Boot.ini file on your hard drive) to point at the mirrored disk and partition that still function, instead of at the disk and partition that failed. (The next section of this chapter discusses how to edit the Boot.ini file.)

Editing the Boot.ini file   The `Boot.ini` file is a read-only file in the root of the active partition on the first hard disk in the computer.

Before you can edit the `Boot.ini` file, you must remove its read-only attribute.

caution   **Remember, you are editing the `Boot.ini` file that has been copied to a floppy disk, not the `Boot.ini` file on your hard drive.**

You can use Windows NT Explorer to deselect this attribute (which is found in the General tab of the Boot.ini Properties dialog box). After you remove the read-only attribute, you can use any text editor, such as Notepad, to edit the `Boot.ini` file.

However, before you go on to edit this file, you might want to take a closer look at it to understand its structure and syntax. I've reproduced below a sample `Boot.ini` file.

LISTING 5-1 Sample Boot.ini file

```
[boot loader]
timeout=30
default=multi(0)disk(0)rdisk(1)partition(1)\WINNT
[operating systems]
multi(0)disk(0)rdisk(1)partition(1)\WINNT="Windows NT
        Server Version 4.00"
multi(0)disk(0)rdisk(1)partition(1)\WINNT="Windows NT
        Server Version 4.00 [VGA mode]" /basevideo /sos
C:\="Microsoft Windows"
```

Note that there are two sections to the `Boot.ini` file: `[boot loader]` and `[operating systems]`.

The first section, `[boot loader]`, contains two entries. The first entry, `timeout`, determines how long, in seconds, the boot loader screen (or boot menu) is displayed when the computer boots. The default timeout is thirty seconds. The second entry, `default`, specifies which operating system loads if no selection is made within the timeout period.

The second section of the `Boot.ini` file, `[operating systems]`, first lists entries consisting of ARC (*Advanced RISC Computing*) pathnames to various operating systems. Only Windows NT uses ARC pathnames in the `Boot.ini` file to indicate which partition, physical disk, and folder contains the files used to start the operating system. Next, the drive letter and path to any other operating systems are listed. The operating system named at the end of each operating systems entry, after the = sign (whether it is an ARC pathname entry or not), is displayed in the boot loader screen.

There are two types of ARC pathname entries: *multi* and *scsi*. The terms multi and SCSI refer to the type of hard disk that is listed in the ARC pathname.

> note 📝 **The term *scsi* is normally presented in lowercase letters when it is used to indicate a type of file entry. It is normally presented in uppercase letters when it is used to refer to a disk, adapter, or controller.**

All hard disks that can be detected by the computer's BIOS, or by the BIOS on a SCSI adapter, are referred to as *multi*. All hard disks connected to SCSI adapters that do not have their BIOS enabled are referred to as *SCSI*. SCSI disks require a device driver to be loaded before the operating system can access the disk. The Windows NT installation program copies the device driver for a SCSI adapter to the root of the system partition and renames the file as `Ntbootdd.sys`.

The syntax of operating systems entries that begin with multi is as follows:

```
multi(W)disk(X)rdisk(Y)partition(Z)\path
```

- W is the ordinal number of the adapter. It should always be zero.
- X is not used for multi. It is always zero.
- Y is the ordinal for the hard disk on the controller. It is always 0 or 1 for disks connected to the primary controller, including SCSI adapters that have their BIOS enabled. It is 0, 1, 2, or 3 on dual channel EIDE controllers.
- Z is the partition number. The range of Z is usually 1–4.

The syntax of operating system entries that begin with scsi is as follows:

```
scsi(W)disk(X)rdisk(Y)partition(Z)\path
```

- W is the ordinal number of the adapter.
- X is the SCSI ID of the disk.
- Y is the logical unit number (LUN) of the disk. It is usually zero.

- o Z is the partition number. The range of Z is usually 1 – 4.

Operating systems entries that begin with scsi are typically used in three types of situations:

- o When the hard disk containing the system partition is on a SCSI adapter that does *not* have its BIOS enabled
- o When the hard disk containing the system partition is on a SCSI adapter *and* has an SCSI ID greater than one
- o When the hard disk containing the system partition is on a SCSI adapter *and* there is an IDE or EIDE controller in the system

Now that you understand the structure of the Boot.ini file, and the types of entries and syntax used in this file, you're ready to edit it.

Suppose that Figure 5-5 represents a computer that has a newly created mirror set (Disk 1 and Disk 2). The boot partition for this computer is located on the second disk (Disk 1), and uses the drive letter F:. The system partition of this computer (which contains the ntldr, Ntdetect.com, Boot.ini, and Bootsect.dos files) is located on the first disk (Disk 0), and uses the drive letter C:. The computer in this example uses a dual-channel EIDE controller.

You want to create a fault tolerance boot disk so you can reboot the computer in the event that Disk 1 fails. You follow the steps outlined in the "Creating a fault tolerance boot disk" section up to the point where you edit the Boot.ini file on the floppy disk. The Boot.ini file looks like this:

LISTING 5-2 Boot.ini file

```
[boot loader]
timeout=30
default=multi(0)disk(0)rdisk(1)partition(1)\WINNT
[operating systems]
multi(0)disk(0)rdisk(1)partition(1)\WINNT="Windows NT
      Server Version 4.00"
multi(0)disk(0)rdisk(1)partition(1)\WINNT="Windows NT
      Server Version 4.00 [VGA mode]" /basevideo /sos
C:\="Microsoft Windows"
```

FIGURE 5-5 New mirror set

In this situation, you must edit the Boot.ini file so it points to Disk 2. (The Boot.ini file must point to Disk 2 because if Disk 1 fails, Disk 2 will be the only disk in the mirror set that still works.) You remove the Boot.ini file's read-only attribute and use a text editor, such as Notepad, to edit the file. The edited version of the Boot.ini file on your newly created fault tolerance boot disk is presented here.

LISTING 5-3 Boot.ini file edited for fault tolerance boot disk

```
[boot loader]
timeout=30
default=multi(0)disk(0)rdisk(2)partition(1)\WINNT
[operating systems]
multi(0)disk(0)rdisk(2)partition(1)\WINNT="Windows NT
     Server Version 4.00"
multi(0)disk(0)rdisk(2)partition(1)\WINNT="Windows NT
     Server Version 4.00 [VGA mode]" /basevideo /sos
C:\="Microsoft Windows"
```

Notice that the ARC pathnames in the operating systems section now point to Disk 2 instead of Disk 1.

Finally, there are several switches you can add at the end of an operating systems entry in the Boot.ini file. Table 5-2 lists and describes these switches.

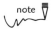 **These switches are not typically used when creating a fault toler-
ance boot disk. However, because they are used frequently during
troubleshooting, and because this is the only section of this book
that addresses the** Boot.ini **file in detail, I've covered the switches
here for completeness.**

Stripe Sets

In a *stripe set*, which is made up of 2 – 32 hard disks, data is stored, a block at a
time, evenly and sequentially among all of the disks in the set. Stripe sets are
sometimes referred to as disk striping. *Disk striping* alludes to the process wherein
a file is written, or striped, one block at a time; first to one disk, then to the next
disk, and then to the next disk, and so on, until all of the data has been evenly distributed among all of the disks.

TABLE 5-2 Boot.ini File Switches	
Switch	*Description*
/BASEVIDEO	This switch causes the computer to use the standard VGA driver when it starts, and is useful in troubleshooting video driver problems.
/BAUDRATE=nnnn	This switch specifies the baud rate used during debugging, and includes all of the functionality of the /DEBUG switch.
/CRASHDEBUG	This switch forces the debugger to load in an inactive state until an error occurs.
/DEBUG	This switch causes the debugger to be loaded. It can be activated by another computer connected to this computer by a modem or null-modem cable.
/DEBUGPORT=comx	This switch specifies which COM port the debugger uses, and includes all of the functionality of the /DEBUG switch.
/MAXMEM:n	This switch specifies the maximum amount of memory that Windows NT can use. It is useful for troubleshooting memory problems.
/NODEBUG	This switch specifies that the debugger will not run, and that no debugging information will be generated.

SWITCH	DESCRIPTION
/NOSERIALMICE=COMx |COMx,y,z... |	This specifies that the indicated serial port will not be tested for the presence of a mouse. Use this switch if you have an uninterruptible power supply (UPS) or some other device connected to a serial port.
/SOS	This switch provides a verbose listing of each device driver as it is loaded during the boot sequence. It is useful for troubleshooting device drivers.

 note

Neither the boot nor the system partition can be on a stripe set.

A stripe set is accessed by using a single drive letter, as if all of its disks were combined into a single drive. A stripe set is created from identical amounts of free space on each of the disks that belong to the set.

Stripe sets provide faster disk access than volume sets or large individual hard disks because the stripe sets store a single file across multiple disks. The various pieces of the file can be read nearly simultaneously from the multiple disks, thus increasing performance. Access speed is the primary advantage and common reason for using a stripe set. The tradeoff or downside to using a stripe set is that the potential disk failure rate is increased because there are more possible points of failure when a file is accessed across several disks.

Stripe sets have no additional cost associated with them because they use the same amount of disk space in which that data would normally be stored. However, stripe sets do not provide any fault tolerance. If one partition or disk in a stripe set fails, all data on the stripe set is lost.

A stripe set (or disk striping) is also known as RAID level 0.

TO CREATE A STRIPE SET, FOLLOW THESE STEPS:

1. Start Disk Administrator.

2. Click an area of free space on one of your computer's hard disks.

3. Press and hold Ctrl while you click one or more additional areas of free space on other hard disks. You can't select more than one area of free space per physical disk.

4. Select Partition ⇒ Create Stripe Set.

5. The Create Stripe Set dialog box is displayed, as shown in Figure 5-6. Note that it shows the minimum and maximum amount of total space that can be used for the stripe set. The maximum total size is the amount of free space from the smallest area of free space you selected, multiplied by the number of disks you selected. (Remember, in stripe sets, the size of the free space areas on the disks used in the set are identical.) You can either accept this number or type in a smaller value in the "Create stripe set of total size" text box. Click OK to create the stripe set.

6. The Disk Administrator main dialog box reappears. Select Partition ⇒ Commit Changes Now. Click Yes to save the changes to disk. Then click OK to acknowledge that the disks were updated successfully.

7. The Disk Administrator main dialog box reappears. Figure 5-7 shows the stripe set at this point. Note that the stripe set is created and uses the drive letter H: on Disks 1, 2, and 3, but it still needs to be formatted.

FIGURE 5-6   Creating a stripe set

FIGURE 5-7   Unformatted stripe set

8. Follow the directions in the "Creating and formatting a primary partition" section earlier in this chapter to format the stripe set. The stripe set is now complete.

Stripe Sets with Parity

A *stripe set with parity* is similar to a stripe set, but it provides a degree of fault tolerance that the stripe set cannot. In a stripe set with parity, data is not only distributed a block at a time, evenly and sequentially among all the disks in the set, but parity information is also written across all of the disks in the set.

 note   **Neither the boot nor the system partition can be on a stripe set with parity.**

A stripe set with parity is made up of 3 – 32 hard disks. Like stripe sets, stripe sets with parity are created from identical amounts of free space on each disk that belongs to the set.

in the real world **Striping with parity, in my experience, is the most common method of fault tolerance. It is less costly than disk mirroring (because data is not replicated on another disk), is faster than disk mirroring, and provides a modest level of data safety.**

A stripe set with parity provides the same read performance as a stripe set, but its write performance is a little slower.

If a single disk in a stripe set with parity fails, the parity information contained in the other disks is used to regenerate the data from the failed disk. (Recovering from a single disk failure in a stripe set with parity is discussed later in this chapter.) You cannot recover your data in a stripe set with parity if more than one disk fails.

Stripe sets with parity (sometimes called *striping with parity*) are also known as RAID level 5.

TO CREATE A STRIPE SET WITH PARITY, FOLLOW THESE STEPS:

1. Start Disk Administrator.

2. Click an area of free space on one of your computer's hard disks.

3. Press and hold Ctrl while you click two or more additional areas of free space on other hard disks. You can't select more than one area of free space per physical disk.

4. Select Fault Tolerance ⇒ Create Stripe Set with Parity.

5. The Create Stripe Set with Parity dialog box is displayed showing the minimum and maximum amount of space that can be used for the stripe set. The maximum amount is the amount of free space from the smallest area of free space you selected, multiplied by the number of disks you selected. You can either accept this number or type in a smaller value in the "Create stripe set of total size" text box. Click OK to create the stripe set with parity.

6. The Disk Administrator main dialog box reappears. Select Partition ⇒ Commit Changes Now. Click Yes to save the changes to disk. Then click OK to acknowledge that the disks were updated successfully. At this point, the stripe set with parity is created, but still needs to be formatted.

7. To format the stripe set with parity, follow the directions presented earlier in this chapter in the "Creating and formatting a primary partition" section.

8. At the conclusion of the formatting process, Disk Administrator performs additional functions on the newly created stripe set with parity. The Disk Administrator main dialog box reappears. Click any disk that is part of the stripe set with parity to view the status of this process. As Figure 5-8 shows, Disk Administrator indicates that it is INITIALIZING the stripe set with parity. Notice that the stripe set with parity uses the drive letter F: and consists of Disks 1, 2, and 3.

The initializing process takes quite a while. (It may take several minutes to an hour or more, depending on the size of the stripe set with parity.)

FIGURE 5-8   **Stripe set with parity (INITIALIZING)**

9. When the initializing process is finally complete, the Disk Administrator main dialog box changes. Figure 5-9 shows the completed stripe set with parity. Notice at the bottom of the dialog box the stripe set with parity is called HEALTHY.

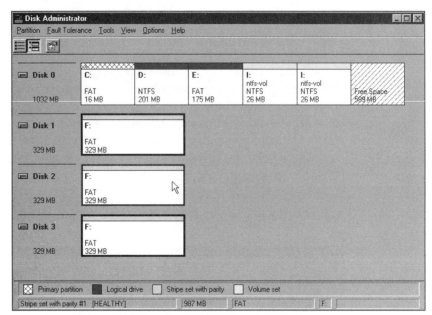

FIGURE 5-9   **Stripe set with parity (HEALTHY) established**

Volume Sets

A *volume set* is a combination of free space areas over 2–32 hard disks that is treated as a single drive. (The free space areas do not need to be of identical size.)

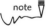 **Neither the boot nor the system partition can be on a volume set.**

The primary purpose and use of a volume set is to access disk space on more than one hard disk by using a single drive letter. A volume set is sometimes used when a drive becomes full and you want to enlarge its capacity.

A volume set is similar to a stripe set. However, a file in a volume set is usually fully contained on a single hard disk, instead of being striped over multiple hard disks.

Volume sets do not involve additional cost, because no additional hard disks are required over the number normally needed to store data.

Volume sets, like stripe sets, do not perform any fault tolerance function. If one disk in a volume set fails, all data on the volume may be lost, because Windows NT can't access data unless all of the disks that make up the volume set are functional.

Volume sets are said to be *created* when areas of free space only (not existing volumes) are combined into a volume set. Volume sets are said to be *extended* when an existing NTFS partition is enlarged.

It's been my experience that extending a volume set is far more common than creating one. It's one way to approach a situation when a drive is filled to capacity and you still need additional space in that volume.

The following sections explain how to create and extend volume sets.

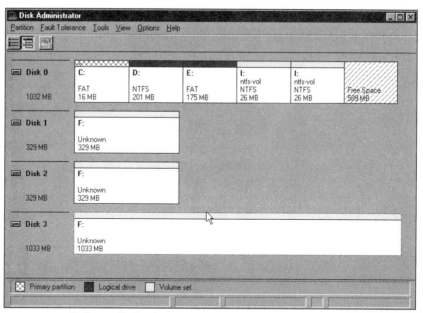

FIGURE 5-10 Unformatted volume set

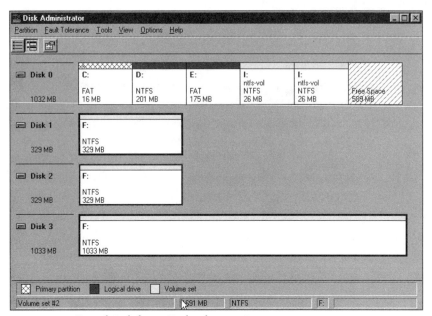

FIGURE 5-11   Completed, formatted volume set

TO CREATE A VOLUME SET, FOLLOW THESE STEPS:

1. Start Disk Administrator.

2. Click an area of free space on one of your computer's hard disks.

3. Press and hold Ctrl while you click one or more additional areas of free space on other disks.

4. Select Partition ⇒ Create Volume Set.

5. The Create Volume Set dialog box is displayed showing the minimum and maximum amount of space that can be used for the volume set. Enter the size you want the volume set to be in the "Create volume set of total size" text box. Click OK to create the volume set.

6. The Disk Administrator main dialog box reappears. Select Partition ⇒ Commit Changes Now. Click Yes to save the changes to disk. Then click OK to acknowledge that the disks were updated successfully.

7. The Disk Administrator main dialog box reappears. Figure 5-10 shows the status of the volume set at this point. Note that the volume set, which uses the drive letter F: over Disks 1, 2, and 3 is created, but still needs to be formatted.

8. To format the volume set, follow the directions from the "Creating and formatting a primary partition" section earlier in this chapter. Figure 5-11 displays the completed, formatted volume set.

TO EXTEND A VOLUME SET, FOLLOW THESE STEPS:

1. Start Disk Administrator.

2. Click an NTFS partition on one of your computer's hard disks. (Only NTFS volumes and volume sets can be extended.)

3. Press and hold Ctrl while you click one or more additional areas of free space on other disks.

4. Select Partition ⇒ Extend Volume Set.

5. The Extend Volume Set dialog box is displayed showing the minimum and maximum amount of space that can be used for the total volume set. Enter the size you would like the total volume set to be in the "Create volume set of total size" text box. Click OK to extend the volume set.

6. The Disk Administrator main dialog box reappears. The volume set is now extended. You don't have to format extensions to volume sets.

7. Exit Disk Administrator and reboot your computer to make the extended volume set effective.

Comparison of Disk Partitioning Schemes

At this point, you've had a chance to examine four different disk partitioning schemes: disk mirroring, stripe sets, stripe sets with parity, and volume sets.

Table 5-3 compares the fault tolerance, cost, and access speed provided by these four disk partitioning schemes. Note that the most expensive scheme, disk mirroring, also provides the highest level of fault tolerance of the methods listed. As with most things in life, you get what you pay for.

DISK PARTITIONING SCHEME	FAULT TOLERANCE	COST	ACCESS SPEED
Disk mirroring	High	High	Normal (Slowest)
Stripe sets with parity	Medium	Medium	Medium-Fast
Stripe sets	Low (None)	Low	Fastest
Volume sets	Low (None)	Low	Normal (Slowest)

TABLE 5-3 COMPARISON OF DISK PARTITIONING SCHEMES

Now that you're familiar with the various disk partitioning schemes, it's appropriate to discuss how to recover from disk failure when each of these schemes is used.

RECOVERING FROM DISK FAILURE

So what do you do when it all comes crashing down—when the remote possibility of disk failure that you planned for, but never thought would actually happen, is a painful reality?

This section provides information on how to recover from a single or multiple hard disk failure. Specifically, you'll learn how to recover from disk failure in situations where disk mirroring, stripe sets, stripe sets with parity, and volume sets are used.

 exam preparation pointer **The preparation guide for the Server exam lists a specific objective in the Troubleshooting section on resolving fault tolerance failures. Because you are unlikely to get a lot of practice at this in real life, I recommend that you study this section carefully, and revisit it just before you take the exam.**

In some cases your disk configuration may enable you to continue operations (but without any fault tolerance) until you can replace the failed hard disk and restore your fault tolerance configuration.

In cases of stripe set, volume set, or multiple hard disk failure, you must repair the hardware and restore your data from tape to continue operations. If you don't have a tape backup in these situations, Windows NT will *not* be able to recover your data.

 concept link

Tape backup is critically important. For more information on data backup and restoration, see Chapter 13.

 tip

When you have a disk failure (or a multiple disk failure in the case of disk mirroring or a stripe set with parity), and you don't have a tape backup, you might consider contacting a third-party data recovery service if the data is extremely important or valuable to you. The data recovery service may be able to retrieve some of your data from the failed disk. Be forewarned, however, that this process is expensive and takes time to complete.

The next several sections explain the detailed steps you can take to recover from disk failure in situations where disk mirroring, stripe sets, stripe sets with parity, and volume sets are involved.

Disk Mirroring

Sometimes a disk that is part of a mirror set fails. Here's what you can do if that happens.

 caution

The steps in this and other how-to sections in this book are meant to be informational, not a lab exercise. Don't delete or reformat any partition that contains data that you don't want to lose. And remember, back up all important data and programs before you make any changes to your computer's configuration.

TO RESTORE YOUR FAULT TOLERANCE DISK CONFIGURATION AFTER ONE DISK IN A MIRROR SET FAILS, FOLLOW THESE STEPS:

1. Boot the computer (by using the fault tolerance boot disk if needed) and then start Disk Administrator.

2. Click the disk in the mirror set that is still operational.

3. Select Fault Tolerance ⇒ Break Mirror. Click Yes in the Confirm dialog box to end mirroring and to create two independent partitions.

4. The Disk Administrator main dialog box reappears. Select Partition ⇒ Commit Changes Now.

5. In the Confirm dialog box, click Yes to save the changes.

6. Disk Administrator indicates that the disks were updated successfully. Click OK.

7. The Disk Administrator main dialog box reappears. Exit Disk Administrator, shut down the computer, and replace the failed hard disk.

8. Restart the computer (by using the fault tolerance boot disk if needed) and then start Disk Administrator.

9. Click the partition that you broke the mirror on in Step 3. (This is the good [non-failed] partition that has your data on it.)

10. Press and hold Ctrl while you click an area of free space on the new hard disk that is at least as large as the partition you want to mirror.

11. From the Fault Tolerance menu, select Establish Mirror.

12. The Disk Administrator main dialog box reappears. Disk activity occurs and may last for some time, depending on the size of the partition to be mirrored and the amount of data on that partition. Your mirror set is now reestablished.

Stripe Sets

Recovering from a failed disk or disks in a stripe set is fairly straightforward.

If you don't have a tape backup of the files on the stripe set, Windows NT can't recover your data. If you have a tape backup, first delete the existing stripe set, and then create a new stripe set. Follow the steps below to recover from a stripe set disk failure.

TO REPLACE THE FAILED DISK AND DELETE THE EXISTING STRIPE SET (INCLUDING ALL REMAINING DATA ON THE DISKS IN THE SET), FOLLOW THESE STEPS:

1. Replace the failed hard disk or disks. Reboot the computer.

2. Start Disk Administrator.

3. Click any of the good (non-failed) partitions in the stripe set. (Clicking any good partition in the stripe set highlights all remaining partitions in the set.) Select Partition ⇒ Delete. Click Yes in the Confirm dialog box to delete the partition.

4. The Disk Administrator main dialog box reappears. Select Partition ⇒ Commit Changes Now.

5. In the Confirm dialog box, click Yes to save the changes.

6. Disk Administrator indicates that the disks were updated successfully. Click OK. The Disk Administrator main dialog box reappears.

THEN, TO CREATE A NEW STRIPE SET (THAT WILL INCLUDE THE NEW DISK) FOLLOW THESE STEPS:

1. To create a new stripe set that will include the new disk, follow the steps presented earlier in this chapter for creating a stripe set.

2. Restore all data from tape.

Stripe Sets with Parity

If you have more than one failed hard disk in a stripe set with parity, follow the steps for recovering from a disk failure in a stripe set (in the previous section). If a single hard disk in your stripe set with parity fails, the following steps explain how to recover.

TO RECOVER FROM A *single* HARD DISK FAILURE IN A STRIPE SET WITH PARITY, FOLLOW THESE STEPS:

1. Replace the failed disk and reboot the computer.

2. Start Disk Administrator.

3. Click any portion of the existing stripe set with parity. Press and hold Ctrl while you click the free space area on the new hard disk.

4. Select Fault Tolerance ⇒ Regenerate.

5. The Disk Administrator main dialog box reappears. Click any disk that is part of the stripe set with parity. A significant amount of disk activity occurs as the computer regenerates the data on the new hard disk.

During the regeneration process, various messages are displayed at the bottom of the Disk Administrator dialog box, including RECOVERABLE, REGENERATING, and HEALTHY. The process is complete when HEALTHY is displayed.

 note **Sometimes it is necessary to reboot the computer during Step 5. For example, if Disk Administrator displays RECOVERABLE for a long period of time (10 minutes or more), you might try rebooting the computer to start the regeneration process.**

Volume Sets

Recovering from a failed disk or disks in a volume set is fairly straightforward.

If you don't have a backup of the files on the volume set, Windows NT can't recover your data. If you have a tape backup, follow these steps to recover from the disk failure.

FIRST, TO DELETE THE EXISTING VOLUME SET (AND ALL REMAINING DATA ON THE DISKS IN THE SET), FOLLOW THESE STEPS:

1. Replace the failed hard disk or disks. Reboot the computer.

2. Start Disk Administrator.

3. Click any of the good (non-failed) partitions in the volume set. (Clicking any partition in the volume set highlights all remaining partitions in the volume set.) Select Partition ⇒ Delete. Click Yes in the Confirm dialog box to delete the partition.

4. The Disk Administrator main dialog box reappears. Select Partition ⇒ Commit Changes Now.

5. In the Confirm dialog box, click Yes to save the changes.

6. Disk Administrator indicates that the disks were updated successfully. Click OK. The Disk Administrator main dialog box reappears.

NEXT, CREATE A NEW VOLUME SET (THAT WILL INCLUDE THE NEW HARD DISK) BY FOLLOWING THESE STEPS:

1. To create a new volume set that will include the new hard disk, follow the steps presented earlier in this chapter for creating a volume set.

2. Restore all data from tape.

UPDATING THE EMERGENCY REPAIR DISK

The *Emergency Repair Disk* is a floppy disk used to restore the Windows NT Registry to the configuration that existed when the Emergency Repair Disk was created (or updated).

If you have made any changes to your computer's system configuration since the Emergency Repair Disk was created or last updated, those changes will be lost during the emergency repair process. For this reason, you should update your Emergency Repair Disk *every time* you make a change to your computer's system configuration, including any changes to your disk configuration. Windows NT will prompt you to update your Emergency Repair Disk every time you make a change to your disk configuration in Disk Administrator. (You'll have a chance to update your Emergency Repair Disk in Lab 5.10 at the end of this chapter.)

concept link

This chapter only discusses updating the Emergency Repair Disk. Chapter 21 explains how to use the Emergency Repair Disk to restore the Registry.

The Emergency Repair Disk is initially created during the installation of Windows NT. To update it at any time after installation (or to create an Emergency Repair disk after installation if one was not created at that time), you must use the `Rdisk.exe` utility.

You won't find the `Rdisk.exe` utility in the Start menu. You will either need to run it from the command line, run it by selecting the Run option from the Start menu, or you can create a shortcut for it on your desktop.

When you run Rdisk.exe, a Repair Disk Utility dialog box is displayed. Figure 5-12 shows the first Repair Disk Utility dialog box.

FIGURE 5-12   The first Repair Disk Utility dialog box

If you click the Update Repair Info command button in the Repair Disk Utility dialog box (and click Yes in the next dialog box displayed to confirm), Rdisk.exe will save all of your Registry (with the exception of the Security hive and the Security Accounts Manager [SAM] database) to the <winntroot>\ repair directory. <winntroot> is the directory that was specified for the installation of Windows NT, usually C:\winnt.

concept link

For additional information on the Windows NT Registry, see Chapter 21, as well as the *Microsoft Windows NT Workstation Resource Kit for version 4.0*, Part V, "Windows NT Registry."

After Rdisk.exe saves your Registry configuration information, it will ask if you want to create an Emergency Repair Disk. Figure 5-13 displays this Repair Disk Utility dialog box. Click Yes to create the Emergency Repair Disk.

**FIGURE 5-13   Creating (Updating) the Emergency
Repair Disk**

note

Don't be thrown because Rdisk.exe asks if you want to *create* an Emergency Repair Disk when what you're really trying to do is to *update* it. Rdisk.exe uses the same process and terminology for both.

At this point, Repair Disk prompts you to insert a labeled 3.5-inch floppy disk into drive A:. If you have the Emergency Repair Disk you created during the installation of Windows NT, use this disk to create an updated Emergency Repair Disk. If you didn't create an Emergency Repair Disk during installation, insert any blank floppy disk to create an Emergency Repair Disk now.

A second way you can update your Emergency Repair Disk is to use the one command line switch that can be used with `Rdisk.exe`, the `/S` switch. The `S` stands for security. Using the `/S` switch causes the entire Registry, including the Security hive and the SAM database, to be backed up. When you run `Rdisk.exe` with the `/S` switch, `Rdisk.exe` automatically begins saving your Registry information to the repair directory and then prompts you to create the Emergency Repair Disk.

 tip
It's a good idea to use the `Rdisk.exe` utility with the `/S` switch. This will provide you with a backup of the SAM database in addition to the one on your regularly scheduled tape backup.

 tip
Another good idea is to write down the Administrator's password *at the time you create a new or updated Emergency Repair Disk*. Because passwords may be changed frequently, and because you will need to enter the Administrator's password (as of the date the Emergency Repair Disk was created or last updated) after you restore the Registry from the Emergency Repair Disk, it's very important to know what the Administrator's password was *at that time*. Personally, I go so far as to write the Administrator's password on the Emergency Repair Disk label.

To use the `Rdisk.exe` utility with the `/S` switch, select the Run option from the Start menu, and then type **rdisk /s** in the text box within the Run dialog box.

KEY POINT SUMMARY

This chapter introduced the three file systems that Windows NT supports, as well as partitions and how to work with them, how to recover from disk failure, and how to update the Emergency Repair Disk.

- Windows NT supports the file allocation table (FAT) file system, the Windows NT file system (NTFS), and the Compact Disc Filing System (CDFS).

  - The *FAT file system* does not support file and folder security in Windows NT. The FAT file system supports the use of long filenames, and normally permits faster access to files on partitions smaller than 500MB than other file systems. The maximum size of a FAT partition is 4GB. The FAT file system does not support file compression.

  - *NTFS* is the most powerful file system supported by Windows NT. NT is the only operating system that supports NTFS. NTFS provides file and folder security. NTFS, like FAT, supports the use of long filenames. NTFS usually provides faster access to files stored on a large partition that contains a large number of files than the FAT file system. The maximum functional size of an NTFS partition is two terabytes. NTFS supports file compression, and is a highly reliable, recoverable file system. You can use the Convert.exe command to convert an existing FAT partition into an NTFS partition. This is a one-way conversion. It is much more difficult to convert an NTFS partition into a FAT partition.

- Marking a disk to identify which parts contain a file system is called *partitioning*. A hard disk can be separated into a maximum of four partitions. Windows NT supports two types of partitions: *primary* and *extended*. The Windows NT 4.0 *system partition* must be located on the active primary partition on the first hard disk in a computer. The *boot partition* can be located on either a primary or extended partition. A hard disk can have more than one primary partition on it, but can have only one extended partition on it.

- *Disk Administrator* is the Windows NT tool that is used to create, format, and otherwise manage partitions. This chapter includes detailed steps explaining how to use Disk Administrator for creating partitions, formatting partitions, establishing disk mirroring, creating a fault tolerance boot disk (including editing the Boot.ini file), and creating stripe sets, stripe sets with parity, and volume sets. Table 5-3 compares the levels of fault tolerance, cost, and access speed provided by four common disk partitioning schemes: *disk mirroring*, *stripe sets with parity*, *stripe sets*, and *volume sets*. Of the four schemes, disk mirroring is the most expensive and provides the highest level of fault tolerance. Stripe sets and volume sets are inexpensive, but neither provide any fault tolerance.

o Specific steps on recovering from single and multiple disk failure in instances of disk mirroring, stripe sets, stripe sets with parity, and volume sets are presented. Tape backup is critically important to this process.

o The `Rdisk.exe` utility is used to update the Emergency Repair Disk. The Emergency Repair Disk is used to restore the Windows NT Registry to the configuration that existed when the Emergency Repair Disk was created (or updated). The Emergency Repair Disk should be updated *every time* you make a change to your computer's system or disk configuration. `Rdisk.exe` can be run with the `/S` switch to backup the Security hive and the SAM database.

APPLYING WHAT YOU'VE LEARNED

Now it's time to regroup, review, and apply what you've learned in this chapter.

The questions in the following Instant Assessment section bring to mind key facts and concepts. Next, two Critical Thinking Labs focus on planning, and give you a chance to apply your knowledge of disk management to real-world situations. Finally, the two Hands-on Labs reinforce what you've learned, and give you an opportunity to practice some of the tasks tested by the Server exam.

Instant Assessment

1. What are the three file systems supported by Windows NT 4.0?

2. If you want your computer to dual boot between Windows NT 4.0 and Windows 95, which file system must your computer's first partition use?

3. Which is easier to accomplish: converting a FAT partition to NTFS, or converting an NTFS partition to a FAT partition?

4. When a computer boots, from which partition on which disk does it attempt to *begin* the process of loading the operating system?

5. When booting from the hard disk, on which partition must the Windows NT 4.0 system partition be located?

6. How many primary partitions can you have on one disk? How many extended partitions? How many total partitions?

7. Which Windows NT tool is used to create, format, and otherwise manage partitions?

8. Which of the four disk partitioning schemes involves making an exact replica of a partition onto a separate hard disk?

9. When is a fault tolerance boot disk used?

10. What two sections make up the `Boot.ini` file?

11. Which disk partitioning scheme involves the distribution of data, a block at a time, evenly and sequentially, among all of the disks in the set?

12. Which of the four disk partitioning schemes discussed provide no fault tolerance (that is to say, if one disk fails, all data is lost)?

13. Which of the four disk partitioning schemes is the most commonly used method of fault tolerance? Why?

14. Which of the four disk partitioning schemes is the most expensive and provides the highest amount of fault tolerance?

15. Which utility can you use to update your Emergency Repair Disk?

16. After starting Disk Administrator, what's the first main step in recovering from a single disk failure when the disk is part of a mirror set?

T/F

17. The FAT file system supports file and folder security in Windows NT. _____

18. The FAT file system supports the use of long filenames. _____

19. The FAT file system supports file compression. _____

20. NTFS provides file and folder security in Windows NT. _____

21. NTFS supports the use of long filenames. _____

22. NTFS does *not* preserve upper- and lowercase in filenames. _____

23. The minimum functional size of an NTFS partition is 2 terabytes. _____

24. NTFS supports a compression attribute for each file. _____

25. NTFS is a highly reliable, recoverable file system.   _____

26. Using NTFS increases the likelihood of fragmentation on partitions. _____

27. You can use NTFS to format a floppy disk.   _____

concept link   **For answers to the Instant Assessment questions see Appendix B.**

Critical Thinking Labs

The following labs challenge your understanding of disk configuration topics.

Lab 5.7 *File system planning exercise*

Planning involves considering the facts and needs of a given situation *before* you make a choice or commitment to a particular path.

exam preparation pointer   **Planning is not only critically important in the real world, it's also tested on the Server exam. So, try to start thinking about planning situations, not just as you do this exercise, but throughout the rest of your study and preparation for the exam.**

For each of the following scenarios, consider the given facts and any expressed needs or goals. Then choose the most appropriate file system for each scenario.

Problem 1   You want to run Windows NT Server on a computer. Your computer's hard disk has one 480MB partition and one 20MB partition. Each folder on the partitions contains a moderate amount of files. You want to optimize access speed to the files. Which file system should you choose?

Problem 2   You want your new computer to dual boot between Windows NT Server and MS-DOS. Your computer's 1GB hard drive has only one partition on it. Which file system should you choose?

Problem 3   Your computer has two hard disks, and each hard disk has a 4GB partition. There are a large number of files in the folders on these partitions. You want to run Windows NT on this computer and optimize access speed to the files. Which file system should you choose?

Problem 4   You plan to install and run Windows NT Server on a computer. Your supervisor informs you that file and folder security are required because of highly sensitive data that is stored on this computer. You also need to be able to utilize file compression because of the amount and size of files on this computer. Which file system should you choose?

concept link   **For answers to the Critical Thinking Lab see Appendix B.**

Lab 5.8 *Disk partitioning and fault tolerance planning exercise*

This chapter introduced four disk partitioning schemes: disk mirroring, stripe sets with parity, stripe sets, and volume sets.

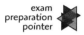

exam
preparation
pointer
The Server exam tests your ability to plan the disk drive configuration for various requirements, including choosing a fault tolerance method.

I know this seems like a lot of stuff to memorize, but for experienced network professionals, making these decisions is almost second nature. It should also be second nature to you by the time you take the exam!

For each of the following scenarios, consider the given facts and any expressed criteria that must be met. Then choose the most appropriate disk partitioning scheme for each scenario.

(Hint: As you may recall, Table 5-3 compares the levels of fault tolerance, cost, and access speed provided by the four schemes.)

Problem 1   You are in charge of planning a new server for your company. Management tells you that protection of data is the most important requirement for this new server, more important than speed and even more important than cost. Which disk partitioning scheme should you choose?

Problem 2   You are planning a new server for your company's network. The server will contain a large database. Speed of access to files on the database is your primary concern. Fault tolerance is not important, but you do need to minimize costs. Which disk partitioning scheme should you choose?

Problem 3   You are planning to add a new server to your organization's network. You want to achieve a moderate amount of fault tolerance and minimize costs. Which disk partitioning scheme should you choose?

 concept link   **For answers to the Critical Thinking Lab see Appendix B.**

Hands-on Labs

The following Hands-on Labs provide you with two different opportunities to use the disk management knowledge you've gained in this chapter.

Lab 5.9 *Managing partitions*

The objective of this lab is for you to gain experience using Disk Administrator to manage partitions.

Follow the steps carefully to successfully partition and format the remaining 10MB of your computer's hard drive with an NTFS partition.

 note   **If you didn't leave enough space on your hard disk to perform this, I recommend that you reinstall NT Server to accommodate this lab. If this is not possible, you should create an NTFS partition somewhere on one of your hard disks so that you can perform the file security labs later in this book.**

 caution   **Don't delete or reformat any partition that contains data that you don't want to lose. As always, make sure you back up all important data and programs *before* you do the lab exercise.**

1. Boot your computer to Windows NT Server. Log on as Administrator.
2. Close the Welcome to NT dialog box if it appears.
3. Select Start ⇒ Programs ⇒ Administrative Tools (Common) ⇒ Disk Administrator.
4. Disk Administrator displays a dialog box indicating that this is the first time Disk Administrator has been run. Click OK to update the system configuration.

5. If this is the first time Disk Administrator has been run, a Confirm dialog box appears, indicating that no signature is found on Disk 0. Click Yes to write a signature on Disk 0.

6. Click the box that indicates a drive with a 10MB partition (to highlight it), and select Partition ⇒ Delete. (Caution! If this partition is displayed as Free Space, don't do this step. Instead, skip to Step 11.)

7. Click Yes in the Confirm dialog box to delete the partition.

8. Select Partition ⇒ Commit Changes Now.

9. Click Yes in the Confirm dialog box to save the changes to your disk.

10. Click OK to return to the Disk Administrator main dialog box.

11. Click the box that indicates the drive with 10MB of free space (to highlight it), and then select Partition ⇒ Create.

12. A Confirm dialog box appears. Click Yes to continue to create the partition.

13. Click OK in the Create Primary Partition dialog box to create a new partition.

14. Select Partition ⇒ Commit Changes Now.

15. Click Yes in the Confirm dialog box to save the changes to your disk.

16. Click OK to return to the Disk Administrator main dialog box.

17. Click the box that indicates the drive with a 10MB partition (labeled Unknown) to highlight it.

18. Select Tools ⇒ Format.

19. Choose NTFS in the File System drop-down list box, accept all the other defaults, and then click Start.

20. A warning dialog box appears. Click OK to format the drive.

21. A dialog box appears indicating that the format is complete. Click OK.

22. Click Close to return to the Disk Administrator main dialog box.

23. Select Partition ⇒ Exit to exit Disk Administrator.

Congratulations! You have now formatted the 10MB partition on your computer with NTFS.

Lab 5.10 *Updating the Emergency Repair Disk*

The purpose of this lab is to provide you with the skills required to update your Emergency Repair Disk and to give you experience performing this task.

In order to do this lab, you need the Emergency Repair Disk you created in Lab 2.2 during the installation of Windows NT.

1. Boot your computer to Windows NT Server. Log on as Administrator.

2. Select Start ⇒ Run.

3. When the Run dialog box appears, type **RDISK** in the drop-down dialog box.

4. Click OK to run `Rdisk.exe`.

5. When the Repair Disk Utility dialog box appears, click Update Repair Info.

6. Click Yes to update your repair information.

7. `Rdisk.exe` saves your current configuration. This takes a couple of minutes. Click Yes to create the Emergency Repair Disk.

8. When prompted, place the Emergency Repair Disk you created in Lab 2.2 in drive A:. Click OK to create the Emergency Repair Disk. (This process erases your original Emergency Repair Disk and creates a new Emergency Repair Disk with your current system configurations.) It takes a couple of minutes for the Repair Disk Utility to complete this process.

9. Click Exit to exit the Repair Disk Utility. Your Emergency Repair Disk is now updated. Remove it from drive A:.

Managing Printing

About Chapter 6

This chapter covers printing from A to Z. It begins with a discussion of Windows NT printing terminology, and then quickly moves to the print process, and then to creating and connecting to a printer.

Chapter 6 explores configuring printer properties extensively. You'll learn how to assign a separator page; how to assign forms to paper trays; and how to use Windows NT printer security to assign printer permissions to users and groups, to audit a user or group's printer usage, and to take ownership of a printer. Other topics discussed in this section include printing to multiple ports (printer pools), scheduling printers, setting printer priorities, and sharing printers.

Finally, this chapter concludes with a practical section on troubleshooting common printing problems.

This chapter includes two Hands-on Labs. In the first lab, you become familiar with the Windows NT `Printers` folder and create and share a local printer. In the second, you install and configure Microsoft TCP/IP Printing.

The material presented in this chapter maps to the "Configure printers" and ". . . resolve printer problems" objectives listed in the Installation and Configuration and Troubleshooting sections in the Preparation Guide for the Server exam.

PRINTING TERMINOLOGY

Before you can fully understand printing with Windows NT, you should first understand a few terms.

In Windows NT, the term *printer* does not represent a physical device that produces printed output. Rather, a printer is the software interface between the Windows NT operating system and the device that produces printed output.

 in the real world **If you are used to working with a different operating system, such as NetWare or UNIX, you may be used to thinking of what Windows NT calls a printer as a combination of a print queue (or print spooler) plus a driver for the device that produces printed output.**

If you aren't used to working with another operating system, feel free to ignore this note, because it may just be confusing at this point.

In Windows NT, the term *print device* refers to the physical device that produces printed output — what is more commonly referred to as a "printer."

exam
preparation
pointer

Be sure that you know the Windows NT printing terminology cold. Otherwise, you may become confused when taking the Server exam.

Remember: a *printer* is software, and a *print* (or *printing*) device is hardware. Beat this into your head with a large wooden mallet!

Now that you have a grasp of the Windows NT printing terminology, you're ready to move on to the nuts and bolts of printing in Windows NT.

WINDOWS NT PRINTING OVERVIEW

This section examines the process of printing in Windows NT. It also explains, in detail, the most commonly used print monitors.

The Print Process

Perhaps the easiest way to understand the Windows NT print process is to follow the steps that occur when a document is printed from an application in Windows NT.

1. A user at a Windows NT computer starts the print process from an application, such as Word, usually by selecting Print from the File menu. This action creates the print job. (A print job is all of the data and commands needed to print a document.)

2. The application hands off the print job to the *Graphics Device Interface* (GDI). (In Windows NT 4.0, the GDI is a kernel mode component.)

3. The GDI initiates a request to the driver for the print device.

4. The driver for the print device converts the application's output (the print job) into either a Windows NT *enhanced metafile* (EMF) or into a RAW format. (The RAW format is ready to print, as is, and no further processing is required.) The driver then returns the converted print job to the GDI.

5. The GDI hands off the print job to the Windows NT spooler.

6. The Windows NT spooler determines whether the print device is managed by the computer that initiated the print job, or by a network-connected computer.

If the print device is managed by the local computer (the computer that initiated this print job), the spooler copies the print job to a temporary storage area on the computer's hard disk.

If the print device is managed by a network-connected computer, the spooler hands off the print job to the spooler on the network-connected computer. Then that spooler copies the print job to a temporary storage area on that computer's hard disk.

7. Once the spooler has copied the file to temporary storage, the print job is handed off to the local print provider on the computer that has the print job spooled to its hard disk.

8. The local print provider initiates a request to the print processor to perform any additional conversions needed on the file, such as from EMF to RAW. (When a print device receives a print job, it always receives it in the RAW format.) The print processor then returns the converted print job to the local print provider.

9. The local print provider adds a separator page to the print job (if it's configured to do so) and then hands off the print job to the print monitor.

10. The print monitor communicates directly with the print device and sends the ready-to-print print job to the print device.

11. The print device produces the printed document.

Figure 6-1 graphically illustrates the steps in the Windows NT print process. Notice that the spooler routes the print job to the local hard disk if the print device is managed by the local computer, and routes the print job to the spooler on the network-connected computer if the print device is managed by the network-connected computer.

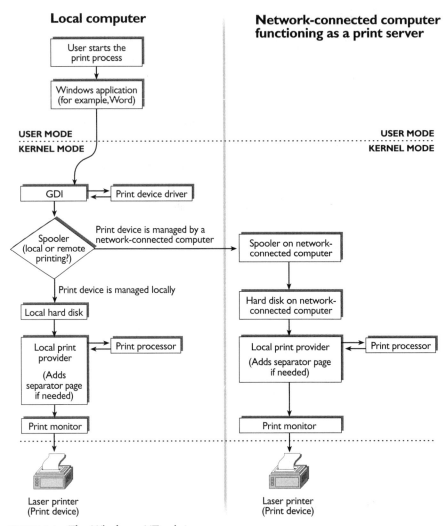

FIGURE 6-1   The Windows NT print process

Using EMFs in network printing

Using Windows NT *enhanced metafiles* (EMFs) can significantly increase the performance of printing across a network for the following reasons:

- Windows NT creates an EMF faster than it can create a RAW format file.

- Windows NT splits the overhead of the print process between the local computer (which creates the EMF) and the network-connected computer (which converts the EMF to the RAW format).

This means that the user who creates the print job experiences faster printing than if the RAW format file was created locally on the user's computer.

CREATING AND CONNECTING TO PRINTERS

There are two ways to install and configure a printer in Windows NT: you can either create a printer, or you can connect to a shared network printer.

Creating a printer involves installing and configuring all of the drivers needed to use a locally managed print device. Connecting to a shared network printer involves installing and configuring all of the drivers needed to use a print device that is managed by another computer on the network. You can either connect to a shared network printer by using the Add Printer Wizard in the `Printers` folder, or you can use drag-and-drop printing to connect to a shared network printer.

Both creating a printer and connecting to a printer are called "adding a printer," because both processes use the Add Printer Wizard.

Steps to Create a Printer

This section explains the steps involved in creating a printer in Windows NT by using the Add Printer Wizard.

TO CREATE A PRINTER IN WINDOWS NT, FOLLOW THESE STEPS:

1. Open the `Printers` folder. You can do this in any of the following four ways:
- Select Start ⇒ Settings ⇒ Printers.
- Double-click My Computer, and then double-click the `Printers` folder.
- Select Start ⇒ Programs ⇒ Windows NT Explorer, and then click the `Printers` folder in the All Folders list box.
- Select Start ⇒ Settings ⇒ Control Panel, and then double-click the Printers icon in Control Panel.

2. Double-click the Add Printers icon.

3. The Add Printer Wizard dialog box appears. To create a printer, select My Computer, and click Next.

4. Select a port in the Available ports list box. If the port you want to use is not listed, click the Add Port command button and follow the directions given. Click Next. Figure 6-2 shows the Available ports list box within the Add Printer Wizard. Notice that the LPT1: port is highlighted and selected.

FIGURE 6-2   **Selecting a port for a print device**

5. Select the appropriate manufacturer and print device model, and click Next. Figure 6-3 shows the Manufacturers and Printers list boxes.

FIGURE 6-3   **Selecting a print device's**
manufacturer and model

6. Type a printer name, or accept the default. Click Next.

7. Choose whether to share the printer. (You can share or stop sharing the printer later if you change your mind. More information is presented in the "Sharing a Printer" section later in this chapter.) Click Next.

8. Choose whether to print a test page. Click Finish.

You can modify a printer's properties any time after the printer is created by right-clicking the printer's icon (in the `Printers` folder), and then selecting Properties from the menu that appears.

concept link

See Lab 6.12 at the end of this chapter for hands-on practice in creating a printer.

Steps to Connect to a Printer

This section explains the steps involved in connecting to a Windows NT shared network printer using the Add Printer Wizard.

TO CONNECT TO A WINDOWS NT SHARED NETWORK PRINTER, FOLLOW THESE STEPS:

1. Open the `Printers` folder. (Select Start ⇒ Settings ⇒ Printers.)

2. Double-click the Add Printers icon.

3. The Add Printer Wizard dialog box appears. To connect to a printer, select Network printer server, and click Next.

4. In the Connect to Printer dialog box, do one of the following:

In the Printer text box, type in a complete path to the network printer to which you want to connect, in the form of
`\\server_name\printer_name`.

Or, use the browse list in the Shared Printers list box to select the network printer to which you want to connect.

Figure 6-4 shows the Connect to Printer dialog box. Notice that when a network printer is selected in the Shared Printers list box, the Add Printer Wizard places the full path to the network printer in the Printer text box.

Then click OK.

note

When you connect to a shared network printer on a Windows NT computer, your local Windows NT computer automatically copies the necessary printer drivers from the Windows NT computer that hosts the shared printer. If the Windows NT computer that hosts the shared printer does not have printer drivers for your version of Windows NT or for your hardware platform (such as Intel, DEC Alpha, MIPS R4000, or PowerPC), then Windows NT prompts you to install printer drivers as the next step in this process.

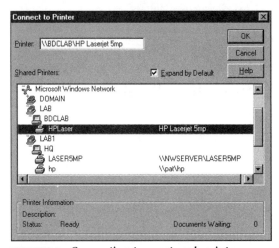

FIGURE 6-4   **Connecting to a network printer**

5. In the Add Printer Wizard dialog box, choose whether you want this printer to be your default printer. Click Next.

6. Click Finish. You are now connected to a shared network printer.

Using drag-and-drop printing to connect to a printer

Drag-and-drop printing is an easy way to connect to a shared network printer, because drag-and-drop printing requires less user interaction than using the Add Printer Wizard interactively.

To use drag-and-drop printing to connect to a shared network printer, you must first use My Computer to locate a file that you want to print. Then use Network Neighborhood to locate the shared network printer (or NetWare print queue) that you want to use.

Figure 6-5 shows two windows open on the desktop. Note that one window shows the shares that are available on a network computer named Bdclab, and that the other window contains files in the `Windows` folder. (If you prefer, instead of using My Computer and Network Neighborhood, you can accomplish the same thing by opening two copies of Windows NT Explorer, and then tiling the windows.)

FIGURE 6-5 **Preparing for drag–and–drop printing**

To connect to the shared network printer and print your document, drag the file from the open window and drop it on the shared network printer in the other window.

Figure 6-6 shows a document being dropped on the shared printer.

Windows NT displays an information dialog box, which is shown in Figure 6-7. The essence of the dialog box message is that Windows NT must connect to the shared network printer and install drivers on your local Windows NT computer before the document can be printed.

If you click No, Windows NT automatically cancels your print job. If you click Yes, Windows NT automatically connects to the shared network printer, installs local printer drivers, opens the application the document was created in, prints the document, and closes the application.

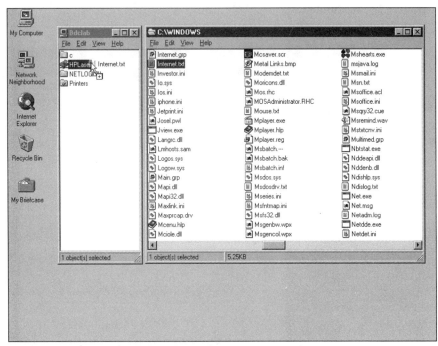

FIGURE 6-6   Dragging and dropping a document on a printer

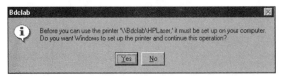

**FIGURE 6-7   Instructing NT to install local drivers
for a shared network printer**

If you click Yes and the Windows NT computer that hosts the shared network printer does *not* have printer drivers for your version of Windows NT or for your hardware platform (such as Intel, DECAlpha, MIPS R4000, or PowerPC), or if you are dragging and dropping a document to a NetWare print queue, then Windows NT prompts you to select and install appropriate printer drivers before it completes the drag-and-drop printing.

note Drag-and-drop printing requires that the printer on which you are dropping files be configured as your default printer. Also, drag-and-drop printing often produces inconsistent results (for example, the process may complete normally, but the document will not print). Sometimes repeating the process will cause everything to work correctly. Sometimes a printer is created in your `Printers` folder, and sometimes not. Maybe drag-and-drop printing's inconsistencies will be fixed in one of the future service packs for Windows NT 4.0.

PRINT MONITORS

Print monitors are software components that run in kernel mode. In Windows NT, print monitors send ready-to-print print jobs to a print device, either locally or across the network. Print monitors are also called *port monitors*.

When you create a printer, you select the port to which the print device is connected. Each port is associated with one specific print monitor.

This section discusses the most commonly used print monitors.

Localmon

The *Localmon print monitor* sends print jobs to print devices that are connected to hardware ports on a local Windows NT computer (local hardware ports include LPT1: and COM1:).

Localmon is the only print monitor that is installed by default during the installation of Windows NT. All other print monitors require that you install additional Windows NT services and/or protocols.

Hpmon

The *Hpmon print monitor* sends print jobs to a network print device via a Hewlett-Packard JetDirect adapter. The HP JetDirect adapter may either be installed in the print device or function as a separate external unit.

Hpmon uses the DLC protocol to communicate with HP JetDirect adapters. Most HP JetDirect adapters support multiple protocols, including: TCP/IP, IPX,

AppleTalk, and DLC. However, Hpmon can only communicate by using the DLC protocol.

The DLC protocol is a non-routable protocol. A Windows NT computer that uses Hpmon can only communicate with HP JetDirect adapters that are located on the same network segment. In other words, the DLC protocol will not be forwarded by a network router to another network segment.

If your network supports bridging, however, you can use DLC to communicate to an HP JetDirect adapter on any network segment that is connected by a bridge.

The Hpmon print monitor is not installed by default during the installation of Windows NT. Hpmon is installed automatically when you install the DLC protocol. You must install DLC before you can connect to an HP JetDirect adapter using Hpmon.

TO CREATE A PRINTER THAT USES HPMON, FOLLOW THESE STEPS:

1. Install the DLC protocol on your computer. (If you need more information on how to do this, refer to the section on "Installing and Configuring Protocols and Services" in Chapter 3.)

2. Open the `Printers` folder. (Select Start ⇒ Settings ⇒ Printers.)

3. Double-click the Add Printers icon.

4. The Add Printer Wizard dialog box appears. To create a printer, select My Computer, and click Next.

5. In the Available ports list box, click the Add Port command button.

6. In the Printer Ports dialog box, click the Hewlett-Packard Network Port. Figure 6-8 shows the Printer Ports dialog box. Notice that the Hewlett-Packard Network Port is selected. Click New Port.

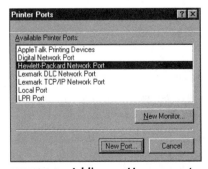

FIGURE 6-8   Adding an Hpmon port

7. The Add Hewlett-Packard Network Peripheral Port dialog box appears. In the lower Card Address list box, double-click the MAC address of the HP JetDirect adapter you want to use. The Add Printer Wizard then places this address in the upper Card Address text box. In the Name text box, type a name for the Hpmon port that will be associated with the HP JetDirect adapter you selected.

Figure 6-9 shows the Hewlett-Packard Network Peripheral Port dialog box. Note that the Hpmon port is named after its association with an HP JetDirect adapter. Click the Timers command button.

FIGURE 6-9   Selecting and configuring
an Hpmon port

8. The HP Network Peripheral Port Timers dialog box appears. Choose either a *Job Based* or *Continuous* connection.

- If you choose *Job Based*, all computers on the network will be able to access the HP JetDirect adapter for printing, because the connection to the HP JetDirect adapter is dropped after each print job. (Only one computer can have a DLC connection to the HP JetDirect adapter at any given time.)

- If you choose *Continuous*, Hpmon will monopolize the HP JetDirect adapter and no other computer on the network will be able to use DLC to access the HP JetDirect adapter for printing.

Figure 6-10 shows the HP Network Peripheral Port Timers dialog box. Notice that Continuous Connection is the default selection. Click OK.

9. Click OK in the Add Hewlett-Packard Network Peripheral Port dialog box.

10. Click Close in the Printer Ports dialog box.

FIGURE 6-10 Selecting Job Based or Continuous connection

11. The Add Printer Wizard dialog box, shown in Figure 6-11, reappears. Note that the Hpmon port that you have added is highlighted and selected in the Available ports list box. Click Next.

FIGURE 6-11 Hpmon/HP JetDirect port added to available ports list

12. Select the appropriate manufacturer and print device model, and click Next.

13. Type in a printer name, or accept the default. Click Next.

14. Choose whether to share the printer. (You can share or stop sharing the printer later if you change your mind.) Click Next.

15. Choose whether to print a test page. Click Finish.

in the real world

Selecting between a job based and continuous connection requires some careful planning and consideration.

If a printer isn't shared and you select a continuous connection, only a single user will have access to the HP JetDirect adapter for printing. In this situation, you should generally select a job based connection.

However, if you share the printer that is associated with the Hpmon port, selecting a continuous connection can make sense. This computer will then function as a print server and manage all print jobs sent to the shared printer. In this situation, all computers on the network that have access to the shared printer, in effect, will have access to the HP JetDirect adapter for printing.

AppleTalk

The *AppleTalk print monitor* sends print jobs to network print devices that support the AppleTalk protocol. The AppleTalk protocol is normally associated with Apple Macintosh computers.

Before you can connect to an AppleTalk print device, you must install Services for Macintosh on your Windows NT Server computer.

AppleTalk is a routable protocol. A Windows NT computer that uses the AppleTalk print monitor can communicate with any AppleTalk print device on any segment of a routed AppleTalk network.

TO CREATE A PRINTER THAT USES THE APPLETALK PRINT MONITOR, FOLLOW THESE STEPS:

1. Install Services for Macintosh. (If you need more information on how to do this, refer to the section "Installing and Configuring Protocols and Services" in Chapter 3.)
2. Open the Printers folder. (Select Start ⇒ Settings ⇒ Printers.)
3. Double-click the Add Printers icon.
4. The Add Printer Wizard dialog box appears. To create a printer, select My Computer, and click Next.
5. In the Available ports list box, click the Add Port command button.
6. In the Printer Ports dialog box, click AppleTalk Printing Devices.

   Figure 6-12 shows the Printer Ports dialog box. Notice that AppleTalk Printing Devices is selected. Click New Port.

FIGURE 6-12   Adding an AppleTalk port

7. When the Available AppleTalk Printing Devices dialog box appears, highlight the AppleTalk print device you want to use.

Figure 6-13 shows the Available AppleTalk Printing Devices dialog box, with an HP LaserJet 5P selected. Click OK.

FIGURE 6-13   Selecting an AppleTalk
print device

8. A dialog box appears asking if you want to *capture* this AppleTalk print device.

If you choose to capture an AppleTalk print device, it is the same as choosing a continuous connection (discussed in the previous section, "Hpmon"). The AppleTalk print monitor will monopolize the connection to the AppleTalk print device, and no other computer on the network will be able to access the AppleTalk print device. In addition, the AppleTalk print monitor instructs the AppleTalk print device not to advertise itself on the network. This is called *hiding.*

If you choose not to capture an AppleTalk print device, it is the same as choosing a job based connection (discussed in the previous section, "Hpmon"). All computers on the network will be able to access the AppleTalk print device for printing, because the connection to the print device is dropped after each print job. Only one computer can connect to an AppleTalk print device at any given time.

Click Yes or No.

9. Click Close in the Printer Ports dialog box.

10. The Available ports list box reappears with your newly created AppleTalk port highlighted and selected. Click Next.

11. Select the appropriate manufacturer and print device model, and click Next.

12. Type in a printer name, or accept the default. Click Next.

13. Choose whether to share the printer. (You can share or stop sharing the printer later if you change your mind.) Click Next.

14. Choose whether to print a test page. Click Finish.

TCP/IP

The *TCP/IP print monitor* sends print jobs to network print devices that both support TCP/IP *and* function as *line printer daemon (LPD)* print servers. TCP/IP and LPD are normally associated with UNIX computers.

 note   *Daemon* **is a UNIX term. A UNIX daemon performs the same function as a Windows NT service. Basically, a UNIX daemon is a program that runs in the background and performs an operating system service.**

Line printer daemon (LPD) is the print server software used in TCP/IP printing. The client print software used in TCP/IP printing is called *line printer remote* (LPR). To connect to a TCP/IP print server that uses LPD, use a TCP/IP print client that uses LPR.

Before you can connect to a TCP/IP print device, you must install TCP/IP and the Microsoft TCP/IP Printing service on your Windows NT computer.

In addition, to share printers on a Windows NT computer as TCP/IP printers, you must also start the TCP/IP Print Server service. The TCP/IP Print Server service is configured for manual startup by default, so you should configure this service to start automatically.

TCP/IP is a routable protocol. A Windows NT computer that uses the TCP/IP print monitor can communicate with any TCP/IP print device on any segment of a routed TCP/IP network.

TO CREATE A PRINTER THAT USES THE TCP/IP PRINT MONITOR, FOLLOW THESE STEPS:

1. Install TCP/IP and the Microsoft TCP/IP Printing service. Optionally, you can configure the TCP/IP Print Server service to start automatically if you want to share your printers as TCP/IP printers. (If you need more information on how to do this, refer to the section "Installing and Configuring Protocols and Services" in Chapter 3.)

2. Open the `Printers` folder. (Select Start ⇒ Settings ⇒ Printers.)

3. Double-click the Add Printers icon.

4. The Add Printer Wizard dialog box appears. To create a printer, select My Computer, and click Next.

5. In the "Available ports" list box, click the Add Port command button.

6. In the Printer Ports dialog box, click LPR Port. (The Lexmark TCP/IP Network Port displayed in this dialog box is for use *only* with Lexmark TCP/IP print devices, and requires you to install additional software.)

Figure 6-14 shows the Printer Ports dialog box. Notice that LPR Port is selected. Then click New Port.

FIGURE 6-14   Adding an LPR port

7. In the Add LPR compatible printer dialog box, type the host name or IP address of the computer or device that provides the LPD service for the print device you want to use. Depending on your network configuration, this could be the host name or IP address of a UNIX computer, a Windows NT computer, or an HP JetDirect adapter that supports TCP/IP printing.

In addition, type in the name of the printer or print queue on the computer or device providing the LPD service.

Figure 6-15 shows the Add LPD compatible printer dialog box. Notice the IP address of the device providing the LPD service (in this case, an HP JetDirect adapter) and the name of the printer have been entered. Click OK.

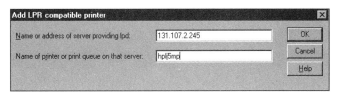

FIGURE 6-15   **Configuring an LPR port**

8. In the Printer Ports dialog box, click Close.

9. The Add Printer Wizard dialog box, shown in Figure 6-16, reappears. Note that the LPR port that you created is displayed in the form of *IP_address:printer_name* and is highlighted and selected in the Available ports list box. Click Next.

FIGURE 6-16   **LPR port added to available ports list**

10. Select the appropriate manufacturer and print device model, and click Next.

11. Type in a printer name, or accept the default. Click Next.

12. Choose whether to share the printer. (You can share or stop sharing the printer later if you change your mind.) Click Next.

13. Choose whether to print a test page. Click Finish.

NetWare

The *NetWare print monitor* sends print jobs to a print queue on a Novell NetWare server. The NetWare server then sends the print job from the print queue to the print device.

 tip **A *print queue* is the NetWare term for a shared printer. A NetWare print queue is designed to handle print jobs that are ready to send to the print device, and that need no additional conversion or formatting.**

Before you can connect to a NetWare print queue, you must install NWLink IPX/SPX Compatible Transport on your Windows NT Server computer. In addition, you must install *Gateway Service for NetWare (GSNW)*.

NWLink IPX/SPX Compatible Transport is a routable protocol. A Windows NT computer that uses the NetWare print monitor can communicate with any NetWare server on any segment of a routed NetWare network.

TO CONNECT A WINDOWS NT SERVER COMPUTER TO A PRINTER THAT USES THE NETWARE PRINT MONITOR, FOLLOW THESE STEPS:

1. Install NWLink IPX/SPX Compatible Transport on your Windows NT Server computer. In addition, install Gateway Service for NetWare. (If you need more information on how to do this, refer to the section "Installing and Configuring Protocols and Services" in Chapter 3.)

2. Open the `Printers` folder. (Select Start ⇒ Settings ⇒ Printers.)

3. Double-click the Add Printers icon.

4. The Add Printer Wizard dialog box appears. To connect to a printer, select Network printer server, and click Next.

5. In the Connect to Printer dialog box, do *one* of the following:

In the Printer text box, type in a complete path to the NetWare print queue you want to connect to, in the form of `\\Netware_server_name\print_queue_name`

Or use the browse list in the Shared Printers list box to select the NetWare print queue to which you want to connect.

Figure 6-17 shows the Connect to Printer dialog box. Notice that a NetWare print queue is selected. Then click OK.

FIGURE 6-17 Connecting to a NetWare print queue

6. A warning message appears, indicating that the server on which the NetWare print queue resides doesn't have the appropriate printer driver installed. Click OK to install a printer driver on your Windows NT computer.

7. Select the appropriate manufacturer and print device model, and click OK.

8. A dialog box appears asking if you want this printer to be your default printer. Click Yes or No, as appropriate, and then click Next to continue.

9. Click Finish. You are now connected to a NetWare print queue.

CONFIGURING PRINT SERVER PROPERTIES

A *print server* is a computer (or network device) that manages print jobs and print devices. The Windows NT Spooler service performs many of the functions of a print server. You can configure several of the Spooler service's properties (which Windows NT calls *print server properties*) including the spool folder, forms, and ports.

TO ACCESS THE PRINT SERVER PROPERTIES DIALOG BOX, FOLLOW THESE STEPS:

1. Select Start ⇒ Settings ⇒ Printers.

2. Then select File ⇒ Server Properties in the Printers dialog box.

The following sections explain how you can configure each of the print server properties.

Changing the Spool Folder

The *spool folder* is used by the Windows NT Spooler service as a temporary storage area for print jobs waiting to be sent to a print device. The default location for the spool folder is `<winntroot>\System32\Spool\Printers`.

If the partition that contains the spool folder does not have enough free space to store print jobs, you may experience print job failures. On a busy Windows NT Server computer with multiple shared printers, for example, you might need between 25MB and several hundred megabytes of free space for the spool folder, depending on the number, type, and size of print jobs that are spooled on this server.

If you experience print job failures due to a lack of free space for your spool folder, you can specify that a different folder on another partition (that has more free space) be used as your spool folder.

To change your spool folder, click the Advanced tab in the Print Server Properties dialog box. Then, edit the contents of the Spool Folder text box. You can specify any folder in any partition as your spool folder, in the format of `Drive_letter:\Folder\Subfolder`.

Figure 6-18 shows the Advanced tab in the Print Server Properties dialog box. Note the default spool folder location, and the additional options that you can configure on this tab.

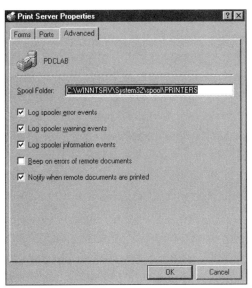

FIGURE 6-18   Configuring advanced
print server properties

Many a network administrator has changed the spool folder on a
Windows NT computer, only to find out that users can no longer
print to shared network printers on this computer.

To solve this problem, the administrator must assign permissions
so that all users who print to any shared printer on the Windows
NT computer have the Change permission to the spool folder.
Users that don't have the Change permission to the spool folder
won't be able to print to any shared network printer on the
Windows NT computer. (Permissions are covered in detail in
Chapter 12.)

Creating Forms

You can create forms on the Forms tab in the Print Server Properties dialog box.
Options that you can configure include form name, paper size, and printer area
margins.

Once you've created a form, you can assign that form to a paper tray on a
printer. (Assigning a form to a paper tray is covered later in this chapter.) Once a
form is assigned to a paper tray, documents that specify that form are automati-

cally printed using that paper tray. This process can be helpful in managing document printing on a network.

For example, suppose a company wants to print all documents that require company letterhead from a specific paper tray. When a user wants to print a document using letterhead paper, the user can select the letterhead form (in the Printer Properties dialog box) in any Windows application when the user creates a print job. Using the Windows NT form capabilities enables the user to print a document on letterhead without necessarily knowing which paper tray in the print device contains the company's letterhead.

Some network administrators create a separate printer for each form and paper tray assignment to ease administration and to enable users to select forms in a more obvious manner.

To create a form, click the Forms tab in the Print Server Properties dialog box. Highlight any existing form in the Forms list box, select the check box next to Create a New Form, and then edit the name of the form, as well as the paper size and printer area margins to meet your new form's specifications. Then click the Save Form command button. The new form is added to the Forms list box, and the old form is not changed or deleted.

Figure 6-19 shows the Forms tab in the Print Server Properties dialog box. Notice that a form called *Letterhead* has been created and now appears in the Forms list box.

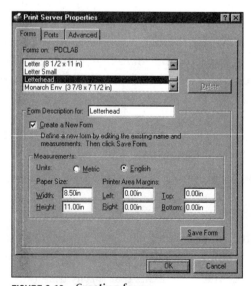

FIGURE 6-19   Creating forms

Managing Ports

You can use the Ports tab in the Print Server Properties dialog box to add, delete, and configure ports. (As you recall, creating and configuring ports by using the Add Printer Wizard was discussed in the "Print Monitors" section earlier in this chapter.)

The capabilities of the Ports tab in the Print Server Properties dialog box are identical to those in the Add Printer Wizard with one exception: ports can only be deleted from the Ports tab in the Print Server Properties dialog box.

Figure 6-20 shows the Ports tab in the Print Server Properties dialog box. Notice the Delete Port command button.

FIGURE 6-20   Managing ports

CONFIGURING PRINTER PROPERTIES

In Windows NT you can configure options for a printer in the printer's Properties dialog box. This dialog box is printer specific, and is titled *Printer_name* Properties.

The following sections explain how you can configure printer properties, including assigning a separator page, assigning forms to paper trays, printer security, printing to multiple ports (printer pools), scheduling printers and setting printer priorities, and sharing a printer.

Assigning a Separator Page

You can configure Windows NT so that a *separator page* is printed at the beginning of every document. Using separator pages at the beginning of print jobs enables users to locate their print jobs at the print device easily. Separator pages are sometimes called *banner pages*.

You can assign a separator page to a printer by using the Properties dialog box for your printer. To do this, click the Separator Page command button on the General tab in your printer Properties dialog box. In the Separator Page dialog box, type in the full path of the separator page file you want to assign to your printer; or click the Browse command button and double-click the separator page file you want to assign from the Separator Page dialog box. Then click OK in the Separator Page dialog box, and exit the Properties dialog box for your printer.

Figure 6-21 shows the Separator Page dialog boxes. Notice that there are three default separator page files shown: `Pcl.sep`, `Pscript.sep`, and `Sysprint.sep`. The `Pcl.sep` separator page file switches a dual language print device to PCL printing, and causes a separator page to be printed at the beginning of each print job. The `Pscript.sep` separator page file switches a dual language print device to PostScript printing, but does *not* cause a separator page to be printed at the beginning of each print job. The `Sysprint.sep` separator page file causes a separator page to be printed at the beginning of each print job, and is only compatible with PostScript print devices.

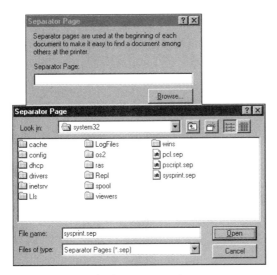

FIGURE 6-21   Assigning a separator page
to a printer

You can create additional separator page files by editing an existing separator
page file and saving it with a different name.

concept link

**For detailed information on editing separator page files and using
custom separator pages, search for "Separator pages, printing" in
NT Books Online (Start ⇒ Programs ⇒ Books Online). Or see
Chapter 7 of the *Microsoft Windows NT Workstation Resource Kit for
version 4.0* (Microsoft Press, 1996).**

Assigning Forms to Paper Trays

As discussed in the section on "Creating Forms" earlier in this chapter, assigning
forms to paper trays can be helpful in managing document printing on a network,
because once a form is assigned to a paper tray, print jobs that specify that form
are automatically printed using that paper tray.

To assign a form to a paper tray, select the Device Settings tab in the
Properties dialog box for your printer. Highlight the paper tray to which you want
to assign the form, and then select the form you want to assign to this paper tray
from the Change Tray Setting list box. Click OK.

Figure 6-22 shows the Device Settings tab in the Properties dialog box for my printer, an HP LaserJet 5MP. Notice that the letterhead form is now assigned to Tray 1.

FIGURE 6-22   Assigning a form to a paper tray

Printer Security

You can use Windows NT printer security to control access to a printer by assigning printer permissions to users and groups. Printer security is configured on the Security tab in a printer's Properties dialog box. In addition, you can take ownership of a printer and configure Windows NT to audit printer usage in this dialog box.

Figure 6-23 shows the Security tab in a printer's Properties dialog box. Note the Permissions, Auditing, and Ownership command buttons.

The next sections discuss printer permissions, auditing printers, and taking ownership of a printer.

FIGURE 6-23   The Security tab in a
printer's Properties dialog box

Printer permissions

Printer permissions control which tasks a user can perform on a specific printer.
Table 6-1 lists and describes the Windows NT printer permissions.

TABLE 6-1 WINDOWS NT PRINTER PERMISSIONS	
PRINTER PERMISSION	*DESCRIPTION AND FUNCTIONALITY*
No Access	A user or group that has the No Access permission cannot access the printer.
Print	The Print permission enables users to create print jobs and also to delete their own print jobs.
Manage Documents	The Manage Documents permission allows users to pause, restart, delete, and control job settings for all print jobs. The Manage Documents permission does not allow users to print to the printer.
Full Control	A user or group that has the Full Control permission can do everything that a user with the Print and Manage Documents permissions can do, and in addition, can also assign printer permissions, delete printers, share printers, and change printer properties.

You can assign printer permissions to users and groups. User and group permissions are additive. In other words, if a user has the Print permission, and a group that the user is a member of has Full Control, then the user has Full Control.

There is one exception to this rule. If a user, or any group that a user is a member of, has the No Access permission, then the user's effective permission is always No Access. For example, a user may have the Full Control permission, but a group that the user is a member of may have the No Access permission. The user's effective permission is No Access, and the user cannot access the printer.

 concept link **For more information on user and group accounts, see Chapter 8.**

To assign printer permissions to users and groups, click the Permissions command button on the Security tab in the Properties dialog box for the printer you want to configure. Figure 6-24 shows the default printer permissions assigned to a newly created printer in the Printer Permissions dialog box. Note that by default the Everyone group has the Print permission, which effectively enables all users to create and delete their own print jobs on this printer.

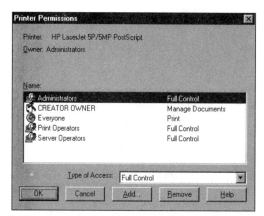

FIGURE 6-24 Assigning printer permissions

To modify permissions in this dialog box, highlight a user or group, and then select the permission you want to assign to this user or group from the Type of Access drop-down list box. Then click OK, and click OK in your printer's Properties dialog box.

To add a user or group to the Name list box, click the Add command button in the Printer Permissions dialog box. The Add Users and Groups dialog box appears. Select the user(s) and/or group(s) you want to add, then click the Add command button. Then click OK to return to the Printer Permissions dialog box. Click OK, and click OK in your printer's Properties dialog box.

To remove a user or group from the Name list box, highlight the user or group and press Delete. Then click OK. Click OK in your printer's Properties dialog box.

Auditing printers

You can use your printer's Properties dialog box to configure Windows NT to audit a user or group's usage (and/or attempted usage) of a printer. Only members of the Administrators group can configure auditing on a Windows NT computer.

When auditing is enabled, Windows NT adds an entry to the Security Log in Event Viewer every time an audited user or group exercises (and/or attempts to exercise) an audited permission on a specific printer. To gain a better understanding of auditing printers, how about a walk through the process of configuring printer auditing?

Auditing printers is accomplished in two parts: first, auditing is enabled in User Manager for Domains; second, printer auditing is configured in a specific printer's Properties dialog box.

The following sections explain how to perform these tasks.

TO ENABLE AUDITING IN USER MANAGER FOR DOMAINS, FOLLOW THESE STEPS:

1. Select Start ⇒ Programs ⇒ Administrative Tools (Common) ⇒ User Manager for Domains.

2. In the User Manager dialog box, select Policies ⇒ Audit.

3. The Audit Policy dialog box appears. Select the option button next to Audit These Events. Then select the events you want to be audited. You *must* select the Success and/or Failure check boxes for File and Object Access to audit printer events.

Success auditing means that Windows NT will report successful attempts to complete the task or event listed.

Failure auditing means that Windows NT will report unsuccessful attempts to complete the task or event listed.

Figure 6-25 shows the Audit Policy dialog box. Note that the option button next to Audit These Events is selected, and that the Success and Failure check boxes for File and Object Access are checked. Click OK.

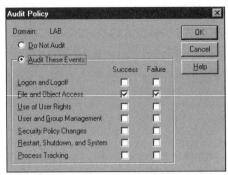

FIGURE 6-25   **Enabling auditing of file and object access**

4. Exit User Manager for Domains.

TO CONFIGURE PRINTER AUDITING, FOLLOW THESE STEPS:

1. Select Start ⇒ Settings ⇒ Printers.

2. In the Printers dialog box, right-click the printer you want to configure.

3. Then select Properties from the menu that appears.

4. Click the Security tab in your printer's Properties dialog box.

5. Click the Auditing command button.

6. The Printer Auditing dialog box appears. You must add the user(s) and/or group(s) you want to audit for this printer to the Name list box. To do this, click the Add command button.

7. The Add Users and Groups dialog box appears. Select the user(s) and/or group(s) you want to add, and then click the Add command button. Then click OK to return to the Printer Auditing dialog box.

8. The user(s) and/or group(s) you added are now listed in the Name list box. Select the Success and/or Failure check boxes for the print events you want to audit. You *must* select at least one event for print auditing to occur.

Figure 6-26 shows the Printer Auditing dialog box. Notice that the check boxes for Success and Failure auditing of Print events are selected for the Everyone group. Click OK.

9. Click OK in your printer's Properties dialog box. Auditing of print events is now enabled and configured.

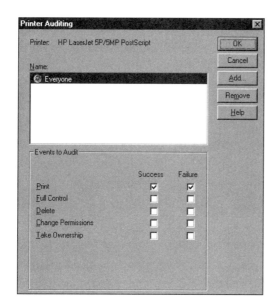

FIGURE 6-26 Configuring print events to audit

To view the events generated by printer auditing, select Start ⇒ Programs ⇒ Administrative Tools (Common) ⇒ Event Viewer. In the Event Viewer dialog box, select Log ⇒ Security. A list of audited events is displayed. You can double-click any event for a detailed description of the event.

in the real world

Auditing printers can generate a significant number of entries in the Security Log. I recommend you don't use printer auditing unless you have a specific need to do so.

Taking ownership of a printer

The owner of a printer has special status — an owner can assign printer permissions for that printer to any user or group, even if the owner has the No Access permission to that printer. A printer can have only one owner at any given time.

There are two ways to become an owner of a printer: either by creating the printer, or by taking ownership of the printer. By default, the user that creates a printer is the owner of that printer (unless the person who creates a printer is a member of the Administrators group, in which case the Administrators group is the owner of that printer). Only certain users can take ownership of a printer. You must either be a member of the Administrators group or have the Full Control permission to take ownership of a printer.

So why would you ever want to take ownership of a printer? Well, assume that a user on your network (I'll call him Fred) who has the Full Control permission to a printer has inadvertently taken ownership and removed *all* users' printer permissions for that printer. As a result of Fred's faux pas, the network administrator — that's you — (and every other user) now have no permissions for the printer. To be able to resolve the problem and assign yourself and other users permissions to the printer again, you need to first take ownership of the printer.

The process of taking ownership is fairly straightforward. First, log on as Administrator. (You must log on as the user that wants to become the new owner of the printer. Normally this is the administrator, but it can be any user with the Full Control permission to that printer.) In the `Printers` folder, right-click the printer you want to take ownership of, then select Properties from the menu that appears. If you have no permissions to the printer (such as in the previous example), a dialog box appears, indicating that you do not have access to this printer, and that only the Security tab will be displayed. Click OK. On the Security tab, click the Ownership command button. A warning dialog box appears, indicating that you do not have permission to view the current owner, but that you may have permission to change it. Click Yes. The Owner dialog box, shown in Figure 6-27, appears.

FIGURE 6-27   Taking ownership of a printer

Click the Take Ownership command button. Then click OK on the Security tab of the printer's Properties dialog box. You are now the new owner of the printer and can assign printer permissions for that printer.

Printing to Multiple Ports (Printer Pools)

When a printer has multiple ports (and multiple print devices) assigned to it, this is called a *printer pool*. Users print to a single printer, and the printer load-balances its print jobs between the print devices assigned to it.

A printer pool is a useful tool when *both* of the following criteria are met:

- All print devices assigned to the printer use the same print device driver. (Usually, this means that identical print devices are used.)

- All print devices assigned to the printer pool are located physically close to each other.

in the
real world

A printer pool can be a good solution when the desired number of printed pages is more output than one print device can produce. When you implement a printer pool, I recommend you use two or more identical print devices, located next to each other. A printer pool is definitely *not* useful if the print devices are located at opposite ends of a building, because users would have to check both locations to find their print jobs.

To configure multiple ports (and their associated print devices) as a printer pool, first create a printer. Then, from the `Printers` folder, right-click this printer and select Properties from the menu that appears. Click the Ports tab of the printer's Properties dialog box. On the Ports tab, click the check box next to "Enable printer pooling." Then select at least one additional port from the Port list box. Figure 6-28 shows the Properties dialog box for a printer that has been configured as a printer pool. Notice that three ports have been selected, and that the check box next to "Enable printer pooling" is checked.

When a user prints to a printer pool, the print job is sent to the first listed print device in the Port list that is not busy printing another print job. The entire print job is sent to the same port (print device). In a printer pool the print spooler — not the user — determines to which print device the print job will be sent.

FIGURE 6-28   Creating a printer pool

Scheduling Printers and Setting Printer Priorities

Scheduling printers and setting printer priorities are two techniques you can use to help manage the flow of print jobs on your Windows NT network. I will discuss both of these approaches in the following sections.

Scheduling printers

Scheduling a printer means assigning the hours a specific print device is available for use by a specific printer. When scheduling a printer, the hours of availability apply only to the print device, not to the printer. This means that users can print to the printer at any time during the day, and the printer then spools the jobs to the hard disk. However, the print jobs are only sent to the print device during the print device's hours of availability. (If you decide to schedule a printer, be sure to reserve plenty of hard disk space to spool print jobs while they wait for the print device to become available.)

So why would you want to schedule a printer? Well, suppose you are the network administrator for a small, 20-computer network. The owner of the company recently bought a laser print device for network printing and doesn't want to spend any more money on print devices. One of the employees occasionally generates a print job that is five to six hundred pages long. This report ties up the one available printer for a long time, frustrating other employees. The large reports are for archival and reference purposes and are not needed immediately.

You solve the problem this way: first, you create a second printer that prints to the laser print device. Then you schedule the new printer so that it only sends print jobs to the print device during non-business hours. You instruct the employee who creates the large print jobs to use the new printer for the large print jobs. The result is that the employee can generate large print jobs at any time without inconveniencing other employees. The large print jobs are spooled to the hard disk and then sent to the print device during non-business hours. (Make sure to stock the print device with plenty of paper just before leaving for the evening!)

To schedule a printer, right-click the printer in the `Printers` folder and select Properties from the menu that is displayed. Then select the Scheduling tab from the printer's Properties dialog box. To set the available hours, click the option button next to From and set the times in the spin boxes next to From and To.

Figure 6-29 shows the Scheduling tab in the HP LaserJet 5MP Properties dialog box. Note that the available hours are from 9:00 p.m. to 5:00 a.m. Print jobs sent to this printer will only be sent to the print device during these non-business hours.

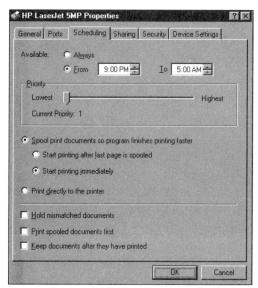

FIGURE 6-29   Scheduling available hours
for a print device

Setting printer priorities

When more than one printer sends print jobs to the same print device, setting printer priorities may be useful. If two printers are configured to use the same print device, and you configure one of these printers to have a higher priority than the other printer, then all print jobs from the higher priority printer will be sent to the print device before any print jobs from the lower priority printer are sent.

The highest printer priority is 99, and the lowest printer priority is 1. All printers have a priority of 1 by default.

Here's one situation in which setting printer priorities could be beneficial: Suppose you have two printers on a Windows NT Server computer that both send print jobs to the print device connected to LPT1:. One printer is named *sales*, and the other printer is named *managers*. Figure 6-30 shows the *sales* and *managers* Properties dialog boxes. Notice that both printers are configured to use LPT1:.

The managers at this company, who think their work is more important than everyone else's, tell you — the network administrator — that they want their print jobs printed before anyone else's.

FIGURE 6-30   The sales and managers printers

So what's a network administrator to do? You decide to configure printer security so that everyone can use the *sales* printer, but only members of the Managers group can use the *managers* printer. Then you set the priority on the *managers* printer to a value higher than one. Once this is done, the managers' print jobs will take priority. Suppose that there are 100 print jobs waiting to print in the *sales* printer, and a manager sends a print job to the *managers* printer. The current print job from the *sales* printer will finish printing, then the manager's print job will be printed, even though there are 100 other print jobs in the *sales* printer that were generated before the manager's print job.

Figure 6-31 shows the Scheduling tab in the Properties dialog boxes for both the *sales* and *managers* printers. Notice that the *sales* printer is set to a priority of 1 (lowest), and that the *managers* printer is set to a priority of 99 (highest).

Also notice in Figure 6-31 that the "Start printing after last page is spooled" option is selected for the *sales* printer. This means that print jobs sent to the *sales* printer are not sent to the print device until the entire print job has been received by the spooler. Finally, notice that the "Start printing immediately" option is selected for the *managers* printer. This causes print jobs sent to the *managers* printer to be sent to the print device as soon as the spooler starts receiving the print job. This setting gives the managers another subtle speed advantage over those who use the *sales* printer.

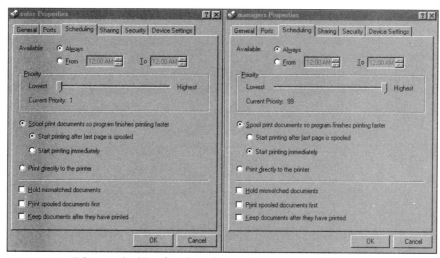

FIGURE 6-31   Printer priorities for the sales and managers printers

Sharing a Printer

The purpose of sharing a printer on a Windows NT computer is to enable users of other computers on the network to connect to and to send print jobs to the shared printer. The computer that hosts the shared printer is called a *print server*. The print server performs all of the spooling, print job management, scheduling, and sending of the final print jobs to the print device.

When you share a printer on your Windows NT computer, the types of computers on the network that can access your shared printer are somewhat dependent upon the protocols and services installed in your computer.

When you install Windows NT, Microsoft Windows Networking is installed by default. If you have not installed any other services and you share a printer on your computer, only computers that support Microsoft Windows Networking can access the shared printer.

If you installed Microsoft TCP/IP Printing *and* started the TCP/IP Print Server service (which is installed with Microsoft TCP/IP Printing), and you share a printer on your computer, then computers that support Microsoft Windows Networking and computers that support TCP/IP printing (such as UNIX computers) can access the shared printer.

If you have installed Services for Macintosh on a Windows NT Server computer and you share a printer on your computer, then computers that support Microsoft Windows Networking and Macintosh computers can access the shared printer.

concept link

For more information on sharing printers in a Macintosh environment, see the section "Sharing AppleTalk printers in Windows NT" later in this chapter.

Microsoft TCP/IP Printing and Services for Macintosh both include components that enable you to share printers. These components are called *print server services*. If you have more than one print server service installed and started on your Windows NT computer, and then you share a printer, the printer is shared on *all* running print server services installed on your computer.

Installing printer drivers for shared printers

When you share a printer on a Windows NT computer, Windows NT permits you to install alternate printer drivers for other versions of Windows NT and Windows 95. You can also install alternate printer drivers for other Windows NT hardware platforms, such as MIPS R4000, PowerPC, and DEC Alpha.

Installing these drivers enables users of Windows NT and Windows 95 computers on your network to automatically download and install the appropriate printer drivers for their operating systems/hardware platforms when they connect to the shared printer. The advantage of being able to install these alternate printer drivers on a shared printer is that the network administrator is spared the time-consuming task of manually installing printer drivers on every computer on the network.

To install alternate drivers on a shared printer, click the Sharing tab in the shared printer's Properties dialog box. Then select the alternate drivers for the operating systems/hardware platforms you want to install. Click OK when you are finished. Windows NT prompts you for the source media and path for each alternate driver you select.

The source media is your Windows NT Server compact disc if you are installing alternate printer drivers for NT Server 4.0. If you are installing alternate drivers for another version of Windows NT, such as NT 3.51, the source media is the Windows NT Server (version 3.51) compact disc. The path is the appropriate platform subdirectory, such as `\I386`, `\MIPS`, `\PPC`, or `\Alpha`.

When installing alternate printer drivers for Windows 95, a more complex task is indicated. First, copy all of the operating system files from the Windows 95 source media (the `Win95` folder on the Windows 95 compact disc) to a folder on your Windows NT computer. Then, in this folder on your Windows NT computer, expand all of the CAB files.

concept link **For more information on how to expand Windows 95 CAB files,** **refer to the Windows 95 product documentation and help files.**

When Windows NT prompts you for the source media for the Windows 95 alternate printer drivers, type the path to the folder that contains the expanded Windows 95 source files.

Figure 6-32 shows a shared printer, named *managers*, with alternate printer drivers for Windows 95 and Windows NT 4.0 *x*86 highlighted. The *x*86 indicates that printer drivers for Intel-based computers that run Windows NT 4.0 will be installed.

FIGURE 6-32   Installing printer drivers for multiple operating systems

Sharing AppleTalk printers in Windows NT

When a Windows NT Server computer that has Services for Macintosh installed on it shares a printer, the printer is accessible from Macintosh computers on the network, because Windows NT Server has full AppleTalk print server capabilities.

Shared printers on a Windows NT Server computer that has Services for Macintosh installed advertise themselves to Macintosh computers on the network as Apple LaserWriters. (An Apple LaserWriter is the original laser print device for Macintosh computers. All Macintosh computers have built-in drivers for the Apple LaserWriter.) This means that a Macintosh computer does not need special drivers to access the shared printer. Windows NT Server converts the PostScript print jobs it receives from Macintosh computers into RAW format print jobs for the print device.

TROUBLESHOOTING COMMON PRINTING PROBLEMS

Printing problems can occur on a Windows NT network for several reasons. Some of the most common printing problems involve users who do not have the permissions they need to access the printer, or users who have the Full Control permission or the Manage Document permission accidentally deleting documents that belong to other users. A good first step, when troubleshooting printer problems, is to ensure that users have appropriate printer permissions.

Table 6-2 lists some common printing problems, along with their probable causes and recommended solutions.

TABLE 6-2 TROUBLESHOOTING PRINTING PROBLEMS	
PROBLEM	*PROBABLE CAUSE/RECOMMENDED SOLUTION*
Print jobs are not being sent from the printer to the print device. A print job with a size of 0 bytes is at the top of the print job list for the printer. Other documents are also listed in the print job list, and users can still send print jobs to the printer. There is plenty of free space on the partition that contains your spool folder.	The most likely cause of this problem is a stalled print spooler. Stop and restart the Spooler service, and printing should resume.
No print events are listed in the Security Log in Event Viewer. You recently configured success auditing for print events in the Properties dialog box for the printer. Several days have passed, and hundreds of documents have been printed.	The most likely cause of this problem is that the success option for auditing file and object access has not been configured in User Manager for Domains. Auditing of printers requires that auditing of file and object access be configured. To resolve the problem, configure the necessary options in User Manager for Domains.
A printer that uses the Hpmon print monitor has stopped sending print jobs to its assigned print device.	This problem usually occurs when another computer on the network is configured to use Hpmon to connect to the print device by using a continuous connection. If you want more than one printer to be able to access a print device by using Hpmon, configure a job based connection for all printers.

continued

TABLE 6-2 *(continued)*

Problem	Probable Cause/Recommended Solution
You are unable to connect a Windows NT computer to a print device that uses TCP/IP and LPD.	Of the many possible causes for this problem, the most common is an incorrect configuration of a TCP/IP parameter on either the Windows NT computer or on the print device that uses TCP/IP and LPD. Ensure that the IP address, subnet mask, and default gateway parameters on both the Windows NT computer and the print device that uses TCP/IP and LPD are set correctly.
You experience a paper jam in the middle of an important print job. You want to reprint the entire print job, but it is not possible to reprint the job from the application that created it because you deleted the document after you created the print job.	The cause of the paper jam is not important here, but being able to reprint the entire print job is. To solve this problem, I recommend that you: 1. Immediately double-click the printer in the Printers folder. 2. The Printers dialog box appears. Select Document ⇒ Pause. This pauses the print job. 3. Clear the paper jam at the print device. 4. Select Document ⇒ Restart to reprint the entire print job. (Do not select Resume from the Document menu, because this will only print the print job from wherever the printer jammed to the end of the document, and the pages jammed in the print device will very likely be lost.)
You receive spooler messages indicating that your print job has been spooled with a size of 0 bytes. Figure 6-33 shows a sample error message of this type.	The most probable cause of this problem is that the partition that contains the printer's spool folder does not have enough free space to print the document in question. You should delete some files from this partition, or move the spool folder to a different partition that has more free space.

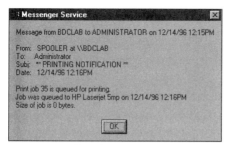

FIGURE 6-33   Spooler error message

   While troubleshooting is sometimes an art, it is more often a methodical, step-by-step process. If you do not quickly see the cause of your problem, I recommend you check all permissions, as well as hardware and software configuration parameters. Be careful here—it's easy to bypass a configuration parameter that looks correct at first glance but has a small error in it. Be very detail-oriented and methodical when troubleshooting, and you will probably resolve most of the problems you encounter in short order.

KEY POINT SUMMARY

Chapter 6 introduced many key Windows NT printing topics.

- It is important to have a solid grasp of Windows NT printing terminology, not only for fully understanding printing in NT, but also for passing the Server exam. A *printer* is the software interface between NT and the device that produces printed output. A *print* (or *printing*) device is the physical device (hardware) that produces the printed output.

- The *print process* begins with the user at an NT computer creating a print job within an application, such as Word. The application then hands off the print job to the *Graphics Device Interface* (GDI). The GDI initiates a request to the driver for the print device. The driver for the print device converts the print job into either a Windows NT *enhanced metafile* (EMF) or into a RAW format. The driver returns the converted print job to the GDI. The GDI hands off the print job to the Windows NT spooler, which determines whether the print device is managed locally or by a network-connected computer. If the print device is managed by the local computer that initiated this print job, the spooler copies the print job to a temporary storage area on the local computer's hard disk. If the print device is managed by a network-connected computer, the spooler hands off the print job to the spooler on the network-connected computer. Then that spooler copies the print job to a temporary storage area on that computer's hard disk. The print job is then handed off to the local print provider on the computer that has the print job spooled to its hard disk. The local print provider calls the print processor to perform any additional necessary conversions. Then the print processor returns the ready-to-print print job to the local print provider. The local print provider adds a separator page to the print job (if it is configured to do so) and then hands off the print job to the print monitor. The print monitor communicates directly with the print device and sends the ready-to-print print job to the print device, which finally produces the printed output. You may want to refer back to Figure 6-1, which shows a graphical illustration of the Windows NT print process.

o There are two ways of installing and configuring a printer in Windows NT: you can either *create a printer* or *connect to a shared network printer*. Both creating a printer and connecting to a printer are called "adding a printer," because both processes use the Add Printer Wizard in the `Printers` folder. You can also connect to a printer by using drag-and-drop printing.

o *Print monitors* (also called *port monitors*) are software components that send ready-to-print print jobs to a print device, either locally or across the network. Each port is associated with one specific print monitor. The most commonly used print monitors are Localmon, Hpmon, AppleTalk, TCP/IP, and NetWare.

o The *Localmon print monitor* sends print jobs to print devices that are connected to hardware ports on a local Windows NT computer. It is the only print monitor that is installed by default during the installation of Windows NT.

o The *Hpmon print monitor* sends print jobs to a network print device via an HP JetDirect adapter. Although HP JetDirect adapters typically support a variety of protocols, Hpmon uses only the DLC protocol to communicate with HP JetDirect adapters. The DLC protocol is a non-routable protocol, although it does support bridging. You must install DLC before you can connect to an HP JetDirect adapter using Hpmon. When you configure an Hpmon port, you must choose between a job based and a continuous connection. A *job based connection* enables all computers on the network to access the HP JetDirect adapter for printing, because the connection to the HP JetDirect adapter is dropped after each print job. A *continuous connection* causes Hpmon to monopolize the HP JetDirect adapter, and no other computer on the network is able to access the HP JetDirect adapter for printing.

o The *AppleTalk print monitor* sends print jobs to network print devices that support the AppleTalk protocol. The AppleTalk protocol is usually associated with Apple Macintosh computers. Before you can connect to an AppleTalk print device, you must install Services for Macintosh on your Windows NT Server computer. AppleTalk is a routable protocol.

o The *TCP/IP print monitor* sends print jobs to network print devices that both support TCP/IP *and* function as *line printer daemon* (LPD) print servers. TCP/IP and LPD are often associated with UNIX computers. LPD is the print server software used in TCP/IP printing, and *line printer remote* (LPR) is the client print software used in TCP/IP printing. Before you can connect to a TCP/IP print device, you must install TCP/IP and the Microsoft TCP/IP Printing service on your Windows NT computer. In addition, you must start the TCP/IP Print Server service to share printers as TCP/IP printers. TCP/IP is a routable protocol.

o The *NetWare print monitor* sends print jobs to a print queue on a NetWare server. The NetWare server then sends the print job from the print queue to the print device. Before you can connect to a NetWare print queue, you must install NWLink IPX/SPX Compatible Transport on your Windows NT Server computer. In addition, you must install Gateway Service for NetWare. NWLink IPX/SPX Compatible Transport is a routable protocol.

o A *print server* is a computer (or network device) that manages print jobs and print devices. The *Windows NT Spooler service* performs many of the functions of a print server. You can configure several of the Spooler service's properties (which Windows NT calls print server properties), including the spool folder, forms, and ports, by using the Print Server Properties dialog box. If you experience print job failures due to lack of free space on the partition where your spool folder is located, you can specify that a different folder on another partition (that has more free space) be used as your spool folder.

- You can use the Properties dialog box for a specific printer to configure numerous options for the printer, including: assigning a separator page, assigning forms to paper trays, printer security, printing to multiple ports (printer pools), scheduling printers and setting printer priorities, and sharing a printer.

- There are four Windows NT *printer permissions* that control which tasks a user can perform on a specific printer. A user or group with the *No Access* permission cannot access the printer. The *Print* permission enables users to create and delete their own print jobs. The *Manage Documents* permission allows users to pause, restart, delete, and control job settings for all print jobs, but does not allow users to print to the printer. A user or group that has the *Full Control* permission can do everything a user with the Print and Manage Documents permissions can do, and in addition, can also assign printer permissions, delete printers, share printers, and change printer properties. User and group permissions are additive, with the exception of the No Access permission. *If a user, or any group that a user is a member of, has the No Access permission, then the user's effective permission is always No Access.*

- Windows NT can be configured to audit a user or group's usage (and/or attempted usage) of a printer. Auditing printers is accomplished in two parts: first, auditing is enabled in User Manager for Domains; and second, printer auditing is configured in a specific printer's Properties dialog box. You *must* select the Success and/or Failure check boxes for File and Object Access (in User Manager for Domains) in order to audit print events.

- The owner of a printer can assign printer permissions for that printer to any user or group, even if the owner has the No Access permission. A printer can have only one owner at any given time. There are two ways to become an owner of a printer: either by creating the printer, or by taking ownership of the printer.

- When a printer has multiple ports (and multiple print devices) assigned to it, this is called a *printer pool*. Users print to a single printer, and the printer load-balances its print jobs between the print devices assigned to it.

o *Scheduling a printer* means assigning the hours that a specific print device
  is available for use by a printer. *Setting printer priorities* (giving one printer
  a higher priority to a print device than another printer) can be useful when
  more than one printer sends print jobs to the same print device. Scheduling
  printers and setting printer priorities are two techniques you can use to
  help manage the flow of print jobs on your Windows NT network.

o The purpose of *sharing a printer* is to enable users of other computers on the
  network to connect to and to send print jobs to that printer. The computer
  that hosts the shared printer is called a print server. When you share a printer
  on your Windows NT computer, the types of computers that can access your
  shared printer are dependent upon the protocols and services installed in your
  computer. If you have more than one print server service installed on your
  Windows NT computer, and then you share a printer, the printer is shared on
  all running print server services installed on your computer.

o When you share a printer on a Windows NT computer, Windows NT
  permits you to install *alternate printer drivers* for other versions of
  Windows NT and Windows 95, and also for other Windows NT hardware
  platforms, such as MIPS R4000, PowerPC, and DEC Alpha. Installing these
  alternate drivers enables users of Windows NT and Windows 95 computers
  on the network to automatically download and install the appropriate
  printer drivers for their operating systems/hardware platforms when they
  connect to the shared printer. This process spares the network
  administrator from having to manually install printer drivers on every
  computer on the network.

o AppleTalk printers can be shared in Windows NT. When a Windows NT
  Server computer that has Services for Macintosh installed on it shares a
  printer, the printer is accessible from Macintosh computers on the network.

o Printing problems can occur on a Windows NT network for several reasons.
  Troubleshooting recommendations for printer problems include: ensuring
  that users have the permissions they need to access the printer, making
  sure configuration parameters are correctly set, and using a methodical,
  step-by-step troubleshooting process.

APPLYING WHAT YOU'VE LEARNED

Now it's time to regroup, review, and apply what you've learned in this chapter.

The questions in the following Instant Assessment section bring to mind key facts and concepts. In addition, the Critical Thinking Lab gives you a chance to solve common Windows NT printing problems. Finally, the Hands-on Labs reinforce what you've learned and provide you with the opportunity to practice some of the tasks tested by the Server exam.

Instant Assessment

1. What is a *printer* in Windows NT terminology?

2. What is a *print device* in Windows NT terminology?

3. Which component in the Windows NT print process determines whether the print device is managed by the local computer that initiated the print job or by a network-connected computer, and routes the print job accordingly?

4. Fill in the blanks: There are two ways to install and configure a printer in Windows NT: you can either _____ a printer or _____ _____ a shared network printer.

5. What is the Windows NT term for software components that send ready-to-print print jobs to a print device?

6. Which print monitor sends print jobs to network print devices that both support TCP/IP and function as LPD print servers?

7. What two things must you install on your Windows NT Server computer before you can connect to a NetWare print queue by using the NetWare print monitor?

8. Which print monitor sends print jobs to a network print device via an HP JetDirect adapter?

9. What are the characteristics of a job based connection?

10. What are the characteristics of a continuous connection?

11. Which print monitor uses only the DLC protocol to communicate?

12. If you experience print job failures due to lack of free space on the partition where your spool folder is located, what can you do to resolve the problem?

13. Which Windows NT printer permission, when combined with other permissions, overrides and takes precedence over all other printer permissions?

14. What are the four Windows NT printer permissions?

15. When auditing a printer, what must you select, in User Manager for Domains, in order to audit print events?

16. What are the two ways to become an owner of a printer?

17. Which Windows NT printing term is defined as a printer having multiple ports (and multiple print devices) assigned to it?

18. What is the purpose of sharing a printer?

19. What is the advantage of being able to install printer drivers for alternate operating systems/hardware platforms on a shared printer on a Windows NT computer?

T/F

20. The DLC protocol is a non-routable protocol that supports bridging. _____

21. AppleTalk, TCP/IP, and NWLink IPX/SPX Compatible Transport are routable protocols.   _____

 concept link   **For answers to the Instant Assessment questions see Appendix B.**

Critical Thinking Lab

The following lab tests your ability to troubleshoot common Windows NT printing problems.

Lab 6.11 *Windows NT printing troubleshooting exercise*

For each of the following problems, explain what you think are the possible causes of the problem, and what course of action you would take to resolve the problem.

Problem 1   Halfway through a print job you discover that the print device's paper tray contains letterhead paper, and you need your document printed on white paper. You want to reprint the entire job, but you have already deleted your document from the spreadsheet application you were using.

Problem 2   Several days ago you configured success and failure auditing for print events in the Properties dialog box for your printer. However, no print events are listed in the Security Log in Event Viewer, even though at least two hundred documents have been printed since you configured auditing.

Problem 3   When you attempt to print a document in a word processing application, an error message is displayed, indicating that your print job has been spooled with a print job size of 0 bytes.

concept link **For answers to the Critical Thinking Lab see Appendix B.**

Hands-on Labs

The following Hands-on Labs provide you with practical opportunities to apply the knowledge you've gained in this chapter about managing printing.

Lab 6.12 *Creating and sharing a local printer*

The purpose of this lab is to familiarize you with the Windows NT Printers folder and its user interface and to provide you with the skills necessary to create and share a local printer.

To begin this lab, boot your computer to Windows NT Server, and log on as Administrator.

There are two parts to this lab:

Part 1: Creating a local printer

Part 2: Sharing a local printer

Part 1: Creating a local printer

1. Select Start ⇒ Programs ⇒ Windows NT Explorer.
2. Highlight (single-click) the Printers folder in the All Folders list box. (You might have to scroll down to find this folder.)
3. Double-click the Add Printer icon in the Contents of 'Printers' list box.
4. The Add Printer Wizard appears. Ensure that the option button next to My Computer is selected. Click Next.
5. Select the check box next to LPT1: in the Available ports list box. Click Next.
6. If you have a print device, select your print device's manufacturer from the Manufacturers list box, and then select your print device's model from

the Printers list box. Then click Next. (If you don't have a print device, accept the defaults in the Add Printer Wizard dialog box and click Next.)

7. Type a name for the new printer in the text box, or accept the default name that Windows NT presents. (If your computer has any additional printers installed, you are presented with another option to configure: Select the option button next to Yes if you want this to be your default printer. Otherwise, select the option button next to No.) Click Next.

8. Ensure that the option button next to Not shared is selected in the Add Printer Wizard dialog box. Click Next.

9. In the Add Printer Wizard dialog box, select the option button next to Yes to print a test page. Click Finish.

10. Windows NT copies files. (Respond to any prompts requesting the location of your Windows NT source files—this means the path to your CD-ROM drive that contains your Windows NT compact disc, such as `e:\I386`.)

11. A dialog box appears indicating that the printer test page is completed. Click Yes.

12. The printer is now created. The Windows NT Explorer dialog box reappears. (If you do not have a print device connected to LPT1, an error message eventually appears, indicating that there was an error printing the test page and that the print device is not ready. Click Cancel.) Continue on to Part 2 to share the printer.

Part 2: Sharing a local printer

1. In the Windows NT Explorer dialog box, with the Contents of 'Printers' list box displayed on the right, right-click the printer you just created. Select Sharing from the menu that appears.

2. A dialog box with your printer's properties appears. Select the option button next to Shared. Edit the text box next to Share Name to read **My Shared Printer**. (Don't type the period at the end.) Don't select any alternate drivers at this time. Click OK.

3. A warning message appears (because the share name you typed is longer than eight characters and has spaces in it) indicating that the share name you entered may not be accessible from MS-DOS workstations. Click Yes.

4. The Windows NT Explorer dialog box reappears. In the Contents of 'Printers' list box, right-click your printer. Select Properties from the menu that appears.

5. In your printer's Properties dialog box, click the Security tab.

6. Click Permissions.

7. In the Printer Permissions dialog box, notice the default permissions for a newly created printer. Click OK.

8. The Printer Permissions dialog box reappears. Click OK. Exit Windows NT Explorer.

Lab 6.13 *Installing and configuring Microsoft TCP/IP Printing*

The purpose of this lab is to give you hands-on experience in installing and configuring Microsoft TCP/IP Printing.

Begin this lab by booting your computer to Windows NT Server, and log on as Administrator.

There are two parts to this lab:

Part 1: Installing Microsoft TCP/IP Printing

Part 2: Configuring Microsoft TCP/IP Printing

Part 1: Installing Microsoft TCP/IP Printing

1. Select Start ⇒ Programs ⇒ Windows NT Explorer.

2. Click Control Panel in the All Folders list box on the left. In the Contents of 'Control Panel' list box on the right, double-click Network.

3. The Network dialog box appears. Click the Services tab.

4. On the Services tab, click the Add command button.

5. The Select Network Service dialog box appears. Click Microsoft TCP/IP Printing in the Network Service list box. Click OK.

6. A Windows NT Setup dialog box appears, requesting the location of Windows NT source files. Type the path to your Windows NT source files on your Windows NT compact disc (for example, e:\I386) and place your Windows NT compact disc in your CD-ROM drive. Click Continue.

7. Windows NT copies the files to your hard drive. The Services tab reappears. Click Close.

8. Several dialog boxes appear while Windows NT configures the new network service. When the Network Settings Change warning dialog box appears, click Yes to restart your computer.

Part 2: Configuring Microsoft TCP/IP Printing

1. When your computer reboots, log on as Administrator. Windows NT Explorer appears.

2. In the Contents of 'Control Panel' list box on the right, double-click Services.

3. Select TCP/IP Print Server from the Service list box. Click the Startup command button.

4. In the Startup Type section of the Service dialog box, select the option button next to Automatic. Click OK.

5. The Services dialog box reappears. Click the Start command button.

6. A Service Control dialog box appears, indicating that Windows NT is attempting to start the service. The Services dialog box reappears. Notice in the Status column that the TCP/IP Print Server service is started. Click Close.

7. The Windows NT Explorer dialog box reappears. Exit Windows NT Explorer. Microsoft TCP/IP Printing is now installed and configured.

Configuring Windows NT Server for Client Computers

About Chapter 7

This chapter tackles the subject of configuring a Windows NT Server computer for various types of client computers, including Windows NT Workstation, Windows 95, and MS-DOS-based client computers.

First, the chapter defines server-based deployment and explains what you need to do to prepare for the server-based deployment process.

Then, Chapter 7 introduces Network Client Administrator, a Windows NT Server tool you can use to create an installation disk set, or to create a network installation startup disk.

Next, you'll discover how to create answer files and Uniqueness Database Files to fully automate the Windows NT installation and setup process.

Finally, this chapter addresses how to automate the installation of applications during an automated installation of Windows NT. The OEM subfolder and Sysdiff.exe are introduced in this section.

The material presented in this chapter maps to the "Install Windows NT Server using various methods . . . including Network Client Administrator . . . " and the "Configure a Windows NT Server computer for various types of client computers" objectives listed in the Installation and Configuration section in the Preparation Guide for the Server exam.

WHAT IS SERVER-BASED DEPLOYMENT?

Server-based deployment is a process that involves automating the installation and setup of Windows NT, other operating systems (Windows 95 and Windows for Workgroups), and applications on multiple computers on a network.

This process is primarily designed for rolling out large networks quickly and efficiently.

In server-based deployment, source files are placed on a centrally located Windows NT Server computer. Then floppy disks are created which, when run on the computers that need to be set up, cause these computers to automatically connect to the server and to run a partially or fully automated installation and setup routine.

Server-based deployment is commonly used in two types of environments. First, *original equipment manufacturers* (OEMs) use this process to install and configure large numbers of computers at the factory prior to shipping these computers to customers and retail outlets. Second, organizations that install a new network or add several new computers to an existing network use this process to install operating systems and applications on their new computers in an efficient manner.

 tip **Using server-based deployment can save you a significant amount of time. Consider using it when you have five or more identical installs to perform.**

Before you can use server-based deployment, you must prepare the Windows NT Server computer that will store the source files used in this process.

PREPARING FOR SERVER-BASED DEPLOYMENT

To prepare your Windows NT Server computer for server-based deployment, you need to place the appropriate files on this server in a prescribed format.

To begin the preparation, copy the Clients folder, including all files and subfolders, from your Windows NT Server compact disc to one of the drives on the Windows NT Server computer. This drive must have enough free space to hold the entire contents of the Clients folder and the source files for any additional operating systems and applications you want to install using server-based deployment.

Then share the Clients folder on the Windows NT Server computer as CLIENTS. At this point, if the only operating system you want to deploy is

Windows 95, you are finished preparing your Windows NT Server computer. If you want to deploy other operating systems, follow the steps below for *each* operating system you want to deploy.

TO PREPARE YOUR WINDOWS NT SERVER COMPUTER FOR SERVER-BASED DEPLOYMENT OF WINDOWS FOR WORKGROUPS, FOLLOW THESE STEPS:

1. Create a subfolder in the Clients folder named Wfw.
2. Create a subfolder in the Clients\Wfw folder named Netsetup.
3. Copy the Windows for Workgroups installation files from your source media (compact disc or floppy disk) to the Netsetup folder.

TO PREPARE YOUR WINDOWS NT SERVER COMPUTER FOR SERVER-BASED DEPLOYMENT OF WINDOWS NT WORKSTATION, FOLLOW THESE STEPS:

1. Create a subfolder in the Clients folder named Winnt.
2. Create a subfolder in the Clients\Winnt folder named Netsetup.
3. Copy the Windows NT Workstation installation files and subfolders from the I386 folder on your Windows NT Workstation compact disc to the Netsetup folder.

TO PREPARE YOUR WINDOWS NT SERVER COMPUTER FOR SERVER-BASED DEPLOYMENT OF WINDOWS NT SERVER, FOLLOW THESE STEPS:

1. Create a subfolder in the Clients folder named Winnt.srv.
2. Create a subfolder in the Clients\Winnt.srv folder named Netsetup.
3. Copy the Windows NT Server installation files and subfolders from the I386 folder on your Windows NT Server compact disc to the Netsetup folder.

Once the Windows NT Server computer is prepared, you're ready to use the Network Client Administrator tool to proceed with the server-based deployment process.

USING NETWORK CLIENT ADMINISTRATOR

Network Client Administrator is a Windows NT Server tool that you can use to create an *installation disk set* to install network clients or services on client computers.

You can also use Network Client Administrator to create a *network installation startup disk*. A network installation startup disk, when run on a computer that needs to be set up (the *target computer*), causes the target computer to automatically connect to the server and start an interactive installation/setup routine.

Creating an Installation Disk Set

You can use Network Client Administrator to create an installation disk set to install network clients or services on client computers.

For example, suppose you want to install TCP/IP on several Windows for Workgroups computers. You can use Network Client Administrator to create a TCP/IP installation disk set, and then use this disk set on each computer on which you want to install TCP/IP.

The network clients and services that you can create an installation disk set for are: Network Client *v*3.0 for MS-DOS and Windows, Remote Access *v*1.1a for MS-DOS, TCP/IP 32 for Windows for Workgroups 3.11, LAN Manager *v*2.2c for MS-DOS, and LAN Manager *v*2.2c for OS/2.

TO CREATE AN INSTALLATION DISK SET, FOLLOW THESE STEPS:

1. Boot your computer to Windows NT Server. Select Start ⇒ Programs ⇒ Administrative Tools (Common) ⇒ Network Client Administrator.

2. The Network Client Administrator dialog box appears, as shown in Figure 7-1. Notice that the option button next to Make Network Installation Startup Disk is selected. Click the option button next to Make Installation Disk Set. Click Continue.

**FIGURE 7-1   Using Windows NT Server
Network Client Administrator**

3. Click the option button next to Use Existing Shared Directory in the Share
Network Client Installation Files dialog box. Type in the name of the
Windows NT Server that you are using for server-based deployment for
the Server Name. Type **clients** for the Share Name. Click OK.

4. In the drop-down list box in the Make Installation Disk Set dialog box, scroll
down and select the network client or service for which you want to
create an installation disk set. This dialog box is shown in Figure 7-2.
Notice that I have selected the TCP/IP 32 for Windows for Workgroups
3.11 network service. Click OK.

FIGURE 7-2   Creating an installation disk set

5. Windows NT prompts you to insert one to four floppy disks, depending
on the network client or service you selected. (These disks will become the
installation disk set.) Use blank disks for this procedure, even though NT
indicates a specifically named disk should be inserted. Insert a disk and
click OK.

6. Windows NT creates the installation disk set.

Creating a Network Installation Startup Disk

You can use Network Client Administrator to create a network installation startup disk.

For example, suppose you want to install Windows NT Workstation on several new client computers on your network. You can use Network Client Administrator to create a single disk that you can use on each of the new client computers to automatically begin an interactive, over-the-network installation of Windows NT Workstation.

You can create a network installation startup disk that can be used to install any of the following operating systems: Windows for Workgroups, Windows 95, Windows NT Workstation, or Windows NT Server. (A separate disk is required for each different operating system.)

TO CREATE A NETWORK INSTALLATION STARTUP DISK, FOLLOW THESE STEPS:

1. Boot your computer to Windows NT Server. Select Start ⇒ Programs ⇒ Administrative Tools (Common) ⇒ Network Client Administrator.

2. The Network Client Administrator dialog box appears. Ensure the option button next to Make Network Installation Startup Disk is selected. Click Continue.

3. Click the option button next to Use Existing Shared Directory in the Share Network Client Installation Files dialog box. Type in the name of the Windows NT Server you are using for server-based deployment for the Server Name. Type **clients** for the Share Name. Click OK.

4. The Target Workstation Configuration dialog box appears. In the Network Client list box, highlight the client or operating system for which you want to create a network installation startup disk. In the Network Adapter Card drop-down list box, select the network adapter that is installed in the target computer. (The target computer is the computer on which you want to install a new operating system.) Figure 7-3 shows the Target Workstation Configuration dialog box. Notice that Windows NT Workstation and a 3Com EtherLink III network adapter card have been selected. Click OK.

FIGURE 7-3   Creating a network installation
startup disk

 You may be wondering, at this point, if the network installation
startup disk works only on computers that have identical network
adapters installed in them. Yep. That's how it is. You must create a
separate network installation startup disk for each network
adapter/operating system combination you plan to install.

5. A warning message appears, indicating that a license for Windows NT
Workstation must be purchased prior to installing and using this operating
system. Click OK.

6. The Network Startup Disk Configuration dialog box appears. Type in a
computer name that will be used by the target computer during the
installation process. Type in a user name to be used to log on to the
Windows NT Server from the target computer during the installation
process. Type in the domain name that the user account is maintained in.
Select a network protocol to be used during the installation process. Enter
any configuration values needed for this protocol (IP address, subnet
mask, default gateway, and so on). Click OK when you are finished. Figure
7-4 shows the Network Startup Disk Configuration dialog box. Note that all
text boxes have been completed.

7. The Confirm Network Disk Configuration dialog box appears. Figure 7-5
shows this dialog box. Note that NT requires you to insert a formatted,
high-density floppy disk. This disk *must* be formatted as an MS-DOS
system disk. (This can be accomplished on any computer that runs MS-
DOS by using the FORMAT /s command.) Insert a formatted system disk
and click OK to continue.

FIGURE 7-4 Configuring network installation startup disk options

8. Windows NT creates the over-the-network installation startup disk. The network installation startup disk is now configured for the operating system you selected. To start an interactive installation, boot the target computer by using the network installation startup disk.

FIGURE 7-5 Confirming network startup disk configuration

To fully automate the Windows NT installation and setup process, you must create an answer file to be used by the Windows NT setup program, and you must edit the `Autoexec.bat` file on the network installation startup disk so that it uses this answer file during the installation. The next section discusses, in detail, automating the Windows NT installation and setup process.

AUTOMATING SETUP OF WINDOWS NT

Until now, you have learned how to automate the start of an interactive Windows NT installation process by creating a network installation startup disk. Now you'll discover how to create and use answer files (Unattend.txt) and Uniqueness Database Files (UDFs) to fully automate the Windows NT installation and setup process.

 You'll probably notice that many of the examples of deployment discussed in this chapter feature the automated installation of Windows NT Workstation rather than Windows NT Server. While I haven't forgotten that this book is about NT Server, in reality, when a lot of identical installations of an operating system on multiple computers are performed, client computers are being set up, and this typically means deploying Windows NT Workstation.

Creating and Using Answer Files (Unattend.txt)

Answer files are text files that contain stylized responses to the queries posed by the Windows NT Setup program during installation. You can use an answer file, in conjunction with a network installation startup disk (discussed in the previous section), to fully automate the installation of Windows NT on a single computer (that is, perform an unattended installation). The default name for an answer file is Unattend.txt, but you can use any filename you want for your answer files. Listing 7-1 presents a sample answer file.

LISTING 7-1 Sample Unattend.txt file

```
[Unattended]
OemPreinstall = yes
NoWaitAfterTextMode = 1
NoWaitAfterGUIMode = 1
FileSystem = ConvertNTFS
ExtendOEMPartition = 0
ConfirmHardware = no
NtUpgrade = no
```

```
Win31Upgrade = no
TargetPath = *
OverwriteOemFilesOnUpgrade = no
KeyboardLayout = "US"

[UserData]
FullName = "MCSE Candidate"
OrgName = "MCSE Candidates Company"
ComputerName = NTW2
ProductId = "975-4769754"

[GuiUnattended]
OemSkipWelcome = 1
OEMBlankAdminPassword = 1
TimeZone = "(GMT-08:00) Pacific Time (US & Canada); Tijuana"

ConfigureAtLogon = 0
BitsPerPel = 8
XResolution = 800
YResolution = 600
VRefresh = 60
AutoConfirm = 1

[Network]
DetectAdapters = ""
InstallProtocols = ProtocolsSection
InstallServices = ServicesSection
InstallInternetServer = InternetParamSection
JoinDomain = LAB
CreateComputerAccount = administrator, password

[ProtocolsSection]
TC = TCParamSection

[TCParamSection]
DHCP = no
```

LISTING 7-1 *(continued)*

```
IPAddress = 192.168.59.7
Subnet = 255.255.255.0
Gateway = 192.168.59.1


[ServicesSection]
```

There are two ways you can create an answer file. You can use any text editor, such as Notepad, to type in all of the appropriate responses in the correct format. Or, you can use Windows NT Setup Manager (Setupmgr.exe) to create an answer file, which is the easiest and preferred method.

 concept link

For additional information on the format and content of answer files, see Appendix A of the *Microsoft Windows NT Workstation Resource Kit for version 4.0* (Microsoft Press, 1996).

To use an answer file, run the Windows NT Setup program (Winnt.exe or Winnt32.exe) with the /U switch.

For example, to use an answer file from the command line, you can type: Z:\Winnt\Netsetup\Winnt.exe /U:Z:\Winnt\Netsetup\Unattend.txt /S:Z:\Winnt\Netsetup

In this example, Winnt.exe starts the installation process with the unattended switch (/U) to specify that Winnt.exe will use a specific answer file (Z:\Winnt\Netstup\Unattend.txt). Winnt.exe uses the /S switch to specify that the source folder for all Windows NT Workstation files is Z:\Winnt\Netsetup.

Using the command line is one way to start the installation process with an answer file. Another more efficient way is using the network installation startup disk in conjunction with an answer file to fully automate the installation of Windows NT on a single computer. To do this, you must first edit the Autoexec.bat file on the network installation startup disk by using Notepad or any other text editor.

For example, the last line of the Autoexec.bat file on a network installation startup disk that has been created for a Windows NT Workstation installation, before editing, is normally: Z:\Winnt\Netsetup\Winnt.exe /B /S:Z:\Winnt\Netsetup

To use the startup disk in conjunction with an answer file, you should edit this line so that it reads: `Z:\Winnt\Netsetup\Winnt.exe /U:Z:\Winnt\Netsetup\Unattend.txt /S:Z:\Winnt\Netsetup`

in the real world

In practice, it often takes several attempts to correctly configure a network installation startup disk and an answer file. I recommend you try these out on a test computer prior to deploying them live on your network.

Now that you understand what an answer file is and how it is used, it's time to discuss how to create an answer file by using Setup Manager.

Using Setup Manager

Windows NT Setup Manager (`Setupmgr.exe`) is a graphical tool that provides an easy way to create an answer file (`Unattend.txt`) that you can use to install Windows NT in unattended mode.

Setup Manager is located on the Windows NT Server compact disc. You can find it in the `\Support\Deptools\I386` folder (for Intel-based computers). To start Setup Manager, double-click `Setupmgr.exe` in Windows NT Explorer.

When you start Setup Manager, the Windows NT Setup Manager main dialog box appears, as shown in Figure 7-6. Notice that you can choose from three options: General Setup, Networking Setup, and Advanced Setup.

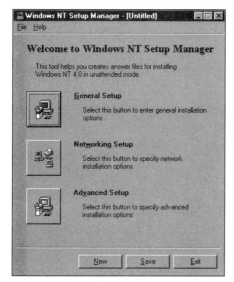

FIGURE 7-6 Windows NT Setup Manager main dialog box

The *General Setup* options in Windows NT Setup Manager are used to configure the user information, computer role, installation directory, display settings, time zone, and license mode entries in an answer file.

The *Networking Setup* options in Windows NT Setup Manager are used to configure the adapters, protocols, services, Internet, and modem entries in an answer file.

The *Advanced Setup* options in Windows NT Setup Manager are used to configure the file system, mass storage, display driver, keyboard, pointing device, and boot files entries in an answer file.

Using Uniqueness Database Files

Uniqueness Database Files (UDFs) are text files, similar to answer files, that make it possible for one answer file to be used for the installation of many computers with different identifying characteristics. For example, each computer has a different computer name and user name. A UDF, used in conjunction with a network installation startup disk and an answer file, makes it possible to fully automate the installation of Windows NT on multiple computers on a network.

The UDF is structured like an answer file, and uses the same types of entries that an answer file uses. The UDF has an additional section, named [UniqueIds]. When the appropriate command-line switch is used, selected entries in the UDF replace entries with the same name in the answer file.

The only types of entries you can't use in a UDF are entries that are used during the text-mode portion (Phase 1) of the installation routine. In other words, entries from the following section headings *must* be specified in the answer file — they can't be used in a UDF:

- [Unattended]
- [OEMBootFiles]
- [MassStorageDrivers]
- [KeyboardDrivers]
- [PointingDeviceDrivers]

 note **If you have computers with different hard disk controllers, keyboards, or mice, you must use a different answer file for each hardware configuration.**

Listing 7-2 presents a sample UDF named `Authors.txt`.

LISTING 7-2 **Sample UDF, Authors.txt**

```
[UniqueIds]
Wshakespeare = Wshakespeare:UserData
Sclemens = Sclemens:UserData
Hmelville = Hmelville:UserData

[Wshakespeare:UserData]
FullName = "William Shakespeare"
OrgName = "Playwrights, Inc."
ComputerName = Willie
ProductId = "975-4769755"

[Sclemens:UserData]
FullName = "Samuel Clemens"
OrgName = "The Mark Twain Book Company"
ComputerName = Huck
ProductId = "975-4769756"

[Hmelville:UserData]
FullName = "Herman Melville"
OrgName = "A Whale of a Story, Inc."
ComputerName = Moby
ProductId = "975-4769757"
```

Notice in the `Authors.txt` UDF that the names listed in the `[UniqueIds]` section map to the other section headings in the UDF.

Using the `Authors.txt` UDF file as an example, assume that you want to use a UDF, an answer file, and a network installation startup disk to install Windows NT Workstation on Samuel Clemens's computer. To configure the network installation startup disk, you must edit the last line of the `Autoexec.bat` file on this disk so that it reads as follows:

```
Z:\Winnt\Netsetup\Winnt.exe /U:Z:\Winnt\Netsetup\Unattend.txt
 /S:Z:\Winnt\Netsetup /UDF:Sclemens, Authors.txt
```

This command instructs `Winnt.exe` to use the entries in the [Sclemens:UserData] section of the `Authors.txt` UDF to replace the entries with the same name in the answer file during the installation. In this case, the user name, organization name, computer name, and product ID specified in the [Sclemens:UserData] section of the `Authors.txt` UDF is used during the installation of Windows NT Workstation; and the user name, organization name, computer name, and product ID specified in the answer file is disregarded.

A UDF can specify that more than one section in a UDF is to be associated with a unique identifier (UniqueId). Continuing along the same line as the previous example, you could specify in the [UniqueIds] section of a UDF that:

```
Wshakespeare = Wshakespeare:UserData, Protocols1
```

This line indicates that the UniqueID Wshakespeare is associated with two sections in the UDF: [Wshakespeare:UserData] and [Protocols1]. The [Wshakespeare:UserData] section contains user specific information, and the [Protocols1] section contains an alternate list of protocols to be installed on William Shakespeare's computer. During installation, `Winnt.exe` will use the entries contained in [Wshakespeare:UserData] and [Protocols1] instead of the same-named entries in the answer file.

concept link **For additional information on UDFs, see Chapter 2 and Appendix A of the *Microsoft Windows NT Workstation Resource Kit*.**

AUTOMATING APPLICATION INSTALLATION DURING SETUP

In addition to automating the installation of Windows NT, you may also want to automate the installation of various applications at the same time.

In this section, you'll learn how the OEM subfolder and `Sysdiff.exe` can be used to automatically install applications at the end of the automated installation/setup process.

The OEM Subfolder

The OEM subfolder is used to store source files that are used to install applications, components, or files that do not ship with Windows NT.

You must create the OEM subfolder — it does not exist as part of Windows NT distribution files.

To create a OEM subfolder to use in conjunction with an automated installation/setup of Windows NT Workstation, create the OEM subfolder in the Clients\Winnt\Netsetup folder.

To create a OEM subfolder to use in conjunction with an automated installation/setup of Windows NT Server, create the OEM subfolder in the Clients\Winnt.srv\Netsetup folder.

You can use the OEM subfolder to store source files of applications that support scripted installation. Scripted installation enables complete installation of an application from a single command line. Most Microsoft applications support scripted installation.

For example, to prepare for automated installation of a scripted application (in conjunction with a Windows NT Workstation automated installation) on your computer's C: drive, first create a OEM subfolder in the Clients\Winnt\Netsetup folder. Then create a subfolder named C in the OEM folder, and a subfolder named *name_of_application* in the OEM\C folder. Then copy the application's source files, including all subfolders, to the Clients\Winnt\Netsetup\OEM\C*name_of_application* folder. Then, create a Cmdlines.txt file in the OEM subfolder that uses the following syntax:

```
[Commands]
"complete command line to install the application"
```

 note The use of quotation marks to surround the command line is required in the Cmdlines.txt **file.**

Finally, add an OemPreinstall = yes entry to the answer file to instruct Winnt.exe to execute the commands in the Cmdlines.txt file. (If the answer file is *not* edited, Winnt.exe will ignore the OEM subfolder and all of its contents during automated installation.)

As an alternative to placing files in a *subfolder* of the OEM folder, particularly when you have only one application to install, you can place files directly into the OEM folder. For instance, suppose that you want to automatically apply Service Pack 3 as part of an automated installation of Windows NT. The next section outlines the steps involved in preparing to automatically apply Service Pack 3.

TO PREPARE FOR AN AUTOMATED APPLICATION OF SERVICE PACK 3 DURING AN UNATTENDED WINDOWS NT INSTALLATION, FOLLOW THESE STEPS:

1. Create a OEM subfolder in the Clients\Winnt\Netsetup (or Clients\Winnt.srv\Netsetup) folder on the NT Server computer that contains the source files for the automated installation of Windows NT.

2. Copy all of the Service Pack 3 files (from the I386 folder on the Service Pack 3 compact disc) to the OEM folder.

3. Copy the Disk1 and Spcdrom.40 files from the root of the Service Pack 3 compact disc to the OEM folder.

4. Use Notepad (or any other text editor) to create a Cmdlines.txt file in the OEM folder that contains the following text:

[Commands]

"update /u /z"

The above commands will cause Service Pack 3 to be applied after the installation of Windows NT is complete. The service pack installation will be done in the "quiet" mode, which means that no user interaction is required.

5. Edit the answer file to instruct Winnt.exe to execute the commands in the Cmdlines.txt file. (If the answer file is *not* edited, Winnt.exe will ignore the OEM subfolder and all of its contents during automated installation.) Using Notepad (or any other text editor) edit the [Unattended] section of the answer file to include the following entry:

OemPreinstall = yes

concept link

For additional information on the `$OEM$` **subfolder, see Chapter 2 of the** *Microsoft Windows NT Workstation Resource Kit,* **and the article titled** "MS Windows NT Workstation Deployment Guide — automating Windows NT Setup" **in** *Microsoft TechNet.*

Applications that don't support scripted installation can be installed by using `Sysdiff.exe`. Using `Sysdiff.exe` is discussed in the next section.

Using Sysdiff.exe

`Sysdiff.exe` is used to automate the installation of applications that don't support scripted installation and that would otherwise require user interaction during the installation process. `Sysdiff.exe` is designed to be used when the same application must be installed on many different computers, and you want to install the application automatically during an unattended installation of Windows NT.

Using `Sysdiff.exe` to automatically install an application requires a fair amount of work in advance of the actual unattended installation. First, you must install Windows NT on a computer, then use `Sysdiff.exe` to take a snapshot of the computer's current configuration, then manually install the application (that you want to automate the installation of), and finally, use `Sysdiff.exe` to create a difference file. This difference file will then be used to automate the installation of this application on future unattended installations of Windows NT.

`Sysdiff.exe` is located on the Windows NT Server compact disc. You can find it in the `\Support\Deptools\I386` folder (for Intel-based computers).

`Sysdiff.exe` is typically used with the following switches:

- `/snap` When this switch is used after Windows NT is installed but before any applications are installed, `Sysdiff.exe` takes a snapshot of a typical target computer's current configuration.

- `/diff` When this switch is used after the desired application is installed, `Sysdiff.exe` creates a difference file that contains all of the files that were added and Registry changes that were made as a result of installing the application.

- `/apply` When this switch is used, `Sysdiff.exe` will apply the difference file to a Windows NT installation.

The following section explains how to use `Sysdiff.exe` to create a snapshot file, a difference file, and finally, to apply the difference file to an unattended Windows NT installation.

─────────────────────────────────────⋀─────────────────────────────────────

TO CREATE A SNAPSHOT FILE, FOLLOW THESE STEPS:

1. Create a folder named **C:\Images** on a newly installed Windows NT computer.

2. Copy `Sysdiff.exe` and `Sysdiff.inf` from the `\SUPPORT\DEPTOOLS\I386` folder on your Windows NT Server compact disc to the `C:\Images` folder.

3. Select Start ⇒ Programs ⇒ Command Prompt.

4. At the command prompt type **C:\images\sysdiff /snap c:\images\appsnap.img** and press Enter.

5. `Sysdiff.exe` creates a snapshot of your current installation. The snapshot information is contained in the `c:\images\appsnap.img` file.

6. After creating a snapshot file, install the application (that you want to automate the installation of) on the Windows NT computer.

TO CREATE A DIFFERENCE FILE, FOLLOW THESE STEPS:

1. Select Start ⇒ Programs ⇒ Command Prompt.

2. At the command prompt, type **C:\images\sysdiff /diff c:\images\appsnap. img c:\images\appdiff.img** and press Enter.

   `Sysdiff.exe` creates a difference file named `appdiff.img`. `Appdiff.img` contains all of the files and Registry settings which were added to the Windows NT computer when the application was installed.

TO CONFIGURE THE DIFFERENCE FILE TO BE APPLIED DURING AN UNATTENDED INSTALLATION OF WINDOWS NT, FOLLOW THESE STEPS:

1. Copy `Sysdiff.exe`, `Sysdiff.inf`, and `appdiff.img` (the difference file) from the `C:\Images` folder to the `$OEM$` folder. (If you have not already done so, before performing this step, create a `$OEM$` subfolder in the `Clients\Winnt\Netsetup` [or `Clients\Winnt.srv\Netsetup`] folder on the NT Server computer that contains the source files for the automated installation of Windows NT.)

2. Edit the answer file to instruct Winnt.exe to execute the commands in the Cmdlines.txt file. (If the answer file is *not* edited, Winnt.exe will ignore the OEM subfolder and all of its contents during automated installation.) Using Notepad (or any other text editor) edit the [Unattended] section of the answer file to include the following entry:

OemPreinstall = yes

3. Use Notepad (or any other text editor) to create a Cmdlines.txt file in the OEM folder that contains the following text:

[Commands]

".\Sysdiff /apply /m .\appdiff.img"

 note You must use quotation marks around all commands in the Cmdlines.txt **file.**

 concept link For additional information on using Sysdiff.exe, **see Chapter 2 of the *Microsoft Windows NT Workstation Resource Kit* and the article** titled "MS Windows NT Workstation Deployment Guide — Automating Windows NT Setup" in *Microsoft TechNet*.

KEY POINT SUMMARY

Chapter 7 explained how to configure a Windows NT Server computer for various types of client computers, including Windows NT Workstation, Windows 95, and MS-DOS-based client computers.

○ *Server-based deployment* is a process that involves automating the installation and setup of Windows NT, other operating systems (Windows 95 and Windows for Workgroups), and applications on multiple computers on a network.

○ You must prepare the Windows NT Server computer that you will use for the server-based deployment process by copying the Clients folder from the Windows NT Server compact disc to this computer. Then you share the Clients folder as CLIENTS and modify this folder depending on the operating system(s) you want to install.

- *Network Client Administrator* is a Windows NT Server tool that you can use to create an installation disk set and a network installation startup disk. An *installation disk set* is used to install network clients or services on client computers. A *network installation startup disk*, when run on a computer that needs to be set up (the target computer), causes the target computer to automatically connect to the Windows NT Server computer and start an interactive installation/setup routine.

- Automating the setup of Windows NT involves creating an *answer file* and *Uniqueness Database File* (UDF) that enable you to fully automate the Windows NT installation and setup process.

  - An *answer file* is a text file that contains stylized responses to the queries posed by the Windows NT Setup program during installation. The default name for an answer file is Unattend.txt. The easiest way to create an answer file is to use Windows NT Setup Manager (Setupmgr.exe). To use an answer file, run the Windows NT Setup program with the /U switch.

  - A *Uniqueness Database File* (UDF) is a text file, similar to an answer file, that allows one answer file to be used for the installation of many computers that have different identifying characteristics (different computer names, user names, and so on). When used in conjunction with a network installation startup disk and an answer file, a UDF makes it possible to fully automate the installation of Windows NT on multiple computers on a network. If you have computers with different hard disk controllers, keyboards, or mice, you must use a different answer file for each hardware configuration, because these entries can only be specified in an answer file, not in a UDF. When the appropriate command-line switch is used, selected entries in the UDF replace same-named entries in the answer file.

- In addition to automating the installation of Windows NT, you may want to automate the installation of various applications at the same time. The OEM subfolder is used to store source files that are used to install scripted applications, components, or files that do not ship with Windows NT. Scripted applications are those that permit complete installation from a single command line. Create the `$OEM$` subfolder in the `Clients\Winnt\Netsetup` folder to use in conjunction with an automated installation of Windows NT Workstation. Create the `$OEM$` subfolder in the `Clients\Winnt.srv\Netsetup` folder to use in conjunction with an automated installation of Windows NT Server.

○ `Sysdiff.exe` is used to automate the installation of applications that don't support scripted installation, and that otherwise would require user interaction during the installation process. `Sysdiff.exe` can be used to perform these three major functions:

  ○ When run with the `/snap` switch after Windows NT is installed but before any applications are installed, `Sysdiff.exe` takes a snapshot of a typical target computer's current configuration.

  ○ When run with the `/diff` switch after the desired application is installed, `Sysdiff.exe` creates a difference file containing all of the application files and Registry changes.

  ○ When run with the `/apply` switch from the `Cmdlines.txt` file, `Sysdiff.exe` applies the difference file during an unattended Windows NT installation.

APPLYING WHAT YOU'VE LEARNED

Now it's time to regroup, review, and apply what you've learned in this chapter.

The questions in the Instant Assessment section that follows bring to mind key facts and concepts. In addition, some of the questions give you a chance to analyze situations and apply your knowledge to that particular situation.

Instant Assessment

1. What is server-based deployment?

2. What is the primary reason for using server-based deployment?

3. What are the two types of environments in which server-based deployment is commonly used?

4. Which folder must be copied from the Windows NT Server compact disc to the Windows NT Server computer that will be used for server-based deployment?

5. You are preparing a Windows NT Server computer to use in deploying Windows NT Workstation to several client computers. You copy the `Clients` folder from the Windows NT Server compact disc to one of the drives on the Windows NT Server computer. What two additional subfolders must you create in the `Clients` folder?

6. You are preparing a Windows NT Server computer to use in deploying Windows NT Server to several other computers. You copy the `Clients` folder from the Windows NT Server compact disc to one of the drives on the Windows NT Server computer. What two additional subfolders must you create in the `Clients` folder?

7. You want to install TCP/IP 32 for Windows for Workgroups 3.11 on twenty computers on your network. What can you create, using Network Client Administrator, to help you accomplish this task efficiently?

8. You are rolling out a new network for a company and want to install Windows NT Workstation on 50 new client computers. What can you create, using Network Client Administrator, to help you accomplish this task efficiently?

9. What is an answer file?

10. What is the easiest way to create an answer file?

11. What switch must you use with the Windows NT Setup program to ensure that an answer file will be utilized?

12. Where is Windows NT Setup Manager (`Setupmgr.exe`) located?

13. Fill in the blank: When the appropriate command-line switch is used, selected entries in the UDF _____ same-named entries in the answer file.

14. You want to use UDFs in conjunction with a network installation startup disk and answer files to automate the installation of Windows NT on multiple computers on your network. However, several of the computers on your network have different hard disk controllers and different keyboards. How many different answer files do you need?

15. You want to automate the installation of various applications at the same time you perform an unattended installation of Windows NT. Which subfolder should you use to store source files that will be used to install applications that support scripted installation?

16. What file must you edit to instruct `Winnt.exe` to execute the commands in the `Cmdlines.txt` file so that applications will be installed during an unattended installation of Windows NT?

17. What are the three major functions of `Sysdiff.exe`?

concept link **For answers to the Instant Assessment questions see Appendix B.**

Managing Resources

Putting it all together and managing what you've got—that's what this part is all about. First, Chapter 8 explains how to create and manage user accounts. Then, we discuss creating and managing groups—complete with in-depth coverage of local groups and global groups.

Next, Chapter 9 explains managing account policy, followed by step-by-step instructions on how to manage user rights and auditing.

Then, Chapter 10 explores how to manage user profiles, including roaming and mandatory user profiles. It also covers managing Windows NT system policy.

Moving right along, Chapter 11 explains how to administer servers remotely from client computers. The use of Client-based Network Administration Tools and Windows NT Server Tools is the major focus of this chapter.

Next, Chapter 12 covers how to share and secure file systems. Both share and NTFS permissions are explained in detail.

Finally, Chapter 13 provides practical information and tips on backing up and restoring data.

Part III maps to the Managing Resources exam objectives for the Implementing and Supporting Microsoft Windows NT Server 4.0 exam.

Managing User and Group Accounts

About Chapter 8

This chapter could be called, "Everything You Always Wanted to Know About Users and Groups but Were Afraid Someone Would Explain to You in Great Detail."

It starts by taking you through the steps to create a user account, including important tips on naming conventions and passwords. Then it outlines how to configure specific Windows NT user account properties. Other common user account tasks are also explained, including how to copy user accounts, how to apply properties to multiple user accounts, and how to rename and delete user accounts.

The remainder of this chapter focuses on creating and managing groups. Local groups and global groups are discussed and compared extensively. You'll not only find out how to create these groups but also how and when to use them to efficiently organize users and to assign rights and permissions to multiple users. Built-in groups and special groups are also addressed.

This chapter includes one comprehensive Hands-on Lab. In this lab you'll practice creating user accounts, managing user account properties, creating group accounts, assigning user accounts to groups, and creating user account templates.

The material presented in Chapter 8 maps to the "Manage user and group accounts" objective listed in the Managing Resources section in the Preparation Guide for the Server exam.

CREATING AND MANAGING USER ACCOUNTS

User accounts are records that contain unique user information, such as user name, password, and any logon restrictions. User accounts enable users to log on to Windows NT computers or domains.

There are two types of user accounts: built-in user accounts, and user accounts that you create. You can configure various user account properties, including group memberships, profile, logon script, logon hours, workstation logon restrictions, account expiration, and dialin permission.

The following sections cover these topics, as well as copying user accounts, applying properties to multiple accounts, and renaming and deleting user accounts.

Built-in User Accounts

There are two built-in user accounts in Windows NT: *Administrator* and *Guest*. Built-in accounts are created automatically during the installation of Windows NT.

The Administrator account has all of the rights and permissions needed to fully administer a Windows NT computer or a Windows NT domain. The Administrator account can be used to perform numerous tasks, including creating and managing users and groups, managing file and folder permissions, and installing and managing printers and printer security. In addition, members of the Administrators local group have the right to take ownership of any file, folder, or printer. The Administrator account's rights and permissions are due solely to its membership in the Administrators local group.

The Administrator account, because of its powerful capabilities, can pose a security risk to your network if a nonauthorized user is able to guess the password for the account. For this reason, you should consider renaming the Administrator account. (Renaming user accounts is covered later in this chapter.)

The Guest account is designed to permit limited access to network resources to occasional users that don't have their own user account. For example, a client visiting your office might want to connect a laptop computer to the network to print a document. The client can log on using the Guest account. You can specify which network resources are available to this account by assigning the appropriate file, folder, and printer permissions to the Guest account.

The Guest account is disabled by default. If your network contains sensitive data I recommend, for security reasons, you leave the Guest account disabled.

Instead of using the Guest account, establish a user account for every person who needs access to network resources.

Creating a User Account

Every person who uses the network should have a user account. You can create user accounts by using User Manager for Domains.

TO CREATE A USER ACCOUNT, FOLLOW THESE STEPS:

1. Select Start ⇒ Programs ⇒ Administrative Tools (Common) ⇒ User Manager for Domains.

2. In the User Manager dialog box, select User ⇒ New User.

3. The New User dialog box, shown in Figure 8-1, appears. Fill in the user name, person's full name (optional), description (this could be a department, location, or job title—it is also optional), and password. Confirm the password by retyping it.

FIGURE 8-1   Creating a user account

4. Select the check box next to User Must Change Password at Next Logon if you want the user to choose and enter a new password the first time the user logs on. This option is selected by default.

Select the check box next to User Cannot Change Password if you—the network administrator—want to manage user passwords.

Select the check box next to Password Never Expires if you are configuring a user account for a Windows NT service to use when it logs in.

Select the check box next to Account Disabled if you are creating a user template.

5. Use the command buttons at the bottom of the New User dialog box to configure group memberships, profile and home folder location, logon hours, logon restrictions, and dialin permission for the new user account. (These options are each discussed in detail later in this chapter.)

6. Click the Add command button. Click the Close command button. The new user account is created.

Naming conventions

When you create user accounts, keep in mind a few simple rules for user account names:

- User account names can be from one to twenty characters long.

- User account names created in a domain must be unique within the domain. User account names created on a non-domain controller (such as a stand-alone server) must be unique within the non-domain controller.

- User account names cannot be the same as a group name within the domain or non-domain controller.

- The following characters may *not* be used in user account names: < > ? * + , = | ; : [ ] \ / "

If you have more than a few people in your organization, it's a good idea to plan your user account naming convention.

There are several possible naming schemes you can use. Often, the overall length of a user account name is limited to eight characters (to be compatible with MS-DOS directory name limitations), although this is not mandatory. Common naming schemes include:

A. The first seven letters of the user's first name plus the first letter of the user's last name

B. The first letter of the user's first name plus the first seven letters of the user's last name

C. The user's initials plus the last four digits of the user's employee number

D. Various hybrid combinations of the above schemes

Table 8-1 shows how three user account names would appear using the naming conventions described in A, B, and C.

TABLE 8-1 USER ACCOUNT NAMING CONVENTIONS			
FULL NAME	SCHEME A	SCHEME B	SCHEME C
Nancy Yates	NancyY	Nyates	NY5500
Robert Jones	RobertJ	Rjones	RJ1234
Jonathan Whitmore	JonathaW	Jwhitmor	JW2266

In addition to choosing a naming convention, you should have a way to handle exceptions. It's quite common, for example, for two users to have the same first name and last initial, such as Mike Smith and Mike Sutherland. If you choose to adopt the naming convention described in A above, you would need to have a way to resolve potential duplicate user names. You could resolve the problem by assigning Mike Smith the user account name of MikeS (assuming he was hired before Mike Sutherland), and assigning Mike Sutherland the user account name of MikeSu.

Passwords

Just a few words about passwords. Everyone knows that using passwords protects the security of the network, because only authorized users can log on.

When user accounts are created, you should have a plan for managing passwords. Will passwords be assigned and maintained by the network administrator? Or will users choose their own passwords?

in the
real world

I almost never recommend that the network administrator maintain user passwords, because it can take an enormous amount of administrator time to maintain passwords for users.

Normally the only time a network administrator should maintain user passwords is when the highest level of network security is required. The administrator can then assign passwords of the appropriate length and complexity.

When users maintain their own passwords, it's a good idea to remind them of a few password security basics:

- Don't use your own name or the names of family members or pets as passwords. (This is a common security loophole on most networks.)

- Never disclose your password to anyone. Don't write your password on a sticky note and stick it to your monitor. Other not-so-hot places to store your password are on or under your keyboard, in your top desk drawer, in your Rolodex, or in your briefcase, wallet, or purse.

- Use a sufficiently long password. I recommend using eight or more characters in a password. The longer a password, the more difficult it is to guess. The maximum password length is 14 characters.

- Use a mix of upper- and lowercase letters, numbers, and special characters. Remember, passwords are case-sensitive.

- If passwords are changed regularly, don't use the same password with an incremental number at the end, such as: Alan01, Alan02, Alan03, and so on. (Don't laugh. This may seem like common sense, but I know several network administrators who actually do this.)

User Account Properties

User accounts have numerous options that can be configured. These options are called *user account properties*.

User account properties that you can configure include group memberships, profile, logon scripts, logon hours, workstation logon restrictions, account expiration, and dialin permission.

User account properties are configured in the User Properties dialog box in User Manager for Domains.

Figure 8-2 shows the User Properties dialog box for Administrator in User Manager for Domains on a Windows NT computer configured as a non-domain controller. *Non-domain controllers* include Windows NT Server computers configured as stand-alone or member servers and Windows NT Workstation computers. Notice the Groups, Profile, and Dialin command buttons along the bottom of the dialog box.

FIGURE 8-2 Administrator's user properties
on a non-domain controller

Figure 8-3 shows the User Properties dialog box for Administrator in User Manager for Domains on a Windows NT Server computer configured as a primary domain controller (PDC). Notice the Groups, Profile, Hours, Logon To, Account, and Dialin command buttons along the bottom of the dialog box. More account properties can be configured on a domain controller than on a non-domain controller.

FIGURE 8-3 Administrator's user properties
on a domain controller

TO ACCESS THE USER PROPERTIES DIALOG BOX, FOLLOW THESE STEPS:

1. Select Start ⇒ Programs ⇒ Administrative Tools (Common) ⇒ User Manager for Domains.

2. In the User Manager dialog box, double-click any user name in the Username list box.

Groups

The Groups command button in the User Properties dialog box is used to config-ure which group(s) a user is a member of. Assigning users to groups is an efficient way to manage permissions for multiple users. (The subject of groups is covered in more detail later in this chapter.)

When you click the Groups command button in the User Properties dialog box, the Group Memberships dialog box appears. Figure 8-4 shows the Group Memberships dialog box for Administrator.

FIGURE 8-4   Administrator's group memberships

To make a user a member of a group, highlight the desired group in the "Not member of" list box. Then click the Add command button. The group now appears in the "Member of" list box.

To remove a user from a group, highlight the group in the "Member of" list box. Then click the Remove command button. The group no longer appears in the "Member of" list box.

You can make any number of group membership changes in this dialog box, but you must click OK when you are finished to make the changes effective.

On Windows NT Server domain controllers, there is an option in the Group Memberships dialog box to set a primary group for a user account. The primary group setting concerns file ownership and permissions and only affects users of Macintosh computers who access files on a Windows NT Server computer and users of Windows NT computers who run POSIX-compliant applications. The default primary group setting is Domain Users. However, you can assign any global group as a user's primary group. In most Windows NT networks, you can simply accept the default setting for this option.

Profile

The Profile command button in the User Properties dialog box is used to configure the user's environment. You can configure the user profile path, logon script name, and home directory location.

When you click the Profile command button in the User Properties dialog box, the User Environment Profile dialog box appears. Figure 8-5 shows the User Environment Profile dialog box for Administrator.

FIGURE 8-5   Administrator's environment profile

The user profile path is used to assign a location for the user's profile. A user's profile contains the user's unique desktop settings, such as screen color, screen saver, desktop icons, fonts, and so on. The default location for a user's profile is the `<winntroot>\Profiles\%USERNAME%` folder. User profile paths must include the complete path to the folder that contains the user's profile, in the format of `\\Server_name\Share_name\Folder\Subfolder`. If no path is entered in the User Profile Path text box, Windows NT uses the default location.

concept link **Profiles and logon scripts are covered in more detail in Chapter 10.**

The Logon Script Name text box is an optional configuration that enables you to enter the user's logon script filename, if the user has one. *Logon scripts* are batch files that run on a user's computer during the logon process. Many Windows NT installations don't use logon scripts. If you choose to use logon scripts, enter the user's logon script filename in the Logon Script Name text box. You should place a copy of each user's logon script file in the Netlogon share on every domain controller in the domain, or use directory replication to replicate the logon script file. Directory replication is covered in detail in Chapter 3.

The Home Directory section of the User Environment Profile dialog box is used to configure either a local home directory on the user's computer, or a server-based home directory.

A *home directory* (either local or server-based) is a user's default directory for the Save As and File Open dialog boxes in most Windows-based applications. Using server-based home directories enables the network administrator to easily backup user-created data files, because the user-created files are stored by default on the server instead of on individual computers. For security reasons, I recommend you place sever-based home directories on an NTFS partition.

If you select the option button next to Local Path, you can enter the user's home directory in the format of *Drive_Letter:\Folder\Subfolder*. This assigns a user's home directory to a folder on the user's local computer.

If you want to use a server-based home directory, select the option button next to Connect. Then select a drive letter to use for the user's home directory. The default drive letter is Z:. Next type a complete path in the form of *\\Server_name\Share_name\Folder\Subfolder* in the To text box. If the last folder in the path you type in this box does not yet exist, Windows NT will create it.

The most common way of assigning a server-based home directory is to first create a shared folder named Users on the server, and then to assign the path *\\Server_name\Users\%USERNAME%* as each user's home directory location. When the %USERNAME% variable is used in a path, Windows NT creates a home directory/folder (that is named using the user's account name) in the Users shared folder. Using this variable can simplify administration when creating a large number of user accounts because you can enter the same path for each new user, and Windows NT creates a unique home directory/folder for each user account.

Hours

The Hours command button in the User Properties dialog box is used to configure the hours that a user is allowed to log on. This command button is only available when managing Windows NT Server computers that are configured as domain controllers.

The logon hours configuration only affects the user's ability to access the domain controller — it does not affect a user's ability to log on to a Windows NT Workstation computer or other non-domain controller.

When you click the Hours command button in the User Properties dialog box, the Logon Hours dialog box appears. Figure 8-6 shows the Logon Hours dialog box for Administrator. Notice that by default all hours are available for logon. This is the default for all users, not just Administrator.

FIGURE 8-6   Administrator's logon hours

To modify the user's logon hours, use your mouse to highlight the hours you do *not* want the user to be able to log on, and click the Disallow command button. Or, you can use your mouse to highlight the entire graph, click the Disallow command button, then highlight the hours you *want* the user to be able to log on, and then click the Allow command button.

Figure 8-7 shows modified logon hours for a user named BillT. Notice that BillT can't log on between the hours of midnight and 3:00 a.m. The administrator of BillT's network normally runs a tape backup during these hours and does not want users to log on and open files (which may not be backed up) during the backup process.

FIGURE 8-7 **User's logon hours restricted**

Restricting a user's logon hours does not disconnect a user from a domain controller when the user's logon hours expire. A logon hours restriction only *prevents* a user from logging on to the domain controller during certain specified hours. If you want to forcibly disconnect users when their logon hours expire, additional steps must be taken.

TO FORCIBLY DISCONNECT ALL USERS FROM THE DOMAIN CONTROLLER(S) WHEN THEIR LOGON HOURS EXPIRE, FOLLOW THESE STEPS:

1. Select Start ⇒ Programs ⇒ Administrative Tools (Common) ⇒ User Manager for Domains.

2. Select Policies ⇒ Account in the User Manager dialog box.

3. The Account Policy dialog box appears. Select the check box next to "Forcibly disconnect remote users from server when logon hours expire." Click OK.

Figure 8-8 shows the Account Policy dialog box. Notice that the check box next to "Forcibly disconnect remote users from server when logon hours expire" is selected. All settings in the Account Policy dialog box apply to all user accounts in the domain — no individual configurations are possible.

FIGURE 8-8   **Disconnecting users from the domain controller when logon hours expire**

Logon To

The Logon To command button in the User Properties dialog box is used to configure the names of computers from which a user can log on to the domain. This command button is only available on Windows NT Server computers that are configured as domain controllers.

When you click the Logon To command button in the User Properties dialog box, the Logon Workstations dialog box appears. Figure 8-9 shows the Logon Workstations dialog box for Administrator. Notice that by default a user may log on to any workstation (computer) on the network. This is the default setting for all users, not just Administrator.

If you want to limit the workstations to which a user can log on, select the option button next to User May Log On To These Workstations, and then enter the computer name for up to eight workstations. The user will only be able to log on to the domain from the computers entered in this dialog box. Click OK.

FIGURE 8-9   Configuring logon workstations

Account

The Account command button in the User Properties dialog box is used to configure account expiration and user account type. This command button is only available on Windows NT Server computers that are configured as domain controllers.

When you click the Account command button in the User Properties dialog
box, the Account Information dialog box appears. Figure 8-10 shows the Account
Information dialog box for Administrator. Notice that by default a user account
never expires. This is the default setting for all users, not just Administrator.

FIGURE 8-10   Configuring account information

You might want to configure a user account expiration date for an employee
working on a temporary or short-term basis. To set an account expiration, select
the option button next to "End of," and then enter the date you want the user's
account to expire. Click OK. The user will not be forcibly disconnected from the
domain controller when the account expires, but will not be able to log on after
the account expiration date. You can't set an account expiration date on the two
built-in user accounts, Administrator and Guest.

There are two options for account type: *global account* and *local account*. By default, all user accounts are configured as global accounts. A global account is designed for regular user accounts in this domain. Users can log on to the domain using a global account. Most Windows NT installations only use global accounts.

A local account is designed to enable users from untrusted domains to access resources on the domain controller(s) in this domain. Users can't log on using a local account.

Dialin

The Dialin command button in the User Properties dialog box is used to configure dialin permission for a user account. The dialin permission allows a user to log on by using a Dial-Up Networking connection.

When you click the Dialin command button in the User Properties dialog box, the Dialin Information dialog box, which is shown in Figure 8-11, appears. Notice that by default a user account is not granted the dialin permission.

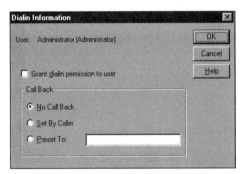

FIGURE 8-11   Granting dialin permission to a user account

The dialin permission should be granted to every user that needs access to the network by using a Dial-Up Networking connection. For example, traveling sales representatives need to access e-mail and other network resources from their laptop computers, and employees who occasionally work from home may need to be able to dial in to access network resources from their home computers.

To grant a user the dialin permission, select the check box next to Grant dialin permission to user.

There are three options in the Call Back section: No Call Back, Set By Caller, and Preset To. The default setting is No Call Back.

If you select No Call Back, the user can dial in to the server, but the user can't request that the server break the connection and call the user back. Selecting No Call Back ensures that the user dialing in — not the server — is billed for any long-distance telephone charges.

If you select Set By Caller, the server prompts the user for a telephone number. The server breaks the connection and calls the user back using this number, and thus the server incurs the bulk of any long-distance telephone charges.

If you select Preset To, you must enter a telephone number that the server will always use to call back this user when the user dials in. This setting reduces the risk of unauthorized access to network resources, because the server always calls a preset telephone number, such as a user's home telephone number. An unauthorized user might be able to dial in and guess a password, but will not be able to direct the server to call back at any other number than the number specified in Preset To, and thus will not be able to connect to the network.

Copying User Accounts

Sometimes the easiest way to create a new user account is to copy an existing user account.

There are basically two ways to accomplish this:

- You can copy any existing user account that has properties that are similar to the desired properties for the new user account.

- You can create a new user account that will be used as a template to create multiple user accounts with the same set of account properties.

For example, suppose that you want to create a user account to be used by an employee to administer the network. You want this user account to have all of the capabilities of the Administrator account, so you decide to copy the Administrator account. When a user account is copied, all properties of the user account are copied to the new user account, with the exception of user name, full name, password, the account disabled option, and user rights and permissions.

To copy the Administrator user account, start User Manager for Domains, then highlight Administrator in the Username list box in the User Manager dialog box. Select User ⇒ Copy, and then type in a new user name and password for the new user account. Make any other desired changes in the User Properties dialog box, then click the Add command button. Then click Close. The newly created user has the same account properties as Administrator.

Suppose, instead, that you are setting up a new network and need to create multiple new user accounts for the accountants at a large CPA firm. All of the accountants at this firm have similar network access needs, and their user accounts will have substantially similar properties. You can create a new user account, named Acct_Template, to use as a template to create these new user accounts.

To create a new user account that will be used as a template, start User Manager for Domains, then select User ⇒ New User in the User Manager dialog box. Assign the user account a name that indicates the type of user account this template will be used to create, such as Acct_Template for the accountants in the previous example. Configure the template user account's group memberships, profile, logon hours, and so on to match the requirements of the user accounts you will create using this template. When you create a user account to be used as a template, I recommend that you select the Account Disabled check box so that no one can log on using this account.

Figure 8-12 shows the User Properties dialog box of a user account that is designed to be used as a template. Note that the Account Disabled check box is selected.

FIGURE 8-12   Configuring a user account to be used as a template

To use a template, highlight the template user account in the User Manager dialog box, then select User ⇒ Copy. Then type in a new user name and password for the new user account. Make any other desired changes in the User Properties dialog box, then click the Add command button. Then click Close.

All properties of the template user account are copied to the new user account, with the exception of user name, full name, password, the account disabled option, and user rights and permissions.

Applying Properties to Multiple Accounts

Occasionally you might want to apply a property to multiple user accounts.

For example, suppose that you recently installed the *Remote Access Service* (RAS) on one of your network servers, and now you want to grant several users the dialin permission so they can connect to the network from their computers at home.

Another situation where you might want to apply properties to multiple user accounts is right after you create several new user accounts. You can create several bare-bones user accounts, consisting only of user names, full names, and passwords. Then you can select all of the new user accounts and configure them all at once with identical properties. You can use this method as an alternative to using a user account as a template.

TO APPLY A PROPERTY (OR PROPERTIES) TO MULTIPLE USER ACCOUNTS, FOLLOW THESE STEPS:

1. Select Start ⇒ Programs ⇒ Administrative Tools (Common) ⇒ User Manager for Domains.

2. Highlight the first user account you want to apply a property to in the User Manager dialog box. Then press and hold Ctrl while you click each additional user account that you want to apply that property to. Then select User ⇒ Properties.

3. The User Properties dialog box appears. The users you selected in Step 1 are listed in the Users list box. Figure 8-13 shows the User Properties dialog box. Notice that multiple users are displayed in the Users list box.

FIGURE 8-13 Selecting multiple user accounts

4. Configure the user account property (or properties) as desired. All changes made will apply to all of the users in the Users list box. Then click OK.

Renaming and Deleting User Accounts

Occasionally you may want to rename or delete a user account.

Renaming a user account retains all of the account properties, including group memberships, permissions, and rights for the new user of the account. You might want to rename a user account when a new staff member replaces an employee who has left the company.

Deleting a user account is just what it sounds like — the user account is permanently removed, and all of its group memberships, permissions, and rights are lost. Normally you only delete a user account when you never plan to use the account again.

The two built-in accounts, Administrator and Guest, can't be deleted, although they can be renamed. The following section details how to rename and delete a user account.

TO RENAME A USER ACCOUNT, FOLLOW THESE STEPS:

1. Select Start ⇒ Programs ⇒ Administrative Tools (Common) ⇒ User Manager for Domains.

2. In the User Manager dialog box, highlight the user account that you want to rename. Select User ⇒ Rename.

3. Type in the new user name for the user account in the Rename dialog box. Click OK.

4. Double-click the renamed user account in the User Manager dialog box.

5. The User Properties dialog box appears. Assign (and confirm) a new password to the renamed user account. Select the check box next to User Must Change Password at Next Logon. Click OK.

6. Exit User Manager for Domains.

7. If the renamed user account has an associated home directory, also rename the home directory using Windows NT Explorer.

TO DELETE A USER ACCOUNT, FOLLOW THESE STEPS:

1. Select Start ⇒ Programs ⇒ Administrative Tools (Common) ⇒ User Manager for Domains.

2. In the User Manager dialog box, highlight the user account you want to delete. Press Delete.

3. A warning message appears. Click OK to continue.

4. Another warning dialog box appears. Click Yes to delete the user account. The user account is deleted.

5. Exit User Manager for Domains.

CREATING AND MANAGING GROUPS

The remainder of this chapter is dedicated to groups. Using groups is a convenient and efficient way to assign rights and permissions to multiple users.

Groups are collections of user accounts. There are four types of groups in Windows NT: *local groups, global groups, built-in groups*, and *special groups*.

Local Groups

Local groups are primarily used to control access to resources. In a typical Windows NT configuration, a local group is assigned permissions to a specific resource, such as a shared folder or a shared printer. Individual user accounts and global groups (discussed later in this chapter) are made members of this local group. The result is that all members of the local group now have permissions to the resource. Using local groups simplifies the administration of resources, because permissions can be assigned once, to a local group, instead of separately to each user account.

In Windows NT, all domain controllers (within a single domain) maintain identical copies of the same directory database, while each non-domain controller maintains its own separate directory database. All user accounts and group accounts are stored in the directory database in which they are created. For example, if you create a local group in the LAB domain, it is stored in the LAB domain directory database. If you create a local group on a Windows NT Workstation computer, it is stored in the NT Workstation computer's local directory database.

Local groups can be created on any Windows NT computer. A local group in the directory database on a domain controller can be assigned permissions to resources on any domain controller in the domain. However, a local group in the directory database on a domain controller cannot be assigned permissions to resources on any non-domain controller. (Remember that non-domain controllers include stand-alone servers, member servers, and all Windows NT Workstation computers.) A local group in the directory database on a non-domain controller can be assigned permissions to resources only on that computer.

A local group can contain various user accounts and global groups, depending on whether the local group is located in the directory database on a domain controller, on a non-domain controller that is a member of a domain, or on a non-domain controller that is not a member of a domain.

A local group in the directory database on a domain controller can contain individual user accounts and global groups from the domain directory database and can also contain user accounts and global groups from the directory database of any trusted domain. A *trusted domain* is a domain whose users can access resources in the domain that "trusts" it.

A local group in the directory database on a non-domain controller that is a member of a domain (such as a member server or a Windows NT Workstation computer that is a member of the domain) can contain individual user accounts from the local directory database, user accounts and global groups from the directory database of the member domain, and user accounts and global groups from the directory database of any trusted domain.

A local group in the directory database on a non-domain controller that is *not* a member of a domain (such as a stand-alone server or a Windows NT

Workstation computer that is a member of a workgroup) can only contain individual user accounts from the local directory database.

Local groups can't contain other local groups.

The next section explains how local groups are created.

TO CREATE A NEW LOCAL GROUP, FOLLOW THESE STEPS:

1. Select Start ⇒ Programs ⇒ Administrative Tools (Common) ⇒ User Manager for Domains.

2. Highlight any of the groups listed in the Groups list box. (The reason for this is the first user in the Username list box is highlighted by default, and if this user is not unhighlighted, the user will automatically become a member of the new local group you create.) Select User ⇒ New Local Group.

3. The New Local Group dialog box appears. In the Group Name text box, type in a name for the new local group. In the Description text box, type a description if you want—such as the name of the resource the group will have permissions to. This text box is optional. Click the Add command button.

4. The Add Users and Groups dialog box appears. Highlight the user accounts and/or global groups from the Names list box that you want to make members of the new local group. Then click the Add command button. The names you selected appear in the Add Names list box. Click OK.

5. The New Local Group dialog box reappears. Figure 8-14 shows the New Local Group dialog box. Notice that several user accounts and one global group are listed as members of the new local group. Also note that the description reflects the resource to which the new local group has permissions. Click OK.

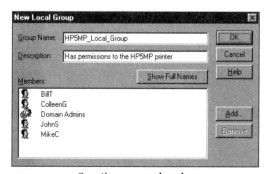

FIGURE 8-14 Creating a new local group

6. The User Manager dialog box reappears. The new local group appears in the Groups list box. Exit User Manager for Domains.

Global Groups

Global groups are primarily used to organize users that perform similar tasks or have similar network access requirements. In a typical Windows NT configuration, user accounts are placed in a global group, the global group is made a member of one or more local groups, and each local group is assigned permissions to a resource. The advantage of using global groups is ease of administration — the network administrator can manage large numbers of users by placing them in global groups.

Suppose when the network was first installed, the administrator created user accounts and placed these user accounts in various global groups depending on the users' job functions. Now, the network administrator wants to assign several users permissions to a shared printer on a member server. The administrator creates a new local group on the member server and assigns the new local group permissions to the shared printer. Then the administrator selects, from the domain directory database, the global groups that contain the user accounts that need access to the shared printer. The administrator makes these global groups members of the new local group on the member server. The result is that all domain user accounts that are members of the selected global groups now have access to the shared printer.

A global group can only be created on a domain controller and can only contain individual user accounts from the domain directory database that contains the global group. Global groups can't contain local groups, other global groups, or user accounts from other domains.

Although it is not a preferred practice, you can assign rights and permissions to global groups. Global groups can be assigned permissions to shared files and folders on domain controllers, member servers, NT Workstation computers that are members of the domain, and computers from trusted domains.

Creating a new global group

The following section explains how to create a new global group.

TO CREATE A NEW GLOBAL GROUP, FOLLOW THESE STEPS:

1. Select Start ⇒ Programs ⇒ Administrative Tools (Common) ⇒ User Manager for Domains.

2. Highlight any of the groups listed in the Groups list box. (The reason for this is that the first user in the Username list box is highlighted by default, and if this user is not unhighlighted, the user will automatically become a member of the new global group you create.) Select User ⇒ New Global Group.

3. The New Global Group dialog box appears. In the Group Name text box, type in a name for the new global group. In the Description text box, type a description of the group. This text box is optional. Highlight the user accounts from the Not Members list box that you want to make members of the new global group. Then click the Add command button. The names you selected appear in the Members list box. Figure 8-15 shows the New Global Group dialog box. Notice that two user accounts are listed as members of the new global group. Click OK.

FIGURE 8-15   Creating a new global group

4. The User Manager dialog box reappears. The new global group appears in the Groups list box. Exit User Manager for Domains.

Comparison of Local and Global Groups

Local and global groups are complex topics that can be confusing.

To help simplify the important information about each type of group, I've prepared a comparison table for you. Table 8-2 summarizes the basic characteristics of local and global groups. Remember that the table is only a summary—you should refer to the detailed descriptions of local and global groups in the previous sections for complete coverage of these topics.

TABLE 8-2 COMPARISON OF LOCAL AND GLOBAL GROUPS

CHARACTERISTIC	LOCAL GROUPS	GLOBAL GROUPS
Primary purpose/use	Used to control access to network resources.	Used to organize users that perform similar tasks or have similar network access requirements.
Where created	On any Windows NT computer.	Only on a domain controller.
Can contain	User accounts and global groups. (The specific user accounts and global groups that can be contained in a local group depend on the type of computer on which the Directory Services database that contains the local group in question is located.)	User accounts from the domain directory database that contains the global group.
Can't contain	Other local groups.	Local groups, other global groups, or user accounts from other domains.
Can be assigned permissions to	Resources on any domain controller in the domain, if the local group is created on a domain controller; otherwise, only resources on the local computer.	Not a preferred practice, but can be assigned permissions to a resource on any computer in the domain, or on any computer in any trusting domain.

Built-in Groups

Built-in groups are groups with preset characteristics that are automatically created during the installation of Windows NT. The actual built-in groups created during installation depend on whether the computer is configured as a domain controller or a non-domain controller.

The members of built-in local groups have the rights and/or permissions to perform certain administrative tasks. You can assign users to the built-in local groups that most closely match the tasks that the users need to perform. If there isn't a built-in local group that has the rights and/or permissions needed to perform a specific task or access a specific resource, then you can create a local group and assign it the necessary rights and/or permissions to accomplish the task or access the resource.

You can use built-in global groups to organize the user accounts in your domain. As you recall from the previous section, you can also create additional global groups to further organize your domain's user accounts by task or network access requirements.

You can assign permissions to and remove permissions from built-in groups. (An exception is the built-in Administrators group — this group always has full rights and permissions to administer the computer or domain.) You can also assign users to and remove users from built-in groups. Built-in groups can't be renamed or deleted.

The following tables list the various built-in groups on Windows NT domain controllers and non-domain controllers and give a brief description of each group's purpose or function. The table of built-in groups on domain controllers indicates whether each built-in group is a local or global group. The table of built-in groups on non-domain controllers contains only local groups.

Table 8-3 lists the built-in groups on domain controllers, and Table 8-4 lists the built-in groups on non-domain controllers.

TABLE 8-3 BUILT-IN GROUPS ON DOMAIN CONTROLLERS

BUILT-IN GROUP NAME	TYPE OF GROUP	DESCRIPTION
Administrators	Local	Has full administrative rights and permissions to administer the domain; initially contains the Domain Admins global group.
Backup Operators	Local	Has permissions to back up and restore files and folders on all domain controllers in the domain.
Guests	Local	Has no initial permissions; initially contains the Domain Guests global group.

continued

TABLE 8-3 *(continued)*

BUILT-IN GROUP NAME	TYPE OF GROUP	DESCRIPTION
Replicator	Local	Used by the Windows NT Directory Replicator service.
Users	Local	Has no initial permissions; initially contains the Domain Users global group.
Account Operators	Local	Can create, delete, and modify user accounts, local groups, and global groups, with the exception of Administrators and Server Operators groups.
Printer Operators	Local	Can create and manage printers on any domain controller in the domain.
Server Operators	Local	Has permissions to back up and restore files and folders on all domain controllers in the domain; can share folders on any domain controller in the domain.
Domain Admins	Global	No initial permissions; initially contains the built-in Administrator user account.
Domain Users	Global	No initial permissions; initially contains the built-in Administrator user account; when new user accounts are created, they are automatically made members of this group.
Domain Guests	Global	No initial permissions; initially contains the built-in Guest user account.

TABLE 8-4 BUILT-IN LOCAL GROUPS ON NON-DOMAIN CONTROLLERS

BUILT-IN LOCAL GROUP NAME	DESCRIPTION
Administrators	Has full administrative rights and permissions to administer the computer; initially contains the built-in Administrator user account.
Backup Operators	Has permissions to back up and restore files and folders on the computer.
Guests	Has no initial permissions; initially contains the built-in Guest user account.
Replicator	Used by the Windows NT Directory Replicator service.

BUILT-IN LOCAL GROUP NAME	DESCRIPTION
Users	Has no initial permissions; when new user accounts are created, they are automatically made members of this group.
Power Users	Can create and modify user and group accounts, with the exception of the Administrator user account and the Administrators group; can share folders and printers.

Special Groups

Special groups are created by Windows NT and are used for specific purposes by the operating system.

These groups don't appear in User Manager for Domains. Special groups are only visible in Windows NT utilities that assign permissions to network resources, such as a printer's Properties dialog box, and Windows NT Explorer.

You can assign permissions to and remove permissions from special groups. You can't assign users to special groups, and you can't rename or delete these groups. Special groups are sometimes called *system groups*.

There are five special groups: *Everyone, Interactive, Network, System*, and *Creator Owner*.

Any user who accesses a Windows NT computer, either interactively or over-the-network, is considered a member of the Everyone special group. This includes all users accessing the computer using authorized user accounts, as well as unauthorized users who accidentally or intentionally breach your system security. If your computer is connected to the Internet, over-the-network also means over-the-Internet. Everyone means *everyone*. You should consider limiting the permissions assigned to the Everyone group to those that you really want everyone to have.

Any user who physically sits at a computer and logs on locally to a Windows NT computer is a member of the Interactive special group. If you want to assign permissions to a resource that is limited to users who have physical access to a computer, consider assigning these permissions to the Interactive group. You are only a member of the Interactive group during the time that you are logged on locally.

Any user who accesses resources on a Windows NT computer over-the-network is a member of the Network special group. If you want to assign permissions to a resource that is limited to users who access the computer over-the-network, consider assigning these permissions to the Network group. You are only a member of the Network group during the time that you access resources on a computer over-the-network.

The System special group is used by the Windows NT operating system. The System special group is not normally assigned any permissions to network resources.

A user who creates a file, folder, or a print job is considered a member of the Creator Owner special group for that object. The Creator Owner special group is used to assign permissions to creators of these objects. For example, by default the Creator Owner special group is assigned the Manage Documents permission to a printer when it is first created, so that creators of print jobs sent to this printer are able to manage their own print jobs.

Renaming and Deleting Groups

I apologize if you envisioned a time-saving solution when you read the above heading, but unfortunately, the fact of the matter is, you can't rename groups. You can delete user-created groups, but you can't delete built-in or special groups. Deleting a group does not delete the user accounts that the group contains.

TO DELETE A GROUP, FOLLOW THESE STEPS:

1. Select Start ⇒ Programs ⇒ Administrative Tools (Common) ⇒ User Manager for Domains.

2. In the User Manager dialog box, highlight the group you want to delete. Press Delete.

3. A warning message appears. Click OK to continue.

4. Another warning message is displayed. Click the Yes command button to delete the group.

5. The group is deleted. Exit User Manager for Domains.

KEY POINT SUMMARY

This chapter explored and outlined the properties, creation, and management of user accounts and groups.

- *User accounts* are records that contain unique user information and enable users to log on to Windows NT. There are two kinds of user accounts: built-in user accounts, and the user accounts that you create. The two built-in user accounts are Administrator and Guest. You can create user accounts by using User Manager for Domains. User account names can be up to twenty characters in length, must be unique within the domain, can't be the same as a group name within the domain (or non-domain controller), and may not contain certain special characters. Often a naming convention for user accounts is adopted, along with a way to handle exceptions that would result in two user names being identical. Using passwords protects the security of the network. Normally, users choose their own passwords, although in some high-security situations the network administrator may maintain user passwords. Common sense security measures should be taken by users to protect their passwords.

- User accounts have numerous options, called *user account properties*, that can be configured, including: group membership, profile, logon scripts, logon hours, workstation logon restrictions, account expiration, and dialin permission. These properties are configured in the User Properties dialog box in User Manager for Domains.

  - The *Groups* command button in the User Properties dialog box is used to configure which group(s) a user is a member of.

  - The *Profile* command button in the User Properties dialog box is used to configure the user's environment, including user profile path, logon script name, and home directory location. The variable %USERNAME% is often used when assigning a server-based home directory to many users, because using the variable enables you to enter the same path for multiple users, and yet results in each user having a unique home directory based on their unique user account name.

  - The *Hours* command button in the User Properties dialog box is used to configure the hours that a user can log on.

- The *Logon To* command button in the User Properties dialog box is used to configure the names of computers from which a user can log on to the domain.

- The *Account* command button in the User Properties dialog box is used to configure account expiration and user account type. You might want to configure a user account expiration date for a temporary employee. You can't set an account expiration date on the two built-in accounts, Administrator and Guest.

- The *Dialin* command button in the User Properties dialog box is used to configure the dialin permission for a user account. This permission enables a user to log on using a Dial-Up Networking connection. There are three options in the Call Back section: No Call Back (the default setting), Set By Caller, and Preset To.

- The Hours, Logon To, and Account command buttons are only available on Windows NT Server computers that are configured as domain controllers.

- User accounts can be copied using User Manager for Domains. You can copy an existing user account that has properties similar to the properties you want the new user account to have, or you can create a new user account that will be used as a template to create multiple user accounts with the same set of account properties.

- You can also use User Manager for Domains to apply a property (or properties) to multiple user accounts at the same time. User accounts can also be renamed and deleted, with the exception of the two built-in accounts, Administrator and Guest.

- Using groups is a convenient and efficient way to assign rights and permissions to multiple users.

- *Local groups* are primarily used to control access to resources. Typically, a local group is assigned permission to a specific resource (such as a shared folder or shared printer), and then user accounts and global groups are made members of the local group. As a result, all members of the local group have permission to the resource. Local groups can contain individual user accounts and global groups. (The specific user accounts and global groups that can be contained in a local group depend on the type of computer that the directory services database is located on that contains the local group in question.) Local groups can't contain other local groups.

Local groups can be assigned permissions to resources on any domain controller in the domain (if the local group is created on a domain controller); otherwise, local groups can be assigned permissions only to resources on the local computer. Local groups can be created on any Windows NT computer.

- *Global groups* are primarily used to organize users who perform similar tasks or have similar network access requirements. Global groups can contain user accounts from the domain directory database that contains the global group; but global groups can't contain local groups, other global groups, or user accounts from other domains. A global group can only be created on a domain controller.

- There are a number of built-in local and global groups that are automatically created during the installation of Windows NT. Built-in local groups can be used to assign users rights and/or permissions to perform certain administrative tasks. Built-in global groups are used to organize the user accounts in a domain. The actual built-in groups present on a Windows NT computer depend on whether the computer is configured as a domain controller or a non-domain controller. The built-in local groups on domain controllers are: Administrators, Backup Operators, Guests, Replicator, Users, Account Operators, Printer Operators, and Server Operators. The built-in global groups on domain controllers are: Domain Admins, Domain Users, and Domain Guests. The built-in groups on non-domain controllers are: Administrators, Backup Operators, Guests, Replicator, Users, and Power Users. All the built-in groups on non-domain controllers are local groups.

- There are five *special groups* (sometimes called *system groups*) created by Windows NT: Everyone, Interactive, Network, System, and Creator Owner. You can assign permissions to and remove permissions from special groups, but you can't assign users to special groups.

- You can't rename groups. You can delete user-created groups by using User Manager for Domains, but you can't delete built-in or special groups.

APPLYING WHAT YOU'VE LEARNED

Now it's time to regroup, review, and apply what you've learned in this chapter.

The questions in the following Instant Assessment section bring to mind key facts and concepts. Then, the Hands-on Lab reinforces what you've learned and gives you an opportunity to practice some of the tasks tested by the Server exam.

Instant Assessment

1. What are the two built-in user accounts?

2. What Windows NT tool can you use to create user accounts?

3. Name two common user account naming conventions.

4. Which groups can be deleted? Which groups can't be deleted?

5. What are the six command buttons in the User Properties dialog box in User Manager for Domains that can be used to configure various user account properties?

6. What variable is often used when assigning a server-based home directory to many users?

7. Suppose that you wanted to create several new user accounts that all had identical properties. What could you do to accomplish this in an efficient manner?

8. What is the primary purpose of local groups? What is the primary purpose of global groups?

9. Where can local groups be created? Where can global groups be created?

10. Suppose that you want to use groups to assign permissions to a shared folder on your network. How could you accomplish this?

11. List the eight built-in local groups on domain controllers and the three built-in global groups on domain controllers.

12. List the six built-in local groups on non-domain controllers.

13. What are the five special groups in Windows NT?

14. Why is it important to limit the permissions assigned to the Everyone group, especially if your computer is connected to the Internet?

15. Which groups can be renamed?

T/F

16. You should pick a name that is familiar to you, such as your own name, or the name of a family member or pet, to use as your password.   ____

concept link **For answers to the Instant Assessment questions see Appendix B.**

Hands-on Lab

The following Hands-on Lab provides you with a practical opportunity to apply the knowledge you've gained in this chapter about managing user and group accounts.

Lab 8.14 *Creating and managing user and group accounts*

The purpose of this lab is to give you hands-on experience in creating user accounts, assigning home directories, managing user account properties, creating group accounts, and assigning user accounts to groups. You will also create user account templates to help simplify the creation of user accounts.

This lab consists of four parts:

Part 1: Creating the Users folder
Part 2: Creating group accounts
Part 3: Creating user account templates
Part 4: Creating and managing user accounts

In this lab you'll create users and groups for the local office of a sales organization. Within this organization there are several employees. Table 8-5 shows the organization's employees and their job titles.

TABLE 8-5 SALES ORGANIZATION EMPLOYEES	
EMPLOYEE	**JOB TITLE**
Pam Rhodes	District Manager
John Spencer	Sales Manager
Robert Jones	Accounting Manager
Colleen Green	Sales Representative
Bill Tracy	Sales Representative

continued

TABLE 8-5 *(continued)*

EMPLOYEE	JOB TITLE
Mike Calhoun	Sales Representative
Nancy Yates	Accounting Staff
Mike Cook	Accounting Staff

The users will select their own passwords when they first access their user accounts. Each user will have a home folder on the primary domain controller named PDCLAB.

Begin this lab by booting your computer to Windows NT Server. Log on as Administrator. (Remember, the password is *password*.)

FOLLOW THE STEPS BELOW CAREFULLY.

Part 1: Creating the Users folder

In this section you create and share a Users folder in Windows NT Explorer. The Users folder will eventually contain a home directory for each user account.

1. Select Start ⇒ Programs ⇒ Windows NT Explorer.

2. In the All Folders list box, highlight the drive on which your NTFS partition is located. (This is probably drive D:.) Select File ⇒ New ⇒ Folder.

3. A folder named New Folder is created and appears in the "Contents of D:." Edit the folder's name so that it is called **Users**. Press Enter.

4. Highlight the Users folder in the Windows NT Explorer dialog box. Select File ⇒ Sharing.

5. In the Users Properties dialog box, select the option button next to Shared As. Accept the default Share Name of Users. Click OK.

6. Exit Windows NT Explorer. Continue to Part 2.

Part 2: Creating group accounts

In this section you create three new global groups: Managers, Sales, and Accounting.

1. Select Start ⇒ Programs ⇒ Administrative Tools (Common) ⇒ User Manager for Domains.

2. Highlight any of the groups listed in the Groups list box. (The reason for this is that the first user in the Username list box is highlighted by default, and if this user is not unhighlighted, the user will automatically become a member of the new global group you create.) Select User ⇒ New Global Group.

3. The New Global Group dialog box appears. In the Group Name text box, type in **Managers**. In the Description text box, type in **Managers of the Sales Organization**. Click OK.

4. The User Manager dialog box reappears. Select User ⇒ New Global Group.

5. The New Global Group dialog box appears. In the Group Name text box, type in **Sales**. In the Description text box, type in **Sales Representatives**. Click OK.

6. The User Manager dialog box reappears. Select User ⇒ New Global Group.

7. The New Global Group dialog box appears. In the Group Name text box, type in **Accounting**. In the Description text box, type in **Accounting Staff**. Click OK.

8. The User Manager dialog box reappears. You have now created three new global groups: Managers, Sales, and Accounting. Continue to Part 3.

Part 3: Creating user account templates

In this section you create two user account templates, one that will be used to create user accounts for sales representatives, and another that will be used to create user accounts for accounting staff.

1. In the User Manager dialog box, select User ⇒ New User.

2. The New User dialog box appears. Type the bolded information below in the appropriate text boxes:

- User Name: **Sales_User**
- Full Name: (Leave this box blank.)
- Description: **Sales Representative**
- Password: **newuser**
- Confirm Password: **newuser**

Ensure that the check box next to User Must Change Password at Next Logon is selected. Select the check box next to Account Disabled. Click the Groups command button.

3. The Group Memberships dialog box appears. In the "Not member of" list box, highlight Sales. Click the Add command button. (Notice that the Sales group, along with Domain Users, is now listed in the "Member of" list box.) Click OK.

4. The New User dialog box reappears. Click the Dialin command button.

5. The Dialin Information dialog box appears. Select the check box next to "Grant dialin permission to user." Accept the default of No Call Back in the Call Back section. Click OK.

6. The New User dialog box reappears. Click the Profile command button.

7. The User Environment Profile dialog box appears. In the Home Directory section, select the option button next to Connect. Accept the Z: in the drop-down list box. In the To text box, type: **\\PDCLAB\USERS\% USERNAME%**. Click OK.

8. The New User dialog box reappears. Click the Add command button.

9. The New User dialog box reappears. Type the following bolded information in the appropriate text boxes:

- User Name: **Acct_User**
- Full Name: (Leave this box blank.)
- Description: **Accounting Staff**
- Password: **newuser**
- Confirm Password: **newuser**

Ensure that the check box next to User Must Change Password at Next Logon is selected. Select the check box next to Account Disabled. Click the Groups command button.

10. The Group Memberships dialog box appears. In the "Not member of" list box, highlight Accounting. Click the Add command button. (Notice that the Accounting group, along with Domain Users, is now listed in the "Member of" list box.) Click OK.

11. The New User dialog box reappears. Click the Hours command button.

12. The Logon Hours dialog box appears. Using your mouse, highlight the entire graph. Click the Disallow command button. Using your mouse, highlight the area on the graph that represents 6:00 a.m. to 9:00 p.m. Monday through Friday. Click the Allow command button. Click OK.

13. The New User dialog box reappears. Click the Profile command button.

14. The User Environment Profile dialog box appears. In the Home Directory section, select the option button next to Connect. Accept the Z: in the drop-down list box. In the To text box, type: **\\PDCLAB\USERS\%USERNAME%**. Click OK.

15. The New User dialog box reappears. Click the Add command button. Click the Close command button. Notice that your two new user account templates, Sales_User and Acct_User, now appear in the Username list box within the User Manager dialog box. Continue to Part 4.

Part 4: Creating and managing user accounts

In this section you create user accounts from scratch and also use the user account templates to create user accounts. You assign some of the new user accounts to groups.

1. In the User Manager dialog box, select User ⇒ New User.

2. The New User dialog box appears. Type the following bolded information in the appropriate text boxes:

- o User Name: **PamR**
- o Full Name: **Pam Rhodes**
- o Description: **District Manager**
- o Password: **newuser**
- o Confirm Password: **newuser**

Ensure that the check box next to User Must Change Password at Next Logon is selected. Click the Groups command button.

3. The Group Memberships dialog box appears. In the "Not member of" list box, highlight Accounting. Then press and hold Ctrl while you scroll down and click Managers and Sales. Click the Add command button. (The Accounting, Managers, and Sales groups, along with Domain Users, should now be listed in the "Member of" list box.) Click OK.

4. The New User dialog box reappears. Click the Add command button.

5. The New User dialog box reappears. Type the following bolded information in the appropriate text boxes:

- o User Name: **JohnS**
- o Full Name: **John Spencer**
- o Description: **Sales Manager**
- o Password: **newuser**
- o Confirm Password: **newuser**

Ensure that the check box next to User Must Change Password at Next Logon is selected. Click the Groups command button.

6. The Group Memberships dialog box appears. In the "Not member of" list box, highlight Managers. Then press and hold Ctrl while you click Sales. Click the Add command button. (The Managers and Sales groups, along with Domain Users, should now be listed in the "Member of" list box.) Click OK.

7. The New User dialog box reappears. Click the Add command button.

8. The New User dialog box reappears. Type the following bolded information in the appropriate text boxes:

- User Name: **RobertJ**

- Full Name: **Robert Jones**

- Description: **Accounting Manager**

- Password: **newuser**

- Confirm Password: **newuser**

Ensure that the check box next to User Must Change Password at Next Logon is selected. Click the Groups command button.

9. The Group Memberships dialog box appears. In the "Not member of" list box, highlight Accounting. Then press and hold Ctrl while you scroll down and click Managers. Click the Add command button. (The Accounting and Managers groups, along with Domain Users, should now be listed in the "Member of" list box.) Click OK.

10. The New User dialog box reappears. Click the Add command button. Click the Close command button.

11. The User Manager dialog box reappears. Notice that the three users you just created are in the Username list box. Highlight JohnS, and then press and hold Ctrl while you click PamR and RobertJ. Select User ⇒ Properties.

12. The User Properties dialog box appears. Notice the three users you selected are listed in the Users list box. Click the Dialin command button.

13. The Dialin Information dialog box appears. Select the check box next to "Grant dialin permission to user." Accept the default of No Call Back in the Call Back section. Click OK.

14. The User Properties dialog box reappears. Click the Profile command button.

15. The User Environment Profile dialog box appears. In the Home Directory section, select the option button next to Connect. Accept the Z: in the drop-down list box. In the To text box, type: **\\PDCLAB\USERS\%USERNAME%**. Click OK.

16. The User Properties dialog box reappears. Click OK. You have now granted dialin permission and assigned home folders to JohnS, PamR, and RobertJ.

17. The User Manager dialog box reappears. Highlight Sales_User. Select User ⇒ Copy.

18. The Copy of Sales_User dialog box appears. Type the following bolded information in the appropriate text boxes:

- User Name: **ColleenG**
- Full Name: **Colleen Green**
- Description: (This is already filled in.)
- Password: **newuser**
- Confirm Password: **newuser**

Ensure that the check box next to User Must Change Password at Next Logon is selected. Click Groups. Notice that the Sales group, as well as Domain Users, is listed in the "Member of" list box. Click OK.

19. In the Copy of Sales_User dialog box, click the Dialin command button. In the Dialin Information dialog box, notice that the check box next to "Grant dialin permission to user" is selected. Click OK.

20. In the Copy of Sales_User dialog box, click the Add command button.

21. The Copy of Sales_User dialog box reappears. Type the following bolded information in the appropriate text boxes:

- User Name. **BillT**
- Full Name: **Bill Tracy**
- Description: (This is already filled in.)
- Password: **newuser**
- Confirm Password: **newuser**

Ensure that the check box next to User Must Change Password at Next Logon is selected. Click the Add command button.

22. The Copy of Sales_User dialog box reappears. Type the bolded information below in the appropriate text boxes:

- User Name: **MikeC**
- Full Name: **Mike Calhoun**
- Description: (This is already filled in.)
- Password: **newuser**
- Confirm Password: **newuser**

Ensure that the check box next to User Must Change Password at Next Logon is selected. Click the Add command button. Click the Close command button.

23. The User Manager dialog box reappears. Notice that your new users now appear in the Username list box. Highlight the Acct_User. Select User ⇒ Copy.

24. The Copy of Acct_User dialog box appears. Type the following bolded information in the appropriate text boxes:

- User Name: **NancyY**
- Full Name: **Nancy Yates**
- Description: (This is already filled in.)
- Password: **newuser**
- Confirm Password: **newuser**

Ensure that the check box next to User Must Change Password at Next Logon is selected. Click the Groups command button. Notice that the Accounting group, in addition to Domain Users, appears in the "Member of" list box. Click OK.

25. In the Copy of Acct_User dialog box, click the Hours command button. In the Logon Hours dialog box, notice that this user will be able to log on between 6:00 a.m. and 9:00 p.m. Monday through Friday. Click OK.

26. In the Copy of Acct_User dialog box, click the Add command button.

27. The Copy of Acct_User dialog box reappears. Type the following bolded information in the appropriate text boxes:

- User Name: **MikeCo**
- Full Name: **Mike Cook**
- Description: (This is already filled in.)
- Password: **newuser**
- Confirm Password: **newuser**

Ensure that the check box next to User Must Change Password at Next Logon is selected. Click the Add command button. Then click the Close command button.

28. The User Manager dialog box reappears. Notice that the new users you created appear in the Username list box. Exit User Manager for Domains.

Managing Account Policy, User Rights, and Auditing

About Chapter 9

This chapter explores the Policies menu in User Manager for Domains, with emphasis on its three major configurable options: Account Policy, User Rights, and Auditing.

Managing account policy, which applies to all users in the domain, is discussed first. Password restrictions and the account lockout feature are also addressed.

Next, the chapter explains how to manage user rights, which enable users to perform tasks. All the Windows NT user rights are listed and described in this section, followed by detailed, step-by-step instructions for assigning user rights.

Finally, Chapter 9 explores auditing, the Windows NT feature that, when enabled, produces a log of specified events and activities.

This chapter includes two Hands-on Labs. In the first lab, you implement Windows NT auditing and then view audit events in the Security Log in Event Viewer. In the second, you set account policy and configure user rights.

The material presented in Chapter 9 is a continuation of the user and group accounts topics introduced in Chapter 8, and maps to the "Manage user and group accounts" objective listed in the Managing Resources section in the Preparation Guide for the Server exam.

MANAGING ACCOUNT POLICY

This chapter focuses on the Policies menu in User Manager for Domains. The Policies menu provides three main configurable options: Account Policy, User Rights, and Auditing. Only members of the Administrators local group have the necessary rights to manage account policy, user rights, and auditing.

The Account Policy dialog box has two main sections: one enables you to configure password restrictions, and another enables you to set the account lockout policy.

Settings in the Account Policy dialog box apply to *all* users in the domain (or to all users on a computer, if it is not a domain controller). You can't set individual account policies.

TO ACCESS THE ACCOUNT POLICY DIALOG BOX, FOLLOW THESE STEPS:

1. Select Start ⇒ Programs ⇒ Administrative Tools (Common) ⇒ User Manager for Domains.

2. In the User Manager dialog box, select Policies ⇒ Account. The Account Policy dialog box appears, as shown in Figure 9-1. Notice the default settings in this dialog box.

FIGURE 9-1   The Account Policy dialog box in User Manager for Domains

Password Restrictions

The Password Restrictions section of the Account Policy dialog box has four configurable options: Maximum Password Age, Minimum Password Age, Minimum Password Length, and Password Uniqueness.

Maximum Password Age

Maximum Password Age determines the maximum number of days a user may use the same password. Two selections are available in this section: Password Never Expires, or Expires In *xx* Days. The default setting is Expires in 42 Days.

When Password Never Expires is selected, users are never required to change their passwords.

When Expires in *xx* Days is selected, Windows NT forces users to change their passwords when the maximum password age setting is exceeded. Normal settings for password expiration are between 30 and 90 days. If users have to change their passwords too frequently, they may be unable to remember their passwords.

If a user's password expires *and* the check box next to "Users must log on in order to change password" (at the bottom of the dialog box) is selected, the user will *not* be able to change his or her own password — the administrator must change the user's password.

 in the
real world

I normally recommend administrators do *not* select the check box next to "Users must log on in order to change password," because Windows NT does not force users to change their passwords before they expire. When users attempt to log on after password expiration, they are unable to log on to change their passwords. This situation creates a lot of hassle and extra work for the administrator.

Minimum Password Age

Minimum Password Age determines the minimum number of days a user must keep the same password. Two selections are available in this section: Allow Changes Immediately, or Allow Changes in *xx* Days. The default setting is Allow Changes Immediately.

If Allow Changes Immediately is selected, users can change their passwords as often as they like, without waiting for any time to pass before selecting a new password.

If Allow Changes in *xx* Days is selected, users must use their passwords for at least the number of days specified before Windows NT lets them change their passwords. Normal settings for Minimum Password Age are from one day to the number of days specified as the Maximum Password Age.

If Minimum Password Age is not set, and Password Uniqueness is set at Remember 8 Passwords, then users are often tempted to bypass the Password Uniqueness setting by changing their passwords nine times, in rapid succession, so they can recycle back to their original, favorite, and easily remembered password.

Minimum Password Length

Minimum Password Length specifies the minimum number of characters required in users' passwords. Two selections are possible in this section: Permit Blank Password, or At Least *xx* Characters.

If Permit Blank Password is selected, users are not required to have a password. This is the default setting.

If At Least *xx* Characters is selected, you can specify the minimum number of characters a user's password must contain. Windows NT will not enable users to choose a password with fewer than the required number of characters. Possible settings for password length are from one to fourteen characters. I recommend you set a minimum of eight characters for Minimum Password Length. With a password length of eight characters or more (assuming basic password security measures are taken), it's statistically almost impossible for an unauthorized user to guess a password.

Password Uniqueness

Password Uniqueness specifies how many different passwords a user must use before an old password can be reused. Two selections are possible in this section: Do Not Keep Password History, or Remember *xx* Passwords. The default setting is Do Not Keep Password History.

If Do Not Keep Password History is selected, users can cycle back and forth between their two favorite passwords each time they are required to change their passwords.

If Remember *xx* Passwords is selected, users must use at least the number of new passwords specified before they can reuse an old password. Possible settings for Password Uniqueness are between 1 and 24 passwords. Normal settings range between 5 and 12 passwords.

You can multiply the number of passwords specified in Password Uniqueness times the number of days specified in Minimum Password Age to determine the number of days that must pass before a user can reuse an old password.

 concept link   **For more password tips, see the "Passwords" section in Chapter 8.**

Account Lockout

The Account lockout section of the Account Policy dialog box specifies how Windows NT treats user accounts after several successive unsuccessful logon attempts have occurred. The default setting is "No account lockout."

Figure 9-2 shows the Account Policy dialog box. Notice the options in the Account lockout section.

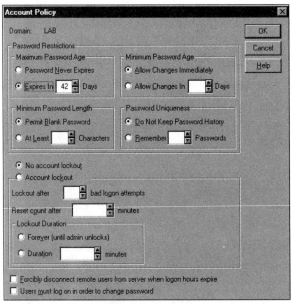

FIGURE 9-2   The Account Policy dialog box in User Manager for Domains

When "No account lockout" is selected, user accounts are never locked out. This means no matter how many unsuccessful logon attempts a user makes, the user's account is not locked out.

When Account lockout is selected, users are locked out after the specified number of successive bad logon attempts is reached. Several configuration options exist for Account lockout: Lockout after *xx* bad logon attempts, Reset count after *xx* minutes, and Lockout Duration.

Lockout after *xx* bad logon attempts specifies the number of successive unsuccessful logon attempts that are acceptable before Windows NT will lock out an account. The possible settings are from 1 to 999 bad logon attempts. Normal settings for this configuration are from 3 to 10 bad logon attempts. This counter is reset after each successful logon. Windows NT maintains a separate counter for each user account.

Reset count after *xx* minutes specifies the number of minutes that must pass without a bad logon attempt in order for the bad logon attempts counter to be reset to zero. (Resetting the counter to zero gives users the full number of possible bad logon attempts before account lockout.) The possible settings are from 1 to 99,999 minutes. Normal settings for this configuration are from 30 to 60 minutes.

Lockout duration specifies how long a user account is locked out after the specified number of bad logon attempts occurs. Two possible settings are in this section: Forever (until admin unlocks), or "Duration *xx* minutes."

If Forever is selected *and* the specified number of bad logon attempts occurs, the administrator must unlock the user account in User Manager for Domains before the user can log on.

If "Duration *xx* minutes" is selected, user accounts that are locked out (because the specified number of bad logon attempts have been exceeded) are unlocked automatically by Windows NT after the specified number of minutes elapses. The possible settings are from 1 to 99,999 minutes. Normal settings for this configuration are from 30 to 60 minutes.

Two additional check boxes are in the Account Policy dialog box: "Forcibly disconnect remote users from server when logon hours expire," and "Users must log on in order to change password." By default, both of these check boxes are *not* selected. The "Forcibly disconnect remote users from server when logon hours expire" check box is only available on Windows NT Server computers configured as domain controllers.

If "Forcibly disconnect remote users from server when logon hours expire" is selected, users whose logon hours expire are automatically disconnected from the domain controllers in the domain. Users are *not* disconnected from Windows NT Workstation computers, however, or from member servers in the domain.

If "Users must log on in order to change password" is selected, and a user's password expires, the administrator must change the user's password (because the user cannot log on with an expired password).

A configuration conflict arises when the "Users must log on in order to change password" option is set in Account Policy *and* new users are configured so that User Must Change Password at Next Logon. This combination of settings places users in a catch-22 situation: Users can't log on without changing their passwords, and users can't change their passwords without logging on. The administrator can resolve this problem by changing the users' passwords and clearing the check box next to User Must Change Password at Next Logon in the users' Properties dialog box in User Manager for Domains.

MANAGING USER RIGHTS

User rights authorize users and groups to perform specific tasks on a Windows NT computer. User rights are not the same as permissions: user rights enable users to *perform tasks*; whereas permissions allow users to *access objects*, such as files, folders, and printers.

User rights are assigned in the User Rights Policy dialog box in User Manager for Domains.

TO ACCESS THE USER RIGHTS POLICY DIALOG BOX, FOLLOW THESE STEPS:

1. Select Start ⇒ Programs ⇒ Administrative Tools (Common) ⇒ User Manager for Domains.

2. In the User Manager dialog box, select Policies ⇒ User Rights.

Figure 9-3 shows the User Rights Policy dialog box. Notice the option to Show Advanced User Rights.

FIGURE 9-3 The User Rights Policy dialog box in User Manager for Domains

The following sections discuss user rights and advanced user rights and examine how user rights are assigned.

User Rights

Each *user right* authorizes a user or group to perform a specific task. User rights, unlike account policy, can be assigned to individual users and groups.

User rights are listed in the User Rights Policy Dialog box. You can choose to display regular user rights or a combination of regular and advanced user rights in the Right drop-down list box. The default configuration displays only non-advanced user rights.

Table 9-1 lists and describes each of the Windows NT Server user rights. The table also indicates whether each right is an advanced user right.

TABLE 9-1 WINDOWS NT SERVER USER RIGHTS

USER RIGHT	ADVANCED USER RIGHT?	DESCRIPTION
Access this computer from the network	No	Authorizes a user to access a computer over the network.
Act as part of the operating system	Yes	Not normally used by administrators. Used by programmers of Windows NT applications. See Microsoft's Win32 Software Development Kit for more information.
Add workstations to domain	No	Authorizes a user to cause workstation computers to join the domain.

continued

TABLE 9-1 *(continued)*

USER RIGHT	ADVANCED USER RIGHT?	DESCRIPTION
Back up files and directories	No	Authorizes a user to back up files and folders. This right supersedes permissions on files and folders.
Bypass traverse checking	Yes	Authorizes a user to change the current folder on the user's computer to a different folder, even if the user or group has no permissions to the newly selected current folder.
Change the system time	No	Authorizes a user to change the time on the Windows NT computer's internal clock.
Create a pagefile	Yes	Not normally used by administrators. Used by programmers of Windows NT applications. See Microsoft's Win32 Software Development Kit for more information.
Create a token object	Yes	Not normally used by administrators. Used by programmers of Windows NT applications. See Microsoft's Win32 Software Development Kit for more information.
Create permanent shared objects	Yes	Not normally used by administrators. Used by programmers of Windows NT applications. See Microsoft's Win32 Software Development Kit for more information.
Debug programs	Yes	Not normally used by administrators. Used by programmers of Windows NT applications. See Microsoft's Win32 Software Development Kit for more information.
Force shutdown from a remote system	No	This right is not currently implemented. It is reserved for future use.
Generate security audits	Yes	Not normally used by administrators. Used by programmers of Windows NT applications. See Microsoft's Win32 Software Development Kit for more information.
Increase quotas	Yes	Not normally used by administrators. Used by programmers of Windows NT applications. See Microsoft's Win32 Software Development Kit for more information.
Increase scheduling priority	Yes	Not normally used by administrators. Used by programmers of Windows NT applications. See Microsoft's Win32 Software Development Kit for more information.

USER RIGHT	ADVANCED USER RIGHT?	DESCRIPTION
Increase scheduling priority	Yes	Not normally used by administrators. Used by programmers of Windows NT applications. See Microsoft's Win32 Software Development Kit for more information.
Load and unload device drivers	No	Authorizes a user to load and unload device drivers for the Windows NT operating system.
Lock pages in memory	Yes	Not normally used by administrators. Used by programmers of Windows NT applications. See Microsoft's Win32 Software Development Kit for more information.
Log on as a batch job	Yes	Not normally used by administrators. Used by programmers of Windows NT applications. See Microsoft's Win32 Software Development Kit for more information.
Log on as a service	Yes	Allows a service or application to log on using a specified user account. (For example, in Chapter 3 you configured the Directory Replicator service to use a specific user account to log on as a service.)
Log on locally	No	Authorizes a user to log on locally (interactively at the computer).
Manage auditing and security log	No	Authorizes a user to view and change the Security Log in Event Viewer. Enables a user to configure auditing of files, folders, and printers. Does *not* enable a user to access the Audit Policy dialog box in User Manager for Domains.
Modify firmware environment values	Yes	Not normally used by administrators. Used by programmers of Windows NT applications. See Microsoft's Win32 Software Development Kit for more information.
Profile single process	Yes	Not normally used by administrators. Used by programmers of Windows NT applications. See Microsoft's Win32 Software Development Kit for more information.
Profile system performance	Yes	Not normally used by administrators. Used by programmers of Windows NT applications. See Microsoft's Win32 Software Development Kit for more information.

continued

TABLE 9-1 *(continued)*

USER RIGHT	ADVANCED USER RIGHT?	DESCRIPTION
Replace a process level token	Yes	Not normally used by administrators. Used by programmers of Windows NT applications. See Microsoft's Win32 Software Development Kit for more information.
Restore files and directories	No	Authorizes a user to restore files and folders. This right supersedes permissions on files and folders.
Shut down the system	No	Authorizes a user to shut down the Windows NT computer the user is logged on to.
Take ownership of files or other objects	No	Authorizes a user to take ownership of files, folders, and printers.

Assigning User Rights

The assigning of user rights is accomplished in the User Rights Policy dialog box. You can add and remove user rights to and from users and groups in this dialog box.

The following sections describe first how to assign a user right to a user or group, and then how to remove a user right from a user or group.

TO ASSIGN A USER RIGHT TO A USER OR GROUP, FOLLOW THESE STEPS:

1. In the User Rights Policy dialog box in User Manager for Domains, select the user right you want to assign from the Right drop-down list box. (If you want to assign an advanced user right, first select the check box next to Show Advanced User Rights.)

Figure 9-4 shows the User Rights Policy dialog box. Notice the "Back up files and directories" user right is selected. Click the Add command button.

2. The Add Users and Groups dialog box appears. If you want to assign a user right to a user, click the Show Users command button. (Otherwise, only groups are listed.) Scroll down through the Names list box and select the user(s) and/or group(s) to which you want to assign a user right.

Figure 9-5 shows the Add Users and Groups dialog box. Notice both users and groups are displayed in the Names list box (because the Show Users command button has been clicked).

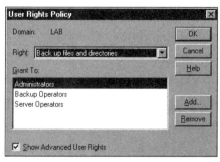

FIGURE 9-4   Assigning the "Back up files and directories" user right

FIGURE 9-5   The Add Users and Groups dialog box

Click the Add command button. (Or, instead of first selecting a user or group and then clicking the Add command button, you can double-click each user or group to which you want to assign the user right.) The name(s) you select appear in the Add Names list box. Click OK.

3. The User Rights Policy dialog box reappears. Click OK.

4. Exit User Manager for Domains.

TO REMOVE A USER RIGHT FROM A USER OR A GROUP, FOLLOW THESE STEPS:

1. In the User Rights Policy dialog box in User Manager for Domains, select the user right you want to remove from the Right drop-down list box. (If you want to remove an advanced user right, first select the check box next to Show Advanced User Rights.)

2. Then highlight the user or group you want to remove the user right from in the Grant To list box. Click the Remove command button. Click OK.

3. Exit User Manager for Domains.

in the real world

Understanding and being able to use Windows NT user rights is important when preparing for the Server exam. Most user rights, however, are not used by administrators in the real world. In my experience, one of the most common "real world" user right assignments is the "Log on locally" user right to users who need to log on interactively to domain controllers.

MANAGING AUDITING

When enabled, Windows NT auditing produces a log of specified events and activities that occur on a Windows NT computer. Audited events are written to the Security Log in Event Viewer. Windows NT auditing is divided into two areas: system access and object access. *System access auditing* is configured by using User Manager for Domains. *Object access auditing* is configured in the Properties dialog boxes for files, folders, and printers. By default, auditing is turned off.

The next section explains how to enable system access auditing using the Audit Policy dialog box in User Manager for Domains.

TO ACCESS THE AUDIT POLICY DIALOG BOX AND TO ENABLE AUDITING, FOLLOW THESE STEPS:

1. Select Start ⇒ Programs ⇒ Administrative Tools (Common) ⇒ User Manager for Domains.

2. In the User Manager dialog box, select Policies ⇒ Audit.

3. The Audit Policy dialog box appears. The default setting for this dialog box is Do Not Audit. To enable auditing, select the option button next to Audit These Events, *and* select at least one Success or Failure check box.

The Audit Policy dialog box is shown in Figure 9-6. Note the option button next to Audit These Events is selected, and the Success and Failure check boxes for File and Object Access are checked. Click OK.

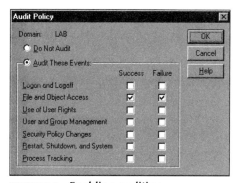

FIGURE 9-6   **Enabling auditing**

4. Exit User Manager for Domains.

When a Success check box is selected, Windows NT generates an audit event each time a user successfully performs the audited task.

When a Failure check box is selected, Windows NT generates an audit event each time a user attempts to perform an audited task but fails (usually because of a lack of rights or permissions).

When both success and failure auditing are selected, an audit event is generated each time a user attempts to perform an audited task, whether successfully or unsuccessfully.

Table 9-2 lists and describes the types of audit events that can be selected in the Audit Policy dialog box.

TABLE 9-2 WINDOWS NT AUDIT EVENTS

EVENT	DESCRIPTION
Logon and Logoff	A user logs on, logs off, or accesses this Windows NT computer over the network.
File and Object Access	A user accesses a file, folder, or printer configured for auditing. Note: To audit file, folder, or print events, you must enable file and object access auditing *in addition to* file, folder, or printer auditing (which is set in Windows NT Explorer or in a printer's Properties dialog box).
Use of User Rights	A user exercises an assigned user right, other than the "Log on locally" or "Access this computer from the network" user rights.
User and Group Management	A user account or group is created, changed, or deleted; or, a user account is renamed, disabled, enabled, or its password is changed.
Security Policy Changes	The user rights, audit, or trust relationship policies are modified or changed.
Restart, Shutdown, and System	A user restarts or shuts down the computer, or a system security or Security Log event occurs.
Process Tracking	An event, such as program activation, some forms of handle duplication, indirect object accesses, or process exit occurs. This event is not often selected for audit by administrators.

tip **Carefully consider which events you need to audit. If you choose to audit everything, your Security Log will fill up quickly, primarily with useless information.**

To view audited events in Windows NT, use Event Viewer. The next section describes how to access Event Viewer and view audited events.

TO ACCESS EVENT VIEWER AND TO VIEW SECURITY LOG EVENTS, FOLLOW THESE STEPS:

1. Select Start ⇒ Programs ⇒ Administrative Tools (Common) ⇒ Event Viewer.

2. In the Event Viewer dialog box, select Log ⇒ Security.

3. The Security Log dialog box appears.

Figure 9-7 shows a Security Log in Event Viewer. Notice some events are marked with keys (these designate success events), and some events are marked with locks (these designate unsuccessful events).

Double-click an event you want to view in greater detail.

Date	Time	Source	Category	Event	User	Computer
6/6/97	4:46:08 PM	Security	Privilege Use	576	Administrator	PDCLAB
6/6/97	4:46:08 PM	Security	Logon/Logoff	528	Administrator	PDCLAB
6/6/97	4:46:08 PM	Security	Privilege Use	577	SYSTEM	PDCLAB
6/6/97	4:46:08 PM	Security	System Event	515	SYSTEM	PDCLAB
6/6/97	4:46:08 PM	Security	Privilege Use	577	SYSTEM	PDCLAB
6/6/97	4:46:08 PM	Security	Privilege Use	577	SYSTEM	PDCLAB
6/6/97	4:46:08 PM	Security	System Event	515	SYSTEM	PDCLAB
6/6/97	4:46:08 PM	Security	System Event	515	SYSTEM	PDCLAB
6/6/97	4:46:08 PM	Security	Privilege Use	576	Administrator	PDCLAB
6/6/97	4:46:08 PM	Security	Logon/Logoff	528	Administrator	PDCLAB
6/6/97	4:45:58 PM	Security	Logon/Logoff	529	SYSTEM	PDCLAB
6/6/97	4:45:55 PM	Security	Logon/Logoff	529	SYSTEM	PDCLAB
6/6/97	4:45:51 PM	Security	Logon/Logoff	529	SYSTEM	PDCLAB
6/6/97	4:45:39 PM	Security	Logon/Logoff	538	Administrator	PDCLAB
6/6/97	4:45:35 PM	Security	Privilege Use	578	Administrator	PDCLAB
6/6/97	4:45:26 PM	Security	System Event	517	SYSTEM	PDCLAB

FIGURE 9-7   **Viewing events in the Security Log dialog box**

4. The Event Detail dialog box appears. Figure 9-8 shows an Event Detail dialog box. Notice the types of information included in this dialog box.

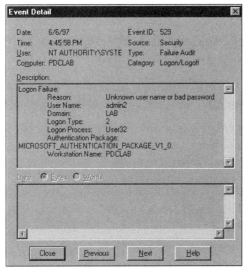

FIGURE 9-8   **Viewing the details of a logon
failure event**

KEY POINT SUMMARY

This chapter focused on the Policies menu in User Manager for Domains, which contains three primary configurable options: *Account Policy, User Rights*, and *Auditing*.

- Only members of the Administrators local group have the necessary rights to manage account policy, user rights, and auditing.

- The Account Policy dialog box in User Manager for Domains has two main sections: One allows you to configure password restrictions, and another allows you to set the account lockout policy. Settings in the Account Policy dialog box apply to *all* users in the domain (or to all users on a computer, if it is not a domain controller.)

  - Four configurable options are in the Password Restrictions section of the Account Policy dialog box: Maximum Password Age, Minimum Password Age, Minimum Password Length, and Password Uniqueness.

  - The Account lockout section of the Account Policy dialog box specifies how Windows NT treats user accounts after several successive bad logon attempts have occurred. Several configurations exist for Account lockout: Lockout after *xx* bad logon attempts, Reset count after *xx* minutes, and Lockout Duration (which can either be set to Forever [until admin unlocks], or Duration *xx* minutes).

  - The two additional check boxes in the Account Policy dialog box include: "Forcibly disconnect remote users from server when logon hours expire," and "Users must log on in order to change password." By default, both of these check boxes are *not* selected.

- *User rights* authorize users or groups to perform specific tasks. User rights, unlike account policy, can be assigned to (and removed from) individual users and groups. User rights are not the same as permissions: User rights enable users to *perform tasks*, whereas permissions allow users to *access objects*, such as files, folders, and printers. User rights are assigned in the User Rights Policy dialog box in User Manager for Domains.

- User rights are made up of advanced and non-advanced rights, such as: Access this computer from the network, Add workstations to domain, Back up files and directories, Change the system time, Force shutdown from a remote system, Load and unload device drivers, Log on locally, Manage auditing and security log, Restore files and directories, Shut down the system, and Take ownership of files or other objects.

- When enabled, *Windows NT auditing* produces a log of specified events and activities that occur on a Windows NT computer. Audited events are written to the Security Log in Event Viewer. Auditing is configured in the Audit Policy dialog box in User Manager for Domains.

  - When *success auditing* is selected, an audit event is generated every time a user successfully performs the audited task. When *failure auditing* is selected, an audit event is generated each time a user tries to perform an audited task, but fails for some reason. When both success and failure auditing are selected, an audit event is generated every time a user attempts to perform an audited task, whether successfully or unsuccessfully.

  - The events that can be selected for audit in the Audit Policy dialog box are Logon and Logoff; File and Object Access; Use of User Rights; User and Group Management; Security Policy Changes; Restart, Shutdown, and System; and Process Tracking. Audited events can be viewed in the Security Log in Event Viewer.

  - To audit file, folder, or print events you *must* enable file and object access auditing *in addition to* file, folder, or printer auditing (which is set in Windows NT Explorer or in a printer's Properties dialog box).

Applying What You've Learned

Now it's time to regroup, review, and apply what you've learned in this chapter.

The questions in the following Instant Assessment section bring to mind key facts and concepts. Then, the Hands-on Labs reinforce what you learned, and give you an opportunity to practice some of the tasks tested by the Server exam.

Instant Assessment

1. What are the two main configurable sections in the Account Policy dialog box?

2. How can you access the Account Policy dialog box?

3. What is the default setting for Maximum Password Age?

4. What does the Minimum Password Age configuration determine?

5. What are the possible settings for Minimum Password Length? What is a recommended setting for Minimum Password Length?

6. What does the Password Uniqueness configuration specify?

7. What does the Account lockout section of the Account Policy dialog box specify?

8. Only members of which local group have the necessary rights to manage account policy, user rights, and auditing?

9. What is the difference between user rights and permissions?

10. When enabled, what does Windows NT auditing produce?

11. Which Windows NT tool can you use to view audited events?

12. In addition to selecting success and/or failure auditing for File and Object Access in the Audit Policy dialog box, what else must you do before you can audit file, folder, or print events?

13. What are the seven specific event types that can be selected for audit in the Audit Policy dialog box?

T/F

14. The settings in the Account Policy dialog box can be configured to apply to individual users.   _____

15. User rights can be assigned to individual users and groups.   _____

concept link   **For answers to the Instant Assessment questions see Appendix B.**

Hands-on Labs

The following Hands-on Labs provide excellent opportunities to apply the knowledge you've gained in this chapter about Windows NT account policy, user rights, and auditing.

Lab 9.15 *Implementing auditing*

The purpose of this lab is to provide you with hands-on experience in using the Windows NT auditing feature.

This lab consists of three parts:

Part 1: Implementing auditing

Part 2: Creating audited events

Part 3: Viewing the Security Log in Event Viewer

Begin this lab by booting your computer to Windows NT Server. Log on as Administrator.

Perform the following steps carefully.

Part 1: Implementing auditing

In this part you implement auditing on a Windows NT Server computer.

1. Select Start ⇒ Programs ⇒ Administrative Tools (Common) ⇒ User Manager for Domains.

2. In the User Manager dialog box, select Policies ⇒ Audit.

3. In the Audit Policy dialog box, select the option button next to Audit These Events, and then select the Success and Failure check boxes for *all* audit events *except* Process Tracking. Click OK.

4. Auditing is now implemented. Exit User Manager for Domains. Proceed to Part 2.

Part 2: Creating audited events

In this part you cause a user to create audited events.

1. Select Start ⇒ Shut Down.

2. In the Shut Down Windows dialog box, select the option button next to Restart the computer. Click the Yes command button. The computer shuts down and restarts.

3. Reboot the computer to Windows NT Server. Press Ctrl + Alt + Delete to log on. When the Logon Information dialog box appears, type in a user name of **PamR** (replacing Administrator) and a password of **wrongo**. Click OK.

4. An error message appears, stating the system could not log you on. Click OK.

5. The Logon Information dialog box reappears. Type in a password of **newuser**. Click OK.

6. A message appears, indicating you are required to change your password at first logon. (You may recall you set this configuration when you created this user in Lab 8.14.) Click OK.

7. Type in a new password of **password**. Confirm the new password by retyping it. Click OK.

8. A dialog box appears, indicating your password has been changed. Click OK.

9. Another dialog box appears, indicating the local policy of this system does not enable you to log on interactively. Click OK.

10. The Logon Information dialog box reappears. Type in a user name of **Administrator**, and a password of **password**. Click OK. You have now created several audited events. Continue to Part 3.

Part 3: Viewing the Security Log in Event Viewer

In this part you view the Security Log in Event Viewer to see the audited events you created in Part 2.

1. Select Start ⇒ Programs ⇒ Administrative Tools (Common) ⇒ Event Viewer.

2. Select Log ⇒ Security.

3. Scroll down the list and double-click the first event marked with a lock (not a key) in the left margin. (A lock marks a failure audit event. A key marks a success audit event.)

4. The Event Detail dialog box appears. Notice the event is a logon failure for PamR, because she was not allowed to log on interactively (locally). Click the Close command button.

5. Scroll down and double-click the next event marked with a lock in the left margin.

6. The Event Detail dialog box reappears. This is also a failure audit event. Notice an unexpected error occurred during PamR's attempted logon. Click the Close command button.

7. Scroll down and double-click the next event marked with a lock in the left margin.

8. The Event Detail dialog box appears. This is a logon failure event for PamR, because an incorrect password (wrongo) was entered. Click the Close command button.

9. Double-click various other events, as desired, and view their event details.

10. Exit Event Viewer.

Lab 9.16 *Managing account policy and user rights*

The purpose of this lab is to provide you with hands-on experience in setting account policy and user rights in Windows NT.

This lab consists of three parts:

Part 1: Setting account policy

Part 2: Creating users and configuring user rights

Part 3: Auditing revisited — clearing the Security Log in Event Viewer

Begin this lab by booting your computer to Windows NT Server. Log on as Administrator.

Follow the steps carefully.

Part 1: Setting account policy

In this section you set account policy that affects all users in the domain.

1. Select Start ⇒ Programs ⇒ Administrative Tools (Common) ⇒ User Manager for Domains.

2. In the User Manager dialog box, select Policies ⇒ Account.

3. The Account Policy dialog box appears. Configure the following:

- ○ Configure the Maximum Password Age to Expires in **30** Days.
- ○ Configure the Minimum Password Age to Allow Changes in **5** Days.
- ○ Configure the Minimum Password Length to be At Least **8** Characters.
- ○ Configure Password Uniqueness to Remember (the last) **6** Passwords.
- ○ Select the option button next to Account lockout.
- ○ Set Lockout after **3** bad logon attempts.
- ○ Set Reset count after **30** minutes.
- ○ Configure Lockout Duration to Forever (until admin unlocks).
- ○ Select the check box next to Users must log on in order to change password.

Figure 9-9 shows the Account Policy dialog box as correctly configured at the close of this step. You can check the configurations you have made against this figure. Click OK.

FIGURE 9-9   Account Policy dialog box as correctly
configured in Lab 9.16

4. In the User Manager dialog box, select Policies ⇒ User Rights.

5. The User Rights Policy dialog box appears. In the Right drop-down list box, select Log on locally. Click the Add command button.

6. The Add Users and Groups dialog box appears. In the Names list box, double-click the Everyone group. (Everyone appears in the Add Names list box.) Click OK. (Granting the "Log on locally" right to the Everyone group enables all users to log on interactively at the Windows NT Server.)

7. In the Users Rights Policy dialog box, click OK.

8. Exit User Manager for Domains.

9. Select Start ⇒ Shut Down. In the Shut Down Windows dialog box, select the option button next to Close all programs and log on as a different user. Click the Yes command button.

10. Press Ctrl + Alt + Delete to log on.

11. In the Logon Information dialog box, type in a user name of **JohnS** and a password of **newuser**. Click OK.

12. A dialog box appears, indicating you are required to change your password at first logon. (You may recall you set this configuration when you created this user in Lab 8.14.) Click OK.

13. The Change Password dialog box appears. Type in a new password of **password**. Confirm the new password by retyping it. Click OK.

14. A warning message appears, indicating you do not have permission to change your password. (This is because in the Account Policy dialog box you selected the check box next to "Users must log on in order to change password" *and*, when you created this user, you selected the option for User Must Change Password at Next Logon. *These two options do not work together*.) Click OK.

15. The Change Password dialog box appears. Click the Cancel command button.

16. The Logon Information dialog box appears. Type in a user name of **PamR** and a password of **wrongo**. Click OK. (Note: In this part of the lab you will attempt to log PamR on several times with an incorrect password to experience the account lockout feature.)

17. A warning message appears, indicating the system could not log you on. Click OK.

18. Repeat Steps 16 and 17 until a warning message appears, indicating NT is unable to log you on because your account has been locked out. You must contact your network administrator to unlock your account. Click OK. (Next, you will log on as administrator and unlock PamR's user account.)

19. In the Logon Information dialog box, type in a user name of **Administrator** and a password of **password**. Click OK.

20. Select Start ⇒ Programs ⇒ Administrative Tools (Common) ⇒ User Manager for Domains.

21. In the User Manager dialog box, double-click the user account PamR in the Username list box.

22. The User Properties dialog box appears. Notice the check box next to Account Locked Out is checked. Deselect this check box. Click OK.

23. Double-click PamR again in the Username list box.

24. The User Properties dialog box appears. Notice the check box next to Account Locked Out is cleared and grayed out. (The Administrator can't lock out a user account—only the system can.) Click the Cancel command button.

25. In the User Manager dialog box, select Policies ⇒ Account.

26. In the Account Policy dialog box, deselect the check box next to "Users must log on in order to change password." (This will enable users to change their passwords during logon.) Click OK.

27. Continue to Part 2.

Part 2: Creating users and configuring user rights

In this section you create two special-use user accounts and configure user rights for these new user accounts.

1. In the User Manager dialog box, select User ⇒ New User.

2. The New User dialog box appears. Type the following bolded text in the appropriate text boxes:

  o User name: **Admin2**

  o Full name: **Administrator's Helper**

  o Description: **User account with limited admin privileges**

  o Password: **password**

  o Confirm password: **password**

  Deselect the check box next to User Must Change Password at Next Logon. Select the check box next to Password Never Expires. Click the Add command button.

3. The New User dialog box reappears. Type the following bolded text in the appropriate text boxes:

  o User name: **Backuponly**

  o Full name: **Backup Operator's Helper**

  o Description: **Only able to back up files, not restore**

  o Password: **password**

  o Confirm password: **password**

  Deselect the check box next to User Must Change Password at Next Logon. Select the check box next to Password Never Expires. Click the Add command button. Click the Close command button.

4. In the User Manager dialog box, select Policies ⇒ User Rights.

5. The User Rights Policy dialog box appears. In the Right drop-down list box, select "Log on locally." Click the Add command button.

6. The Add Users and Groups dialog box appears. Click the Show Users command button. Double-click Backuponly. Click OK.

7. In the Right drop-down list box, select Back up files and directories. Click the Add command button.

8. The Add Users and Groups dialog box appears. Click the Show Users command button. Scroll down and double-click Backuponly. Click OK. (The Backuponly user is now able to log on to the Windows NT Server and is able to back up the server's files.)

9. The User Rights Policy dialog box reappears. Using the sequence you used in Steps 7 and 8, grant the following rights to the Admin2 user:

- Add workstations to domain
- Back up files and directories
- Change the system time
- Log on locally
- Manage auditing and security log
- Restore files and directories
- Shut down the system
- Take ownership of files or other objects

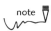 note **You must go through all the steps for each user right you want to assign. No shortcuts exist here.**

Click OK in the User Rights Policy dialog box when you finish.

10. Exit User Manager for Domains. Continue to Part 3.

Part 3: Auditing revisited – clearing the Security Log in Event Viewer

In this section you explore the capabilities of the "Manage auditing and security log" user right, and clear the Security Log in Event Viewer.

1. Press Ctrl + Alt + Delete. Click the Logoff command button. Click OK to close all programs and log off.

2. Press Ctrl + Alt + Delete. In The Logon Information dialog box, type in a user name of **Admin2** and a password of **password**. Click OK. (If a Welcome to Windows NT screen is displayed, click the Close command button.)

3. Select Start ⇒ Programs ⇒ Administrative Tools (Common) ⇒ User Manager for Domains.

4. In the User Manager dialog box, select Policies. Notice all the options in the Policies menu are grayed out. These options are only available to members of the Administrators group — The "Manage auditing and security log" user right does *not* give you the rights needed to set account policy, to configure user rights, or to enable auditing. Exit User Manager for Domains.

5. Select Start ⇒ Programs ⇒ Administrative Tools (Common) ⇒ Event Viewer.

6. In the Event Viewer dialog box, select Log ⇒ Security.

7. Select Log ⇒ Clear All Events.

8. Click Yes in the Clear Event Log dialog box.

9. In the Save As dialog box, type **old security log** in the File name text box. Click the Save command button.

10. Click the Yes command button to clear the Security Log. The "Manage auditing and security log" user right authorizes a user to view and change the Security Log in Event Viewerw and enables a user to configure auditing of files, directories, and printers (in Windows NT Explorer, or in a printer's Properties dialog box, and so forth). But this user right does *not* enable a user to access the Audit Policy dialog box in User Manager for Domains.

11. Exit Event Viewer.

Managing User Profiles and System Policy

About Chapter 10

This chapter explores managing user profiles and system policy in a Windows NT environment.

After a quick look at the benefits of using user profiles, the chapter details the contents of a user profile and the steps involved in creating a user profile. Two special types of user profiles—roaming user profiles and mandatory user profiles—are also discussed.

Next, Chapter 10 focuses on managing system policy, which is actually a collection of user, group, and computer policies. The System Policy Editor is introduced. The section wraps up with an explanation of the systematic manner in which system policy is applied, and step-by-step instructions for creating a system policy file.

Finally, this chapter presents a brief discussion of logon scripts and how to assign a logon script to a user.

This chapter includes two Hands-on Labs. In the first lab, you create and copy user profiles, and configure roaming and mandatory user profiles. In the second, you create and configure both a Windows 95 system policy and a Windows NT system policy.

The material presented in Chapter 10 maps to the "Create and manage policies and profiles. . ." objective listed in the Managing Resources section in the Preparation Guide for the Server exam.

Managing User Profiles

In Windows NT, a *user profile* is a collection of settings and options that specify a user's desktop and all other user-definable settings for a user's work environment.

Both users and administrators can benefit from user profiles.

Benefits to users include:

o When a user logs on, the same desktop is displayed as when the user last logged off.

o When there's more than one user on the same computer, a customized desktop is displayed for each at logon.

o Roaming user profiles can be saved on a Windows NT Server computer, and thereby apply to a user no matter which Windows NT computer on the network the user logs on at.

Benefits to administrators include:

o Administrators can develop and assign user profiles that are customized, so each user has a desktop and work environment that complies with established company standards, and can assign user profiles that are suitable for the tasks that each particular user needs to perform.

o If desired or necessary, administrators can forcibly prevent certain users from changing any of their desktop or work environment settings by assigning them mandatory user profiles.

o User profiles make it possible for administrators to assign common program items and shortcuts to all users by customizing the `All Users` profile folder.

The following sections discuss the contents of a user profile, how a user profile is created, customizing the `Default User` and the `All Users` profile folders, roaming and mandatory user profiles, and deleting user profiles.

Contents of a User Profile

Various settings are saved in a user profile. The contents of a user profile include:

o All user-specific settings for Windows NT Explorer, Notepad, Paint, HyperTerminal, Clock, Calculator, and other built-in Windows NT applications;

- User-specific desktop settings, including: screen saver, background color, background pattern, wallpaper, and other display settings;

- User-specific settings for applications written to run on Windows NT;

- User-specific settings for network drive and printer connections;

- User-specific settings for the Start menu, including program groups, applications, and recently accessed documents.

A user profile is normally stored in a subfolder of the `<winntroot>`\Profiles folder on the local computer. Each user's profile is stored in a separate folder named after the user's account. For example, the Administrator's user profile is stored in the `<winntroot>`\Profiles\Administrator folder. Figure 10-1 shows, in Windows NT Explorer, the location and contents of the Administrator's profile folder.

FIGURE 10-1   Contents of the Administrator's profile folder

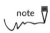 note   **All user profiles have the same contents as those shown for the Administrator.**

Note in Figure 10-1 that there are several subfolders and files contained in the Administrator's profile folder. Table 10-1 lists and describes each of these folders and files. All users' profile folders (not just the Administrator's) contain the folders and files listed in Table 10-1.

TABLE 10-1 WINDOWS NT USER PROFILE FOLDER CONTENTS

FOLDER OR FILE	DESCRIPTION
Application Data	This folder contains any user-specific application data that an application vendor has chosen to store here. For example, a word processing application could store the user's custom dictionary in this subfolder. Currently, use of this folder is not widely implemented by application vendors.
Desktop	This folder contains all shortcuts, files, and folders stored on the user's desktop.
Favorites	This folder contains shortcuts from the user's Favorites folder in various applications. For example, when you add an Internet site to your Favorites folder in Internet Explorer, a shortcut to that site is created in this folder.
NetHood	This folder contains any shortcuts a user has created to network servers or shared folders. These shortcuts are displayed in the Network Neighborhood dialog box.
Personal	This folder contains any shortcuts a user has created to program items.
PrintHood	This folder contains any shortcuts a user has created to network printers. These shortcuts are displayed in the Printers dialog box.
Recent	This folder contains shortcuts to document files that the user has recently accessed. These shortcuts can be displayed by selecting Start ⇒ Documents.
SendTo	This folder contains shortcuts to folders, briefcases, mail, and so on. These shortcuts are displayed when a user right-clicks any file or folder, and then selects Send To from the menu that appears.
Start Menu	This folder contains the Programs folder from a user's Start menu, and any additional shortcuts to programs that the user has created in the Start Menu folder or any of its subfolders. These shortcuts are displayed in the Start menu, or in the Programs folder in the Start menu, depending on where the shortcut was created.
Templates	This folder contains shortcuts to template items.

continued

TABLE 10-1 *(continued)*	
FOLDER OR FILE	DESCRIPTION
Ntuser.dat	This file contains all of the Registry settings that are specific to a user account. When a user logs on, the settings in this file are copied to the HKEY_CURRENT_USER Registry settings on the local computer.
ntuser.dat.LOG	This file is used by Windows NT to recover the user's original ntuser.dat file if an error occurs while updating the ntuser.dat file.

How a User Profile Is Created

Windows NT automatically creates a user profile for every new user the first time the new user logs on. After that point, an Administrator can create and assign a user profile to an existing user (a user who has previously logged on and been assigned a user profile by Windows NT) by copying an existing user profile over that user's profile.

 There is a way to assign a user profile to a new user in Windows NT — the Administrator can assign a new user a *server-based* (roaming) user profile. Roaming user profiles make it possible for the Administrator to copy and assign a user profile to a new user and have that profile be effective the first time the new user logs on. See the section on "Roaming User Profiles" later in this chapter for more information.

The next section explains how an Administrator can copy a user profile.

TO ASSIGN A USER PROFILE TO A USER BY COPYING AN EXISTING USER PROFILE, FOLLOW THESE STEPS:

 If you have Internet Explorer 4.0 installed on your Windows NT computer, you will not be able to successfully copy user profiles by using the steps listed below. See Microsoft TechNet article Q175667 for information on how to copy user profiles when Internet Explorer 4.0 has been installed.

1. Select Start ⇒ Settings ⇒ Control Panel.

2. Double-click the System icon.

3. In the System Properties dialog box, click the User Profiles tab.

4. On the User Profiles tab, highlight the existing user profile that you want to copy. Figure 10-2 shows the User Profiles tab in the System Properties dialog box. Notice that the user profile for ColleenG is highlighted. Click the Copy To command button.

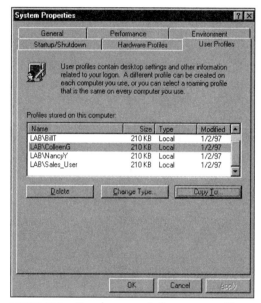

FIGURE 10-2 Copying an existing user profile

5. In the Copy To dialog box, type in the full path to the user's profile folder. For example, to assign a user profile to FrankG, you might type the path `<winntroot>\Profiles\FrankG` in the Copy profile to text box. (Remember, `<winntroot>` is the drive letter and folder in which you installed Windows NT.) Figure 10-3 shows the Copy To dialog box. Notice the user listed in the Permitted to use section of this dialog box. Click the Change command button.

6. The Choose User dialog box appears. Click the Show Users command button. Scroll down and highlight the user (FrankG in the previous example), and then click the Add command button. Click OK.

FIGURE 10-3   Specifying the new user's profile path

7. The Copy To dialog box reappears. Figure 10-4 shows the Copy To dialog box at this point in the process. Notice that FrankG is now permitted to use this profile. Click OK.

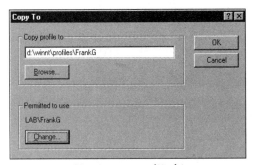

FIGURE 10-4   New user permitted to use copied profile

8. The User Profiles tab reappears. Click OK.

9. Exit Control Panel.

tip **You can't use Windows NT Explorer to copy user profiles. You can only copy user profiles using the System application in Control Panel.**

As mentioned earlier in this section, when a new user logs on for the first time, Windows NT creates a new user profile folder for the user. Windows NT accomplishes this by copying the entire contents of the Default User profile folder to a new folder named after the user's account. When Windows NT creates a new user's profile, the new user's initial profile is an exact copy of the Default User profile folder.

The `Default User` profile folder can also be customized by an Administrator, as described in the next section.

Customizing the Default User Profile Folder

Administrators can customize the `Default User` profile folder so new users, at first logon, have the appropriate desktop and work environment settings. For example, you might want to place a shortcut to a network application on the desktop of all new users. Or, you might want to add a shortcut that will appear in the Start menu for all new users.

You can customize the local `Default User` profile folder on a Windows NT computer, or you can create a domain-wide `Default User` profile folder for all Windows NT Workstation computers and member servers in a domain. Changes to the local `Default User` profile folder on a Windows NT computer affect only new users that log on to that computer. The domain-wide `Default User` profile folder affects all new domain users when they log on to Windows NT Workstation computers (that are domain members) and member servers.

To customize the local `Default User` profile folder on a Windows NT computer, an Administrator can either copy an existing user profile to the local `Default User` profile folder or create shortcuts in the `Default User` profile subfolders.

TO CREATE SHORTCUTS IN THE DEFAULT USER PROFILE SUBFOLDERS, FOLLOW THESE STEPS:

1. Select Start ⇒ Programs ⇒ Windows NT Explorer.

2. In the All Folders section of the Exploring dialog box, click the + sign next to the drive letter that you installed Windows NT on. (This is often the C: drive.) Then click the + sign next to the folder in which Windows NT is installed. (This folder is \`Winnt` by default, but you installed Windows NT Server in \`Winntsrv` in Lab 2.2 earlier in this book.) Next click the + sign next to the `Profiles` folder, and then click the + sign next to `Default User`. Figure 10-5 shows the `Default User` profile folder in Windows NT Explorer.

FIGURE 10-5 The `Default User` **profile folder**

3. Highlight the subfolder of the `Default User` profile folder that you want to create shortcuts in. Select File ⇒ New ⇒ Shortcut

4. In the Create Shortcut dialog box, type in the full path to the application in the Command line text box. Click the Next command button.

5. In the Select a Title for the Program dialog box, type the name of the shortcut the way you want it to appear on the new users' desktops. Click the Finish command button.

6. Repeat Steps 3–5 until you have created all the shortcuts you want in the `Default User` profile folder. Exit Windows NT Explorer.

To create a domain-wide `Default User` profile folder for all Windows NT Workstation computers and member servers in a domain, customize and copy an existing user profile to a subfolder named `Default User` in the `<winntroot>` `\System32\Repl\Import\Scripts` folder on the *primary domain controller* (PDC). (Remember, the `Import\Scripts` folder is shared as `Netlogon`.)

If you have configured directory replication on your PDC, copy the existing user profile to the <*winntroot*>\System32\Repl\Export\ Scripts\Default User **folder on the PDC,** *not* **to the** <*winntroot*> \System32\Repl\Import\Scripts\DefaultUser **folder. If you copy it to the** Import\Scripts **folder and directory replication is configured, the Directory Replicator service will delete any files or folders in the** Import\Scripts **folder that do not exist in the** Export\Scripts **folder.**

To copy an existing user profile, use the steps outlined in the section on "How a User Profile is Created" earlier in this chapter. When choosing the user that is permitted to use this copied profile in the Choose User dialog box, select the Everyone group, and ensure that the Everyone group is listed in the Permitted To Use section of the Copy To dialog box.

After a Default User profile folder is created on the Netlogon share on the PDC, the domain-wide Default User profile folder is available to all Windows NT computers that are members of the domain. When a Windows NT Workstation computer (that is a member of the domain) or a member server is rebooted, it copies the domain-wide Default User profile folder from the PDC to a subfolder named Default User (Network) in its local Profiles folder. This member computer now has two Default User profile folders: one named Default User and one named Default User (Network).

note ⬚ **The domain-wide** Default User **profile folder is** *not* **copied to the local** Profiles **folder on any domain controller in the domain. It is only copied to the local** Profiles **folder on** *non*-**domain controllers that are members of the domain.**

Figure 10-6 shows the Profiles folder and its subfolders on a Windows NT Workstation computer that is a member of the LAB domain. Notice the Default User and Default User (Network) folders.

When a user logs on to a member computer that has two Default User profile folders by using a *local user account*, and that user does not have a profile folder on this local computer, Windows NT creates a new user profile for the user on the local computer by using the Default User profile folder.

FIGURE 10-6   Two *Default User* **profile folders on a member computer**

When a user logs on to a member computer that has two `Default User` profile folders by using a *user account from the domain*, and that user does not have a profile folder on this local computer, Windows NT creates a new user profile for the user on the local computer by using the `Default User (Network)` profile folder.

Customizing the All Users Profile Folder

The `All Users` profile folder is a subfolder of the `Profiles` folder on all Windows NT computers. The `All Users` profile folder contains only two subfolders: `Desktop` and `Start Menu`. **Figure 10-7** shows the `All Users` profile folder and its subfolders in Windows NT Explorer.

The purpose of the `All Users` profile folder is to enable an administrator to create shortcuts and install applications that are made available to *all* — not just new — users of a particular Windows NT computer. Whenever a user logs on to a Windows NT computer, any shortcuts or applications placed in the `Desktop` and `Start Menu` subfolders of the local `All Users` profile folder appear on the user's desktop and/or Start Menu, as appropriate. Only members of the Administrators group on the local computer can customize the `All Users` profile folder.

FIGURE 10-7   The All Users **profile folder**

Currently, there is no method to create a domain-wide All Users profile folder on a server. This means that an Administrator must customize the All Users profile folder on each individual Windows NT computer.

To customize the All Users profile folder, follow the same steps you would use to customize the Default User profile folder, except select the All Users profile folder in Windows NT Explorer instead of the Default User profile folder.

Roaming User Profiles

Roaming user profiles are user profiles that are stored on a server. Because these profiles are stored on a server instead of a local computer, they are available to users regardless of which Windows NT computer on the network they log on to.

The benefit of using roaming user profiles is that users retain their own customized desktop and work environment settings even though they may use several different Windows NT computers.

Roaming user profiles are implemented by first creating a shared folder on a server, and then assigning a server-based user profile path to a user account.

TO IMPLEMENT ROAMING USER PROFILES, FOLLOW THESE STEPS:

1. Choose a server on your network on which to store roaming user profiles. (This is usually the PDC.)

2. Create a shared folder on the server. To do this, select Start ⇒ Programs ⇒ Windows NT Explorer.

3. In the All Folders section of the Exploring dialog box, highlight one of the drives on the server. (This drive must have enough free space to contain your roaming user profiles.) Select File ⇒ New ⇒ Folder.

4. Assign the new folder a name. (I recommend you use the name *Profiles*.) Right-click the newly created folder. Select Sharing from the menu that appears.

5. In the Profiles Properties dialog box, select the option button next to Shared As. Accept the default share name of Profiles in the Share Name text box. Click OK.

6. Exit Windows NT Explorer.

7. Select Start ⇒ Programs ⇒ Administrative Tools (Common) ⇒ User Manager for Domains.

8. In the User Manager dialog box, double-click the user account to which you want to assign a roaming profile.

9. In the User Properties dialog box for that user, click the Profile command button.

10. In the User Profile Path text box in the User Environment Profile dialog box, type in the path to the share that you created in Steps 4 and 5, and append the user name to the end of this path. (For example, on a server named PDCLAB you might use the path \\pdclab\Profiles\BillT. If you highlighted multiple users in Step 8, you could use the path \\server_name\Profiles\%USERNAME% to assign a unique profile path to each user account. Click OK.

11. In the User Properties dialog box, click OK.

12. Exit User Manager for Domains.

At this point, all you have done is assign a location for the user's roaming user profile. Now the user must log on and log off to create a roaming user profile folder on the server. (When the user logs off, the user's local user profile is saved to the server and becomes the user's roaming user profile.) The roaming user profile is then available to the user from any Windows NT computer to which the user logs on. From this point, every time the user logs off, the user's roaming user profile will be updated with any changes the user has made during the time the user was logged on.

Both new and existing users can be assigned roaming user profiles. If you assign an existing user a roaming user profile, the next time the user logs on and then logs off, the user's local user profile will be copied, intact, at logoff to the server, and will become the user's roaming user profile.

You can also preconfigure a new or existing user's roaming user profile, so that the next time the user logs on, the properties of the preconfigured server-based roaming user profile are applied to the user. The advantage of using preconfigured roaming user profiles is that the administrator can provide users with all the shortcuts and program items users need to perform their day-to-day tasks.

To preconfigure a user's roaming user profile, assign a server-based profile path to a user account, and then copy an existing user profile (that you have customized with all of the shortcuts and applications you want the user to have) to the user's roaming user profile path.

Mandatory User Profiles

Mandatory user profiles are user profiles that, when assigned to a user, cannot be changed by the user. A user can make changes to desktop and work environment settings during a single logon session, but these changes are *not* saved to the mandatory user profile when the user logs off. Each time the user logs on, the user's desktop and work environment settings revert to those contained in the mandatory user profile.

In most cases, an administrator permits users to change and customize their own user profiles. There are instances, however, when you might want to use mandatory user profiles:

- When problem users require a significant amount of administrator time
- When an administrator has a large number of users to administer

Occasionally, a problem user modifies his or her profile so that needed shortcuts and applications are deleted, and the administrator must constantly fix the user's profile by reinstalling the necessary items. After repairing the user's profile, the administrator might choose to assign the user a mandatory user profile. To make an individual user's profile (either local or roaming) a mandatory user profile, rename the user's Ntuser.dat file in the user's profile folder as Ntuser.man. The mandatory profile becomes effective the next time the user logs on.

Sometimes an administrator needs to create a standardized desktop and work environment for a large number of users with similar job tasks. To accomplish this, the administrator can assign a single, customized mandatory profile to multiple user accounts.

TO ASSIGN A MANDATORY USER PROFILE TO MULTIPLE USER ACCOUNTS, FOLLOW THESE STEPS:

1. Log on as Administrator. Use User Manager for Domains to create a new user account. (You will use this user account to create the customized mandatory profile.) Log off.

2. Log on as the new user you created in Step 1. Customize desktop and work environment settings as desired. Install shortcuts and applications in the new user's Start Menu and Desktop folders as desired. (These are subfolders of the user's Profile folder.) Log off.

3. Log on as Administrator.

4. Choose a server on your network on which to store the mandatory user profile. (This is usually the PDC.) In the next steps, you create and share a Profiles folder on the server. (If you have already created and shared a Profiles folder on your server, skip to Step 10 now.)

5. Select Start ⇒ Programs ⇒ Windows NT Explorer.

6. In the All Folders section of the Exploring dialog box, highlight one of the drives on the server. (This drive must have enough free space to contain the mandatory user profile.) Select File ⇒ New ⇒ Folder.

7. Assign the new folder a name. (I recommend you use the name *Profiles*.) Right-click the newly created folder. Select Sharing from the menu that appears.

8. In the Profiles Properties dialog box, select the option button next to Shared As. Accept the default share name of Profiles in the Share Name text box. Click OK.

9. Exit Windows NT Explorer.

10. Select Start ⇒ Programs ⇒ Administrative Tools (Common) ⇒ User Manager for Domains.

11. In the User Manager dialog box, highlight the first user to whom you want to assign the mandatory user profile. Then press and hold Ctrl while you click each additional user to whom you want to assign the mandatory user profile. When you have selected all the users that you want, select User ⇒ Properties.

12. In the User Properties dialog box, click the Profile command button.

13. In the User Profile Path text box in the User Environment Profile dialog box, type in the path to the share you created in Steps 7 and 8, and add a subfolder name to the end of this path that describes the group of users the mandatory user profile is being assigned to (such as accountants or sales reps, and so on). An example of a path you might use on a server named PDCLAB when assigning a mandatory profile to several accountants is `\\pdclab\Profiles\accountants`. Click OK.

14. In the User Properties dialog box, click OK.

15. Exit User Manager for Domains.

16. Using the steps to copy a user profile listed in the "How a User Profile is Created" section earlier in this chapter, copy the customized user profile you created in Steps 1 and 2 to the folder specified by the path that you entered in the User Environment Profile dialog box in Step 13. Ensure that the Everyone group is permitted to use the new profile.

17. Using Windows NT Explorer, highlight the folder specified by the path you entered in Step 13. Within this folder, rename the `Ntuser.dat` file as `Ntuser.man`. The mandatory profile is assigned and becomes effective for each assigned user at each user's next logon.

If you have a need for the capabilities of mandatory user profiles, consider using a system policy instead. The Windows NT system policy provides the administrator with much more control over users' environment settings than mandatory user profiles. System policy is covered later in this chapter.

Deleting User Profiles

You should consider deleting user profiles for user accounts that have been deleted. Deleting a user profile removes the entire user profile folder for the specified user and also removes any Windows NT Registry entries related to that user profile. Simply deleting the user profile folder by using Windows NT Explorer does *not* completely delete all settings related to the user profile.

TO DELETE A USER PROFILE, FOLLOW THESE STEPS:

1. Select Start ⇒ Settings ⇒ Control Panel.

2. Double-click the System icon in Control Panel.

3. Click the User Profiles tab in the System Properties dialog box.

4. On the User Profiles tab, highlight the user profile you want to delete. Click the Delete command button.

5. In the Confirm Delete dialog box, click the Yes command button.

6. On the User Profiles tab, click OK.

7. Exit Control Panel.

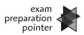

exam
preparation
pointer

Profiles in Windows NT 4.0 have changed significantly from profiles in Windows NT 3.51. Additionally, NT 4.0 now has Windows 95-style system policy. You should become familiar with all of the nuances of user profiles and system policy, when each should be used, which settings take precedence when policies are combined with a user profile, and which settings take precedence when multiple policies apply.

MANAGING SYSTEM POLICY

The Windows NT *system policy* file is a collection of user, group, and computer policies. System policy restricts the user's ability to perform certain tasks on any Windows NT computer on the network to which the user logs on. System policy can also be used to enforce certain mandatory display settings, such as wallpaper and color scheme. You can also create a system policy file that applies to users of Windows 95 computers.

System policy, like a mandatory profile, enables an administrator to control the work environment of users on the network. System policy, however, gives the administrator far more configurable options than a mandatory profile. Administrators can use system policy to provide a consistent environment for a large number of users, or to enforce a specified work environment for problem users who demand a significant amount of administrator time.

In addition to enabling the administrator to limit the changes users can make to their work environments, system policy can be used as a security measure to limit access to parts of the network; to restrict the use of specific tools, such as the Registry Editor; and to remove the Run command option from the Start menu.

System policy is managed and configured by using the System Policy Editor. You can use System Policy Editor to create both Windows NT and Windows 95 system policy files. The administrator must create a system policy file — a system policy file is not installed by default.

After a system policy file is created, it should be saved in the `Netlogon` share on each domain controller. When a user logs on to the domain, Windows NT or Windows 95 retrieves the system policy file from the `Netlogon` share on the domain controller that authenticates the user's logon.

Because system policy is comprised of user, group, and computer policies, it can be applied to all users and computers; or it can be applied to individual users, groups, and computers.

User Policy

A *user policy* is a collection of settings that restrict a user's program and network options and/or enforce a specified configuration of the user's work environment. A user policy is created by an Administrator — it does not exist by default.

There are two types of user policies: an individual user policy and the Default User policy.

An *individual user policy* applies to a single, specific user. Normally, an individual user policy is created only when a user requires a unique policy that differs from any existing Default User or group policy.

The *Default User policy*, contrary to what its name implies, does not exist by default. Rather, it is created when a system policy file is initially created. When the Default User policy is initially created, it doesn't contain any settings that restrict users. The Administrator must configure any desired user restrictions in the Default User policy. The Default User policy applies to a user only if the user does not have an individual user policy.

There are a variety of settings that you can configure in a user policy. Figure 10-8 shows all of the configurable options for a Windows NT individual user policy. The same list of configurable options is available for the Default User policy. Notice the options available in the Desktop and Shell sections.

FIGURE 10-8 **Configurable settings in a Windows NT individual user policy**

The actual process of configuring the check boxes in this list is covered in the "Creating a System Policy File" section later in this chapter.

When a user logs on, Windows NT (or Windows 95) permanently overwrites the existing settings in the HKEY_CURRENT_USER section of the Registry on the local computer with the settings contained in the user policy.

Group Policy

A *group policy* is a policy that applies to a group of users. Group policies apply to all users that are members of a group (that has a group policy) and that do not have individual user policies. Group policies have the same configurable options as user policies. Like user policies, group policies don't exist by default — group policies must be created.

A group policy should be created when more than one user requires the same settings. It takes far less time to create one group policy than to create multiple individual user policies.

A user often belongs to multiple groups that have group policies. In this situation, the Administrator can configure group policy priorities. Figure 10-9 shows the Group Priority dialog box in System Policy Editor. Notice the Move Up and Move Down command buttons that are used to arrange the group priority order. The group at the top of the Group Order list box has the highest priority.

FIGURE 10-9   Configuring group priority

Assume that a user named JohnS, a Sales Manager with administrative duties, belongs to three of the groups listed in Figure 10-9: Domain Admins, Managers, and Sales. Also assume that JohnS does *not* have an individual user policy. When JohnS logs on to the domain, the group policy for the Sales group (which has the lowest group priority) is applied first, and then the group policy for the Managers group is applied, and finally the group policy for the Domain Admins group (which has the highest group priority) is applied to JohnS. As each group policy is applied, it overwrites the settings from previously applied group policies. The last group policy applied (the Domain Admins group policy, in this case) takes precedence over the lower priority group policies.

Computer Policy

A *computer policy* is a collection of settings that specifies a local computer's configuration. A computer policy enforces the specified configuration on all users of a particular Windows NT (or Windows 95) computer. A computer policy is created by an Administrator — it does not exist by default.

There are two types of computer policies: an individual computer policy and the Default Computer policy.

An *individual computer policy* applies to a single, specific computer. Normally, an individual computer policy is created only when a computer requires a unique policy that differs from the Default Computer policy.

The *Default Computer policy*, like the Default User policy, is created when a system policy file is initially created. The Default Computer policy applies to a computer only if the computer does *not* have an individual computer policy.

There are a variety of settings that you can configure in a computer policy. Figure 10-10 shows the configurable options for a Windows NT individual computer policy. The same list of configurable options is available for the Default Computer policy. Notice the options available in the Windows NT System Logon and File system sections.

The actual process of configuring the check boxes in this list is covered in the "Creating a System Policy File" section in this chapter.

When a user logs on, Windows NT (or Windows 95) permanently overwrites the existing settings in the HKEY_LOCAL_MACHINE section of the Registry on the local computer with the settings contained in the computer policy.

How System Policy Is Applied

A Windows NT system policy is applied to a user or computer in a predefined, systematic manner. When a user logs on, the user's roaming or local profile is applied first, and then the system policy is applied. If settings in the system policy conflict with settings in the user profile, the system policy settings take precedence. System policy is applied in the following sequence:

○ If a user has an individual user policy, it is applied.

FIGURE 10-10   **Configurable settings in a Windows NT individual computer policy**

- If a user does *not* have an individual user policy, and the user is a member of a group that has a group policy, then the group policy (or policies, if the user is a member of multiple groups that have group policies) is applied.

- If a user does *not* have an individual user policy, then the Default User policy is applied. (If a user that does not have an individual user policy has a group policy that conflicts with the Default User policy, then the settings in the Default User policy take precedence.)

- If the computer the user logs on to has an individual computer policy, it is applied.

- If the computer the user logs on to does *not* have an individual computer policy, then the Default Computer policy is applied.

The end result is that a user has one of the following user/group policy combinations applied: an individual user policy only, a Default User policy only, or a combination of the Default User policy and a group policy (or policies, if the user is a member of multiple groups that have group policies). In addition, the computer to which the user logs on has either an individual computer policy or the Default Computer policy applied.

Creating a System Policy File

A *system policy file* is created by using the System Policy Editor. After a system policy file is created, it is normally saved in the `Netlogon` share on each domain controller. Only an Administrator can create and save a system policy file to the `NetLogon` share on a domain controller.

caution

If you have configured directory replication on your domain, copy the system policy file to the `<winntroot>\System32\Repl\Export\Scripts\` **folder on the PDC, not to the** `<winntroot>\System32\Repl\Import\Scripts\` **folder that is shared as** `Netlogon`. **If you copy it to the** `Import\Scripts` **folder and directory replication is configured, the Directory Replicator service will delete any files or folders in the** `Import\Scripts` **folder that do not exist in the** `Export\Scripts` **folder.**

The steps for creating a Windows NT system policy file and a Windows 95 system policy file are similar, but have a few important differences.

Windows NT system policy

The following section explains, in detail, how to create and configure a Windows NT system policy file.

TO CREATE, CONFIGURE, AND SAVE A WINDOWS NT SYSTEM POLICY FILE, FOLLOW THESE STEPS:

1. Select Start ⇒ Programs ⇒ Administrative Tools (Common) ⇒ System Policy Editor.

2. In the System Policy Editor dialog box, select Options ⇒ Policy Template.

3. In the Policy Template Options dialog box, ensure that both the COMMON.ADM and winnt.adm files are listed. If one of these files is missing, click the Add command button. In the Open Template File dialog box, type **%SystemRoot%\inf*filename*** (either COMMON.ADM or winnt.adm) in the File name text box. Click the Open command button. The Policy Template Options dialog box reappears. (If any files other than COMMON.ADM and winnt.adm are listed in the Policy Template Options dialog box, highlight the extra file(s), and click the Remove command button.) Click OK.

4. In the System Policy Editor dialog box, select File ⇒ New Policy.

5. Two icons are displayed in the System Policy Editor dialog box: Default Computer and Default User. Figure 10-11 shows the System Policy Editor dialog box.

FIGURE 10-11   Creating a Windows NT system policy file

6. Customize the Default Computer and Default User policies as desired. To customize a policy, double-click the policy icon in the System Policy Editor dialog box. On the Policies tab, click the + sign next to the option that you want to configure. Then configure the check boxes that appear. Each check box has three possible configurations:

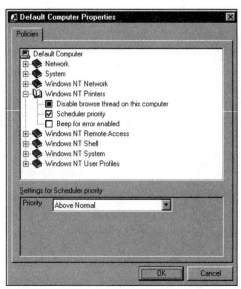

FIGURE 10-12   **Configuring check boxes**
                 for the Default Computer
                 policy

- Grayed out—causes the current setting for this option on the local
  computer to be retained.

- Checked—causes this option to be applied on the local computer.

- Cleared (white)—causes the *opposite* of this option to be applied on the
  local computer.

Figure 10-12 shows the Policies tab in the Default Computer Properties
dialog box. Notice the three check boxes listed under Windows NT
Printers. In Figure 10-12, the gray check box next to "Disable browse
thread on this computer" causes the current setting for this option on the
local computer to be retained. The check in the box next to "Scheduler
priority" causes the priority listed in the Settings For Scheduler priority list
box to be applied on the local computer. The clear (white) check box next
to "Beep for error enabled" causes the "Beep for error" setting to be
disabled on the local computer. After configuring all check boxes
appropriately, click OK.

7. Create and customize individual user and group policies, and create
   individual computer policies as desired:

- To create an individual user policy, select Edit ⇒ Add User in the System
  Policy Editor dialog box. In the Add User dialog box, type the name of the
  user you want to create an individual user policy for. Click OK.

- To create a group policy, select Edit ⇒ Add Group in the System Policy Editor dialog box. In the Add Group dialog box, type the name of the group you want to create a group policy for. Click OK.

- To create an individual computer policy, select Edit ⇒ Add Computer in the System Policy Editor dialog box. In the Add Computer dialog box, type the name of the computer you want to create an individual computer policy for. Click OK.

To customize your new policies, follow the directions in Step 6.

8. After you create and customize all of the user, group, and computer policies, save the system policy file. Select File ⇒ Save As in the System Policy Editor dialog box. Save the file to the Netlogon share on all domain controllers as Ntconfig.pol. (However, if directory replication is configured on your domain, save the Ntconfig.pol file to the <winntroot>\system32\repl\export\scripts folder on the PDC instead.)

9. Exit System Policy Editor.

Windows 95 system policy

To create, configure, and save a Windows 95 system policy file, follow the steps in the previous section on "Windows NT system policy," with the following exceptions:

- In Step 3, substitute the windows.adm file for all references to the winnt.adm file. In other words, ensure that the COMMON.ADM and windows.adm files are the only files listed in the Policy Template Options dialog box.

- In Step 8, substitute the Config.pol file for all references to the Ntconfig.pol file. In other words, save the customized system policy file to the Netlogon share on the PDC as Config.pol.

Windows 95 system policy can also be configured for load balancing. By default, Windows 95 computers take system policy only from the Netlogon share on the PDC. This can place a significant load on the PDC if your network has a large number of Windows 95 computers. To enable Windows 95 computers to take system policy from the domain controller that authenticates the user, configure load balancing for all computer policies (both individual computer policies and the Default Computer policy) in the Windows 95 system policy file.

Figure 10-13 shows load balancing configured for the Windows 95 Default Computer policy. Notice that the check box next to Remote update is checked, and that the check box next to Load balancing (in the Settings For Remote update section) is selected.

FIGURE 10-13   **Configuring load balancing for Windows 95 system policy**

LOGON SCRIPTS

A *logon script* is a batch file or executable file that runs during the user's logon process. An administrator can configure logon scripts to connect network drives and printers, or to run a program during logon. Many Windows NT networks don't use logon scripts at all. However, some Microsoft BackOffice products, such as Systems Management Server, use logon scripts extensively.

You can create a logon script by using any text editor, such as Notepad. All MS-DOS 5.0 (and earlier) batch commands can be used in logon scripts. Logon scripts should be saved in the `Netlogon` share on all domain controllers. (Remember, if directory replication is configured on your domain, save the logon script to the `<winntroot>\system32\repl\export\scripts` folder on the PDC instead of the `Netlogon` share on all domain controllers.)

Administrators can assign a unique logon script to each user, or one logon script to multiple users.

TO ASSIGN A LOGON SCRIPT TO A USER, FOLLOW THESE STEPS:

1. Select Start ⇒ Programs ⇒ Administrative Tools (Common) ⇒ User Manager for Domains.

2. In the User Manager dialog box, highlight the user(s) you want to assign the logon script to. Select User ⇒ Properties.

3. In the User Properties dialog box, click the Profile command button.

4. In the User Environment Profile dialog box, type the name of the logon script file (*not* the full path) in the Logon Script Name text box. Click OK.

5. In the User Properties dialog box, click OK.

6. Exit User Manager for Domains.

---

concept link

For more information on logon scripts, see Logon Scripts and associated topics in the Windows NT Books Online program that ships with Windows NT Server. To access Books Online, select Start ⇒ Programs ⇒ Books Online.

KEY POINT SUMMARY

Chapter 10 explored the various types of user profiles and explained the steps involved in creating, customizing, and deleting user profiles. This chapter also covered Windows NT system policy, and how system policy is applied and created.

- A *user profile* is a collection of settings and options that specify a user's desktop and all other user-definable settings for a user's work environment. In an environment where user profiles are implemented, when a user logs on, the same desktop is displayed as when the user last logged off, even when more than one user uses the same computer.

- The contents of a user profile include user-specific settings for: Windows NT Explorer, Notepad, Paint, Calculator, and other built-in NT applications;

various display settings; applications written to run on Windows NT; network drive and printer connections; and the Start menu. A user profile is normally stored in a subfolder of the `<winntroot>\Profiles` folder. Each user's profile is stored in a separate folder named after the user's account name.

o Each user profile folder contains various subfolders and files. Subfolders include: `Application Data`, `Desktop`, `Favorites`, `NetHood`, `Personal`, `PrintHood`, `Recent`, `SendTo`, `Start Menu`, and `Templates`. Files contained in a user profile folder include `Ntuser.dat` and `Ntuser.dat.LOG`.

o Windows NT automatically creates a user profile for every new user the first time the new user logs on. After that point, an Administrator can create and assign a user profile to an existing user by copying an existing user profile over that user's profile. Remember: user profiles are copied by using the System application in Control Panel. *You can't use Windows NT Explorer to copy user profiles*.

o Administrators can customize the `Default User` profile folder so that new users, at first logon, have the appropriate desktop and work environment settings. You can customize the *local* `Default User` profile folder on a Windows NT computer to affect only new users that log on to that computer; or, you can create a *domain-wide* `Default User` profile folder on the `Netlogon` share on the PDC to affect all new domain users when they log on to a member computer.

o Administrators can customize the `All User` profile folder so that specific shortcuts and applications are made available to *all* users of a particular Windows NT computer. Currently, there is no method available to create a domain-wide `All Users` profile folder on a server.

o *Roaming user profiles* are user profiles that are stored on a server and are available to users regardless to which Windows NT computer on the network they log on. Roaming profiles, which can be assigned to new or existing users, make it possible for users to retain their own customized desktop and work environment settings even though they may use different Windows NT computers. Roaming user profiles are implemented by first creating a shared folder on a server, and then assigning a server-based user profile path to a user account. At this point in the process, a location is assigned for the user's roaming user profile, but the roaming user profile is not actually created until the next time the user logs on and logs off. When the user logs off, the user's local profile is saved to the server and becomes the user's roaming profile. From this point on, every time the user logs off, the user's roaming user profile is updated with any changes the user has made during the logon session.

○ *Mandatory user profiles*, when assigned to a user, cannot be changed by the user. Although normally administrators permit users to change and customize their own user profiles, administrators may decide to use mandatory user profiles when problem users require a significant amount of administrator time, or when there are a large number of users with similar job tasks to administer. To make an individual user's profile (either local or roaming) a mandatory user profile, rename the user's `Ntuser.dat` file in the user's profile folder as `Ntuser.man`. The mandatory profile becomes effective the next time the user logs on.

○ You should consider deleting user profiles for user accounts that have been deleted. Use the System application in Control Panel to delete user profiles, because Windows NT Explorer does not completely delete all settings related to a user profile.

○ The *Windows NT system policy file* is an Administrator-created collection of user, group, and computer policies that restrict the user's ability to perform certain tasks on any Windows NT computer to which the user logs on. System policy can also be used to enforce certain mandatory display settings. You can also create a system policy file that applies to users of Windows 95 computers. System policy is created and configured by using System Policy Editor. After a system policy file is created, it should normally be saved in the `Netlogon` share on each domain controller.

○ A *user policy* restricts a user's program and network options and/or enforces a specified configuration of the user's work environment. There are two types of user policies: an *individual user policy* and the *Default User policy*. There are a variety of settings that can be configured in a user policy. When a user logs on, the existing settings in the HKEY_CURRENT_ USER section of the Registry on the local computer are permanently overwritten with the settings contained in the user policy.

○ *Group policies* apply to all users that are members of a group (that has a group policy) and that do *not* have individual user policies. If a user belongs to multiple groups that have group policies, an Administrator can configure group policy priorities. When multiple group policies are applied, the group policy of the group that has the *lowest* priority is assigned first. As each next-highest priority group policy is applied, it overwrites settings from previously applied group policies. The last group policy applied takes precedence over the lower priority group policies.

o There are two types of computer policies: *individual computer policies* and the *Default Computer policy*. An individual computer policy applies to a single, specific computer. The Default Computer policy applies to a computer only if the computer does *not* have an individual computer policy. When a user logs on, the existing settings in the HKEY_LOCAL_MACHINE section of the Registry on the local computer are overwritten by the settings contained in the computer policy.

o When a user logs on, the user's profile is first applied, and then the system policy is applied. If settings in the system policy conflict with settings in the user profile, the system policy settings take precedence. System policy is applied in the following sequence:

  o If a user has an individual user policy, it is applied.

  o If a user does *not* have an individual user policy, and the user is a member of a group that has a group policy, then the group policy (or policies, if the user is a member of multiple groups that have group policies) is applied.

  o If a user does *not* have an individual user policy, then the Default User policy is applied. (If a user that does not have an individual user policy has a group policy that conflicts with the Default User policy, then the Default User policy takes precedence.)

  o If the computer the user logs on to has an individual computer policy, it is applied.

  o If the computer the user logs on to does *not* have an individual computer policy, then the Default Computer policy is applied.

o A *logon script* is a batch file or executable file that runs during the user's logon process. Logon scripts can be created with any text editor, such as Notepad. Logon scripts are normally saved in the `Netlogon` share on all domain controllers. Administrators can assign a unique logon script to each user, or one logon script to multiple users. Many Windows NT networks don't use logon scripts at all.

Applying What You've Learned

Now it's time to regroup, review, and apply what you've learned in this chapter.

The questions in the Instant Assessment section that follows bring to mind key facts and concepts. Then, the Hands-on Labs reinforce what you've learned and give you a chance to practice some of the tasks tested by the Server exam.

Instant Assessment

1. What is a user profile?

2. Where is a user profile normally stored?

3. What are the subfolders and files contained in a user profile folder?

4. What Windows NT application should you use to copy a user profile?

5. What Windows NT program *can't* you use to copy user profiles?

6. You want all new users, at first logon to a domain member computer, to have the appropriate desktop and work environment settings. What should you do to accomplish this?

7. What is a roaming user profile?

8. What is a logon script?

9. What is a mandatory user profile?

10. Name two situations where the use of mandatory user profiles might be considered.

11. Which file in a user's profile folder must be renamed in order to make the user profile into a mandatory user profile? What must the file be renamed as?

12. What Windows NT application should you use to delete a user profile?

13. What is the Windows NT system policy file?

14. What Windows NT tool is used to create and configure system policy?

15. Where is a system policy file normally saved after it is created?

16. What are the two types of user policies?

17. When multiple group policies are applied, which group policy takes precedence?

18. A user named SusanH has an individual user policy. She is also a member of a group that has a group policy. Which policy is applied to SusanH when she logs on?

19. What are the two types of computer policies?

20. When a user logs on to a Windows NT computer that does *not* have an individual computer policy, what kind of computer policy is applied?

T/F

21. Roaming user profiles can only be assigned to new users. _____

concept link **For answers to the Instant Assessment questions see Appendix B.**

Hands-on Labs

The following Hands-on Labs provide you with practical opportunities to apply the knowledge you've gained in this chapter about managing user profiles and Windows NT system policy.

Lab 10.17 *Implementing user profiles*

The purpose of this lab is to give you hands-on experience in creating and copying user profiles, and experience in configuring roaming and mandatory user profiles.

This lab consists of five parts:

Part 1: Creating and sharing a Profiles folder

Part 2: Configuring a user profile

Part 3: Copying a user profile

Part 4: Configuring server-based profiles

Part 5: Testing profiles

caution **If you have Internet Explorer 4.0 installed on your Windows NT computer, you will *not* be able to successfully copy user profiles by using the steps listed in Part 3 of this lab. See *Microsoft TechNet* article Q175667 for information on how to copy user profiles when Internet Explorer 4.0 has been installed.**

Article Q175667 can also be accessed at http://support.microsoft .com/support/kb/articles/q175/6/67.asp

Begin this lab by booting your computer to Windows NT Server. Log on as Administrator.

Follow the steps below carefully.

Part 1: Creating and sharing a Profiles folder

In this section, you create a shared folder that contains users' profiles.

1. Select Start ⇒ Programs ⇒ Windows NT Explorer.
2. In the All Folders section of the Exploring dialog box, highlight the NTFS volume on your computer—this is most likely drive D:. Select File ⇒ New ⇒ Folder.
3. In the Contents of the NTFS Volume section, type the new folder name: **Profiles**. Press Enter.
4. Right-click the newly created `Profiles` folder. Select Sharing from the menu that appears.
5. In the Profiles Properties dialog box, select the option button next to Shared As. Accept the default Share Name of Profiles. Click OK.
6. Notice that a hand appears under the `Profiles` folder in the Exploring dialog box, indicating that it is a shared folder. Exit Windows NT Explorer. Continue to Part 2.

Part 2: Configuring a user profile

In this section, you configure a profile that will be used by all sales representatives.

1. Select Start ⇒ Programs ⇒ Administrative Tools (Common) ⇒ User Manager for Domains.
2. In the User Manager dialog box, double-click Sales_User in the Username list box. (You will use this user account to create the profile that you will copy to the user account of each sales representative.)
3. In the User Properties dialog box, clear the check boxes next to User Must Change Password at Next Logon and Account Disabled. Select the check box next to Password Never Expires. Click OK.
4. Exit User Manager for Domains.
5. Select Start ⇒ Shut Down.
6. In the Shut Down Windows dialog box, select the option button next to "Close all programs and log on as a different user." Click the Yes command button.
7. Press Ctrl + Alt + Delete to log on.
8. In the Logon Information dialog box, type in a user name of **Sales_User** and a password of **newuser**. Click OK.

9. If the Welcome to Windows NT dialog box appears, click the Close command button.

10. Right-click the desktop. Select Properties from the menu that appears.

11. In the Display Properties dialog box, click the Appearance tab.

12. In the Scheme drop-down list box, select the Red, White, and Blue (VGA) scheme. Click the Background tab.

13. In the Pattern drop-down list box, select the Scottie pattern. Click OK.

14. Right-click the desktop. Select New ⇒ Shortcut from the menus that appear.

15. In the Create Shortcut dialog box, type **calc.exe** in the Command line text box. Click the Next command button.

16. In the "Select a name for the shortcut" text box, type **Calculator**. Click the Finish command button.

17. Right-click the desktop. Select New ⇒ Shortcut from the menus that appear.

18. In the Create Shortcut dialog box, type **notepad.exe** in the Command line text box. Click the Next command button.

19. In the "Select a name for the shortcut" text box, type **Notepad**. Click the Finish command button.

20. Right-click the desktop. Select Arrange Icons ⇒ Auto Arrange from the menus that appear. Notice that the new shortcuts are neatly arranged on your desktop.

21. Select Start ⇒ Shut Down.

22. In the Shut Down Windows dialog box, select the option button next to "Close all programs and log on as a different user." Click the Yes command button.

23. Press Ctrl + Alt + Delete to log on.

24. In the Logon Information dialog box, type in a user name of **Administrator** and a password of **password**. Click OK. Continue to Part 3.

Part 3: Copying a user profile

In this section, you copy the user profile you created in Part 2 to a profile folder for each sales representative. You also configure one of the sales representative's user profiles as a mandatory user profile.

1. Select Start ⇒ Settings ⇒ Control Panel.

2. In the Control Panel dialog box, double-click the System icon.

3. In the System Properties dialog box, click the User Profiles tab.

4. Scroll down the Profiles stored on this computer list box. Select the LAB\Sales_User profile. Click the Copy To command button.

5. In the Copy profile to text box, type **\\pdclab\profiles\BillT**. (Don't type the period at the end.) Click the Change command button.

6. In the Choose User dialog box, click the Show Users command button. Scroll down the Names list box and select BillT. Click the Add command button. Click OK.

7. In the Copy To dialog box, click OK.

8. The System Properties dialog box reappears, with LAB\Sales_User highlighted. Click the Copy To command button.

9. In the Copy profile to text box, type **\\pdclab\profiles\MikeC**. (Don't type the period at the end.) Click the Change command button.

10. In the Choose User dialog box, click the Show Users command button. Scroll down the Names list box and select MikeC. Click the Add command button. Click OK.

11. In the Copy To dialog box, click OK.

12. The System Properties dialog box reappears, with LAB\Sales_User highlighted. Click the Copy To command button.

13. In the Copy profile to text box, type **\\pdclab\profiles\ColleenG**. (Don't type the period at the end.) Click the Change command button.

14. In the Choose User dialog box, click the Show Users command button. Scroll down the Names list box and select ColleenG. Click the Add command button. Click OK.

15. In the Copy To dialog box, click OK.

16. In the System Properties dialog box, click OK.

17. Exit Control Panel.

18. Select Start ⇒ Programs ⇒ Windows NT Explorer.

19. In the All Folders section of the Exploring dialog box, click the + sign next to the NTFS volume (probably drive D:). Click the + sign next to the Profiles folder. Highlight the BillT folder. In the Contents of 'BillT' section of the dialog box, highlight the Ntuser.dat file. Select File ⇒ Rename. Rename the Ntuser.dat file as Ntuser.man. Press Enter. (Renaming BillT's Ntuser.dat file as Ntuser.man causes BillT's profile to be a mandatory user profile.)

20. Exit Windows NT Explorer. Continue to Part 4.

Part 4: Configuring server-based profiles

In this section, you configure the user accounts of the sales representatives to use the server-based profiles you created for them in Parts 2 and 3. Additionally, you configure the user accounts of the accounting staff to use roaming user profiles.

1. Select Start ⇒ Programs ⇒ Administrative Tools (Common) ⇒ User Manager for Domains.

2. In the User Manager dialog box, highlight BillT, and then press and hold Ctrl while you click ColleenG and MikeC in the Username list box. Select User ⇒ Properties.

3. In the User Properties dialog box, click the Profile command button.

4. In the User Environment Profile dialog box, type **\\pdclab\profiles\% USERNAME%** in the User Profile Path text box. Click OK. (This step assigns a copied profile to each selected user account.)

5. In the User Properties dialog box, click OK.

6. In the User Manager dialog box, double-click Sales_User in the Username list box.

7. In the User Properties dialog box, select the check box next to Account Disabled. (Remember that in Part 2 you deselected this check box so that you could use the account to create a profile. Now you want to disable the account again so that no one can use it to log on.) Click OK.

8. In the User Manager dialog box, highlight MikeCo, and then press and hold Ctrl while you click NancyY. Select User ⇒ Properties.

9. In the User Properties dialog box, click the Profile command button.

10. In the User Environment Profile dialog box, type **\\pdclab\profiles\% USERNAME%** in the User Profile Path text box. Click OK. (This step assigns a roaming user profile to MikeCo and NancyY.)

11. In the User Properties dialog box, click the Hours command button.

12. In the Logon Hours dialog box, highlight the entire chart, so that all hours are selected. Click the Allow command button. (You are changing the hours now in case you're doing this lab during nonbusiness hours. This change permits you to log on as MikeCo or NancyY anytime.) Click OK.

13. In the User Properties dialog box, click OK.

14. In the User Manager dialog box, select Policies ⇒ User Rights.

15. In the User Rights Policy dialog box, select "Shut down the system" from the Right drop-down list box. Click the Add command button.

16. In the Names list box (in the Add Users and Groups dialog box), double-click the Everyone group. Click OK.

17. In the User Rights Policy dialog box, click OK.

18. Exit User Manager for Domains. Continue to Part 5.

Part 5: Testing profiles

In this section, you try out the sales representatives' profiles, including the mandatory user profile. Additionally, you try out the roaming user profiles for one of the accounting staff.

1. Select Start ⇒ Shut Down.

2. In the Shut Down Windows dialog box, select the option button next to "Close all programs and log on as a different user." Click the Yes command button.

3. Press Ctrl + Alt + Delete to log on.

4. In the Logon Information dialog box, type in a user name of **ColleenG** and a password of **newuser**. Click OK.

5. A message appears indicating that you are required to change your password at first logon. Click OK.

6. In the Change Password dialog box, type in a new password of **password**, and confirm the new password by retyping it. Click OK.

7. A message is displayed, indicating that your password has been changed. Click OK.

8. If a Welcome to Windows NT screen appears, deselect the check box next to Show this Welcome Screen next time you start Windows NT, and then click the Close command button.

9. Notice that the background pattern (Scottie dogs) and color scheme (Red, white, and blue) that you configured for the Sales_User profile and copied to ColleenG's profile appear on the desktop. Right-click the desktop. Select Properties from the menu that appears.

10. In the Display Properties dialog box, select (None) from the Pattern drop-down list box. Select a Wallpaper of lanmannt. Click the Appearance tab.

11. In the Scheme drop-down list box, select Rose. Click OK.

12. Select Start ⇒ Shut Down.

13. In the Shut Down Windows dialog box, select the option button next to "Close all programs and log on as a different user." Click the Yes command button.

14. Press Ctrl + Alt + Delete to log on.

15. In the Logon Information dialog box, type in a user name of **ColleenG** and a password of **password**. Click OK.

16. Notice that the changes you made to ColleenG's desktop (the rose scheme and the lanmannt wallpaper) appear on the desktop. These settings have been successfully saved to ColleenG's user profile, because her profile is not a mandatory user profile.

17. Select Start ⇒ Shut Down.

18. In the Shut Down Windows dialog box, select the option button next to "Close all programs and log on as a different user." Click the Yes command button.

19. Press Ctrl + Alt + Delete to log on.

20. In the Logon Information dialog box, type in a user name of **BillT** and a password of **newuser**. Click OK.

21. A message appears indicating that you are required to change your password at first logon. Click OK.

22. In the Change Password dialog box, type in a new password of **password**, and confirm the new password by retyping it. Click OK.

23. A message is displayed, indicating that your password has been changed. Click OK.

24. If a Welcome to Windows NT screen appears, deselect the check box next to Show this Welcome Screen next time you start Windows NT. Click the Close command button.

25. Notice that the background pattern (Scottie dogs) and color scheme (Red, white, and blue) that you configured for the Sales_User profile and copied to BillT's profile appear on the desktop. Right-click the desktop. Select Properties from the menu that appears.

26. In the Display Properties dialog box, select Critters from the Pattern drop-down list box. Click the Appearance tab.

27. In the Scheme drop-down list box, select Pumpkin (large). Click OK.

28. Select Start ⇒ Shut Down.

29. In the Shut Down Windows dialog box, select the option button next to "Close all programs and log on as a different user." Click the Yes command button.

30. Press Ctrl + Alt + Delete to log on.

31. In the Logon Information dialog box, type in a user name of **BillT** and a password of **password**. Click OK.

32. If a Welcome to Windows NT screen appears, deselect the check box next to "Show this Welcome Screen next time you start Windows NT." Click the Close command button.

33. Notice that the desktop changes that you made for BillT's desktop in Steps 26 and 27 were *not* saved to BillT's profile. (This is because in an earlier part of this lab you configured BillT to have a mandatory user profile.) Select Start ⇒ Shut Down.

34. In the Shut Down Windows dialog box, select the option button next to "Close all programs and log on as a different user." Click the Yes command button.

35. Press Ctrl + Alt + Delete to log on.

36. In the Logon Information dialog box, type in a user name of **NancyY** and a password of **newuser**. Click OK.

37. A Logon Message is displayed, indicating that you are required to change your password at first logon. Click OK.

38. In the Change Password dialog box, type in a new password of **password**, and confirm the new password by retyping it. Click OK.

39. A message indicating that your password has been changed appears. Click OK.

40. If a Welcome to Windows NT screen appears, click the Close command button.

41. Right-click the desktop. Select New ⇒ Shortcut from the menus that appear.

42. In the Create Shortcut dialog box, type **calc.exe** in the Command line text box. Click the Next command button.

43. In the Select a name for the shortcut text box, type **Calculator**. Click the Finish command button.

44. Right-click the desktop. Select Arrange Icons ⇒ Auto Arrange.

45. Select Start ⇒ Shut Down.

46. In the Shut Down Windows dialog box, select the option button next to "Close all programs and log on as a different user." Click the Yes command button.

47. Press Ctrl + Alt + Delete to log on.

48. In the Logon Information dialog box, type in a user name of **Administrator** and a password of **password**. Click OK.

49. Select Start ⇒ Programs ⇒ Windows NT Explorer.

50. In the All Folders section of the Exploring dialog box, click the + sign next to the NTFS volume (probably drive D:). Click the Profiles folder. Notice that a profile folder has been created for NancyY. (It is displayed in the Contents of 'Profiles' section.) Also notice that there is not a folder for MikeCo, because he has not logged on since you assigned him a roaming profile. Exit Windows NT Explorer.

Lab 10.18 *Configuring a system policy*

The purpose of this lab is to give you hands-on experience in creating and configuring a Windows 95 system policy; and experience in creating, configuring, and testing a Windows NT system policy.

This lab consists of three parts:

Part 1: Creating a system policy and configuring load balancing for all Windows 95 computers

Part 2: Creating a system policy for all Windows NT computers

Part 3: Testing the Windows NT system policy

Begin this lab by booting your computer to Windows NT Server. Log on as Administrator.

Follow these steps carefully.

Part 1: Creating a system policy and configuring load balancing for all Windows 95 computers

1. Select Start ⇒ Programs ⇒ Administrative Tools (Common) ⇒ System Policy Editor.

2. In the System Policy Editor dialog box, select Options ⇒ Policy Template.

3. In the Policy Template Options dialog box, click the Add command button.

4. In the Open Template File dialog box, type **\winntsrv\inf\windows.adm** in the File name text box. Click the Open command button.

5. The Policy Template Options dialog box reappears. Highlight the C:\WINNTSRV\INF\Winnt.adm file. Click the Remove command button. Click OK.

6. In the System Policy Editor dialog box, select File ⇒ New Policy.

7. Double-click Default Computer.

8. On the Policies tab, click the + sign next to Network. Then click the + sign next to System policies update. Select the check box next to Remote update. In the Settings For Remote Update section, select Automatic (use default path) in the Update Mode drop-down list box. Scroll to the bottom of the section, and select the check box next to "Load balancing."

9. On the Policies tab, click the + sign next to Windows 95 Network. Then click the + sign next to Microsoft Client for Windows networks. Select the check box next to Log on to Windows NT. In the Settings for Log on to Windows NT section, select the check boxes next to Display domain logon confirmation and Disable caching of domain password. Type **LAB** in the Domain name text box.

10. On the Policies tab, click the + sign next to Windows 95 System. Then click the + sign next to Profiles. Select the check box next to "Enable user profiles." Click OK.

11. In the System Policy Editor dialog box, double-click Default User.

12. On the Policies tab, click the + sign next to Shell. Then click the + sign next to Restrictions. Then select the check boxes next to "Remove Run command from Start menu" and "Don't save settings at exit."

13. On the Policies tab, click the + sign next to System. Then click the + sign next to Restrictions. Next, select the check box next to Disable Registry editing tools. Click OK.

14. In the System Policy Editor dialog box, select File ⇒ Save As. In the File name text box, type **\\pdclab\repl$\scripts\config**. (Don't type the period at the end.) Click the Save command button.

15. In the System Policy Editor dialog box, select File ⇒ Close. Continue to Part 2.

Part 2: Creating a system policy for all Windows NT computers

1. In the System Policy Editor dialog box, select Options ⇒ Policy Template.

2. In the Policy Template Options dialog box, click the Add command button.

3. In the Open Template File dialog box, double-click the `Winnt.adm` file.

4. In the Policy Template Options dialog box, highlight `C:\WINNTSRV\INF\windows.adm`. Click the Remove command button. Click OK.

5. In the System Policy Editor dialog box, select File ⇒ New Policy.

6. Double-click Default Computer.

7. On the Policies tab, click the + sign next to Windows NT System. Click the + sign next to Logon. Then select the check box next to Logon banner.

8. On the Policies tab, click the + sign next to Windows NT User Profiles. Then select the check box next to "Delete cached copies of roaming profiles."

9. On the Policies tab, click the + sign next to Windows NT Network. Then click the + sign next to Sharing. Then select the check box next to "Create hidden drive shares (server)." Then select the same check box again, so it turns white (not gray), *without* a check in it. Click OK.

10. In the System Policy Editor dialog box, double-click Default User.

11. On the Policies tab, click the + sign next to Windows NT System. Then select the check box next to Parse Autoexec.bat. Click OK.

12. In the System Policy Editor dialog box, select File ⇒ Save As.

13. In the Save As dialog box, type **\\pdclab\repl$\scripts\ntconfig** in the File name text box. Click the Save command button.

14. Exit System Policy Editor.

15. Select Start ⇒ Programs ⇒ Windows NT Explorer.

16. In the All Folders section of the Exploring dialog box, click the + sign next to the `Winntsrv` folder. Then click the + sign next to the `System 32` folder. Next, click the + sign next to the `Repl` folder, and then click the + sign next to the `Export` folder. Highlight the `Scripts` folder. Notice in the Contents of 'Scripts' section that both the policy files you created (`config.POL` and `ntconfig.POL`) are listed. Click the + sign next to the `Import` folder. Highlight the `Scripts` folder under `Import`. Wait until the `ntconfig.POL` file appears (is replicated) to the Contents of 'Scripts' section.

17. Exit Windows NT Explorer. Continue to Part 3.

Part 3: Testing the Windows NT system policy

1. Select Start ⇒ Shut Down.

2. In the Shut Down Windows dialog box, select the option button next to "Close all programs and log on as a different user." Click the Yes command button.

3. Press Ctrl + Alt + Delete to log on.

4. In the Logon Information dialog box, type in a user name of **Administrator** and a password of **password**. Click OK. (Logging on has implemented the Default Computer and Default User policies. These policies will take effect the next time you log on.)

5. Select Start ⇒ Shut Down.

6. In the Shut Down Windows dialog box, select the option button next to "Close all programs and log on as a different user." Click the Yes command button.

7. Press Ctrl + Alt + Delete to log on.

8. Notice that a logon banner (Important Notice) is displayed. (Remember, you configured a logon banner in Part 2 of this lab.) Click OK.

9. In the Logon Information dialog box, type in a user name of **Administrator** and a password of **password**. Click OK. This step completes Lab 10.18.

CHAPTER

Administering Servers from Client Computers

11

About Chapter 11

This chapter explores how to manage Windows NT Server computers remotely from client computers by using Client-based Network Administration Tools.

First, the chapter describes the utilities that make up Client-based Network Administration Tools. Then it explains how to install Windows NT Server Tools on Windows 95 computers and how to install Client-based Network Administration Tools on Windows NT Workstation computers.

Next, the chapter discusses how a user at a client computer can use Client-based Network Administration Tools to manage an NT Server computer remotely on the network.

The chapter wraps up with an illustrative example of an Administrator who uses Client-based Network Administration Tools (installed on a Windows NT Workstation client computer) to remotely promote a backup domain controller to a primary domain controller.

This chapter includes an optional Hands-on Lab, in which you install Client-based Network Administration Tools on a Windows NT Workstation computer.

The material presented in Chapter 11 maps to the "Administer remote servers from various types of client computers" objective listed in the Managing Resources section in the Preparation Guide for the Server exam.

CLIENT-BASED NETWORK ADMINISTRATION TOOLS

Client-based Network Administration Tools (often referred to as *Windows NT Server Tools*, particularly when used on a Windows 95 client computer) are a collection of Windows NT Server utilities that, when installed on a Windows 95 or Windows NT Workstation client computer, make it possible for a user at the client computer to remotely manage an NT Server computer on the network.

Client-based Network Administration Tools make remote administration of an NT Server computer practical and convenient for many administrators.

Because Client-based Network Administration Tools, and their installation, differ on Windows 95 and Windows NT Workstation computers, they are discussed separately in the following sections.

Windows NT Server Tools for Windows 95 Computers

The Windows NT Server Tools that can be installed on Windows 95 client computers are: *User Manager for Domains, Server Manager, Event Viewer*, and *security extensions for Windows Explorer* (to manage file and printer security on a remote Windows NT Server). These tools are Windows 95 versions of the same tools that ship with Windows NT Server and that are discussed throughout this book.

Table 11-1 shows the Windows NT Server Tools that can be installed on Windows 95 client computers and the basic functions that they enable an administrator to perform remotely from the client computer.

TABLE 11-1 WINDOWS NT SERVER TOOLS FOR WINDOWS 95 CLIENT COMPUTERS

WINDOWS NT SERVER TOOL	FUNCTIONALITY
User Manager for Domains	Enables remote management of users, groups, domain security policy, and trust relationships on a Windows NT Server computer.

continued

TABLE 11-1 *(continued)*

WINDOWS NT SERVER TOOL	FUNCTIONALITY
Server Manager	Enables remote management of shared folders, remote starting and stopping of services, remote management of Directory Replication, remote viewing of which users are accessing shared resources, and remote disconnection of users from shared resources on a Windows NT Server computer.
Event Viewer	Enables remote viewing, archiving, and management of the system, security, and application logs in Event Viewer on a Windows NT Server computer.
Security tab extensions for Windows Explorer	This feature adds a Security tab to the "file," "folder," or "printer" Properties dialog boxes (tabs that normally exist on NT Server but aren't present on Windows 95 computers); enables remote management of file, folder, and printer security on a Windows NT Server computer.

Before you install and run Windows NT Server Tools on a Windows 95 client computer, ensure that the computer has the following minimum required hardware and software installed:

Hardware required:

- 486DX/33 processor
- 8MB of RAM
- 3MB of available hard disk space on the system partition

Software required:

- Windows 95
- Client for Microsoft Networks

Installing Windows NT Server Tools on a Windows 95 computer

In addition to the minimum required hardware and software, installing Windows NT Server Tools on a Windows 95 client computer requires either a CD-ROM drive on the client computer *and* the Windows NT Server 4.0 compact disc, or access to a shared folder containing a copy of Windows NT Server Tools on an available network server.

You can't pick and choose which Windows NT Server Tools to install — they are all installed as a single package. The next section describes how to install Windows NT Server Tools on a Windows 95 client computer.

TO INSTALL WINDOWS NT SERVER TOOLS ON A WINDOWS 95 CLIENT COMPUTER (USING A CD-ROM DRIVE), FOLLOW THESE STEPS:

1. Boot the client computer to Windows 95. Place the Windows NT Server 4.0 compact disc in the computer's CD-ROM drive.

2. Windows 95 automatically starts the CD-ROM device. Minimize the Windows NT CD-ROM dialog box.

3. Select Start ⇒ Settings ⇒ Control Panel.

4. The Control Panel dialog box appears. Double-click the Add/Remove Programs icon.

5. The Add/Remove Programs Properties dialog box appears. Click the Windows Setup tab.

6. On the Windows Setup tab, click the Have Disk command button.

7. The Install From Disk dialog box appears. Click the Browse command button.

8. The Open dialog box appears. In the Drives drop-down list box, select the computer's CD-ROM drive. In the Folders list box, double-click the Clients folder. Then scroll down and double-click the Srvtools folder. Double-click the Win95 folder. Srvtools.inf appears in the File Name list box, as shown in Figure 11-1. Click OK.

FIGURE 11-1   Selecting Windows NT Server
Tools from the compact disc

9. The Install From Disk dialog box reappears, as shown in Figure 11-2. Notice the full path to the Windows NT Server Tools. Click OK.

**FIGURE 11-2   Preparing to install Windows NT
Server Tools from the compact disc**

10. The Have Disk dialog box reappears. Select the check box next to Windows
NT Server Tools in the Components list box. The dialog box's appearance,
at this point, is as shown in Figure 11-3. Click the Install command button.

**FIGURE 11-3   Installing Windows NT
Server Tools**

11. Windows 95 copies files and updates shortcuts, and then displays the
Add/Remove Programs Properties dialog box again, as shown in Figure
11-4. Notice the Components list box shows that Windows NT Server Tools
are installed on the computer. Click OK.

12. Before the Windows NT Server Tools can be used on this computer, you
must edit the computer's `autoexec.bat` file. To start this process, select
Start ⇒ Programs ⇒ MS-DOS Prompt.

13. At the C:\WINDOWS> prompt, type **edit c:\autoexec.bat** and press Enter.

14. The contents of the `autoexec.bat` file are displayed. (If you did not
previously have an `autoexec.bat` file, the window will be blank.) After
the last entry listed, type the following line: **SET PATH=%PATH%;C:\
SRVTOOLS** and press Enter. Select File ⇒ Exit.

FIGURE 11-4   Windows NT Server Tools
installed

15. The Save File dialog box appears. Click the Yes command button.

16. The C:\WINDOWS> prompt reappears. Type **exit** and press Enter.

17. Restart Windows, and the new path takes effect. Windows NT Server Tools
will appear in the Start ⇒ Programs menu.

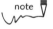 note ▌ **If you want to install Windows NT Server Tools on a Windows 95
computer over the network (instead of using a CD-ROM drive),
connect to the shared folder that contains the Windows NT Server
Tools source files, and select that folder during the installation
process.**

Client-based Network Administration Tools for Windows NT Workstation Computers

The Client-based Network Administration Tools that can be installed on Windows
NT Workstation computers are: *User Manager for Domains, Server Manager,
System Policy Editor, Remote Access Admin, DHCP Administrator, WINS
Manager*, and *Remoteboot Manager*. These tools are Windows NT Workstation

versions of the same tools that ship with Windows NT Server, and that are discussed throughout this book.

Because Event Viewer and Windows NT Explorer are already installed on a Windows NT Workstation computer, they are not part of the Client-based Network Administration Tools add-on package.

Table 11-2 shows the Client-based Network Administration Tools that can be installed on Windows NT Workstation client computers and the basic functions that they enable an administrator to perform remotely from the client computer.

TABLE 11-2 CLIENT–BASED NETWORK ADMINISTRATION TOOLS FOR WINDOWS NT WORKSTATION CLIENT COMPUTERS

CLIENT-BASED NETWORK ADMINISTRATION TOOL	FUNCTIONALITY
User Manager for Domains	Enables remote management of users, groups, domain security policy, and trust relationships on a Windows NT Server computer.
Server Manager	Enables remote management of shared folders, remote starting and stopping of services, remote management of directory replication, remote viewing of which users are accessing shared resources, and remote disconnection of users from shared resources on a Windows NT Server computer.
System Policy Editor	Enables remote creation and editing of policy files on a Windows NT Server computer.
Remote Access Admin	Enables remote configuration and management of the Remote Access Service (RAS) on a Windows NT Server computer.
DHCP Administrator	Enables remote configuration and management of the DHCP service on a Windows NT Server computer.
WINS Manager	Enables remote configuration and management of the WINS service on a Windows NT Server computer.
Remoteboot Manager	Enables remote configuration and management of the Remoteboot service on a Windows NT Server computer.

Before you can install and run Client-based Network Administration Tools on a Windows NT Workstation client computer, you should ensure that the computer has the following minimum required hardware and software installed:

Hardware required:

- 486DX/33 processor

- 12MB of RAM

- 2.5MB of available hard disk space on the boot partition

Software required:

- Windows NT Workstation

- Server service

- Workstation service

Installing Client-based Network Administration Tools on a Windows NT Workstation computer

In addition to the minimum required hardware and software, installing Client-based Network Administration Tools on a Windows NT Workstation client computer requires either a CD-ROM drive on the client computer *and* the Windows NT Server 4.0 compact disc or access to a shared folder containing a copy of the Client-based Network Administration Tools on an available network server.

You can't pick and choose which Client-based Network Administration Tools to install — they are all installed as a single package. The next section explains how to install Client-based Network Administration Tools on a Windows NT Workstation computer.

TO INSTALL CLIENT-BASED NETWORK ADMINISTRATION TOOLS ON A WINDOWS NT WORKSTATION CLIENT COMPUTER (BY USING A CD-ROM DRIVE), FOLLOW THESE STEPS:

1. Start Windows NT Workstation on the computer. Log on as Administrator. Place the Windows NT Server 4.0 compact disc in the CD-ROM drive.

2. Select Start ⇒ Programs ⇒ Windows NT Explorer.

3. In the Exploring dialog box, click the + sign next to the CD-ROM drive. Under the CD-ROM drive, click the + sign next to the `Clients` folder. Click the + sign next to the `Srvtools` folder. Highlight the `Winnt` folder. Figure 11-5 shows the Exploring dialog box at this point. Notice the `Setup.bat` file in the "Contents of Winnt" section.

FIGURE 11-5   Installing Client-based Network Administration
Tools on a Windows NT Workstation computer

4. In the "Contents of Winnt" section in the right-hand window, double-click
`Setup.bat.`

5. A window appears, as shown in Figure 11-6, indicating that the Client-
based Network Administration Tools have been installed. Press any key to
continue.

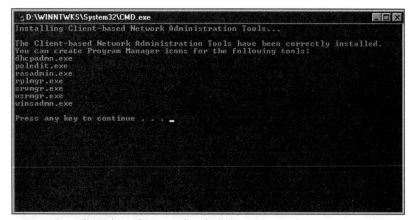

FIGURE 11-6   Client-based Network Administration Tools
installed on an NT Workstation computer

6. The Exploring dialog box reappears. The Client-based Network Administration Tools are now installed. Continue on to Step 7 to create icons for these tools.

7. In the Exploring dialog box, click the + sign next to the drive on your computer on which you originally installed Windows NT Workstation (if it is not already expanded). Often, this is the C: drive. Click the + sign next to the `<winntroot>` folder. (Remember, `<winntroot>` is the folder in which Windows NT Workstation is installed.) Click the + sign next to the `Profiles` folder. Click the + sign next to the `All Users` folder. Click the + sign next to the `Start Menu` folder. Click the + sign next to the `Programs` folder. Highlight the `Administrative Tools (Common)` folder.

8. Select File ⇒ New ⇒ Shortcut.

9. In the Create Shortcut dialog box, type **c:\<*winntroot*>\system32\usrmgr.exe** in the command line text box. (Replace `<winntroot>` with the name of the folder in which NT Workstation is installed.) If Windows NT Workstation is installed on a different drive than the C: drive, substitute the correct drive letter in this path. Click the Next command button.

10. In the Select A Title For The Program dialog box, type **User Manager for Domains** in the Select A Name For The Shortcut text box. Click the Finish command button.

11. The Exploring dialog box reappears. Repeat Steps 8 – 10 to create icons for each of the following Client-based Network Administration Tools:

Filename:	**Shortcut name:**
`c:\<winntroot>\system32\srvmgr.exe`	Server Manager
`c:\<winntroot>\system32\poledit.exe`	System Policy Editor
`c:\<winntroot>\system32\rasadmin.exe`	Remote Access Admin
`c:\<winntroot>\system32\dhcpadmn.exe`	DHCP Administrator
`c:\<winntroot>\system32\winsadmn.exe`	WINS Administrator
`c:\<winntroot>\system32\rplmgr.exe`	Remoteboot Manager

12. The Exploring dialog box reappears. Exit Windows NT Explorer.

USING CLIENT-BASED NETWORK ADMINISTRATION TOOLS TO MANAGE AN NT SERVER COMPUTER

Client-based Network Administration Tools make it possible for a user at a client computer to remotely manage an NT Server computer on the network. In effect, Client-based Network Administration Tools turn an administrator's desktop into an NT Server management station, even if the administrator's desktop runs Windows 95 or Windows NT Workstation.

For the most part, Client-based Network Administration Tools are used in the same way on a client computer as they are when they are run on a Windows NT Server computer. (The main differences on a client computer typically consist of an extra step or two to select the appropriate domain and/or computer on which the action will be performed.)

The next section discusses a practical, real-life example of how Client-based Network Administration Tools can be used by a network administrator.

Using Server Manager to Remotely Promote a BDC to a PDC

Suppose that an Administrator wants to remotely promote a *backup domain controller* (BDC) on the network to a *primary domain controller* (PDC) so that a scheduled upgrade can be performed on the original PDC. The following steps explain how an Administrator can use Client-based Network Administration Tools (installed on a Windows NT Workstation client computer) to accomplish this.

TO REMOTELY PROMOTE A BDC TO A PDC, PERFORM THE FOLLOWING STEPS ON A WINDOWS NT WORKSTATION CLIENT COMPUTER ON WHICH CLIENT-BASED NETWORK ADMINISTRATION TOOLS HAVE BEEN INSTALLED:

1. Select Start ⇒ Programs ⇒ Administrative Tools (Common) ⇒ Server Manager. The Server Manager dialog box appears, as shown in Figure 11-7. Note that the computer named BDCLAB is currently a Windows NT 4.0 BDC.

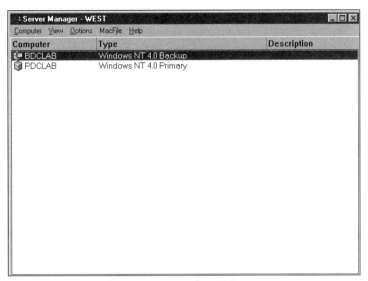

FIGURE 11-7 Preparing to promote the BDC

2. Highlight the BDC in the Server Manager dialog box. Select Computer ⇒ Promote to Primary Domain Controller, as shown in Figure 11-8. Notice the available options in this menu.

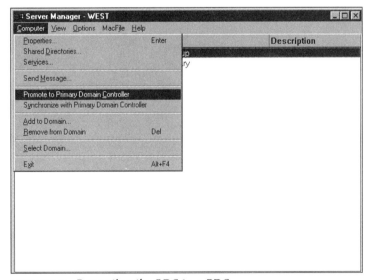

FIGURE 11-8 Promoting the BDC to a PDC

3. Confirm that you want to promote the BDC by clicking the Yes command button in the Server Manager warning dialog box. Server Manager remotely promotes the BDC to a PDC and simultaneously demotes the PDC to a BDC. The process takes a few minutes. Finally, the Server Manager dialog box reappears, as shown in Figure 11-9. Notice that the computer named BDCLAB is now a Windows NT 4.0 primary domain controller (PDC).

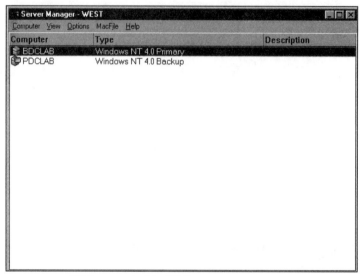

FIGURE 11-9   BDC promoted to PDC

KEY POINT SUMMARY

This chapter explored how to manage Windows NT Server computers remotely on a network by using Client-based Network Administration Tools.

o *Client-based Network Administration Tools* are a collection of Windows NT Server utilities that, when installed on a Windows 95 or Windows NT Workstation client computer, enable a user at the client computer to manage an NT Server computer remotely on the network. Client-based Network Administration Tools are also referred to as *Windows NT Server Tools*, particularly when they are used on a Windows 95 client computer.

- The Windows NT Server Tools that can be installed on Windows 95 client computers are: *User Manager for Domains, Server Manager, Event Viewer*, and *security extensions for Windows Explorer* (to manage file and printer security on a remote Windows NT Server).

  - The minimum hardware and software required to install and run Windows NT Server Tools on a Windows 95 computer is: a 486DX/33 processor with 8MB of RAM and 3MB of available hard disk space, with Windows 95 and Client for Microsoft Networks installed. Additionally, you need either a CD-ROM drive on the client computer and the Windows NT Server 4.0 compact disc, or you must have access to a shared folder containing a copy of the Windows NT Server Tools on an available network server.

  - You can't pick and choose which Windows NT Server Tools to install—they are all installed as a single package.

  - After you install Windows NT Server Tools on a Windows 95 computer, you must edit the computer's `autoexec.bat` file before using the tools.

- The Client-based Network Administration Tools that can be installed on Windows NT Workstation computers are: *User Manager for Domains, Server Manager, System Policy Editor, Remote Access Admin, DHCP Administrator, WINS Manager*, and *Remoteboot Manager*.

  - The minimum hardware and software required to install and run Client-based Network Administration Tools on a Windows NT Workstation computer is: a 486DX/33 processor with 12MB of RAM and 2.5MB of available hard disk space on the boot partition, with Windows NT Workstation, the Server service, and the Workstation service installed. Additionally, you need either a CD-ROM drive on the client computer and the Windows NT Server 4.0 compact disc, or you must have access to a shared folder containing a copy of the Client-based Network Administration Tools on an available network server.

  - After you install Client-based Network Administration Tools on a Windows NT Workstation client computer, you need to create icons for the individual tools.

- Client-based Network Administration Tools, in effect, turn an administrator's desktop into an NT Server management station—even if the administrator's desktop runs Windows 95 or Windows NT Workstation. An example of the steps an Administrator takes to use the Server Manager tool to remotely promote a BDC to a PDC is discussed.

APPLYING WHAT YOU'VE LEARNED

Now it's time to regroup, review, and apply what you've learned in this chapter.

The following Instant Assessment questions bring to mind key facts and concepts. Then, an optional Hands-on Lab reinforces what you've learned and gives you an opportunity to practice some of the tasks that may be tested by the Server exam.

Instant Assessment

1. What is the primary purpose of Client-based Network Administration Tools?

2. Which Windows NT Server Tools can be installed on a Windows 95 client computer?

3. Which Client-based Network Administration Tools can be installed on a Windows NT Workstation client computer?

4. What is the minimum amount of RAM required to install and run Windows NT Server Tools on a Windows 95 client computer? How much RAM is required to install and run Client-based Network Administration Tools on a Windows NT Workstation client computer?

5. Which Client-based Network Administration Tool should you use to remotely promote a BDC to a PDC?

6. Which Windows NT Server Tool should you use to manage a shared folder on an NT Server computer remotely from a Windows 95 client computer?

7. Which Client-based Network Administration Tool should you use to manage users on an NT Server computer remotely from a Windows NT Workstation client computer?

8. Which Windows NT Server Tool should you use to share the CD-ROM drive on an NT Server computer remotely from a Windows 95 client computer?

9. Which Windows NT Server Tool should you use to manage file, folder, and printer security on an NT Server computer remotely from a Windows 95 client computer?

concept link **For answers to the Instant Assessment questions see Appendix B.**

Hands-on Lab

The following Hands-on Lab provides you with a practical opportunity to apply your knowledge of Client-based Network Administration Tools.

Lab 11.19 *Installing Client-based network administration tools*

 This lab is optional because it requires that you have a copy of Windows NT Workstation and adequate space on your computer's hard drive to install it.

The purpose of this lab is to give you hands-on experience in installing Client-based Network Administration Tools on a Windows NT Workstation computer.

In order to install Windows NT Workstation on your Windows NT Server computer, your computer must have 117MB of available hard disk space. In addition, before you can install and run Client-based Network Administration Tools on your computer, you will need an additional 2.5MB of available hard disk space on the boot partition.

This lab consists of two parts:

Part 1: Installing Windows NT Workstation on your Windows NT Server computer

Part 2: Installing Client-based Network Administration Tools

Follow the steps below carefully.

Part 1: Installing Windows NT Workstation on your Windows NT Server computer

Place the Windows NT Workstation compact disc in your CD-ROM drive. You will need one blank, 3.5-inch high-density floppy disk for this lab.

PRE-COPY PHASE

1. Boot your computer to Windows NT Server. Log on as Administrator.
2. Select Start ⇒ Programs ⇒ Command Prompt.
3. At the command prompt, change the default drive to your CD-ROM drive by typing in the CD-ROM drive letter followed by a colon (for example, **D:**). Then press Enter.
4. Type **cd I386**, and then press Enter.

5. Type **winnt32 /b**, then press Enter. (This command performs the installation without creating the Setup Boot Disk set.)

6. The Windows NT 4.00 Upgrade/Installation dialog box appears. Click Continue to accept the default path for the location of your Windows NT files.

7. The Installation program copies files to your hard disk. (This process takes a few minutes.)

8. When Setup displays the Windows NT 4.00 Installation/Upgrade dialog box, click Restart Computer and continue the installation.

PHASE 0

1. After a couple of minutes, the Windows NT Workstation Setup screen appears, welcoming you to Setup. Press Enter to set up Windows NT now.

2. Setup displays a screen indicating any mass storage devices, such as SCSI adapters, CD-ROM drives, and so on. Some older IDE controllers are not displayed here, but they will still function and be recognized by NT. Specify additional devices by making changes on this screen if you need to. When you have completed all necessary changes, press Enter to continue.

3. The Windows NT Licensing Agreement screen appears. Read the licensing agreement, pressing PgDn to view additional screens. When you reach the bottom of the agreement, press F8 to continue setup.

4. Setup displays a screen indicating your computer's hardware and software components. Make any changes necessary. When you are finished, highlight "The above list matches my computer" and press Enter.

5. If you have a previous version of Microsoft Windows installed on your computer, Setup displays a screen indicating that it has found a previous version. If this screen appears, press N to install Windows NT Workstation in a different directory.

6. Setup displays a screen listing your computer's hard disk partitions. Highlight the partition on which you want to install Windows NT Workstation, then press Enter. (Make sure the partition you choose has at least 117MB free.)

7. Setup asks you to select the type of file system you want on this partition. Highlight "Leave the current file system intact <no changes>," and press Enter.

8. Setup displays a location where it will install the NT Workstation files. In the highlighted area, edit the text so that it reads: **\WINNTWKS**. (Don't type the period at the end.) Then press Enter.

9. Setup offers to examine your computer's hard disk for corruption. Press Enter to allow this. (This takes a few minutes.)

10. Setup displays a screen indicating that this portion of Setup is complete. If you have a floppy disk inserted in drive A:, remove it now. Then press Enter to restart your computer and to continue with setup.

PHASE 1

1. After your computer reboots, the Windows NT Workstation Setup dialog box appears. Click Next to continue.

2. A Setup Options screen appears. Select Custom. Click Next to continue.

3. Type in your name, press Tab, and then type in the name of your organization. Click Next to continue.

4. Type in the ten-digit CD key number from the back of your Windows NT Workstation compact disc case (press Tab after you type the first three digits). Click Next to continue.

5. When Setup prompts you to type in a computer name, type **NTW40**. Click Next to continue.

6. Type **password** when Setup prompts you to enter an administrator password. Press Tab. Confirm the password by retyping it. Click Next to continue.

7. Setup asks you if you want to create an Emergency Repair Disk. Accept the Yes default. Click Next to continue.

8. Setup displays a screen indicating you are to Select Components. Add any components that you want to install, but do *not* deselect any components that are selected by default. Click Next to continue.

PHASE 2

1. Setup displays a screen indicating that Phase 2, Installing Windows NT Networking, is about to begin. Click Next to continue.

2. Select "This computer will participate on a network." Then click the check box next to "Wired to the network." (It's OK to select these options even if you don't have a network adapter in your computer.) Click Next to continue.

3. Setup displays the Network Adapters box. If you have a network adapter, click Start Search. Your network adapter should appear in the Network Adapters window. If your network adapter did not appear, or if you do not have a network adapter in your computer, click Select from list. If your network adapter is shown in the list, highlight it and click OK. If your network adapter is not on the list, and you have a driver disk from its

manufacturer, highlight any network adapter and click Have Disk. Setup then prompts you to insert this disk. Do so and click OK. Highlight your network adapter from the list and click OK. If you do not have a network adapter, highlight MS Loopback Adapter and click OK. You should now have either the MS Loopback Adapter or your network adapter displayed in the Network Adapters box. Click Next to continue.

4. Setup displays the Network Protocols list box. Accept the default selection of TCP/IP Protocol. Click Next to continue.

5. Setup displays the Network Services list box. Accept all of the defaults selected in this list box. Click Next to continue.

6. Click Next to continue and to have Setup install the selected components.

7. Setup prompts you to enter your network adapter card settings. (This screen may not appear for some network adapters.) Verify that the settings shown match the ones that you used when you installed and configured your network adapter. Make changes only as needed. Click Continue.

8. A TCP/IP Setup warning screen appears. If you are on a network that has a DHCP server, click Yes. Otherwise, click No.

9. The Microsoft TCP/IP Properties dialog box eventually appears if you clicked No in the previous step. *If you are on a network that uses TCP/IP, or if you are connected to the Internet, obtain an IP address, subnet mask, and default gateway from your network administrator.* Otherwise, type an IP address of **192.168.59.5** and a subnet mask of **255.255.255.0**.

caution **Do *not* use this IP address if you are on a network that uses TCP/IP, or if you are connected to the Internet.**

10. Leave the Default Gateway blank. Click OK to continue.

11. Setup displays a screen showing network binding information. Click Next to continue.

12. Click Next to start the network.

13. Setup displays a screen asking you to choose whether your computer will participate in a workgroup or domain configuration. Accept the default selection of Workgroup, and the default workgroup name WORKGROUP. Click Next to continue.

PHASE 3

1. Click Finish to continue the setup process.

2. In the drop-down list box under the Time Zone tab, highlight and click your time zone. As an option, you may also click the Date & Time tab and set the correct date and time. Click Close to continue when you are finished.

3. Setup displays a screen indicating that it has found your video display adapter. Click OK in the Detected Display dialog box to continue.

4. Adjust the display settings to suit your preferences. Click Test. The Testing Mode dialog box appears. Click OK to test. When the Testing Mode dialog box reappears, click Yes if you saw the test bitmap. When the Display Settings dialog box appears, click OK to continue. Click OK in the Display Properties dialog box to complete the installation. (This takes a few minutes.)

5. When prompted, label and insert a blank 3.5-inch floppy disk into drive A:. Setup formats this disk and makes it into your Emergency Repair Disk. Click OK to continue. (This takes a couple of minutes.)

6. Setup displays a window indicating that Windows NT 4.0 is successfully installed. Remove your newly created Emergency Repair Disk from drive A: (and save it for future use). Also remove the compact disc from your CD-ROM drive. Then click Restart Computer to reboot and start Windows NT Workstation. The setup is complete.

Part 2: Installing Client–based Network Administration Tools

1. Boot your computer to Windows NT Workstation. Log on as Administrator. Place your Windows NT Server 4.0 compact disc in your CD-ROM drive.

2. Select Start ⇒ Programs ⇒ Windows NT Explorer.

3. In the Exploring dialog box, click the + sign next to your CD-ROM drive. Under your CD-ROM drive, click the + sign next to the `Clients` folder. Click the + sign next to the `Srvtools` folder. Highlight the `Winnt` folder.

4. In the Contents of 'Winnt' section in the right-hand window, double-click `Setup.bat`.

5. A window appears, indicating that the Client-based Network Administration Tools are being installed. When you are prompted to press any key to continue, do so.

6. The Exploring dialog box reappears. The Client-based Network Administration Tools are now installed. Continue to Step 7 to create icons for the various tools.

7. In the Exploring dialog box, click the + sign next to the drive on your computer on which you originally installed Windows NT Workstation (if it is not already expanded). Normally, this is the C: drive. Click the + sign next to the `Winntwks` folder. Click the + sign next to the `Profiles` folder.

Click the + sign next to the `All Users` folder. Click the + sign next to the `Start Menu` folder. Click the + sign next to the `Programs` folder. Highlight the `Administrative Tools (Common)` folder.

8. Select File ⇒ New ⇒ Shortcut.

9. In the Create Shortcut dialog box, type **c:\winntwks\system32\usrmgr.exe** in the Command line text box. (If you installed Windows NT Workstation on a different drive than C:, substitute the correct drive letter in this path.) Click the Next command button.

10. In the Select a Title for the Program dialog box, type **User Manager for Domains** in the Select a name for the shortcut text box. Click the Finish command button.

11. The Exploring dialog box reappears. Select File ⇒ New ⇒ Shortcut.

12. In the Create Shortcut dialog box, type **c:\winntwks\system32\srvmgr.exe** in the Command line text box. (If you installed Windows NT Workstation on a different drive than C:, substitute the correct drive letter in this path.) Click the Next command button.

13. In the Select A Title For The Program dialog box, type **Server Manager** in the Select a name for the shortcut text box. Click the Finish command button.

14. The Exploring dialog box reappears. Select File ⇒ New ⇒ Shortcut.

15. In the Create Shortcut dialog box, type **c:\winntwks\system32\poledit.exe** in the Command line text box. (If you installed Windows NT Workstation on a different drive than C:, substitute the correct drive letter in this path.) Click the Next command button.

16. In the Select a Title for the Program dialog box, type **System Policy Editor** in the Select a name for the shortcut text box. Click the Finish command button.

17. The Exploring dialog box reappears. Notice the three shortcuts you have just created are listed in the Contents of 'Administrative Tools (Common).' Exit Windows NT Explorer. The icons you have just created will now appear in the Start ⇒ Programs ⇒ Administrative Tools (Common) menu.

The Client-based Network Administration Tools are now installed on your computer and are available for use.

Sharing and Securing File Systems

About Chapter 12

This chapter focuses on sharing and securing files and folders on a network. After some introductory information about file and folder attributes, we'll get right to the nitty-gritty of sharing folders. You'll learn how to share a folder and how to modify a share. Share permissions are explained, including how to assign them, and how user and group permissions combine.

Next, we explore NTFS permissions. You'll learn how to assign NTFS permissions to files and folders; how NTFS permissions are applied to new, moved, and copied files and folders; and how NTFS and share permissions interact.

Then this chapter presents tips for planning a strategy for sharing and securing your network resources. Finally, we discuss auditing files and folders on NTFS partitions, and tips for troubleshooting common resource access and permission problems.

This chapter includes a Critical Thinking Lab and two Hands-on Labs. You'll have an opportunity, in these labs, to troubleshoot common resource access and permission problems, plan and implement a strategy for sharing and securing resources, and establish file and folder auditing.

The material presented in Chapter 12 maps to the "Manage disk resources" and "Choose the appropriate course of action to take to resolve resource access problems and permission problems" objectives listed in the Managing Resources and Troubleshooting sections in the Preparation Guide for the Server exam.

MANAGING FILE AND FOLDER ATTRIBUTES

Windows NT files and folders have various *attributes*, some of which the administrator can use to provide a limited amount of data protection. For example, administrators often use the read-only file attribute to prevent accidental deletion of files, such as application files. Other file and folder attributes are applied by Windows NT system files automatically during installation.

File attributes can be used on both FAT and NTFS partitions, with the exception of the Compress attribute, which is only available on NTFS partitions.

Table 12-1 lists and describes the five Windows NT file and folder attributes.

TABLE 12-1 WINDOWS NT FILE AND FOLDER ATTRIBUTES

ATTRIBUTE	DESCRIPTION
Archive	Indicates that the file or folder has been modified since the last backup. Is applied by the operating system when a file or folder is saved or created, and is commonly removed by backup programs after the file or folder has been backed up. Is normally not changed by the administrator.
Compress	Indicates that Windows NT has compressed the file or folder. Is only available on NTFS partitions. Uses the same compression algorithm as the MS–DOS 6.0 DoubleSpace utility. Can be set on individual files. Is applied by administrators to control which files and folders will be compressed.
Hidden	Indicates that the file or folder can't be seen in a normal directory scan. Files or folders with this attribute can't be copied or deleted. Is applied to various files and folders by NT automatically during installation.
Read-only	Indicates that the file or folder can only be read. It can't be written to or deleted. Is often applied by administrators to prevent accidental deletion of application files.
System	Indicates that the file or folder is used by the operating system. Files or folders with this attribute can't be seen in a normal directory scan. Files or folders with this attribute can't be copied or deleted. Is applied to various files and folders by NT automatically during installation.

Any user who can access a file or folder on a FAT partition can modify that file or folder's attributes. Any user who has the Write (W) NTFS permission (or any permission that includes the Write (W) permission) to a file or folder on an NTFS partition can modify that file or folder's attributes. (NTFS permissions are covered later in this chapter.)

On NTFS volumes, when a file or folder has the Read-only attribute, and the file or folder also has the Write (W) NTFS permission for a user or group, the Read-only attribute takes precedence. The Read-only attribute must be removed before the file can be modified or deleted. The next section describes how to change file or folder attributes, and how to assign file or folder attributes.

TO CHANGE OR ASSIGN FILE OR FOLDER ATTRIBUTES, FOLLOW THESE STEPS:

1. Select Start ⇒ Programs ⇒ Windows NT Explorer.

2. In the Exploring dialog box, highlight the file or folder on which you want to change attributes or to which you want to assign attributes.

3. Select File ⇒ Properties. (Or, you can right-click the file or folder, and select Properties from the menu that appears.)

4. The *File_name* or *Folder_name* Properties dialog box appears, as shown in Figure 12-1. Notice the System attribute is grayed out and can't be changed using this interface. Also notice the four attributes that are available: Read-only, Archive, Compress, and Hidden.

FIGURE 12-1   Setting file or folder attributes

5. Select the check boxes next to the attributes you want to assign. (Or, clear the check boxes next to attributes you want to remove.) Click OK.

6. Exit Windows NT Explorer.

Managing Shared Folders

In Windows NT, folders are *shared* to enable users to access network resources. A folder can't be accessed by users across the network until it is shared or placed within another folder that is shared. Once a folder is shared, users with the appropriate permissions can access the shared folder (and all folders and files that the shared folder contains) over the network.

A shared folder appears in Windows NT Explorer and My Computer as a folder with a hand under it. A shared folder is often referred to as a *share*.

Only members of the Administrators, Server Operators, and Power Users built-in local groups can share folders.

The following sections discuss how to share a folder, shared folder permissions and how to assign them, how to modify a share, how to stop sharing a folder, and administrative shares and how to prevent their automatic creation by Windows NT.

Sharing a Folder

Only certain users can share folders. Members of the Administrators local group can share folders on any Windows NT computer; members of the Server Operators group can share folders on all Windows NT domain controllers; and members of the Power Users group can share folders on all Windows NT non-domain controllers, including Windows NT Workstation computers.

When a folder is shared, its *entire contents* (including all files and subfolders) are available to users who have the appropriate permissions to the share. Because all files and subfolders are accessible when a folder is shared, you should consider which groups and users need access to folders when you design your server's folder structure.

When sharing a folder, it's a good idea to assign it a share name that is easily recognized by users, and one that appropriately describes the resources contained in the folder. Otherwise, users can become frustrated trying to find the specific network resources they need.

Additionally, keep in mind when you assign a name to a shared folder that a long share name may *not* be readable by all client computers on your network. MS-DOS computers, for example, can only read share names up to eight characters (plus a three-character extension), and Windows 95 computers can only read share names up to 12 characters. Share names in Windows NT can be as long as 80 characters.

You can use either Windows NT Explorer or Server Manager to share folders.

The next sections explain the steps involved in sharing a folder, first by using Windows NT Explorer, and then by using Server Manager.

 note **You can use Windows NT Explorer to share folders only on the local computer; however, you can use Server Manager to share folders both locally and on remote computers.**

TO SHARE A FOLDER USING WINDOWS NT EXPLORER, FOLLOW THESE STEPS:

1. Select Start ⇒ Programs ⇒ Windows NT Explorer.

2. In the Exploring dialog box, highlight the folder you want to share. Select File ⇒ Properties. (Or, right-click the folder and select Sharing from the menu that appears. Skip to Step 4.)

3. In the *Folder_name* Properties dialog box, click the Sharing tab.

4. On the Sharing tab, select the option button next to Shared As. Either accept the default name in the Share Name text box or type in the name you want to use for the share. Figure 12-2 shows the Sharing tab in the Data Properties dialog box. Note that the option button next to Shared As is selected.

FIGURE 12-2   Using Windows NT Explorer to share a folder

You can add a descriptive comment about the share in the Comment text box if you so choose. (This is an optional setting.)

If you want to limit the number of users who can connect to this share simultaneously (because of licensing limitations and such) you can configure the User Limit section on the Sharing tab. The default User Limit setting is Maximum Allowed.

Click OK.

5. The Exploring dialog box reappears. A hand appears under the folder you shared, indicating that it is a shared folder. Exit Windows NT Explorer.

TO SHARE A FOLDER USING SERVER MANAGER, FOLLOW THESE STEPS:

1. Select Start ⇒ Programs ⇒ Administrative Tools (Common) ⇒ Server Manager.

2. In the Server Manager dialog box, highlight the computer that contains the folder you want to share. Select Computer ⇒ Shared Directories.

3. In the Shared Directories dialog box, click the New Share command button.

4. The New Share dialog box appears, as shown in Figure 12-3. Notice the various configuration options in the dialog box.

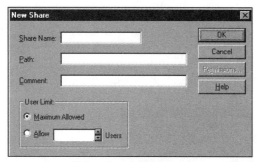

FIGURE 12-3   **Using Server Manager
to share a folder**

In the Share Name text box, type in the name you want to assign to the new share. Then, in the Path text box, type in the full path to the share, in the form of *Drive_letter*:*Folder**subfolder*\\... For example, to share the CD-ROM drive on a remote Windows NT computer that uses E: as the drive letter, you would type **E:** in the Path text box.

You can enter a descriptive comment about the share in the Comment text box if you so choose. If you want to limit the number of users that can connect to this share simultaneously you can configure the User Limit section. Click OK.

5. The new share appears (with a hand under it) in the Shared Directories dialog box. Click the Close command button.

6. Exit Server Manager.

If you want to restrict user access to the folders that you have shared, you can assign shared folder permissions.

Shared Folder Permissions

Shared folder permissions control user access to shared folders. Shared folder permissions only apply when users connect to the folder over the network — they do not apply when users access the folder from the local computer.

Shared folder permissions (commonly called *share permissions*) apply to the shared folder, its files, and subfolders (in other words, to the *entire* directory tree under the shared folder).

Share permissions are the only folder and file security available on a FAT partition (with the exception of file attributes), and control only over-the-network access to the share — local access is totally unrestricted on a FAT partition.

Table 12-2 lists and describes the Windows NT share permissions, from the most restrictive to the least restrictive.

Share permissions are assigned by adding a user or group to the permissions list for the share. From an administrative standpoint, it's much more efficient to add groups to the permissions list for a particular share than to add individual users. By default, the Everyone group is granted the Full Control permission to all newly created shared folders.

When assigning permissions to a share, you should consider assigning the most restrictive permission that still allows users to accomplish the tasks they need to perform. For example, on shares that contain applications, consider assigning the Read permission so that users can't accidentally delete application files.

TABLE 12-2 WINDOWS NT SHARE PERMISSIONS

PERMISSION	DESCRIPTION
No Access	Permits a user to connect to a share only, but prevents a user from accessing the shared folder and its contents.
Read	Permits a user to view file and folder names. Permits a user to change current folder to a subfolder of the share. Permits a user to view data in files; and to run application files.
Change	Permits a user to perform all tasks included in the Read permission. Permits a user to create files and folders within the share; to edit data files and save changes; and to delete files and folders within the share.
Full Control	Permits a user to perform all tasks included in the Change permission. Permits a user to change NTFS permissions (discussed later in this chapter) – this only applies to shares on NTFS partitions; and Permits a user to take ownership of files and folders – this only applies to shares on NTFS partitions.

You can assign share permissions by using Windows NT Explorer or Server Manager. The next section explains how to assign share permissions using Windows NT Explorer.

TO ASSIGN SHARE PERMISSIONS BY USING WINDOWS NT EXPLORER, FOLLOW THESE STEPS:

1. Select Start ⇒ Programs ⇒ Windows NT Explorer.

2. In the Exploring dialog box, highlight the shared folder to which you want to assign permissions. Select File ⇒ Properties.

3. In the *Folder_name* Properties dialog box, click the Sharing tab.

4. On the Sharing tab, click the Permissions command button.

5. The Access Through Share Permissions dialog box appears, as shown in Figure 12-4. Notice that, by default, the Everyone group has Full Control. Click the Add command button.

FIGURE 12-4 Assigning share permissions

6. The Add Users and Groups dialog box appears, as shown in Figure 12-5. Notice that only group names from the WEST domain appear in the Names list box.

FIGURE 12-5 Adding users and groups to the permissions list for the share

If you want to add global groups and users from other trusted domains, click the arrow in the List Names From drop-down list box and select the domain you want. If you want to add individual users, click the Show Users command button. Double-click the group or user you want to add to the permissions list for the share. Then select the appropriate permission from the Type of Access drop-down list box. Click OK.

7. In the Access Through Share Permissions dialog box, highlight any users or groups you want to remove from the permissions list for the share. Click the Remove command button.

(Once you have assigned the appropriate user and groups to the permissions list for the share, I recommend you remove the Everyone group from the list, so that only authorized users can access the share.) Click OK.

8. Click OK in the *Folder_name* Properties dialog box.

9. Exit Windows NT Explorer.

in the real world If you share folders on a FAT partition, I recommend you assign appropriate share permissions. However, if you share folders on an NTFS partition, I recommend you assign the Domain Users group the Full Control share permission, delete the Everyone group's Full Control share permission, and then manage security by assigning the appropriate NTFS permissions (covered later in this chapter).

How user and group permissions combine

It is not uncommon for a user to have permission to a share and to be a member of multiple groups that have different permissions to that share. When this occurs, the user and group permissions are additive, and the *least* restrictive permission is the user's effective permission. For example, a user has the Read permission to a share, and a group that the user is a member of has the Change permission to the share. The user's effective share permission is Change.

The exception to this rule is the No Access permission. *No Access always overrides all other share permissions.* If a user has the Full Control permission, but is a member of a group that has the No Access permission, the user's effective permission is No Access. *No Access always means no access.*

Here are two examples that illustrate how user and group share permissions combine.

Example 1   A user, RomanB, manages a shared folder named SalesData that contains Sales Department data. RomanB is a member of three groups. Table 12-3 shows the SalesData share permissions assigned to RomanB and to the three groups of which he is a member.

USER OR GROUP	*SalesData* **SHARE PERMISSION ASSIGNED**
RomanB	Full Control
Sales	Change
Everyone	Read
Domain Users	Read

TABLE 12-3 ROMANB'S GROUP MEMBERSHIPS AND SHARE PERMISSIONS

Because share permissions are additive, RomanB's effective permission to the `SalesData` share is Full Control.

Example 2   Until recently, a user, PennyL, was a design analyst in the Marketing Department. She has just been promoted to a management position in the Human Resources Department. PennyL's network has a shared folder named `HRData` that contains Human Resources Department data, including employee performance reviews. PennyL is a member of three groups. Table 12-4 shows the `HRData` share permissions assigned to the three groups of which PennyL is a member.

GROUP	*HRData* **SHARE PERMISSION ASSIGNED**
Managers	Read
HR	Change
Marketing	No Access

TABLE 12-4 PENNYL'S GROUP MEMBERSHIPS AND THEIR HRDATA SHARE PERMISSIONS

Because the No Access permission always overrides all other share permissions, PennyL's effective permission to the `HRData` share is No Access. The administrator should remove PennyL from the Marketing group so that she can access the `HRData` share.

Modifying a Share

After a share is created, you may want to modify its properties. You can assign multiple share names to a share, change the name of a share, or stop sharing a share.

Assigning multiple share names to a share

To aid different users in locating or recognizing a share, you can assign multiple names to the same share.

For example, a group of technical support engineers might routinely access a share called CIM (CompuServe Information Manager), and less technical personnel at a help desk might access this same share using the name CompuServe.

When you assign an additional name to a share, you can assign a new set of share permissions that apply only to the new share name.

TO ASSIGN AN ADDITIONAL NAME TO A SHARE, FOLLOW THESE STEPS:

1. Select Start ⇒ Programs ⇒ Windows NT Explorer.
2. In the Exploring dialog box, highlight the share to which you want to assign an additional name. Select File ⇒ Properties.
3. In the *Folder_name* Properties dialog box, click the Sharing tab.
4. On the Sharing tab, click the New Share command button.
5. In the New Share dialog box, type in the additional name you want to assign to the share. Type in a descriptive comment if you so choose. Configure the share permissions and user limit as desired. Click OK.
6. In the *Folder_name* Properties dialog box, click OK.
7. Exit Windows NT Explorer.

Changing a share name

Occasionally, you may need to change a share name. Perhaps you want to assign a more intuitive share name for users, or you might need to comply with a newly established set of naming conventions.

TO CHANGE A SHARE NAME, FOLLOW THESE STEPS:

1. Select Start ⇒ Programs ⇒ Windows NT Explorer.

2. In the Exploring dialog box, highlight the share with the name you want to change. Select File ⇒ Properties.

3. In the *Folder_name* Properties dialog box, click the Sharing tab.

4. On the Sharing tab, click the New Share command button.

5. In the New Share dialog box, type a new name for the share in the Share Name text box. You should configure the share permissions and user limit to match those assigned to the original share name (assuming no permission or user limit changes are desired). Click OK when you are finished.

6. The *Folder_name* Properties dialog box reappears. Click the arrow in the Share Name drop-down list box to display all names assigned to the share. Figure 12-6 shows the Sharing tab in the Data Properties dialog box. Notice that two names are assigned to the Data folder: Data and Spreadsheets. (In this example, the Data share is being renamed as Spreadsheets because it is a more intuitive name for users to recognize.)

FIGURE 12-6 Changing the name of a share

Select the original name (not the new name) of the share in the Share Name drop-down list box. Click the Remove Share command button. (This deletes the original share.) Click OK.

7. Exit Windows NT Explorer.

How to stop sharing a folder

You might decide to stop sharing a folder because it is no longer needed, or for other reasons.

TO STOP SHARING A FOLDER, FOLLOW THESE STEPS:

1. Select Start ⇒ Programs ⇒ Windows NT Explorer.

2. In the Exploring dialog box, highlight the share you want to stop sharing. Select File ⇒ Properties.

3. In the *Folder_name* Properties dialog box, click the Sharing tab.

4. On the Sharing tab, select the option button next to Not Shared. Then click OK.

5. Exit Windows NT Explorer.

Administrative Shares

Every time you start Windows NT on a computer, NT automatically creates several hidden shares that only members of the Administrators group have permission to access. These shares are referred to as *administrative shares* because they are used by Administrators to perform administrative tasks.

The Windows NT administrative shares are: C$, D$, E$, and so on (one share for the root of each hard disk partition on the computer); and a share named Admin$, which corresponds to the folder in which NT is installed (<*winntroot*>). The $ at the end of each administrative share causes the share to be hidden from users when they browse the network.

Administrative shares make it possible for an Administrator to connect to any hard drive on a computer and access all of its files and folders, regardless of whether regular shares exist on that hard drive. In this way an Administrator can perform back up, restore, and other administrative functions on a Windows NT computer.

Any share can be configured as a hidden share by placing a $ at the end of its share name. However, hiding a share by appending a $ to the share name does *not* limit user access to the share. The hidden share retains its assigned share permissions. Only access to the hidden *administrative* shares is restricted, by default, to Administrators only.

If you do not want administrative shares available on a Windows NT computer, you can configure NT to prevent the creation of administrative shares.

Preventing the creation of administrative shares

To configure Windows NT so it does not automatically create administrative shares each time it is started, you can edit the Registry. You can edit the Registry directly using `regedt32.exe`, or you can use the System Policy Editor to turn off the default administrative shares. The steps below explain how to turn off administrative shares by using the Registry editor, `regedt32.exe`.

TO PREVENT THE AUTOMATIC CREATION OF ADMINISTRATIVE SHARES, FOLLOW THESE STEPS:

1. Select Start ⇒ Run.

2. In the Open text box, type **Regedt32**. (Don't type the period at the end.)

3. In the Registry Editor dialog box, select Window ⇒ HKEY_LOCAL_MACHINE on Local Machine.

4. Double-click the `System` folder under HKEY_LOCAL_MACHINE. Double-click the `CurrentControlSet` folder. Double-click the `Services` folder. Double-click the `LanmanServer` folder, then click the `Parameters` folder.

5. In the window on the right-hand side of the dialog box, double-click AutoShareServer. (If this value is not present, select Edit ⇒ Add Value. In the Add Value dialog box, type **AutoShareServer** in the Value Name text box. In the Data Type drop-down list box, select REG_DWORD. Click OK.)

6. In the DWORD Editor dialog box, edit the Data text box so that it has a value of **0** (zero). Click OK.

7. The Registry Editor dialog box reappears. The AutoShareServer REG_DWORD setting is changed to 0. Exit Registry Editor.

MANAGING NTFS FILE AND FOLDER SECURITY

When files and folders are stored on an NTFS volume, NTFS permissions can be assigned to provide a greater level of security than share permissions, because

o NTFS permissions, unlike share permissions, can be assigned to individual files as well as folders. This gives an administrator a much finer level of control over shared files and folders than is possible by using only share permissions.

o NTFS permissions apply to local users as well as to users who connect to a shared folder over the network. This fills the large security loophole left when files and folders on FAT partitions are secured only by share permissions.

The following sections discuss NTFS permissions, including how they are assigned to files and folders, how NTFS permissions are applied, and how NTFS and share permissions interact.

NTFS Permissions

NTFS permissions, which can only be assigned to files and folders on NTFS volumes, protect data from authorized access when users connect to the share locally or over the network.

The NTFS permissions that can be assigned, and how each permission applies to folders and files, are shown in Table 12-5.

To make the assignment of NTFS permissions easier, Microsoft has created a set of standard directory (folder) permissions and a set of standard file permissions. These *standard permissions* consist of the most commonly used combinations of NTFS permissions.

Standard permissions are used in most situations. Individual NTFS permissions are typically only used when a unique combination of permissions must be assigned. The individual NTFS permissions are sometimes referred to as *Special Access Directory permissions* and *Special Access File permissions*.

Table 12-6 shows the standard NTFS directory permissions. The permissions specified within the first set of parentheses following the permission name apply to the *folder*, and the permissions specified within the second set of parentheses following the permission name apply to *files* within the folder.

TABLE 12-5 WINDOWS NT NTFS PERMISSIONS		
PERMISSION	*WHEN APPLIED TO A FOLDER,* *A USER IS ABLE TO...*	*WHEN APPLIED TO A FILE,* *AS USER IS ABLE TO...*
Read (R)	View folder attributes, permissions, and owner; view names of files and subfolders.	View file attributes, permissions, owner, and file contents.
Write (W)	View folder attributes, permissions, and owner; change folder attributes; add files and subfolders.	View file attributes, permissions, and owner; change file attributes; change file contents.
Execute (X)	View folder attributes, permissions, and owner; change the current folder to a subfolder.	View file attributes, permissions, and owner; run the file if it is an executable program.
Delete (D)	Delete the folder.	Delete the file.
Change Permissions (P)	Assign NTFS permissions to the folder.	Assign NTFS permissions to the file.
Take Ownership (O)	Take ownership of the folder	Take ownership of the file.

Table 12-7 shows the standard NTFS file permissions. NTFS file permissions apply only to the individual file they are assigned to. Other files in the same folder are *not* affected.

Sometimes a user has a different set of NTFS permissions to a file than to the folder that contains the file. When the user wants to access a file, and the NTFS file and folder permissions conflict, the file permissions are applied. *File permissions take precedence over folder permissions.* For example, if a user has the Change (RWXD) (RWXD) permission to the folder, and has the Read (RX) permission to the file, the user's effective permission to the file is Read (RX).

If a user has permission to access a file, but does *not* have permission to access the folder that contains the file, the user can access the file by typing the file's full path name (in an application, in the Run dialog box, or at the command prompt). The user can't see the file when browsing in Windows NT Explorer.

TABLE 12-6 STANDARD NTFS DIRECTORY (FOLDER) PERMISSIONS

STANDARD PERMISSION	DESCRIPTION
No Access (None) (None)	Prevents access to the folder, and to any file in the folder. When the permission is initially assigned, the administrator can choose whether to apply the permission to existing files and subfolders.
List (RX) (Not Specified)	Assigns the Read and Execute permissions to the folder, but no permissions are assigned to any files in the folder.
Read (RX) (RX)	Assigns the Read and Execute permissions to the folder and to *new* files created in the folder. When the permission is initially assigned, the administrator can choose whether to apply the permission to all *existing* files and subfolders.
Add (WX) (Not Specified)	Assigns the Write and Execute permissions to the folder, but no permissions are assigned to any files in the folder.
Add & Read (RWX) (RX)	Assigns the Read, Write, and Execute permissions to the folder, and assigns the Read and Execute permissions to *new* files created in the folder. When the permission is initially assigned, the administrator can choose whether to apply the permission to all *existing* files and subfolders.
Change (RWXD) (RWXD)	Assigns the Read, Write, Execute, and Delete permissions to the folder and to *new* files created in the folder. When the permission is initially assigned, the administrator can choose whether to apply the permission to all *existing* files and subfolders.
Full Control (All) (All)	Assigns all NTFS permissions (Read, Write, Execute, Delete, Change Permissions, and Take Ownership) to the folder and to *new* files created in the folder. When the permission is initially assigned, the administrator can choose whether to apply the permission to all *existing* files and subfolders.

TABLE 12-7 STANDARD NTFS FILE PERMISSIONS

STANDARD FILE PERMISSION	DESCRIPTION
No Access (None)	Prevents access to the file.
Read (RX)	Assigns the Read and Execute permissions to the file.
Change (RWXD)	Assigns the Read, Write, Execute, and Delete permissions to the file.
Full Control (All)	Assigns all NTFS permissions (Read, Write, Execute, Delete, Change Permissions, and Take Ownership) to the file.

caution **The Full Control (All) (All) standard directory permission has a feature that you should be aware of. Because it is designed to support POSIX applications, the Full Control (All) (All) permission allows a user to delete any file in the folder,** *even if the user has the No Access (None) standard file permission to the file.* **(This is the only exception to the rule that file permissions take precedence over folder permissions.) To prevent this, I recommend that you assign all of the individual (Special Access) NTFS permissions instead of the Full Control (All) (All) standard directory permission.**

As with share permissions, it is not uncommon for a user to have one set of NTFS permissions to a file or folder, and to be a member of multiple groups that have different NTFS permissions to the file or folder. When this occurs, the user and group permissions are additive, and the *least* restrictive combination of permissions applies. The exception to this rule is the No Access permission. *No Access always overrides all other NTFS permissions.*

NTFS permissions are assigned by adding a user or group to the *access control list* (ACL) for the file or folder. From an administrative standpoint, it's much more efficient to add groups to the ACL for a particular file or folder than to add individual users. By default, the Everyone group is granted the Full Control (All) (All) NTFS permission to the root of all newly created NTFS volumes.

Assigning NTFS Permissions to Files and Folders

A user can assign NTFS permissions to a file or folder only if one or more of the following criteria are met:

- The user is the owner of the file or folder.
- The user has the Change Permissions NTFS permission to the file or folder.
- The user has the Full Control NTFS permission to the file or folder. (The Full Control permission includes the Change Permissions NTFS permission.)

The following sections explain how to assign NTFS permissions — first to a file, and second, to a folder.

TO ASSIGN NTFS PERMISSIONS TO A FILE, FOLLOW THESE STEPS:

1. Select Start ⇒ Programs ⇒ Windows NT Explorer.

2. In the Exploring dialog box, highlight the file to which you want to assign NTFS permissions. (To assign identical permissions to multiple files, highlight more than one file.) Select File ⇒ Properties.

3. The *File_name* Properties dialog box appears. Click the Security tab. On the Security tab, click the Permissions command button.

4. The File Permissions dialog box appears, as shown in Figure 12-7. Notice the complete path to the file and the owner of the file are listed.

Click the Add command button.

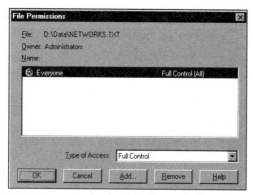

FIGURE 12-7 Assigning NTFS permissions to the Networks.txt file

5. The Add Users and Groups dialog box appears.

To add users or groups from trusted domains, click the arrow in the List Names From drop-down list box, and select the appropriate domain from the list.

To add individual users, click the Show Users command button to display individual users, as well as groups, in the Names list box.

Double-click each user and/or group you want to add to the ACL (permissions list) for the file. Select the NTFS file permission you want to assign from the Type of Access drop-down list box. Click OK.

6. The File Permissions dialog box reappears. If you want to assign individual (Special Access) NTFS file permissions (as opposed to the standard NTFS permissions):

Highlight the user(s) or group(s) to which you want to assign the individual NTFS permissions. Select Special Access from the Type of Access drop-down list box.

The Special Access dialog box appears, as shown in Figure 12-8. Notice the individual NTFS permissions that can be assigned.

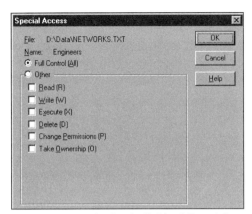

FIGURE 12-8 Assigning individual (Special Access) NTFS permissions

Select the option button next to Other. Check the check box next to the individual NTFS permission(s) you want to assign. Click OK. The File Permissions dialog box reappears.

If you want to remove any users or groups from the ACL for the file (such as the Everyone group), highlight the user or group and click the Remove command button.

Figure 12-9 shows the File Permissions dialog box after NTFS permissions have been assigned. Notice the various NTFS permissions assigned, and how they appear in the Name list box. Click OK.

FIGURE 12-9 NTFS permissions assigned to the Networks.txt file

7. In the *File_name* Properties dialog box, click OK.

8. Exit Windows NT Explorer.

TO ASSIGN NTFS PERMISSIONS TO A FOLDER, FOLLOW THESE STEPS:

1. Select Start ⇒ Programs ⇒ Windows NT Explorer.

2. In the Exploring dialog box, highlight the folder to which you want to assign NTFS permissions. (To assign identical permissions to multiple folders, highlight more than one folder.) Select File ⇒ Properties.

3. The *Folder_name* Properties dialog box appears. Click the Security tab. On the Security tab, click the Permissions command button.

4. The Directory Permissions dialog box appears, as shown in Figure 12-10. Note the two check boxes available. Also note that the check box next to Replace Permissions on Existing Files is selected by default.

Click the Add command button.

**FIGURE 12-10   Assigning NTFS permissions
to the** `D:\Data` **folder**

5. The Add Users and Groups dialog box appears. To add users or groups from trusted domains, click the arrow in the List Names From drop-down list box, and select the appropriate domain from the list.

To add individual users, click the Show Users command button to display individual users, as well as groups, in the Names list box.

Double-click each user and/or group you want to add to the ACL (permissions list) for the folder. Select the NTFS folder permission you want to assign from the Type of Access drop-down list box. Click OK.

6. The Directory Permissions dialog box reappears. If you want to assign individual (Special Access) NTFS folder permissions (as opposed to the standard NTFS permissions):

Highlight the user(s) or group(s) to which you want to assign the individual NTFS permissions. Select Special Directory Access (to assign individual *directory* [folder] permissions) or Special File Access (to assign individual *file* permissions within the folder) from the Type of Access drop-down list box.

The Special Directory Access (or Special File Access) dialog box appears. Select the option button next to Other. Then check the check box next to the individual NTFS permission(s) you want to assign. Click OK. The Directory Permissions dialog box reappears.

If you want to remove any users or groups from the ACL for the folder (such as the Everyone group), highlight the user or group and click the Remove command button.

7. In the Directory Permissions dialog box, select the check box next to Replace Permissions on Subdirectories if you want these NTFS permissions assigned to all subfolders.

Clear the check box next to Replace Permissions on Existing Files if you do *not* want these NTFS permissions assigned to each existing file within the folder.

note   **The Replace Permissions on Existing Files option is selected by default for a good reason. It can become very cumbersome for an administrator to have to manage individual file permissions. Therefore, it is a good practice to accept the default to Replace Permissions on Existing Files so that all files will have the same permissions as set on the folder. If different permissions are required, a different folder can be created.**

If both check boxes are selected, these NTFS permissions will be assigned to all files within the folder, all subfolders, and their files. If both check boxes are cleared, these NTFS permissions will be assigned only to the folder and to new files created in the folder. Existing subfolders and the files they contain will not be affected.

Figure 12-11 shows the Directory Permissions dialog box after NTFS permissions have been assigned. Notice that both check boxes are selected.

Click OK.

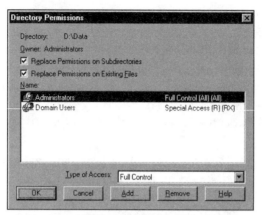

FIGURE 12-11 NTFS permissions assigned
to the D:\Data **folder**

8. If you checked the check box next to Replace Permissions on
Subdirectories, a warning message appears, asking if you want to replace
the security information on all existing subfolders. Click the Yes command
button. (If both check boxes were selected, this could take a while. You
might want to consider performing this task during nonbusiness hours.)

9. In the *Folder_name* Properties dialog box, click OK.

10. Exit Windows NT Explorer.

There are a few common administrative practices you should consider when
assigning NTFS permissions to files or folders:

- Consider assigning the most restrictive NTFS permission that still makes it
  possible for users to accomplish necessary tasks.

- After assigning the appropriate NTFS permissions, consider removing the
  Everyone group, which by default is granted the Full Control permission.

- When you want all users to be able to access a file or folder, consider
  assigning the NTFS permissions to the Domain Users group instead of to
  the Everyone group. (The Everyone group includes not only all domain
  users, but also *anyone* [authorized or not] who can access your network,
  including those who connect via the Internet.)

How NTFS Permissions Are Applied to New, Moved, and Copied Files and Folders

When files are created in a folder on an NTFS volume, the new files inherit the NTFS permissions of the folder in which they are created. For example, if you create a new file in the `Public` folder, and the `Public` folder has the Change (RWXD) (RWXD) NTFS permission for the Everyone group, the new file inherits the Change (RWXD) permission for the Everyone group.

note **The permissions in the *second* set of parentheses following the NTFS folder permission name are the permissions that are assigned to the new *file*. So, if you create a new file in the `Data` folder, and the `Data` folder has the Add & Read (RWX) (RX) NTFS permission for the Domain Users group, the file inherits the Read (RX) permission for the Domain Users group.**

When new subfolders are created on an NTFS volume, they inherit the NTFS permissions of the folder that contains them. For example, if you create a new subfolder in the `Data` folder, and the `Data` folder has the Add & Read (RWX) (RX) NTFS permission for the Everyone group, the new subfolder inherits the Add & Read (RWX) (RX) permission for the Everyone group.

When files or folders are moved or copied, their NTFS permissions often change. Normally, when files or folders are moved or copied, they inherit the NTFS permissions of the destination folder. The only exception to this rule is when files or folders are *moved* to a new folder on the *same* NTFS volume — in this case, the moved files or folders retain their original NTFS permissions.

The following examples illustrate how NTFS permissions are applied to moved or copied files:

Example 1:   Moving a file to a folder on a different volume You *move* the `D:\Public\Readme.txt` file (that has the Read (RX) NTFS permissions for the Everyone group) to the `E:\Data` folder (that has the Full Control (All) (All) NTFS permission for the Everyone group). When the file is moved to a folder on a different volume, it inherits the NTFS permissions from the `E:\Data` folder (the destination folder), so the moved file's permissions are now Full Control (All) for the Everyone group.

Example 2:   Copying a file to a different folder on the same volume You *copy* the D:\Data\Busplan.doc file (that has the Read (RX) NTFS permissions for the Managers group) to the D:\Public folder (that has the Change (RWXD) (RWXD) NTFS permissions for the Everyone group). When the file is copied, it inherits the NTFS permissions from the D:\Public folder (the destination folder), so the copied file's permissions are now Change (RWXD) for the Everyone group.

Example 3:   Moving a file to a different folder on the same volume You *move* the D:\Data\Busplan.doc file (that has the Read (RX) NTFS permissions for the Managers group) to the D:\Public folder (that has the Change (RWXD) (RWXD) NTFS permissions for the Everyone group). When the file is moved to a folder on the *same* NTFS volume, it retains its original NTFS permissions. In this case, the moved file's NTFS permissions are still Read (RX) for the Managers group.

 tip **Because FAT partitions can't support NTFS permissions, any files that you copy or move to a FAT partition lose all their NTFS permissions, along with the security that those permissions provided.**

How NTFS and Share Permissions Interact

When users access a share on an NTFS volume over the network, *both* NTFS and share permissions are used to determine the user's effective permission to the file or folder in the share.

When NTFS and share permissions differ, the *most* restrictive permission becomes the user's effective permission to the file or folder in the share. This means that if *either* the NTFS or the share permissions deny a user access, access is denied.

The following examples illustrate how NTFS and share permissions interact:

Example 1:   A folder named Documents is shared on an NTFS volume. The Documents share has the Change share permission for the Everyone group, and the files and folders in the share all have the Full Control NTFS permission for the Everyone group. Users who access the Documents share over the network only have the Change permission to the files and folders, because Change is the most restrictive permission.

Example 2: A folder named `Apps` is shared on an NTFS volume. The `Apps` share has the Full Control share permission assigned to the Everyone group, and the files and folders in the share all have the Read NTFS permission for the Everyone group. Users who access the `Apps` share over the network only have the Read permission to the files and folders, because Read is the most restrictive permission.

Remember, share permissions only apply when users connect to a shared folder *over the network*. NTFS permissions are the only permissions that apply to users who log on locally to the computer that contains the share.

PLANNING STRATEGIES FOR SHARING AND SECURING RESOURCES

There is no one right way to share and secure your network resources. However, there are several common practices that you can use when planning your network sharing-and-securing strategy. Consider using some or all of the following tips to provide security for network resources and to simplify administration.

- Assign share names that are easily recognized by users, that appropriately describe the resources contained in the share, and that are of appropriate length, so that users of all client computers can access the share.

- When assigning permissions, use groups, rather than individual users, when possible, to simplify administration.

- Consider using the Domain Users group instead of the Everyone group when assigning permissions to all users in the domain to close up the security loophole that the Everyone group allows.

- Consider storing important data on NTFS volumes instead of on FAT volumes, because of the greater security possible on NTFS volumes.

- Consider storing operating systems on a separate volume from data files, home folders, and applications. This makes backup, restore, and administration easier.

- Always store data files and application files in different folders. This helps prevent accidental deletion of application files and simplifies backup and restore procedures.

- Consider making it a practice to always assign the most restrictive permission that still allows a user to accomplish the tasks they need to perform.

- Consider assigning administrators the Full Control permission to all shares, with the exception of users' home folders (directories).

- When assigning both share and NTFS permissions, consider assigning the Full Control share permission to the Domain Users group and using the appropriate NTFS permissions to secure the resource. (After you assign the Domain Users group the Full Control share permission, you can remove the Everyone group's Full Control permission from the share.) This prevents the administrative nightmare of always having to determine the most restrictive combination of share and NTFS permissions for a given user or group to a resource.

Planning Form: Sharing and Securing Resources

You can use this form to help you plan how to apply share and/or NTFS permissions to shared resources on your network. (Find an enlarged version of this form in Appendix E.)

Resource (Include path)	Share Name	Share Permissions Applied		NTFS Permissions Applied	
		User/Group	Permission	User/Group	Permission
(Example) D:\Data\Sales	Sales Data	Domain Users (Remove the Everyone group)	Full Control	Sales Administrators	Change Full Control

TAKING OWNERSHIP OF FILES AND FOLDERS

The creator of a file or folder is its *owner* (except that when a member of the Administrators group creates a file or folder, the Administrators *group*, not the user, is the owner of the file or folder). The owner of a file or folder can always assign permissions to that file or folder. Only files and folders on NTFS partitions have owners.

Occasionally, you may need to change or assign permissions to a file or folder, but not have the Change Permissions NTFS permission (or the Full Control NTFS permission, which includes the Change Permissions NTFS permission) to the file or folder. Without being the owner of the file or folder or having the Change Permissions NTFS permission, the only way you can accomplish changing or assigning permissions to the file or folder is to *take ownership* of the file or folder.

A common situation where taking ownership becomes necessary is when a user (who created a folder and was its owner) leaves the company, and no one else has the Change Permissions NTFS permission (or the Full Control NTFS permission) to the folder. To change the permissions on the folder, the Administrator must first take ownership of it.

A user can take ownership of a file or folder only if one or more of the following criteria are met:

o The user is a member of the Administrators group.

o The user has the Take Ownership NTFS permission to the file or folder (or has the Full Control NTFS permission, which includes the Take Ownership permission).

o The user has the "Take ownership of files or other objects" user right.

The next section describes the steps involved in taking ownership of a file or folder.

TO TAKE OWNERSHIP OF A FILE OR FOLDER, FOLLOW THESE STEPS:

1. Select Start ⇒ Programs ⇒ Windows NT Explorer.

2. Highlight the file or folder that you want to take ownership of. Select File ⇒ Properties.

3. The *File_name* or *Folder_name* Properties dialog box appears. Click the Security tab.

4. On the Security tab, click the Ownership command button.

5. If you currently have no permissions to the file or folder, a warning dialog box appears, as shown in Figure 12-12. Notice that the message asks if you want to try overwriting the current owner.

Click the Yes command button.

FIGURE 12-12   Taking ownership warning message

6. The Owner dialog box appears, as shown in Figure 12-13. Note that the owner of the folder is listed as "Unable to retrieve."

Click the Take Ownership command button.

**FIGURE 12-13   Taking ownership of
                   a folder**

7. If you are taking ownership of a folder, Windows NT displays an informational dialog box, asking if you want to take ownership of all the files and subfolders contained in the selected folder. Click the Yes or No command button, as appropriate. (Yes is usually the appropriate response.)

8. If prior to taking ownership you had no permissions to the file or folder, Windows NT displays an informational dialog box, as shown in Figure 12-14. Note that you can choose to grant yourself the Full Control permission to the folder.

Click the Yes command button.

**FIGURE 12-14   Replacing folder permissions
                   while taking ownership**

9. The *File_name* or *Folder_name* Properties dialog box reappears. Click OK.

10. You are now the owner of the file or folder. Exit Windows NT Explorer.

AUDITING FILES AND FOLDERS
ON NTFS PARTITIONS

You can't be sure that your network is secure until you know that the permissions and other security measures you've put in place haven't been breached. Windows NT auditing makes it possible for you to determine whether unauthorized users have accessed or attempted to access sensitive data.

Windows NT auditing is *only* available on NTFS partitions. You can't audit files or folders that are located on FAT partitions.

Because auditing generates a large amount of data, it's important that you determine what is really necessary to audit. Not only does auditing data take up space in the Security Log, it also takes administrative time to review the events in the log. In general, if you won't use the information obtained by auditing a given event, you probably shouldn't choose to audit it.

You can choose to audit both successful and unsuccessful (failure) events. For example, you can audit all successful attempts to access a particular program, or you can audit all unsuccessful attempts to access a file that contains confidential data. Success auditing is often performed to gather information about how resources, such as programs and printers, are used. Failure auditing is normally performed to determine whether unauthorized users are attempting to access restricted files or folders. Sometimes success and failure auditing are used simultaneously to determine if any unauthorized users have been successful in breaching the system's security.

When you choose to audit a sensitive resource to determine if your network security has been compromised, consider auditing the Everyone group's success and failure access to the resource. This way, you can track *all* attempts to access the resource, not just attempts made by Domain Users (in other words, the users that you know about).

Configuring Auditing for Files and Folders on NTFS Partitions

Configuring Windows NT auditing for files and folders on NTFS partitions is a two-part process. First, the audit policy is configured in User Manager for Domains. Then, auditing is configured for each file and folder individually using Windows NT Explorer.

Only members of the Administrators group can configure the audit policy. Users with the "Manage auditing and Security Log" user right can establish file and folder auditing, and view and manage the Security Log in Event Viewer, but can't set audit policy.

Auditing is configured on an individual computer basis. If you want to audit an event that takes place on a domain controller, such as access to a particular folder, you need to set the audit policy for the domain and configure the folder for auditing on the domain controller. If you want to audit an event that takes place on a non-domain controller, such as access to a particular file, you need to set the audit policy on the non-domain controller and configure the particular file for auditing on the non-domain controller, as well.

The next sections describe how to configure audit policy in User Manager for Domains, and then how to configure file or folder auditing in Windows NT Explorer.

TO CONFIGURE AUDIT POLICY, FOLLOW THESE STEPS:

1. Select Start ⇒ Programs ⇒ Administrative Tools (Common) ⇒ User Manager for Domains.

2. In the User Manager dialog box, select Policies ⇒ Audit.

3. The Audit Policy dialog box appears, as shown in Figure 12-15. Notice that Success and Failure auditing are selected for File and Object Access.

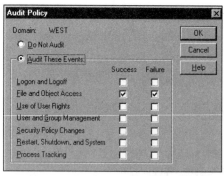

FIGURE 12-15   Configuring audit policy

You must select File and Object Access auditing to audit files and folders. If you configure file and folder auditing, but don't configure the audit policy for File and Object Access, no auditing will occur on the files and folders.

Select the option button next to Audit These Events, and check the check boxes to configure success and/or failure auditing of the events you want to audit. Click OK.

4. Exit User Manager for Domains.

TO CONFIGURE FILE OR FOLDER AUDITING, FOLLOW THESE STEPS:

1. Select Start ⇒ Programs ⇒ Windows NT Explorer.

2. In the Exploring dialog box, highlight the file or folder you want to audit. Select File ⇒ Properties.

3. In the *File_name* or *Folder_name* Properties dialog box, click the Security tab.

4. On the Security tab, click the Auditing command button.

5. In the Directory Auditing dialog box, click the Add command button.

6. The Add Users and Groups dialog box appears. If you want to audit global groups and users from other trusted domains, click the down arrow in the List Names From drop-down list box and select the domain you want. If you want to audit individual users, click the Show Users command button. Double-click each of the groups or users whose access or attempted access to this resource you want to audit. Click OK.

7. The Directory Auditing dialog box reappears. Select the Success and/or Failure check boxes next to each NTFS permission you want to track for this resource. For example, if you want to know who has viewed or attempted to view a confidential file, you could select Success and Failure auditing for the Read permission.

If you are configuring auditing for a folder, you have the option of choosing to replace the existing auditing configuration on all files and/or subfolders with the settings you are configuring now. Select or deselect the check boxes next to Replace Auditing on Subdirectories and Replace Auditing on Existing Files as desired. Figure 12-16 shows the configured Directory Auditing dialog box for the D:\New Products Research Data folder. Notice that success and failure auditing for the Read permission is configured for the Everyone group.

Click OK.

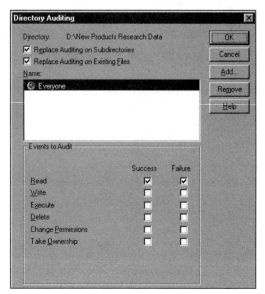

FIGURE 12-16   Configuring folder auditing

8. If you are configuring folder auditing, *and* if you selected the Replace Auditing on Subdirectories check box, a warning dialog box appears, as shown in Figure 12-17.

Click the Yes command button.

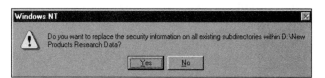

FIGURE 12-17   Replacing auditing configuration on subfolders

9. The *File_name* or *Folder_name* Properties dialog box reappears. Click OK.

10. Exit Windows NT Explorer.

Using Event Viewer to View Auditing Results

You can use Event Viewer to view the results of the auditing you have configured. Event Viewer has three logs: the System Log, the Application Log, and the Security Log. The Security Log contains the data generated by auditing.

You can view the Security Log in its entirety, or you can filter events by date and type of audit event. You can clear the Security Log when it is full; and you can save (archive) the log to be viewed at a later date by using Event Viewer, a text editor, or a spreadsheet or database program. You can also configure the size of the log and event log wrapping (how the log handles additional auditing data when it becomes full).

An important consideration, from an administrative standpoint, is scheduling time to regularly view auditing events in the Security Log. The data gathered by auditing is of no value if it is not used.

The sections that follow explain how to access the Security Log in Event Viewer and how to filter audit events, how to save (archive) and clear the Security Log, and how to configure the maximum size of the Security Log and event log wrapping.

TO ACCESS THE SECURITY LOG, AND TO FILTER AND VIEW AUDIT EVENTS, FOLLOW THESE STEPS:

1. Select Start ⇒ Programs ⇒ Administrative Tools (Common) ⇒ Event Viewer.

2. In the Event Viewer dialog box, select Log ⇒ Security. This accesses the Security Log.

Figure 12-18 shows the Security Log dialog box in Event Viewer. Notice that both success and failure events are listed. (Remember, success events are denoted by a key, and failure events are denoted by a lock in the left margin.)

Date	Time	Source	Category	Event	User	Computer
6/20/97	7:46:45 PM	Security	Object Access	562	Administrator	PDCLAB
6/20/97	7:46:45 PM	Security	Object Access	560	Administrator	PDCLAB
6/20/97	7:46:45 PM	Security	Object Access	562	Administrator	PDCLAB
6/20/97	7:46:45 PM	Security	Object Access	560	Administrator	PDCLAB
6/20/97	7:46:24 PM	Security	Privilege Use	577	SYSTEM	PDCLAB
6/20/97	7:46:24 PM	Security	System Event	515	SYSTEM	PDCLAB
6/20/97	7:46:24 PM	Security	System Event	515	SYSTEM	PDCLAB
6/20/97	7:46:24 PM	Security	Privilege Use	577	SYSTEM	PDCLAB
6/20/97	7:46:24 PM	Security	System Event	515	SYSTEM	PDCLAB
6/20/97	7:46:24 PM	Security	Privilege Use	577	SYSTEM	PDCLAB
6/20/97	7:46:24 PM	Security	Privilege Use	576	Administrator	PDCLAB
6/20/97	7:46:24 PM	Security	Logon/Logoff	528	Administrator	PDCLAB
6/20/97	7:45:47 PM	Security	Logon/Logoff	535	SYSTEM	PDCLAB
6/20/97	7:45:44 PM	Security	Logon/Logoff	529	SYSTEM	PDCLAB
6/20/97	7:45:39 PM	Security	Logon/Logoff	529	SYSTEM	PDCLAB
6/20/97	7:45:32 PM	Security	Privilege Use	577	SYSTEM	PDCLAB
6/20/97	7:45:32 PM	Security	System Event	515	SYSTEM	PDCLAB
6/20/97	7:45:20 PM	Security	Logon/Logoff	535	SYSTEM	PDCLAB
6/20/97	7:45:18 PM	Security	Logon/Logoff	529	SYSTEM	PDCLAB
6/20/97	7:45:15 PM	Security	Logon/Logoff	529	SYSTEM	PDCLAB
6/20/97	7:45:09 PM	Security	Logon/Logoff	538	Administrator	PDCLAB
6/20/97	7:44:54 PM	Security	Privilege Use	578	Administrator	PDCLAB
6/20/97	7:44:45 PM	Security	Privilege Use	578	Administrator	PDCLAB

FIGURE 12-18 Viewing the Security Log

3. To filter Security Log events by date or type of event, select View ⇒ Filter Events.

4. The Filter dialog box appears, as shown in Figure 12-19. Notice the filter configuration options available.

FIGURE 12-19   **Filtering events in the Security Log**

If you need more information on filtering events, click the Help command button. Configure filtering as desired. Click OK.

5. To view details for a specific audit event, double-click the event.

TO SAVE (ARCHIVE) AND CLEAR THE SECURITY LOG, FOLLOW THESE STEPS:

1. In Event Viewer, select Log ⇒ Clear All Events.

2. A dialog box appears, asking if you want to save the log before clearing it. Click the Yes command button to save the log.

3. The Save As dialog box appears, as shown in Figure 12-20. Notice the three types of files that you can save the log as.
If you want to view the log later by using Event Viewer, save (archive) the log as an Event Log File (*.EVT). If you want to view the log later by using a text editor, save the log as a Text File (*.TXT). If you want to export the file for analysis in a spreadsheet or database program, save the log as a Comma Delimited Text file (*.TXT)

Type in a file name for the log you are saving, then select a type of file in the "Save as type" drop-down list box. Click the Save command button.

FIGURE 12-20   Saving the Security Log

4. A dialog box appears, asking you to confirm that you want to clear the Security Log. Click the Yes command button. The log is cleared.

TO CONFIGURE THE MAXIMUM SIZE OF THE SECURITY LOG AND EVENT LOG WRAPPING, FOLLOW THESE STEPS:

1. Select Log ⇒ Log Settings in the Event Viewer dialog box.

2. The Event Log Settings dialog box appears, as shown in Figure 12-21. Notice the available event log wrapping settings. This feature determines how Event Viewer handles new audit events when the Security Log has reached its maximum size.

FIGURE 12-21   Configuring Event Log settings

Configure the maximum log size as desired. The available range for this setting is from 64KB to 4,194,176KB. The default maximum log size is 512KB.

Select one of the three event log wrapping configuration options. Click OK.

TROUBLESHOOTING COMMON RESOURCE ACCESS AND PERMISSION PROBLEMS

When a user can't access a resource (that he or she is supposed to be able to access), the administrator must determine why this is happening and correct the problem. Most resource access problems are caused by incorrectly configured and/or conflicting permissions.

Here are some recommended troubleshooting tips to help you to determine why a user can't access a shared network resource:

○ **Look for conflicting share and NTFS permissions.** Determine which groups the user is a member of (including groups in other domains), and determine the user's effective share permission and effective NTFS permissions to the resource.

○ **Look for the No Access permission.** If the user, or any group of which the user is a member, has been assigned the No Access permission to the share or has been assigned the No Access NTFS permission to the resource, the user will not be able to access the resource.

○ If you have just assigned the user permission to the resource, and the user can't access the resource, **try having the user log off and log on again**, so the user's access token will be updated.

KEY POINT SUMMARY

This chapter discussed how to share and secure file systems in a Windows NT environment.

○ The Windows NT file and folder attributes are: Archive, Compress, Hidden, Read-only, and System. The file attributes can be used on both FAT and NTFS partitions, with the exception of the Compress attribute, which is only available on NTFS partitions.

○ In Windows NT, folders are *shared* to make it possible for users to access network resources. Only members of the Administrators, Server Operators, and Power Users groups can share folders. When a folder is shared, the folder's entire contents, including all files and subfolders (in other words, the entire directory tree under the shared folder), are available to users that have the appropriate permissions to the share. You can use either Windows NT Explorer or Server Manager to share folders.

○ *Shared folder permissions* control access to shared folders. Share permissions only apply when users connect to the folder over the network — they do *not* apply when users access the folder from the local computer.

○ The Windows NT share permissions, from most restrictive to least restrictive, are: No Access, Read, Change, and Full Control. Share permissions are assigned by adding a user or group to the permissions list for the share. You can assign share permissions by using Windows NT Explorer or Server Manager.

○ It's not uncommon for a user to be a member of multiple groups that have different permissions to a share. When this occurs, the user and group permissions are additive, and the *least* restrictive permission is the user's effective permission. The exception to this rule is the No Access permission. No Access always overrides other share permissions.

○ After a share is created, you may want to modify its properties. You can assign multiple share names to it, change the name of it, or stop sharing it.

○ Every time you start Windows NT on a computer, NT automatically creates several hidden shares that only members of the Administrators group have permission to access. These shares are referred to as *administrative shares*. The Windows NT administrative shares are: C$, D$, E$, and so on (one share for the root of each hard disk partition on the computer), and Admin$ (which corresponds to the folder in which NT is installed). The $ at the end of each administrative share causes the share to be hidden from users when they browse the network. Any share can be configured as a hidden share by appending a $ to the share name, but only access to the hidden administrative shares is automatically restricted to Administrators only. If you don't want administrative shares available on a Windows NT computer, you can configure the Registry so that NT does not create these shares each time Windows NT is started.

○ When files and folders are stored on an NTFS volume, *NTFS permissions* can be assigned to provide a greater level of security than share permissions. This is because NTFS permissions can be assigned to individual files and folders, and they apply to local users as well as to users who connect to a shared folder over the network.

o The NTFS permissions are: Read (R), Write (W), Execute (E), Delete (D), Change Permissions (P), and Take Ownership (O). The individual NTFS permissions are sometimes referred to as *Special Access Directory permissions* and *Special Access File permissions*. To make the assignment of NTFS permissions easier, Microsoft has created a set of standard directory (folder) permissions and a set of standard file permissions. Standard permissions, which are combinations of the most commonly used NTFS permissions, are used in most situations.

o The standard NTFS directory (folder) permissions are: No Access (None) (None), List (RX) (Not Specified), Read (RX) (RX), Add (WX) (Not Specified), Add and Read (RWX) (RX), Change (RWXD) (RWXD), and Full Control (All) (All). The permissions specified within the first set of parentheses following the permission name apply to the *folder*, and the permissions specified within the second set of parentheses following the permission name apply to *files* within the folder.

o The standard NTFS file permissions are No Access (None), Read (RX), Change (RWXD), and Full Control (All). NTFS file permissions apply only to the individual file to which they are assigned. Other files in the same folder are not affected.

o When a user wants to access a file, and the NTFS file and folder permissions conflict, the file permissions are applied. *File permissions take precedence over folder permissions.*

o As with share permissions, user and group NTFS permissions are additive, and the *least* restrictive combination of permissions applies. The exception to this rule is the No Access permission. No Access always overrides all other NTFS permissions.

o Only a user who is the owner of the file or folder, or who has the Change Permissions or Full Control NTFS permissions, can assign NTFS permissions to the file or folder. NTFS permissions are assigned to files and folders by using Windows NT Explorer.

o When files are created in a folder on an NTFS volume, the new files inherit the NTFS permissions of the folder they are created in. When new subfolders are created on an NTFS volume, the new subfolders inherit the NTFS permissions of the folder that contains the new subfolder.

o   When files or folders are moved or copied, their NTFS permissions often change. Normally, when files or folders are moved or copied, they inherit the NTFS permissions of the destination folder. The only exception to this rule is when files or folders are *moved* to a new folder on the *same* NTFS volume — in this case, the moved files or folders retain their original NTFS permissions.

o   When NTFS and share permissions differ, the *most restrictive* permission becomes the user's effective permission to the file or folder in the share. This means that if either the NTFS or the share permissions deny a user access, access is denied.

o   The creator of a file or folder is its *owner* (except that when a member of the Administrators group creates a file or folder, the Administrators *group*, not the user, is the owner of the file or folder). Without being the owner of a file or folder or having the Change Permissions NTFS permission, the only way you can change or assign permissions to the file or folder is to *take ownership* of the file or folder.

o   A user must either be a member of the Administrators group, have the Take Ownership NTFS permission to the file or folder (or have the Full Control permission, which includes the Take Ownership permission), or have the "Take ownership of files or other objects" user right in order to take ownership of a file or folder.

o   *Windows NT auditing is available only on NTFS partitions.* Success auditing is often performed to gather information about how resources are used. Failure auditing is normally performed to determine whether unauthorized users are attempting to access restricted files or folders.

o   There are two parts involved in configuring auditing: first, the audit policy is configured in User Manager for Domains; second, auditing is configured for each file and folder individually by using Windows NT Explorer. Only members of the Administrators group can configure audit policy. When configuring audit policy, you *must* select File and Object Access auditing to audit files and folders. If you configure file and folder auditing, but don't configure the audit policy for File and Object Access, no auditing of files and folders will occur.

o You can view the results of auditing that are contained in the Security Log in Event Viewer. In Event Viewer, you can filter events by date and type, you can clear the Security Log when it is full, and you can save (archive) the log to be viewed at a later date. The size of the log and event log wrapping (how the log handles additional auditing data when it becomes full) can also be configured.

o Most resource access problems are caused by incorrectly configured and/or conflicting permissions. Some troubleshooting tips for dealing with resource access problems are:

  o Look for conflicting share and NTFS permissions. Determine which groups the user is a member of (including groups in other domains), and determine the user's effective share permission and effective NTFS permissions to the resource.

  o Look for the No Access permission.

  o If you have just assigned the user permission to the resource, and the user can't access the resource, try having the user log off and log on again.

APPLYING WHAT YOU'VE LEARNED

Now it's time to regroup, review, and apply what you've learned in this chapter.

The Instant Assessment questions bring to mind key facts and concepts. Next, the Critical Thinking Lab challenges your ability to troubleshoot common resource access and permission problems. Finally, the two Hands-on Labs reinforce what you've learned about sharing and securing file systems and allow you to practice some of the tasks tested by the Server exam.

Instant Assessment

1. What Windows NT file attribute can you use to prevent the accidental deletion of application files?

2. What Windows NT file attribute is only available on NTFS partitions?

3. On a Windows NT network, what is the purpose of sharing folders?

4. List the Windows NT share permissions — from most restrictive to least restrictive.

5. When user and group share permissions are combined, which permission always overrides all others?

6. A user, JohnZ, belongs to three groups, whose respective share permissions are Change, Read, and Full Control. What is JohnZ's effective share permission?

7. A user, PaulS, belongs to two groups, whose respective share permissions are Full Control and No Access. What is PaulS's effective share permission?

8. What are the Windows NT administrative shares?

9. How can you configure a share to be a hidden share?

10. How do NTFS permissions provide a higher level of security than share permissions?

11. List the NTFS (individual) permissions.

12. What are the standard NTFS folder permissions?

13. What are the standard NTFS file permissions?

14. When a user wants to access a file, and the NTFS file and folder permissions conflict, which permissions are applied?

15. When a file is created in a folder on an NTFS volume, what NTFS permissions does the file have?

16. Fill in the blank: Normally, when files or folders are moved or copied, they inherit the NTFS permissions of the _____ folder.

17. What NTFS permissions are applied to a file that is *moved* to a different folder on the *same* NTFS volume?

18. When NTFS and share permissions differ, which permission becomes the user's effective permission to the file or folder in the share?

19. Who is the owner of a file or folder?

20. Why would a user want to take ownership of a file or folder?

21. What are the two parts involved in configuring auditing?

22. What *must* be configured in the Audit Policy dialog box in order to audit files and folders?

23. Which Windows NT utility is used to examine the results of auditing?

24. What is the cause of most resource access problems?

T/F

25. Only members of the Administrators group can share folders.   _____

26. When a folder is shared, the folder's entire contents, including all files and subfolders (that is, the entire directory tree under the shared folder) are available to users that have the appropriate permissions to the share.   _____

27. User and group NTFS permissions, when combined, are *not* additive. _____

28. Share permissions *don't* apply when a user accesses files in a shared folder on the local computer, but NTFS permissions *do* apply when a user accesses files in a shared folder on the local computer.   _____

29. Windows NT auditing is only available on FAT partitions.   _____

concept link   **For answers to the Instant Assessment questions see Appendix B.**

Critical Thinking Lab

The following Critical Thinking Lab tests your ability to troubleshoot resource access and permission problems.

Lab 12.20 *Troubleshooting resource access and permission problems*

The purpose of this lab is to provide you with hands-on experience in troubleshooting some common resource access and permission problems.

For each problem presented, consider the troubleshooting information provided and determine:

1. The cause of the problem

2. What steps you would take to resolve the problem

Problem 1 A user, NancyY, reports that she can't save files to the `AccountingData` share located on an NTFS volume on a Windows NT computer. You begin the troubleshooting process by using User Manager for Domains and Windows NT Explorer to obtain NancyY's group memberships, and the share and NTFS permissions assigned to the `AccountingData` share.

Figure 12-22 shows the Group Memberships dialog box, which lists NancyY's group memberships.

FIGURE 12-22 Group memberships for NancyY

Figure 12-23 shows the Access Through Share Permissions dialog box, which lists the share permissions assigned to the `AccountingData` share.

FIGURE 12-23 Share permissions for
AccountingData **share**

Figure 12-24 shows the Directory Permissions dialog box. This dialog box lists the NTFS permissions assigned to the `D:\Data\Accounting` folder, which is shared as `AccountingData`.

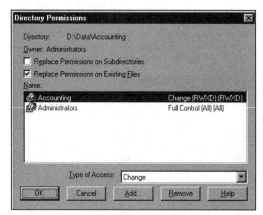

FIGURE 12-24   NTFS permissions for
AccountingData **share**

What is the cause of the problem?

What would you do to resolve the problem?

Problem 2   A user, JohnS, reports he can't access the ManagersData share
located on an NTFS volume on a Windows NT computer. You begin the troubleshooting process by using User Manager for Domains and Windows NT
Explorer to obtain JohnS's group memberships, and the share and NTFS permissions assigned to the ManagersData share.

Figure 12-25 shows the Group Memberships dialog box, which lists JohnS's
group memberships.

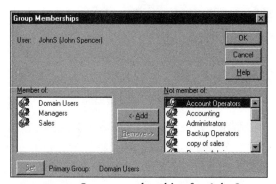

FIGURE 12-25   **Group memberships for JohnS**

Figure 12-26 shows the Access Through Share Permissions dialog box, which lists the share permissions assigned to the `ManagersData` share.

FIGURE 12-26 **Share permissions for**
ManagersData **share**

Figure 12-27 shows the Directory Permissions dialog box. This dialog box lists the NTFS permissions assigned to the `D:\Data\Managers` folder, which is shared as `ManagersData`.

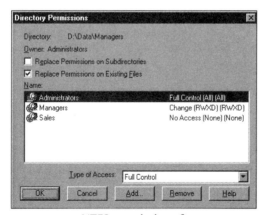

FIGURE 12-27 **NTFS permissions for**
ManagersData **share**

What is the cause of the problem?

What would you do to resolve the problem?

concept link   **For answers to the Critical Thinking Lab see Appendix B.**

Hands-on Labs

The following Hands-on Labs provide you with practical opportunities to apply the knowledge you've gained in this chapter about sharing and securing file systems.

Lab 12.21 *Sharing and securing resources*

The purpose of this lab is to provide you with hands-on experience in planning a strategy for sharing and securing resources, and in performing the tasks of sharing and securing resources in Windows NT.

This lab consists of three parts:

Part 1: Planning a strategy for sharing and securing resources

Part 2: Sharing and securing folders

Part 3: Establishing NTFS permissions

Begin this lab by booting your computer to Windows NT Server. Log on as Administrator.

Follow the ensuing steps carefully.

Part 1: Planning a strategy for sharing and securing resources

In this section, you plan a strategy for sharing and securing folders on a Windows NT Server computer given a particular scenario.

Scenario: SalesPros, Inc. is a sales organization. (It's the same company you created users and groups for in Lab 8.14). Table 12-8 shows some of SalesPros, Inc.'s employees, their user names, job titles, and respective group membership(s):

The resources to be shared are located on two partitions on a Windows NT Server computer. The C: drive is a FAT partition that contains applications, and the D: drive is an NTFS partition that contains data folders. The following resources exist:

Use the following criteria for determining your strategy to share and secure resources:

1. All employees need to be able to access all three applications: Word, Excel, and Access. However, employees should *not* be able to save data files to the application folders or to change or delete files in the application folders.

TABLE 12-8 SALESPROS, INC.'S USER AND GROUP ACCOUNTS

EMPLOYEE	USER NAME	JOB TITLE	GROUP MEMBERSHIP(S)
Pam Rhodes	PamR	District Manager	Managers, Sales, Accounting, Users
John Spencer	JohnS	Sales Manager	Managers, Sales, Users
Robert Jones	RobertJ	Accounting Manager	Managers, Accounting, Users
Colleen Green	ColleenG	Sales Rep	Sales, Users
Bill Tracy	BillT	Sales Rep	Sales, Users
Mike Calhoun	MikeC	Sales Rep	Sales, Users
Nancy Yates	NancyY	Accounting Staff	Accounting, Users
Mike Cook	MikeCo	Accounting Staff	Accounting, Users

C: DRIVE – FAT PARTITION	D: DRIVE – NTFS PARTITION
`C:\Apps\Word`	`D:\Data\Managers`
`C:\Apps\Excel`	`D:\Data\Accounting`
`C:\Apps\Access`	`D:\Data\Sales`
	`D:\Data\AllUsers`

2. Employees should be able to access (create, read, write, and delete files) only the data folders that correspond to the groups to which they belong. For example, only members of the Accounting group should be able to access the `D:\Data\Accounting` folder. Furthermore, members of the Accounting group should not be able to access data folders that correspond to groups of which they are not members.

3. All employees need to be able to access (create, read, write, and delete files) the `D:\Data\AllUsers` folder.

4. Members of the Administrators group require Full Control to all shared resources on the NTFS partition.

Plan a strategy for sharing and securing folders by assigning a share name to each resource (folder), and then choosing the appropriate share and/or NTFS permissions for each resource listed.

Use the following worksheet for your answers:

Resource (Include path)	Share Name	Share Permissions Applied		NTFS Permissions Applied	
		User/Group	Permission	User/Group	Permission
(Example) D:\Data\Sales	Sales Data	Domain Users (Remove the Everyone group)	Full Control	Sales Administrators	Change Full Control
C:\Apps\Word					
C:\Apps\Excel					
C:\Apps\Access					
D:\Data\Managers					
D:\Data\ Accounting					
D:\Data\AllUsers					

concept link **For answers to the Hands–on Lab, see Appendix B.**

Continue to Part 2.

Part 2: Sharing and securing folders

In this section, you create several folders to share, and then apply appropriate share permissions to each of the folders.

1. Select Start ⇒ Programs ⇒ Windows NT Explorer.

2. In the Exploring dialog box, highlight the C: drive (or the drive that contains your FAT partition — this is the drive that you installed Windows NT Server on). Select File ⇒ New ⇒ Folder.

3. The new folder appears in the Contents of 'D' list box. Type in a new folder name of **Apps**. Press Enter. Double-click the Apps folder.

4. Select File ⇒ New ⇒ Folder.

5. The new folder appears in the Contents of 'Apps' list box. Type in a new folder name of **Word**. Press Enter.

6. Select File ⇒ New ⇒ Folder.

7. The new folder appears in the Contents of 'Apps' list box. Type in a new folder name of **Excel**. Press Enter.

8. Select File ⇒ New ⇒ Folder.

9. The new folder appears in the Contents of 'Apps' list box. Type in a new folder name of **Access**. Press Enter.

10. Highlight the `Word` folder in the Contents of 'Apps' list box. Select File ⇒ Properties.

11. In the Word Properties dialog box, click the Sharing tab. Select the option button next to Shared As. In the Share Name text box, accept the default name of Word. Click the Permissions command button.

12. The Access Through Share Permissions dialog box appears. Click the Add command button.

13. The Add Users and Groups dialog box appears. Double-click the Domain Users group. In the Type of Access drop-down list box, select Change. Click OK.

14. In the Access Through Share Permissions dialog box, highlight the Everyone group. Click the Remove command button. Click OK.

15. In the Word Properties dialog box, click OK.

16. In the Exploring dialog box, highlight the `Excel` folder in the Contents of 'Apps' list box. Select File ⇒ Properties.

17. In the Excel Properties dialog box, click the Sharing tab. Select the option button next to Shared As. In the Share Name text box, accept the default name of Excel. Click the Permissions command button.

18. The Access Through Share Permissions dialog box appears. Click the Add command button.

19. The Add Users and Groups dialog box appears. Double-click the Domain Users group. In the Type of Access drop-down list box, select Change. Click OK.

20. In the Access Through Share Permissions dialog box, highlight the Everyone group. Click the Remove command button. Click OK.

21. In the Excel Properties dialog box, click OK.

22. In the Exploring dialog box, highlight the `Access` folder in the Contents of 'Apps' list box. Select File ⇒ Properties.

23. In the Access Properties dialog box, click the Sharing tab. Select the option button next to Shared As. In the Share Name text box, accept the default name of Access. Click the Permissions command button.

24. The Access Through Share Permissions dialog box appears. Click the Add command button.

25. The Add Users and Groups dialog box appears. Double-click the Domain Users group. In the Type of Access drop-down list box, select Change. Click OK.

26. In the Access Through Share Permissions dialog box, highlight the Everyone group. Click the Remove command button. Click OK.

27. In the Access Properties dialog box, click OK.

28. The Exploring dialog box reappears. Notice that all three folders (Word, Excel, and Access) appear in the Contents of 'Apps' list box, and that all three appear with a hand under the folder, indicating that they are shared folders.

29. Highlight the D: drive (or the drive that contains your NTFS partition). Select File ⇒ New ⇒ Folder.

30. The new folder appears in the Contents of 'D' list box. Type in a new folder name of **Data**. Press Enter. Double-click the Data folder.

31. Select File ⇒ New ⇒ Folder.

32. The new folder appears in the Contents of 'Data' list box. Type in a new folder name of **Managers**. Press Enter.

33. Select File ⇒ New ⇒ Folder.

34. The new folder appears in the Contents of 'Data' list box. Type in a new folder name of **Accounting**. Press Enter.

35. Select File ⇒ New ⇒ Folder.

36. The new folder appears in the Contents of 'Data' list box. Type in a new folder name of **Sales**. Press Enter.

37. Select File ⇒ New ⇒ Folder.

38. The new folder appears in the Contents of 'Data' list box. Type in a new folder name of **AllUsers**. Press Enter.

39. In the Exploring dialog box, highlight the Managers folder in the Contents of 'Data' list box. Select File ⇒ Properties.

40. In the Managers Properties dialog box, click the Sharing tab. Select the option button next to Shared As. In the Share Name text box, type **ManagersData**. Click the Permissions command button.

41. The Access Through Share Permissions dialog box appears. Notice that the Everyone group is listed and has the Full Control share permission. (Because this folder is located on an NTFS partition, you will use NTFS permissions to secure this folder, and accept the default share permission.) Click OK.

42. In the Managers Properties dialog box, Click OK.

43. A warning message appears, indicating that the new share name may not be accessible from some MS-DOS workstations. (This is because the name you assigned is longer than eight characters.) Click the Yes command button.

44. In the Exploring dialog box, highlight the `Accounting` folder in the Contents of 'Data' list box. Select File ⇒ Properties.

45. In the Accounting Properties dialog box, click the Sharing tab. Select the option button next to Shared As. In the Share Name text box, type in **AccountingData**. Click OK.

46. In the Sharing warning dialog box, click the Yes command button.

47. In the Exploring dialog box, highlight the `Sales` folder in the Contents of 'Data' list box. Select File ⇒ Properties.

48. In the Sales Properties dialog box, click the Sharing tab. Select the option button next to Shared As. In the Share Name text box, type in **SalesData**. Click OK.

49. In the Sharing warning dialog box, click the Yes command button.

50. In the Exploring dialog box, highlight the `AllUsers` folder in the Contents of 'Data' list box. Select File ⇒ Properties.

51. In the AllUsers Properties dialog box, click the Sharing tab. Select the option button next to Shared As. In the Share Name text box, type in **AllUsersData**. Click OK.

52. In the Sharing warning dialog box, click the Yes command button.

53. The Exploring dialog box reappears. Notice that all four folders (`Managers`, `Accounting`, `Sales`, and `All Users`) appear in the Contents of 'Data' list box, and that all four appear with a hand under each folder, indicating that they are shared folders.

In the next section, you assign NTFS permissions to these folders. Continue to Part 3.

Part 3: Establishing NTFS permissions

In this section, you assign the appropriate NTFS permissions to the `Managers`, `Accounting`, `Sales`, and `AllUsers` folders that you created and shared in Part 2.

1. In the Exploring dialog box, highlight the `Managers` folder in the Contents of 'Data' list box. Select File ⇒ Properties.

2. In the Managers Properties dialog box, click the Security tab. Click the Permissions command button.

3. In the Directory Permissions dialog box, click the Add command button.

4. In the Add Users and Groups dialog box, double-click the Managers group. In the Type of Access drop-down list box, select Change. Click OK.

5. Click the Add command button.

6. In the Add Users and Groups dialog box, double-click Administrators. In the Type of Access drop-down list box, select Full Control. Click OK.

7. In the Directory Permissions dialog box, highlight the Everyone group. Click the Remove command button. Click OK.

8. In the Managers Properties dialog box, click OK.

9. In the Exploring dialog box, highlight the `Accounting` folder in the Contents of 'Data' list box. Select File ⇒ Properties.

10. In the Accounting Properties dialog box, click the Security tab. Click the Permissions command button.

11. In the Directory Permissions dialog box, click the Add command button.

12. In the Add Users and Groups dialog box, double-click the Accounting group. In the Type of Access drop-down list box, select Change. Click OK.

13. Click the Add command button.

14. In the Add Users and Groups dialog box, double-click Administrators. In the Type of Access drop-down list box, select Full Control. Click OK.

15. In the Directory Permissions dialog box, highlight the Everyone group. Click the Remove command button. Click OK.

16. In the Accounting Properties dialog box, click OK.

17. In the Exploring dialog box, highlight the `Sales` folder in the Contents of 'Data' list box. Select File ⇒ Properties.

18. In the Sales Properties dialog box, click the Security tab. Click the Permissions command button.

19. In the Directory Permissions dialog box, click the Add command button.

20. In the Add Users and Groups dialog box, double-click the Sales group. In the Type of Access drop-down list box, select Change. Click OK.

21. Click the Add command button.

22. In the Add Users and Groups dialog box, double-click Administrators. In the Type of Access drop-down list box, select Full Control. Click OK.

23. In the Directory Permissions dialog box, highlight the Everyone group. Click the Remove command button. Click OK.

24. In the Sales Properties dialog box, click OK.

25. In the Exploring dialog box, highlight the `AllUsers` folder in the Contents of 'Data' list box. Select File ⇒ Properties.

26. In the AllUsers Properties dialog box, click the Security tab. Click the Permissions command button.

27. In the Directory Permissions dialog box, click the Add command button.

28. In the Add Users and Groups dialog box, double-click the Domain Users group. In the Type of Access drop-down list box, select Change. Click OK.

29. Click the Add command button.

30. In the Add Users and Groups dialog box, double-click Administrators. In the Type of Access drop-down list box, select Full Control. Click OK.

31. In the Directory Permissions dialog box, highlight the Everyone group. Click the Remove command button. Click OK.

32. In the AllUsers Properties dialog box, click OK. This completes the assigning of NTFS permissions. Exit Windows NT Explorer.

Lab 12.22 *Establishing file and folder auditing*

The purpose of this lab is to provide you with hands-on experience in establishing file and folder auditing.

This lab consists of two parts:

Part 1: Establishing file and folder auditing

Part 2: Testing file and folder auditing

Begin this lab by booting your computer to Windows NT Server. Log on as Administrator.

Follow the ensuing steps carefully.

Part 1: Establishing file and folder auditing

In this section, you establish file and folder auditing on the `Managers`, `Accounting`, `Sales`, and `AllUsers` subfolders in the `D:\Data` folder that you created and shared in Lab 12.21.

In Lab 9.15, you implemented success and failure auditing for File and Object Access by using User Manager for Domains. That was the first step in auditing files and folders. This lab completes the process of establishing auditing on files and folders.

1. Select Start ⇒ Programs ⇒ Windows NT Explorer.

2. In the All Folders section of the Exploring dialog box, click the + sign next to the drive that contains your NTFS partition (usually this is the D: drive). Highlight the `Data` folder. In the Contents of 'Data' list box, highlight the `Accounting` folder. Select File ⇒ Properties.

3. In the Accounting Properties dialog box, click the Security tab. Click the Auditing command button.

4. In the Directory Auditing dialog box, click the Add command button. Double-click the Domain Users group. Click OK.

5. In the Directory Auditing dialog box, select the Success and Failure check boxes next to Read, Write, and Execute. Click OK.

6. In the Accounting Properties dialog box, click OK.

7. In the Exploring dialog box, highlight the `AllUsers` folder in the Contents of 'Data' list box. Select File ⇒ Properties.

8. In the AllUsers Properties dialog box, click the Security tab. Click the Auditing command button.

9. In the Directory Auditing dialog box, click the Add command button. Double-click the Domain Users group. Click OK.

10. In the Directory Auditing dialog box, select the Success and Failure check boxes next to Delete. Click OK.

11. In the AllUsers Properties dialog box, click OK.

12. In the Exploring dialog box, highlight the `Managers` folder in the Contents of 'Data' list box. Select File ⇒ Properties.

13. In the Managers Properties dialog box, click the Security tab. Click the Auditing command button.

14. In the Directory Auditing dialog box, click the Add command button. Double-click the Domain Users group. Click OK.

15. In the Directory Auditing dialog box, select the Success and Failure check boxes next to Read, Write, Execute, Delete, Change Permissions, and Take Ownership. Click OK.

16. In the Managers Properties dialog box, click OK.

17. In the Exploring dialog box, highlight the `Sales` folder in the Contents of 'Data' list box. Select File ⇒ Properties.

18. In the Sales Properties dialog box, click the Security tab. Click the Auditing command button.

19. In the Directory Auditing dialog box, click the Add command button. Double-click the Domain Users group. Click OK.

20. In the Directory Auditing dialog box, select the Success and Failure check boxes next to Read, Write, and Execute. Click OK.

21. In the Sales Properties dialog box, click OK. Exit Windows NT Explorer. Continue on to Part 2.

Part 2: Testing file and folder auditing

In this section, you clear the Security Log in Event Viewer, then log on as NancyY and attempt to access each of the data folders you created and shared in Lab 12.21. Then you use Event Viewer to view the results of the auditing that you established in Part 1.

1. Select Start ⇒ Programs ⇒ Administrative Tools (Common) ⇒ Event Viewer.
2. In the Event Viewer dialog box, select Log ⇒ Security. Select Log ⇒ Clear All Events. (You are clearing the Security Log to make room for new auditing events.)
3. In the Clear Event Log dialog box, click the No command button, so as to not save the log to a file.
4. In the Clear Event Log dialog box, click the Yes command button to clear the Security Log.
5. Exit Event Viewer.
6. Select Start ⇒ Shut Down.
7. In the Shut Down Windows dialog box, select the option button next to "Close all programs and log on as a different user." Click the Yes command button.
8. Press Ctrl + Alt + Delete to log on.
9. Click OK in the Important Notice dialog box.
10. Type in a user name of **NancyY**, and a password of **password**. Click OK.
11. A warning message may appear, indicating that your password will expire in *xx* days. If this message appears, click the No command button.
12. If a Welcome to Windows NT dialog box appears, clear the check box next to "Show this Welcome Screen next time you start Windows NT." Click the Close command button.
13. Select Start ⇒ Programs ⇒ Windows NT Explorer.
14. In the Exploring dialog box, click the plus sign next to the drive that contains your NTFS partition (usually this is the D: drive). Click the plus sign next to the `Data` folder on this drive. Highlight the `Accounting` folder. Notice that there are no files in this folder.
15. Highlight the `AllUsers` folder. Notice that there are no files in this folder.
16. Highlight the `Managers` folder. A dialog box appears, indicating that access has been denied. (This is because NancyY is not a member of the Managers group and does not have the appropriate permission to access this folder.) Click the Cancel command button.

17. Highlight the `Sales` folder. A dialog box appears, indicating that access has been denied. (This is because NancyY is not a member of the Sales group and does not have the appropriate permission to access this folder.) Click the Cancel command button. Exit Windows NT Explorer.

18. Select Start ⇒ Shut Down.

19. In the Shut Down Windows dialog box, select the option button next to "Close all programs and log on as a different user." Click the Yes command button.

20. Press Ctrl + Alt + Delete to log on.

21. Click OK in the Important Notice dialog box.

22. Type in a user name of **Administrator**, and a password of **password**. Click OK.

23. Select Start ⇒ Programs ⇒ Administrative Tools (Common) ⇒ Event Viewer.

24. In the Event Viewer dialog box, select Log ⇒ Security. Scroll down the log and double-click the first event that lists NancyY in the User column *and* Logon/Logoff in the Category column.

25. The Event Detail dialog box appears. Notice that this is a Success audit of the Logon/Logoff event. Click the Close command button.

26. Scroll down and double-click the event that has a lock (rather than a key) in the left-hand margin, lists NancyY in the User column, *and* Object Access in the Category column. (This event should be approximately eleven events down from the top of the list.)

27. The Event Detail dialog box appears. Notice that this is a Failure audit event of the Object Access type. (This audit event occurred when NancyY attempted to access the `D:\Data\Sales` folder and was denied access.) Click the Next command button to view the next audit event.

28. Continue clicking on the Next command button to view several more audit events. When you are finished viewing audit events, click the Close command button.

29. Exit Event Viewer.

Backing Up and Restoring Data

13

About Chapter 13

This chapter covers the basics of backing up and restoring your Windows NT computer's data.

Chapter 13 begins by explaining the importance of performing and testing regular backups. Various backup types, such as normal, differential, and incremental are considered; and common backup strategies are presented. Security considerations are presented, as well as tape rotation schemes and tips for documenting backups.

Next, the chapter takes you through the steps to perform a backup using Windows NT Backup. Backing up the local Registry is included in this section. Finally, the chapter outlines the steps to perform a restore by using Windows NT Backup.

This chapter includes one optional Hands-on Lab that requires the use of a tape drive. In this lab you practice using Windows NT Backup to back up files and folders on your Windows NT computer.

If you're reading this book, it's probably important for you to know how to back up and restore data. Additionally, this chapter maps to the "Choose the appropriate course of action to take to resolve fault-tolerance failures" objective listed in the Troubleshooting section in the Preparation Guide for the Server exam.

BACKING UP FILES AND FOLDERS

Backing up files and folders is an important part of your network fault tolerance plan. Planning and adhering to a regular backup schedule can make recovering from a corrupt file or a failed hard drive a straightforward, if somewhat painful, task. Failing to make regular backups of your system's critical data can be harmful (or even fatal) to your business and/or to your employment status.

A tape backup is *not* a replacement for other fault tolerance methods, such as disk mirroring and striping with parity. It is an additional safety precaution to use when other fault tolerance methods fail. I don't recommend that you rely solely on disk mirroring, striping with parity, or tape backup. A comprehensive fault tolerance policy typically should include two or more of these strategies.

Always remember that a tape backup is your last line of defense against data loss. If the data on the tape is too old to be of value, or if it is corrupt, or if the tape has been damaged due to fire or other causes, then you have nothing. And having nothing is very hard to explain to upper management.

 in the real world

It's been my sorry duty, on more than one occasion, to have to explain to a client that both disks in a mirrored pair have failed *and* that their most recent tape backup is corrupt. I can't stress enough the importance of carefully performing regular tape backups and periodically testing the validity of those backups. If you've ever experienced a partial or total disk failure, you know why I'm saying this. Have a hard disk fail on you — and you will never regret the time it takes you to perform backups again.

This chapter covers the basics about backing up and restoring data, including what to back up, backup types, using Windows NT Backup to perform a backup, using the Schedule service to automate backups, and restoring files and folders.

What to Back Up

Before you can create a backup strategy, you need to determine which data on your network will be backed up. I recommend that all network data be backed up regularly to tape. This includes operating systems, applications, the Registry, and user-created data files.

In general, operating systems and applications need to be backed up less frequently than user-created data files. You may find it sufficient to back up operating systems and applications once a week, once a month, or even less often. I recommend that you back up operating systems and applications, on separate tapes, initially and every time you modify the operating system or install a new application.

Depending on the importance of the data, user-created data files can be backed up once a week, once a day, once an hour, or at any frequency that meets your organization's needs. When determining which files to back up and how often, the main question you need to ask yourself is *how much data can you afford to lose?* For example, if you decide to back up only once a week, can you afford to lose six days of sales information and other employee-created data?

Backup Types

Before the specific backup types are presented, a short discussion on the archive attribute, and how the operating system and backup programs use this attribute, is in order.

The *archive attribute* is a marker that the operating system automatically assigns to all files and folders when they are first installed or created. Depending on the backup type, backup programs *remove* the archive attribute from a file or folder to indicate that the file or folder has been backed up. If a file or folder is modified after it is backed up, the operating system reassigns the archive attribute to it.

There are five standard types of backups that you can perform:

○ **Normal (full):** A *normal backup* backs up all selected files and folders. It removes the archive attribute from the backed up files and folders. A normal backup is a full, complete backup — it is the backbone of your backup plan or strategy.

○ **Differential:** A *differential backup* backs up all selected files and folders that have changed since the last normal (full) backup. A differential backup does *not* remove the archive attribute from any files or folders. A differential backup is a *cumulative* backup since the last normal (full) backup. Because the differential backup does not remove the archive attribute, if a normal backup is performed on Sunday, and differential backups are performed Monday through Friday, Monday's differential backup will contain all changes made to data on Monday; Tuesday's differential backup will contain all changes made to data on Monday and Tuesday, Wednesday's differential backup will contain all changes made to data on Monday, Tuesday, and Wednesday, and so on. A differential backup is often used in between normal backups, because it takes less time to perform a differential backup than a normal backup.

o **Incremental:** An *incremental backup* backs up all selected files and folders that have changed since the last normal or incremental backup. An incremental backup removes the archive attribute from the backed up files and folders. An incremental backup is *not* cumulative like a differential backup. It contains only changes made since the last normal or incremental backup. If a normal backup is performed on Sunday, Monday's incremental backup will contain all changes made to data on Monday; Tuesday's incremental backup will contain all changes made to data only on Tuesday; Wednesday's incremental backup will contain all changes made to data only on Wednesday, and so on. Because less data is backed up, an incremental backup takes even less time to perform than a differential backup.

o **Copy:** A *copy backup* backs up all selected files and folders. It does not remove or otherwise affect the archive attribute. The copy backup can be performed without disrupting the normal backup schedule, because it does not affect the archive attribute. You could use a copy backup to create an extra backup to store off-site.

o **Daily:** A *daily backup* backs up all selected files and folders that have changed during the day the backup is made. It does not remove or otherwise affect the archive attribute.

Companies often use a combination of the standard backup types in their backup strategy.

Backup Strategies

There are a number of acceptable backup strategies, and three fairly common ones:

- *Perform a normal (full) backup every day.* This is the most time-consuming of the three common strategies. However, should a restore be necessary, only the last normal backup is required, and restore time is generally less than either of the other two strategies.

- *Perform a weekly normal backup and daily differential backups.* As the week progresses, the time required to perform the differential backups increases. However, should a restore be necessary, only two backups will be needed — the most recent normal backup, and the most recent differential backup. (This is because the most recent differential backup contains *all* files and folders that have changed since the last normal backup.) The restore can be accomplished relatively quickly.

- *Perform a weekly normal backup and daily incremental backups.* Incremental backups tend to take about the same amount of time each day and are considered the fastest backup method. However, should a restore be necessary, multiple backup sets will be required — the most recent normal backup, and *every* incremental backup since the most recent normal backup. (This is because the incremental backups each contain different data and are not cumulative.) The restore will typically take more time than if a differential backup had been used.

When planning your backup strategy, the big trade-off you need to consider is time — the time it takes to perform backups versus the time it takes to restore data.

Security considerations

When planning your company's backup strategy, there are a few security considerations to take into account:

- If the data is of a sensitive nature, consider physically securing the tape drive and the backup tapes. While your server may require a password and permissions to access confidential data, when a backup tape is taken and restored on another server, your server's security measures are defeated.

- Consider rotating backup tapes to an off-site location. This can prevent or minimize data loss due to a single catastrophic event, such as a theft, fire, flood, or earthquake. Consider using a third-party company that will store your data tapes in a secure, climate-controlled environment.

- If you store backup tapes in a fireproof safe, remember that *fireproof* does not necessarily mean heat- or smoke-proof. Make sure the safe is capable of protecting magnetic media as well as papers and other important items.

- Finally, depending on your organization's security needs, consider who should perform backups. In very high security environments, consider allowing only administrators to perform backups. In medium-to-low-security situations, consider separating the backup and restore functions by designating certain personnel to perform only backups, and other employees to perform only restores.

Tape rotation

Most organizations rotate their magnetic tapes in order to reduce the cost of backups. Instead of using a new tape every day, tapes are reused in a systematic manner.

There are probably almost as many tape rotation methods as there are network administrators. Consider the following tape rotation example, which is illustrated in Table 13-1.

TABLE 13-1 SAMPLE BACKUP TAPE ROTATION SCHEME

MONDAY	TUESDAY	WEDNESDAY	THURSDAY	FRIDAY
Tape # 1	Tape # 2	Tape # 3	Tape # 4	Tape # 5
Tape # 1	Tape # 2	Tape # 3	Tape # 4	Tape # 6
Tape # 1	Tape # 2	Tape # 3	Tape # 4	Tape # 7
Tape # 1	Tape # 2	Tape # 3	Tape # 4	Tape # 8-Archived

This example requires eight tapes for a four-week period. Tapes one through four are reused each week, with the Monday tape used again the following Monday, and so on. Depending on the amount of data backed up and the tape's capacity, the data from the previous backup can be appended or replaced. The eighth tape is permanently archived and removed from the tape rotation scheme.

When choosing a tape rotation method, consider the following:

- The useful life of a tape. Eventually tapes need to be removed from the rotation scheme and replaced with new tapes. The number of times a magnetic tape can be reused depends on the tape's quality and storage conditions.
- Tape cost versus the cost of lost data. Many tapes are guaranteed for life — but for only the cost of the tape. The cost of lost data is not guaranteed.
- Removing a tape from the rotation schedule weekly, monthly, or quarterly to provide a permanent, long-term archive of your data.

Documenting backups

Documenting your backups will make restoring after a failure a much easier task.

You should consider keeping a backup log book that documents each backup procedure performed. You should record the date and time the backup was performed, a brief description of the data backed up, the name of the person who performed the backup, the tape number used, and its storage location. You can also include a detailed or summarized printed log of the backup. If you have this information readily available, the person performing the restore will be able to quickly identify and locate the most recent backup tape(s) needed.

 tip **Most backup programs can be configured to create detailed logs that list the individual files and folders backed up. These logs can be quite helpful if a user tells you that he or she has accidentally deleted an important file and asks you to restore it from tape. A log (either printed, or written to a file on disk) will enable you to locate the appropriate tape needed to restore the file quickly and easily.**

Performing a Backup Using Windows NT Backup

Windows NT ships with a backup program called *Windows NT Backup*. Windows NT Backup is a basic tape backup program that gives you full capability to back up and restore a Windows NT computer, including the local Registry. It does not back up the Registry on computers other than the one in which the tape device is installed. Windows NT Backup does not provide the extensive scheduling and automation features included in more sophisticated third-party backup programs.

In order to perform a backup, you need a tape drive that is compatible with NT (check the Windows NT *Hardware Compatibility List* [HCL]). If possible, select a tape drive that has the capacity to back up your entire server on a single tape. This is a big help, especially if you perform unattended tape backups.

Before you perform a tape backup using Windows NT Backup, you need to install a tape device and driver, if you haven't already done so, by using the Tape Devices application in Control Panel. Also, make sure that you have the appropriate user rights to perform a backup — you need to either be a member of the Administrators, Backup Operators, or Server Operators groups; or, you need to have the "Back up files and directories" user right assigned to you.

Consider the time of day when performing backups. Because of the utilization of processor and memory during backup, it's normally best to perform backups during the periods of lowest server and/or network usage — often after business hours.

TO PERFORM A BACKUP USING WINDOWS NT BACKUP, FOLLOW THESE STEPS:

1. Place a tape in the tape drive.

2. Start ⇒ Programs ⇒ Administrative Tools (Common) ⇒ Backup.

3. The Backup dialog box appears. Select Window ⇒ Drives.

4. Maximize the Drives dialog box. Select the drive(s) and/or files and/or folders that you want to back up.

- To back up an entire drive, select the check box next to the drive.

- To back up individual files and folders, double-click the drive that contains those files and folders, and then select the check boxes next to the files and/or folders that you want to back up. Click the Backup command button.

5. The Backup Information dialog box appears, as shown in Figure 13-1. Notice the various backup configuration options available.

FIGURE 13-1   **Configurable options in Windows NT Backup**

○ Tape Name: In the Tape Name text box, either accept the default name listed or type in a new name for the tape.

○ Verify After Backup: Select the check box next to Verify After Backup if you want Windows NT Backup to verify the files and folders it has backed up. It's a good idea to verify after a backup, even though selecting this option approximately doubles the time the backup takes.

○ Backup Local Registry: Select the check box next to Backup Local Registry (if it is not grayed out) if you want Windows NT Backup to include the Registry on the computer that the tape drive is installed on in its backup. In order to back up the Registry, you must select at least one file or folder for backup on the drive on which Windows NT is installed.

○ Restrict Access to Owner or Administrator: Select the check box next to Restrict Access to Owner or Administrator if you want Windows NT Backup to only enable the owner of the tape, an Administrator, or a member of the Backup Operators group to read, write, or erase the tape using Windows NT Backup.

○ Hardware Compression: Select the check box next to Hardware Compression if you want the backup data compressed as it is backed up, and if your tape backup hardware supports this feature.

○ Operation: In the Operation section, you have two options: you can choose to have this backup appended to the last backup on the tape, or you can choose to have Windows NT Backup write over (replace) any existing data on the tape. (Replace is the default operation.)

- Backup Set Information: In the Backup Set Information section, you can type a description of the backup. I recommend that you enter the date, a brief description of the data backed up, and the type of backup performed.

- Backup Type: In the Backup Type drop-down list box, select the backup type you want to perform: Normal, Copy, Differential, Incremental, or Daily.

- Log Information: In the Log Information section, Windows NT Backup shows the location to which it will write a backup log. Modify this location if necessary.

- Log Options: Select the option button next to one of the three log options, depending on the type of log you want NT Backup to create: Full Detail, Summary Only, or Don't Log. (Summary Only is the default log option.) Click OK.

6. The Backup Status dialog box appears. If the tape has been used before, a Replace Information dialog box appears. These dialog boxes are shown in Figure 13-2. Click the Yes command button to have Windows NT Backup replace the data on the tape with the backup you are preparing to perform.

FIGURE 13-2   Performing a backup using Windows NT Backup

7. Windows NT Backup performs the backup. (This process takes several minutes to several hours, depending on the amount of data being backed up and your tape drive speed.)

8. The Verify Status dialog box appears if you selected Verify After Backup. Windows NT Backup verifies that all files and folders were backed up correctly. (This process takes approximately the same amount of time as the backup.) Figure 13-3 shows the Verify Status dialog box after the verify has been completed. Notice the information presented in the Summary list box. Click OK after the verify is completed.

**Figure 13-3   Windows NT Backup
verification completed**

9. Exit Windows NT Backup.

Using the Schedule Service to Automate Backups

You can use the Schedule service in Windows NT to schedule unattended (automated) backups.

To do this, you must first configure the Schedule service to start automatically (by default, it is started manually) by using the Services application in Control Panel.

Then you must use the `At.exe` command-line utility to schedule and configure the unattended backup. All options of Windows NT Backup can be configured and scheduled by using this utility in conjunction with the `NTBackup.exe` (Windows NT Backup) utility's command-line switches.

concept link

A detailed discussion of the command-line syntax and switches is beyond the scope of this book. For more information on the At.exe command-line utility, type a /? at the command prompt. For more information on the NTBackup.exe utility's command-line switches, type ntbackup /? at the command prompt. You might also want to check out the Command Scheduler, a graphical scheduler utility on the compact disc that ships with the *Microsoft Windows NT Server Resource Kit* (Microsoft Press, 1996). Command Scheduler is a graphical version of the At.exe command-line utility.

RESTORING FILES AND FOLDERS

Hopefully, you'll never have to restore files and folders after a catastrophic data loss. Nevertheless, it's a good practice to be comfortable with the process of restoring data to your system, just in case.

For this reason, and also to ensure that your backup tapes contain valid copies of your data files, you should periodically test your backup by performing a trial restore.

The following sections discuss testing your backup with a trial restore and performing a restore using Windows NT Backup.

Test Your Backup with a Trial Restore

To test the validity of the data contained on a backup tape, you should restore at least one folder that contains several data files to a *different* folder than it was originally backed up from. The folder you restore to is a test folder and shouldn't contain other files. For example, you could restore the D:\Public folder to D:\Public2 or to E:\Public2. This process verifies that the tape can be read, and that files and folders can be restored from it.

Once you've restored the folder, compare its contents with the original folder (on your hard drive) to find out whether the files are the same by using the Comp.exe command-line utility. If there are no differences between the files compared, then presumably all of the files on the backup tape are valid and not corrupt.

Another resource you can use to compare files is the Windiff.exe graphical utility that ships with the *Microsoft Windows NT Server Resource Kit*. An advantage of using Windiff.exe is that it enables you to specify multiple files and folders for comparison, as opposed to Comp.exe, which only enables you to specify a single file at a time for comparison.

Performing a Restore Using Windows NT Backup

You can use Windows NT Backup to perform a full or partial restore of data from a tape backup created by using NT Backup.

TO PERFORM A RESTORE USING WINDOWS NT BACKUP, FOLLOW THESE STEPS:

1. Place the backup tape that contains the data you want to restore in the tape drive. (If the tape backup consisted of more than one tape, insert the *last* tape in the backup set into the tape drive, because NT Backup wrote a catalog of the backup to this tape.)

2. Select Start ⇒ Programs ⇒ Administrative Tools (Common) ⇒ Backup.

3. The Backup dialog box appears. Select Window ⇒ Tapes.

4. Maximize the Tapes window that is displayed. If you want to perform a full restore, select the check box next to the backup set you want to restore in the right-hand window. If you want to perform a partial restore, double-click the backup set in the right-hand window. Windows NT Backup loads a catalog list of the files and folders in the backup. Then select the check boxes next to the individual files and folders you want to restore.

Click the Restore command button.

5. The Restore Information dialog box appears, as shown in Figure 13-4. Notice the available configuration options.

   o Restore to Drive and Alternate Path: If you want the selected files to be restored to their original drive location, accept the default in the Restore to Drive drop-down list box. Otherwise, you can specify a new drive letter, and then specify a folder that you want the files restored to in the Alternate Path text box. (You might want to do this if you're doing a trial restore to test your backup.)

- o Restore Local Registry: Select the check box next to Restore Local Registry only if you want the current Registry on your server replaced with the Registry on the backup tape. Use great caution when exercising this option.

- o Restore File Permissions: Select the check box next to Restore File Permissions if you want to keep the file permissions as they were stored on the tape backup. Otherwise, the restored files will be assigned their file permissions based on the permissions of the folder to which they are restored.

- o Verify After Restore: Select the check box next to Verify After Restore if you want NT Backup to verify files after it restores them. (Selecting this option approximately doubles the time it takes to perform a restore.)

- o Log Information: Configure the Log Information section. (The options are the same for performing restores as they are for performing backups.) Click OK.

Figure 13-4   Restore options available in
Windows NT Backup

6. The Restore Status dialog box appears. NT Backup rewinds the tape and restores the files and/or folders selected and verifies the files and folders selected if configured to do so. (This process can take a while.) The Restore Status dialog box, after the restore is completed, is shown in Figure 13-5. Notice the information presented in the Summary list box. Click OK.

FIGURE 13-5   Restore completed

7. Exit Windows NT Backup.

KEY POINT SUMMARY

This chapter covered the importance of backing up files and folders, how to decide which data to back up, and various backup types and strategies. Performing a backup using Windows NT Backup and utilizing the Schedule service were also outlined. Finally, Chapter 13 covered restoring files and folders.

o Backup is an important part of your network fault tolerance plan. Backup is not a substitute for other fault tolerance methods, such as disk mirroring and striping with parity, but is an additional safety precaution. A tape backup is your last line of defense against data loss.

o All network data should be regularly backed up to tape, including: operating systems, applications, the Registry, and user-created data files. It's a good idea to back up operating systems and applications on separate tapes, and separately from data file backups, to make the restore process easier. Determining the frequency of backup is often based on the answer to the question: How much data can you afford to lose?

o The *archive attribute* is a marker that, when removed from a file or folder, indicates that the file or folder has been backed up.

o There are five standard types of backups:

- *Normal (full):* Backs up all selected files and folders, and removes the archive attribute from the backed up files and folders.

- *Differential:* Backs up all selected files and folders that have changed since the last normal backup, and does *not* remove the archive attribute from files or folders. A differential backup is a *cumulative* backup, and because of this fact, takes more time to perform than an incremental backup, but less time to perform than a normal backup.

- *Incremental:* Backs up all selected files and folders that have changed since the last normal or incremental backup, and removes the archive attribute from the backed up files and folders. An incremental backup is *not* cumulative, and because of this fact, takes less time to perform than a differential backup.

- *Copy:* Backs up all selected files and folders, and does *not* remove the archive attribute. This backup type can be used without disrupting the normal backup schedule.

- *Daily:* Backs up all selected files and folders that have changed during the day the tape backup is made, and does *not* remove the archive attribute.

- Often, a combination of the standard backup types is used.

- There are three fairly common backup strategies. The trade-off that needs to be considered, when planning a backup strategy, is the time it takes to perform backups versus the time it takes to restore data.

  - One strategy is to perform a normal backup every day. This strategy is time consuming in terms of backup, but requires the least amount of effort should a restore be necessary, because only the most recent normal backup is required.

  - A second strategy is to perform a weekly normal backup and daily differential backups. This strategy takes more backup time than performing daily incremental backups, but requires only the last normal backup and the most recent differential backup should a restore be necessary.

  - A third strategy is to perform a weekly normal backup and daily incremental backups. This strategy takes the least amount of time in terms of backup, and potentially the most amount of time to perform a restore, because the last normal backup, in addition to *all* incremental backups since the last normal backup, are required.

o When planning a backup strategy and procedure, remember to take into account *security considerations*, *tape rotation*, and the *documentation* you should keep on your backups. It is beneficial to keep a detailed logbook that contains the date and time each backup was performed, a brief description of the data backed up, the person who performed the backup, the tape number used, and its storage location. It's also helpful to keep a detailed log of each backup so that individual files can be restored from tape quickly and easily.

o You can use Windows NT Backup to back up and restore data.

o Performing a tape backup requires the use of a tape drive device. Make sure to use a tape drive that is on the HCL, and if possible, one that has the capacity to back up your entire server on a single tape.

o You can use the Schedule service and the At.exe command-line utility in conjunction with Windows NT Backup (NTBackup.exe) command-line switches to configure and schedule unattended backups.

o To ensure that your backup tapes contain valid copies of your data, you should periodically test your backup by performing a trial restore. When performing a trial restore, restore files from a backup tape to a different folder (that is only used as a test folder and that contains no other files). Then compare the files to the original files (on your hard disk) using the Comp.exe command-line utility (or Winndiff.exe, a graphical utility included in the *Microsoft Windows NT Server Resource Kit*). If there are no differences between the files compared, then presumably all of the files on the backup tape are valid and not corrupt.

Applying What You've Learned

Now it's time to regroup, review, and apply what you've learned in this chapter.

The Instant Assessment questions bring to mind key facts and concepts. Then, the Hands-on Lab reinforces what you've learned and allows you to practice some of the tasks that may be tested by the Server exam.

Instant Assessment

1. Which Windows NT utility can you use to perform backups and restores?

2. What is the archive attribute, and how can it be affected during backup?

3. Briefly list and describe the five standard types of backups.

4. What two items should be considered when selecting a tape drive device?

5. What should you do periodically to ensure that your backup tapes contain valid copies of your data?

6. Which backup combination listed below, A or B, takes more time *in terms of the amount of time it takes to perform backups?*

   A. A weekly normal backup and daily differential backups

   B. A weekly normal backup and daily incremental backups

7. Which backup combination listed below, A or B, typically takes more time *in terms of amount of time it takes to perform restores?*

   A. A weekly normal backup and daily differential backups

   B. A weekly normal backup and daily incremental backups

8. How does selecting the Verify After Backup option in Windows NT Backup affect the amount of time it takes to perform a backup?

9. Which Windows NT Service must be configured before an unattended backup can be performed using Windows NT Backup?

10. What can you do to minimize data loss from a single catastrophic event, such as a theft, fire, flood, or earthquake?

 concept link   **For answers to the Instant Assessment questions see Appendix B.**

Hands-on Lab

The following Hands-on Lab provides you with an opportunity to apply the knowledge you've gained in this chapter about backing up and restoring data.

Lab 13.23 *Performing a backup*

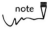 *This lab is optional* because it requires a tape drive.

The purpose of this lab is to give you hands-on experience using Windows NT Backup to back up files and folders on a Windows NT computer. You will also view the detailed log created during the backup by using Windows NT Explorer and Notepad.

Begin this lab by booting your computer to Windows NT Server. Log on as Administrator. If you haven't already done so, install a driver for your tape drive by using the Tape Devices application in Control Panel. Place a tape in the tape drive.

FOLLOW THE STEPS BELOW CAREFULLY:

1. Start ⇒ Programs ⇒ Administrative Tools (Common) ⇒ Backup.

2. The Backup dialog box appears. Select Window ⇒ Drives.

3. Maximize the Drives dialog box. Double-click the C: drive (or the drive that you have installed Windows NT Server on). Select the check box next to the Winntsrv folder. (If you wanted to back up the entire C: drive instead of selected folders only, when the Drives dialog box first appears, select the check box next to the C: drive instead of double-clicking it.)

Click the Backup command button.

4. The Backup Information dialog box appears. Select the check boxes next to the following: Verify After Backup, Hardware Compression (if the box is not grayed out), and Backup Local Registry.

In the Operation section, ensure that the option button next to Replace is selected.

In the Description text box, type Winntsrv folder *current_date* normal backup.

In the Backup Type drop-down list box, select Normal.

In the Log Information section, select the option button next to Full Detail. Click OK.

5. The Backup Status dialog box appears. If the tape has been used before, a Replace Information dialog box appears. Click the Yes command button to have Windows NT Backup replace the data on the tape with the backup you are preparing to perform.

6. Windows NT Backup performs the backup. (This process takes several minutes.)

7. The Verify Status dialog box appears. Windows NT Backup verifies that all files and folders were backed up correctly. (This process also takes several minutes.) After the verify is completed, click OK.

8. The Backup-(Drives) dialog box appears. Select Window ⇒ Tapes.

9. The Backup-(Tapes) dialog box appears. Double-click the + sign next to the C: in the right-hand window (or the letter of the drive on which you installed Windows NT Server).

10. Double-click the `Winntsrv` folder in the left-hand window.

11. Windows NT Backup displays the contents of the `Winntsrv` folder from the tape backup that you just created. Notice that, for restore purposes, you can select individual files and subfolders by selecting the check boxes next to the files and subfolders that you want to restore.

    Exit Windows NT Backup.

12. To view the log for the backup you just created, select Start ⇒ Programs ⇒ Windows NT Explorer.

13. In the Exploring dialog box, click the + sign next to the C: drive (or the drive on which you installed Windows NT Server). Highlight the `Winntsrv` folder. In the Contents of 'Winntsrv,' double-click `Backup.log`.

14. View the backup log that is displayed in Notepad. Exit Notepad.

15. Exit Windows NT Explorer.

Connectivity

As the title implies, the emphasis of Part IV is on connectivity—specifically, how Windows NT functions in a network environment. This part begins with Chapter 14, which is all about networking using TCP/IP. Chapter 14 explains IP addressing in depth. It also introduces publishing on the Internet using Microsoft Internet Information Server. Then, we discuss some practical suggestions for troubleshooting common TCP/IP connectivity problems.

Next, Chapter 15 explains how Windows NT computers can coexist with NetWare computers. We discuss the NWLink IPX/SPX Compatible Transport protocol and Gateway Service for NetWare, as well as troubleshooting common NetWare connectivity problems. Chapter 16 then covers how to use the Migration Tool for NetWare to migrate data from a NetWare server to a Windows NT Server computer.

Finally, Chapter 17 explores Remote Access Service (RAS). Step-by-step instructions show you how to install and configure RAS, and how to configure Dial-Up Networking connections. Troubleshooting information is also included.

This part maps to the Connectivity exam objectives for the Implementing and Supporting Microsoft Windows NT Server 4.0 exam.

Networking Using TCP/IP

About Chapter 14

This chapter is a concise, practical primer on TCP/IP and related subjects.

After a brief overview of TCP/IP, this chapter discusses IP addressing, including how IP addresses are assigned.

Then the chapter turns its attention to publishing on the Internet. Microsoft's primary tool, Microsoft Internet Information Server (IIS) is featured. Complete steps to install this product are included.

Finally, Chapter 14 presents tips on troubleshooting common TCP/IP connectivity problems.

This chapter includes a Critical Thinking Lab and a Hands-on Lab. In these labs, you'll identify and resolve some common TCP/IP connectivity problems, and configure Microsoft Internet Information Server (IIS).

Chapter 14 maps to numerous objectives for the Server exam, including protocol objectives that include the TCP/IP protocol, and the "Choose the appropriate course of action to take to resolve connectivity problems" objective.

OVERVIEW OF TCP/IP

The *Transmission Control Protocol/Internet Protocol* (TCP/IP) is a widely used transport protocol that provides robust capabilities for Windows NT networking.

TCP/IP is a fast, routable enterprise protocol that is used on the Internet. TCP/IP is supported by many other operating systems, including: Windows 95, Macintosh, UNIX, MS-DOS, and IBM mainframes. TCP/IP is typically the recommended protocol for large, heterogeneous networks.

 concept link

This chapter covers only the basics of TCP/IP that are required for the Server exam. Volumes have been written on this subject! For more information on TCP/IP, see the TCP/IP topics in Books Online, and *TCP/IP MCSE Study Guide* by Greg Bulette (IDG Books Worldwide, 1998).

A good place to begin a basic discussion of TCP/IP is with IP addressing — including subnet masks and default gateway addresses.

IP ADDRESSING

An *IP address* is a 32-bit binary number, broken into four 8-bit sections (often called *octets*), that uniquely identifies a computer or other network device on a network that uses TCP/IP. IP addresses must be unique — *no two computers or other network devices on an internetwork should have the same IP address*. If two computers have the same IP address, one or both of the computers may be unable to communicate over the network. An IP address is *not* the same as a network adapter's hardware (or MAC) address.

Although an IP address is a 32-bit binary number, it is normally represented in a dotted decimal format. Each 8-bit octet is represented by a whole number between 0 and 255. The following numbers are sample IP addresses:

192.168.59.5

172.31.151.1

An IP address contains two important identifiers: a *network ID* and a *host ID*.

One portion of each IP address identifies the network segment on which a computer (or other network device) is located. This portion is called the network

ID. *All computers located on the same network segment have the same network ID.* The length of the network ID within an IP address is variable and is specified by the subnet mask used in conjunction with the IP address. (Subnet masks are discussed in more detail in the next section.)

The second portion of each IP address identifies the individual computer or network device. This portion is called the host ID. *Each computer or other network device on a given network segment must have a unique host ID.*

To ensure that unique IP addresses are used, if you plan to connect your network to the Internet, you should contact your Internet service provider or InterNIC to obtain a range of valid IP addresses for your network.

web links **InterNIC, which manages domain names as well as IP addresses, can be reached by e-mail at** info@internic.net.

Subnet Masks

A *subnet mask* specifies which portion of an IP address represents the network ID and which portion represents the host ID. A subnet mask allows TCP/IP to determine whether network traffic destined for a given IP address should be transmitted on the local subnet, or whether it should be routed to a remote subnet. *A subnet mask should be the same for all computers and other network devices on a given network segment.*

A subnet mask is a 32-bit binary number, broken into four 8-bit sections (octets), that is normally represented in a dotted decimal format. Each 8-bit section is represented by a whole number between 0 and 255.

A common subnet mask is 255.255.255.0. This particular subnet mask specifies that TCP/IP will use the first three octets of an IP address as the network ID, and will use the last octet as the host ID.

Another common subnet mask is 255.255.0.0. This subnet mask specifies that TCP/IP will use the first two octets of an IP address as the network ID, and use the last two octets as the host ID. (Without getting into too much binary math, an octet number of 255 specifies the entire octet is part of the network ID; and an octet number of 0 specifies the entire octet is part of the host ID. Numbers between 0 and 255 specify that part of the octet corresponds to the network ID, and the remaining part corresponds to the host ID.)

If subnet masks are incorrectly configured, network communications problems due to routing errors may occur. For example, TCP/IP may incorrectly determine that a computer on the local subnet is located on a remote subnet and attempt to route a packet to the remote subnet. In this instance, the computer on the local subnet would never receive the packet intended for it.

Default Gateway Addresses

A *default gateway address* specifies the IP address of a router on the local network segment. When a computer that uses TCP/IP determines that the computer it wants to communicate with is located on a remote subnet, it sends all network messages intended for the remote computer to the default gateway address, instead of directly to the destination computer. Then the router on the local subnet specified by the default gateway address forwards the messages to the destination computer on the remote subnet, either directly or via other routers.

If a computer's default gateway address does *not* specify a router on the local subnet, then that computer will be *unable* to communicate with computers or other network devices located on other network segments.

When a router is used to connect two network segments, it has two network cards and two IP addresses. Figure 14-1 illustrates how default gateway addresses are used to specify the IP address of a router on the local subnet.

FIGURE 14-1 Default gateway addresses specify local router

Notice in Figure 14-1, the default gateway address of Computer_A matches the IP address of its local router, and the default gateway address of Computer_B matches the IP address of its local router.

ASSIGNING IP ADDRESSES

IP addresses must be configured on each computer when TCP/IP is installed. You can assign an IP address to a Windows NT computer in one of two ways: by configuring a computer to obtain an IP address automatically from a DHCP server, or by manually specifying a computer's IP address configuration.

IP addresses are assigned to Windows NT computers in the Microsoft TCP/IP Properties dialog box. Instructions for accessing and configuring this dialog box are covered later in this chapter.

Assigning IP Addresses by Using a DHCP Server

The most convenient method for assigning IP addresses to multiple computers, in terms of administration time required, is to configure each of the computers to obtain its IP address from a *Dynamic Host Configuration Protocol* (DHCP) server.

This section discusses the advantages of using a DHCP server, the process of installing and configuring Microsoft DHCP Server, and configuring a client computer to obtain its IP address from a DHCP server.

Advantages of using a DHCP server

Assigning IP addresses by using a DHCP server is the preferred method because

- Using a DHCP server makes it possible for you to manage IP addresses centrally, thus ensuring addresses are valid and are *not* duplicated.

- Using a DHCP server reduces the amount of administration time required to manage and maintain IP addresses for each computer on the network.

- Using a DHCP server reduces the likelihood of human error when IP addresses are assigned because no need exists to enter an IP address manually on every individual computer.

○ Using a DHCP server enables you to regain the use of an IP address no longer assigned to a host when the DHCP lease period for this IP address expires.

Before you can assign an IP address to a Windows NT computer by using a DHCP server, you must first install and configure a DHCP server on your network.

Installing and configuring Microsoft DHCP Server

Microsoft includes a DHCP server product with Windows NT Server. *Microsoft DHCP Server* is an NT Server service that provides centralized management of IP address assignment. Microsoft DHCP Server can be installed on any Windows NT Server computer that has a manually configured IP address for each network adapter installed in it. The next sections explain how to install and configure Microsoft DHCP Server on a Windows NT Server computer.

TO INSTALL MICROSOFT DHCP SERVER, FOLLOW THESE STEPS:

1. Select Start ⇒ Settings ⇒ Control Panel.

2. In the Control Panel dialog box, double-click Network.

3. In the Network dialog box, click the Services tab.

4. On the Services tab, click the Add command button.

5. In the Select Network Service dialog box, highlight Microsoft DHCP Server. Click OK.

6. A Windows NT Setup dialog box appears. Ensure the correct path to the Windows NT Server source files (normally the I386 folder on your Windows NT Server compact disc) is displayed in the text box. Edit the text box as necessary. Click the Continue command button.

7. Windows NT copies and installs the appropriate files. An informational dialog box appears, indicating all network adapters in this computer must have manually configured IP addresses. (At the end of the DHCP Server installation process, Windows NT prompts you to assign IP addresses manually to the computer's network adapters if you have not already done so.) Click OK.

8. The Network dialog box reappears. Click the Close command button. (Manually configure IP addresses only if prompted to do so.)

9. Windows NT performs various bindings operations.

10. The Network Settings Change dialog box is displayed, indicating you must shut down and restart the computer for the new settings to take effect. Click the Yes command button to restart the computer. You are now ready to configure Microsoft DHCP Server.

TO CONFIGURE MICROSOFT DHCP SERVER, FOLLOW THESE STEPS:

1. Log on as Administrator.

2. Select Start ⇒ Programs ⇒ Administrative Tools (Common) ⇒ DHCP Manager.

3. The DHCP Manager dialog box appears. Select Server ⇒ Add.

4. In the Add DHCP Server to Server List, type the IP address of the computer you installed Microsoft DHCP Server on. Click OK.

5. Highlight the IP address you entered in Step 4 in the DHCP Servers list box. Select Scope ⇒ Create.

6. In the Create Scope dialog box, enter a starting and ending IP address (in the Start Address and End Address text boxes) to create a scope — a range of IP addresses also called an IP address pool. All IP addresses in the pool must have the same network ID. Enter a subnet mask in the Subnet Mask text box. This subnet mask will be used for all IP addresses assigned from this IP address pool. Figure 14-2 shows a configured Create Scope dialog box. Notice the IP Address Pool configurations. Click OK.

7. The DHCP Manager dialog box appears, indicating the scope has been created, but not yet activated. Click the Yes command button. If a dialog box is displayed indicating no more information is available, click OK to clear it.

8. If you want the DHCP Server to assign a predefined default gateway address along with every IP address it assigns from this scope, select DHCP Options ⇒ Scope in the DHCP Manager dialog box. Continue on to Steps 9, 10, and 11.

If you *don't* want the DHCP server to assign a default gateway address when it assigns IP addresses, skip to Step 12.

FIGURE 14-2 Creating a DHCP scope

9. The DHCP Options: Scope dialog box appears. In the Unused Options list box, highlight 003 Router.

 note **You can configure several other options in the DHCP Options: Scope dialog box. A detailed discussion of these options is beyond the scope of this book and the objectives for the Server exam. For more information on the configurable options in this dialog box, see the various Help screens in DHCP Manager, the *Microsoft Windows NT Server Resource Kit for version 4.0* (Microsoft Press, 1996), and *TCP/IP MCSE Study Guide* by Greg Bulette (IDG Books Worldwide, 1998).**

Click the Add command button. Click the Value command button. Then click the Edit Array command button.

10. The IP Address Array Editor dialog box appears. Type in the IP address of the router you want assigned as the default gateway address in the New IP Address text box. Click the Add command button. Click OK.

11. In the DHCP Options: Scope dialog box, click OK.

12. Exit DHCP Manager.

Configuring a computer to obtain an IP address from a DHCP server

Now that you've installed and configured a DHCP server, you're ready to configure a client computer to obtain its IP address from a DHCP server.

TO CONFIGURE A WINDOWS NT CLIENT COMPUTER TO OBTAIN AN IP ADDRESS FROM A DHCP SERVER, FOLLOW THESE STEPS:

1. Select Start ⇒ Settings ⇒ Control Panel.

2. In the Control Panel dialog box, double-click Network.

3. In the Network dialog box, click the Protocols tab.

4. On the Protocols tab, double-click the TCP/IP Protocol in the Network Protocols list box. (Or, if you prefer, highlight the TCP/IP Protocol in the Network Protocols list box and click the Properties command button.)

5. The Microsoft TCP/IP Properties dialog box appears. Ensure the option button next to "Obtain an IP address from a DHCP server" is selected.

Figure 14-3 shows the Microsoft TCP/IP Properties dialog box.

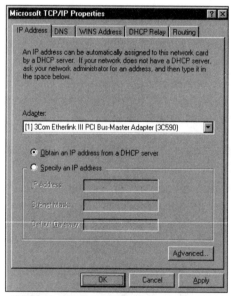

FIGURE 14-3   Using a DHCP server to assign an IP address

6. If the option button next to "Obtain an IP address from a DHCP server" was *not* selected by default and you selected it, Windows NT displays a Microsoft TCP/IP warning dialog box, asking if you want to enable DHCP. Click the Yes command button to continue.

7. If only one network adapter is installed in the computer, click OK.

If additional network adapters are installed in the computer you are configuring to obtain IP addresses from a DHCP server, select each adapter (one at a time) from the Adapter drop-down list box, and select the option button next to "Obtain an IP address from a DHCP server." When you have configured all network adapters, click OK.

8. The Network dialog box reappears. Click the Close command button.

9. A Network Settings Change dialog box is displayed, indicating you must shut down and restart the computer for the new settings to take effect. Click the Yes command button to restart the computer.

Assigning IP Addresses Manually

If you don't have a DHCP server, you must assign IP addresses manually. This method is both more time-consuming than using a DHCP server and more prone to error, because an IP address must be manually typed on each individual computer. The following section explains the steps involved in assigning an IP address manually.

TO ASSIGN AN IP ADDRESS MANUALLY TO A WINDOWS NT COMPUTER, FOLLOW THESE STEPS:

1. Select Start ⇒ Settings ⇒ Control Panel.

2. In the Control Panel dialog box, double-click Network.

3. In the Network dialog box, click the Protocols tab.

4. On the Protocols tab, double-click the TCP/IP Protocol in the Network Protocols list box. (Or, if you prefer, highlight the TCP/IP Protocol in the Network Protocols list box and click the Properties command button.)

5. The Microsoft TCP/IP Properties dialog box appears. Select the option button next to "Specify an IP address." Then complete the following text boxes:

- o IP Address: Enter the IP address you want to assign in the IP Address text box. (The IP address is a mandatory setting.) Press Tab.

- o Subnet Mask: Either accept the default subnet mask displayed or type in the subnet mask you want to assign in the Subnet Mask text box. (The subnet mask is a mandatory setting.) Press Tab.

- o Default Gateway: Type in a default gateway address in the Default Gateway text box. (The default gateway setting is optional.)

Figure 14-4 shows a manually configured IP address for a Windows NT Server computer.

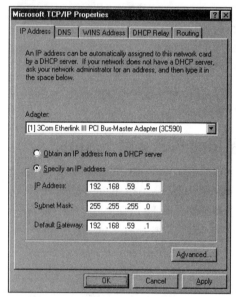

**FIGURE 14-4   Assigning an IP address
                manually**

If only one network adapter is installed in the computer, click OK.
If additional network adapters are installed in the computer to which you want to manually assign IP addresses at this time, select each adapter (one at a time) from the Adapter drop-down list box and select the option button next to "Specify an IP address." Type in an IP address, subnet mask, and default gateway (if desired) for each network adapter. When you have configured IP addresses for all network adapters, click OK.

6. The Network dialog box reappears. Click the Close command button.

7. A Network Settings Change dialog box is displayed, indicating you must shut down and restart the computer for the new settings to take effect. Click the Yes command button to restart the computer.

PUBLISHING ON THE INTERNET

Publishing World Wide Web pages on the Internet is becoming more popular every day. Many companies and organizations, from small, home-based businesses to multimillion-dollar concerns, use the Web to advertise their products and services. Web pages can be made available to anyone who has an Internet connection and a Web browser, such as Internet Explorer or Netscape Navigator.

Microsoft's primary tool for publishing on the Internet is Microsoft Internet Information Server (IIS) The following sections discuss this product in detail.

Microsoft Internet Information Server (IIS)

Microsoft Internet Information Server (IIS) is a Windows NT Server service that provides World Wide Web (WWW), File Transfer Protocol (FTP), and Gopher publishing services.

Internet Information Server uses *Hypertext Transfer Protocol* (HTTP) to publish WWW documents on the Internet. FTP enables users to transfer files between computers on the Internet. The FTP service included with IIS replaces the FTP service included in previous versions of Windows NT Server. Gopher is a complicated publishing service that is not used extensively anymore and is not included in the objectives for the Server exam.

Internet Information Server (IIS) requires the use of TCP/IP. You *must* have TCP/IP installed in your Windows NT Server computer to install and use IIS. No additional hardware is required to install and use IIS on an internal intranet.

The following sections discuss the basics of IIS, including: connecting your Internet Information Server to the Internet, installing and configuring IIS, using Internet Service Manager, configuring the WWW service, and configuring a virtual server.

Connecting your Internet Information Server to the Internet

If you want to connect your Internet Information Server to the Internet instead of just using it on your company's internal network (intranet), additional hardware is required.

Different hardware is required for different types of Internet connections. When determining the type of Internet connection to use, you should consider how many people will access your Internet Information Server, the frequency and duration of those accesses, and the size of documents and files being accessed.

Table 14-1 shows some of the Internet connection types, their speeds, and the additional hardware each requires.

You may want to consult with your Internet service provider (ISP) when determining the type of connection you need and when configuring the hardware and software used to establish your Internet connection.

TABLE 14-1 INTERNET CONNECTION TYPES

CONNECTION TYPE	SPEED	ADDITIONAL HARDWARE REQUIRED
Modem	28.8 – 56Kbps	A modem and standard telephone line
ISDN	64 – 128Kbps	An ISDN adapter card with either an internal or external network terminating unit (NT1), and an ISDN line
Digital Leased Line	56Kbps – 44.7Mbps	A router, a DSU/CSU, a network adapter, and a digital leased line – 56Kbps, fractional T1, T1, or T3

Installing and configuring Microsoft Internet Information Server (IIS)

Before installing and configuring Microsoft Internet Information Server (IIS), you should install Windows NT Server and TCP/IP. Additionally, you may want to install and configure the computer's Internet connection, including the additional hardware required, before you install IIS.

You can install IIS either during the Windows NT Server installation process or at a later time. The following steps explain how to install IIS on a computer after Windows NT Server and TCP/IP have been installed.

TO INSTALL AND CONFIGURE MICROSOFT INTERNET INFORMATION SERVER (IIS), FOLLOW THESE STEPS:

1. Select Start ⇒ Settings ⇒ Control Panel.

2. In the Control Panel dialog box, double-click Network.

3. In the Network dialog box, click the Services tab.

4. On the Services tab, click the Add command button.

5. The Select Network Service dialog box appears. Highlight Microsoft Internet Information Server.

Figure 14-5 shows the Select Network Service dialog box. Notice Microsoft Internet Information Server is highlighted. Click OK.

FIGURE 14-5   **Installing Microsoft Internet Information Server**

6. An Internet Information Server Installation dialog box appears. Ensure the correct path to your Windows NT Server source files (usually the I386 folder on your Windows NT Server compact disc) is listed in the text box. Edit the text box as necessary. Click OK.

7. A Microsoft Internet Information Server 2.0 Setup dialog box appears. Click OK.

8. The Microsoft Internet Information Server 2.0 Setup dialog box appears, as shown in Figure 14-6. Notice the options that can be installed with IIS.

Select all the options you want installed with IIS. Deselect any undesired options. Click OK.

9. If a Microsoft Internet Information Server 2.0 Setup dialog box appears prompting you to confirm the creation of the inetsrv folder, click the Yes command button.

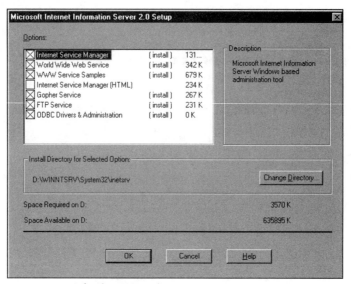

FIGURE 14-6   Selecting IIS options

10. The Publishing Directories dialog box appears, as shown in Figure 14-7. Note the default publishing directories.

FIGURE 14-7   Configuring publishing directories for the WWW, FTP, and Gopher services

Configure the publishing directories as desired, or accept the default publishing directories presented. Click OK.

11. If a Microsoft Internet Information Server 2.0 Setup dialog box appears prompting you to create the publishing directories, click the Yes command button.

12. Windows NT installs Microsoft Internet Information Server and the options you selected. (This process takes a few minutes.)

13. If you installed the Gopher service and you have not yet assigned an Internet domain name to the computer, a dialog box appears, indicating you should assign an Internet domain name to your computer. Click OK.

14. If you installed ODBC drivers and administration, a dialog box may appear indicating you need to close Control Panel to continue the ODBC installation. Click OK to close Control Panel.

15. The Install Drivers dialog box appears. Highlight the ODBC drivers you want to install, and click OK.

16. The Microsoft Internet Information Server 2.0 Setup dialog box appears, indicating IIS was successfully installed. Click OK.

17. The Network dialog box reappears. Click the Close command button.

Microsoft Internet Information Server is now installed, and all its services have been started. You needn't restart your computer at this time.

Using Internet Service Manager
Once you have installed Microsoft Internet Information Server, you can use Internet Service Manager to manage IIS.

Internet Service Manager can be used to configure the IIS services, to configure IIS security, and to start and stop the individual IIS services.

Internet Service Manager can be accessed by selecting Start ⇒ Programs ⇒ Microsoft Internet Server (Common) ⇒ Internet Service Manager.

The next section discusses configuring the WWW service.

note **Because configuring the FTP and Gopher services is substantially similar to configuring the WWW service, detailed configuration instructions for the FTP and Gopher services are not included. For more information on the FTP and Gopher services, see the Help screens in Microsoft Internet Service Manager.**

TO CONFIGURE THE WWW SERVICE, FOLLOW THESE STEPS:

1. Start Internet Service Manager by selecting Start ⇒ Programs ⇒ Microsoft Internet Server (Common) ⇒ Internet Service Manager. Figure 14-8 shows the Microsoft Internet Service Manager dialog box. Notice the WWW service is listed in the Service column and is running.

FIGURE 14-8   Using Internet Service Manager to configure IIS services

2. To access the Properties dialog box for the WWW service, highlight the computer on the same line as the WWW service, and select Properties ⇒ Service Properties. The WWW Service Properties dialog box appears, as shown in Figure 14-9. Note the configurable options on the Service tab.

3. Configure options for the WWW service on the Service tab. Many of the options on this tab are security features. The most commonly configured options are

- Anonymous Logon: This section should be configured if the check box next to Allow Anonymous is selected in the Password Authentication section. When a user name and password are entered in the Anonymous Logon section, the user rights and permissions assigned to this user name are applied to all anonymous users of the WWW service. In this way, IIS security is integrated with Windows NT security. The default user name listed is IUSR_*Computer_name*.

FIGURE 14-9 Configuration options on the WWW
Service Properties Service tab

- Password Authentication: The three options in this section are Allow
  Anonymous, Basic (Clear Text), and Windows NT Challenge/Response.

  - Allow Anonymous: If you select the check box next to Allow
    Anonymous, anyone with Internet access can access the WWW service
    on your server anonymously. These users will not be required to supply
    a user name and password. If you clear the check box next to Allow
    Anonymous, all users will be required to supply a user name and a
    password to access the WWW service. The Allow Anonymous option is
    selected by default.

  - Basic (Clear Text): If you select the check box next to Basic (Clear
    Text), user names and passwords can be sent over the Internet in an
    unencrypted format. Selecting this option is not normally desirable
    because it compromises the security of your server. If this check box is
    cleared, unencrypted user names and passwords will not be accepted by
    the WWW service. The Basic (Clear Text) option is not selected by default.

  - Windows NT Challenge/Response: If you select the check box next to
    Windows NT Challenge/Response, user names and passwords can be
    sent over the Internet in an encrypted format. If this check box is
    cleared, encrypted user names and passwords will not be accepted by
    the WWW service. This security feature is selected by default and should
    be used in high-security environments.

4. Configure advanced options for the WWW service as desired on the Advanced tab in the WWW Service Properties dialog box, as shown in Figure 14-10. Note: most of the options on the Advanced tab are used to manage access security for the WWW service.

FIGURE 14-10   **Configuration options on the WWW Service Properties Advanced tab**

The Advanced tab is primarily used to control access to the WWW service by the IP address of the computer attempting to access the service. The most commonly configured options on the Advanced tab are

- Granted Access: If you select the option button next to this option, all computers on the Internet will be allowed to access the WWW service *except* those explicitly listed, by IP address, in the following list box. To add computers to the list box, click the Add command button.

- Denied Access: If you select the option button next to this option, all computers on the Internet will be denied access to the WWW service *except* those explicitly listed, by IP address, in the following list box. To add computers to the list box, click the Add command button.

This completes the configuration of the WWW service

Configuring a virtual server   A virtual server is a pseudo WWW server with its own unique domain name and IP address. To the Internet user accessing the virtual server, a virtual server appears to be a separate server; but in reality, a virtual server is not a separate server, but more like an extra shared folder on an Internet Information Server accessed by specifying a different domain name and IP address. A single Internet Information Server can be configured to accommodate multiple virtual servers. Each virtual server is assigned a separate publishing directory.

For example, an Internet service provider could use one Internet Information Server to host virtual servers for several customers. Each customer could have its own domain name, such as `www.company_a.com`, `www.company_b.com`, `www.company_c.com`, and so forth. To Internet users accessing these companies' WWW services, each domain name appears to be on a separate server.

Configuring a virtual server consists of two parts: first, you must configure an additional IP address for your network adapter; second, you use Internet Service Manager to configure the virtual server. The following sections describe how to accomplish these tasks.

TO CONFIGURE AN ADDITIONAL IP ADDRESS FOR A NETWORK ADAPTER, FOLLOW THESE STEPS:

1. Select Start ⇒ Settings ⇒ Control Panel.

2. In the Control Panel dialog box, double-click Network.

3. In the Network dialog box, click the Protocols tab.

4. On the Protocols tab, double-click TCP/IP Protocol in the Network Protocols list box.

5. The Microsoft TCP/IP Properties dialog box appears. Click the Advanced command button.

6. The Advanced IP Addressing dialog box appears. In the Adapter drop-down list box, select the network adapter to which you want to assign an additional IP address. Click the Add command button in the IP Addresses section.

7. The TCP/IP Address dialog box appears. Type in the additional IP address and subnet mask you want to assign to the network adapter. Click the Add command button.

8. The Advanced IP Addressing dialog box reappears.

Figure 14-11 shows the Advanced IP Addressing dialog box with two IP addresses configured for a single network adapter. Click OK.

FIGURE 14-11   Multiple IP addresses assigned
to a single network adapter

9. In the Microsoft TCP/IP Properties dialog box, click OK.

10. In the Network dialog box, click the Close command button.

11. A Network Settings Change warning dialog box appears, asking if you want to restart your computer now for the new settings to take effect. Click the Yes command button.

TO USE INTERNET SERVICE MANAGER TO CONFIGURE THE VIRTUAL SERVER, FOLLOW THESE STEPS:

1. Select Start ⇒ Programs ⇒ Microsoft Internet Server (Common) ⇒ Internet Service Manager.

2. In the Microsoft Internet Service Manager dialog box, highlight the computer on the same line as the WWW service, and select Properties ⇒ Service Properties.

3. The WWW Service Properties dialog box appears. Click the Directories tab.

4. The Directories tab appears, as shown in Figure 14-12. Note the check box next to Directory Browsing Allowed. When selected, this option permits users to browse all files and folders published by the WWW service. For security reasons, this option is not normally selected. Click the Add command button.

FIGURE 14-12 **Configuration options on the WWW Service Properties Directories tab**

5. In the Directory Properties dialog box, select the option button next to Home Directory. In the Directory text box, type the full path to the home directory that will be used by the virtual server, for example: c:\inetpub\wwwroot_2. (This directory need *not* be an existing directory— entering a new directory in this text box will cause NT to create it when you click OK.) Then select the check box next to Virtual Server. Type in the additional IP address you assigned to your network adapter in the Virtual Server IP Address text box. Click OK.

Figure 14-13 shows the Directory Properties dialog box configured to implement a virtual server.

6. The WWW Service Properties dialog box reappears. The virtual server's home directory and IP address now appear in the list box. Click OK.

7. Exit Microsoft Internet Service Manager.

FIGURE 14-13   **Configuring a virtual server**

TROUBLESHOOTING COMMON TCP/IP CONNECTIVITY PROBLEMS

There are several common TCP/IP connectivity problems. Most TCP/IP connectivity problems are caused by incorrectly configured TCP/IP settings on the computer that has the problem.

TCP/IP connectivity problems commonly reported by users include

- A user is unable to access a computer located on another subnet.

- A user is unable to access the Internet.

- A user is unable to access computers on both the local and remote subnets.

- TCP/IP fails to initialize on the user's computer.

When troubleshooting a TCP/IP connectivity problem, carefully check the TCP/IP settings on the computer experiencing the problem, including IP address, subnet mask, and default gateway:

- **IP address:** Make sure the computer's IP address is *not* a duplicate of another IP address used on the network, and that it is an appropriate IP address for the local subnet (the network ID portion of the IP address must be the same for all computers on the local subnet).

- **Subnet mask:** Ensure the computer's subnet mask is the same subnet mask used by all computers and routers located on that subnet.

- **Default gateway:** Ensure the computer's default gateway address matches the IP address of a router on the local subnet.

Two command-line utilities exist that can help you when you're troubleshooting TCP/IP connectivity problems: `Ipconfig.exe` and `ping.exe`.

`Ipconfig.exe` displays the computer's current IP configuration settings, including IP address, subnet mask, and default gateway. To use `Ipconfig.exe`, select Start ⇒ Programs ⇒ Command Prompt. At the command prompt, type **ipconfig /all** and press Enter.

`Ping.exe` verifies network communications between the local computer and any other computer specified on the network. To use `ping.exe`, select Start ⇒ Programs ⇒ Command Prompt. At the command prompt, type **ping *ip_address*** and press Enter. (The IP address entered is the IP address of the computer with which you are attempting to communicate.) If your computer is able to communicate with the remote computer specified, `ping.exe` will display four replies from the remote computer's IP address. The following is an example of a successful ping response:

```
Reply from 192.168.59.5: bytes=32 time<10ms TTL=128
Reply from 192.168.59.5: bytes=32 time<10ms TTL=128
Reply from 192.168.59.5: bytes=32 time<10ms TTL=128
Reply from 192.168.59.5: bytes=32 time<10ms TTL=128
```

If your computer is unable to communicate with the remote computer specified, `ping.exe` usually displays `Request timed out` four times.

You can ping your own computer's IP address to determine whether TCP/IP is correctly configured and initialized on your local computer. If TCP/IP is correctly configured on your local computer, `ping.exe` will display four replies from your local computer's IP address.

KEY POINT SUMMARY

This chapter explored how to network Windows NT using TCP/IP.

- The *Transmission Control Protocol/Internet Protocol* (TCP/IP) is a fast, routable, transport protocol that provides robust capabilities for Windows NT networking. TCP/IP is the protocol used on the Internet. TCP/IP is an enterprise protocol that is supported by many other operating systems. TCP/IP is typically the recommended protocol for large, heterogeneous networks.

- An *IP address* is a 32-bit binary number, broken into four 8-bit sections, which uniquely identifies a computer or other network device on a network that uses TCP/IP. *No two computers or other devices on an internetwork should have the same IP address.* An IP address contains two important identifiers: a *network ID* and a *host ID*. All computers located on the same network subnet have the same network ID. Each computer or other network device on a given network subnet must have a unique host ID.

- A *subnet mask* specifies which portion of an IP address represents the network ID and which portion represents the host ID. A subnet mask allows TCP/IP to determine whether network traffic destined for a given IP address should be transmitted on the local subnet, or whether it should be routed to a remote subnet. *A subnet mask should be the same for all computers on a given network segment.* If subnet masks are incorrectly configured, network communications problems due to routing errors may occur.

- A *default gateway address* specifies the IP address of a router on the local network segment. If a computer's default gateway address does not specify a router on the local subnet, then that computer will be unable to communicate with computers or other network devices located on other network segments.

- IP addresses must be configured on each computer when TCP/IP is installed. You can assign an IP address to a Windows NT computer in one of two ways: by configuring a computer to obtain an IP address from a DHCP server, or by manually specifying a computer's IP address configuration.

- The advantages of using a DHCP server to assign IP addresses are as follows:

  - It allows central management of IP addresses, and ensures addresses are valid and are not duplicated.

  - It reduces the amount of administration time required to manage and maintain IP addresses for each computer on the network.

  - It reduces the likelihood of human error when IP addresses are assigned, because no need exists to enter an IP address manually on each individual computer.

- Microsoft's primary tool for publishing on the Internet is *Microsoft Internet Information Server* (IIS). This product requires the use of TCP/IP. IIS provides WWW, FTP, and Gopher publishing services. No additional hardware is required to install IIS on an internal intranet. If you want to connect your IIS to the Internet, however, you need additional hardware to support this connection.

- *Internet Service Manager* is a Windows NT tool you can use to manage IIS. You can use Internet Service Manager to configure the IIS services, configure IIS security, and start and stop the individual IIS services.

- Many of the configuration options on the WWW service enable you to manage security. When configuring password authentication, you can clear the check box next to Basic (Clear Text) and select the check box next to Windows NT Challenge/Response to prevent user names and passwords from being transmitted in an unencrypted format over the Internet. You can control access by IP address. You can ensure directory browsing is not selected, and you can require users to supply user names and passwords by not permitting anonymous users to access the WWW service.

- A *virtual server* is a pseudo WWW server with its own unique domain name and IP address. To the Internet user accessing the virtual server, a virtual server appears to be a separate server; but in reality, a virtual server is not a separate server, but more like an extra shared folder on an Internet Information Server. A single Internet Information Server can be configured to accommodate multiple virtual servers. Before you can configure a virtual server, you must configure an additional IP address for the network adapter in the Windows NT Server computer.

- When troubleshooting a TCP/IP connectivity problem, carefully check the TCP/IP settings on the computer experiencing the problem, including IP address, subnet mask, and default gateway:
  - Make sure the computer's IP address is *not* a duplicate of another IP address used on the network, and that it is an appropriate IP address for the local subnet. (The network ID portion of the IP address must be the same for all computers on the local subnet.)
  - Ensure the computer's subnet mask is the same subnet mask used by all computers and routers located on that subnet.
  - Ensure the computer's default gateway address matches the IP address of a router on the local subnet.
  - Also consider using the `Ipconfig.exe` and `ping.exe` command-line utilities when troubleshooting TCP/IP connectivity problems.

APPLYING WHAT YOU'VE LEARNED

Now it's time to regroup, review, and apply what you've learned in this chapter.

The questions in the following Instant Assessment section bring to mind key facts and concepts. Then, a Critical Thinking Lab gives you a chance to analyze two situations and apply your troubleshooting knowledge of TCP/IP to those situations. Finally, a Hands-on Lab reinforces what you've learned and provides an opportunity for you to practice some of the tasks that may be tested by the Server exam.

Instant Assessment

1. What does TCP/IP stand for?
2. Which transport protocol is typically recommended for use in large, heterogeneous networks?
3. What is an IP address?
4. What problem can occur if subnet masks are incorrectly configured?
5. What problem will occur if a computer's default gateway address does not specify a router on the local subnet?

6. What are the two methods you can use to assign IP addresses to Windows NT computers?

7. What is Microsoft's primary tool for publishing on the Internet?

8. Your company plans to connect its Internet Information Server to the Internet over a fractional T1 leased line. What additional hardware is required to implement the connection?

9. You want to connect your Internet Information Server to the Internet using an ISDN line. What additional hardware is required to implement the connection?

10. Your company operates in a high-security environment. What steps can you take to secure access to the WWW service on your Microsoft Internet Information Server?

11. What is a virtual server?

12. How must you configure the network adapter in your computer before you can configure a virtual server?

13. Which three TCP/IP settings should you check when troubleshooting a computer that has a TCP/IP connectivity problem?

14. You want to determine whether TCP/IP is correctly configured and initialized on a Windows NT computer. Which command-line utility can you use to help you determine this?

15. You want to verify TCP/IP network communications between two Windows NT Server computers. Which command-line utility can you use to help you determine this?

16. You want to display the TCP/IP configuration of a Windows NT computer. Which command-line utility can you use to accomplish this?

T/F

17. All computers located on the same network segment have the same network ID. _____

18. Each computer or other network device on a given network segment must have the same host ID. _____

19. A subnet mask should be the same for all computers and other network devices on a given network segment. _____

concept link   **For answers to the Instant Assessment questions see Appendix B.**

Critical Thinking Lab

The following Critical Thinking Lab is designed to allow you to practice the connectivity troubleshooting skills you have learned in the chapter.

Lab 14.24 *Identifying and resolving TCP/IP connectivity problems*

The purpose of this lab is to give you hands-on experience in identifying and resolving common TCP/IP connectivity problems.

In each of the following situations:

1. Identify the TCP/IP connectivity problem (for example, an invalid or duplicate IP address).

2. Describe what you would do to resolve the problem.

Situation 1   Several components on a network subnet are configured as shown in Figure 14-14:

FIGURE 14-14   Network subnet configuration for Situation 1

What is the TCP/IP connectivity problem in this situation?

What would you do to resolve the problem?

Situation 2   Several components on a network subnet are configured as shown in Figure 14-15.

IP address: 10.105.232.8
Default gateway: 10.105.232.1

IP address: 10.105.232.9
Default gateway: 10.105.232.1

IP address: 10.105.232.1
Default gateway: 10.105.232.1

Client_A

Client_B

Router

The Internet

Ethernet

Client_C

Client_D

Server_A

IP address: 10.105.232.8
Default gateway: 10.105.232.1

IP address: 10.105.232.12
Default gateway: 10.105.232.1

IP address: 10.105.232.18
Default gateway: 10.105.232.1

FIGURE 14-15   **Network subnet configuration for Situation 2**

What is the TCP/IP connectivity problem in this situation?

What would you do to resolve the problem?

 concept link   **For answers to the Critical Thinking Lab see Appendix B.**

Hands–on Lab

The following Hands-on Lab provides you with a practical opportunity to apply the TCP/IP knowledge you've gained in this chapter.

Lab 14.25 *Configuring Microsoft Internet Information Server (IIS)*

The purpose of this lab is to give you hands-on experience in configuring Microsoft Internet Information Server (IIS).

Begin this lab by booting your computer to Windows NT Server. Log on as Administrator.

COMPLETE THE FOLLOWING STEPS CAREFULLY:

1. Select Start ⇒ Programs ⇒ Microsoft Internet Server (Common) ⇒ Internet Information Server Setup.

2. The Microsoft Internet Information Server 2.0 Setup dialog box appears. Click OK.

3. In the next Microsoft Internet Information Server 2.0 Setup dialog box that appears, click the Add/Remove command button.

4. Ensure the correct source file location is displayed in the text box. (This is probably the `C:\WINNTSRV\system32\inetsrv` folder on your Windows NT Server computer.) It should be unnecessary to edit this text box. Click OK.

5. In the Microsoft Internet Information Server 2.0 Setup dialog box, *deselect* the check box next to Gopher Service. (This will deinstall the Gopher Service, which is not used in most NT installations.) Click OK.

6. The Microsoft Internet Information Server 2.0 Setup dialog box appears. Click the Yes command button to stop the Gopher Publishing Service.

7. In the Microsoft Internet Information Server 2.0 Setup dialog box, click OK.

8. Select Start ⇒ Programs ⇒ Microsoft Internet Server (Common) ⇒ Internet Service Manager.

9. In the Microsoft Internet Service Manager dialog box, double-click the first computer listed in the Computer list box.

10. The "WWW Service Properties for pdclab" dialog box appears. Notice the configuration options available on the Service tab. Click the Directories tab.

11. On the Directories tab, notice the configuration options available. Click the Logging tab.

12. On the Logging tab, notice the configuration options available. Click the Advanced tab.

13. Notice the configuration options available. Click OK.

14. In the Microsoft Internet Service Manager dialog box, highlight the first computer listed in the Computer list box. Select Properties ⇒ Stop Service.

15. Notice the state of the WWW service has changed to Stopped. Select Properties ⇒ Start Service.

16. Notice the state of the WWW service has changed to Running. Exit Microsoft Internet Service Manager.

17. Double-click Internet Explorer on your desktop.

18. The Microsoft Internet Explorer Home Page dialog box appears. Edit the Address text box (which becomes the Open text box as soon as you begin to edit it) so it reads pdclab and press Enter.

19. The Microsoft Internet Information Server home page is displayed. You have successfully configured and accessed the Microsoft Internet Information Server. Exit Internet Explorer.

Coexistence with NetWare

About Chapter 15

This chapter is all about the Windows NT Server components that increase the interoperability of Windows NT with NetWare.

The chapter describes NWLink IPX/SPX Compatible Transport, which provides protocol compatibility between Windows NT and NetWare computers. Next, Gateway Service for NetWare, which enables users of NT Server computers to access resources on a NetWare server, is explored.

Finally, Chapter 15 presents tips on troubleshooting common NetWare connectivity problems.

This chapter includes a Hands-on Lab, in which you'll install and configure NWLink IPX/SPX Compatible Transport and Gateway Service for NetWare.

Chapter 15 maps to numerous objectives for the Server exam, including: protocol objectives that include the NWLink IPX/SPX Compatible Transport protocol, the "Configure Windows NT Server for interoperability with NetWare servers…" objective, and the "Choose the appropriate course of action to take to resolve connectivity problems" objective.

WINDOWS NT IN A NETWARE ENVIRONMENT

Microsoft includes components with Windows NT Server that enable Windows NT Server computers to coexist with Novell NetWare servers and client computers on the same network.

In a nutshell, these features enable Windows NT Server computers to utilize the resources on NetWare servers in a heterogeneous networking environment. These components can be used for long-term integration in a mixed network operating system environment, or for the short-term during a migration from NetWare to Windows NT.

When you consider the large number of existing Novell NetWare networks, particularly when Windows NT was first released, it's not too surprising that Microsoft has developed and included these components with Windows NT. Solutions that enable both Windows NT and NetWare to be used on the same network were critical to Windows NT's wide acceptance in the network operating system arena.

Microsoft has addressed this challenge by developing a protocol and a service that increase the interoperability of Windows NT with NetWare:

- NWLink IPX/SPX Compatible Transport
- Gateway Service for NetWare (GSNW)

This protocol and service are discussed in detail in the following sections.

exam preparation pointer

If you don't regularly use a NetWare server on your network, plan to review this chapter just before you take the Server exam. The details in this chapter are *very* important! Plan on doing some brute memorization.

NWLINK IPX/SPX COMPATIBLE TRANSPORT

NWLink IPX/SPX Compatible Transport is a routable transport protocol typically used in a combined Windows NT and NetWare environment. NWLink IPX/SPX Compatible Transport is Microsoft's version of Novell's IPX/SPX protocol. (*IPX/SPX* is the protocol used on most Novell NetWare networks.) NWLink provides protocol compatibility between Windows NT and NetWare computers. In addition to its functionality in a NetWare environment, NWLink also fully supports Microsoft networking.

NWLink IPX/SPX Compatible Transport, which is included with Windows NT Server, must be installed on NT Server computers in order to enable them to communicate over the network with NetWare computers.

There are two important topics that need to be discussed before moving on to the installation of NWLink IPX/SPX Compatible Transport: frame types and network numbers. Because frame types and network numbers must be configured during installation, it's important to have a solid grasp of these basic network concepts.

Frame Types

Frame types (also called *frame formats*) are accepted, standardized structures for transmitting data packets over a network. All frame types include certain common components, such as source address, destination address, data field, and cyclic redundancy check — but the various frame types include different combinations of additional fields beyond the common components.

Windows NT and NWLink IPX/SPX Compatible Transport support nine different frame types, which are described in Table 15-1.

TABLE 15-1 NWLink IPX/SPX Compatible Transport Frame Types

FRAME TYPE	DEFAULT/COMMON USAGE	NETWORK ADAPTERS THAT SUPPORT THIS FRAME TYPE
Ethernet 802.2	Default frame type for NetWare 3.12 and later NetWare versions on Ethernet networks	Ethernet
Ethernet 802.3	Default frame type for NetWare 3.11 and earlier NetWare versions on Ethernet networks	Ethernet
Ethernet II	Commonly associated with the TCP/IP protocol; not commonly used with NWLink IPX/SPX Compatible Transport	Ethernet
Ethernet SNAP	Commonly associated with the AppleTalk protocol; not commonly used with NWLink IPX/SPX Compatible Transport	Ethernet, FDDI

FRAME TYPE	DEFAULT/COMMON USAGE	NETWORK ADAPTERS THAT SUPPORT THIS FRAME TYPE
ARCNET	Default frame type for all versions of NetWare on ARCNET networks	ARCNET
Token Ring	Default frame type for all versions of NetWare on Token Ring networks	Token Ring
Token-Ring SNAP	Commonly associated with the AppleTalk protocol; not commonly used with NWLink IPX/SPX Compatible Transport	Token Ring
FDDI	Default frame type for NetWare 3.12 and later NetWare versions on FDDI networks	FDDI
FDDI 802.3	Default frame type for NetWare 3.11 and earlier NetWare versions on FDDI networks	FDDI

Before you select a frame type when installing and configuring NWLink IPX/SPX Compatible Transport, you should determine which frame type(s) are already in use on the network. You should select a frame type that *matches* the frame type already in use, or use the Windows NT auto frame type detection feature to automatically select a frame type. You can assign more than one frame type to an individual network adapter.

Frame type mismatching is a common cause of communications problems on networks that use NWLink IPX/SPX Compatible Transport. (This issue is covered in more depth in the "Troubleshooting Common NetWare Connectivity Problems" section later in this chapter.)

Network Numbers

Network numbers are 32-bit binary numbers that uniquely identify an NWLink IPX/SPX Compatible Transport network segment for routing purposes. Because network numbers uniquely identify a network segment, they are used by IPX routers to correctly forward data packets from one network segment to another.

Network numbers are only assigned to Windows NT computers that use NWLink IPX/SPX Compatible Transport. Network numbers are assigned during the installation and configuration of NWLink IPX/SPX Compatible Transport.

Network numbers are commonly presented in an eight-digit hexadecimal format. (In a hexadecimal format, the numbers 0 through 9 and the letters A through F can be used.) Don't confuse a network number with a TCP/IP network ID or a computer's MAC (hardware) address.

There are two types of network numbers: *external network numbers* (network numbers that are assigned to network adapters) and *internal network numbers*. A Windows NT computer that uses NWLink IPX/SPX Compatible Transport can have one or more external network number(s) and an internal network number, as well.

When NWLink IPX/SPX Compatible Transport is used, an external network number is assigned to each network adapter installed in a computer. An external network number uniquely identifies the network segment to which the network adapter is connected. (If more than one frame type is assigned to a network adapter, then each frame type is assigned its own external network number.) Windows NT can automatically detect and use the external network number in use on a network segment. However, you can manually assign any unique eight-digit external network number to a network adapter during the configuration of NWLink IPX/SPX Compatible Transport. External network numbers are sometimes referred to simply as network numbers.

An internal network number must be assigned to a Windows NT computer that uses NWLink IPX/SPX Compatible Transport when more than one network adapter is installed in it. (If there is only one network adapter installed in a computer, Windows NT does not require you to assign an internal network number, although you can assign an internal network number if you want.) An internal network number is an additional unique eight-digit network number that is used by the computer's operating system — an internal network number does *not* correspond to a specific network adapter installed in the computer. A Windows NT computer has only one internal network number, regardless of the number of network adapters installed in it.

Installing and Configuring NWLink IPX/SPX Compatible Transport

Installing and configuring NWLink IPX/SPX Compatible Transport is a fairly straightforward process. You should be prepared to enter the appropriate frame type(s) and network number(s) when prompted. If you have multiple adapters installed in your Windows NT computer, you will also have to assign an internal network number. Finally, only install this protocol at a time when you can shut down and restart the computer.

TO INSTALL AND CONFIGURE NWLINK IPX/SPX COMPATIBLE TRANSPORT, FOLLOW THESE STEPS:

1. Select Start ⇒ Settings ⇒ Control Panel.

2. In the Control Panel dialog box, double-click Network.

3. In the Network dialog box, click the Protocols tab.

4. On the Protocols tab, click the Add command button.

5. In the Select Network Protocol dialog box, highlight NWLink IPX/SPX Compatible Transport in the Network Protocol list box. Figure 15-1 shows the Select Network Protocol dialog box. Notice NWLink IPX/SPX Compatible Transport is highlighted. Click OK.

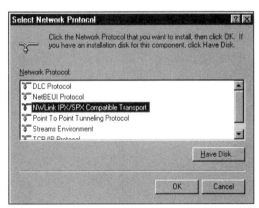

FIGURE 15-1   Installing NWLink IPX/SPX Compatible Transport

6. A Windows NT Setup dialog box appears. Ensure that the correct path to your Windows NT Server source files (usually the I386 folder on your Windows NT Server compact disc) is listed in the text box. Edit the text box as necessary. Click the Continue command button.

7. Windows NT installs NWLink IPX/SPX Compatible Transport. The Network dialog box reappears. Click the Close command button.

8. Windows NT performs various bindings operations.

9. If there is more than one network adapter installed in your computer, an NWLink IPX/SPX warning dialog box appears, indicating that you need to configure your computer's internal network number, as shown in Figure 15-2. Click the Yes command button.

FIGURE 15-2   Multiple network adapter warning

10. The NWLink IPX/SPX Properties dialog box appears, as shown in Figure 15-3.

FIGURE 15-3   Configuring the internal network number

Notice that you can configure the internal network number and the frame type in this dialog box. The configurable options in this dialog box are

o Internal Network Number: Change the Internal Network Number to a unique nonzero hexadecimal number up to eight digits long.

- Auto Frame Type Detection: If you want Windows NT to automatically detect and assign a frame type to a network adapter, select the option button next to Auto Frame Type Detection. Skip to Step 12.

- Manual Frame Type Detection: If you want to manually assign a frame type to a network adapter, select the option button next to Manual Frame Type Detection, and click the Add command button.

11. If you selected Manual Frame Type Detection, the Manual Frame Detection dialog box appears, as shown in Figure 15-4. Note the Frame Type drop-down list box and the Network Number text box. Select the desired frame type from the Frame Type drop-down list box. Type in a unique nonzero hexadecimal number up to eight digits long in the Network Number text box. Click the Add command button. (Note: All computers on a single subnet should use the *same* network number.)

FIGURE 15-4   **Manually assigning a frame type and network number to a network adapter**

12. The NWLink IPX/SPX Properties dialog box reappears. If you want to configure a frame type and network number for an additional network adapter(s), select the network adapter from the Adapter drop-down list box, and then follow the instructions in Steps 10 and 11 to configure a frame type and network number for the network adapter.

 You can assign multiple frame types and network numbers to an individual network adapter.

Figure 15-5 shows the NWLink IPX/SPX Properties dialog box after the configuration process is complete. Notice that two frame types and two network numbers are assigned to a single network adapter. Click OK.

13. A Network Settings Change dialog box appears, indicating you must shut down and restart the computer in order for the new settings to take effect. Click the Yes command button to restart the computer.

FIGURE 15-5   Multiple frame types assigned to a network adapter

GATEWAY SERVICE FOR NETWARE (GSNW)

Gateway Service for NetWare (GSNW) is a Windows NT Server service that, when installed and configured on a Windows NT Server computer, allows users to access resources (such as files, folders, and printers) on a NetWare server. GSNW enables access to resources on NetWare 4.x servers as well as NetWare 3.x servers. GSNW also enables users to run NetWare login scripts during the Windows NT logon process.

Additionally, GSNW enables the Windows NT Server computer to transparently share resources (files, folders, and printers) located on a NetWare server to client computers of the Windows NT Server computer. GSNW accomplishes this by converting the *Server Message Blocks* (SMBs) from the client computers of the Windows NT Server computer into *NetWare Core Protocol* (NCP) requests that are recognized by the NetWare server.

GSNW does *not* enable a Windows NT Server computer to share its resources with NetWare client computers.

GSNW is included with Windows NT Server and requires the use of NWLink IPX/SPX Compatible Transport.

Installing Gateway Service for NetWare (GSNW)

You should install NWLink IPX/SPX Compatible Transport *before* you install GSNW on your Windows NT Server computer.

I recommend you only install this service at a time when you can shut down and restart the Windows NT Server computer.

**TO INSTALL GATEWAY SERVICE FOR NETWARE (GSNW),
FOLLOW THESE STEPS:**

1. Select Start ⇒ Settings ⇒ Control Panel.

2. In the Control Panel dialog box, double-click Network.

3. In the Network dialog box, click the Services tab.

4. On the Services tab, click the Add command button.

5. In the Select Network Service dialog box, highlight Gateway (and Client) Services For NetWare. Figure 15-6 shows the Select Network Service dialog box. Note that Gateway (and Client) Services for NetWare is highlighted. Click OK.

FIGURE 15-6   Installing Gateway Service for NetWare

6. A Windows NT Setup dialog box appears. Ensure that the correct path to your Windows NT Server source files (usually the I386 folder on your Windows NT Server compact disc) is listed in the text box. Click the Continue command button.

7. Windows NT installs Gateway Service for NetWare. The Network dialog box reappears, as shown in Figure 15-7. Notice that Gateway Service for NetWare is listed in the Network Services list box. Click the Close command button.

FIGURE 15-7   Gateway Service for NetWare installed

8. Windows NT performs various bindings operations.

9. A Network Settings Change dialog box appears, indicating that you must shut down and restart the computer in order for the new settings to take effect. Click the Yes command button to restart the computer.

Configuring Gateway Service for NetWare (GSNW)

You can either configure GSNW the first time you log on after installing GSNW, or you can configure GSNW at a later time by using the GSNW application in Control Panel.

When configuring GSNW, you should be prepared to enter either the name of a preferred NetWare 3.x server you want to use or your tree and context for a NetWare 4.x server.

Pay particular attention to the gateway configuration options, including the user account used to configure the gateway. The user account on the NetWare server *must* be a member of the NTGATEWAY group on the NetWare server, and the NTGATEWAY group *must* have the appropriate NetWare permissions to the share.

The following sections explain the steps necessary to perform some common GSNW configurations. The first section discusses how to configure GSNW and then how to share a folder on the NetWare server with client computers of the Windows NT Server computer. The second section explains how to share a printer on a NetWare server (with client computers of a Windows NT Server computer) from a Windows NT Server computer that is running GSNW.

TO CONFIGURE GATEWAY SERVICE FOR NETWARE (GSNW) AND SHARE A FOLDER ON THE NETWARE SERVER, FOLLOW THESE STEPS:

1. The next time you boot your computer after installing GSNW, the Select NetWare Logon dialog box appears. (Note: This dialog box only appears the *first* time you log on after installing GSNW.)

   o If you want to configure GSNW now, skip to Step 4.

   o If you choose to configure GSNW at a later time, click OK in the Select NetWare Logon dialog box. When you decide to initially configure or change the configuration of GSNW, begin the configuration process at Step 2.

2. Select Start ⇒ Settings ⇒ Control Panel.

3. In the Control Panel dialog box, double-click the GSNW icon.

4. The Gateway Service for NetWare dialog box appears, as shown in Figure 15-8. Notice the various configuration options available.

   To configure GSNW, you must select from one of two primary options: Preferred Server, or Default Tree and Context. You can also select print, login script, and gateway options in this dialog box.

   o Preferred Server: Select the option button next to Preferred Server if you primarily access resources on NetWare 3.*x* servers. Then select the NetWare server of your choice from the Select Preferred Server drop-down list box.

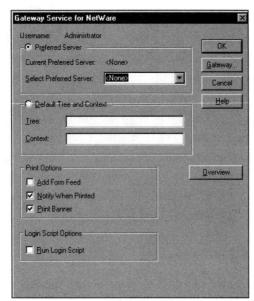

FIGURE 15-8   Configuring Gateway
Service for NetWare

- **Default Tree and Context:** Select the option button next to Default Tree
  and Context if you primarily access resources on NetWare 4.*x* servers. Then
  enter the tree name and context that contain your NetWare 4.*x* user
  account in the Tree and Context text boxes. (Note: You have to know this
  information — browsing is not supported in this section.)

- **Print Options:** If you print to a printer on a NetWare server, you can
  configure the Print Options section of the Gateway Service for NetWare
  dialog box. There are three options you can select:

  - **Add Form Feed:** Selecting this check box causes an additional form feed
    to be sent at the end of each print job. Deselect this check box if an
    additional blank page is printing at the end of each of your print jobs.
    By default, this check box is not selected.

  - **Notify When Printed:** Selecting this check box causes a pop-up message
    to appear on your screen after a print job is sent by the NetWare server
    to the print device. Clear this check box if you no longer want to
    receive these messages. This check box is selected by default.

  - **Print Banner:** Selecting this check box causes an additional sheet of
    paper that identifies the user that initiated the print job (called a banner
    page) to be printed at the beginning of each print job. If you want to
    save paper, deselect this check box. This check box is selected by
    default.

- Login Script Options: Selecting the check box next to Run Login Script in this section causes the NetWare login script to run during the Windows NT logon process. By default, this check box is not selected.

- Gateway: You can configure the gateway if you want to share resources located on NetWare servers with clients of your Windows NT Server computer. To configure the gateway, proceed to Step 5. If you don't want to configure the gateway at this time, click OK and skip to Step 11.

5. To configure the gateway, click the Gateway command button.

6. The Configure Gateway dialog box appears, as shown in Figure 15-9. Note the check box next to Enable Gateway.

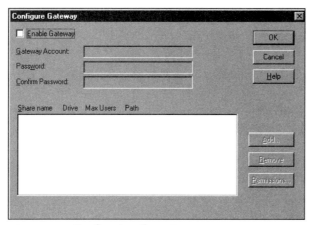

FIGURE 15-9   Configuring the gateway

You can configure the following items in this dialog box:

- Enable Gateway: Before you can share any resources located on a NetWare server with client computers of your Windows NT Server computer, the check box next to Enable Gateway must be selected. (If you enable the gateway and you login to the NetWare server, GSNW uses two user connections on the NetWare server: one for you, and one for the gateway. When using a five-user client license on the NetWare server, logging in and using the gateway leaves you only three connections.)

- Gateway Account: Enter a user account on the NetWare Server that you want to share resources from in the Gateway Account text box. If the user account is on a NetWare 4.*x* server, enter the complete account name, in the format .*user_name.organizational_unit.organization_name*. This user account *must* be a member of a group on the NetWare server called NTGATEWAY. The gateway won't function correctly if the user account listed in this text box is not a member of this group. Also, the NTGATEWAY group must have the appropriate NetWare permissions to the resources that you want to share by using the gateway.

o Password and Confirm Password: Enter the password (and confirm it by retyping it) for the user account on the NetWare Server (that you entered in the Gateway Account text box) in the Password and Confirm Password text boxes. To share a folder from a NetWare server, click the Add command button.

7. The New Share dialog box appears, as shown in Figure 15-10.

FIGURE 15-10   Creating a gateway share

The following options can be configured in this dialog box.

o Share Name: Type in the name of the share, as you want it to appear to client computers of the Windows NT Server computer, in the Share Name text box.

o Network Path: Type in the complete UNC path to the NetWare folder that you are sharing in the Network Path text box. (For more information on UNC paths for NetWare resources, see the section in this chapter on "Using GSNW to Access Resources on NetWare Servers.")

o Comment: Type in a comment that will appear in the browse list of the client computers of the Windows NT Server computer. This configuration is optional.

o Use Drive: Select a drive letter that GSNW will use to connect to the NetWare server. This drive letter can't already be in use on this computer.

o User Limit: In the User Limit section, select the option button next to either Unlimited or Allow *xx* Users. If you select Allow *xx* Users, enter the maximum number of concurrent users that will be allowed to access the share.

Click OK.

8. The Configure Gateway dialog box reappears. Click the Permissions command button if you want to configure share permissions on the gateway share.

9. The Access Through Share Permissions dialog box appears, as shown in Figure 15-11. Note that this is the standard NT Share Permissions dialog box. Configure the share permissions as desired. (Note: The most restrictive combination of share permissions and NetWare file and folder permissions applies.) Click OK.

FIGURE 15-11   **Setting permissions on a gateway share**

10. The Configure Gateway dialog box reappears. Click OK.

11. If you are configuring GSNW by using the GSNW application in Control Panel, a Gateway Service for NetWare dialog box appears, indicating that your configuration changes will take effect the next time you log in. Click OK.

12. The Control Panel dialog box reappears (if you are configuring GSNW by using the GSNW application in Control Panel). Exit Control Panel.

TO SHARE A PRINTER ON A NETWARE SERVER (WITH CLIENT COMPUTERS OF A WINDOWS NT SERVER COMPUTER) FROM A WINDOWS NT SERVER COMPUTER USING GSNW, FOLLOW THESE STEPS:

1. Enable the gateway, if you haven't already done so, as explained in Steps 5 and 6 in the previous section.

2. Select Start ⇒ Settings ⇒ Printers.

3. In the Printers dialog box, double-click Add Printer.

4. The Add Printer Wizard dialog box appears. Select the option button next to Network Printer Server. Click the Next command button.

5. The Connect to Printer dialog box appears. In the Printer text box, type the UNC path to the NetWare printer. Or, browse the shared network printers in the Shared Printers list box. Click OK.

6. A Connect to Printer warning dialog box appears, indicating that you need to install a printer driver. Click OK.

7. The Add Printer Wizard dialog box appears. Select the manufacturer and printer model from the list boxes. Click OK.

8. The Add Printer Wizard dialog box appears, asking whether you want your Windows-based programs to use this printer as the default printer. Select the appropriate option button. Click the Next command button.

9. Click the Finish command button.

10. In the Printers dialog box, highlight the printer you just created. Select File ⇒ Properties.

11. In the Printer Properties dialog box, click the Sharing tab.

12. On the Sharing tab, select the option button next to Shared. Enter a share name in the Share Name text box. Click OK.

13. Close the Printers dialog box.

USING GSNW TO ACCESS RESOURCES ON NETWARE SERVERS

Resources on NetWare 3.x servers and NetWare 4.x servers are accessed by using two different types of UNC path names.

To access resources on NetWare 3.x servers from a Windows NT Server computer that is running GSNW, you can use standard UNC path names in the format

```
\\server_name\share_name
```

For example, to connect to a volume named SYS on a NetWare 3.x server named NWSERVER, use the following UNC path name:

```
\\nwserver\sys
```

You can use these UNC path names when

- Configuring the gateway by using the GSNW application in Control Panel
- Connecting to a printer by using the Add Printer Wizard
- Connecting to a shared folder in Windows NT Explorer

To access resources on NetWare 4.*x* servers from a Windows NT Server computer that is running GSNW, you can use UNC path names in the format

```
\\tree_name\volume_name.organizational_unit.organization_name\
 folder_name
```

For example, to connect to the `Public` folder in a volume named `NWSERVER_SYS` (on a NetWare 4.*x* server) in the Sales organizational unit in the Widgets organization in a tree named CORP, use the following UNC path name:

```
\\corp\nwserver_sys.sales.widgets\public
```

You can use these UNC path names when

- Configuring the gateway by using the GSNW application in Control Panel
- Connecting to a printer by using the Add Printer Wizard
- Connecting to a shared folder in Windows NT Explorer

TROUBLESHOOTING COMMON NETWARE CONNECTIVITY PROBLEMS

There are several common NetWare connectivity problems. Most NetWare connectivity problems are caused by incorrectly configuring NWLink IPX/SPX Compatible Transport or GSNW on the computer that is experiencing the problem. Most user-reported problems relate to an inability to connect a Windows NT computer to resources on NetWare servers.

Table 15-2 shows the most common configuration errors that cause NetWare connectivity problems and recommended solutions to these problems.

TABLE 15-2 COMMON NETWARE CONFIGURATION ERRORS AND RECOMMENDED SOLUTIONS	
CONFIGURATION ERROR	*RECOMMENDED SOLUTION*
Frame type mismatch/network number mismatch	Both the NT client and the NetWare server normally must use the same frame type. Additionally, these computers must use the same network number if they are located on the same network segment. To find out what frame type and network number are being used on the NetWare server, type **config** at the : prompt on the NetWare server. Normally, you can use the NT autodetect feature for frame type selection on an NT computer. However, if you are unable to connect to a resource while using the autodetect feature, try manually configuring the frame type and network number on the NT computer to match those of the NetWare server. Remember, NetWare 3.11 and earlier versions use the Ethernet 802.3 frame type by default on Ethernet networks. NetWare 3.12 and later versions use the Ethernet 802.2 frame type by default on Ethernet networks.
Gateway user account is not a member of the NTGATEWAY group on the NetWare server	Make the gateway user account a member of the NTGATEWAY group on the NetWare server.
The gateway user account has permissions to access the resource on the NetWare server, but the NTGATEWAY group does not have these permissions	The NTGATEWAY group must have the appropriate permissions to access the shared resource on the NetWare server. Assign permissions to the NTGATEWAY group using the appropriate NetWare administration utility on the NetWare server. Remember that the most restrictive combination of gateway share permissions and NetWare file and folder permissions applies.
You have shared a NetWare printer, but have not enabled the gateway	Enable the gateway, even though you are not sharing any files or folders on the NetWare server.

KEY POINT SUMMARY

This chapter explored the Windows NT Server components that increase the interoperability of Windows NT with NetWare. These components enable Windows NT Server computers to utilize resources on NetWare servers in a heterogeneous networking environment.

- *NWLink IPX/SPX Compatible Transport* is a routable transport protocol that is typically used in a combined Windows NT and NetWare environment and provides compatibility between Windows NT and NetWare computers. NWLink IPX/SPX Compatible Transport, which is included with NT Server, must be installed on NT computers in order to enable them to communicate over the network with NetWare computers.

- *Frame types* (also called *frame formats*) are accepted, standardized structures for transmitting data packets over a network. A frame type must be configured during the installation and configuration of NWLink IPX/SPX Compatible Transport. It is important that the frame type you select matches the frame type already in use on the network. Frame type mismatching is a common cause of communications problems on networks that use NWLink IPX/SPX Compatible Transport.

- *Network numbers* are 32-bit binary numbers that uniquely identify an NWLink IPX/SPX Compatible Transport network segment for routing purposes. Network numbers are only assigned to Windows NT computers that use NWLink IPX/SPX Compatible Transport and are assigned during the installation and configuration of this protocol. Network numbers are commonly presented in an eight-digit hexadecimal format.

- There are two types of network numbers: *external network numbers* and *internal network numbers*. An *external network number* is assigned to each network adapter installed in the computer. Additionally, an *internal network number* must be assigned to a Windows NT computer when more than one network adapter is installed in it. The internal network number does *not* correspond to a specific network adapter, but rather is used by the computer's operating system. A Windows NT computer has only one internal network number, regardless of the number of network adapters installed in it.

- *Gateway Service for NetWare* (GSNW) is a Windows NT Server service that allows users to access resources (such as files, folders, and printers) on a NetWare server. GSNW enables access to resources on NetWare 4.*x* servers as well as NetWare 3.*x* servers. GSNW also enables users to run NetWare login scripts during the Windows NT logon process. Additionally, GSNW enables the Windows NT Server computer to transparently share resources (files, folders, and printers) located on a NetWare server to client computers of the Windows NT Server computer. GSNW is included with Windows NT Server and requires the use of IPX/SPX Compatible Transport.

- GSNW does *not* enable a Windows NT Server to share its resources with NetWare client computers. You should install File and Print Services for NetWare (FPNW) if you want to accomplish this.

- When configuring GSNW, pay particular attention to the gateway configuration options. The user account on the NetWare server *must* be a member of the NTGATEWAY group on the NetWare server, and the NTGATEWAY group *must* have the appropriate NetWare permissions to the gateway share.

- To access resources on NetWare 3.x servers from a Windows NT Server computer that is running GSNW, use standard UNC path names in the format \\server_name\share_name.

- To access resources on NetWare 4.x servers from a Windows NT Server computer that is running GSNW, use UNC path names in the format \\tree_name\volume_name.organizational_unit.organization_name\folder_name.

- Most NetWare connectivity problems are caused by incorrectly configuring NWLink IPX/SPX Compatible Transport or GSNW on the computer that is experiencing the problem. Most user-reported problems relate to an inability to connect to resources on NetWare servers. The most common configuration errors that cause NetWare connectivity problems include frame type mismatch and/or network number mismatch, the gateway user account is not a member of the NTGATEWAY group, the NTGATEWAY group does not have the necessary permissions to access the resource, and the gateway is not enabled.

APPLYING WHAT YOU'VE LEARNED

Now it's time to regroup, review, and apply what you've learned in this chapter.

The Instant Assessment questions bring to mind key facts and concepts. Then, the Hands-on Lab reinforces what you've learned and gives you an opportunity to practice some of the tasks that may be tested by the Server exam.

Instant Assessment

1. Which routable transport protocol is typically used in a combined Windows NT and NetWare environment because it provides compatibility between Windows NT and NetWare computers?

2. What are frame types?

3. What frame type configuration error is a common cause of NetWare connectivity problems?

4. What is a network number?

5. What are the two types of network numbers?

6. Which Windows NT Server service enables users to access resources (such as files, folders, and printers) on NetWare servers, and also permits resources located on a NetWare server to be transparently shared with client computers of the Windows NT Server computer?

7. What are the three print options you can configure in GSNW?

8. What conversion does GSNW perform to enable client computers of a Windows NT Server computer to access resources on a NetWare server?

9. When configuring the gateway using GSNW, of what group on the NetWare server must the gateway user account on the NetWare server be a member?

10. What UNC path name format must you use to access resources on NetWare 3.*x* servers from a Windows NT Server computer that is running GSNW?

11. What UNC path name format must you use to access resources on NetWare 4.*x* servers from a Windows NT Server computer that is running GSNW?

12. What are two common configuration errors that cause NetWare connectivity problems?

T/F

13. GSNW does *not* allow a Windows NT Server computer to share its resources with NetWare client computers.   _____

14. GSNW requires the use of NWLink IPX/SPX Compatible Transport.   _____

concept link   **For answers to the Instant Assessment questions see Appendix B.**

Hands-on Lab

The following Hands-on Lab provides you with a practical opportunity to apply the knowledge you've gained in this chapter about the components that increase the interoperability of Windows NT with NetWare.

Lab 15.26 *Installing and configuring NWLink and Gateway Service for NetWare*

The purpose of this lab is to give you hands-on experience in installing and configuring NWLink IPX/SPX Compatible Transport, and also in installing and configuring Gateway Service for NetWare on a Windows NT Server computer.

This lab consists of two parts:

Part 1: Installing NWLink and Gateway Service for NetWare

Part 2: Configuring Gateway Service for NetWare

Begin this lab by booting your computer to Windows NT Server. Log on as Administrator. Place your Windows NT Server compact disc in your computer's CD-ROM drive.

Follow the steps below carefully.

Part 1: Installing NWLink and Gateway Service for NetWare

In this section, you install NWLink IPX/SPX Compatible Transport and Gateway Service for NetWare on a Windows NT Server computer. Additionally, you configure NWLink IPX/SPX Compatible Transport.

1. Select Start ⇒ Settings ⇒ Control Panel.

2. In the Control Panel dialog box, double-click Network.

3. In the Network dialog box, click the Protocols tab.

4. On the Protocols tab, click the Add command button.

5. In the Select Network Protocol dialog box, highlight NWLink IPX/SPX Compatible Transport in the Network Protocol list box. Click OK.

6. A Windows NT Setup dialog box appears. Ensure that the correct path to your Windows NT Server source files (usually the I386 folder on your

Windows NT Server compact disc) is listed in the text box. Edit the text box as necessary. Click the Continue command button.

7. Windows NT installs NWLink IPX/SPX Compatible Transport. The Network dialog box reappears. Click the Services tab.

8. On the Services tab, click the Add command button.

9. In the Select Network Service dialog box, highlight Gateway (and Client) Services for NetWare. Click OK.

10. A Windows NT Setup dialog box appears. Ensure that the correct path to your Windows NT Server source files (usually the I386 folder on your Windows NT Server compact disc) is listed in the text box. Click the Continue command button.

11. Windows NT installs Gateway Service for NetWare. The Network dialog box reappears. Click the Close command button.

12. Windows NT performs various bindings operations.

13. A Network Settings Change dialog box appears, indicating that you must shut down and restart the computer in order for the new settings to take effect. Click the Yes command button to restart the computer. Continue to Part 2.

Part 2: Configuring Gateway Service for NetWare

In this section, you configure Gateway Service for NetWare on a Windows NT Server computer.

1. When the computer restarts, reboot to Windows NT Server. Log on as Administrator.

2. When the Select NetWare Logon dialog box appears, click OK.

3. The Control Panel dialog box appears. (If Control Panel doesn't appear, select Start ⇒ Settings ⇒ Control Panel.)

4. In the Control Panel dialog box, double-click the GSNW icon.

5. The Gateway Service for NetWare dialog box appears.

   o If your computer is connected to a network that has a NetWare server, configure the Select Preferred Server option, or Default Tree and Context option, as appropriate. (Obtain the appropriate configuration settings from your network administrator.) Configure the Print Options and Login Script Options as desired or as instructed by your network administrator.

   o If your computer is *not* connected to a network that has a NetWare server, ensure that the option button next to Preferred Server is selected, and accept the default Select Preferred Server option of <None>.

Click the Gateway command button.

6. The Configure Gateway dialog box appears. Notice the various options in this dialog box. Click OK.

7. The Gateway Service for NetWare dialog box reappears. Click OK.

8. If you made any changes in the Gateway Service for NetWare dialog box in Step 5, another Gateway Service for NetWare dialog box appears, indicating that the changes you made will take effect the next time you login. Click OK.

9. The Control Panel dialog box reappears. Exit Control Panel.

Migrating to Windows NT from NetWare

About Chapter 16

This chapter is all about migration. No, we're not talking about flying south for the winter. What we're talking about is converting from Novell NetWare to Microsoft Windows NT, and the process of copying accounts, files, and folders from the NetWare server to the Windows NT Server computer.

Chapter 16 takes you through this migration process from start to finish. It explains how to start the Migration Tool for NetWare; how to select the source NetWare server and destination Windows NT Server computer; and how to configure the way user accounts, group accounts, files, and folders will be migrated. Next, the process of performing one or more trial migrations is outlined. Then the actual migration is performed. Finally, Chapter 16 explains how NetWare client computers must be configured after the migration to enable them to access the Windows NT Server computer.

The material presented in this chapter maps to the "Configure Windows NT Server for interoperability with NetWare servers by using various tools . . . including Migration Tool for NetWare" objective listed in the Connectivity section in the Preparation Guide for the Server exam.

MIGRATING TO WINDOWS NT FROM NETWARE

When an organization decides to replace one or more of its Novell NetWare servers with a Windows NT Server computer, a *migration* to Windows NT from NetWare is performed. The migration process involves copying user and group accounts, files, and folders from the NetWare server(s) to the Windows NT Server computer.

Microsoft supplies an administrative tool with Windows NT Server, called the *Migration Tool for NetWare*, that makes migrating to Windows NT from NetWare possible. The Migration Tool for NetWare can be used to migrate user accounts, group accounts, files, and folders from NetWare 2.*x*, 3.*x*, and 4.*x* servers to a Windows NT Server computer. You can choose to migrate only users, only files, only groups, or any combination of the three.

The migration process involves the following steps:

- Starting the Migration Tool for NetWare
- Selecting the source NetWare server and destination Windows NT Server computer
- Configuring how user and group accounts will be migrated
- Configuring how files and folders will be migrated
- Performing one or more trial migrations to test your configurations
- Performing an actual migration
- Configuring NetWare client computers to access the Windows NT Server computer

Each of these steps is discussed in the sections that follow.

MIGRATION TOOL FOR NETWARE

You don't have to install the Migration Tool for NetWare — it is automatically installed on a Windows NT Server computer during the installation process.

However, before you can use the Migration Tool for NetWare, several prerequisites must be satisfied:

○ NWLink IPX/SPX Compatible Transport must be installed and configured on the Windows NT Server computer.

○ Gateway Service for NetWare (GSNW) must be installed and configured on the Windows NT Server computer.

○ The user who performs the migration must have Administrator privileges on the Windows NT Server computer and must also have Supervisor privileges on the NetWare server(s).

○ An NTFS partition must be configured on the Windows NT Server computer and must be specified as the destination volume if you want to retain file permissions on migrated files.

○ If you are migrating from a NetWare 4.x server, the NetWare server must be configured for bindery emulation.

When planning a migration from NetWare to Windows NT, it's helpful to know exactly what can and can't be migrated. Table 16-1 lists this information.

TABLE 16-1 WHAT CAN AND CAN'T BE MIGRATED

WHAT CAN BE MIGRATED	*WHAT CAN'T BE MIGRATED*
User accounts and their properties	User account passwords
Group accounts and their properties	Print servers, print queues, and their configurations — all printing must be configured manually on the Windows NT Server computer *after* the migration is complete
Files and their permissions	Workgroup managers and user account managers
Folders (directories) and their permissions	Application — defined bindery objects Login scripts — NetWare login scripts don't run on client computers of Windows NT Server computers

Using the Migration Tool for NetWare

Using the Migration Tool for NetWare is fairly straightforward. The following section explains how to start and use this tool.

TO START THE MIGRATION TOOL FOR NETWARE AND TO SELECT THE SOURCE AND DESTINATION SERVERS, FOLLOW THESE STEPS:

1. Select Start ⇒ Programs ⇒ Administrative Tools (Common) ⇒ Migration Tool for NetWare.
2. The Migration Tool for NetWare dialog box appears with the Select Servers For Migration dialog box on top of it, as shown in Figure 16-1. Notice that you must configure a source and destination server before you can continue.

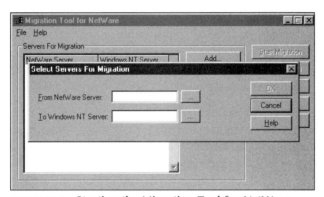

FIGURE 16-1 Starting the Migration Tool for NetWare

Fill in the following text boxes:

- From NetWare Server — Type in the name of the NetWare server to be migrated in the From NetWare Server text box, or click the . . . command button to browse for the NetWare server to be migrated.
- To Windows NT Server — Type in the name of the Windows NT Server computer that will be the destination for the user accounts, group accounts, files, and folders that will be migrated in the To Windows NT Server text box. Or, click the . . . command button to browse for the destination Windows NT Server computer.

Click OK.

3. The Migration Tool for NetWare dialog box appears, as shown in Figure 16-2. Note that the NetWare Server and Windows NT Server list boxes display the source and destination servers.

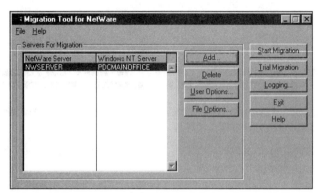

FIGURE 16-2   Source and destination servers configured for migration

- If you want to add additional source and/or destination servers, click the Add command button.

- If you want to delete a server pair from the Servers For Migration list box, highlight the pair of servers you want to delete and click the Delete command button.

- To configure user and group account migration options, click the User Options command button. (Specific configuration of user options is discussed in the next section.)

- To configure file and folder migration options, click the File Options command button. (Specific configuration of file options is discussed in a later section in this chapter.)

The next sections discuss the remaining steps in the migration process, including configuring the Migration Tool for NetWare to migrate user and group accounts, configuring the Migration Tool for NetWare to migrate files and file permissions, and performing a trial migration.

Migrating user and group accounts

An important consideration is determining how duplicate user and group account names will be treated during the migration. If you are migrating more than one NetWare server, it is likely that users have accounts on more than one NetWare server. This is because each NetWare server maintains its own user account data-base, much like a stand-alone Windows NT Server computer.

An efficient way to deal with duplicate user and group account names is to create a mapping file. A *mapping file* specifies every source NetWare user and group account name that is being migrated and specifies a corresponding user or group account name that will be created on the destination Windows NT Server computer during the migration for each specified NetWare user or group. A map-ping file can also specify unique passwords for all user accounts being migrated. The following section explains how to configure user and group account migra-tion options.

TO CONFIGURE USER AND GROUP ACCOUNT OPTIONS IN MIGRATION TOOL FOR NETWARE, FOLLOW THESE STEPS:

1. After starting Migration Tool for NetWare and configuring the source and destination servers, click the User Options command button in the Migration Tool for NetWare dialog box.

2. The User and Group Options dialog box appears, as shown in Figure 16-3. Notice the check boxes next to Transfer Users and Groups and Use Mappings in File.

FIGURE 16-3   **Configuring options for migrating users and groups**

There are several configurable options in this dialog box:

- o Transfer Users and Groups: Select the check box next to Transfer Users and Groups if you want to migrate user and group accounts from the NetWare server. Clear this check box if you don't want to migrate user and group accounts. This check box is selected by default.

- Use Mappings in File: Select the check box next to Use Mappings in File if you want to use a mapping file to migrate user and group accounts. You don't need to select this check box if you are only migrating one NetWare server and you want to retain the same user and group account names on the NT Server computer that were used on the NetWare server. This check box is not selected by default.

  For more information on creating a mapping file, click the Help command button in the User and Group Options dialog box.

- Passwords tab: Because NetWare user passwords can't be migrated, you can choose from one of three password options to be applied to the migrated user accounts:

  - No Password: Select the option button next to No Password if you want user accounts to be migrated without passwords. This option is selected by default.

  - Password is Username: Select the option button next to Password is Username if you want each migrated user account to have a password consisting of the user account name.

  - Password is: Select the option button next to Password is if you want to specify one password that will be assigned to all user accounts that are migrated. If you select this option, type in the password you want to be assigned.

  - User Must Change Password: In addition to choosing from the three option buttons on the Passwords tab, you can select the check box next to User Must Change Password. When this check box is selected, users whose user accounts are migrated will have to change their password the first time they log on to the Windows NT Server computer. This check box is selected by default.

3. To configure user name options, click the Usernames tab in the User and Group Options dialog box. The Usernames tab appears, as shown in Figure 16-4.

   There are four option buttons you can choose from to configure how duplicate user account names will be handled:

   - Log Error: Selecting this option button causes an error to be logged to a log file when a duplicate user account is encountered during the migration process. Once a user account is migrated, each additional occurrence of an identical user account name will be logged to a log file but will not be migrated. This option button is selected by default.

FIGURE 16-4 Configuring options for duplicate
user account names

- Ignore: Selecting this option button causes duplicate user account names to be ignored during the migration process. Once a user account is migrated, each additional occurrence of an identical user account name will be ignored.

- Overwrite with new info: Selecting this option button causes Windows NT to overwrite existing user account information with the account information from the duplicate user account(s) encountered during migration.

- Add prefix: Selecting this option button causes a prefix to be added to duplicate user account names encountered during the migration process.

4. To configure group name options, click the Group Names tab in the User and Group Options dialog box. The Group Names tab appears, as shown in Figure 16-5. Notice the options available for handling duplicate group names encountered during the migration process.

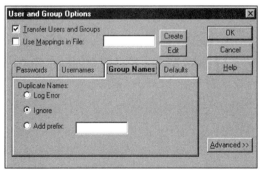

FIGURE 16-5 Configuring options for
duplicate group account names

You can choose from three duplicate name options: Log Error, Ignore, and Add prefix. These options have the same effect as the identical options on the Usernames tab, except that they are applied to group accounts rather than to user accounts.

5. To configure defaults, click the Defaults tab. The Defaults tab appears, as shown in Figure 16-6. Notice the three check boxes on the tab. Select or deselect the defaults options check boxes, as appropriate:

FIGURE 16-6   Configuring default account migration options

- Use Supervisor Defaults — To migrate global NetWare account policy settings, such as password length and expiration, to the Windows NT Server account policy, select the check box next to Use Supervisor Defaults. This check box is selected by default.

If you are *not* migrating to a "clean" Windows NT Server computer that was installed expressly for the purpose of migration, use caution here — selecting this check box can cause your existing Windows NT Server account policy to be overwritten.

- Add Supervisors to the Administrators Group — Selecting the check box next to Add Supervisors to the Administrators Group causes the NetWare Supervisor user account, and all NetWare user accounts with Supervisor equivalence, to be added to the Administrators group on the Windows NT Server computer. This check box is *not* selected by default.

- Migrate NetWare Specific Account Information — If you select the check box next to Migrate NetWare Specific Account Information, all user account properties, such as group memberships, will be migrated to equivalent properties on the Windows NT Server computer. (Note: Not all NetWare account properties have equivalent properties in Windows NT. Account properties with no equivalents will not be migrated.)

6. When you have finished configuring all user and group account options, click OK to return to the Migration Tool for NetWare dialog box.

Migrating files and folders

When migrating files from a NetWare server to a Windows NT Server computer, the files must be migrated to an NTFS partition on the Windows NT Server computer for the file permissions to be retained.

NetWare file and folder permissions are *not* the same as Windows NT file and folder permissions. During migration, each NetWare file and folder permission is translated into its closest equivalent Windows NT permission. For more information on how NetWare file and folder permissions are applied during the migration process, select the Help menu in the Migration Tool for NetWare dialog box.

By default, certain files and folders on the NetWare server are *not* migrated. Hidden files, system files, and the contents of the \SYSTEM, \MAIL, \LOGIN, and \ETC directories are not migrated. You can override these defaults, however, by configuring the file options in the Migration Tool for NetWare. The next section explains how to configure file and folder migration options.

 tip Because potentially large volumes of data are transferred during a migration, you should consider performing the migration during nonbusiness hours, so that network performance is not impaired.

TO CONFIGURE FILE MIGRATION OPTIONS IN MIGRATION TOOL FOR NETWARE, FOLLOW THESE STEPS:

1. After starting Migration Tool for NetWare, configuring the source and destination servers, and configuring user options (if desired), click the File Options command button in the Migration Tool for NetWare dialog box.

2. The File Options dialog box appears, as shown in Figure 16-7. Note the check box next to Transfer Files.

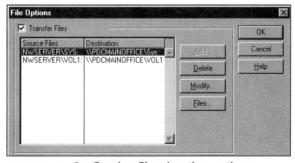

FIGURE 16-7   Configuring file migration options

- If you *don't* want to migrate files, clear the check box next to Transfer Files. This check box is selected by default.

- To modify, delete, or add NetWare volumes on the source NetWare server to be transferred during the migration, select the Modify, Delete, or Add command buttons, as appropriate.

- If you want to select or deselect specific files and/or folders for migration, highlight the source NetWare volume in the Source Files list box, and click the Files command button.

- If you don't want to select or deselect specific files, click OK to return to the Migration Tool for NetWare dialog box. You are finished configuring file migration options.

3. The Files To Transfer dialog box appears, as shown in Figure 16-8. Notice the check boxes next to each file and folder.

FIGURE 16-8 **Selecting individual files and folders for migration**

There are two primary configurable options in this dialog box — Tree and Transfer.

- Tree options: To expand your view of subdirectories and files on the volume you have selected, select Tree and then choose the appropriate option from the menu that appears. The Tree options are Expand One Level, Expand Branch, Expand All, and Collapse Branch.

Figure 16-9 shows the Files To Transfer dialog box after the Tree ⇒ Expand All option has been selected. Note that the full tree is expanded and displayed on the left side of the dialog box.

    To select or deselect individual files or folders to be migrated, select or deselect the check box next to the file or folder, as appropriate.

FIGURE 16-9 Expanded tree view

○ Transfer options: To migrate hidden or system files (which are not migrated by default), select Transfer ⇒ Hidden Files or Transfer ⇒ System Files, as appropriate, in the Files To Transfer dialog box.

When you finish configuring the files to transfer, click OK.

4. The File Options dialog box reappears. Repeat Steps 2 and 3 to configure file options on the remaining volumes as desired. When you finish configuring file options on all volumes selected for migration, click OK to return to the Migration Tool for NetWare dialog box.

This completes the configuration of file options. You can save your completed migration configurations for use at a later time by selecting File ⇒ Save Configuration.

Now you're ready to proceed with a trial migration to test your configurations.

PERFORMING TRIAL MIGRATIONS AND AN ACTUAL MIGRATION

The Migration Tool for NetWare enables you to perform one or more trial migrations that simulate a migration without actually completing the migration process.

The purpose of performing trial migrations is to test your migration configurations and to resolve any errors that occur *before* the actual migration is performed. The Migration Tool for NetWare can be configured so that errors that occur during a trial (or actual) migration are written to a log file and/or displayed on screen. It is recommended that you perform as many trial migrations as necessary until you are satisfied that no critical errors will occur during the actual migration. The next section discusses the steps involved in performing a trial migration.

TO PERFORM A TRIAL MIGRATION, FOLLOW THESE STEPS:

1. Start the Migration Tool for NetWare. After configuring all user, group, and file migration options, the Migration Tool for NetWare dialog box appears, as shown in Figure 16-10. Notice the Logging, Trial Migration, and Start Migration command buttons.

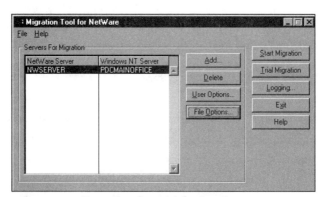

FIGURE 16-10   **Preparing for a trial migration**

To configure error logging options, click the Logging command button. Figure 16-11 shows the Logging dialog box.

FIGURE 16-11   **Configuring logging options**

Notice the three logging configuration options available, and select the options you want applied during the trial migration:

- Popup on errors: Selecting this check box causes the migration process to pause and to display a message on the screen when an error occurs during the migration process. This check box is not selected by default. This option can require extensive amounts of user intervention, and can significantly increase the amount of time involved in a trial migration.

- Verbose User/Group Logging: Selecting this check box causes all user and group migration errors to be written to the log file, in addition to recording a complete list of users and groups migrated. This check box is selected by default.

- Verbose File Logging: Selecting this check box causes all file and folder migration errors to be written to the log file, in addition to recording a complete list of files migrated. This check box is not selected by default.

When you are finished configuring logging options, click OK.

2. In the Migration Tool for NetWare dialog box, click the Trial Migration command button to begin a trial migration.

3. A Verifying Information dialog box appears, as shown in Figure 16-12.

FIGURE 16-12 **Trial migration in process – part 1**

After some time, the Converting dialog box appears, as shown in Figure 16-13.

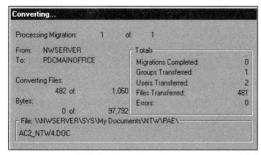

FIGURE 16-13 **Trial migration in process – part 2**

4. At the completion of the trial migration, the Transfer Completed dialog box appears, as shown in Figure 16-14. Notice the summary migration statistics presented.

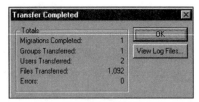

FIGURE 16-14   Trial migration completed

If errors are displayed in the Totals section of the Transfer Completed dialog box, you can click the View Log Files command button to view the three logs created during the trial migration: Error.LOG, Summary.LOG, and LogFile.LOG. When you are finished viewing the log files, close the LogView dialog box. Click OK in the Transfer Completed dialog box.

5. The trial migration is complete. Resolve any errors that occurred, such as duplicate user or group account names, or disk space limitations on the destination Windows NT Server computer. Perform additional trial migrations as necessary.

 note

Some migration errors are more serious than others. You might choose to ignore some errors and clean up the Windows NT Server after the migration. Sometimes performing a migration in this way involves less work than eliminating all migration errors.

Not all errors are detected by a trial migration. Some errors will be detected only when the migration utility performs the actual migration.

When you are satisfied with the results of a trial migration, you can click the Start Migration command button in the Migration Tool for NetWare dialog box to perform an actual migration. The process of performing an actual migration is the same as performing a trial migration.

If you're not ready to perform an actual migration at this time, select File ⇒ Save Configuration to save your current settings for later use in an actual migration.

CONFIGURING NETWARE CLIENT COMPUTERS TO ACCESS THE WINDOWS NT SERVER COMPUTER AFTER MIGRATION

After the migration is performed, the existing NetWare client computers must be reconfigured to enable them to access the Windows NT Server computer.

If the existing NetWare client computers will no longer access any NetWare servers, their NetWare client software should be removed and a Microsoft redirector (Microsoft client software that enables client computers to access resources on the Windows NT Server computer) should be installed on each of the client computers.

Examples of Microsoft client software include Network Client *v*3.0 for MS-DOS and Windows, TCP/IP 32 for Windows for Workgroups 3.11, and LAN Manager *v*2.2c for OS/2. Microsoft client software is included with Windows for Workgroups, Windows 95, Windows NT Workstation, and Windows NT Server.

If the existing NetWare client computers will continue to access NetWare servers, and will also access the Windows NT Server computer, their NetWare client software should be left intact, and a Microsoft redirector should be installed on each of the client computers.

KEY POINT SUMMARY

This chapter explored migrating from NetWare to Windows NT.

- When an organization decides to replace one or more of its Novell NetWare servers with a Windows NT Server computer, a *migration* to Windows NT from NetWare is performed. The migration process entails copying user accounts, group accounts, files, and folders from the NetWare server(s) to the Windows NT Server computer. Microsoft supplies an administrative tool with NT Server, called the *Migration Tool for NetWare*, that makes migrating to Windows NT from NetWare possible.

- Migration involves several steps:
  - Starting and configuring the Migration Tool for NetWare
  - Selecting the source NetWare server and destination Windows NT Server computer

- Configuring how user and group accounts will be migrated
- Configuring how files and folders will be migrated
- Performing a trial migration to test your configurations
- Performing an actual migration
- Configuring NetWare client computers to access the Windows NT Server computer

- Several prerequisites that must be satisfied *before* a migration can successfully be performed:
  - NWLink IPX/SPX Compatible Transport and Gateway Service for NetWare must be installed and configured on the Windows NT Server computer.
  - The user who performs the migration must have Administrator privileges on the Windows NT Server computer, and must also have Supervisor privileges on the NetWare server(s).
  - An NTFS partition must be configured on the Windows NT Server computer and must be specified as the destination volume if you want to retain file permissions on migrated files.
  - If you are migrating from a NetWare 4.*x* server, the NetWare server must be configured for bindery emulation.

- User and group accounts and their properties, and files and folders and their permissions *can* be migrated. User account passwords, print servers and print queues and their configurations, workgroup managers and user account managers, application-defined bindery objects, and login scripts *cannot* be migrated.

- An important consideration when migrating user and group accounts is determining how duplicate user and group account names will be treated during the migration. An efficient way to handle duplicate user and group account names is to create a mapping file. A *mapping file* specifies every source NetWare user and group account name that is being migrated, and specifies a corresponding user or group account name that will be created on the destination Windows NT Server computer, during the migration, for each specified NetWare user or group.

- When migrating files from a NetWare server to a Windows NT Server computer, the files must be migrated to an NTFS partition on the Windows NT Server computer for the file permissions to be retained. By default, hidden files, system files, and the contents of the \SYSTEM, \MAIL, \LOGIN, and \ETC directories are *not* migrated. You can override these defaults, however, by configuring the file options in the Migration Tool for NetWare.

o The purpose of performing trial migrations is to test migration configurations and to resolve any errors that occur before the actual migration is performed. The Migration Tool for NetWare can be configured so that errors that occur during a trial (or actual) migration are written to a log file and/or displayed on screen. Perform as many trial migrations as necessary until you are satisfied that no critical errors will occur during the actual migration. When you are satisfied with the results of a trial migration, the actual migration can be performed. The process of performing an actual migration is identical to performing a trial migration.

o After the migration is performed, the existing NetWare client computers must be reconfigured to enable them to access the Windows NT Server computer. A Microsoft redirector (Microsoft client software) must be installed on each NetWare client computer to enable it to access resources on the Windows NT Server computer.

APPLYING WHAT YOU'VE LEARNED

Now it's time to regroup, review, and apply what you've learned in this chapter. The following Instant Assessment questions bring to mind the key facts and concepts presented in Chapter 16.

Instant Assessment

1. What are the steps involved in performing a migration from NetWare to Windows NT?

2. Which Windows NT protocol and which Windows NT Server service must be installed and configured on the Windows NT Server before a migration is performed?

3. What privileges must the user who performs the migration have?

4. What type of partition must be configured on the Windows NT Server computer and specified as the destination volume if you want to retain file permissions on migrated files?

5. What items can be migrated?

6. What items cannot be migrated?

7. What type of file can you use to efficiently manage duplicate user and group account names during a migration?

8. What should you always do before you perform an actual migration?

9. Which Windows NT Server tool should you use to accomplish a migration from Novell NetWare to Windows NT?

10. How must you reconfigure existing NetWare client computers *after* a migration is performed to enable them to access resources on the Windows NT Server computer?

 For answers to the Instant Assessment questions see Appendix B.

concept link

Installing and Configuring Remote Access Service (RAS)

About Chapter 17

The focus of this chapter is on Remote Access Service (RAS), the Windows NT service that enables dial-up network connections between a RAS server and a Dial-Up Networking client computer.

First, the chapter explains the various RAS connection types, and the connection and transport protocols supported by RAS. The RAS NetBIOS gateway and RAS name resolution are also introduced.

Next, the steps to install and configure RAS are outlined. Then the chapter discusses how to use Remote Access Admin to manage a RAS server.

Next, Chapter 17 details how to configure Dial-Up Networking connections. Dial-Up Networking is the client/dial out component of RAS. Configuring Dial-Up Networking to connect to the Internet is also addressed.

Finally, Chapter 17 presents tips on troubleshooting common RAS problems.

This chapter includes a Critical Thinking Lab that will give you practice troubleshooting RAS problems. It also includes a Hands-on Lab in which you'll install and configure RAS and Dial-Up Networking on a Windows NT Server computer.

The material presented in Chapter 17 maps to the "Install and configure Remote Access Service (RAS)" and the "Choose the appropriate course of action to take to resolve RAS problems" objectives listed in the Connectivity and Troubleshooting sections of the Preparation Guide for the Server exam.

RAS OVERVIEW

Remote Access Service (RAS) is a Windows NT service that enables dial-up network connections between a RAS server and a Dial-Up Networking client computer. RAS includes software components for both the RAS server and the Dial-Up Networking client in a single Windows NT service.

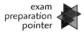
exam
preparation
pointer

RAS is a complex topic. Even Administrators who manage RAS servers on a daily basis are well advised to study the details and nuances presented in this chapter before taking the Server exam. Become familiar with the various dialog boxes and configuration options. I recommend you review this chapter just prior to taking the exam.

RAS enables users of remote computers to use the network as though they were directly connected to it. Once the dial-up connection is established, there is no difference in network functionality, except the speed of the link is often much slower than a direct connection to the LAN.

RAS is an important networking function in light of today's highly mobile workforce. With RAS and Dial-Up Networking, users can connect to their company's network from home, from a hotel room, or from a client's remote office.

Windows NT Server RAS can support up to 256 simultaneous dial-in connections.

Client computers that run MS-DOS, Windows 3.1*x*, Windows for Workgroups, Windows 95, and Windows NT can be configured as Dial-Up Networking or RAS client computers. These clients can all connect to a Windows NT RAS server.

RAS supports multiple connection types, connection protocols, and transport protocols. These features are discussed in the following sections.

RAS Connection Types

Dial-Up Networking client computers can connect to a RAS server by using a variety of connection types, including

- A standard telephone line (also called a *Public Switched Telephone Network* or PSTN) and modem
- ISDN
- X.25
- Point-to-Point Tunneling Protocol (PPTP)

Probably the most common connection type is a standard analog telephone line (also called *plain old telephone service* or POTS) and modem. This service is inexpensive and widely available.

Many modems are supported by Windows NT. You can determine if your modem is supported by checking the Windows NT *Hardware Compatibility List* (HCL), or by trying to have Windows NT autodetect your modem. Unsupported modems can generally be used by adding an entry for that modem to the `Modem.inf` file in the `<winntroot>\System32\Ras` folder. (Instructions for adding a new entry to this file are contained in the file.)

Integrated Services Digital Network (ISDN) is a digital, dial-up telephone service that supports much faster data transmission rates than a standard analog telephone line. The standard ISDN connection is called an ISDN *Basic Rate Interface* (BRI) line. An ISDN BRI line consists of three separate data channels. Two of these channels (called *B channels*) support telephone or data communications at a rate of 64Kbps. The third channel is called a *D channel* and is used to establish and maintain the connection. If both B channels are used together, data transmission rates of up to 128Kbps can be supported.

ISDN lines must be installed at both the dial-up server and Dial-up Networking client locations. Additionally, an ISDN adapter card with either an internal or external network terminating unit (NT1) must be installed in the dial-up server and in the Dial-Up Networking client. (The ISDN adapter card takes the place of a modem.) Finally, you may need a *Service Provider Identification* (SPID) number to configure the ISDN adapter cards. If needed, you can obtain the SPID from the telephone company that provides your ISDN service.

X.25 is a packet-switching protocol that is used on dial-up or leased lines. X.25 is available in most countries. An X.25 connection requires a fair amount of hardware, including an X.25 adapter card, with either a built-in or external *Packet Assembler/Disassembler* (PAD) in the dial-up server and in the Dial-Up Networking client. Additionally, access to an X.25 packet-switched network is required at both the dial-up server and the Dial-Up Networking client locations.

Point-to-Point Tunneling Protocol (PPTP) is not a physical connection type. Rather, it is a virtual network connection that is "tunneled" inside of an existing TCP/IP network connection. RAS encryption can be used with PPTP to provide a secure, private connection over a public TCP/IP network, such as the Internet. Because PPTP uses an existing TCP/IP network connection, no additional hardware is required.

Connection Protocols Supported by RAS

RAS communications can be carried out over several connection protocols. These protocols provide the data-link connectivity for Dial-Up Networking in much the same way as Ethernet, ARCNET, or Token Ring provide the data-link connectivity on a local area network. Each of these protocols has different features and capabilities. The connection protocols commonly used by RAS include Serial Line Internet Protocol (SLIP), Point-to-Point Protocol (PPP), Point-to-Point Multilink Protocol, and Point-to-Point Tunneling Protocol (PPTP). These protocols are discussed in the following sections.

Serial Line Internet Protocol (SLIP)

The *Serial Line Internet Protocol* (SLIP) is an older connection protocol, commonly associated with UNIX computers, that only supports one transport protocol —TCP/IP. SLIP connections don't support NWLink IPX/SPX Compatible Transport or NetBEUI.

The version of SLIP supported by Windows NT 4.0 requires a static IP address configuration at the client computer — dynamic IP addressing is not supported. Additionally, password encryption is not supported by this version of SLIP. A script file is usually required to automate the connection process when SLIP is used.

Windows NT RAS can't be used as a SLIP server. Only the Dial-Up Networking portion of RAS (the client side) supports SLIP. This means that only dial-out SLIP connections are supported — such as when a Dial-Up Networking client computer dials out to connect to a UNIX SLIP server. (The Dial-Up Networking client computer, in this case, can be either a Windows NT Server or Windows NT Workstation computer that has RAS installed on it.)

Point-to-Point Protocol (PPP)

Point-to-Point Protocol (PPP) is a newer connection protocol that was designed to overcome the limitations of SLIP. PPP is currently the industry standard remote connection protocol and is recommended for use by Microsoft.

PPP connections support multiple transport protocols, including TCP/IP, NWLink IPX/SPX Compatible Transport, and NetBEUI. Additionally, PPP supports dynamic server-based IP addressing (such as DHCP).

PPP supports password encryption, and the PPP connection process does not usually require a script file.

PPP is supported over both dial-in and dial-out connections. Windows NT computers that have RAS installed on them can function either as Dial-Up Networking clients or as RAS servers when using PPP.

Point-to-Point Multilink Protocol

Point-to-Point Multilink Protocol is an extension of PPP. Point-to-Point Multilink Protocol combines the bandwidth from multiple physical connections into a single logical connection. This means that multiple modem, ISDN, or X.25 connections can be bundled together to form a single logical connection with a much higher bandwidth than a single connection can support.

In order to implement Point-to-Point Multilink Protocol, multiple modems and telephone lines (or multiple ISDN adapter cards and lines; or multiple X.25 adapters, PADs, and connections) are required at *both* the RAS server and at the Dial-Up Networking client locations. Additionally, both sides of the connection must be configured to use Point-to-Point Multilink Protocol.

Point-to-Point Tunneling Protocol (PPTP)

Point-to-Point Tunneling Protocol (PPTP) permits a virtual private encrypted connection between two computers over an existing TCP/IP network connection. The existing TCP/IP network connection can be over a LAN or over a Dial-up Networking TCP/IP connection (including the Internet). All standard transport protocols are supported within the PPTP connection, including NWLink IPX/SPX Compatible Transport, NetBEUI, and TCP/IP.

A primary reason for choosing to use PPTP is that it supports the RAS encryption feature over standard, unencrypted TCP/IP networks, such as the Internet.

Transport Protocols Supported by RAS

All Windows NT standard transport protocols are supported by RAS. Client computers can connect to a RAS server by using

- NetBEUI

- TCP/IP

- IPX — including NWLink IPX/SPX Compatible Transport

The DLC protocol is *not* supported by RAS.

Client computers can use one or more of these transport protocols on a RAS connection. For example, a client computer that needs to access a NetWare server and a UNIX host via a RAS server can use both NWLink IPX/SPX Compatible Transport and TCP/IP during a single RAS session.

A RAS server acts as a router for client computers that use TCP/IP or IPX, enabling these clients to access other computers on the network via the RAS server's routing functionality. Access to NetBIOS-based resources (such as shared folders and printers, Lotus Notes servers, SQL Servers, and SNA Servers) and protocol-specific resources (such as NetWare servers and World Wide Web servers) is possible because of the RAS server's routing capability. The RAS server can only route protocols that are installed on the RAS server. For example, if a client computer has NWLink IPX/SPX Compatible Transport installed, but the RAS server doesn't, the client computer won't be able to access IPX-based resources, such as a NetWare server.

A RAS server acts as a NetBIOS gateway for client computers that use the NetBEUI protocol.

RAS NetBIOS Gateway

The *RAS NetBIOS gateway* is a function of the RAS server. The RAS NetBIOS gateway enables client computers that use NetBEUI to access shared resources on other servers located on the RAS server's local network. These other servers can use TCP/IP, NWLink IPX/SPX Compatible Transport, or NetBEUI. In a nutshell, the RAS NetBIOS gateway performs protocol translation for the remote NetBEUI client computer so it can access shared resources on the RAS server's local network.

Only NetBIOS-based services (such as shared folders and printers, Lotus Notes servers, SQL Servers, and SNA Servers) can be accessed by NetBEUI client computers via the RAS NetBIOS gateway. Protocol-specific services (such as NetWare servers and World Wide Web servers) can't be accessed by NetBEUI client computers via the RAS NetBIOS gateway.

Even though RAS enables up to 256 simultaneous connections, the NetBIOS gateway has a maximum connection limit of 250 simultaneous connections. This is a NetBIOS limitation, not a RAS limitation.

RAS Name Resolution

The same methods that are used for NetBIOS name resolution and browsing functionality on a Windows NT network are supported by RAS and are used by Dial-Up Networking client computers that connect to a RAS server. Supported NetBIOS name resolution methods include

o NetBIOS broadcasts

o WINS servers

o DNS servers

o LMHOSTS files

o HOSTS files

INSTALLING AND CONFIGURING RAS

Before installing RAS, you should install and configure all of the transport protocols you plan to use on the RAS server. Also, you should install and configure at least one connection device, such as a modem, ISDN adapter card, or X.25 adapter card in the Windows NT computer that you plan to install RAS on. Or, you can install the Point-to-Point Tunneling Protocol (PPTP).

 If you don't install a connection device or PPTP before installing RAS, the RAS installation program will prompt you to do so during installation.

The following sections explore the various steps involved in installing RAS, including configuring modems, ports, protocols, and encryption.

Installing RAS

This section explains how to install RAS on a Windows NT computer.

TO INSTALL RAS, FOLLOW THESE STEPS:

1. Select Start ⇒ Settings ⇒ Control Panel.

2. In the Control Panel dialog box, double-click Network.

3. In the Network dialog box, click the Services tab.

FIGURE 17-1 Installing RAS

4. On the Services tab, click the Add command button.

5. In the Select Network Service dialog box, highlight Remote Access Service, as shown in Figure 17-1. Click OK.

6. A Windows NT Setup dialog box appears. Ensure the correct path to your Windows NT Server source files (usually the I386 folder on your Windows NT Server compact disc) is listed in the text box. Edit this text box if necessary. Click the Continue command button.

7. Windows NT copies source files.

After copying the RAS source files, Windows NT prompts you to configure modems and ports. These tasks are explained in the following section.

Configuring Modems and Ports

Configuring modems and ports is an integral part of the RAS installation and configuration process.

TO CONFIGURE MODEMS AND PORTS, FOLLOW THESE STEPS:

1. After Windows NT copies source files, the Add RAS Device dialog box appears, as shown in Figure 17-2. Notice that a Sportster modem is listed in the RAS Capable Devices drop-down list box. Select the modem, ISDN adapter card, X.25 adapter card, or PPTP virtual LAN connection that you installed prior to beginning the RAS installation from the RAS Capable Devices drop-down list box. Click OK.

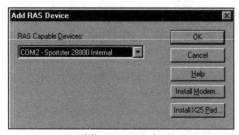

FIGURE 17-2   Adding a RAS device/port

2. The Remote Access Setup dialog box appears, as shown in Figure 17-3.

To add additional RAS ports, click the Add command button.

To remove a listed port, highlight the port and click the Remove command button.

To configure a port's dial-in/dial-out properties, highlight the port and click the Configure command button.

FIGURE 17-3   Managing a RAS port

3. The Configure Port Usage dialog box appears, as shown in Figure 17-4. Note the three port usage options available.

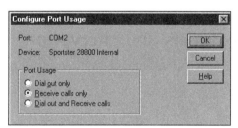

FIGURE 17-4   Configuring dial-in/dial-out port settings

4. Choose one of three options for the port:

- Dial-out only: If you select the option button next to "Dial-out only," the port will *only* be available for use by the Dial-Up Networking client. Selecting this option button for *all* ports effectively selects a client-only role for this computer. This computer won't be able to function as a RAS server if this option button is selected for all ports.

- Receive calls only: If you select the option button next to "Receive calls only," the port will *only* be available for use by the RAS server. Selecting this option button for *all* ports effectively selects a RAS server-only role for this computer. This computer won't be able to function as a Dial-Up Networking client if this option button is selected for all ports.

• Dial out and Receive calls: If you select the option button next to "Dial out and Receive calls," the port will be available for use by both the RAS server and the Dial-Up Networking client. This computer will be able to function both as a RAS server and as a Dial-Up Networking client.

5. Click OK.

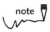 **Each port is configured individually. If one port is configured to dial out only, another can be configured to receive calls only or to dial out and receive calls.**

6. The Remote Access Setup dialog box reappears. Add and configure additional ports as desired.

When you are finished configuring ports, you are ready to configure the RAS network settings for both the RAS server and the Dial-Up Networking client. The next section explains how these network settings, including protocols and encryption, are configured.

Configuring Protocols and Encryption

The next part of the RAS installation/configuration process involves configuring protocols and encryption.

TO CONFIGURE PROTOCOLS AND ENCRYPTION, FOLLOW THESE STEPS:

1. After configuring RAS ports, the Remote Access Setup dialog box reappears. Click the Network command button.

2. The Network Configuration dialog box appears, as shown in Figure 17-5. Notice the Dial-out Protocols and Server Settings sections.

This is the primary RAS configuration dialog box. In this dialog box, select dial-out protocols (if you configured any ports for dial-out usage), configure dial-in protocols and RAS server settings (if you configured any ports for dial-in usage), select RAS encryption features, and enable the RAS server side of Point-to-Point Multilink Protocol connections, if desired.

FIGURE 17-5 Configuring protocols and security

 Configuration options selected in the Network Configuration dialog box are global settings that apply to *all* ports. No individual port protocol or encryption settings are available.

- Dial-out Protocols: If you configured any ports for dial-out usage, you can select any or all three dial-out protocols: NetBEUI, TCP/IP, and/or IPX (NWLink IPX/SPX Compatible Transport). If you *didn't* configure any ports for dial-out usage, these options are grayed out and not available. All installed protocols are selected by default.

- Server Settings: Allow remote clients running: If you configured any ports for dial-in (RAS server) usage, you can select any or all of three dial-in protocols: NetBEUI, TCP/IP, and/or IPX (NWLink IPX/SPX Compatible Transport). If you didn't configure any ports for dial-in usage, the Server Settings configuration section is not displayed. All installed protocols are selected by default.

  You can configure individual protocol-specific options for each of the three protocols in this section. (Configuring each of these protocols is discussed in detail later in this chapter.)

- Server Settings: Encryption settings: Select one of the three possible password authentication encryption options:

- Allow any authentication including clear text: If you select the option button next to "Allow any authentication including clear text," the RAS server will authenticate user passwords in clear text or in any encryption format supported by the RAS server. Selecting this option button, in effect, enables the Dial-Up Networking client to determine the level of password encryption.

- Require encrypted authentication: If you select the option button next to "Require encrypted authentication," Dial-Up Networking clients will be required to send encrypted user passwords in any encryption format supported by the RAS server. The RAS server won't authenticate user passwords that are sent in clear text.

- Require Microsoft encrypted authentication: If you select the option button next to "Require Microsoft encrypted authentication," Dial-Up Networking clients must send user passwords that are encrypted using Microsoft encrypted authentication. The RAS server won't authenticate user passwords sent in clear text or in any encryption format other than Microsoft encrypted authentication. This is the most secure password authentication option and is selected by default. If the "Require Microsoft encrypted authentication" option button is selected, the "Require data encryption" check box is available.

- Require data encryption: If you select this check box, in addition to requiring Microsoft encrypted password authentication, the RAS server requires that all data sent to the RAS server from the Dial-Up Networking client be transmitted in an encrypted format. This check box is not selected by default. Currently, only Windows NT Dial-Up Networking clients support data encryption. If you want to use the RAS server to establish secure, private PPTP connections, ensure that you select the option button next to "Require Microsoft encrypted authentication" *and* the check box next to "Require data encryption."

- Server Settings: Enable Multilink: Selecting the check box next to Enable Multilink enables the RAS server side of Point-to-Point Multilink Protocol connections. Selecting this check box enables the RAS server to support Multilink connections if requested to do so by the Dial-Up Networking client computer. This check box is not selected by default. Don't click the OK command button just yet—you still need to configure the dial in protocol(s) you selected. Configuring these three dial in protocols (NetBEUI, TCP/IP, and IPX) is explained in detail in the next three sections.

Configuring NetBEUI

Once you have selected dial out protocol(s) in the Server Settings section of the Network Configuration dialog box, you are ready to configure the protocols.

If you selected NetBEUI as a dial out protocol, it must be configured.

TO CONFIGURE NETBEUI, FOLLOW THESE STEPS:

1. Click the Configure command button next to NetBEUI in the Server Settings section of the Network Configuration dialog box.

2. The RAS Server NetBEUI Configuration dialog box appears, as shown in Figure 17-6. Notice the two configuration options available.

FIGURE 17-6   Configuring RAS server NetBEUI options

Choose one of the two possible NetBEUI configuration options:

o Entire network: If you select the option button next to "Entire network," the RAS server's NetBIOS gateway will be enabled, and remote NetBEUI clients will be able to access shared resources on all servers on the RAS server's local network, even servers that use TCP/IP or NWLink IPX/SPX Compatible Transport. This option button is selected by default.

o This computer only: If you select the option button next to "This computer only," the RAS server's NetBIOS gateway will be disabled, and remote NetBEUI clients will only be able to access shared resources located on the RAS server. This option is sometimes used in high security environments to prevent unauthorized access to other computers on the corporate network.

 note   Selections made in this dialog box apply to *all* Dial-Up Networking client computers that access the RAS server using NetBEUI. You either choose to allow all remote NetBEUI client computers to access the entire network, or you choose to allow all remote NetBEUI client computers to access *only* the RAS server.

3. Click OK to return to the Network Configuration dialog box.

Configuring TCP/IP

If you selected TCP/IP as a dial-out protocol, it must be configured.

TO CONFIGURE TCP/IP, FOLLOW THESE STEPS:

1. Click the Configure command button next to TCP/IP in the Server Settings section of the Network Configuration dialog box.

2. The RAS Server TCP/IP Configuration dialog box appears, as shown in Figure 17-7. Notice the options to configure IP address assignment for remote Dial-Up Networking clients.

 Selections made in this dialog box apply to *all* **Dial-Up Networking client computers that access the RAS server using TCP/IP.**

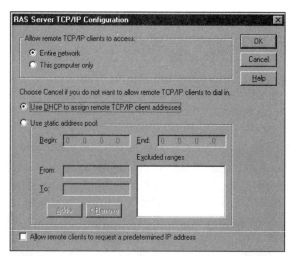

FIGURE 17-7   Configuring RAS server TCP/IP options

3. In the Allow remote TCP/IP clients to access section, choose one of the two possible TCP/IP configuration options:

- Entire network: If you select the option button next to "Entire network," the RAS server will function as a router for Dial-Up Networking client computers, and remote TCP/IP clients will be able to access resources on all servers that use TCP/IP on the RAS server's local network. This option button is selected by default.

- This computer only: If you select the option button next to "This computer only," the RAS server will not function as a router for Dial-Up Networking client computers, and remote TCP/IP clients will only be able to access resources located on the RAS server. This option is sometimes used in high-security environments to prevent unauthorized access to other computers on the corporate network.

4. The remainder of this dialog box is concerned with the assignment of IP addresses to remote Dial-Up Networking client computers that use TCP/IP. Choose one of the two primary IP address assignment options:

- Use DHCP to assign remote TCP/IP client addresses: If you select the option button next to "Use DHCP to assign remote TCP/IP client addresses," the RAS server will request an IP address for the remote TCP/IP client from the DHCP server on its local network when the remote TCP/IP client connects to the RAS server. This option should be selected if a DHCP server is available. This option button is selected by default.

- Use static address pool: If you select the option button next to "Use static address pool," the RAS server will assign an IP address to the remote TCP/IP client from the range of IP addresses specified in the Begin and End text boxes.

note **Even though "Use DHCP to assign remote TCP/IP client addresses" is the default option, I recommend that you use a specific address pool for RAS IP address assignments. When you use DHCP, the IP address is assigned to a specific client for the length of the lease, whereas if you use an IP address pool, the IP address is only assigned to the client during the connection time period.**

5. If you want to exclude specific IP addresses from the range, type the IP address (or range of IP addresses) you want to exclude in the From and To text boxes, and then click the Add command button. The excluded IP addresses will appear in the Excluded Ranges list box.

6. Select the "Allow remote clients to request a predetermined IP address" check box when remote TCP/IP clients have been configured so that their Dial-Up Networking software requests a specific IP address from the RAS server. This option is not selected by default, and is not commonly used.

7. Click OK to return to the Network Configuration dialog box.

Configuring IPX (NWLink IPX/SPX Compatible Transport)

If you selected IPX (NWLink IPX/SPX Compatible Transport) as a dial-out protocol, it must be configured.

TO CONFIGURE IPX, FOLLOW THESE STEPS:

1. Click the Configure command button next to IPX in the Server Settings
section of the Network Configuration dialog box.

note   **References to IPX in the various RAS configuration dialog boxes
include NWLink IPX/SPX Compatible Transport and other versions
of IPX.**

2. The RAS Server IPX Configuration dialog box appears, as shown in Figure
17-8. Notice the network number configuration options.

note   **Selections made in this dialog box apply to** *all* **Dial-Up Networking
client computers that access the RAS server by using IPX.**

FIGURE 17-8 Configuring RAS server
IPX options

3. In the "Allow remote IPX clients to access" section, choose one of the two
possible configuration options:

    o Entire network: If you select the option button next to "Entire network,"
the RAS server will function as a router for Dial-Up Networking client
computers, and remote IPX clients will be able to access resources on all
servers that use IPX on the RAS server's local network. This option button
is selected by default.

- This computer only: If you select the option button next to "This computer only," the RAS server will not function as a router for Dial-Up Networking client computers, and remote IPX clients will only be able to access resources located on the RAS server. This option is sometimes used in high-security environments to prevent unauthorized access to other computers on the corporate network.

4. The remainder of this dialog box concerns the assignment of network numbers and node numbers to remote IPX client computers. Select one of the two primary network number assignment options:

- Allocate network numbers automatically: If you select the option button next to "Allocate network numbers automatically," the RAS server assigns a network number that is not currently in use to a remote IPX client computer when it connects to the RAS server. This option button is selected by default.

- Allocate network numbers: If you select the option button next to "Allocate network numbers," the RAS server assigns a network number from the specified range of numbers listed in the From and To text boxes to a remote IPX client computer when it connects to the RAS server. You must specify a range of network numbers in the From and To text boxes if you select this option button.

5. Two additional check boxes are available in this section, regardless of the network number allocation method you selected above:

- Assign same network number to all IPX clients: If you select the check box next to "Assign same network number to all IPX clients," the RAS server assigns the same network number to all remote IPX client computers. This check box is selected by default.

- Allow remote clients to request IPX node number: Select the check box next to "Allow remote clients to request IPX node number" when remote IPX clients have been configured so that their Dial-Up Networking software requests a specific IPX node number from the RAS server. This option is not selected by default and is not commonly used.

6. Click OK to return to the Network Configuration dialog box.

Completing the RAS Installation

Once you have completed all configurations in the Network Configuration dialog box, you are ready to complete the RAS installation.

TO COMPLETE THE RAS INSTALLATION, FOLLOW THESE STEPS:

1. In the Network Configuration dialog box, click OK.

2. The Remote Access Setup dialog box reappears. Click the Continue command button.

3. Windows NT installs RAS. If you selected the IPX dial-in protocol, the RIP for NWLink IPX Configuration dialog box appears, as shown in Figure 17-9.

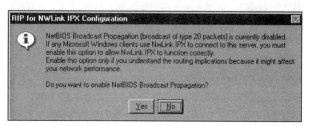

FIGURE 17-9   Configuring NetBIOS Broadcast Propagation

- Select the Yes command button if remote IPX clients will be accessing shared NetBIOS resources on servers (that use IPX) on the RAS server's local network. Selecting the Yes command button causes RAS to automatically forward NetBIOS broadcasts from IPX clients.

- Select the No command button if remote IPX clients will only be accessing resources on the RAS server, and/or will only be accessing resources on NetWare servers on the RAS server's local network. Selecting the No command prevents the RAS server from automatically forwarding NetBIOS broadcasts from IPX clients.

4. A Setup Message is displayed, indicating that RAS has been successfully installed. Click OK.

5. The Network dialog box reappears. Click the Close command button.

6. Windows NT performs various bindings operations.

7. A Network Settings Change dialog box appears, indicating that you must shut down and restart the computer in order for the new settings to take effect. Click the Yes command button to restart the computer.

USING REMOTE ACCESS ADMIN
TO MANAGE THE RAS SERVER

Remote Access Admin is a Windows NT administrative tool that is primarily used to start and stop the Remote Access Service (RAS), to assign the dialin permission to users, and to configure a call back security level for each user. Remote Access Admin can also be used to view COM port status and statistics, to disconnect users from individual ports, and to remotely manage RAS on other Windows NT computers.

Remote Access Admin is available on all Windows NT computers that have RAS installed. In addition, because Remote Access Admin is a component of Client-based Network Administration Tools, it is also available on Windows NT Workstation computers that have these tools installed.

To access Remote Access Admin, select Start ⇒ Programs ⇒ Administrative Tools (Common) ⇒ Remote Access Admin.

When you start Remote Access Admin, the Remote Access Admin dialog box appears, as shown in Figure 17-10. Notice the RAS server condition and other information displayed.

FIGURE 17-10   Starting Remote Access Admin

To start, stop, or pause RAS on a server, highlight the server in the Server list box and select the appropriate option from the Server menu, as shown in Figure 17-11.

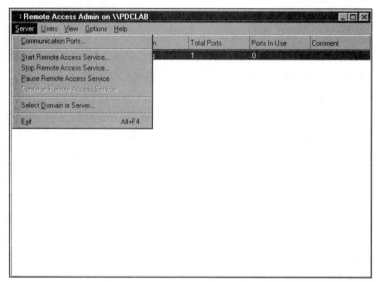

FIGURE 17-11   Starting, stopping, or pausing RAS

In addition to starting, stopping, or pausing RAS, Remote Access Admin is also used to manage the assignment of the dialin permission and to configure call back security. These tasks are discussed in the next section.

Assigning the Dialin Permission and Configuring Call Back Security

Before remote users can dial in and connect to a RAS server, they must be assigned the dialin permission. Until this permission is assigned to at least one user account, RAS connections and RAS functionality can't be established.

TO ASSIGN THE DIALIN PERMISSION TO USERS AND TO CONFIGURE CALL BACK SECURITY, FOLLOW THESE STEPS:

1. Select Start ⇒ Programs ⇒ Administrative Tools (Common) ⇒ Remote Access Admin to start Remote Access Admin. In the Remote Access Admin dialog box, select Users ⇒ Permissions.

2. The Remote Access Permissions dialog box appears, as shown in Figure 17-12. Notice the Grant All command button.

FIGURE 17-12   Assigning the dialin permission and configuring call back security

- To assign the dialin permission to *all* users, click the Grant All command button.
- To remove the dialin permission from *all* users, click the Revoke All command button.
- To assign the dialin permission to an *individual* user account, highlight the user account in the Users list box, then select the check box next to Grant dialin permission to user.

note   The dialin permission and call back security can also be configured by selecting the Dialin command button in the User Properties dialog box in User Manager for Domains. (See Chapter 8 to refresh yourself on how to use User Manager for Domains to manage the dialin permission for user accounts.)

3. Call back security is configured on an individual user basis in the Remote Access Permissions dialog box. To configure call back security, highlight the user account, then select one of the following three options:

- No Call Back: If you select the option button next to No Call Back, the user can dial in to the RAS server, but the user can't request that the RAS server break the connection and call the user back. Selecting this option ensures that the user dialing in—not the server—is billed for any long-distance telephone charges. Selecting this option provides no security other than user account and password authentication. This option button is selected by default.

- Set By Caller: If you select the option button next to Set By Caller, the RAS server prompts the remote user for a telephone number to dial back. The RAS server then breaks the connection and dials the user back at the number specified by the remote user. This setting is typically used when remote employees must make a long-distance call to connect to the RAS server. Selecting this option button enables the company, rather than the remote employee, to incur the bulk of the long-distance telephone charges. There is no real security (other than user account and password authentication) provided when this option is selected, because the RAS server will dial back to *any* telephone number specified by a user, whether authorized or unauthorized.

- Preset To: If you select the option button next to Preset To, you must also specify a telephone number that the RAS server will always use to call back whenever this remote user dials in. This configuration provides the highest amount of call back security, because only a predetermined telephone number (such as an employee's home telephone number) will be used by the RAS server. Unauthorized remote users calling from a different location, even if they can provide a valid user name and password, won't be able to maintain a connection, because the RAS server will break the connection and call back only the prespecified number.

4. When you have finished configuring call back security, click OK to return to the Remote Access Admin dialog box.

5. Exit Remote Access Admin.

CONFIGURING DIAL–UP NETWORKING CONNECTIONS

Dial-Up Networking is the client/dial-out component of RAS. The Dial-Up Networking accessory is installed during the RAS installation. Dial-Up Networking enables Windows NT computers to connect to dial-up servers and to establish network connections through those servers. Dial-up servers include Windows NT RAS servers; UNIX computers that are configured as SLIP or PPP servers; and any other computers, routers, or front-end processors that are configured as SLIP or PPP servers.

Before the Dial-Up Networking functionality on a Windows NT computer can be used, RAS must be installed and configured, and at least one of the computer's RAS ports must be configured for dial-out usage. Additionally, you must create at least one phonebook entry that contains various dialing information and instructions. Phonebook entries are created by using the Windows NT Dial-Up Networking accessory and are explained in detail in the next section.

Configuring and Using Phonebook Entries

Phonebook entries contain all of the information and instructions required by Dial-Up Networking to connect to a dial-up server. You can select, create, or edit a phonebook entry by using the Dial-Up Networking accessory.

To access the Dial-Up Networking accessory, select Start ⇒ Programs ⇒ Accessories ⇒ Dial-Up Networking. Figure 17-13 shows the Dial-Up Networking dialog box.

To use an existing phonebook entry to connect to a dial-up server, select the phonebook entry you want to use from the "Phonebook entry to dial" drop-down list box. Then select your current location from the "Dialing from" drop-down list box. Then click the Dial command button.

To create a new phonebook entry, click the New command button in the Dial-Up Networking dialog box. The New Phonebook Entry dialog box appears, as shown in Figure 17-14. Notice the five configuration tabs in this dialog box: Basic, Server, Script, Security, and X.25.

FIGURE 17-13   The Dial-Up Networking accessory main dialog box

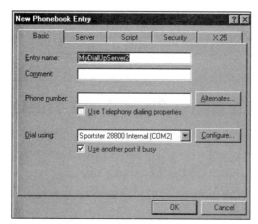

FIGURE 17-14   Creating a new phonebook entry

 tip   To configure the Telephony settings for the location you are dialing from, use the Telephony application in Control Panel; or, click the Location command button in the Dial-Up Networking dialog box. (Telephony settings include your area code, country, number used to access an outside line, and calling card settings for each location that you configure.)

The Telephony application is decidedly more user friendly than the Location Settings dialog box in Dial-Up Networking.

The first time the you start Dial-Up Networking, a dialog box appears stating that the phonebook is empty.

To complete the new phonebook entry, select the appropriate configuration options on the various tabs in the New Phonebook Entry dialog box. Each of the five configuration tabs are discussed in detail in the following sections.

 If you are editing an existing phonebook entry (rather than creating a new phonebook entry) the five configuration tabs — Basic, Server, Script, Security, and X.25 — are the same. The only difference is that the dialog box is titled Edit Phonebook Entry instead of New Phonebook Entry.

Configuring basic properties

The Basic tab in the New Phonebook Entry dialog box is used to configure the phonebook entry name, the phone number to be used, and the modem/port to be used to establish the connection to the dial-up server. The Basic tab contains several configurable options:

- **Entry name:** Type in a name that describes the connection in the "Entry name" text box. The default name is MyDialUpServer. Entry name is a mandatory setting.

- **Comment:** You can enter a comment about the phonebook entry in the Comment text box if you want to. This entry is optional.

- **Phone number:** Type in the phone number to be dialed to access the dial-up server in the "Phone number" text box. Alternate phone numbers for the dial-up server can be entered by clicking the Alternates command button. If this dial-up connection will use PPTP, enter the IP address of the RAS server in the "Phone number" text box instead of a phone number. (Remember, PPTP tunnels its connection *inside* of an existing TCP/IP network connection.)

- **Use Telephony dialing properties:** If you select the check box next to "Use Telephony dialing properties," Dial-Up Networking will use your location telephony settings (area code, number to dial to get an outside line, and so on) when dialing the phone number entered in the "Phone number" text box to establish a connection. If you don't select this check box, the location telephony settings won't be used — only the phone number listed in the "Phone number" text box will be used. This check box is not selected by default.

o **Dial using:** Select the modem, other connection device, or PPTP RAS port you want to use for this connection from the "Dial using" drop-down list box. After you highlight your selection, click the Configure command button to configure the modem, device, or port. Modems can also be configured by using the Modems application in Control Panel.

o **Use another port if busy:** Select the check box next to "Use another port if busy" if you want Dial-Up Networking to use a different port to establish a connection if the primary port you selected is busy.

Configuring a Multilink connection   When you need more throughput than a single line can provide, you might consider using multiple lines to establish a Point-to-Point Multilink Protocol connection.

TO CONFIGURE A POINT-TO-POINT MULTILINK PROTOCOL CONNECTION, FOLLOW THESE STEPS:

1. Select the Multiple Lines option from the "Dial using" drop-down list box, as shown in Figure 17-15. Notice that the "Phone number" text box is grayed out when the Multiple Lines option is selected.

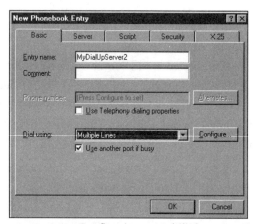

FIGURE 17-15   Configuring a Multilink connection

2. To configure the phone numbers to be dialed to establish the Multilink connection, click the Configure command button. The Multiple Line Configuration dialog box appears, as shown in Figure 17-16. Notice the text in the dialog box that indicates that multiple lines simultaneously connected to a PPP Multilink server behave like a single, faster connection.

3. Select two or more modems, devices, or ports from those listed, and individually configure a phone number for each by highlighting the modem, device, or port and clicking the Phone numbers command button. Click OK when you are finished to return to the Basic tab in the New Phonebook Entry dialog box.

FIGURE 17-16   Selecting the modems, devices, or ports
to be used in a Multilink connection

 To establish a Multilink connection, both the Dial-Up Networking client and the RAS server must be configured to support Multilink.

 Call back security should normally *not* be configured on RAS servers that support Multilink connections. The reason for this is that only one phone number can be stored in the call back configuration, and if the RAS server breaks the connection and calls this number back, only a single line will be used for the connection. This effectively eliminates any Multilink functionality.

Configuring server properties

To configure server properties, including dial-up server type and network protocols, click the Server tab in the New Phonebook Entry dialog box. The Server tab
appears, as shown in Figure 17-17.

FIGURE 17-17   Configuring dial-up server type
and network protocols

Select from the many options presented on the Server tab:

o **Dial-up server type:** Select the type of dial-up server you want to connect
to from the "Dial-up server type" drop-down list box.

o **Network protocols:** Select the transport protocols that you want to use for
this dial-up connection. Protocols available include TCP/IP, (NWLink)
IPX/SPX Compatible (Transport), and NetBEUI. You can select more than
one protocol. All installed protocols are selected by default.

o **TCP/IP Settings:** If you select TCP/IP, click the TCP/IP Settings command
button to configure TCP/IP settings for this connection. The PPP TCP/IP
Settings dialog box appears, as shown in Figure 17-18. Notice that you can
either accept a server-assigned IP address or specify an IP address.

FIGURE 17-18 Configuring TCP/IP
address assignment
options

o **Enable software compression:** Select the check box next to "Enable
software compression" if you want the Dial-Up Networking software to
compress all data before it is transmitted to the RAS server. You should
disable modem compression if you select this option. This check box is
selected by default.

o **Enable PPP LCP extensions:** Select the check box next to "Enable PPP
LCP extensions" if you want to enable the newer PPP features. Deselect
this check box only if you are unable to connect with it selected. This
check box is selected by default.

Configuring script properties

To configure script properties, click the Script tab in the New Phonebook Entry
dialog box. The Script tab appears, as shown in Figure 17-19. Notice that only
"After dialing" script options are shown. To configure script options that will be
used prior to dialing, click the Before dialing command button.

FIGURE 17-19   Configuring Dial-Up Networking
scripts

Scripts are often used to connect to dial-up servers that require interactive logon sequences, and/or have special menu options that must be selected during the connection process. Scripts are typically associated with SLIP servers, or with servers that support both SLIP and PPP.

By default, this tab is configured so that Dial-Up Networking will *not* use a script. Unless you are connecting to a dial-up server that requires the use of a script, you do not need to configure this tab.

To configure script properties, select one of the three script options:

- **None:** If you select the option button next to None, no script or pop-up terminal will be used. This option is selected by default.

- **Pop up a terminal window:** Select the option button next to "Pop up a terminal window" if you don't want to create or use a script, but you still need to make interactive selections during the logon process. Experienced users often select this option to determine which settings need to be placed in a script file.

- **Run this script:** Select the option button next to "Run this script" to automate the connection process to a dial-up server that requires the use of a script. If you select this option, either select a script from the drop-down list box or click the Edit script command button to create a new script file. When you click the Edit script command button, a copy of the

`Switch.inf` file is displayed by the Notepad text editor. The `Switch.inf` file includes instructions for creating new script files.

Configuring security properties

To configure security, including password authentication and encryption options, click the Security tab in the New Phonebook Entry dialog box. The Security tab appears, as shown in Figure 17-20. Notice that the authentication and encryption options are similar to the Server Settings that are configured for dial-in connections during the installation of RAS.

FIGURE 17-20   Configuring password authentication and encryption options

Options selected in this dialog box will be applied to the Dial-Up Networking client only, not to the RAS server.

Select one of the three authentication and encryption policy options:

o **Accept any authentication including clear text:** If you select the option button next to "Accept any authentication including clear text," Dial-Up Networking will connect to a dial-up server using the lowest password authentication option accepted by the server. For example, if the dial-up server is configured to enable any authentication including clear text, and this option is selected, Dial-Up Networking transmits the password to the dial-up server by using clear text. This option is selected by default.

○ **Accept only encrypted authentication:** If you select the option button next to "Accept only encrypted authentication," Dial-Up Networking will not be able to connect to a dial-up server that does not support some form of encrypted authentication.

○ **Accept only Microsoft encrypted authentication:** If you select the option button next to "Accept only Microsoft encrypted authentication," Dial-Up Networking will not be able to establish a connection with a dial-up server unless that server supports Microsoft encrypted authentication. You must select this option if you want to use data encryption. If you select this option, two additional check boxes are available:

  ○ **Require data encryption:** If you select the check box next to "Require data encryption," the Dial-Up Networking client will encrypt all data sent over this connection. You should select this check box if you are configuring a PPTP connection. This check box is only available if you selected the option button next to Accept only Microsoft encrypted authentication. This check box is not selected by default.

  ○ **Use current username and password:** If you select the check box next to "Use current username and password," Dial-Up Networking will not prompt you for a user name or password when establishing a connection with the dial-up server. This check box is only available if you selected the option button next to "Accept only Microsoft encrypted authentication." This check box is not selected by default.

Configuring X.25 connection properties

To configure an X.25 connection, click the X.25 tab in the New Phonebook Entry dialog box. The X.25 tab appears, as shown in Figure 17-21.

Contact your X.25 provider to obtain the information you should use to configure this dialog box. You should obtain the network provider type (such as CompuServe, InfoNet, or Transpac), and X.25 address to be used.

FIGURE 17-21 Configuring X.25 settings

CONFIGURING DIAL-UP NETWORKING TO CONNECT TO THE INTERNET

There are several circumstances when you might want to use Dial-Up Networking to connect your Windows NT computer to the Internet:

o When users need to access the Internet to perform research, browse Web pages, and so on

o When you want to connect your Windows NT WWW server (that is also a Dial-Up Networking client) to the Internet, and you expect only a few concurrent users to access your WWW server

o When you want to establish a TCP/IP connection to the Internet so that you can use PPTP to access a remote RAS server over the Internet

To establish a Dial-Up Networking connection to the Internet, you normally need to use the services of an *Internet Service Provider* (ISP). The ISP has a local network connection directly to the Internet. The ISP uses dial-up servers, such as RAS servers, SLIP servers, or front-end processors to enable remote users to connect to the Internet via the ISP's network.

Before you can establish a connection to the Internet via your ISP, you need to know how to configure your Dial-Up Networking client so that it is compatible with the ISP's dial-up server. Configuration information you should obtain from your ISP includes

- Type of dial-up server used by the ISP (SLIP or PPP connection protocol)
- Whether the ISP's dial-up server supports software compression
- Whether you will specify an IP address when you connect to the ISP, or the ISP's dial-up server will assign you an IP address
- Whether the ISP will provide the IP address of a DNS server during the connection process
- Whether the ISP's dial-up server uses IP header compression (IP header compression is also referred to as Van Jacobson header compression or VJ header compression)
- Type of modem you will be connecting to at the ISP and recommended settings that you should use for your modem
- The phone number you should use to connect to the ISP

CONFIGURING PPTP SECURITY

If your RAS server is connected to the Internet via a router and an ISP, and you want to allow only PPTP connections to your server, you can configure TCP/IP to only accept PPTP packets. To accomplish this, a TCP/IP PPTP option, called *PPTP filtering*, must be individually configured for each network adapter installed in the RAS server that has a routed connection to the Internet.

TO CONFIGURE PPTP FILTERING FOR A NETWORK ADAPTER, FOLLOW THESE STEPS:

1. Select Start ⇒ Settings ⇒ Control Panel.

2. In Control Panel, double-click the Network application.

3. In the Network dialog box, click the Protocols tab.

4. On the Protocols tab, double-click the TCP/IP Protocol in the Network Protocols list box.

5. In the Microsoft TCP/IP Properties dialog box, click the Advanced command button.

6. The Advanced IP Addressing dialog box appears, as shown in Figure 17-22. Notice the check box next to Enable PPTP Filtering. Select the network adapter you want to configure from the Adapter drop-down list box. Then select the check box next to Enable PPTP Filtering. Click OK.

7. In the Microsoft TCP/IP Properties dialog box, click OK.

8. In the Network dialog box, click the Close command button.

9. A Network Settings Change dialog box appears, indicating that you must shut down and restart the computer in order for the new settings to take effect. Click the Yes command button to restart the computer.

FIGURE 17-22   **Enabling PPTP filtering for a network adapter**

TROUBLESHOOTING COMMON RAS PROBLEMS

Most common RAS problems reported by users involve an inability to connect to a RAS server, a third-party SLIP server, or a front-end processor from a Dial-Up Networking client computer.

Table 17-1 shows some common causes of RAS connection problems, and recommended solutions.

TABLE 17-1 COMMON CAUSES OF RAS PROBLEMS AND RECOMMENDED SOLUTIONS

COMMON CAUSES OF RAS PROBLEMS	*SUGGESTED/RECOMMENDED SOLUTIONS*
Modem configuration or compatibility problem	If you suspect that your modem is the problem, first determine the type of modem to which you are attempting to connect; and then reconfigure your modem settings to the most compatible option, or as recommended by your ISP. If you are using an unsupported modem (for example, one that is not on the HCL), verify that your settings in the Modem.inf file are appropriate for your modem. If you have selected RAS software compression, ensure that your modem is not configured to compress data. If you are still unable to connect, you can configure your modem to record a log file of all attempted connections. To configure a modem log file, use the Modems application in Control Panel to access your modem's Properties dialog box. Select the Connection tab and then the Advanced Connection Settings dialog box.
Password authentication problem	If you suspect a password authentication problem, configure Dial-Up Networking to accept any authentication including clear text, and/or configure the RAS server to enable any authentication including clear text. (Note: Clear text passwords are usually required by SLIP servers.)
TCP/IP configuration problem	If you suspect a TCP/IP configuration problem, contact the manager of the dial-up server you are attempting to connect to and determine the dial-up server's TCP/IP configuration. Configure Dial-Up Networking so that the client's TCP/IP configuration settings match those of the dial-up server.
Dial-Up Networking configuration problem	Verify that you have chosen the appropriate dial-up server type (SLIP or PPP connection type) by contacting the manager of the dial-up server, if necessary.
Script problem	If you are using a script and your modem makes contact with the dial-up server, but you are *not* able to successfully complete a connection to the dial-up server, try editing your script file or try using a pop-up terminal window instead of the script file.

KEY POINT SUMMARY

This chapter focused on *Remote Access Service* (RAS) — a Windows NT service that enables dial-up network connections between a RAS server and a Dial-Up Networking client computer.

- Dial-Up Networking client computers can connect to a RAS server by using a variety of connection types, including a standard telephone line and modem, ISDN, X.25, and Point-to-Point Tunneling Protocol (PPTP).

- The most common connection type is a standard analog telephone line and modem. This service is inexpensive and widely available.

- *ISDN* is a digital, dial-up telephone service that supports faster data transmission rates than a standard telephone line. An ISDN Basic Rate Interface (BRI) line consists of two B channels and a D channel. If both B channels are used together, data can be transmitted at up to 128Kbps.

- *X.25* is a packet-switching protocol that is used on dial-up or leased lines. This service is available in most countries and requires a fair amount of hardware to implement.

- *PPTP* is not a physical connection type. Rather, it is a virtual network connection that is "tunneled" inside of an existing TCP/IP network connection. RAS encryption can be used with PPTP to provide a secure, private connection over a public TCP/IP network, such as the Internet.

- RAS communications can be carried out over several connection protocols, including Serial Line Internet Protocol (SLIP), Point-to-Point Protocol (PPP), Point-to-Point Multilink Protocol (PPMP), and Point-to-Point Tunneling Protocol (PPTP).

- *SLIP* is an older connection protocol, commonly associated with UNIX computers, that supports only the TCP/IP transport protocol.

- *PPP* is a newer connection protocol designed to overcome the limitations of SLIP. PPP is currently the industry standard remote connection protocol and is recommended for use by Microsoft. PPP supports password encryption, multiple transport protocols (including TCP/IP, NWLink IPX/SPX Compatible Transport, and NetBEUI), and dynamic, server-based IP addressing.

- *Point-to-Point Multilink Protocol* combines the bandwidth from multiple physical connections into a single logical connection.

- *PPTP* supports the RAS encryption feature over standard, unencrypted TCP/IP networks, such as the Internet. PPTP supports all standard transport protocols, including NWLink IPX/SPX Compatible Transport, NetBEUI, and TCP/IP.

- All Windows NT standard transport protocols are supported by RAS. Client computers can connect to a RAS server by using NetBEUI, TCP/IP, or NWLink IPX/SPX Compatible Transport. The DLC protocol is *not* supported by RAS. A RAS server acts as a router for client computers that use TCP/IP or NWLink IPX/SPX Compatible Transport, enabling these clients to access other computers on the network via the RAS server's routing capability.

- The *RAS NetBIOS gateway* enables client computers that use NetBEUI to access shared resources on other servers located on the RAS server's local network. The RAS NetBIOS gateway performs protocol translation for the remote NetBEUI client computers. Only NetBIOS-based services (such as shared folders and printers, Lotus Notes servers, SQL Servers and SNA Servers) can be accessed by NetBEUI client computers via the RAS NetBIOS gateway. The NetBIOS gateway has a maximum connection limit of 250 simultaneous connections.

- RAS supports the following NetBIOS name resolution methods: NetBIOS broadcasts, WINS servers, DNS servers, `LMHOSTS` files, and `HOSTS` files.

- Before installing RAS, you should install and configure all of the transport protocols you plan to use, and you should also install and configure at least one connection device, such as a modem or ISDN adapter card.

- RAS is installed using the Services tab in the Network application in Control Panel. Many items are configured during the RAS installation, including modems, ports, protocols, password encryption, and enabling Multilink. All settings in the Network Configuration dialog box are global settings that apply to all ports. When each protocol is configured, you must choose whether to allow remote clients connecting via that protocol access to all computers on the RAS server's local network (Entire network), or to limit remote clients' access to only the RAS server (This computer only).

- *Remote Access Admin* is a Windows NT administrative tool that is commonly used to start, stop, and pause RAS; to assign the dialin permission to users; and to configure call back security. Before remote users can establish a dial-up connection with a RAS server, they must be assigned the dialin permission. (The dialin permission can also be assigned by selecting the Dialin command button in the User Properties dialog box in User Manager for Domains.) Call back security is configured on an individual user basis in Remote Access Admin. The Preset To configuration offers the highest level of call back security.

- *Dial-Up Networking* is the client/dial out component of RAS. The Dial-Up Networking accessory is installed during the RAS installation. Before Dial-Up Networking functionality on a Windows NT computer can be used, RAS must be installed and configured, and at least one of the computer's RAS ports must be configured for dial-out usage. Additionally, you must create at least one phonebook entry that contains dialing information and instructions. Phonebook entries are created, edited, and selected by using the Dial-Up Networking accessory.

- When a new phonebook entry is created (or an existing phonebook entry is edited) by using the Dial-Up Networking accessory, there are five tabs on which configurations can be made: Basic, Server, Script, Security, and X.25. The phonebook entry name, phone number to be used, and modem/port to be used are configured on the Basic tab. A Multilink connection can also be configured on the Basic tab. The dial-up server type and network protocols are configured on the Server tab. Scripts, which are typically associated with SLIP servers, are configured on the Script tab. Password authentication and encryption policy is configured on the Security tab. X.25 connection settings are configured on the X.25 tab.

- To establish a Dial-Up Networking connection to the Internet, you normally need to use the services of an *Internet service provider* (ISP). Configuration information you should obtain from your ISP includes the following:

  - Type of dial-up server used by the ISP (SLIP or PPP connection protocol)

  - Whether the ISP's dial-up server supports software compression

  - Whether you will specify an IP address when you connect to the ISP, or the ISP's dial-up server will assign you an IP address

- o Whether the ISP will provide the IP address of a DNS server during the connection process

- o Whether the ISP's dial-up server uses IP header compression (IP header compression is also referred to as Van Jacobson header compression or VJ header compression)

- o Type of modem to which you will be connecting at the ISP and recommended settings that you should use for your modem

- o The phone number you should use to connect to the ISP

- o If your RAS server has a routed connection to the Internet, you can configure *PPTP filtering* so that TCP/IP will only accept PPTP packets. To accomplish this, use the Network application in Control Panel.

- o Most common RAS problems reported by users involve an inability to connect to a RAS server, a third-party SLIP server, or a front-end processor from a Dial-Up Networking client computer. Common causes of RAS connection problems are modem compatibility or configuration problems, password authentication problems, TCP/IP configuration problems, Dial-Up Networking configuration problems, and script problems.

APPLYING WHAT YOU'VE LEARNED

Now it's time to regroup, review, and apply what you've learned in this chapter.

The questions in the Instant Assessment section that follows bring to mind key facts and concepts. Next, the Critical Thinking Lab gives you an opportunity to test your troubleshooting skills. Finally, a Hands-on Lab reinforces what you've learned and gives you a chance to practice some of the tasks that may be tested by the Server exam.

Instant Assessment

1. What is the "server component" of RAS called?

2. What is the "client component" of RAS called?

3. Up to how many simultaneous dial-in connections can Windows NT Server RAS support?

4. How many simultaneous dial-in connections can the RAS NetBIOS gateway support on a Windows NT Server computer?

5. List the four types of connection types that Dial-Up Networking client computers can use to connect to a RAS server.

6. List the four connection protocols that RAS communications can be carried out over.

7. Which connection protocol is older, commonly associated with scripts and with UNIX computers, and supports only the TCP/IP transport protocol?

8. Which connection protocol is newer, is currently the industry standard, and supports multiple transport protocols (including TCP/IP, NWLink IPX/SPX Compatible Transport, and NetBEUI)?

9. Describe the Point-to-Point Multilink Protocol.

10. What is PPTP?

11. Which transport protocols are supported by RAS?

12. What does the RAS NetBIOS gateway do?

13. Which NetBIOS name resolution methods does RAS support?

14. Assuming that RAS and Dial-Up Networking are installed and configured, what must be assigned before remote users can establish a dial-up connection with a RAS server?

15. What entries in Dial-Up Networking contain dialing information and instructions that are used to establish the connection to the dial-up server?

16. List three configuration information items you should obtain from your ISP before you establish a Dial-Up Networking connection to the Internet.

17. Which Windows NT tool should you use to configure RAS call back security, and which configuration option offers the highest level of security?

 concept link   **For answers to the Instant Assessment questions see Appendix B.**

Critical Thinking Lab

The following Critical Thinking Lab gives you a chance to apply your RAS knowledge in two common real-life troubleshooting situations.

Lab 17.27 *Troubleshooting common RAS problems*

The purpose of this lab is to give you experience in troubleshooting common RAS problems.

In each of the situations below, propose a solution to the reported problem.

Problem 1   A user reports that he can't establish a connection with the dial-up server from his Dial-Up Networking client computer. You suspect a modem problem.

Recommend a course of action to solve the reported problem:

Problem 2   A user reports that she is unable to connect to a SLIP server from her Dial-Up Networking client computer. The phonebook entry on the user's computer is configured as shown in Figure 17-23.

FIGURE 17-23   Password authentication configuration for Dial-Up Networking client computer in Problem 2

Recommend a course of action to solve the reported problem:

 concept link   **For answers to the Critical Thinking Lab see Appendix B**.

Hands-on Lab

The following Hands-on Lab provides you with an opportunity to apply the RAS knowledge you've gained in this chapter.

Lab 17.28 *Installing and configuring RAS and Dial-Up Networking*

The purpose of this lab is to give you hands-on experience in installing and configuring RAS and Dial-Up Networking on a Windows NT Server computer.

Begin this lab by booting your computer to Windows NT Server. Log on as Administrator. Place your Windows NT Server compact disc in your CD-ROM drive.

 note **This lab assumes that you have installed a modem in your computer by using the Modems application in Control Panel. You probably performed this task in Lab 3.5. If you *haven't* installed a modem in your computer, see Part 3 of Lab 3.5 and perform the steps in the Modem section prior to doing this lab. You can perform these steps even if you don't have a modem in your computer.**

FOLLOW THE STEPS BELOW CAREFULLY:

1. Select Start ⇒ Settings ⇒ Control Panel.

2. In the Control Panel dialog box, double-click Network.

3. In the Network dialog box, click the Services tab.

4. On the Services tab, click the Add command button.

5. In the Select Network Service dialog box, highlight Remote Access Service. Click OK.

6. A Windows NT Setup dialog box appears. Ensure that the correct path to your Windows NT Server source files (usually the I386 folder on your Windows NT Server compact disc) is listed in the text box. Edit this text box if necessary. Click the Continue command button.

7. Windows NT copies source files. The Add RAS Device dialog box appears. Select the modem that you installed in Lab 3.5 (or any other modem that you have installed by using the Modems application in Control Panel) from the RAS Capable Devices drop-down list box. Click OK.

8. The Remote Access Setup dialog box appears. Click the Configure command button.

9. The Configure Port Usage dialog box appears. Select the option button next to "Dial out and Receive calls." Click OK.

10. The Remote Access Setup dialog box reappears. Click the Network command button.

11. The Network Configuration dialog box appears. Select the check box next to Enable Multilink at the bottom of the dialog box. Click the Configure command button next to the TCP/IP option in the Server Settings section.

12. The RAS Server TCP/IP Configuration dialog box appears. Click the option button next to "Use static address pool." In the Begin text box, enter an IP address of 192.168.58.1, and in the End text box, enter an IP address of 192.168.58.255. Click OK.

13. The Network Configuration dialog box reappears. Click the Configure command button next to the IPX option in the Server Settings section.

14. The RAS Server IPX Configuration dialog box appears. Notice that IPX clients are configured, by default, to access the entire network. Click OK.

15. The Network Configuration dialog box reappears. Click OK.

16. The Remote Access Setup dialog box reappears. Click the Continue command button.

17. Windows NT installs and configures RAS. If the RIP for NWLink IPX Configuration dialog box appears, asking if you want to enable NetBIOS Broadcast Propagation, click the Yes command button.

18. A Setup Message dialog box appears, indicating that RAS has been successfully installed. Click OK.

19. The Network dialog box reappears. Click the Close command button.

20. Windows NT performs various bindings operations.

21. A Network Settings Change dialog box appears, indicating that you must shut down and restart the computer in order for the new settings to take effect. Click the Yes command button to restart the computer.

22. Reboot your computer to Windows NT Server. Log on as Administrator. If the Control Panel dialog box appears, close it.

23. Select Start ⇒ Programs ⇒ Administrative Tools (Common) ⇒ Remote Access Admin.

24. The Remote Access Admin dialog box appears. Notice that RAS is running on your server. Select Users ⇒ Permissions.

25. The Remote Access Permissions dialog box appears. Click the Grant All command button to assign the dialin permission to all user accounts.

26. The Remote Access Admin warning dialog box appears, asking you to confirm that you want to grant the dialin permission to all users. Click the Yes command button.

27. The Remote Access Permissions dialog box reappears. Click OK.

28. The Remote Access Admin dialog box reappears. Close Remote Access Admin.

29. Select Start ⇒ Programs ⇒ Accessories ⇒ Dial-Up Networking.

30. A Dial-Up Networking dialog box appears, indicating that the phonebook is empty. Click OK.

31. The New Phonebook Entry Wizard appears. Accept the default of MyDialUpServer in the "Name the new phonebook entry" text box. Click the Next command button.

32. The Server dialog box appears. Select the check boxes next to "I am calling the Internet" and "Send my plain text password, if that's the only way to connect." Click the Next command button.

33. The Phone Number dialog box appears. Type 555-5425 in the "Phone number" text box. Click the Next command button.

34. Click the Finish command button in the New Phonebook Entry Wizard dialog box.

35. The Dial-Up Networking dialog box reappears. Exit Dial-Up Networking.

Monitoring and Optimization

Part V explores how to monitor and optimize the performance of your Windows NT computer or Windows NT network. This part begins with Chapter 18, which focuses on Performance Monitor, a Windows NT tool that can be used to identify performance problems, determine current usage of resources, track performance trends over time, predict future usage of resources, and determine how configuration changes affect performance. You'll learn how and when to use each of the four Performance Monitor "views" to gather and view statistics.

Then, Chapter 19 presents practical information on performance optimization. This chapter explains what you can do to increase the performance of your system and how to identify and resolve bottlenecks.

Part V maps to the Monitoring and Optimization exam objectives for the Implementing and Supporting Microsoft Windows NT Server 4.0 exam.

Using Performance Monitor

About Chapter 18

The focus of this chapter is on Performance Monitor, a Windows NT tool that can be used to identify bottlenecks, determine usage of system resources, track performance trends over time, predict future usage of system resources, and determine how system configuration changes affect system performance.

The chapter begins by explaining Performance Monitor objects, instances, and counters. Then it details how to install the SNMP Service and Network Monitor Agent to obtain various objects and their counters. It also describes how to enable the PhysicalDisk and LogicalDisk objects and their counters.

The remainder of the chapter is all about using Performance Monitor to gather and view statistics. Each of the four Performance Monitor views — Chart view, Alert view, Report view, and Log view — are explored.

This chapter includes one Hands-on Lab. In this lab, you'll install Network Monitor Agent and SNMP Service, use Performance Monitor Chart view and Alert view, create a Performance Monitor log file, and import a Performance Monitor log file into Report view and Chart view.

The material presented in Chapter 18 maps to the "Monitor performance of various functions by using Performance Monitor" objective listed in the Monitoring and Optimization section of the Preparation Guide for the Server exam.

WHAT IS PERFORMANCE MONITOR?

Performance Monitor is a Windows NT tool that ships with Windows NT Server. You don't need to install Performance Monitor — it's installed automatically when you install Windows NT Server.

Performance Monitor has several uses. It can be used to:

- Identify performance problems and/or bottlenecks
- Determine current usage of system resources
- Track performance trends over time
- Predict future usage of system resources (capacity planning)
- Determine how system configuration changes affect system performance

Performance Monitor is often used when there's a problem to be resolved, but it can also be used for planning purposes.

The rest of this chapter discusses the basics of how to use Performance Monitor.

concept link

This chapter covers only the basics of monitoring performance. Using Performance Monitor to detect common bottlenecks is featured in Chapter 19.

A good place to start when discussing Performance Monitor is with an explanation of Performance Monitor objects, instances, and counters — the things Performance Monitor can measure.

PERFORMANCE MONITOR OBJECTS, INSTANCES, AND COUNTERS

The system components that Performance Monitor can measure, such as processor, memory, and physical disk, are called *objects*.

If a system has more than one of a particular object, such as multiple processors or multiple physical disks, there is said to be more than one *instance* of that object. Some objects, such as memory, do not have instances. This is because there can't be more than one of the particular object.

Each instance of an object can be measured in different ways. Each possible measurement of an object is called a *counter*. For example, the PhysicalDisk object has multiple possible counters, including Disk Reads/sec (second), Disk Writes/sec, % Disk Time, % Disk Read Time, and % Disk Write Time. Each counter is selected individually. An object can be selected multiple times with a different counter for each selection, as shown in Figure 18-1. Notice the Performance Monitor report shows multiple counters selected for the PhysicalDisk object.

FIGURE 18-1   Measuring multiple counters for a single object

Many different objects and counters can be measured in Performance Monitor. Table 18-1 shows some of the most commonly used Performance Monitor objects and counters.

TABLE 18-1 COMMONLY USED PERFORMANCE MONITOR OBJECTS AND COUNTERS		
OBJECT	*COUNTER*	*DESCRIPTION*
Memory	Pages/sec	This counter measures how often data is written to and read from the paging file. I use this counter to obtain an overall view of how memory is utilized by Windows NT.
		A consistently high number (greater than 2-3) indicates that the current amount of RAM may be insufficient for the computer.

OBJECT	COUNTER	DESCRIPTION
Network Segment	%Network utilization	This counter measures the total network utilization on a given network segment as a percentage of the maximum amount of network traffic possible on that segment. A consistently high number (a number approaching 100 percent) may indicate that there is too much traffic on that network segment, and that an additional network adapter may need to be installed in the server, or a router installed to further segment the network.
PhysicalDisk	Avg. Disk Queue Length	This counter measures the average number of disk reads and writes waiting to be performed. A consistently high number (greater than 2-3) may indicate that a faster hard disk and/or hard disk controller, or a different disk configuration (such as a stripe set or a stripe set with parity) may be required for adequate system performance.
PhysicalDisk	% Disk Time	This counter measures the percentage of time the disk performs reads and writes. A consistently high number (a number approaching 100 percent) may indicate that a faster hard disk and/or hard disk controller, or a different disk configuration (such as a stripe set or a stripe set with parity) may be required for adequate system performance.
Processor	% Processor Time	This counter measures the percentage of time that the processor is actively used by processes other than the Idle process. (The *Idle process* can be defined as the time the processor spends waiting to be assigned tasks.) A consistently high number (a number approaching 100 percent) may indicate that a faster processor (or an additional processor) may be required for adequate system performance.

continued

OBJECT	COUNTER	DESCRIPTION
		TABLE 18-1 *(continued)*
Server	Bytes Total/sec	This counter measures the total amount of network utilization of a Windows NT Server computer. Specifically, it measures the total number of bytes sent to and received from all network adapters in the Windows NT computer by the Server process.
		The measurement can be used to compare utilization of two similar servers for load balancing purposes. It can also be used in conjunction with other measurements to determine network segment utilization.

Not all Performance Monitor objects and counters are available when Windows NT is first installed. For example, the TCP (Transmission Control Protocol) object is not available until the *Simple Network Management Protocol* (SNMP) Service is installed, and the Network Segment object is not available until the Network Monitor Agent is installed. Additionally, some objects and counters must be enabled before they can be effectively used in Performance Monitor.

The following sections explain how to add and enable certain Performance Monitor objects and counters.

Installing the SNMP Service to Obtain TCP/IP Objects and Their Counters

By default, Performance Monitor does *not* make available TCP/IP objects and their counters, even when TCP/IP is installed and configured on the Windows NT computer. The SNMP Service must be installed before you can monitor TCP/IP objects and counters in Performance Monitor.

Installing the SNMP Service adds four objects and their counters to Performance Monitor:

o IP (Internet Protocol)

o ICMP (Internet Control Message Protocol)

○ TCP (Transmission Control Protocol)

○ UDP (User Datagram Protocol)

These four objects and their counters are used by developers to optimize network usage of applications, and by administrators of large networks to troubleshoot and optimize TCP/IP network traffic.

The following section explains how to install the SNMP Service on a Windows NT computer.

TO INSTALL THE SNMP SERVICE, FOLLOW THESE STEPS:

1. Select Start ⇒ Settings ⇒ Control Panel.

2. The Control Panel dialog box appears. Double-click the Network icon.

3. The Network dialog box appears. Click the Services tab.

4. The Services tab appears. Click the Add command button.

5. The Select Network Service dialog box appears. Highlight SNMP Service, as shown in Figure 18-2. Click OK.

FIGURE 18-2   Installing the SNMP Service

6. A Windows NT Setup dialog box appears. Ensure that the correct path to your Windows NT Server source files (usually the I386 folder on your Windows NT Server compact disc) is listed in the text box. Edit this text box if necessary. Click the Continue command button.

7. Windows NT copies source files and installs the SNMP Service.

8. The Microsoft SNMP Properties dialog box appears, as shown in Figure 18-3. Notice the three tabs available: Agent, Traps, and Security. Configure the SNMP Service as desired. Click OK.

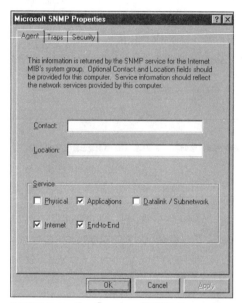

FIGURE 18-3   Configuring SNMP Properties

 If you are installing the SNMP Service only to obtain TCP/IP objects and their counters for use in Performance Monitor, no configuration is required.

9. The Network dialog box reappears. Click the Close command button.

10. Windows NT performs various bindings operations.

11. A Network Settings Change dialog box appears, indicating that you must shut down and restart the computer for the new settings to take effect. Click the Yes command button to restart the computer.

Installing Network Monitor Agent to Obtain the Network Segment Object and Its Counters

By default, the Network Segment object and its counters are *not* available in Performance Monitor. The Network Monitor Agent must be installed to make this object and its counters available.

The counters that are installed with the Network Segment object include: % Broadcast Frames, % Network Utilization, Total Bytes Received/second, and Total Frames Received/second.

The Network Segment object has an instance for each network adapter installed in the Windows NT computer. You can monitor counters for each instance of the Network Segment object. In other words, you can monitor network traffic on each network segment that your Windows NT computer is connected to.

The Network Segment object and its counters are used by network administrators to determine network utilization on individual network segments. In addition, this object and its counters are often used for network capacity planning. The following section explains how to install Network Monitor Agent to obtain the Network Segment object and its counters.

TO INSTALL NETWORK MONITOR AGENT, FOLLOW THESE STEPS:

1. Select Start ⇒ Settings ⇒ Control Panel.

2. The Control Panel dialog box appears. Double-click the Network icon.

3. The Network dialog box appears. Click the Services tab.

4. The Services tab appears. Click the Add command button.

5. The Select Network Service dialog box appears. Highlight Network Monitor Agent, as shown in Figure 18-4. Click OK.

6. A Windows NT Setup dialog box appears. Ensure that the correct path to your Windows NT Server source files (usually the I386 folder on your Windows NT Server compact disc) is listed in the text box. Edit this text box if necessary. Click the Continue command button.

7. Windows NT copies source files and installs the Network Monitor Agent.

8. The Network dialog box reappears. Click the Close command button.

9. Windows NT performs various bindings operations.

FIGURE 18-4   Installing the Network Monitor Agent

10. A Network Settings Change dialog box appears, indicating that you must shut down and restart the computer for the new settings to take effect. Click the Yes command button to restart the computer.

Enabling the PhysicalDisk and LogicalDisk Objects and Their Counters

By default, the PhysicalDisk and LogicalDisk objects and their counters are installed, but *not* enabled. Although you can select these objects and their counters in Performance Monitor, until they are enabled, the counters will always display a value of zero.

The reason these objects and their counters are not enabled by default is that monitoring these objects can cause up to a one-and-a-half-percent increase in processor utilization on an Intel 486 computer. On a Pentium computer, enabling these objects and their counters usually causes a negligible (less than one half of one percent) increase in processor utilization.

The Windows NT `Diskperf.exe` command-line utility is used to enable the PhysicalDisk and LogicalDisk objects and their counters. You must reboot the computer after running `Diskperf.exe` before these objects and their counters will be usable in Performance Monitor.

Table 18-2 shows how the `Diskperf.exe` command-line utility can be used to enable and disable the PhysicalDisk and LogicalDisk objects and their counters.

TABLE 18-2 THE WINDOWS NT DISKPERF.EXE COMMAND

DISKPERF.EXE COMMAND	*DESCRIPTION*
diskperf-y	Enables the PhysicalDisk and LogicalDisk objects and their counters.
diskperf-ye	Enables the PhysicalDisk and LogicalDisk objects and their counters for stripe sets and stripe sets with parity.
diskperf-n	Disables the PhysicalDisk and LogicalDisk objects and their counters.

The remainder of this section explains how to enable the PhysicalDisk and LogicalDisk objects and their counters by using the Diskperf.exe command-line utility.

TO USE DISKPERF.EXE TO ENABLE THE PHYSICALDISK AND LOGICALDISK OBJECTS AND THEIR COUNTERS, FOLLOW THESE STEPS:

1. Select Start ⇒ Programs ⇒ Command Prompt.

2. The Command Prompt dialog box appears. At the command prompt, type **diskperf -y** and press Enter.

3. Diskperf.exe displays a message, as shown in Figure 18-5. Notice that you must reboot the computer before these changes will become effective. At the command prompt, type **exit** and press Enter.

FIGURE 18-5   Using Diskperf.exe to enable disk performance objects and counters

4. Shut down and restart the computer.

Using Performance Monitor to Gather and View Statistics

Now that you have a basic understanding of the Performance Monitor objects and their counters, you're ready to use the Performance Monitor tool.

In this section, you'll learn how to start Performance Monitor and how to use the "views" within Performance Monitor to gather and view statistics on a Windows NT computer's performance.

To start Performance Monitor, select Start ⇒ Programs ⇒ Administrative Tools (Common) ⇒ Performance Monitor.

The Performance Monitor dialog box appears, as shown in Figure 18-6. Notice that no objects are monitored when Performance Monitor is first started.

FIGURE 18-6   Starting Performance Monitor

There are four possible views in Performance Monitor: Chart, Alert, Report, and Log. By default, Performance Monitor starts in Chart view. The other views can be selected from the View menu, as shown in Figure 18-7.

The following sections explain how to use each of the four Performance Monitor views.

FIGURE 18-7   The four views available in Performance Monitor

Chart View

The Performance Monitor Chart view displays activity in a graphical format. It can be used to view current performance activity, or to view archived performance activity from a Performance Monitor log file. (Log files are discussed later in this chapter.)

Before you can view performance statistics in a Performance Monitor chart, you must first select one or more objects and their counters to be measured and displayed in a Chart view.

To select objects and their counters to be displayed in a Performance Monitor chart, you need to access the Add to Chart dialog box. You can access this dialog box in one of two ways: selecting Edit ⇒ Add To Chart, or clicking the + command button in the toolbar at the top of the Performance Monitor dialog box.

The Add to Chart dialog box is shown in Figure 18-8. Notice that you can select objects, counters, and instances in this dialog box.

FIGURE 18-8   Selecting objects, counters, andinstances in the
Add to Chartdialog box

TO SELECT OBJECTS AND COUNTERS (IN THE ADD TO CHART DIALOG BOX) TO BE DISPLAYED IN A PERFORMANCE MONITOR CHART, FOLLOW THESE STEPS:

1. In the Computer text box, type in the name of the computer you want to monitor the performance of in the format *computer_name*, for example, \\PDCLAB. (The name of the computer you are running Performance Monitor on is displayed by default.) You can browse for the computer you want to monitor by clicking the . . . command button to the right of the Computer text box.

 note   **You can view objects and counters from more than one computer on a single Performance Monitor chart.**

2. Select the object you want to monitor from the list in the Object drop-down list box.

3. Select the instance of the object you selected in Step 2 (if an instance is available for this object) from the Instance list box.

4. Select a counter to be monitored for the object you selected in Step 2 from the Counter list box.

tip When you are configuring the Add to Chart dialog box, you can click the Explain command button at any time to display a detailed description of the highlighted object and counter combination. This description is displayed in the Counter Definition box at the bottom of the Add to Chart dialog box, as shown in Figure 18-9.

The Explain command button is also available in the Add to Alert, Add to Report, and Add To Log dialog boxes.

FIGURE 18-9 Obtaining a counter definition by clicking the Explain command button

5. In the Color drop-down list box, select the color you want Performance Monitor to use to display the counter's activity in the chart.

6. In the Scale drop-down list box, accept the default or select the multiplier you want Performance Monitor to apply to the counter's measurement in the chart. For example, if the counter's activity normally varies between 0 and 1, you might select a scale setting of 100.0. This will enable you to view a larger picture of the counter's activity in the chart.

Normally the default scale setting is the appropriate setting for the selected counter.

7. In the Width drop-down list box, select the line width you want Performance Monitor to use to display the counter's activity in the chart.

8. In the Style drop-down list box, select the style of the line you want Performance Monitor to use to display the counter's activity in the chart.

9. When you have configured all of the settings for a particular object, instance, and counter combination, click the Add command button to begin displaying the counter's activity on the Performance Monitor chart.

10. Repeat Steps 1 – 9 if you want to add additional objects, instances, and counter combinations to your Performance Monitor chart.

11. When you are finished adding counters to your chart, click the Done command button to return to the Performance Monitor Chart view.

Figure 18-10 shows a Performance Monitor chart with several objects and counters selected. Notice the Last, Average, Min, Max, and Graph Time boxes toward the bottom of the chart.

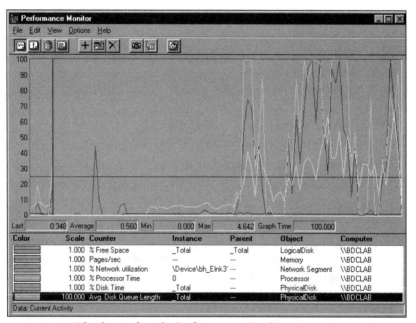

FIGURE 18-10   Viewing a chart in Performance Monitor

When you highlight any counter in the section at the bottom of the dialog box, that counter's statistics are displayed in the Last, Average, Min, Max, and Graph Time boxes directly below the chart. Table 18-3 explains the statistics displayed in each of these text boxes.

TABLE 18-3 STATISTICS DISPLAYED IN PERFORMANCE MONITOR CHART VIEW	
STATISTIC	*DESCRIPTION*
Last	This is the most recent measurement of the counter.
Average	This is an average of the counter's measurement over the period of time represented by the chart.
Min	This is the lowest (minimum) measurement of the counter during the period of time represented by the chart.
Max	This is the highest (maximum) measurement of the counter during the period of time represented by the chart.
Graph Time	This is the number of seconds represented by the entire chart. This is the total amount of time it takes Performance Monitor to graph from one side of the chart to the other.

If you have difficulty determining which line on the chart represents the highlighted counter, you can press Ctrl + H to highlight that counter's line. Press Ctrl + H again to stop highlighting the counter's line on the chart.

To export a Performance Monitor chart for review at a later time in a spreadsheet or database application, select File ⇒ Export Chart. You can export the chart data in either a tab separated value (tsv) file, or a comma separated value (csv) file.

Alert View

The Performance Monitor Alert view is used to display an alert when a monitored counter's value exceeds or drops below a prespecified value.

Performance Monitor has no preset alerts. Alerts must be created in Alert view by selecting one or more counters to be monitored, and by entering a threshold value for each counter. When this threshold value is exceeded or falls below a minimum level (depending on how the alert is configured), an alert is triggered.

To access Alert view in Performance Monitor, select View ⇒ Alert.

To add counters to be monitored in Alert view you need to access the Add to Alert dialog box. You can access this dialog box in one of two ways: either by selecting Edit ⇒ Add To Alert, or by clicking the + command button in the toolbar at the top of the Performance Monitor dialog box.

The Add to Alert dialog box is shown in Figure 18-11. Notice that you can select objects, counters, and instances in this dialog box. The next section explains how to create an alert by using this dialog box.

FIGURE 18-11   **Selecting objects, counters, and instances in the Add to Alert dialog box**

TO CREATE AN ALERT BY USING THE ADD TO ALERT DIALOG BOX, FOL-LOW THESE STEPS:

1. In the Computer text box, type in the name of the computer you want to monitor using the format *computer_name*, for example, \\PDCLAB. (The name of the computer on which you are running Performance Monitor is displayed by default.) You can browse for the computer you want to monitor by clicking the ... command button to the right of the Computer text box.

2. Select the object you want to monitor from the list in the Object drop-down list box.

3. Select the instance of the object you selected in Step 2 (if an instance is available for this object) from the Instance list box.

4. Select a counter to be monitored for the object you selected in Step 2 from the Counter list box.

5. In the Color drop-down list box, select the color of dot you want Performance Monitor to use next to the text description when displaying the alert.

6. In the Alert If section:

- Select the option button next to Over if you want Performance Monitor to generate an alert when the counter being monitored *exceeds* the value you specify.

- Select the option button next to Under if you want Performance Monitor to generate an alert when the counter being monitored ***drops below*** the value you specify.

  In the text box in the Alert If section, type in a number for the value you want Performance Monitor to use as the threshold value.

7. If you want Performance Monitor to run a program automatically when an alert is generated, type the full path to the program in the "Run Program on Alert" text box.

   - If you want this program to be run only the first time an alert is generated for this counter, select the option button next to First Time.

   - If you want this program to be run every time an alert is generated for this counter, select the option button next to Every Time.

8. When you have configured all of the settings for a particular object, instance, and counter combination, click the Add command button to begin monitoring the counter.

9. Repeat Steps 1 – 8 if you want to create additional alerts.

10. When you are finished creating alerts, click the Done command button.

Figure 18-12 shows a Performance Monitor alert. Notice the Alert Legend at the bottom of the dialog box. In this situation, I configured Performance Monitor to generate an alert when the amount of free space on my computer's hard disk dropped below 30 percent.

By default, Performance Monitor measures each specified counter in five-second intervals and compares each measurement with the threshold value. If the threshold value is exceeded or falls below a minimum level (depending on how the alert is configured), Performance Monitor generates an alert. If the threshold value is consistently exceeded or consistently falls below a minimum level, an alert will be generated every five seconds. You can change the alert interval by selecting Options ⇒ Alert (in the Alert view) and then configuring the Alert Options dialog box that appears.

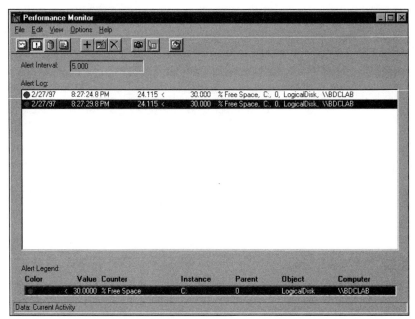

FIGURE 18-12   Viewing an alert in Performance Monitor

Report View

The Performance Monitor Report view displays activity in a report format. It can be used to view current performance activity, or to view archived performance activity from a Performance Monitor log file. (Log files are discussed later in this chapter.)

To access Report view in Performance Monitor, select View ⇒ Report.

Before you can view Performance Monitor statistics in Report view, you must select one or more objects and their counters to be measured and displayed in the report.

To select objects and their counters to be displayed in a Performance Monitor report, you need to access the Add to Report dialog box. You can access this dialog box in one of two ways: selecting Edit ⇒ Add To Report or clicking the + command button in the toolbar at the top of the Performance Monitor dialog box.

The Add to Report dialog box is shown in Figure 18-13. Notice that there are fewer options in this dialog box than are in the Add to Chart and Add to Alert dialog boxes.

FIGURE 18-13 Selecting objects and counters to be included in a Performance Monitor report

TO SELECT OBJECTS AND COUNTERS (IN THE ADD TO REPORT DIALOG BOX) TO BE INCLUDED IN A PERFORMANCE MONITOR REPORT, FOLLOW THESE STEPS:

1. In the Computer text box, type the name of the computer you want to monitor using the format *computer_name*, for example, \\PDCLAB. (The name of the computer on which you are running Performance Monitor is displayed by default.) You can browse for the computer you want to monitor by clicking the ... command button to the right of the Computer text box.

2. Select the object you want to monitor from the list in the Object drop-down list box.

3. Select the instance of the object you selected in Step 2 (if an instance is available for this object) from the Instance list box.

4. Select a counter to be monitored for the object you selected in Step 2 from the Counter list box.

5. When you have selected an object, instance, and counter combination, click the Add command button to begin displaying the counter's activity in a Performance Monitor report.

6. Repeat Steps 1 – 5 if you want to add additional objects, instances, and counter combinations to your Performance Monitor report.

7. When you are finished adding counters to your report, click the Done command button to return to the Performance Monitor Report view.

Figure 18-14 shows a Performance Monitor report with several objects and counters selected.

The value displayed for each counter in the Report view represents an average of the last two Performance Monitor measurements for that counter. However, the value is not an average from the time Performance Monitor was started. Performance Monitor, by default, updates the report every five seconds. You can change the report interval by selecting Options ⇒ Report (in Report view) and then configuring the Report Options dialog box that appears.

FIGURE 18-14   Viewing a report in Performance Monitor

Log View

The Performance Monitor Log view is used to save statistics gathered by Performance Monitor to a log file. The Performance Monitor log file can be viewed at a later time in Chart, Alert, or Report view.

To access Performance Monitor Log view, select View ⇒ Log.

Before you can create a log file, you must select one or more objects to be monitored. To select objects, you need to access the Add To Log dialog box. You can access this dialog box in one of two ways: selecting Edit ⇒ Add To Log, or clicking the + command button in the toolbar at the top of the Performance Monitor dialog box.

The Add To Log dialog box is shown in Figure 18-15. Notice you can only select a computer and the objects to be monitored in this dialog box. The next section explains how to select objects for a Performance Monitor log in this dialog box.

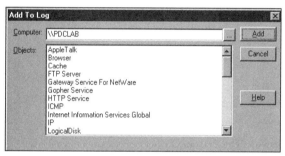

FIGURE 18-15   **Selecting objects to be monitored for a Performance Monitor log**

TO SELECT OBJECTS TO BE MONITORED (IN THE ADD TO LOG DIALOG BOX) FOR A PERFORMANCE MONITOR LOG, FOLLOW THESE STEPS:

1. In the Computer text box, type in the name of the computer you want to log using the format *computer_name*, for example, \\PDCLAB. (The name of the computer on which you are running Performance Monitor is displayed by default.) You can browse for the computer you want to monitor by clicking the ... command button to the right of the Computer text box.

2. Select the objects you want to monitor from the list in the Objects drop-down list box. (You can select more than one object at a time.)

 note   You *can't* select individual counters for the objects you select. All counters for the selected object will be monitored and logged.

3. Click the Add command button.

4. Repeat Steps 1 – 3 until all computers and objects that you want to select have been selected.

5. Click the Done command button to return to Performance Monitor Log view.

6. In the Performance Monitor dialog box (Log view), select Options ⇒ Log.

7. The Log Options dialog box appears, as shown in Figure 18-16.

FIGURE 18-16   Starting a Performance Monitor log

Use the Explorer view in the top half of the Log Options dialog box to select the folder in which you want to store the log file.

8. In the File name text box, type in a name for the log file that uses the .log extension.

9. In the Interval (seconds) drop-down list box, select the interval, in seconds, that you want Performance Monitor to use for measuring the selected objects and logging their activity.

Click the Start Log command button to begin logging.

Performance Monitor begins monitoring the selected objects and logging the statistics it gathers to the log file. It will continue to collect and log this data until you stop the process.

Figure 18-17 shows Performance Monitor in the process of collecting data for the log file. Notice the Status and File Size text boxes.

FIGURE 18-17   Logging data to a Performance Monitor log file

10. When you have collected all the data you want and are ready to stop the logging process, select Options ⇒ Log.

11. The Log Options dialog box appears. Click the Stop Log command button. The Performance Monitor log file has been created. Performance Monitor Log view reappears.

The next section explains how to import the log file you've created into Performance Monitor Chart, Alert, or Report views.

Viewing data from log files

Performance Monitor log files can be viewed in Performance Monitor Chart, Alert, and Report views.

To change Performance Monitor's input from current activity to activity archived in a log file, select Options ⇒ Data From. The Data From dialog box appears, as shown in Figure 18-18.

FIGURE 18-18   **Changing Performance Monitor's input type from current activity to activity archived in a log file**

Select the option button next to Log File and type in the complete path to the Performance Monitor log file you want to view data from. (You can browse for the file name by clicking the ... command button.) Click OK.

The Performance Monitor dialog box reappears. Select the type of view from the View menu (Chart, Alert, or Report) that you want to use to view log file data.

Once you have selected the view that you want to use, you must select objects, counters, and instances to be viewed. The steps to create a chart, alert, or report from a log file are the same as those used to create a chart, alert, or report from current activity. However, only the objects which were logged are available for selection in the Add to Chart, Add to Alert, and Add to Report dialog boxes.

The next section explains how to view a Performance Monitor report created by using data from a log file.

TO VIEW A PERFORMANCE MONITOR REPORT CONSISTING OF DATA FROM A LOG FILE, FOLLOW THESE STEPS:

1. Start Performance Monitor. Select View ⇒ Report.

2. Select Options ⇒ Data From.

3. In the Data From dialog box, select the option button next to Log File, and type in the complete path to the Performance Monitor log file you want to use. Click OK.

4. Select Edit ⇒ Add To Report.

5. The Add to Report dialog box appears. Select the computer, object, instance, and counter you want to view in the report. Click the Add command button.

6. Repeat Step 5 until you have selected all of the counters you want to view in the report. Click the Done command button to view the report.

When you have finished viewing data from a log file, you should change Performance Monitor's input back to current activity. To change Performance Monitor's input from log file to current activity, select Options ⇒ Data From. In the Data From dialog box, select the option button next to Current Activity and click OK.

KEY POINT SUMMARY

This chapter focused on how to use Performance Monitor.

o *Performance Monitor* is a Windows NT tool that can be used to identify performance problems and/or bottlenecks, determine current usage of system resources, track performance trends over time, predict future usage of system resources (capacity planning), and determine how system configuration changes affect system performance.

o The system components that Performance Monitor can measure, such as processor, memory, and physical disk, are called *objects*. If there is more than one of a particular object in the system (such as multiple processors or multiple physical disks) there is said to be more than one *instance* of that object. Some objects, such as memory, do not have instances, because there can't be more than one of the particular object. Each instance of an object can be measured in different ways. Each possible measurement of an object is called a *counter*.

o Commonly used Performance Monitor objects and counters include the following:

Object	Counter(s)
Memory	Pages/sec
Network Segment	% Network utilization
PhysicalDisk	Avg. Disk Queue Length, % Disk Time
Processor	% Processor Time
Server	Bytes Total/sec

- Not all Performance Monitor objects and counters are available when Windows NT is first installed. For example, TCP/IP-related objects (and their related counters) are not available until the *SNMP Service* is installed, and the Network Segment object (and its counters) is not available until the *Network Monitor Agent* is installed. Additionally, some objects and their counters must be enabled by using the `Diskperf.exe` command before they can be effectively used to monitor performance.

- Performance Monitor has four possible views: Chart, Alert, Report, and Log.

  - *Chart view* displays activity in a graphical format. One or more objects and their counters must be selected (in the Add to Chart dialog box) to be measured and displayed in Chart view. Chart view not only displays a graph of activity, but also displays several statistics for each counter, including: *Last, Average, Min, Max,* and *Graph Time.*

  - *Alert view* is used to display an alert when a monitored counter's value exceed or drops below a prespecified value. Alerts must be created in Alert view by selecting one or more counters to be monitored and by entering a threshold value that will trigger an alert.

  - *Report view* displays activity in a report format. One or more objects and their counters must be selected (in the Add to Report dialog box) to be measured and displayed in Report view. The value displayed for each counter in the report represents an average of the last two Performance Monitor measurements for that counter.

  - *Log view* is used to save statistics gathered by Performance Monitor to a Performance Monitor log file. The log file can be viewed at a later time in Chart, Alert, or Report view. One or more objects must be selected to be monitored and their activity logged to a file. The Start Log command button (in the Log Options dialog box) is used to begin logging, and the Stop Log command button is used to stop the logging process.

- To view data from Performance Monitor log files in Performance Monitor Chart, Alert, and Report views, you must change Performance Monitor's input from current activity to log file. Then you select the type of view (Chart, Alert, or Report) and proceed as though you were creating a chart, alert, or report of current activity. When you finish viewing data from a log file, you should change Performance Monitor's input back to current activity.

Applying What You've Learned

Now it's time to regroup, review, and apply what you've learned in this chapter.

The following Instant Assessment questions bring to mind key facts and concepts. Then, the Hands-on Lab reinforces what you've learned and gives you an opportunity to practice some of the tasks that may be tested by the Server exam.

Instant Assessment

1. What command button do you click to cause Performance Monitor to *end* the process of gathering data for a Performance Monitor log file?

2. List five uses of Performance Monitor.

3. What are the system components that Performance Monitor can measure, such as processor and memory, called?

4. What is each possible measurement of a Performance Monitor object called?

5. When does more than one instance of a Performance Monitor object exist?

6. You want to obtain an overall view of how memory is being used on a particular Windows NT computer. Which Performance Monitor object and counter should you use?

7. You want to measure the percentage of time that the processor is actively used by processes (other than the Idle process) on a Windows NT computer. Which Performance Monitor object and counter should you use?

8. You want to measure the percentage of total network utilization on a given network segment as a percentage of the maximum amount of network traffic possible on that segment. Which Performance Monitor object and counter should you use?

9. You want to measure the total amount of network utilization on a particular Windows NT Server computer. Which Performance Monitor object and counter should you use?

10. What must you install on your Windows NT computer before the IP, TCP, ICMP, and UDP objects (and their counters) are available for use in Performance Monitor?

11. What must you install on your Windows NT computer before the Network Segment object (and its counters) is available for use in Performance Monitor?

12. What should you type at the command prompt to enable the PhysicalDisk and LogicalDisk Performance Monitor objects and their counters?

13. What are the four possible views in Performance Monitor?

14. Besides a graph, what other statistics are presented for a highlighted counter in Performance Monitor Chart view?

15. What value must you enter in the Alert If section of the Add to Alert dialog box for a Performance Monitor alert to be created?

16. What command button do you click to cause Performance Monitor to *begin* the process of gathering data for a Performance Monitor log file?

17. When Performance Monitor's input is current activity, what value is displayed for each selected counter in Performance Monitor Report view?

18. What is Performance Monitor Log view used for?

T/F

19. You can view either current performance activity or archived performance activity from a Performance Monitor log file in Performance Monitor Report view.   _____

20. Before you can view data from a Performance Monitor log file, you must change Performance Monitor's input from log file to current activity.   _____

concept link   **For answers to the Instant Assessment questions see Appendix B.**

Hands-on Lab

The following Hands-on Lab provides you with an opportunity to apply the knowledge you've gained in this chapter about Performance Monitor.

Lab 18.29 *Using Performance Monitor*

The purpose of this lab is to provide you with experience in using Performance Monitor on a Windows NT Server computer.

This lab consists of four parts:

Part 1: Adding objects and counters by installing Network Monitor Agent and SNMP Service, and enabling the PhysicalDisk and LogicalDisk objects and their counters using `Diskperf.exe`

Part 2: Using Performance Monitor Chart view and Alert view

Part 3: Creating a Performance Monitor log file

Part 4: Importing a Performance Monitor log file into Report view and Chart view

Begin this lab by booting your computer to Windows NT Server. Log on as Administrator. Place your Windows NT Server compact disc in your computer's CD-ROM drive.

Follow these steps carefully.

Part 1: Adding objects and counters by installing Network Monitor Agent and SNMP Service, and enabling the PhysicalDisk and LogicalDisk objects and their counters by using Diskperf.exe

In this section, you check for the existence of Performance Monitor objects. Then you install Network Monitor Agent and SNMP Service on your Windows NT Server computer. Finally, you use `Diskperf.exe` to enable the PhysicalDisk and LogicalDisk objects and their disk counters on your Windows NT Server computer.

1. Select Start ⇒ Programs ⇒ Administrative Tools (Common) ⇒ Performance Monitor.

2. The Performance Monitor dialog box appears. Select View ⇒ Chart.

3. Click the **+** command button located in the toolbar at the top of the dialog box.

4. The Add to Chart dialog box appears. Click the down arrow in the Object drop-down list box. Look for each of the following objects: ICMP, IP, Network Segment, TCP, and UDP. Notice that *none* of these objects appear in the Object drop-down list box. Click the Cancel command button.

5. The Performance Monitor dialog box reappears. Exit Performance Monitor.

6. Select Start ⇒ Settings ⇒ Control Panel.

7. The Control Panel dialog box appears. Double-click the Network icon.

8. The Network dialog box appears. Click the Services tab.

9. The Services tab appears. Click the Add command button.

10. The Select Network Service dialog box appears. Highlight Network Monitor Agent. Click OK.

11. A Windows NT Setup dialog box appears. Ensure that the correct path to your Windows NT Server source files (usually the I386 folder on your Windows NT Server compact disc) is listed in the text box. Edit this text box if necessary. Click the Continue command button.

12. Windows NT copies source files and installs Network Monitor Agent.

13. The Network dialog box reappears. Click the Add command button.

14. The Select Network Service dialog box appears. Highlight SNMP Service. Click OK.

15. A Windows NT Setup dialog box appears. Ensure that the correct path to your Windows NT Server source files (usually the I386 folder on your Windows NT Server compact disc) is listed in the text box. Edit this text box if necessary. Click the Continue command button.

16. Windows NT copies source files and installs the SNMP Service.

17. The Microsoft SNMP Properties dialog box appears. Click OK.

18. The Network dialog box reappears. Click the Close command button.

19. Windows NT performs various bindings operations.

20. A Network Settings Change dialog box appears. Click the No command button.

21. The Control Panel dialog box reappears. Exit Control Panel.

22. Select Start ⇒ Programs ⇒ Command Prompt.

23. The Command Prompt dialog box appears. At the command prompt, type **diskperf -y** and press Enter.

Notice that Windows NT indicates that disk performance counters on your computer are now set to start at boot and will become effective after the computer is restarted.

24. At the command prompt, type **exit** and press Enter.

25. The Windows NT desktop reappears. Select Start ⇒ Shut Down.

26. In the Shut Down Windows dialog box, select the option button next to "Restart the computer". Click the Yes command button.

27. Reboot the computer to Windows NT Server. Log on as Administrator. Continue to Part 2.

Part 2: Using Performance Monitor Chart view and Alert view

In this section, you install games (if you haven't already done so) on your Windows NT Server computer, and use Performance Monitor Chart view and Alert view to chart server performance and to create an alert.

1. If you have already installed games (including Solitaire and Pinball) on your Windows NT Server computer, skip to Step 8.

   If you have **not** already installed games on your Windows NT Server computer, select Start ⇒ Settings ⇒ Control Panel, and continue to Step 2.

2. The Control Panel dialog box appears. Double-click the Add/Remove Programs icon.

3. The Add/Remove Programs dialog box appears. Click the Windows NT Setup tab.

4. The Windows NT Setup tab appears. Select the check box next to Games. (Or if you have one or two games installed but Solitaire or Pinball is **not** yet installed, deselect and then reselect this check box.) Click OK.

5. The Add/Remove Programs Properties — Copying Files dialog box appears.

   If the Files Needed dialog box appears, ensure that the correct path to your Windows NT Server source files (usually the I386 folder on your Windows NT Server compact disc) is listed in the "Copy files from" text box. Edit the text box as necessary. Click OK.

6. Windows NT installs games.

7. The Control Panel dialog box reappears. Exit Control Panel.

8. Select Start ⇒ Programs ⇒ Administrative Tools (Common) ⇒ Performance Monitor.

9. The Performance Monitor dialog box appears. Select View ⇒ Chart.

10. Click the **+** command button located in the toolbar at the top of the dialog box.

11. The Add to Chart dialog box appears. Click the down arrow in the Object drop-down list box. Look for each of the following objects: ICMP, IP, Network Segment, TCP, and UDP. Notice that after installing Network Monitor Agent and the SNMP Service (which you did in Part 1), all of these objects now appear in the Object drop-down list box.

    Click Memory in the Object drop-down list box. Select Pages/sec from the Counter list box. Click the Add command button.

12. Click the down arrow in the Object drop-down list box. Click Processor in the Object drop-down list box. Select % Processor Time from the Counter list box. Click the Add command button.

13. Click the down arrow in the Object drop-down list box. Click PhysicalDisk in the Object drop-down list box. Select % Disk Time from the Counter list box. Click the Add command button.

14. Click the down arrow in the Object drop-down list box. Click Server in the Object drop-down list box. Select Bytes Total/sec from the Counter list box. Click the Add command button. Click the Done command button.

You have just configured the four most commonly used Performance Monitor counters that monitor server performance.

15. The Performance Monitor dialog box reappears. In the list box at the bottom of the dialog box, highlight % Processor Time in the Counter column. Note the color assigned to the % Processor Time counter.

16. Move your mouse rapidly in a sweeping circular pattern on your mouse pad for several (at least five) seconds. Notice the increase in % Processor time usage, as depicted on the graph, from just moving your mouse.

17. Minimize (*don't* close) Performance Monitor.

18. Select Start ⇒ Programs ⇒ Accessories ⇒ Games ⇒ Solitaire.

19. Play Solitaire for a minute or two.

(If you've never played Solitaire before, select Help ⇒ Contents to find out how to play.)

When you finish playing, exit Solitaire, and quickly select Performance Monitor from the taskbar.

20. The Performance Monitor dialog box appears. Notice the counters and their levels during your Solitaire game, as depicted on the Performance Monitor chart.

21. Highlight Pages/sec (in the Counter column). Press Delete.

Highlight % Disk Time (in the Counter column). Press Delete.

Highlight Bytes Total/sec (in the Counter column). Press Delete.

Highlight % Processor Time (in the Counter column). Press Delete.

22. Select Edit ⇒ Add To Chart.

23. The Add to Chart dialog box appears. Click the down arrow in the Object drop-down list box. Click LogicalDisk in the Object drop-down list box. Select % Free Space from the Counter list box. Highlight 0==>C: in the Instance list box. Click the Add command button. Click the Done command button.

24. The Performance Monitor dialog box reappears. Write the number that appears in the Last box here: _____

25. Add 5 to the number that you entered in Step 24, and write the resulting number here: _____

26. Highlight % Free Space (in the Counter column), and press Delete.

27. Select View ⇒ Alert.

28. The Alert View appears. Select Edit ⇒ Add To Alert.

29. The Add to Alert dialog box appears. Click the down arrow in the Object drop-down list box. Click LogicalDisk in the Object drop-down list box. Select % Free Space from the Counter list box. Select 0==>C: in the Instance list box. Select the option button next to Under in the Alert If section. Type the number you entered in Step 25 in the text box in the Alert If section. Click the Add command button. Click the Done command button.

30. The Performance Monitor dialog box reappears. Every five seconds an alert should appear in the Alert Log list box, indicating that the % Free Space on your C: drive has fallen below the level that you entered in the previous step.

Press Delete to stop logging this alert.

Continue to Part 3.

Part 3: Creating a Performance Monitor log file

In this section, you create a Performance Monitor log file. (You will view the data in this Performance Monitor log file in Part 4.)

1. In the Performance Monitor dialog box, select View ⇒ Log.

2. Select Edit ⇒ Add To Log.

3. The Add To Log dialog box appears. Highlight Memory in the Objects list box. Click the Add command button.

4. Highlight PhysicalDisk in the Objects list box. Click the Add command button.

5. Highlight Processor in the Objects list box. Click the Add command button.

6. Highlight Server in the Objects list box. Click the Add command button. Click the Done command button.

7. The Performance Monitor dialog box reappears. Select Options ⇒ Log.

8. The Log Options dialog box appears. In the File Name text box, type **practice.log**. Select **1** from the Interval (Seconds) drop-down list box. Click the Start Log command button.

9. Minimize (*don't* close) Performance Monitor.

10. Select Start ⇒ Programs ⇒ Accessories ⇒ Games ⇒ Pinball.

11. Play one game of Pinball.

(Hold down the space bar for a couple of seconds and then release it to launch the ball. The z key on the keyboard controls the left flipper. The ? key on the keyboard controls the right flipper.)

When you finish playing, exit Pinball, and quickly select Performance Monitor from the taskbar.

12. The Performance Monitor dialog box reappears. Select Options ⇒ Log.

13. The Log Options dialog box appears. Click the Stop Log command button. Continue to Part 4.

Part 4: Importing a Performance Monitor log file into Report view and Chart view

In this section, you import the Performance Monitor log file you created in Part 3 into Performance Monitor Report view and Chart view.

1. In the Performance Monitor dialog box, select View ⇒ Report.

2. Select Options ⇒ Data From.

3. The Data From dialog box appears. Select the option button next to Log File. Type **practice.log** in the text box. Click OK.

4. Select Edit ⇒ Add to Report in the Performance Monitor dialog box.

5. The Add to Report dialog box appears. Click the down arrow in the Object drop-down list box. Notice that only four objects appear in this list, because you only chose to log four objects when you created the log file. Click Memory. Select Pages/sec in the Counter list box. Click the Add command button.

6. Click the down arrow in the Object drop-down list box. Click PhysicalDisk. Select % Disk Time in the Counter list box. Click the Add command button.

7. Click the down arrow in the Object drop-down list box. Click Processor. Select % Processor Time in the Counter list box. Click the Add command button.

8. Click the down arrow in the Object drop-down list box. Click Server. Select Bytes Total/sec in the Counter list box. Click the Add command button. Click the Done command button.

9. The Performance Monitor dialog box reappears.

The report values displayed represent an average of the last two Performance Monitor measurements for each of the four counters you selected.

Now let's look at the same four counters in a Chart view (instead of a Report view).

10. Select View ⇒ Chart.

11. Select Options ⇒ Data From.

12. The Data From dialog box appears. Select the option button next to Log File. Ensure that `practice.log` appears in the text box. Click OK.

13. Select Edit ⇒ Add To Chart in the Performance Monitor dialog box.

14. The Add to Chart dialog box appears. Click the down arrow in the Object drop-down list box. Click Memory. Select Pages/sec in the Counter list box. Click the Add command button.

15. Click the down arrow in the Object drop-down list box. Click PhysicalDisk. Select % Disk Time in the Counter list box. Click the Add command button.

16. Click the down arrow in the Object drop-down list box. Click Processor. Select % Processor Time in the Counter list box. Click the Add command button.

17. Click the down arrow in the Object drop-down list box. Click Server. Select Bytes Total/sec in the Counter list box. Click the Add command button. Click the Done command button.

18. The Performance Monitor dialog box reappears.

   The chart displayed shows the values for each of the four counters you selected, from the time you initially created the log file until after you finished your Pinball game and clicked on the Stop Log command button in Performance Monitor.

19. Exit Performance Monitor.

About Chapter 19

This chapter is all about getting the fastest server and/or network response out of your hardware and software combination. The technical term for this is performance optimization.

Because bottlenecks slow down system performance, Chapter 19 begins by explaining how to identify a bottleneck. Specific Performance Monitor counters are recommended.

The remainder of this chapter focuses on practical things you can do to resolve bottlenecks and optimize system performance. Various techniques, including adding RAM, optimizing paging files, optimizing or upgrading disks, upgrading or adding a processor, optimizing the server, and optimizing network traffic are discussed.

This chapter includes a Critical Thinking Lab in which you analyze Performance Monitor statistics in order to identify a bottleneck.

The material presented in Chapter 19 maps to the "Identify performance bottlenecks" objective listed in the Monitoring and Optimization section in the Preparation Guide for the Server exam.

WHAT IS PERFORMANCE OPTIMIZATION?

Performance optimization is the process of modifying server and/or network hardware and software configurations with the intent of speeding up server and/or network response.

Performance optimization is performed for several reasons:

- To get the most performance out of existing hardware
- When planning for a new server or network
- In response to user or administrator observations of slow system performance

Performance optimization should be performed with a specific goal in mind. Your primary goal might be to provide the fastest possible file services to client computers. Or your goal might be to remedy slow system response by identifying the problem and implementing a solution. In short, your goal can be almost anything that focuses on improving efficiency and speed of system performance.

For most network administrators, performance optimization usually means resolving user reports of slow system performance. Determining the cause of the slow performance is referred to as *identifying a bottleneck*. This chapter focuses on identifying bottlenecks, as well as on ways to optimize system performance and to resolve bottlenecks.

IDENTIFYING BOTTLENECKS

A *bottleneck* is the component in the system that is slowing system performance. In a networking environment, the bottleneck is the part of the system that is performing at peak capacity while other components in the system are not. In other words, if it weren't for the limiting component, the rest of the system could go faster.

When you are attempting to identify the bottleneck in your system, use Performance Monitor to measure performance of the server's memory, processor, and disk. You can also use Performance Monitor to gather statistics about your network that may help you identify network bottlenecks.

The following tables contain Performance Monitor counters that may help you in identifying bottlenecks. Table 19-1 shows the counters you can use to monitor the server's memory.

TABLE 19-1 PERFORMANCE MONITOR MEMORY COUNTERS		
OBJECT	**COUNTER**	**DESCRIPTION AND HOW TO INTERPRET**
Memory	Pages/sec	Measures the amount of 4KB memory pages that are read from or written to the paging file during a one-second time period. This counter is used to obtain an overall view of how memory is utilized by Windows NT. If the server does not have enough memory, then excessive paging will occur. A consistently high number for this counter (greater than 2 – 3) indicates that the current amount of RAM may be insufficient for the computer.
Paging File	% Usage	This counter measures the percentage of paging file utilization. A consistently high percentage for this counter (approaching 100%) may indicate that you should add RAM to the system or enlarge the paging file. Enlarging the paging file won't speed up the system – only adding RAM will do that.

Table 19-2 shows the counters you can use to monitor the server's processor.

TABLE 19-2 PERFORMANCE MONITOR PROCESSOR COUNTERS		
OBJECT	**COUNTER**	**DESCRIPTION AND HOW TO INTERPRET**
Processor	% Processor Time	Measures the percentage of time that the processor is actively being used by processes other than the Idle process. This counter only measures one processor – if your system has multiple processors, use the System % Total Processor Time counter instead. A consistently high number for this counter (approaching 100%) may indicate that a faster processor (or an additional processor) may be required for adequate system performance. Check the memory counters *before* upgrading your processor – if the memory counters are consistently high, you might just need more RAM.

OBJECT	COUNTER	DESCRIPTION AND HOW TO INTERPRET
System	% Total Processor Time	This counter measures the percentage of time that *all* processors in the computer are actively being used by processes other than the Idle process. A consistently high number for this counter (approaching 100%) may indicate that faster processors (or an additional processor) may be required for adequate system performance. Check the memory counters *before* upgrading your processor(s) — if the memory counters are consistently high, you might just need more RAM.

Table 19-3 shows the counters you can use to monitor the server's disk.

TABLE 19-3 PERFORMANCE MONITOR DISK COUNTERS

OBJECT	COUNTER	DESCRIPTION AND HOW TO INTERPRET
PhysicalDisk	Avg. Disk Queue Length	This counter measures the average number of disk reads and writes waiting to be performed. A consistently high number for this counter (greater than 2 – 3) may indicate that a faster hard disk and/or disk controller, or a different disk configuration (such as a stripe set or a stripe set with parity) may be required for adequate system performance. Check the memory counters *before* upgrading your disk(s) — if the memory counters are consistently high, you might just need more RAM.
PhysicalDisk	% Disk Time	This counter measures the percentage of time that the disk is actually busy performing reads and writes. A consistently high number for this counter (approaching 100%) may indicate that a faster hard disk and/or disk controller, or a different disk configuration (such as a stripe set or a stripe set with parity) may be required for adequate system performance. Check the memory counters *before* upgrading your disk(s) — if the memory counters are consistently high, you might just need more RAM.

continued

TABLE 19-3 *(continued)*

OBJECT	COUNTER	DESCRIPTION AND HOW TO INTERPRET
LogicalDisk	% Free Space	This counter measures the percentage of unused disk space. A consistently high or gradually increasing number for this counter (approaching 100%) indicates that the server does *not* have sufficient disk space available. An additional disk or a replacement disk that has more capacity may be required.

Table 19-4 shows the counters you can use to monitor the network.

TABLE 19-4 PERFORMANCE MONITOR NETWORK COUNTERS

OBJECT	COUNTER	DESCRIPTION AND HOW TO INTERPRET
Network Segment	% Network utilization	This counter measures the total network utilization on a given network segment as a percentage of the maximum amount of network traffic possible on that segment. A consistently high number for this counter (approaching 100%) may indicate that there are too many computers or too much network traffic on that network segment. An additional network adapter may need to be installed in the server, or a router may need to be installed on the network to further segment the network.

OBJECT	COUNTER	DESCRIPTION AND HOW TO INTERPRET
Server	Bytes Total/sec	This counter measures the total amount of network utilization of a Windows NT Server computer. Specifically, it measures the total number of bytes sent to and received from all network adapters in the Windows NT computer by the Server process. *This counter should only be used to measure network utilization when there is only one server on a network segment, and there is only one network adapter in that server.* A consistently high number for this counter (approaching the maximum number of bytes that can be sent on the network segment in one second) may indicate that there are too many computers or too much network traffic on that network segment. An additional network adapter may need to be installed in the server, or a router may need to be installed on the network to further segment the network.

Once you've interpreted the Performance Monitor statistics and have identified the bottleneck in your system, you're ready to take steps to resolve that bottleneck. The next section covers ways to optimize performance and to resolve bottlenecks.

 concept link

To refresh yourself on how to use Performance Monitor, review Chapter 18.

OPTIMIZING PERFORMANCE AND RESOLVING BOTTLENECKS

Performance optimization involves getting the most speed out of your existing hardware and software combination. It can also involve adding to or upgrading specific components to resolve bottlenecks.

You don't have to make a large number of configuration or Registry setting changes to optimize the performance of Windows NT. Windows NT is designed to automatically tune itself for providing the best performance it can with the hardware resources available in the computer. For example, Windows NT automatically adjusts the amount of memory assigned to cache, the amount of memory assigned to buffering network packets, and prioritizes processor allocation as needed.

However, the administrator can modify hardware and software configurations to optimize system performance and to resolve bottlenecks. You can add RAM, optimize paging files, optimize or upgrade disks, upgrade or add a processor, optimize the server, and optimize network traffic. Depending on your situation, implementing one or more of these options may improve your system's performance or resolve a bottleneck.

Adding RAM

Perhaps the single most inexpensive and effective upgrade you can make to your server is to add additional RAM. I've never heard an administrator whine that he or she "just had too much RAM in his or her server." You can *never* have too much RAM.

 in the real world

Operating systems and applications are constantly being updated and revised. Each new version seems to need more RAM and a faster processor just to perform basic tasks.

Adding RAM can reduce how often the server reads or writes virtual memory pages to or from the paging file on the hard disk. This is called *reducing paging*. Because paging uses both processor time and disk time, when paging is reduced, the performance of the processor and the disk can also be improved.

When RAM is added to the server, Windows NT automatically increases the allocation of RAM made available to the disk cache. The disk cache temporarily stores user requested files from the hard disk. Because the disk doesn't need to be accessed when a file is retrieved from the cache, files in the cache are more quickly available to users than files on the disk. Thus, increasing the size of the cache can improve disk performance because the number of disk accesses is reduced.

Optimizing Paging Files

The best method for optimizing a paging file is adding more RAM. The more RAM in the computer, the less paging activity will occur.

That said, there are a few additional things you can do to optimize paging file performance. If the Performance Monitor Paging File % Usage and Paging File % Usage Peak counters indicate that the paging file is being used a consistently high percentage of the time, you might consider trying one or more of the following:

o Configure the paging file so that its initial size and maximum size are equal. This prevents fragmentation of the paging file.

o Place the paging file on the physical disk in your system that has the least amount of activity.

o Place the paging file on a stripe set.

o Place multiple, smaller paging files on multiple physical disks in your system.

o Place the paging file on any other partition than the boot partition.

caution **If you have configured Windows NT to create a memory dump file** (memory.dmp) **when a stop error occurs, you *must* have a paging file on the boot partition that is at least as large as the amount of RAM in the computer. If the paging file isn't large enough or has been moved from the boot partition, a memory dump file won't be created.**

The next section explains how to move and configure paging files.

TO MOVE AND/OR CONFIGURE PAGING FILE(S), FOLLOW THESE STEPS:

1. Select Start ⇒ Settings ⇒ Control Panel.

2. In the Control Panel dialog box, double-click the System icon.

3. In the System Properties dialog box, click the Performance tab.

4. On the Performance tab, click the Change command button in the Virtual Memory section.

5. The Virtual Memory dialog box appears, as shown in Figure 19-1. Notice that *all* logical drives are listed in the Drive list box, regardless of whether a paging file exists on each drive.

FIGURE 19-1   Configuring a paging file

- **To move a paging file to another disk,** create a new paging file on the disk to which you want to move the paging file (see instructions on how to create a paging file in the next step), and then reconfigure the original paging file with an initial size and maximum size of 0.

- **To configure or create an additional paging file,** highlight the logical drive you want to configure or create the paging file on in the Drive list box.

  Next, configure the Initial Size and Maximum Size of the paging file in the Paging File Size for Selected Drive section of the dialog box. Click the Set command button.

When you're finished configuring paging files, click OK.

6. The System Properties dialog box reappears. Click the Close command button.

7. A System Settings Change dialog box appears, indicating that you must restart your computer before the new settings will take effect. Click the Yes command button to restart your computer.

 tip   When deciding how large to make your paging files, check out the Total Paging File Size for All Drives section of the Virtual Memory dialog box. This section shows the minimum required paging file size, as well as the recommended and currently allocated sizes. Be aware that the numbers shown in this section are totals for all paging files on your system, not recommended settings for each individual paging file.

Optimizing and/or Upgrading Disks

Optimizing disks is the process of speeding up hard disk response. Upgrading disks involves either adding to or replacing the existing disk(s) in a computer.

Consider optimizing disks when planning for a new Windows NT Server computer that will perform a specific task, such as file services.

Consider optimizing and/or upgrading disks when you determine, through performance monitoring, that the Windows NT computer's disk is a bottleneck to system performance. Before you upgrade a disk(s), ensure that memory (RAM) is *not* the bottleneck in your system.

You can increase disk performance by doing the following:

- Defragmenting the hard disk(s) in your computer

- Upgrading to a faster disk controller and/or a faster hard disk(s)

- Configuring a stripe set with parity across three or more disks

- Configuring a stripe set across two or more disks

 Configuring disk mirroring does not necessarily improve disk performance. However, it does significantly improve fault tolerance.

Upgrading and/or Adding a Processor

When you determine, through performance monitoring, that the Windows NT computer's processor is a bottleneck to system performance, you should consider upgrading and/or adding a processor to the computer.

Before you upgrade and/or add a processor, ensure that memory (RAM) is *not* the bottleneck in your system.

The following are ways to improve processor performance, all of which involve replacing and/or adding hardware:

- Replacing the existing processor with a faster processor

- Replacing the existing motherboard and processor with a faster motherboard and processor

- Upgrading from a single processor system to a multiprocessor system

- Adding a processor to a multiprocessor system

Optimizing the Server

Optimizing your server enables you to get the most out of what you've got.

There are four primary ways to optimize a server. You can optimize a server by doing the following:

- Configuring load balancing across multiple servers
- Disabling unused services, protocols, and drivers
- Scheduling large, server-intensive tasks for nonpeak hours
- Optimizing the Server service

The following sections explain each of these server optimization methods in detail.

Configuring load balancing across multiple servers

Configuring load balancing across multiple servers involves spreading server tasks among more than one server so that no one server is overburdened.

Say you have two servers that are primarily used for file and print services. One of these servers is functioning near peak capacity, while the other server is hardly being used. To improve overall server performance, consider moving a portion of the busy server's files to the other server. This will reduce some of the load on the busy server, and "balance the load" with the second server.

Disabling unused services, protocols, and drivers

Another way to improve server performance is to disable unused services, protocols, and drivers. Each installed service, protocol, and driver uses processor time and memory space. Also, some services and protocols generate additional network traffic. If an installed service, protocol, or driver is no longer being used, consider removing the service, protocol, or driver; or, consider configuring the service, protocol, or driver to start manually (instead of automatically) when Windows NT starts.

Scheduling server-intensive tasks for nonpeak hours

Another way to improve server performance is to schedule large, server-intensive tasks to be performed during nonpeak hours.

For example, if you must update a large database or generate a large report on a daily basis, and it is *not* critical that this task be done during business hours, consider scheduling the task to run after business hours (and before the tape backup is run for the night). If the task *must* be done during business hours, consider scheduling it to run during a period of lower activity, such as during a lunch hour.

Optimizing the Server service

Finally, you can optimize the Server service on Windows NT Server computers for the type of tasks the server normally performs, and for the number of client computers that normally access the server.

The Server service has the following four possible optimization options:

- **Minimize Memory Used:** Select this option when fewer than 10 users will be accessing the Windows NT Server computer at the same time, and a user will sit at the server and use the server as his or her desktop computer.

- **Balance:** Select this option when fewer than 64 users will be accessing the Windows NT Server computer at the same time. This option is also a good choice when the server is used for file and print services as well as by a distributed application that performs its own memory caching, such as Microsoft SQL Server.

- **Maximize Throughput for File Sharing:** Select this option when more than 64 users will be accessing the Windows NT Server computer at the same time, and when the server is primarily used as a file and print server. *This is the default option for Windows NT Server*, and is a good selection whenever the server functions primarily as a file and print server, even if there are fewer than 64 users.

- **Maximize Throughput for Network Applications:** Select this option when more than 64 users will be accessing the Windows NT Server computer at the same time, and when the server is primarily used for a distributed application that performs its own memory caching, such as SQL Server. This is a good selection whenever the server functions primarily as an application server, even if there are fewer than 64 users.

 If a Windows NT Server computer is primarily used as a WINS server, a DHCP server, or is the PDC for a large network, configur-

ing the Server service to Maximize Throughput For Network Applications should yield the best server performance.

TO OPTIMIZE THE SERVER SERVICE ON A WINDOWS NT SERVER COMPUTER, FOLLOW THESE STEPS:

1. Select Start ⇒ Settings ⇒ Control Panel.

2. In the Control Panel dialog box, double-click the Network icon.

3. In the Network dialog box, click the Services tab.

4. On the Services tab, highlight Server in the Network Services list box. Click the Properties command button.

5. The Server dialog box appears, as shown in Figure 19-2. Notice the four options available for optimizing the Server service. Select the option button next to the option that will provide the best performance for your server. Click OK.

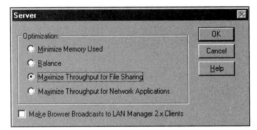

FIGURE 19-2   Optimizing the Server service

6. In the Network dialog box, click the Close command button.

7. A Network Settings Change dialog box appears, indicating that you must restart your computer before the new settings will take effect. Click the Yes command button to restart your computer.

Optimizing Network Traffic

There are two common situations when optimizing network traffic may be beneficial: when there is too much traffic on a network segment, and when a server is on the wrong side of a WAN link from the client computers it services.

When Performance Monitor indicates a high percentage of network utilization on a network segment, you might consider further segmenting that network segment. You can accomplish this by adding an additional network adapter to the server, or by installing a router on the network.

When users of client computers report slow response time from a server that is physically located on the other side of a WAN link, consider one of the following options:

o *Move* the server to the other side of the WAN link so client computers can access the server directly, without having to send network traffic across the WAN link.

o *Add* an additional server of the appropriate type (BDC, DHCP, or WINS) on the other side of the WAN link to service the client computers on that side of the link and to minimize WAN traffic.

For example, when users access a server for logon authentication, IP address assignment, or NetBIOS name resolution across a WAN link (such as a BDC, a DHCP server, or a WINS server), and slow server response time is reported, consider placing an additional server of the appropriate type on the same side of the WAN link as the client computers that need to access that type of server. Placing the server physically close to the client computers will improve server response time and reduce WAN link traffic.

KEY POINT SUMMARY

Chapter 19 described *performance optimization* — the process of modifying server and/or network hardware and software configurations with the intent of speeding up server and/or network response. This chapter provided information on how to best optimize performance, including identifying and resolving bottlenecks.

o For most network administrators, performance optimization most often means resolving user reports of slow system performance. Determining the cause of the slow performance is referred to as identifying a bottleneck. A *bottleneck* is the component in the system that is slowing system performance. In a networking environment, the bottleneck is the part of the system that is performing at peak capacity while other components in the system are *not* working at peak capacity. In other words, if it weren't for the limiting component, the rest of the system could go faster.

o To identify the bottleneck in your system, use Performance Monitor to measure performance of the server's memory, processor, and disk. You can also use Performance Monitor to gather statistics about your network that may help you identify network bottlenecks. Once you've interpreted the statistics and have identified the bottleneck in your system, you're ready to take steps to resolve that bottleneck.

o *Performance optimization* involves getting the most speed out of your existing hardware and software combination. It can also involve adding to or upgrading specific components to resolve bottlenecks.

o *Adding RAM* is often the single most inexpensive and effective upgrade you can make to your server. A beneficial by-product of adding RAM is that processor and disk performance may be improved, as well, because paging is reduced and the disk cache size is increased when RAM is added.

o The best method for *optimizing a paging file* is adding more RAM. Additionally, you can configure the paging file so that its initial size and maximum size are equal; place the paging file on the disk that has the least amount of activity, on a stripe set, or on a partition other than the boot partition; or place multiple, smaller paging files on multiple disks in the system. To move the paging file to a different disk or partition, or to configure and/or add additional paging files, use the System application in Control Panel.

o Consider *optimizing disks* when planning for a new Windows NT Server computer that will perform a specific task, such as file services. Consider optimizing and/or upgrading disks when you determine that the disk is a bottleneck to system performance. Before you upgrade a disk(s), ensure that RAM is *not* the bottleneck in your system.

o You can increase disk performance by defragmenting the hard disk(s) in your computer, upgrading to a faster disk controller and/or a faster hard disk(s), configuring a stripe set with parity across three or more disks, or configuring a stripe set across two or more disks.

- When you determine that the processor is a bottleneck to system performance, you should consider upgrading and/or adding a processor to the computer. Before you upgrade and/or add a processor, ensure that RAM is *not* the bottleneck in your system.

- To improve processor performance, consider replacing the existing processor with a faster processor, replacing the existing motherboard and processor with a faster motherboard and processor, upgrading from a single processor system to a multiprocessor system, or adding a processor to a multiprocessor system.

- There are four primary ways to optimize a server. You can optimize a server by: configuring load balancing across multiple servers; disabling unused services, protocols, and drivers; scheduling large, server-intensive tasks during nonpeak hours; and by optimizing the Server service. The Server service is optimized by using the Network application in Control Panel.

- There are two common situations when optimizing network traffic may be beneficial: when there is too much traffic on a network segment, and when a server is on the wrong side of a WAN link from the client computers that it services.

  - When Performance Monitor indicates a high percentage of network utilization on a network segment, consider further segmenting that network segment.

  - When users of client computers report slow response time from a server that is physically located on the other side of a WAN link, consider either moving the server to the other side of the WAN link, or adding an additional server of the appropriate type (BDC, DHCP, or WINS) on the other side of the WAN link.

APPLYING WHAT YOU'VE LEARNED

Now it's time to regroup, review, and apply what you've learned in this chapter.

The Instant Assessment questions bring to mind key facts and concepts. Then, a Critical Thinking Lab reinforces what you've learned, and gives you an opportunity to practice some of the tasks that may be tested by the Server exam.

Instant Assessment

1. What is performance optimization?

2. In a networking environment, what is a bottleneck?

3. Which Windows NT tool can you use to help identify a bottleneck in your Windows NT system?

4. Which four components should you monitor when attempting to identify a bottleneck in your Windows NT system?

5. What is perhaps the single most inexpensive and effective upgrade that you can make to your Windows NT Server computer?

6. Name one beneficial by-product of adding RAM to a Windows NT Server computer.

7. You decide you want to move the paging file on your Windows NT computer to a different disk. Which Control Panel application should you use to move/configure the paging file?

8. You determine that the disk is the bottleneck in your Windows NT Server computer. List three ways to increase disk performance.

9. You determine that the processor is the bottleneck in your Windows NT Server computer. List three ways to improve processor performance.

10. List four ways to optimize a Windows NT Server computer.

11. Users of client computers report slow server response time for logon authentication from a BDC that is located on the other side of a WAN link. What should you do to improve server response time?

 concept link   **For answers to the Instant Assessment questions see Appendix B.**

Critical Thinking Lab

The following Critical Thinking Lab provides you with a practical opportunity to apply the knowledge you've gained in this chapter about performance optimization.

Lab 19.30 *Finding and resolving bottlenecks*

The purpose of this lab is to give you experience in analyzing Performance Monitor statistics in order to identify the bottlenecks in a system, and also to give you experience in making recommendations to resolve a bottleneck.

Each problem below presents a situation and a set of statistics. In the space provided, supply the requested response to the problem.

Problem 1 Users of your network report slow response times when accessing files from a Windows NT Server computer. The server has a 486/66MHz processor with 20MB of RAM and a 2GB IDE hard disk. You run Performance Monitor on that server and obtain the statistics shown in the following table:

OBJECT	COUNTER	STATISTIC
Processor	% Processor Time	55%
Memory	Pages/sec	125
PhysicalDisk	% Disk Time	85%
Network Segment	% Network utilization	15%

There is enough money left in your annual equipment budget to enable you to do any *one* of the following:

o Upgrade the processor to a Pentium 166MHz processor

o Upgrade memory to 64MB of RAM

o Upgrade to a faster hard disk and a faster hard disk controller

o Install a second network adapter in the server and segment the network

Which upgrade would you perform, and why?

_____

_____

_____

_____

Problem 2 (begin) Users of your network report slow response times when accessing files from a Windows NT Server computer. The server has a Pentium 100MHz processor with 64MB of RAM and a 4GB SCSI hard disk. You run Performance Monitor on that server and obtain the following statistics:

OBJECT	COUNTER	STATISTIC
Processor	% Processor Time	15%
Memory	Pages/sec	4
PhysicalDisk	% Disk Time	90%
Network Segment	% Network utilization	15%

There is enough money left in your annual equipment budget to enable you to do any *one* of the following:

- Upgrade to a multiprocessor system with 2 Pentium PRO 200MHz processors
- Upgrade memory to 128MB of RAM
- Upgrade to a hardware-based RAID 5 (disk striping with parity) disk subsystem
- Install a second network adapter in the server to segment the network

Which upgrade would you perform, and why?

_____

_____

_____

_____

concept link   **For answers to the Critical Thinking Lab see Appendix B.**

Troubleshooting

I t happens to the best of us. Sooner or later, something on our computer or network doesn't work the way we expected it to, and we end up having to troubleshoot it. From basic to advanced troubleshooting, this part covers it.

Chapter 20 begins with an overview of troubleshooting, followed by an in-depth discussion of the troubleshooting process. Next, numerous resources for troubleshooting Windows NT are recommended. You'll even find step-by-step instructions on how to use some of these resources.

Chapter 21 is devoted entirely to advanced Windows NT troubleshooting, including topics such as troubleshooting the boot sequence and using Event Viewer and Windows NT Diagnostics. You'll also learn about the Windows NT Registry structure and how to use the Registry editors.

Part VI maps to the Troubleshooting exam objectives for the Implementing and Supporting Microsoft Windows NT Server 4.0 exam.

CHAPTER

The Troubleshooting Process

20

About Chapter 20

Have you ever wondered where to begin when faced with a tough troubleshooting problem? Or wondered where to get help when you just couldn't find a workable solution? Chapter 20 holds the answers to these questions and more.

After a brief overview of troubleshooting, this chapter explains my recommended five-step approach to troubleshooting.

The process basically boils down to gathering information, defining the problem, listing the probable causes of the problem, identifying possible solutions and attempting to fix the problem, and finally, resolving and documenting the problem.

The last half of this chapter is jam-packed with resources that can help you when you're troubleshooting basic or advanced Windows NT problems. You'll be introduced to *Microsoft TechNet*, the *Micro House Technical Library*, the Microsoft Technical Support Web site, the Microsoft Download Service, as well as several additional troubleshooting resources.

The Preparation Guide for the Server exam devotes an entire objective category to the topic of troubleshooting. For this reason, Chapter 20 is a "must read" for thorough exam preparation.

OVERVIEW OF TROUBLESHOOTING

Some say that troubleshooting is a science. Others say it's a fine art. I guess it's really a bit of both — a methodical approach to solving a problem that's devised from a person's base of knowledge, experience, and intuition.

Perhaps the best preparation for becoming an outstanding troubleshooter is to gain an in-depth understanding of how what you're troubleshooting works — in this case, Windows NT. In addition to understanding Windows NT, you also need to have an intimate understanding of networking and PC hardware. This combined knowledge will form the backbone of your troubleshooting capability.

You can gain this understanding and knowledge in several ways. This book is a great place to start. You can also attend classes, read other books, and work in the Windows NT networking world. One of the best ways to obtain understanding and knowledge is through on-the-job experience.

When you're faced with a tough troubleshooting problem, remember that you're probably *not* the first or only person who's ever had this problem. Don't be afraid to call your friends, colleagues, and professional contacts. Troubleshooting a critical system at 2:00 a.m. is no time to be a Lone Ranger. (Okay, maybe you shouldn't call your friends *then*.) Above all, especially if you've never encountered a problem like it before, use *all* of the troubleshooting resources and technical references available to you — your problem and its solution are probably out there; you just have to find them.

Finally, there's no substitute for experience. If you've seen the problem before, hopefully a little light will come on, and you will remember how you solved it before.

THE TROUBLESHOOTING PROCESS

There are many effective troubleshooting methods. Different people use different methods to arrive at the same solution.

While there may not be one "best" troubleshooting method out there, there are some basic steps you can take to simplify and organize the troubleshooting process.

The basic steps I use when troubleshooting Windows NT are as follows:

- Gather information
- Define the problem
- List probable causes
- Identify possible solutions and attempt to fix the problem
- Resolve and document the problem

The following sections discuss each of these steps in detail.

Gather Information

The troubleshooting process typically starts by a user reporting a problem to you. In this step, you gather specific information that will help you identify the problem.

Talk to the user(s) who is experiencing the problem. Ask a *lot* of questions. Specifically, find out:

- What *exactly* is the problem?

  Sometimes it's painstakingly difficult and time-consuming to identify the problem. A user's description of a problem, such as "I can't get on the network," can mean anything from "I can't log on" to "I can't get my e-mail." Be patient with the user, and encourage him or her to be as specific as possible.

- If the problem is experienced regularly, *when* does the problem occur?

- If an error message was displayed, *what* did the message say?

  Ask the user to write the error message down verbatim, if possible. A paraphrased or otherwise interpreted error message can be extremely difficult to research in a knowledge base.

- Did the user correctly perform all necessary steps to complete the task?

  Consider walking the user through the correct steps to see if you can recreate the problem.

- Has whatever is not working now *ever* worked before?

- If it did work before, when did it *stop* working?

- What has changed since the last time it worked?

This may be the single most important question you can ask. I usually ask this question several times during the troubleshooting process. Often, problems are created by users, administrators, or consultants who have changed, fixed, optimized, or otherwise fiddled with a perfectly good, functional system.

Define the Problem

Once you've gathered information, you're ready to define the problem. Sometimes the problem is glaringly obvious from the information you've gathered. Other times, you'll need to piece together bits and pieces of information from various users before you can identify the problem.

Identifying the problem as accurately as you can is an important step, because all of your efforts to resolve the problem, from that point, will be based on this diagnosis.

List Probable Causes

Once you've defined the problem, make a list of all the hardware and software components, configurations, and common user errors that could be a probable cause of the problem. Don't overlook the obvious here. Is it plugged in? Is it turned on? Is the computer cabled to the network?

Sometimes it's difficult to identify probable causes. For example, if an application fails and Windows NT displays an obscure error message, you might have to do extensive research just to come up with one or more probable causes of the problem.

After you've listed all the probable causes you can, place the items on your list in order, from the most likely cause of the problem to the least likely cause of the problem. If your intuition or experience tells you that one or two of the items may be the culprit, place these at the top of your list.

Identify Possible Solutions and Attempt to Fix the Problem

Starting at the top of your list, identify possible solutions for the first one or two probable causes.

Many causes, by their very nature, imply a solution. For example, if you suspect that the cause of the problem is a bad network cable, it's fairly obvious that replacing the network cable should resolve the problem. Other causes, such as a hardware component that's not on the *Hardware Compatibility List* (HCL), may involve significant amounts of research to come up with a workable solution.

Next, starting at the top of your list of probable causes, implement one of the possible solutions that you identified for the most likely cause of the problem. This may involve repairing, replacing, or reconfiguring the suspected offending component or remedying the suspected user error.

Test the system after this step to determine whether the problem is fixed. If this change *doesn't* fix the problem, restore the system to its original configuration and proceed to the next item on the list. Continue this process until you are satisfied that you have identified the cause and solution to the problem.

 tip **Don't change more than one component at a time or you may have a difficult time determining what's broken and what isn't.**

Resolve and Document the Problem

Once you have positively identified the problem's cause and solution, permanently implement the solution. If the solution to the problem is a configuration change, no more work is required here — you have already implemented a permanent fix to the problem. However, if you determined that a segment of network cable in a wall (or ceiling) was defective by temporarily bypassing this segment, you will have to have the cable segment in the wall (or ceiling) replaced to fix the situation permanently.

Test the system again to make sure the problem is really fixed, and that you have not created any new problems in the system. If the problem only occurred at specific times, test the system during those times to ensure that the problem has been remedied.

Once you're satisfied that you have resolved the problem, document the problem, the date it occurred, and its solution in a trouble log. This will aid you and other engineers in your company if and when this problem reoccurs.

in the
real world

I can't tell you how many times I've spent four hours solving a problem, only to remember afterward that I had solved the exact same problem six months or a year before. If I'd documented the problem the first time, I would have saved myself four hours of troubleshooting the second time around.

RESOURCES FOR TROUBLESHOOTING

Several resources are available to help you when you're troubleshooting Windows NT. Use these resources — they are your friends.

Using outside resources enables you to draw on the experience of others. Typically, you won't be the first person to have encountered a particular problem. If others have had this same problem before you, it is likely that this problem (and its solution) is documented in a knowledge-base resource.

Troubleshooting resources come in many flavors. Knowledge bases are often chock-full of white papers, configuration hints and tips, and problem-specific troubleshooting information. If you have a modem and/or an Internet connection, you can access download services and FTP sites to obtain the latest patches, fixes, drivers, and white papers. You can also access technical support forums via modem or the World Wide Web. On these forums you can post a question, and other professionals may read it and reply to you.

The next sections discuss some of the most helpful and common Windows NT troubleshooting resources: *Microsoft TechNet*, the *Micro House Technical Library*, the Microsoft Technical Support Web site, the Microsoft Download Service, and other troubleshooting resources.

Microsoft TechNet

Microsoft TechNet is an invaluable knowledge base — I recommend using it as your first and primary troubleshooting resource. *TechNet* is published monthly by Microsoft on multiple compact discs. In my opinion, the price of an annual subscription is money well spent.

TechNet includes a complete set of all Microsoft operating system Resource Kits (currently in a help file format), the entire Microsoft Knowledge Base, and supplemental compact discs full of patches, fixes, and drivers (so you don't have to spend time downloading them).

TechNet is particularly helpful when troubleshooting a specific problem. When Microsoft Technical Support helps a client troubleshoot a problem, that problem and its solution are documented. All significant problems and their solutions are then placed in the *TechNet* resource. *TechNet* includes thousands of problems and their respective solutions.

Using *TechNet* is fairly straightforward. Figure 20-1 shows the opening dialog box for *TechNet*. Notice the categories that are displayed in the Entire Contents list box.

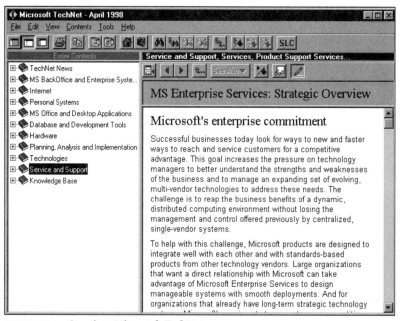

FIGURE 20-1   Starting *Microsoft TechNet*

You can search the entire contents of *TechNet*, or a specific subset of the contents for information on a specific topic. To begin a search, click the Query icon (which appears in the toolbar as a pair of binoculars). The Query dialog box appears, as shown in Figure 20-2.

FIGURE 20-2   Performing a search in *Microsoft TechNet*

Type the topic you want information on in the Query drop-down list box. Be as specific as you can. Even when you are specific, don't be surprised to see numerous articles that include the words you searched for. You can include multiple words in your query, and you can use the logical operators AND, OR, and NOT within the query. If you need more information on constructing a query, click the Help command button in this dialog box. When you're ready to execute the search, click the Run Query command button.

I can't recommend this resource highly enough. When you're troubleshooting, think *TechNet* first.

 You can order *Microsoft TechNet* by calling (800)-344-2121 in the United States. If you're a Microsoft Certified Professional or an MCSE, discounts or special promotions may be offered for first-year subscriptions.

Micro House Technical Library

The *Micro House Technical Library* is a useful CD-ROM-based set of encyclopedias that contains hardware configuration information. This resource can be particularly helpful when you need to configure a specific hardware device, such as a motherboard, I/O card, or network adapter.

Have you ever lost the documentation for a hard drive (or any other piece of hardware)? I have. If you have access to the *Micro House Technical Library*, it could save you a lengthy phone call to product support to obtain jumper switch settings and other configuration information.

An evaluation copy of this product is included on the compact disc that accompanies this book. The *Micro House Technical Library* can be purchased from Micro House International. Their phone number for sales (in the United States) is 1-800-920-8299.

Microsoft Technical Support Web Site

Microsoft Technical Support has its own site on the World Wide Web. You can access this site by first accessing the Microsoft Support home page at: `http://www.microsoft.com/support/`. Figure 20-3 shows the Microsoft Support home page.

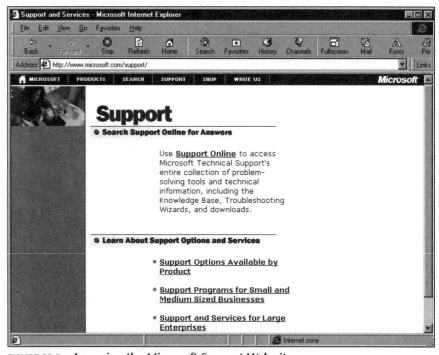

FIGURE 20-3   Accessing the Microsoft Support Web site

Click the Microsoft Technical Support link to access the Microsoft Technical Support home page. A list of several topics/options is displayed on the Technical Support home page, including

- Support Online

- Support Options Available by Product

- Support Programs for Small and Medium Sized Businesses

- Support and Services for Large Enterprises

You can search the Knowledge Base; download service packs, patches, and drivers; or post a question for a support engineer. You can also obtain a phone number to access Microsoft Technical Support engineers directly.

 Be aware that Microsoft charges a fee for most calls to their Technical Support engineers.

The Microsoft Technical Support Web site is a great resource, especially if you don't have *TechNet*.

The Microsoft Download Service

The Microsoft Download Service is a *bulletin board service* (BBS). Through this BBS, you can download patches, fixes, and drivers.

You can access the Microsoft Download Service by using the Windows NT HyperTerminal application. The phone number for the Microsoft Download Service is (425)-936-6735.

The modem settings for accessing the Microsoft Download Service are

- Data bits = 8

- Parity = 0

- Stop bits = 1

- Flow control = 0

When you first connect to the Microsoft Download Service, a welcome screen appears asking you to enter your full name. After you've entered your name, you'll be prompted to enter the city and state from which you are calling. A scrolling screen containing new user information is displayed. Finally, the main screen appears, as shown in Figure 20-4.

At the main menu, type **B** to access the file index and to search for a file.

Most of the files you can access from the Microsoft Download Service are the same files available on the *TechNet* compact discs and from the Microsoft Technical Support Web site. This resource can be helpful, but it is the least user friendly of the three Microsoft resources mentioned in this chapter.

FIGURE 20-4   The Microsoft Download Service main menu

Additional Troubleshooting Resources

Other troubleshooting resources are available, including online service forums, Microsoft Solution Providers, a Microsoft FTP site, Internet search tools, and professional contacts and colleagues.

Many online services host forums where you can post a question that will be read by many people, a few of whom may even respond with some free advice.

Some helpful forums include:

- The MS WinNT Forum and the MS Win32 Forum on CompuServe
- The Windows NT Server Forum on MSN (The Microsoft Network)

Other resources may be as close as your telephone. For example, when I worked for a national computer reseller, I could send a voice mail message requesting help with a specific problem to all the engineers in the company, nationwide. That one call would usually generate five to ten responses within twenty-four hours.

Microsoft Solution Providers usually have multiple MCSEs on staff. These consultants, who are typically available for an hourly fee, can assist you not only with troubleshooting but also with system design and implementation.

Microsoft has another site on the Internet for those who use FTP to download files. You can access this site at `ftp.microsoft.com`. This site has most of the same files that you can access by using *TechNet*, the Microsoft Technical Support Web site, and the Microsoft Download Service.

Several other Internet sites contain Windows NT information. You can find these sites using Internet search tools such as AltaVista, Lycos, and Yahoo!.

Last but not least, don't forget your professional contacts and colleagues. Many times someone you've worked with or met at a conference will have just the bit of information you need to solve a problem. You might consider joining a professional organization or users group where you can meet and network with other industry professionals.

 tip **If you want people to freely and willingly share their time and expertise with you, it's a good idea if you're willing to do the same yourself.**

KEY POINT SUMMARY

This chapter defined and described the troubleshooting process.

- Troubleshooting is a methodical approach to solving a problem. The best preparation for becoming an outstanding troubleshooter is to understand intimately what you're troubleshooting — in this case, Windows NT, and the computer hardware and networking environment in which it runs.

- The basic steps suggested for troubleshooting are as follows:

  - Gather information

  - Define the problem

- List probable causes

- Identify possible solutions and attempt to fix the problem

- Resolve and document the problem

- Several resources can help you when you're troubleshooting Windows NT, including knowledge bases, Web sites, download services, and others.

- *Microsoft TechNet* is a CD-ROM-based knowledge base. It contains a complete set of all the Microsoft Resource Kits, the entire Microsoft Knowledge Base, and supplemental compact discs full of patches, fixes, and drivers.

- The *Micro House Technical Library* is a CD-ROM-based set of encyclopedias that contains hardware configuration information.

- The Microsoft Technical Support Web site, which can be accessed at `http://www.microsoft.com/support/`, is also a great resource. On this site you can search the Microsoft Knowledge Base; download service packs, patches, and drivers; obtain support telephone numbers; or post a question for a support engineer.

- The Microsoft Download Service is a BBS. Through this service you can download patches, fixes, and drivers.

- Additional troubleshooting resources include online service forums, Microsoft Solution Providers, a Microsoft FTP site, Internet search tools, and professional contacts and colleagues.

APPLYING WHAT YOU'VE LEARNED

Now it's time to regroup, review, and apply what you've learned in this chapter.

The questions in the following Instant Assessment section bring to mind key troubleshooting facts and concepts.

Instant Assessment

1. What is troubleshooting?

2. List the five basic steps suggested for troubleshooting.

3. Which troubleshooting resource is published monthly by Microsoft in a multiple compact disc format?

4. What Microsoft Web site can you access to download help files and service packs, or to post a question to a support engineer?

5. Which Microsoft troubleshooting resource is a bulletin board service (BBS)?

 concept link **For answers to the Instant Assessment questions see Appendix B.**

Advanced Troubleshooting

About Chapter 21

C hapter 21 explores a number of advanced Windows NT troubleshooting topics.

This chapter begins with a discussion of the Windows NT boot sequence and recommends solutions to several common boot sequence problems. Included in this section are detailed instructions for performing the Emergency Repair process.

Next, this chapter explains how to use Event Viewer, which can be used to determine why a service or driver failed during system startup. Windows NT Diagnostics, which enables you to view detailed configuration information, is also covered.

Finally, this chapter outlines the structure of the Windows NT Registry and explains how to use the Registry editors to search and modify the Registry.

This chapter includes one Hands-on Lab in which you practice advanced Windows NT troubleshooting techniques, including using Windows NT Diagnostics and using the Registry editors.

The material presented in Chapter 21 maps to the "Choose the appropriate course of action to take to resolve boot failures" and the "Choose the appropriate course of action to take to resolve fault-tolerance failures" objectives listed in the Troubleshooting section in the Preparation Guide for the Server exam.

TROUBLESHOOTING THE BOOT SEQUENCE

The *boot sequence* refers to the process of starting Windows NT, including initializing all of its services and completing the logon process. There are several common problems that can occur during the boot sequence, and in order to successfully troubleshoot them, you need to have an understanding of the steps that occur during the boot sequence.

The following sections identify and explain the steps that occur during the boot sequence, list common boot sequence problems and recommended solutions, and discuss how to perform the Emergency Repair process, which is a solution to several common boot sequence problems.

Overview of the Boot Sequence

The Windows NT boot sequence consists of a sequential series of steps, beginning with powering on the computer and ending with completion of the logon process. Understanding the individual steps that make up the boot sequence will help you to troubleshoot problems that may occur during this process.

The boot sequence steps vary according to the hardware platform you are using. The boot sequence steps discussed in this section apply to the Intel platform only.

The Windows NT boot sequence (Intel platform) is as follows:

1. **Power On Self Test:** The *Power On Self Test* (POST) is performed by the computer's BIOS every time the computer is powered on to test for the existence of specific components, such as processor, RAM, and video adapter. If any errors are detected during this phase, an error message or onscreen diagnostics is typically displayed.

2. **Initial Startup:** In this step, the computer's BIOS attempts to locate a startup disk, such as a floppy disk, or the first hard disk in the computer.

   If the startup disk is the first hard disk, the BIOS reads the *Master Boot Record* from the startup disk, and the code in the Master Boot Record is run. The Master Boot Record then determines which partition is the active partition and loads sector 0 (also called the partition boot sector) from the active partition into memory. Then the code contained in sector 0 is run. This causes the `ntldr` file to be loaded into memory from the root folder of the active partition. `Ntldr` is then run.

If the startup disk is a floppy disk, the code from sector 0 on the floppy disk is loaded into memory. Then the code contained in sector 0 is run. This causes `ntldr` to be loaded into memory from the root folder of the floppy disk. `Ntldr` is then run.

3. **Selecting an operating system:** `Ntldr` switches the processor into a 32-bit flat memory mode. `Ntldr` then initializes the appropriate minifile system (either FAT or NTFS) to enable `ntldr` to locate and load the `Boot.ini` file. `Ntldr` uses the `Boot.ini` file to create the *boot loader screen*.

A typical Window NT 4.0 boot loader screen appears as follows:

```
OS Loader V4.00
Please select the operating system to start:
      Windows NT Server Version 4.00
      Windows NT Server Version 4.00 [VGA mode]
      MS-DOS
Use ↑ and ↓ to move the highlight to your choice.
Press Enter to choose.
Seconds until highlighted choice will be started automatically: 30
```

At this point, either the user selects an operating system from the boot loader menu, or the default operating system is automatically started after a specified number of seconds has elapsed.

If an operating system *other* than Windows NT is selected, the `Bootsect.dos` file is loaded into memory and run, and the appropriate operating system is started. (If an operating system other than Windows NT is selected, the remaining steps of the Windows NT boot sequence do not apply.)

If Windows NT is selected, `ntldr` loads `Ntdetect.com` and executes it.

4. **Detecting hardware:** `Ntdetect.com` searches for computer ID, bus type (ISA, EISA, PCI, or MCA), video adapter, keyboard, serial and parallel ports, floppy disk(s), and pointing device (mouse).

As it checks, the following is displayed onscreen:

```
NTDETECT V4.0 Checking Hardware . . .
```

`Ntdetect.com` creates a list of the components it finds and passes this information to `ntldr`.

5. Selecting hardware profile and loading the kernel: Ntldr displays the following message:

```
OS Loader V4.0
Press spacebar now to invoke Hardware Profile/Last Known Good menu.
```

Ntldr gives you approximately three to five seconds to press the spacebar. If you press the spacebar at this time, the Hardware Profile/Last Known Good menu is displayed as shown:

```
Hardware Profile/Configuration Recovery Menu
This menu enables you to select a hardware profile
to be used when Windows NT is started.
If your system is not starting correctly, then you may switch to a
previous system configuration, which may overcome startup problems.
IMPORTANT: System configuration changes made since the last
successful startup will be discarded.
                Original Configuration
                Some other hardware profile
Use the up and down arrow keys to move the highlight
to the selection you want. Then press Enter.
To switch to the Last Known Good Configuration, press 'L'.
To Exit this menu and restart your computer, press F3.
Seconds until highlighted choice will be started automatically: 5
```

If you press **L** while this screen is displayed, the Last Known Good control set will be used, and any configuration changes made during the last logon session will be discarded.

If you don't press the spacebar and have only one hardware profile, the default hardware profile is loaded.

If you don't press the spacebar and have more than one hardware profile, the Hardware Profile/Configuration Recovery Menu is displayed.

Once you've selected a hardware profile, ntldr loads Ntoskrnl.exe and executes the Windows NT kernel.

6. **Kernel initialization:** When the kernel starts, a screen similar to the following is displayed:

```
Microsoft (R) Windows NT (TM) Version 4.0 (Build 1381)
1 System Processor (32 MB Memory)
```

This screen indicates that the kernel has successfully started.

7. **Initializing device drivers:** At this point, the kernel loads either the default control set or, if you selected the Last Known Good Configuration, it loads the Last Known Good control set. Then the kernel initializes all of the device drivers listed in the control set.

8. **Initializing services:** The kernel loads and starts the services listed in the control set being used.

9. **Logon process:** The Begin Logon dialog box is displayed, prompting the user to press Ctrl + Alt + Delete to log on. Then the user logs on, supplying an appropriate user name and password.

Once a user has successfully logged on, the boot sequence is complete, and the control set currently in use is copied to the Last Known Good Configuration.

Troubleshooting Common Boot Sequence Problems

There are many common problems that can occur during the Windows NT boot sequence. Table 21-1 lists these problems, along with their possible causes and recommended solutions.

TABLE 21-1 TROUBLESHOOTING THE WINDOWS NT BOOT SEQUENCE

PROBLEM	POSSIBLE CAUSE	RECOMMENDED SOLUTION
An error message is displayed during the POST.	This message most likely indicates a hardware failure.	Use the error message (or onscreen diagnostics) displayed to determine the offending hardware device. Repair, replace, or reconfigure the hardware device as necessary.

PROBLEM	POSSIBLE CAUSE	RECOMMENDED SOLUTION
An error message, such as "Invalid partition table" or "Missing operating system" is displayed after the POST.	This type of error message often indicates that either sector 0 of the active partition is damaged, or that important operating system files (such as `ntldr`) are missing.	Perform the Emergency Repair process (as explained in the next section of this chapter) and select the inspect boot sector option during this process. If you suspect that there are missing files, also select the Verify Windows NT system files option during the Emergency Repair process.
After you select MS-DOS from the boot loader menu, the following error is displayed: "I/O error accessing boot sector…"	This message indicates that `ntldr` can't find the `Bootsect.dos` file.	Restore this file from tape; or, perform the Emergency Repair process, selecting the Inspect boot sector option during the process.
During the boot sequence, NT displays a message indicating that it cannot find a specific file, such as `Ntoskrnl.exe` or `ntldr`.	There are two possible causes for this problem: the specified file is missing or corrupt, or the `Boot.ini` file does not specify the correct path to system files.	To restore a missing or corrupt file (except for the `Boot.ini` file), perform the Emergency Repair process, selecting the Verify Windows NT system files option during the process. If the `Boot.ini` file is missing, perform the Emergency Repair process, selecting the Inspect startup environment option during the process, which will create a new `Boot.ini` file. To repair a `Boot.ini` file, do one of the following: • Boot to MS-DOS and edit the `Boot.ini` file (assuming that the `Boot.ini` file is on a FAT partition) • Create a Windows NT boot diskette with the appropriate `Boot.ini`, `ntldr`, `Ntdetect.com`, and `Bootsect.dos` files on it. Use this diskette to boot the computer to Windows NT, and then edit the `Boot.ini` file. • Reinstall Windows NT (this is definitely *not* the preferred option).

TABLE 21-1 *(continued)*

PROBLEM	POSSIBLE CAUSE	RECOMMENDED SOLUTION
Your Windows NT computer crashes during a power outage. When you reboot the computer, a blue screen is displayed during the boot sequence.	The most likely cause of this problem is a corrupt file. Power outages can easily corrupt files on the hard disk.	Perform the Emergency Repair process, selecting the Inspect boot sector and Verify Windows NT system files options during the process.
You make several configuration changes and then reboot your Windows NT computer. A blue screen is displayed during the boot sequence.	The most likely cause of this problem is the configuration changes made during the last logon session.	Reboot the computer, and select the Last Known Good Configuration during the boot sequence. If this does *not* repair the problem, perform the Emergency Repair process, selecting the Inspect Registry files option during the process.
A STOP error (blue screen) is displayed during the device driver or service initialization steps of the boot sequence.	The most probable causes of this error are a corrupt Registry entry, a corrupt device driver, or a corrupt service file.	Perform the Emergency Repair process, selecting the Inspect Registry files and Verify Windows NT system files options during the process.

Performing the Emergency Repair Process

Sometimes the only way to restore a malfunctioning Windows NT system to an operable state is to perform the Emergency Repair process. The Emergency Repair process is primarily used when you are unable to successfully boot your Windows NT computer.

The Emergency Repair process involves using the Windows NT Setup Boot Disk set, the Windows NT compact disc, and the Emergency Repair disk created during (or after) the installation process to repair a damaged or corrupt Windows NT installation.

 note **If you didn't create an Emergency Repair disk during (or after) the Windows NT installation, an Emergency Repair disk from any other Windows NT installation on the same hardware platform (such as Intel) can be used for *most* repair options but *can't* be used to inspect Registry files. Also see the following caution.**

caution

Never replace or repair the Registry with an Emergency Repair disk from another computer. Only repair the Registry using that specific computer's Emergency Repair Disk. Using another computer's Emergency Repair Disk can damage your computer's Windows NT installation, possibly to the point where it won't even start. This is because Registry entries are specific for an individual computer's hardware, software, policy, and user account information. No two computers have identical Registries.

The Emergency Repair process has four different repair options. During the Emergency Repair process, you are prompted to select one or more of these options. These four options are detailed in Table 21-2.

TABLE 21-2 WINDOWS NT EMERGENCY REPAIR PROCESS REPAIR OPTIONS

REPAIR OPTION	DESCRIPTION
Inspect Registry files	This option enables you to select any or all of the Registry files for replacement, including ○ System (System configuration) ○ Software (Software information) ○ Default (Default user profile) ○ Ntuser.dat (New user profile) ○ Security (Security policy) ○ SAM (Security Accounts Manager user accounts database) All selected files will be replaced during the Emergency Repair process.
Inspect startup environment	Selecting this option causes Emergency Repair to verify the files in the Windows NT system partition, including ntldr, Ntdetect.com, Ntbootdd.sys, and Boot.ini. If any of these files are missing or corrupt, they will be replaced.
Verify Windows NT system files	Selecting this option causes Emergency Repair to verify the files in the Windows NT install folder and to replace any missing or corrupt files from the Windows NT compact disc.
Inspect boot sector	Selecting this option causes Emergency Repair to verify that sector 0 on the active partition (also called the partition boot sector) contains the code to start ntldr. If the partition boot sector is corrupt, Emergency Repair will repair it if the partition boot sector is the active partition on the first hard disk in the computer.

TO PERFORM THE EMERGENCY REPAIR PROCESS, FOLLOW THESE STEPS:

1. Start the computer using the Windows NT Setup Book Disk. Ensure that the Windows NT compact disc is in the computer's CD-ROM drive.

2. Insert Windows NT Setup Disk #2 when prompted.

3. When prompted to choose whether to repair an existing installation or to install a new copy of Windows NT, press **R** to start the Emergency Repair process.

4. The Emergency Repair menu is displayed. By default, all four options listed in Table 21-2 are selected. Deselect any options that you don't want to perform. When you're finished selecting options, select Continue from the menu.

5. Insert Windows NT Setup Disk #3 when prompted.

6. Insert the Emergency Repair Disk when prompted.

7. When the Emergency Repair process is completed, remove the floppy disk and reboot the computer to Windows NT.

If the Emergency Repair process doesn't repair your system, you may need to reinstall Windows NT.

 tip **If you don't have the Windows NT Setup Boot Disk set, you can create one on an MS-DOS or Windows NT computer that has a CD-ROM drive.**

To create the Windows NT Setup Boot Disk set, place the Windows NT compact disc in the computer's CD-ROM drive. Then, from an MS-DOS command prompt, type winnt /ox and press Enter to create the disk set. Or, on a Windows NT computer, type winnt32 /ox at the command prompt and press Enter to create the disk set.

USING EVENT VIEWER

Event Viewer is a Windows NT administrative tool that is used to view the System, Security, and Application Logs. These logs contain success, failure, and informational messages generated by the operating system, auditing, and applications.

The most common troubleshooting application of Event Viewer is determining why a service or device driver failed during system startup. After booting the computer, Windows NT notifies the user of such a failure by displaying a Service Control Manager warning dialog box. Figure 21-1 shows a typical Service Control Manager warning dialog box.

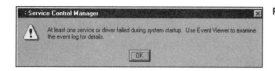

FIGURE 21-1 **Notification of service or driver failure during startup**

When a Service Control Manager warning is displayed, you can use the Event Viewer System Log to determine which service or driver failed and to view a detailed description of the failure. This information will often help you to determine the cause of the failure and an appropriate solution.

TO ACCESS THE SYSTEM LOG IN EVENT VIEWER, FOLLOW THESE STEPS:

1. Select Start ⇒ Programs ⇒ Administrative Tools (Common) ⇒ Event Viewer.

2. The Event Viewer dialog box appears. If the System Log is not displayed, select Log ⇒ System.

3. The Event Viewer System Log dialog box appears, as shown in Figure 21-2. Notice the many stop errors listed in the dialog box.

Date	Time	Source	Category	Event	User	Co
3/17/97	5:41:17 PM	Print	None	13	FPNW Service	
3/17/97	5:39:42 PM	EI59x	None	3	N/A	
3/17/97	5:39:42 PM	EI59x	None	2	N/A	
3/17/97	5:39:42 PM	EI59x	None	5	N/A	
3/17/97	5:39:37 PM	EventLog	None	6005	N/A	
3/17/97	5:39:42 PM	EI59x	None	258	N/A	
3/17/97	5:35:55 PM	BROWSER	None	8015	N/A	
3/17/97	5:35:50 PM	BROWSER	None	8015	N/A	
3/17/97	5:35:48 PM	RemoteAccess	None	20085	N/A	
3/17/97	5:35:48 PM	RemoteAccess	None	20085	N/A	
3/17/97	5:35:45 PM	DhcpServer	None	1024	N/A	
3/17/97	5:35:45 PM	Service Control Mar	None	7023	N/A	
3/17/97	5:35:45 PM	Wins	None	4165	N/A	
3/17/97	5:35:45 PM	Print	None	13	FPNW Service	
3/17/97	5:34:38 PM	EI59x	None	3	N/A	
3/17/97	5:34:38 PM	EI59x	None	2	N/A	
3/17/97	5:34:38 PM	EI59x	None	5	N/A	
3/17/97	5:34:38 PM	EI59x	None	258	N/A	
3/17/97	5:34:34 PM	NetBT	None	4311	N/A	
3/17/97	5:34:34 PM	NetBT	None	4307	N/A	
3/17/97	5:34:34 PM	NetBT	None	4311	N/A	
3/17/97	5:34:32 PM	EventLog	None	6005	N/A	

FIGURE 21-2 Viewing the System Log in Event Viewer

A *stop error* in the System Log is identified by a red stop sign preceding the event on the left-hand side of the dialog box. A stop error indicates that the service or driver listed in the Source column was unable to initialize correctly during system startup.

Examining stop error event details is the key to troubleshooting failed services or drivers. When multiple stop errors are listed, it's usually best to start your troubleshooting by examining the *oldest* stop error in the list first. The oldest stop error is the *first* stop error that occurred during the boot process — it is also the last stop error on the System Log list. This stop error is probably the cause of all the later stop errors listed.

To view stop error event detail, double-click the stop error in the System Log in Event Viewer. When you double-click the stop error, the Event Detail dialog box is displayed, as shown in Figure 21-3. Notice the description of the stop error in the Description text box.

FIGURE 21-3   Viewing stop error
event detail

The stop error detailed in Figure 21-3 indicates that initialization of the NetBT service failed because the driver device could not be created.

Sometimes the event detail provides specific information that can be used to correct the problem. Other times, further investigation using a resource such as *Microsoft TechNet* may be necessary. (When using *TechNet*, I recommend searching by the complete text listed in the Event Detail Description box.)

In this case, further research determined that the NetBT device driver was corrupt, and needed to be replaced. To solve the problem, I restored the device driver from tape. Incidentally, fixing the NetBT service stop error repaired all of the other stop errors in the list.

Remember, when using Event Viewer for troubleshooting, *always* **view the Event Detail for the** *last* **stop error in the list (the event that happened** *first* **chronologically during the boot process) first. Resolving this error will often take care of most or all of the other stop errors listed.**

USING WINDOWS NT DIAGNOSTICS

Windows NT Diagnostics is a Windows NT administrative tool that enables you to view detailed system configuration information and statistics. This tool can help you troubleshoot system configuration problems. It is also very useful for determining service and device driver dependencies. Windows NT Diagnostics does not actually diagnose anything — it simply displays your current system configuration information.

To access Windows NT Diagnostics, at the desktop select Start ⇒ Programs ⇒ Administrative Tools (Common) ⇒ Windows NT Diagnostics.

The Windows NT Diagnostics dialog box appears, as shown in Figure 21-4. Notice the nine different tabs in this dialog box: Version, System, Display, Drives, Memory, Services, Resources, Environment, and Network.

The various tabs in Windows NT Diagnostics contain different options and are used for different purposes:

- **Version:** The Version tab, shown in Figure 21-4, displays this Windows NT installation's version, build number, and service pack number. It also displays the serial number and registered owner. Clicking the Print command button on any Windows NT Diagnostics tab will print details contained on *all* of the tabs in Windows NT Diagnostics. This list can be quite extensive.

FIGURE 21-4   The Windows NT Diagnostics initial
                 dialog box

o **System:** The System tab, which is shown in Figure 21-5, displays the type
  of *Hardware Abstraction Layer* (HAL) being used; BIOS information,
  including BIOS date and manufacturer; and a specific processor description
  for each processor in the computer.

o **Display:** The Display tab, shown in Figure 21-6, displays the display adapter
  configuration and the Windows NT display driver in use.

o **Drives:** The Drives tab, shown in Figure 21-7, displays all drives connected
  to this Windows NT computer, including network connected drives, if any.
  You can double-click any drive listed to view specific drive properties,
  including number of bytes free, number of bytes in use, and total number
  of bytes. You can also view specific file system information about the drive,
  such as file system type.

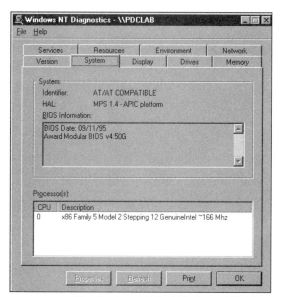

FIGURE 21-5   The System tab in Windows NT Diagnostics

FIGURE 21-6   The Display tab in Windows
                    NT Diagnostics

FIGURE 21-7   The Drives tab in Windows
NT Diagnostics

o **Memory:** The Memory tab, shown in Figure 21-8, displays various statistics
on memory and paging file(s) in this computer. You can use these statistics
to help you determine if the computer has enough memory and large
enough paging files for optimum performance.

o **Services:** The Services tab, shown in Figure 21-9, displays the status of all
services and device drivers installed on this Windows NT computer. Using
this tab is a quick way to determine whether a particular service is
running.

You can double-click any service or device driver to obtain detailed information about that service or driver.

I use this feature primarily to determine service dependencies and group
dependencies for a specific service or driver — it's a lot quicker and easier than
searching the Registry. *Service dependencies* show which services and drivers
must be running before the service in question can start. *Group dependencies*
show which groups of services or drivers must be running before the service in
question can start. Once you have determined what the service and group dependencies for a particular service or driver are, you can then verify that all of these
services and drivers (that are required to be running *before* a particular service or
driver can start) are, in fact, running.

FIGURE 21-8   The Memory tab in Windows
NT Diagnostics

FIGURE 21-9   The Services tab in Windows
NT Diagnostics

To determine service and group dependencies, double-click the service or driver you want to research, and then click the Dependencies tab in the Service Properties dialog box that is displayed. Figure 21-10 shows the Dependencies tab for the Computer Browser service. Notice the services that must be running before the Computer Browser service can start.

FIGURE 21-10   **Using Windows NT Diagnostics to determine service and group dependencies**

○ **Resources**: The Resources tab, shown in Figure 21-11, displays the *interrupt requests* (IRQs) used by various devices in this computer. You can use this information to troubleshoot interrupt conflicts. You can also click the I/O Port, DMA, and Memory command buttons to obtain listings of all devices in this computer, by the I/O Port addresses, DMA addresses, and Memory addresses that they use. You can click the Devices command button for a listing of all devices in this computer.

FIGURE 21-11   The Resources tab in
Windows NT Diagnostics

- **Environment:** The Environment tab, shown in Figure 21-12, displays the
  system environment variables, such as the path, in use on this Windows NT
  computer. To obtain a list of environment variables for the user that is
  currently logged on to this computer, click the Local User command button.

- **Network:** The Network tab, shown in Figure 21-13, displays various
  network information, such as domain name and computer name. If you
  click the Transports or Settings command buttons, additional network
  configuration is displayed.

  If you click the Statistics command button, numerous network utilization
statistics are displayed, as shown in Figure 21-14. These statistics are not updated
automatically — you must click the Refresh command button each time you want
to update these statistics. These network statistics are sometimes helpful when
troubleshooting network problems.

FIGURE 21-12   The Environment tab in Windows
NT Diagnostics

FIGURE 21-13   The Network tab in Windows NT
Diagnostics

FIGURE 21-14   Viewing network utilization statistics in Windows NT Diagnostics

USING THE REGISTRY EDITORS

Registry editors are tools that enable you to search and modify the Windows NT Registry. There are two primary tools for editing the Windows NT Registry:

- Windows NT Registry Editor (`regedt32.exe`)
- Windows 95 Registry Editor (`regedit.exe`)

Additionally, you can use the Windows NT System Policy Editor (`poledit.exe`) to modify a limited number of settings in the Registry. However, you can't use System Policy Editor to search the Registry.

The Registry editors are primarily used for three types of tasks:

- To change Registry settings that can't be changed with any other user interface (such as Control Panel)
- To modify the Registry as directed by *Microsoft TechNet* or by Microsoft Technical Support to resolve a particular problem or to provide a particular feature
- To troubleshoot various startup problems

The focus of this section is on using the Registry editors for troubleshooting purposes. Specifically, you'll learn how to use the Registry editors to determine service and group dependencies of various Windows NT services and device drivers.

Before explaining the specifics of how to use the Registry editors, it will be helpful for you to understand the basics of how the Windows NT Registry is structured.

Registry Structure Overview

The Windows NT Registry is a database that contains all of the information required to correctly configure an individual Windows NT computer, its user accounts, and its applications. Registries are unique to each computer — you shouldn't use the Registry from one computer on another computer. The Registry is organized in a tree structure consisting of five subtrees and their keys and value entries. Within the subtrees, keys are similar to folders in a file system, and value entries are similar to files.

Figure 21-15 shows the five subtrees within the Windows NT Registry.

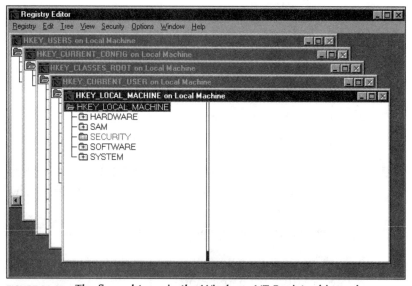

FIGURE 21-15   The five subtrees in the Windows NT Registry hierarchy

Each subtree in the Registry contains different types of information:

- **HKEY_LOCAL_MACHINE:** This subtree contains various configuration information specific to the local computer, including hardware, software, device driver, and services startup configurations. Windows NT accesses this information during system startup and uses it to correctly configure the computer.

 When troubleshooting Windows NT, check the HKEY_LOCAL_ MACHINE subtree *first*, because this subtree contains most of the service and driver configuration information for the operating system.

- **HKEY_CURRENT_USER:** This subtree contains the entire user profile for the user that is currently logged on. This includes the user's individual desktop settings, network drive and printer connections, and so on. HKEY_CURRENT_USER is a replica of the keys and values stored in `HKEY_USERS\security identifier (SID) of currently logged on user`.

- **HKEY_CURRENT_CONFIG:** The subtree contains the hardware configuration currently being used by Windows NT. This subtree consists of a replica of the keys and values stored in `HKEY_LOCAL_MACHINE\System\ CurrentControlSet\HardwareProfiles\Current`.

- **HKEY_CLASSES_ROOT:** This subtree contains all of the associations between applications and their specific filename extensions. For example, files ending in `.doc` are associated with Microsoft Word. This association is what makes it possible for you to double-click a `.doc` file and have Word start automatically and open that file. This subtree also contains all of the *object linking and embedding* (OLE) information used by various Windows applications and consists of a replica of the keys and values stored in `HKEY_LOCAL_MACHINE\Software\Classes`.

- **HKEY_USERS:** This subtree contains the user profile for the user that is currently logged on (the current user profile), as well as the default user profile.

In the Windows NT Registry, various keys and their values are grouped together and stored in a single file. This file is called a hive. All of the Windows NT Registry hives are stored in the `<winntroot>\System32\Config` folder.

Table 21-3 shows the six hives and their respective Windows NT Registry locations.

TABLE 21-3 WINDOWS NT REGISTRY HIVES

HIVE FILE NAME	LOCATION IN THE REGISTRY
SAM	HKEY_LOCAL_MACHINE\SAM
Security	HKEY_LOCAL_MACHINE\Security
Software	HKEY_LOCAL_MACHINE\Software
System	HKEY_LOCAL_MACHINE\System and HKEY_CURRENT_CONFIG
Ntuser.dat	HKEY_CURRENT_USER
Default	HKEY_USERS\.DEFAULT

Now that you've got a basic understanding of the Windows NT Registry structure, you're almost ready to begin using the Registry editors. But first, it's important to back up the Registry before you use a Registry editor to modify it.

Backing Up the Registry

Always back up the Registry before you use the Registry editors to modify it — if you don't, you could end up with a system that won't boot.

There are three primary tools you can use to back up the Windows NT Registry:

- The Windows NT Backup program
- The Regback.exe utility (included in the *Microsoft Windows NT Workstation Resource Kit)*
- The Rdisk.exe utility

When you back up the Registry using the Windows NT Backup program, you must choose to back up at least one file on the boot partition, and you must select the check box next to the Backup Local Registry option.

When you back up the Registry using the `Rdisk.exe` utility, two backup copies are made. First, `Rdisk` makes a backup copy of the Registry and stores it in the `<winntroot>\Repair` folder. Then `Rdisk` prompts you to insert a floppy disk (which will become the Emergency Repair Disk) and copies the contents of the `<winntroot>\Repair` folder to the floppy disk. This process is known as *updating the Emergency Repair Disk*. Be sure to update your computer's Emergency Repair Disk every time you make a successful configuration change to your Windows NT computer.

 tip

Always run `Rdisk` using the `/s` switch, because using this switch will cause the `SAM` and `Security` hives to be backed up. If you *don't* use the `/s` switch, these two hives won't be backed up.

 in the real world

It's a good idea to write the Administrator's current password on the Emergency Repair Disk when you create or update this disk. The reason for this practice is when you restore the Registry from the Emergency Repair Disk, Emergency Repair replaces whatever the Administrator's current password is with the password that was in effect when the Emergency Repair Disk was created or last updated. If the password has changed since that time, and the old password isn't written down or remembered, the Administrator won't be able to log on after the Registry is restored.

Searching the Registry

Now that you understand the structure of the Windows NT Registry and the importance of backing it up before you modify it, you can begin using the Registry editors to search and modify the Registry.

As mentioned previously, there are two primary tools you can use to edit the Windows NT Registry: the Windows NT Registry Editor (`regedt32.exe`) and the Windows 95 Registry Editor (`regedit.exe`).

I recommend you use the Windows 95 Registry Editor (`regedit.exe`) for searching the Windows NT Registry, because this editor can search the Registry by key, by value, or by the data contained in the value. As a Registry search tool, I find this editor more effective than the Windows NT Registry Editor, which can only search the Registry by key. You can manually wade your way through the various Registry folders and subfolders by using the Windows NT Registry Editor, and you can use this editor to modify any Registry value — it's just more cumbersome to use as a search tool than the Windows 95 Registry Editor.

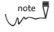 **note**   **While the Windows 95 Registry Editor is a better search tool, the Windows NT Registry Editor has a couple of features not included in the Windows 95 version, including the capability to connect to and edit a remote Windows NT computer's Registry, and the capability to set security on various Registry keys.**

Suppose that you recently bought a used computer that came with Windows NT installed. You want to change the Registry so that your name (not the previous owner's) is displayed as the registered owner. You are unsure where in the Registry this data is stored. However, you know the previous owner's name.

In this example, you could use the Windows 95 Registry Editor (`regedit. exe`) to search and modify the Registry.

To access the Windows 95 Registry Editor, select Start ⇒ Run. Type **regedit** in the Open drop-down list box in the Run dialog box, as shown in Figure 21-16, and click OK.

FIGURE 21-16   Starting the Windows 95 Registry Editor

The Registry Editor dialog box appears, as shown in Figure 21-17. Notice the various subtrees displayed in this dialog box.

 note   **Notice the HKEY_DYN_DATA subtree in the Registry Editor dialog box. This subtree only exists on Windows 95 computers. So, while this subtree is shown, it can't be opened when editing a Windows NT Registry.**

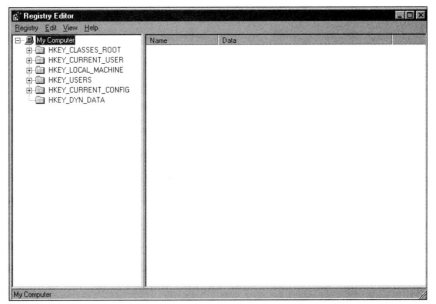

FIGURE 21-17 The Windows 95 Registry Editor dialog box

Now that the Registry Editor is started, you can use it to search the Registry for the previous owner's name.

 tip **The following example shows you how to search the Windows NT Registry for values that contain the previous owner's name.** *However, you can use these same steps to search the Registry for any key, value, or data.*

TO SEARCH THE WINDOWS NT REGISTRY, FOLLOW THESE STEPS:

1. Select Edit ⇒ Find in the Registry Editor dialog box.

2. The Find dialog box appears, as shown in Figure 21-18. Notice that three check boxes give you the option of searching by keys, values, and/or data. (You can select any or all of these options.) Type in the previous owner's name in the "Find what" text box, and click the Find Next command button.

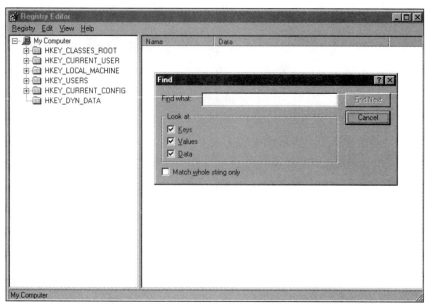

FIGURE 21-18   Configuring the search parameters

3. Registry Editor searches the Registry. Registry Editor displays the first
instance of the previous owner's name, as shown in Figure 21-19. Notice
that the complete path to the key that contains this value is shown across
the bottom of the Registry Editor dialog box.

FIGURE 21-19   Registry Editor displays search results

If you want to edit the displayed value, double-click the value and edit the value's data in the Edit String dialog box that appears. Figure 21-20 shows the Edit String dialog box. Click OK when you're finished.

FIGURE 21-20   Editing a value in Registry Editor

4. The Registry Editor dialog box reappears. To search for additional instances of the previous owner's name, select Edit ⇒ Find Next. Registry Editor searches the Registry again and displays the next instance it finds of the previous owner's name.

5. Repeat Steps 3 and 4 as needed to replace all instances of the previous owner's name.

6. Exit Registry Editor when your search is completed.

Another common type of search that is performed in Registry Editor is a search for a specific service or driver, with the intent of determining the service and group dependencies of that service or driver. The next section explains how to perform such a search, and how to determine the dependencies of the service or driver.

Finding service and group dependencies

As mentioned previously, *service dependencies* show which services and drivers must be running before a particular service (or driver) can start. *Group dependencies* show which groups of services or drivers must be running before the service (or driver) in question can start. For troubleshooting purposes, once you have determined what the service and group dependencies for a particular service (or driver) are, you can then verify that all of these services and drivers (that are required to be running *before* a particular service or driver can start) are, in fact, running.

The easiest way to determine a particular service's or driver's service and group dependencies is using the Services tab in Windows NT Diagnostics, as described earlier in this chapter.

That said, you can search the Windows NT Registry to locate a particular service or driver for the purpose of determining that service's or driver's service and group dependencies.

Although you can use either Registry editor to find dependencies, only the Windows NT Registry Editor (`regedt32.exe`) presents this information in a usable format. (The Windows 95 Registry Editor presents service and group dependencies in hexadecimal format.)

If you don't know the name of the Registry key that is used to store a particular service's or driver's information, you can use the Windows 95 Registry Editor to find the key in the Registry, and then use the Windows NT Registry Editor to view the data. For example, you probably wouldn't think to look for Registry entries for the WINS Client (TCP/IP) service in a key named NetBT, but that's exactly where they are. If you didn't know this up front, you'd have to use the Windows 95 Registry Editor to determine the name of the key in which this service's entries are stored before using the Windows NT Registry Editor to view the specific data.

All service and driver Registry entries are stored in subkeys of `HKEY_LOCAL_MACHINE\System\CurrentControlSet\Services`.

Suppose you want to use a Registry editor to determine service and group dependencies of the Messenger service. (You want to do this because Event Viewer indicates that the Messenger service failed to start because a dependency service of the Messenger service was not running.)

**TO USE THE WINDOWS NT REGISTRY EDITOR TO DETERMINE SERVICE
AND GROUP DEPENDENCIES, FOLLOW THESE STEPS:**

1. Start the Windows NT Registry Editor by selecting Start ⇒ Run from the
desktop, and by then typing **regedt32** in the Open drop-down list box in
the Run dialog box. Then click OK.

2. If the HKEY_LOCAL_MACHINE window is not displayed, select Window ⇒
HKEY_LOCAL_MACHINE on Local Machine.

3. The HKEY_LOCAL_MACHINE window is displayed. Double-click the SYSTEM
folder. Double-click the CurrentControlSet folder. Double-click the
Services folder.

4. Highlight the service or driver for which you want to determine service
and group dependencies. In the example, this is the Messenger service.
Various Registry entries for the highlighted service or driver are displayed
on the right-hand side of the window, as shown in Figure 21-21. Notice
the DependOnGroup and DependOnService entries.

FIGURE 21-21   Viewing the Messenger service's Registry entries

You can ignore the REG_MULTI_SZ: portion of the DependOnGroup and
DependOnService entries — REG_MULTI_SZ just identifies the type of data
that will be placed in the Registry, in this case, multiple string values.

In this example, notice that the Messenger service's DependOnGroup entry does not contain any data (other than the ignored REG_MULTI_SZ). This means this service has no group dependencies.

Also notice that the Messenger's service DependOnService entry lists the LanmanWorkstation and NetBios services as its service dependencies. This means the Messenger service will not start if the LanmanWorkstation (Workstation) and the NetBios services are not running.

5. When you've finished determining a service's dependencies, exit Registry Editor.

KEY POINT SUMMARY

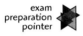
exam
preparation
pointer

Many of the topics in this chapter are very dry. Hopefully you will not need to use this information very often. However, you should study this entire chapter carefully before you take the Server exam.

Chapter 21 covered advanced troubleshooting topics, including solutions to common boot sequence problems, how and when to use the Event Viewer and Windows NT diagnostics, and how to search and modify the Registry.

o The *boot sequence* refers to the process of starting Windows NT, including initializing all of its services and completing the logon process. To successfully troubleshoot problems that can occur during this process, you need an understanding of the steps that occur during the boot sequence. The steps in the Windows NT boot sequence (for the Intel platform only) are:

  o Power On Self Test (POST)

  o Initial Startup

  o Selecting an operating system

  o Detecting hardware

  o Selecting hardware profile (or Last Known Good Configuration) and loading the kernel

  o Kernel initialization

  o Initializing device drivers

  o Initializing services

o Logon process

o Table 21-1, *Troubleshooting the Windows NT Boot Sequence*, lists many common problems that can occur during the boot sequence, along with their possible causes and recommended solutions. Refer to this table now and review it. Review it again just before taking the Server exam. Note that the Emergency Repair process is part of many solutions to boot sequence problems.

o The *Emergency Repair process* involves using the Windows NT Setup Boot Disk set, the Windows NT compact disc, and the Emergency Repair disk created during (or after) the installation process to repair a damaged or corrupt Windows NT installation. There are four different repair options in the Emergency Repair Process. You can select one or more of these options: Inspect Registry files, Inspect startup environment, Verify Windows NT system files, and Inspect boot sector.

o *Event Viewer* is a Windows NT administrative tool used to view the system, security, and application logs. When a Service Control Manager warning message is displayed during bootup, indicating that a service or driver failed to start, you can use the Event Viewer System Log to determine which service or driver failed, and to view a detailed description of the failure. When examining stop errors in the System Log, it's usually most efficient to examine the event that took place first — the last event in the list — first. Solving the oldest error often solves all other errors listed.

o *Windows NT Diagnostics* is a Windows NT administrative tool that enables you to view detailed system configuration information and statistics. This tool can help you troubleshoot system configuration problems and also help you determine service and device driver dependencies. The Services tab in Windows NT Diagnostics is particularly useful for determining service and group dependencies for a specific service or driver.

o *Registry editors* are tools that enable you to search and modify the Windows NT Registry. There are two primary tools for editing the Windows NT Registry: the Windows NT Registry Editor (regedt32.exe) and the Windows 95 Registry Editor (regedit.exe). Before getting into the specifics of how to use the Registry editors, it's helpful to have a basic understanding of how the Windows NT Registry is structured.

- The Windows NT Registry is a database that contains all of the information required to correctly configure an individual Windows NT computer, its user accounts, and applications. The Registry is organized in a tree structure consisting of five subtrees and their keys and value entries. The five subtrees of the Registry are HKEY_LOCAL_MACHINE, HKEY_CURRENT_USER, HKEY_CURRENT_CONFIG, HKEY_CLASSES_ROOT, and HKEY_USERS. The HKEY_LOCAL_MACHINE subtree is the most helpful subtree in terms of troubleshooting because it contains most of the service and driver configuration information for the operating system.

- *Always* back up the Registry before you use the Registry editors to modify it. You can use the Windows NT Backup program, the Regback.exe utility, or the Rdisk.exe utility to back up the Registry on your Windows NT computer. If you use Rdisk, always run this utility using the /s switch, so that the SAM and Security hives will be backed up.

- Use the Windows 95 Registry Editor to search the Registry, because this editor can search the Registry by key, by value, or by the data contained in the value. The Windows NT Registry, on the other hand, can only search the Registry by key. To access the Windows 95 Registry Editor, select Start ⇒ Run from the desktop. Then type **regedit** in the Open drop-down list box in the Run dialog box, and click OK.

- *Service dependencies* show which services and drivers must be running before a particular service (or driver) can start. *Group dependencies* show which groups of services or drivers must be running before the service (or driver) in question can start. For troubleshooting purposes, once you have determined what the service and group dependencies for a particular service (or driver) are, you can then verify that all of these services and drivers (that are required to be running *before* a particular service or driver can start) are, in fact, running.

- The easiest way to determine a particular service's or driver's service and group dependencies is to use Windows NT Diagnostics. However, you can also determine dependencies by using the Windows NT Registry Editor (regedt32.exe). To access the Windows NT Registry Editor, select Start ⇒ Run from the desktop. Then type **regedt32** in the Open drop-down list box in the Run dialog box, and click OK.

- All service and driver Registry entries are stored in subkeys of `HKEY_LOCAL_MACHINE\System\CurrentControlSet\Services`

APPLYING WHAT YOU'VE LEARNED

Now it's time to regroup, review, and apply what you've learned in this chapter.

The review questions in the following Instant Assessment section bring to mind key facts and concepts. Then, the Hands-on Lab reinforces what you've learned and provides an opportunity for you to practice some of the tasks that may be tested by the Server exam.

Instant Assessment

1. Briefly list the nine major steps in the Windows NT boot sequence.

2. Your Windows NT computer crashes during a power outage. When you reboot the computer, a blue screen is displayed during the boot sequence. What is the most likely cause of this problem, and what should you do to resolve it?

3. You make several configuration changes and then reboot your Windows NT computer. A blue screen is displayed during the boot sequence. What is the most likely cause of this problem, and what should you do to resolve it?

4. What does the Emergency Repair process involve?

5. You receive a Service Control Manager warning message that indicates that a service or device driver failed during system startup. Which Windows NT administrative tool should you use to obtain more information about the failure?

6. When using the System Log in Event Viewer for troubleshooting, for which stop error should you view the Event Detail first?

7. What are service dependencies and group dependencies?

8. Which tab in Windows NT Diagnostics is useful for determining service and group dependencies for a specific service or driver?

9. Name the two Registry editors.

10. When you are troubleshooting Windows NT, which subtree in the Registry should you normally check first?

11. What should you always do to the Registry before you modify it?

12. Which switch must you use with the Rdisk utility if you want the SAM and Security hives to be backed up?

13. Which of the two Registry editors is a better tool for searching the Registry, and why?

14. Which of the two Registry editors is more useful for viewing the service and group dependencies of a particular service?

 concept link   **For answers to the Instant Assessment questions see Appendix B.**

Hands-on Lab

The following Hands-on Lab provides you with a practical opportunity to apply the Windows NT troubleshooting knowledge you've gained in this chapter.

Lab 21.31 *Troubleshooting Windows NT*

The purpose of this lab is to give you experience in using advanced Windows NT troubleshooting techniques.

This lab consists of two parts:

Part 1: Using Windows NT Diagnostics

Part 2: Using the Registry editors

Begin this lab by booting your computer to Windows NT Server. Log on as Administrator.

Follow these instructions carefully.

Part 1: Using Windows NT Diagnostics

In this section you use Windows NT Diagnostics to examine your Windows NT Server system configuration and to view service dependencies and group dependencies.

1. Select Start ⇒ Programs ⇒ Administrative Tools (Common) ⇒ Windows NT Diagnostics.

2. The Windows NT Diagnostics dialog box appears. Click the System tab.

3. The System tab appears. Notice the BIOS and CPU information displayed on this tab. Click the Display tab.

4. The Display tab appears. Notice the display adapter and driver settings. Click the Drives tab.

5. The Drives tab appears. Click the + sign next to Local hard drives. Highlight drive D: (or the letter of your NTFS drive, if not D:). Click the Properties command button.

6. The Properties dialog box appears. Notice the statistics on the number of bytes free, used, and total that are presented. Click OK. Click the Memory tab.

7. The Memory tab appears. Notice the memory and pagefile statistics displayed. Click the Network tab.

8. The Network tab appears. Notice the various network information that is displayed. Click the Statistics command button. Notice the statistics that are displayed. These statistics are not updated automatically—you must click the Refresh command button to update these statistics. Click the Resources tab.

9. The Resources tab appears. Notice that you can obtain Interrupt (IRQ), I/O Port, DMA, and memory information on this tab. Click the Devices command button. Double-click Floppy (or any other device listed) in the Device list box.

10. The Floppy Properties (or other device that you selected Properties) dialog box appears. Notice the resource settings displayed. Click OK. Click the Services tab.

11. The Services tab appears. Click the Devices command button.

12. In the Device list box, scroll down and double-click Parallel.

13. The Parallel Properties dialog box appears. Click the Dependencies tab.

14. The Dependencies tab appears. Notice the Service Dependencies and Group Dependencies listed. In the space provided, write down the following, as shown on your monitor:

Service Dependencies:_____

Group Dependencies:_____

Click OK.

15. The Services tab reappears. Click the Services command button.

16. Double-click the Server service.

17. The Server Properties dialog box appears. Click the Dependencies tab.

18. The Dependencies tab appears.

In the space provided, write down the following, as shown on your monitor:

Service Dependencies:_____

Group Dependencies:_____

Click OK.

19. The Services tab reappears. Click OK. Proceed to Part 2.

Part 2: Using the Registry editors

In this section you use the `Regedit.exe` and `Regedt32.exe` Registry Editors to search the Registry and to view service dependencies and group dependencies.

1. Select Start ⇒ Run.

2. The Run dialog box appears. In the Open drop-down list box, type **regedit** and click OK. (This starts the Windows 95 Registry Editor.)

3. The Registry Editor dialog box appears. Select Edit ⇒ Find.

4. The Find dialog box appears. In the Find what text box, type **WINS Client**. Ensure that the check boxes next to Keys, Values, and Data are checked. Click the Find Next command button.

5. Registry Editor searches the Registry. (This may take a few minutes.) The Registry Editor dialog box reappears. Notice that the Title value is highlighted on the right-hand side of the screen. Also notice that the Registry location of the highlighted value is displayed across the bottom of the dialog box.

6. Select Edit ⇒ Find Next.

7. Registry Editor searches the Registry. The Registry Editor dialog box reappears. Notice that a different value, DeviceDesc, is highlighted. Again, notice that the Registry location of this value is displayed across the bottom of the dialog box.

8. Exit Registry Editor.

9. Select Start ⇒ Run.

10. The Run dialog box appears. In the Open drop-down list box, type **regedt32** and click OK. (This starts the Windows NT Registry Editor.)

11. The Registry Editor dialog box appears. Select Window ⇒ HKEY_LOCAL_MACHINE on Local Machine.

12. Maximize the Registry Editor dialog box and the HKEY_LOCAL_MACHINE on Local Machine window.

13. Double-click the `SYSTEM` folder.

14. Double-click the `CurrentControlSet` folder.

15. Double-click the `Services` folder.

16. Scroll down and highlight the `Parallel` folder. Notice the DependOnGroup and DependOnService entries on the right-hand side of the dialog box.

In the space provided, write down the entries that follow these values: (You can ignore the REG_MULTI_SZ: portion of the entries—this just identifies the type of data that will be placed in the Registry, in this case, multiple string values.)

DependOnGroup:_____

DependOnService:_____

Notice that the DependOnGroup and DependOnService values are the same as the Group Dependencies and Service Dependencies that you found using Windows NT Diagnostics in Step 14 in Part 1 of this lab.

17. On the left side of the Registry Editor dialog box, scroll up and highlight the `LanmanServer` folder. Notice the DependOnGroup and DependOnService entries on the right-hand side of the dialog box.

In the space provided, write down the entries that follow these values: (You can ignore the REG_MULTI_SZ: portion of the entries.)

DependOnGroup:_____

DependOnService:_____

Notice that the DependOnGroup and DependOnService values are the same as the Group Dependencies and Service Dependencies that you found using Windows NT Diagnostics in Step 18 in Part 1 of this lab.

Also notice the DisplayName value on the right-hand side of the dialog box. The LanmanServer service is the same as the Server service.

18. Exit Registry Editor.

Resources

Exam Objectives

This appendix consists of three parts:

- The first part contains vital information about Exam 70-067: Implementing and Supporting Microsoft Windows NT Server 4.0. It outlines the credit toward certification that a passing score on this exam earns, the real-world skills being measured by the exam, and a complete list of the exam's objectives.

- The second part lists the basic facts for this exam, including the number of questions, passing score, and time allowed to take the exam.

- The third part is an exhaustive exam objectives cross-reference chart for study purposes. Every exam objective is linked to the corresponding materials (text and labs) in this book.

EXAM CREDIT, SKILLS MEASURED, AND OBJECTIVES

 This section contains portions of Microsoft's *Preparation Guide for Exam 70-067: Implementing and Supporting Microsoft Windows NT Server 4.0* (Microsoft Corporation, 1998).

 This exam information is current as of the date this book went to press, but is subject to change by Microsoft at any time. You can ensure that you have the most current version of this exam's objectives by accessing the Microsoft Training and Certification Web site at: http://www.microsoft.com/train_cert/

Credit Toward Certification

When you pass this exam, you achieve Microsoft Certified Professional status. You also earn core credit toward Microsoft Certified Systems Engineer certification and core credit toward Microsoft Certified Systems Engineer + Internet certification.

Skills Being Measured

This certification exam measures your ability to implement, administer, and troubleshoot information systems that incorporate Windows NT Server version 4.0 in a simple computing environment. A simple computing environment is typically a homogeneous LAN. It might include one or more servers, a single domain, and a single location; and it might have file-sharing and print-sharing capabilities. Before taking the exam, you should be proficient in the following job skills.

Exam Objectives

Planning

Plan the disk drive configuration for various requirements. Requirements include:

- Choosing a file system
- Choosing a fault-tolerance method

Choose a protocol for various situations. Protocols include:

- o TCP/IP
- o NWLink IPX/SPX Compatible Transport
- o NetBEUI

Installation and Configuration

Install Windows NT Server on Intel-based platforms.

Install Windows NT Server to perform various server roles. Server roles include:

- o Primary domain controller
- o Backup domain controller
- o Member server

Install Windows NT Server by using various methods. Installation methods include:

- o CD-ROM
- o Over-the-network
- o Network Client Administrator
- o Express versus custom

Configure protocols and protocol bindings. Protocols include:

- o TCP/IP
- o NWLink IPX/SPX Compatible Transport
- o NetBEUI

Configure network adapters. Considerations include:

- o Changing IRQ, IObase, and memory addresses
- o Configuring multiple adapters

Configure Windows NT Server core services. Services include:

- o Directory Replicator
- o License Manager
- o Other services

Configure peripherals and devices. Peripherals and devices include:
- Communication devices
- SCSI devices
- Tape device drivers
- UPS devices and UPS service
- Mouse drivers, display drivers, and keyboard drivers

Configure hard disks to meet various requirements. Requirements include:
- Allocating disk space capacity
- Providing redundancy
- Improving performance
- Providing security
- Formatting

Configure printers. Tasks include:
- Adding and configuring a printer
- Implementing a printer pool
- Setting print priorities

Configure a Windows NT Server computer for various types of client computers. Client computer types include:
- Windows NT Workstation
- Microsoft Windows 95
- Microsoft MS-DOS-based

Managing Resources

Manage user and group accounts. Considerations include:
- Managing Windows NT user accounts
- Managing Windows NT user rights
- Managing Windows NT groups
- Administering account policies
- Auditing changes to the user account database

Create and manage policies and profiles for various situations. Policies and profiles include:

- Local user profiles

- Roaming user profiles

- System policies

Administer remote servers from various types of client computers. Client computer types include:

- Windows 95

- Windows NT Workstation

Manage disk resources. Tasks include:

- Copying and moving files between file systems

- Creating and sharing resources

- Implementing permissions and security

- Establishing file auditing

Connectivity

Configure Windows NT Server for interoperability with NetWare servers by using various tools. Tools include:

- Gateway Service for NetWare

- Migration Tool for NetWare

Install and configure Remote Access Service (RAS). Configuration options include:

- Configuring RAS communications

- Configuring RAS protocols

- Configuring RAS security

- Configuring Dial-Up Networking clients

Monitoring and Optimization

Monitor performance of various functions by using Performance Monitor. Functions include:

- Processor

- Memory

- Disk

- Network

Identify performance bottlenecks.

Troubleshooting

Choose the appropriate course of action to take to resolve installation failures.

Choose the appropriate course of action to take to resolve boot failures.

Choose the appropriate course of action to take to resolve configuration errors.

Choose the appropriate course of action to take to resolve printer problems.

Choose the appropriate course of action to take to resolve RAS problems.

Choose the appropriate course of action to take to resolve connectivity problems.

Choose the appropriate course of action to take to resolve resource access problems and permission problems.

Choose the appropriate course of action to take to resolve fault-tolerance failures. Fault-tolerance methods include:

- Tape backup

- Mirroring

- Stripe set with parity

- Disk duplexing

EXAM FACTS

Number of questions on this exam:	55
Passing score:	764
Time allowed to take exam:	90 minutes

EXAM OBJECTIVES CROSS-REFERENCE CHART

Table A-1 lists the stated objectives for Exam 70-067, Implementing and Supporting Microsoft Windows NT Server 4.0, in a cross-reference chart for study purposes. For each and every exam objective, you can see exactly where in this book the objective is covered.

TABLE A-1 IMPLEMENTING AND SUPPORTING MICROSOFT WINDOWS NT SERVER 4.0 EXAM OBJECTIVES CROSS-REFERENCE CHART

EXAM OBJECTIVE	CHAPTER(S)	SECTION(S)	LAB(S)
Planning			
Plan the disk drive configuration for various requirements. Requirements include: ○ Choosing a file system ○ Choosing a fault-tolerance method	Chapter 5 — Configuring Disks	File Systems (and all subsections) Working with Partitions (and all subsections)	Lab 5.7 File System Planning Exercise Lab 5.8 Disk Partitioning and Fault Tolerance Planning Exercise
Choose a protocol for various situations. Protocols include: ○ TCP/IP ○ NWLink IPX/SPX Compatible Transport ○ NetBEUI	Chapter 2 — Installing Windows NT Server Chapter 3 — Using Control Panel	Network Protocols Protocols and Services (and all subsections)	

continued

TABLE A-1 *(continued)*

Exam Objective	Chapter(s)	Section(s)	Lab(s)
	Chapter 14 — Networking Using TCP/IP	Overview of TCP/IP	
	Chapter 15 — Coexistence with NetWare	Windows NT in a NetWare Environment NWLink IPX/SPX Compatible Transport	
Installation and Configuration			
Install Windows NT Server on Intel-based platforms.	Chapter 2 — Installing Windows NT Server	Hardware Requirements for Installation Information Required to Install Windows NT Server (and all subsections) The Installation Process	Lab 2.2 Installing Windows NT Server
Install Windows NT Server to perform various server roles. Server roles include: o Primary domain controller o Backup domain controller o Member server	Chapter 2 — Installing Windows NT Server Chapter 3 — Using Control Panel	Server Type Phase 1 Changing the Computer/Domain Name of a Domain Controller Changing the Computer/Domain/ Workgroup Name of a Stand-Alone or Member Server Joining a Domain	Lab 2.2 Installing Windows NT Server
Install Windows NT Server by using various methods. Installation methods include:	Chapter 2 — Installing Windows NT Server	The Installation Process (and all subsections)	Lab 2.2 Installing Windows NT Server

EXAM OBJECTIVE	CHAPTER(S)	SECTION(S)	LAB(S)
o CD-ROM o Over-the-network o Network Client Administrator o Express versus custom	Chapter 7 — Configuring Windows NT Server for Client Computers	What Is Server-Based Deployment? Preparing for Server-Based Deployment Using Network Client Administrator (and all subsections)	
Configure protocols and protocol bindings. Protocols include: o TCP/IP o NWLink IPX/SPX Compatible Transport o NetBEUI	Chapter 3 — Using Control Panel	Protocols and Services Planning for Protocols and Services Installing and Configuring Protocols and Services Configuring Bindings and Network Access Order	
	Chapter 14 — Networking Using TCP/IP	IP Addressing (and all subsections) Assigning IP Addresses (and all subsections)	
	Chapter 15 — Coexistence with NetWare	Installing and Configuring NWLink IPX/SPX Compatible Transport	Lab 15.26 Installing and Configuring NWLink and Gateway Service for NetWare
Configure network adapters. Considerations include: o Changing IRQ, IObase, and memory addresses	Chapter 3 — Using Control Panel	Configuring Network Adapters	Lab 2.2 Installing Windows NT Server

continued

TABLE A-1 *(continued)*

Exam Objective	Chapter(s)	Section(s)	Lab(s)
o Configuring multiple adapters			
Configure Windows NT Server core services. Services include: o Directory Replicator o License Manager o Other services	Chapter 3 — Using Control Panel Chapter 4 — Browsing and the Computer Browser Service	Licensing Configuring Directory Replication Configuring the Computer Browser Service	Lab 3.4 Configuring Directory Replication Lab 4.6 Configuring the Computer Browser Service
Configure peripherals and devices. Peripherals and devices include: o Communication devices o SCSI devices o Tape device drivers o UPS devices and UPS service o Mouse drivers, display drivers, and keyboard drivers	Chapter 3 — Using Control Panel	Managing Peripherals and Devices (and all subsections)	Lab 3.5 Exploring Control Panel
Configure hard disks to meet various requirements. Requirements include: o Allocating disk space capacity o Providing redundancy o Improving performance o Providing security o Formatting	Chapter 5 — Configuring Disks	File Systems (and all subsections) Working with Partitions (and all subsections)	Lab 5.9 Managing Partitions
Configure printers. Tasks include: o Adding and configuring a printer o Implementing a printer pool	Chapter 6 Managing Printing	Creating and Connecting to Printers (and all subsections)	

Exam Objective	Chapter(s)	Section(s)	Lab(s)
o Setting print priorities		Print Monitors (and all subsections) Configuring Print Server Properties (and all subsections) Configuring Printer Properties (and all subsections)	Lab 6.12 Creating and Sharing a Local Printer Lab 6.13 Installing and Configuring Microsoft TCP/IP Printing
Configure a Windows NT Server computer for various types of client computers. Client computer types include: o Windows NT Workstation o Microsoft Windows 95 o Microsoft MS-DOS-based	Chapter 7 – Configuring Windows NT Server for Client Computers	What Is Server-Based Deployment? Preparing for Server-Based Deployment Using Network Client Administrator (and all subsections)	
Managing Resources			
Manage user and group accounts. Considerations include: o Managing Windows NT user accounts o Managing Windows NT user rights o Managing Windows NT groups o Administering account policies o Auditing changes to the user account database	Chapter 8 – Managing User and Group Accounts Chapter 9 – Managing Account Policy, User Rights, and Auditing	All Sections All Sections	Lab 8.14 Creating and Managing User and Group Accounts Lab 9.15 Implementing Auditing

continued

TABLE A-1 *(continued)*

Exam Objective	Chapter(s)	Section(s)	Lab(s)
Create and manage policies and profiles for various situations. Policies and profiles include: o Local user profiles o Roaming user profiles o System policies	Chapter 10 — Managing User Profiles and System Policy	Managing User Profiles (and all subsections) Managing System Policy (and all subsections)	Lab 10.17 Implementing User Profiles Lab 10.18 Configuring a System Policy
Administer remote servers from various types of client computers. Client computer types include: o Windows 95 o Windows NT Workstation	Chapter 11 — Administering Servers from Client Computers	All Sections	Lab 11.19 Installing Client-based Network Administration Tools
Manage disk resources. Tasks include: o Copying and moving files between file systems o Creating and sharing resources o Implementing permissions and security o Establishing file auditing	Chapter 12 — Sharing and Securing File Systems	Managing File and Folder Attributes Managing Shared Folders (and all subsections) Managing NTFS File and Folder Security (and all subsections) Planning Strategies for Sharing and Securing Resources (and all subsections) Taking Ownership of Files and Folders Auditing Files and Folders on NTFS Partitions (and all subsections)	Lab 12.21 Sharing and Securing Resources Lab 12.22 Establishing File and Folder Auditing

Exam Objective	Chapter(s)	Section(s)	Lab(s)
Connectivity			
Configure Windows NT Server for interoperability with NetWare servers by using various tools. Tools include: ○ Gateway Service for NetWare ○ Migration Tool for NetWare	Chapter 15 – Coexistence with NetWare	Windows NT in a NetWare Environment NWLink IPX/SPX Compatible Transport (and all subsections) Gateway Service for NetWare (GSNW) (and all subsections) Using GSNW to Access Resources on NetWare Servers	Lab 15.26 Installing and Configuring NWLink and Gateway Service for NetWare
	Chapter 16 – Migrating to Windows NT from NetWare	All Sections	
Install and configure Remote Access Service (RAS). Configuration options include: ○ Configuring RAS communications ○ Configuring RAS protocols ○ Configuring RAS security ○ Configuring Dial–Up Networking clients	Chapter 17 – Installing and Configuring Remote Access Service (RAS)	RAS Overview (and all subsections) Installing and Configuring RAS (and all subsections) Using Remote Access Admin to Manage the RAS Server (and all subsections) Configuring Dial–Up Networking Connections (and all subsections) Configuring Dial–Up Networking to Connect to the Internet Configuring PPTP Security	Lab 17.28 Installing and Configuring RAS and Dial–Up Networking

continued

TABLE A-1 *(continued)*

EXAM OBJECTIVE	CHAPTER(S)	SECTION(S)	LAB(S)
Monitoring and Optimization			
Monitor performance of various functions by using Performance Monitor. Functions include: ○ Processor ○ Memory ○ Disk ○ Network	Chapter 18 – Using Performance Monitor	All Sections	Lab 18.29 Using Performance Monitor
Identify performance bottlenecks.	Chapter 19 – Performance Optimization	Identifying Bottlenecks Optimizing Performance and Resolving Bottlenecks (and all subsections)	Lab 19.30 Finding and Resolving Bottlenecks
Troubleshooting			
Choose the appropriate course of action to take to resolve installation failures.	Chapter 2 – Installing Windows NT Server	Troubleshooting Common Installation Problems	Lab 2.1 Troubleshooting Windows NT Installation Problems
Choose the appropriate course of action to take to resolve boot failures.	Chapter 21 – Advanced Troubleshooting	Troubleshooting the Boot Sequence (and all subsections)	
Choose the appropriate course of action to take to resolve configuration errors.	Chapter 3 – Using Control Panel	Troubleshooting Common Configuration Problems	
Choose the appropriate course of action to take to resolve printer problems.	Chapter 6 – Managing Printing	Troubleshooting Common Printing Problems	Lab 6.11 Windows NT Printing Troubleshooting Exercise

Exam Objective	*Chapter(s)*	*Section(s)*	*Lab(s)*
Choose the appropriate course of action to take to resolve RAS problems.	Chapter 17 – Installing and Configuring Remote Access Service (RAS)	Troubleshooting Common RAS Problems	Lab 17.27 Troubleshooting Common RAS Problems
Choose the appropriate course of action to take to resolve connectivity problems.	Chapter 14 – Networking Using TCP/IP	Troubleshooting Common TCP/IP Connectivity Problems	Lab 14.24 Identifying and Resolving TCP/IP Connectivity Problems
	Chapter 15 – Coexistence with NetWare	Troubleshooting Common NetWare Connectivity Problems	
Choose the appropriate course of action to take to resolve resource access problems and permission problems.	Chapter 12 – Sharing and Securing File Systems	Troubleshooting Common Resource Access and Permission Problems	Lab 12.20 Troubleshooting Resource Access and Permission Problems
Choose the appropriate course of action to take to resolve fault-tolerance failures. Fault-tolerance methods include: o Tape backup o Mirroring o Stripe set with parity o Disk duplexing	Chapter 5 – Configuring Disks	Recovering from Disk Failure (and all subsections) Updating the Emergency Repair Disk	Lab 5.10 Updating the Emergency Repair Disk
	Chapter 13 – Backing Up and Restoring Data	All Sections	Lab 13.23 Performing a Backup
	Chapter 21 – Advanced Troubleshooting	Performing the Emergency Repair Process Backing Up the Registry	

Answers to Instant Assessment Questions, Critical Thinking Labs, and Hands–on Labs

CHAPTER 1: OVERVIEW OF WINDOWS NT SERVER

Answers to Instant Assessment

1. On an Intel-based computer, the minimum hardware required to run Windows NT Server 4.0 is a 486/33 processor, 16MB of RAM, 124MB of free hard disk space, and a VGA graphics card.

2. Windows NT Server is optimized as a network file, print, and/or application server.

3. Workgroup

4. Domain

5. Kernel mode

6. A virtual memory model

7. See Figure B-1 for answers.

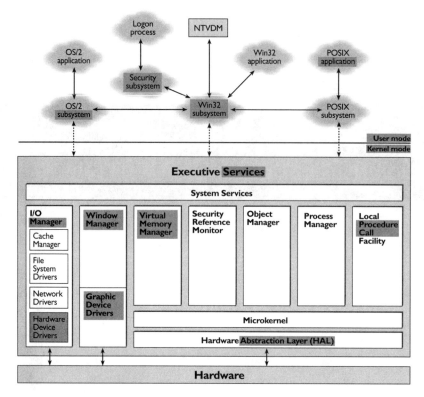

FIGURE B-1   Answers to Question 7: Microsoft Windows NT 4.0 modular
architecture activity

CHAPTER 2: INSTALLING WINDOWS NT SERVER

Answers to Instant Assessment

1. The HCL is the Windows NT Hardware Compatibility List.

2. 486/33 processor with 16MB of RAM and 124MB of free hard disk space

3. The NTHQ is the NT Hardware Qualifier utility. It is used to examine and
identify a computer's hardware configuration.

4. Windows NT 4.0 will automatically configure itself to dual boot between
Windows NT 4.0 and the previously installed operating system.

5. The system partition

6. The boot partition

7. FAT and NTFS

8. Windows NT

9. Winnt.exe

Answers to Critical Thinking Lab

Lab 2.1 *Troubleshooting Windows NT installation problems*

Problem 1   Some possible causes of this problem are hardware conflicts (or incompatibilities), a corrupt boot sector, or a boot sector virus.

Possible courses of action you could take to resolve this problem include using the NTHQ to examine your hardware configuration, checking for two pieces of hardware with the same settings (same I/O Port, interrupt, and so on) and reconfiguring hardware if conflicts are found, and repairing the boot sector by using `Fdisk/mbr` from MS-DOS or by using a virus detection utility.

Problem 2   Probably the most common cause of this problem is that the domain name or the Administrator's user account name or password has been typed incorrectly, or typed in the wrong case. *Remember that all passwords in Windows NT are case-sensitive*. Is the Caps Lock key on? Other possible causes of this problem are incorrect network hardware or software settings, a bad cable or connection, or a PDC that is inaccessible.

Possible courses of action you could take to resolve this problem include retyping the domain name, Administrator's user account name or password (making sure to use the proper case and making sure the Caps Lock key is turned off); and ensuring that all network hardware and software settings are correct. You might also check the network cable and connections and verify that the PDC is up and accessible on the network.

CHAPTER 3: USING CONTROL PANEL

Answers to Instant Assessment

1. Select Start ⇒ Settings ⇒ Control Panel, or Select Control Panel in Windows NT Explorer, or Open the My Computer dialog box, then double-click Control Panel.

2. The Accessibility Options application is used to configure the keyboard, sound, and mouse options on a computer to accommodate users that are physically challenged, including persons who have difficulty striking multiple keys simultaneously on a keyboard, persons with hearing disabilities, or persons who have difficulty holding or clicking a mouse.

3. Display

4. You must change the domain name of all other domain controllers member servers, and Windows NT Workstation computers in that domain to match the new domain name that you have assigned.

5. NWLink IPX/SPX Compatible Transport

6. AppleTalk Protocol

7. TCP/IP Protocol

8. The protocol and service used most often should be at the *top* of their respective lists.

9. Here are the four steps to configure the Directory Replicator service:

   o Create and configure a user account for the Directory Replicator service by using User Manager for Domains. This account must be a member of the Backup Operators group and the Replicator group. This user account must also be granted the "Log on as a service" user right, and must be configured so that its password never expires.

   o Configure the startup type of the Directory Replicator service as Automatic (by using the Services application). Configure the Directory Replicator service to log on using the user account created in Step 1.

- Configure replication by using the Server application. Remember that the PDC should be configured to replicate to itself.

- Stop and restart the Directory Replicator service by using the Services application.

10. At least as large as the amount of RAM in your computer

11. System

12. Make sure that all steps in a configuration process have been completed, verify that all configuration options are set correctly, and ensure that hardware devices do not have conflicting interrupt, I/O port address, or DMA addresses.

13. True

Answers to Critical Thinking Lab

Lab 3.3 *Control Panel application matching exercise*

The correct answers are

1. B

2. F

3. J

4. I

5. N

6. N

7. N

8. V

9. U

10. X

11. X

12. X

CHAPTER 4: BROWSING AND THE COMPUTER BROWSER SERVICE

Answers to Instant Assessment

1. The Computer Browser service

2. A browse list

3. Domain master browser, master browser, backup browser, potential browser, and non-browser

4. The PDC

5. One

6. Computers can be non-browsers either because they are configured to not function as a browser, or because their network software does not provide them with the capability to maintain a browse list.

7. How a browse list is built and maintained:

- When a master browser first comes online, its browse list is empty. To build its browse list initially, the master browser sends a broadcast to all computers on the subnet requesting that all network servers announce their presence. (Remember for the purpose of discussing browsing in this chapter, *network servers include all computers that either have shared resources or are capable of sharing their resources.*)

- All available network servers respond to this request by announcing their presence, within thirty seconds. The master browser incorporates this information into its initial browse list. The master browser then distributes this browse list to the domain master browser and to the backup browsers.

- After initial creation of the browse list, when a Windows computer that functions as a network server is first booted, it broadcasts its presence to the network. The master browser receives this announcement and places the information in its browse list.

- During normal operations, a Windows computer that functions as a network server continues to announce its presence to the network every 12 minutes. If the master browser does *not* receive a broadcast from a network server after three consecutive 12-minute time periods, it removes the computer from its browse list.

- (This is how the master browser maintains its browse list — it assumes that all network servers in its initial browse list are available until it fails to receive a broadcast announcement from a computer for three consecutive 12-minute periods, at which time it updates its browse list by removing this computer from its list. Therefore, it is possible for a network server to remain on the browse list for some time after it is no longer available to network users.)

- During normal operations, backup browsers request an updated browse list from the master browser every 12 minutes. If the master browser does not respond to an update request from the backup browser, the backup browser initiates the master browser election process (covered in more detail in the next section of this chapter).

- During normal operations, the master browser sends an updated browse list to the domain master browser every 12 minutes. The domain master browser, in response, sends an updated domain browse list to the master browser. Additionally, every 15 minutes, the master browser announces its presence to master browsers of other workgroups and domains located on the same subnet.

8. When a user browses the network

- When a user of a Windows NT computer attempts to access browse information by double-clicking Network Neighborhood or by selecting Tools ⇒ Map Network Drive in Windows NT Explorer, the user's computer contacts the master browser and retrieves a list of available backup browsers.

- (This step occurs only the first time a user accesses browse information — the Computer Browser service on the local computer then retains the list of available backup browsers until the computer is rebooted or until the backup browsers on the list are no longer available.)

o The user's computer then contacts a backup browser to request a list of available network servers. The backup browser processes this request and returns a list of available network servers in the requesting computer's workgroup or domain, plus a list of available workgroups and domains. The user's computer then displays this information to the user.

o If the user selects an available network server, the user's computer contacts the selected server and requests a list of shared network resources. The selected server then sends a list of shared resources to the requesting computer, which is then displayed for the user.

o If the user selects an available workgroup or domain, the user's computer contacts the master browser in the selected workgroup or domain and requests a browse list. The master browser sends a list of backup browsers for the workgroup or domain to the requesting computer. Then the user's computer contacts a backup browser in the selected workgroup or domain for a list of available network servers, which is then returned by the backup browser to the requesting computer and displayed for the user. The user then selects an available network server, and the user's computer contacts the selected server and requests a list of shared network resources. The selected server then sends a list of shared resources to the requesting computer, which is displayed for the user.

o The user selects the specific shared resource he or she wants to access from the list that is displayed.

9. Because the master browser does not remove a network server from its browse list until *after* it has failed to receive a broadcast announcement from the network server for three consecutive 12-minute periods, *it is possible for a network server to remain on the browse list for some time after it is no longer available to network users.* This could result in a situation where a user sees a resource on a browse list that is no longer available.

10. The master browser

11. The computer's election criteria value

12. The MaintainServerList entry, which is located in `\HKEY_LOCAL_MACHINE\SYSTEM\CurrentControlSet\Services\Browser\Parameters`

13. The IsDomainMaster entry, which is located in
`\HKEY_LOCAL_MACHINE\SYSTEM\CurrentControlSet\Services\`
`Browser\Parameters`

14. NetBIOS broadcasts

15. `LMHOSTS` files or a WINS server

16. `\\Server_name\Share_name\Subfolder_name\File_name`

17. `Server_name.Domain_name.Root_domain_name`

18. You can replace the `Server_name` in a UNC with an FQDN (if your network uses TCP/IP and DNS servers).

19. True

Chapter 5: Configuring Disks

Answers to Instant Assessment

1. The FAT (File Allocation Table) file system, the Windows NT file system (NTFS), and the Compact Disc Filing System (CDFS)

2. The FAT file system

3. Converting a FAT partition to NTFS

4. From the active primary partition on the first hard disk in the computer

5. On the active primary partition on the first hard disk in the computer

6. You can have up to four primary partitions on one disk, only one extended partition, and a maximum total of four partitions on a disk.

7. Disk Administrator

8. Disk mirroring

9. A fault tolerance boot disk is used to boot a computer after one hard disk in a mirrored set fails.

10. The boot loader section and the operating systems section

11. Stripe sets

12. Stripe sets and volume sets

13. Striping with parity, because it is faster and cheaper than disk mirroring, and provides a modest level of data safety

14. Disk mirroring

15. Rdisk.exe

16. Break the mirror

17. False

18. True

19. False

20. True

21. True

22. False

23. False

24. True

25. True

26. False

27. False

Answers to Critical Thinking Labs

Lab 5.7 *File system planning exercise*

Problem 1   The FAT file system is probably the best choice for this scenario, because it enables NT to access files on partitions smaller than 500MB faster than it could by using NTFS.

Problem 2   You must use the FAT file system in this situation in order to accommodate both NT and MS-DOS.

Problem 3   NTFS is probably the best choice for this scenario. NTFS usually provides faster access to files stored on a large partition that contains a large number of files than the FAT file system provides.

Problem 4   NTFS is the obvious choice for this scenario because it is the only file system supported by Windows NT 4.0 that provides the required file and folder security and also supports file compression.

Lab 5.8 Disk partitioning and fault tolerance planning exercise

Problem 1   Disk mirroring is the best answer because it provides the most fault tolerance of the four disk partitioning schemes.

Problem 2   A stripe set is the best answer because it provides the fastest access speed to files.

Problem 3   A stripe set with parity is the best choice, because it provides moderate fault tolerance and a moderate price tag.

CHAPTER 6: MANAGING PRINTING

Answers to Instant Assessment

1. A printer is the software interface between Windows NT and the device that produces the printed output.

2. A print (or printing) device is the physical hardware device that produces the printed output.

3. The spooler

4. Create, connect to

5. Print monitors

6. The TCP/IP print monitor

7. NWLink IPX/SPX Compatible Transport, plus Gateway Service for NetWare

8. Hpmon

9. A job-based connection enables all computers on the network to access an HP JetDirect adapter for printing, because the connection to the HP JetDirect adapter is dropped after each print job.

10. A continuous connection does not permit any other computer on the network to access an HP JetDirect adapter for printing, because the Hpmon print monitor monopolizes the HP JetDirect adapter when a continuous connection is used.

11. Hpmon

12. You can specify that a different folder on another partition (that has more free space) be used as your spool folder.

13. No Access

14. No Access, Print, Manage Documents, Full Control

15. You must select the Success and/or Failure check boxes for File and Object Access.

16. By creating a printer

    By taking ownership of a printer

17. A printer pool

18. The purpose of sharing a printer is to enable users of other computers on the network to connect to and send print jobs to that printer.

19. The advantage is that the network administrator is spared the time-consuming task of manually installing printer drivers on every computer on the network.

20. True

21. True

Answers to Critical Thinking Lab

Lab 6.11 *Windows NT printing troubleshooting exercise*

Problem 1   To reprint the entire print job

1. Immediately double-click the printer in the `Printers` folder.

2. When the printer's dialog box appears, select Document ⇒ Pause.

3. Make sure that the correct paper is in the paper tray.

4. Select Document ⇒ Restart to reprint the entire print job.

Problem 2   The most likely cause of this problem is that the success and failure options for auditing file and object access have not been configured in User Manager for Domains. Auditing of printers requires that auditing of file and object access be configured.

To solve the problem, configure these options in User Manager for Domains. Print events should begin to appear in the Security Log in Event Viewer.

Problem 3   The most likely cause of this problem is that the partition that contains the printer's spool folder doesn't have enough free space.

To solve the problem, you can delete some files from this partition, or move the spool folder to a different partition that has more free space.

CHAPTER 7: CONFIGURING WINDOWS NT SERVER FOR CLIENT COMPUTERS

Answers to Instant Assessment

1. Server-based deployment involves automating the installation and setup of Windows NT, other operating systems (Windows 95 and Windows for Workgroups), and applications on multiple computers on a network.

2. To save time

3. First, original equipment manufacturers (OEMs) use server-based deployment to install and configure large numbers of computers at the factory. Second, organizations that install a new network or add several new computers to their existing network use server-based deployment to efficiently perform these tasks.

4. The `Clients` folder

5. You must create a subfolder in the `Clients` folder named `Winnt`. Then you must create a subfolder in the `Clients\Winnt` folder named `Netsetup`.

6. You must create a subfolder in the `Clients` folder named `Winnt.srv`. Then you must create a subfolder in the `Clients\Winnt.srv` folder named `Netsetup`.

7. An installation disk set

8. A network installation startup disk

9. An answer file is a text file that contains stylized responses to the queries posed by the Windows NT Setup program during installation.

10. By using Windows NT Setup Manager (`Setupmgr.exe`)

11. The `/U` switch

12. Setup Manager is located on the Windows NT Server compact disc. You can find it in the `\Support\Deptools\I386` folder (on Intel-based computers).

13. Replace

14. You need a different answer file for each hardware configuration, so you need as many answer files as you have different hardware configurations.

15. The `$OEM$` subfolder

16. The answer file

17. When run with the `/snap` switch after Windows NT is installed but before any applications are installed, `Sysdiff.exe` takes a snapshot of a typical target computer's current configuration.

When run with the `/diff` switch after the desired application is installed, `Sysdiff.exe` creates a difference file that contains all of the application files and registry changes.

When run with the `/apply` switch from the `Cmdlines.txt` file, `Sysdiff.exe` applies the difference file during an unattended Windows NT installation.

CHAPTER 8: MANAGING USER AND GROUP ACCOUNTS

Answers to Instant Assessment

1. Administrator and Guest

2. User Manager for Domains

3. Use the first seven letters of the user's first name, plus the first letter of the user's last name.

Use the first letter of the user's first name, plus the first seven letters of the user's last name.

4. You can delete user-created groups, but you can't delete built-in or special groups.

5. Groups, Profile, Hours, Logon To, Account, and Dialin

6. `%USERNAME%`

7. Create a user account to be used as a template.

8. The primary purpose of local groups is to control access to resources.

The primary purpose of global groups is to organize users that perform similar tasks or have similar network access requirements.

9. Local groups can be created on any Windows NT computer.

A global group can only be created on a domain controller.

10. First, create a local group and assign the local group permission to the shared folder. Then, make individual user accounts and/or global groups members of the local group that you created. The result is that all members of the local group will have permission to the shared folder.

11. The built-in local groups on domain controllers are Administrators, Backup Operators, Guests, Replicator, Users, Account Operators, Printer Operators, and Server Operators.

The built-in global groups on domain controllers are Domain Admins, Domain Users, and Domain Guests.

12. The built-in local groups on non-domain controllers are Administrators, Backup Operators, Guests, Replicator, Users, and Power Users.

13. The five special groups are Everyone, Interactive, Network, System, and Creator Owner.

14. It's important to limit the permissions assigned to the Everyone group, especially if your computer is connected to the Internet, because everyone includes all users accessing your computer by using authorized user accounts, as well as unauthorized users who accidentally or intentionally breach your system security — this even includes individuals who access your computer via the Internet.

15. No groups can be renamed.

16. False

CHAPTER 9: MANAGING ACCOUNT POLICY, USER RIGHTS, AND AUDITING

Answers to Instant Assessment

1. The Password Restrictions section, and the Account lockout section

2. Select Start ⇒ Programs ⇒ Administrative Tools (Common) ⇒ User Manager for Domains.

Then, in the User Manager dialog box, select Policies ⇒ Account.

3. Expires in 42 Days

4. The Minimum Password Age configuration determines the minimum number of days a user must keep the same password.

5. The possible settings are from one to 14 characters.

The author's recommended setting is a minimum of eight characters.

6. The Password Uniqueness configuration specifies how many different passwords a user must use before an old password can be reused.

7. The Account lockout section of the Account Policy dialog box specifies how Windows NT treats user accounts after several successive unsuccessful logon attempts have occurred.

8. The Administrators local group

9. User rights allow users to perform certain tasks; whereas permissions allow users to access objects, such as files, folders, and printers.

10. Auditing produces a log of specified events and activities that occur on a Windows NT computer.

11. Event Viewer

12. You must also configure file, folder, or printer auditing (which is set in Windows NT Explorer or in a printer's Properties dialog box.)

13. Logon and Logoff; File and Object Access; Use of User Rights, User and Group Management; Security Policy Changes; Restart, Shutdown, and System; and Process Tracking

14. False

15. True

CHAPTER 10: MANAGING USER PROFILES AND SYSTEM POLICY

Answers to Instant Assessment

1. In Windows NT, a user profile is a collection of settings and options that specify a user's desktop environment and all other user-definable settings for a user's work environment.

2. A user profile is normally stored in a subfolder of the `<winntroot>\Profiles` folder.

3. The subfolders contained in a user profile folder include `Application Data`, `Desktop`, `Favorites`, `NetHood`, `Personal`, `PrintHood`, `Recent`, `SendTo`, `Start Menu`, and `Templates`. The files contained in a user profile folder include `Ntuser.dat` and `ntuser.dat.LOG`.

4. The System application in Control Panel

5. Windows NT Explorer

6. Create a domain-wide `Default User` profile folder on the `Netlogon` share on the PDC.

7. A roaming user profile is a user profile that is stored on a server and is available to a user regardless of which Windows NT computer on the network the user logs onto. Roaming profiles enable users to retain their own customized desktop and work environment settings even though they may use different Windows NT computers.

8. A logon script is a batch file or executable file that runs during a user's logon process.

9. A mandatory user profile is a user profile that, when assigned to a user, cannot be changed by the user.

10. When "problem users" require a significant amount of administrator time

    When an administrator has a large number of users with similar job tasks to administer

11. The `Ntuser.dat` file must be renamed as `Ntuser.man`.

12. The System application in Control Panel

13. The Windows NT system policy file is an Administrator-created collection of user, group, and computer policies that restrict the user's ability to perform certain tasks on any Windows NT computer that the user logs on to. System policy can also be used to enforce certain mandatory display settings.

14. System Policy Editor

15. In the `Netlogon` share on each domain controller

16. Individual user policies and the Default User policy

17. The last group policy applied (which is the group policy of the group that has the highest priority)

18. SusanH's individual user policy

19. Individual computer policies and the Default Computer policy

20. The Default Computer policy

21. False

CHAPTER 11: ADMINISTERING SERVERS FROM CLIENT COMPUTERS

Answers to Instant Assessment

1. The primary purpose of Client-based Network Administration Tools is to enable a user at a client computer to manage an NT Server computer remotely on the network.

2. The Windows NT Server Tools that can be installed on a Windows 95 client computer are User Manager for Domains, Server Manager, Event Viewer, and security extensions for Windows Explorer to manage file and printer security on a remote Windows NT Server.

3. The Client-based Network Administration Tools that can be installed on a Windows NT Workstation computer are User Manager for Domains, Server Manager, System Policy Editor, Remote Access Admin, DHCP Administrator, WINS Manager, and Remoteboot Manager.

4. The minimum RAM required to install and run Windows NT Server Tools on a Windows 95 computer is 8MB.

   The minimum RAM required to install and run Client-based Network Administration Tools on a Windows NT Workstation computer is 12MB.

5. Server Manager

6. Server Manager

7. User Manager for Domains

8. Server Manager

9. Windows Explorer — use the added Security tabs on the file, folder, and printer Properties dialog boxes

---

CHAPTER 12: SHARING AND SECURING FILE SYSTEMS

Answers to Instant Assessment

1. Read-only

2. Compress

3. The purpose of sharing folders is to make it possible for users to access network resources.

4. No Access, Read, Change, and Full Control

5. No Access

6. Full Control

7. No Access

8. The Windows NT administrative shares are the hidden shares that Windows NT automatically creates every time you start NT on a computer. Only members of the Administrators group have permission to access these shares. The administrative shares are `C$`, `D$`, `E$`, and so on (one share for the root of each hard disk partition on the computer), and `Admin$` (which corresponds to the folder that NT is installed in).

9. Any share can be configured as a hidden share by appending a `$` to the share name.

10. NTFS permissions provide a greater level of security than share permissions because

- NTFS permissions can be assigned to individual files and folders
- NTFS permissions apply to local users as well as to users who connect to a shared folder over-the-network

11. The NTFS permissions are Read (R), Write (W), Execute (E), Delete (D), Change Permissions (P), and Take Ownership (O).

12. The standard NTFS directory (folder) permissions are No Access (None) (None), List (RX) (Not Specified), Read (RX) (RX), Add (WX) (Not Specified), Add and Read (RWX) (RX), Change (RWXD) (RWXD), and Full Control (All) (All).

13. The standard NTFS file permissions are No Access (None), Read (RX), Change (RWXD), and Full Control (All).

14. File permissions

15. The new file inherits the NTFS permissions of the folder that contains the new file.

16. Destination

17. The file retains its original NTFS permissions.

18. The *most* restrictive permission

19. The user who created it (except that when a member of the Administrators group creates a file or folder, the Administrators *group*, not the user, is the owner of the file or folder)

20. A user might want to take ownership of a file or folder if the user wanted to assign or change permissions on the file or folder, but wasn't the owner of the file or folder and didn't have the Change Permissions NTFS permission (or the Full Control permission, which includes the Change Permissions NTFS permission) to the file or folder.

21. First, the audit policy is configured in User Manager for Domains. Then, auditing is configured for each file and folder individually by using Windows NT Explorer.

22. You must select success and/or failure auditing of File and Object access in order to audit files and folders.

23. Event Viewer

24. Most resource access problems are caused by incorrectly configured and/or conflicting permissions.

25. False

26. True

27. False

28. True

29. False

Answers to Critical Thinking Lab

Lab 12.20 *Troubleshooting resource access and permission problems*

The following are the causes and suggested solutions to resolve the given problems.

Problem 1   The cause of the problem is that the Everyone group is assigned the Read permission for the `AccountingData` share. When share permissions combine with NTFS permissions, the *most restrictive* permission applies. Even though NancyY is a member of the Accounting group and the Accounting group has the NTFS Change permission, NancyY's effective permission is limited to the Read permission because of the share permission.

To resolve the problem, assign the Everyone group the Full Control share permission for the `AccountingData` share. Access to this share will then be controlled by NTFS permissions.

Problem 2   The cause of the problem is that JohnS is a member of the Sales group, which has been assigned the No Access NTFS permission for the D:\Data\Managers folder. Even though JohnS is appropriately a member of the Managers group, which has been assigned the NTFS Change permission for the D:\Data\Managers folder, *when the NTFS No Access permission is assigned to any group the user is a member of, the user's effective permission is always No Access.*

To resolve the problem, remove the Sales group from the Name list box in the Directory Permissions dialog box.

Answers to Hands-on Lab

Lab 12.21 *Sharing and securing resources*
Suggested answer:

Resource	Share Name	Share Permissions Applied		NTFS Permissions Applied	
		User/Group	Permission	User/Group	Permission
D:\Data\Sales	SalesData	Domain Users	Full Control	Sales	Change
				Administrators	Full Control
C:\Apps\Word	Word	Domain Users	Read	N/A	N/A
C:\Apps\Excel	Excel	Domain Users	Read	N/A	N/A
C:\Apps\Access	Access	Domain Users	Read	N/A	N/A
D:\Data\ Managers	Managers Data	Domain Users	Full Control	Managers	Change
				Administrators	Full Control
D:\Data\ Accounting	Accounting Data	Domain Users	Full Control	Accounting	Change
				Administrators	Full Control
D:\Data\ AllUsers	AllUsers Data	Domain Users	Full Control	Domain Users	Change
				Administrators	Full Control

CHAPTER 13: BACKING UP AND RESTORING DATA

Answers to Instant Assessment

1. Windows NT Backup

2. The archive attribute is a marker that the operating system automatically assigns to all files and folders when they are first installed or created. Depending on the backup type, backup programs *remove* the archive attribute from a file or folder to indicate that the file or folder has been backed up. If a file or folder is modified after it has been backed up, the operating system reassigns the archive attribute to it.

3. There are five standard types of backups:

Normal (full): backs up all selected files and folders, and removes the archive attribute from the backed up files and folders.

Differential: backs up all selected files and folders that have changed since the last normal backup, and does *not* remove the archive attribute from files or folders. A differential backup is a *cumulative* backup, and because of this fact, takes more time to perform than an incremental backup, but less time to perform than a normal backup.

Incremental: backs up all selected files and folders that have changed since the last normal or incremental backup, and removes the archive attribute from the backed up files and folders. An incremental backup is *not* cumulative, and because of this fact, takes less time to perform than a differential backup.

Copy: backs up all selected files and folders, and does *not* remove the archive attribute. This backup type can be used without interrupting the normal backup schedule.

Daily: backs up all selected files and folders that have changed during the day the tape backup is made, and does *not* remove the archive attribute.

4. When selecting a tape drive device, you should consider both of the following:

Be sure to select a tape drive that is on the Hardware Compatibility List.

If possible, select a tape drive that has the capacity to back up your entire server on a single tape.

5. Perform a trial restore

6. A

7. B

8. Selecting the verify option approximately doubles the time it takes to perform a backup.

9. The Schedule service

10. Store a current normal (full) backup off-site — preferably at a location that is secure and that has a controlled-climate environment.

CHAPTER 14: NETWORKING USING TCP/IP

Answers to Instant Assessment

1. Transmission Control Protocol/Internet Protocol

2. TCP/IP

3. An IP address is a 32-bit binary number, broken into four 8-bit octets, that uniquely identifies a computer or other network device on a network that uses TCP/IP. An IP address is normally represented in a dotted decimal format, with each octet being represented by a whole number between zero and 255. An IP address contains two important identifiers: a network ID and a host ID.

4. If subnet masks are incorrectly configured, network communications problems due to routing errors may occur. For example, TCP/IP may incorrectly determine that a computer on the local subnet is located on a remote subnet, and attempt to route a packet to the remote subnet. In this instance, the computer on the local subnet would never receive the packet intended for it.

5. If a computer's default gateway address does not specify a router on the local subnet, then that computer will *not* be able to communicate with computers or other network devices located on other network segments.

6. You can assign an IP address to a Windows NT computer in one of two ways: by configuring a computer to obtain an IP address from a DHCP server or by manually specifying a computer's IP address configuration.

7. Microsoft Internet Information Server (IIS)

8. A router, a DSU/CSU, a network adapter, and a fractional T1 leased line

9. An ISDN adapter card with either an internal or external network terminating unit (NT1) and an ISDN line

10. Steps you can take to increase security include the following:

- When configuring password authentication, you can clear the check box next to Basic (Clear Text) and select the check box next to Windows NT Challenge/Response to prevent user names and passwords from being transmitted in an unencrypted format over the Internet.

- You can control access by IP address.

- You can ensure that directory browsing is not selected.

- You can require that users supply user names and passwords by not enabling anonymous users to access the WWW service.

11. A virtual server is a pseudo WWW server that has its own unique domain name and IP address. To the Internet user accessing the virtual server, a virtual server appears to be a separate server; but in reality, a virtual server is *not* a separate server, but more like an extra shared folder on an Internet Information Server. A single Internet Information Server can be configured to accommodate multiple virtual servers.

12. You must assign and configure an additional IP address to the network adapter in your computer.

13. IP address, subnet mask, and default gateway

14. `ping.exe`

15. `ping.exe`

16. `Ipconfig.exe`

17. True

18. False

19. True

Answers to Critical Thinking Lab

Lab 14.24: *Identifying and resolving TCP/IP connectivity problems*

Situation 1   The problem in this situation is that Client_2 has an incorrect default gateway. (It is incorrect because it specifies Server_1's IP address.) If left in its current configuration, users of Client_2 won't be able to access the Internet.

To resolve the problem, Client_2's default gateway should be changed to match the router's IP address: 172.31.151.1

Situation 2   The problem in this situation is that Client_A has the same IP address as Client_C. Duplicate IP addresses are *not* permitted.

To resolve the problem, either Client_A's or Client_C's IP address should be changed so that it is a *unique* IP address.

CHAPTER 15: COEXISTENCE WITH NETWARE

Answers to Instant Assessment

1. NWLink IPX/SPX Compatible Transport

2. Frame types (also called frame formats) are accepted, standardized structures for transmitting data packets over a network.

3. Frame type mismatching

4. A network number is a 32-bit binary number that uniquely identifies an NWLink IPX/SPX Compatible Transport network segment for routing purposes. Network numbers are commonly presented in an 8-digit hexadecimal format.

5. External network numbers and internal network numbers

6. Gateway Service for NetWare (GSNW)

7. Add Form Feed, Notify When Printed, and Print Banner

8. It converts Server Message Blocks (SMBs) into NetWare Core Protocol (NCP) requests that are recognized by the NetWare server.

9. NTGATEWAY

10. `\\server_name\share_name`

11. `\\tree_name\volume_name.organizational_unit.`
`organization_name\folder_name`

12. The correct answer consists of any two of the following common
configuration errors that cause NetWare connectivity problems:

- The NTGATEWAY group does not have the necessary permissions to access
  the resource

- The gateway is not enabled

- Frame type mismatch and/or network number mismatch

- The gateway user account is not a member of the NTGATEWAY group

13. True

14. True

CHAPTER 16: MIGRATING TO WINDOWS NT FROM NETWARE

Answers to Instant Assessment

1. The migration process involves several steps:
- Starting and configuring the Migration Tool for NetWare
- Selecting the source NetWare server and destination Windows NT Server
  computer
- Configuring how user and group accounts will be migrated
- Configuring how files and folders will be migrated
- Performing a trial migration to test your configurations
- Performing an actual migration
- Configuring NetWare client computers to access the Windows NT Server
  computer

2. NWLink IPX/SPX Compatible Transport and Gateway Service for NetWare

3. The user who performs the migration must have Administrator privileges on the Windows NT Server computer, and must also have Supervisor privileges on the NetWare server(s).

4. An NTFS partition

5. User and group accounts and their properties, and files and folders and their permissions

6. User account passwords, print servers and print queues and their configurations, workgroup managers and user account managers, application defined bindery objects, and login scripts

7. A mapping file

8. Perform a trial migration

9. Migration Tool for NetWare

10. A Microsoft redirector (Microsoft client software) must be installed on each NetWare client computer to enable it to access resources on the Windows NT Server computer.

CHAPTER 17: INSTALLING AND CONFIGURING REMOTE ACCESS SERVICE (RAS)

Answers to Instant Assessment

1. RAS, or the RAS server

2. Dial-Up Networking

3. 256

4. 250

5. Standard analog telephone line and modem, ISDN, X.25, and Point-to-Point Tunneling Protocol (PPTP)

6. Serial Line Internet Protocol (SLIP), Point-to-Point Protocol (PPP), Point-to-Point Multilink Protocol, and Point-to-Point Tunneling Protocol (PPTP)

7. SLIP

8. PPP

9. Point-to-Point Multilink Protocol is an extension of PPP. Point-to-Point Multilink Protocol combines the bandwidth from multiple physical connections into a single logical connection. This means that multiple modem, ISDN, or X.25 connections can be bundled together to form a single logical connection with a much higher bandwidth than a single connection can support.

10. Point-to-Point Tunneling Protocol (PPTP) permits a virtual private encrypted connection between two computers over an existing TCP/IP network connection. The existing TCP/IP network connection can be over a local area network or over a dial-up networking TCP/IP connection (including the Internet).

    All standard transport protocols are supported within the Point-to-Point Tunneling Protocol connection, including NWLink IPX/SPX Compatible Transport, NetBEUI, and TCP/IP.

    A primary reason for choosing to use PPTP is that it supports the RAS encryption feature over standard, unencrypted TCP/IP networks, such as the Internet.

11. RAS supports the following transport protocols: NetBEUI, TCP/IP, and NWLink IPX/SPX Compatible Transport.

12. The RAS NetBIOS gateway is a function of the RAS server. The RAS NetBIOS gateway enables client computers that use NetBEUI to access shared resources on other servers located on the RAS server's local network. These other servers can use TCP/IP, NWLink IPX/SPX Compatible Transport, or NetBEUI. In a nutshell, the RAS NetBIOS gateway performs protocol translation for the remote NetBEUI client computer so that it can access shared resources on the RAS server's local network.

13. The NetBIOS name resolution methods supported by RAS include NetBIOS broadcasts, WINS servers, DNS servers, `LMHOSTS` files, and `HOSTS` files.

14. Remote users must be assigned the dialin permission before they can establish a dial-up connection with a RAS server.

15. Phonebook entries

16. Any three of the following:

    o Type of dial-up server used by the ISP (SLIP or PPP connection protocol)

    o Whether the ISP's dial-up server supports software compression

- Whether you will specify an IP address when you connect to the ISP, or the ISP's dial-up server will assign you an IP address

- Whether the ISP will provide the IP address of a DNS server during the connection process

- Whether the ISP's dial-up server uses IP header compression (IP header compression is also referred to as Van Jacobson header compression or VJ header compression)

- Type of modem you will be connecting to at the ISP and recommended settings that you should use for *your* modem

- The phone number you should use to connect to the ISP

17. RAS call back security is configured by using Remote Access Admin. (It can also be configured by using User Manager for Domains.) Call back security is configured on an individual user basis. The Preset To configuration option offers the highest level of call back security.

Answers to Critical Thinking Lab

Lab 17.27 *Troubleshooting common RAS problems*

Problem 1   First, determine the type of modem to which the user is attempting to connect; then reconfigure the user's modem settings to the most compatible option, or as recommended by the manager of the dial-up server the user is attempting to connect to.

If the user is using an unsupported modem (that is, one that is *not* on the Hardware Compatibility List), verify that the settings in the user's Modem.inf file are appropriate for the modem.

Determine whether the user's computer is configured for RAS software compression — if it is, ensure that the modem is configured to *not* compress data.

If the user is still unable to connect, configure the modem to record a log file of all attempted connections.

Problem 2   Because SLIP servers normally require clear text passwords, try changing the authentication and encryption policy configuration on the Dial-Up Networking client computer. Select the option button next to "Accept any authentication including clear text" on the Security tab of the Edit Phonebook Entry dialog box (instead of the current configuration of "Accept only Microsoft-encrypted authentication").

CHAPTER 18: USING PERFORMANCE MONITOR

Answers to Instant Assessment

1. The Stop Log command button in the Log Options dialog box

2. Performance Monitor is used to

- Identify performance problems and/or bottlenecks
- Determine current usage of system resources
- Track performance trends over time
- Predict future usage of system resources (capacity planning)
- Determine how system configuration changes affect system performance

3. Objects

4. A counter

5. There is more than one instance of a Performance Monitor object when there is *more than one* of that particular object (such as a physical disk or a processor) in the system.

6. Memory — Pages/sec

7. Processor — % Processor Time

8. Network Segment — % Network utilization

9. Server — Bytes Total/sec

10. The SNMP Service

11. The Network Monitor Agent

12. diskperf-y

13. Chart, Alert, Report, and Log

14. Last, Average, Min, Max, and Graph Time

15. A *threshold value* that will cause Performance Monitor to generate an alert if the specified counter *exceeds* or *drops below* this value (depending on whether the Over or Under option button is selected)

16. The Start Log command button in the Log Options dialog box

17. The value displayed is an average of the last two Performance Monitor measurements for each selected counter.

18. Performance Monitor Log view is used to save statistics gathered by Performance Monitor to a log file. The Performance Monitor log file can be viewed at a later time in a Chart, Alert, or Report view.

19. True

20. False

CHAPTER 19: PERFORMANCE OPTIMIZATION

Answers to Instant Assessment

1. Performance optimization is the process of modifying server and/or network hardware and software configurations with the intent of *speeding up* server and/or network response.

2. A bottleneck is the component in the system that is slowing system performance. The bottleneck in a networking environment is the part of the system that is performing at peak capacity while other components in the system are *not* working at peak capacity. In other words, if it weren't for the limiting component, the rest of the system could go faster.

3. Performance Monitor

4. Memory, processor, disk, and network

5. Adding RAM

6. A beneficial by-product of adding RAM is that processor and disk performance may be improved, as well, because paging is reduced and the disk cache size is increased when RAM is added.

7. The System application in Control Panel

8. Any three of the following:

- Defragment the hard disk(s) in your computer
- Upgrade to a faster disk controller and/or a faster hard disk(s)
- Configure a stripe set with parity across three or more disks
- Configure a stripe set across two or more disks

9. Any three of the following:

- Replace the existing processor with a faster processor
- Replace the existing motherboard and processor with a faster motherboard and processor
- Upgrade from a single-processor system to a multi-processor system
- Add a processor to a multi-processor system

10. The four ways to optimize a Windows NT Server computer are

- Configuring load balancing across multiple servers
- Disabling unused services, protocols, and drivers
- Scheduling large, server-intensive tasks during nonpeak hours
- Optimizing the Server service

11. Either move the BDC to the other side of the WAN link, so it is physically close to the client computers that it services; or, add an additional BDC on the other side of the WAN link.

Answers to Critical Thinking Lab

Lab 19.30 *Finding and resolving bottlenecks*

Problem 1   The statistics in this problem seem to indicate that the processor, memory, and disk all need upgrading. However, if you upgrade RAM to 64MB, the amount of paging would be significantly reduced. Reducing paging would also decrease the % Processor Time and % Disk Time statistics to reasonable levels. This server should probably have all of the possible upgrades presented, *but adding memory (RAM) is the best choice if only one upgrade can be performed.*

Problem 2   The statistics in this problem seem to indicate that the *disk* is the biggest bottleneck to optimum system performance. If only one of the possible upgrades can be performed, upgrading to a hardware-based RAID 5 disk subsystem should yield the most significant increase in disk performance for this server.

CHAPTER 20: THE TROUBLESHOOTING PROCESS

Answers to Instant Assessment

1. Troubleshooting is a methodical approach to solving a problem. The approach is often the result of a person's knowledge, experience, and intuition.

2. The five basic steps suggested for troubleshooting are

   - Gather information
   - Define the problem
   - List probable causes
   - Identify possible solutions and attempt to fix the problem
   - Resolve and document the problem

3. *Microsoft TechNet*

4. Microsoft Technical Support Web site, at
   `http://www.microsoft.com/support/`

5. Microsoft Download Service

CHAPTER 21 ADVANCED TROUBLESHOOTING

Answers to Instant Assessment

1. The nine major steps in the Windows NT boot sequence are
   - Power On Self Test (POST)
   - Initial Startup

- Selecting an operating system
- Detecting hardware
- Selecting hardware profile (or Last Known Good Configuration) and loading the kernel
- Kernel initialization
- Initializing device drivers
- Initializing services
- Logon process

2. The most likely cause of this problem is a corrupt file. Power outages can easily corrupt files on the hard disk.

   To resolve the situation, perform the Emergency Repair process, selecting the Inspect boot sector and Verify Windows NT system files options during the process.

3. The most likely cause of this problem is the configuration changes made during the last logon session.

   To resolve the situation, reboot the computer, and select the Last Known Good Configuration during the boot sequence.

   If this does *not* repair the problem, perform the Emergency Repair process, selecting the Inspect Registry files option during the process.

4. The Emergency Repair process involves using the Windows NT Setup Boot Disk set, the Windows NT compact disc, and the Emergency Repair disk created during (or after) the installation process to repair a damaged or corrupt Windows NT installation.

5. Event Viewer (specifically, the System Log in Event Viewer)

6. View the Event Detail for the *last* stop error in the list (the event that happened *first* chronologically during the boot process) *first*. Resolving this error will often take care of most or all of the other stop errors listed.

7. *Service dependencies* show which services and drivers must be running before the service in question can start. *Group dependencies* show which groups of services or drivers must be running before the service in question can start. Once you have determined what the service and group dependencies for a particular service or driver are, you can then verify that

all of these services and drivers (that are required to be running *before* a particular service or driver can start) are, in fact, running.

8. The Services tab

9. Windows NT Registry Editor (`regedt32.exe`) and
Windows 95 Registry Editor (`regedit.exe`)

10. HKEY_LOCAL_MACHINE

11. Back it up

12. `/s`

13. The Windows 95 Registry Editor (`regedit.exe`) is a better tool for *searching* the Windows NT Registry because this editor can search the Registry by key, by value, or by data contained in the value. As a Registry search tool, this editor is more effective than the Windows NT Registry Editor, which can only search the Registry by key. You can manually wade your way through the various folders and subfolders; in the Windows NT Registry Editor, and you can edit any Registry value, it's just more cumbersome to use as a search tool than the Windows 95 Registry Editor.

14. The Windows NT Registry Editor (`regedt32.exe`)

Exam Preparation Tips

This whole book has focused on giving you the knowledge and skills you need to successfully take a Microsoft certification exam—an exam that is *not* easy and that requires a great deal of preparation. To even further increase your preparedness and your chances of passing the exam, I recommend you read the Microsoft Step-by-Step Guide, which is discussed in the following section, and also put into practice the test-preparation and test-taking tips listed in this appendix.

Step-by-Step Guide

Microsoft publishes, online at their Web site, a Step-by-Step Guide designed to help you prepare for a Microsoft certification exam. (Directions on how to access this guide are listed at the end of this section.) In the Step-by-Step Guide, Microsoft recommends a six-step approach for preparing for a Microsoft certification exam:

1. Choose the certification you plan to pursue
2. Get an exam preparation guide
3. Choose the training you need
4. Apply your skills in a real-world environment
5. Take a practice test
6. Register for an exam

Numerous Web site links are included in the Step-by-Step Guide so that you can easily access the exam preparation guide for the exam you want to take, download a free practice test, find out how to register for an exam, and more. I also recommend you take the time to check out the links listed in the Other Information section at the end of the Step-by-Step Guide, specifically

- How Exams Are Developed
- What to Expect at the Testing Center
- Your Exam Results

You'll definitely want to read this guide before you take the exam.

TO ACCESS THE STEP-BY-STEP GUIDE, FOLLOW THESE STEPS:

1. Access the Step-by-Step Guide directly at `http://www.microsoft.com/mcp/certstep/steps.htm`. Or, if this doesn't work, follow Steps 2 – 4.
2. Access the Microsoft Training and Certification Web site at `http://www.microsoft.com/train_cert/`.
3. Click the MCP Online icon. The MCP home page appears.
4. Click How Do I Get Started in the left sidebar. The Step-by-Step Guide appears.

The Step-by-Step Guide is a great resource, and because the Web site is constantly updated, you can be sure of getting the most current exam information available.

Test-Preparation and Test-Taking Tips

I know that test-taking is more difficult for some people than it is for others. Whether test-taking comes easily to you or not, there *are* several things you can do to improve your chances of passing a Microsoft certification exam. Here are some tips that I hope are helpful to you:

Before the exam

o Take the test-preparation process seriously. Microsoft certification exams aren't for the faint of heart.

o As you read this book, do the Critical Thinking Labs and the Hands-on Labs. Don't even think about skipping them! Remember, the exam measures real-world skills that you can't obtain unless you actually use Windows NT.

o Review the Key Point Summary sections *and* answer the Instant Assessment questions at the end of the chapters just before taking the exam.

o Pay special attention to the Exam Preparation Pointers scattered throughout this book — these pointers will help you focus on important exam-related topics.

o After you've finished reading this book (and have done all the labs), take a practice test to assess your readiness for the exam. Most practice tests will tell you what your weak areas are. Use this information to go back and study.

o Take as many practice exams as you can get your hands on before taking the exam. This will help you in two ways. First, some practice exam questions are quite similar to the real thing, and if you do enough practice exams, some of the questions you see on the exam might look familiar. Second, taking practice exams will make you more comfortable with the computer-based testing environment/process. This will reduce your stress when you take the actual exam. You can't take too many practice exams. It's virtually impossible to be *too* prepared for the exam.

o Consider joining (or becoming an associate member of) a professional organization or user group in your area that focuses on Windows NT. Some user groups have a computer lab and/or lending library that can help you with your exam preparation. The meetings are a great place to meet people with similar interests, and potential employers, too.

o Consider subscribing to *Microsoft Certified Professional Magazine*. This magazine, which is an independent publication that is not associated with Microsoft, features an Exam Spotlight section where new Microsoft Certified Professional exams are critically reviewed as they are released. For more information about this magazine or to subscribe, visit the magazine's Web site at www.mcpmag.com.

- If possible, talk to friends or colleagues who have taken the exam for which you're preparing. Or check out the Internet for newsgroups or forums where people sometimes share their exam experiences. The experiences of others can shed some light on your potential weak areas that might benefit from further study. The MCSE list server at www.saluki.com is one example. Don't share (or ask friends to share with you) specific exam questions. However, it's fair game to share general topics that were strongly emphasized on the exam, and/or areas that had particularly detailed or tough questions.

- Consider forming a study group with friends or coworkers who are also preparing for one or more of the Windows NT certification exams. As a group, you can share hardware and software resources, thus reducing your out-of-pocket costs for exam preparation.

- Speaking of reducing costs . . . check out the Internet for good software deals. From time to time, Microsoft offers free 120-day evaluation copies of Windows NT on their Web site at http://www.microsoft.com. These evaluation copies are often offered in conjunction with a new product release, such as Microsoft Internet Information Server, and so on. A free evaluation copy is a great study tool.

- Don't study all night before the test. A good night's sleep is often better preparation than the extra studying.

- Try to schedule the exam during your own "peak" time of day. In other words, if you're a morning person, try not to schedule the exam for 3:00 p.m.

- Know your testing center. Call ahead. Ask about the hardware they use for their testing computers. If some computers are faster than others, ask for the seat numbers of the faster computers and request one of those seat numbers when scheduling your testing appointment with Sylvan Prometric. Consider visiting a testing center before you schedule an exam there. This will give you an opportunity to see what the testing environment will be like.

On exam day

- Dress casually and comfortably if at all possible.

- Arrive at the testing center early (10 to 15 minutes should be adequate), and don't forget your photo ID.

- If you have questions about the exam rules or procedures, ask the exam administrator *before* the exam begins. Avoid using exam time for questions you could have asked earlier.

- Don't drink a lot of coffee or other beverages before taking the exam. Remember, the exam lasts ninety minutes, and you don't want to spend precious exam time running back and forth to the restroom.

During the exam

- Answer the easy questions first. The testing software permits you to move forward and backward through the exam. Go through all the items on the test once, answering the items you are certain of first; then go back to the tougher questions.

- Remember, there are no trick questions on the exam. The correct answer will always be among the list of choices.

- Eliminate the most obviously wrong answers first. This will make it easier for you to select the correct answer.

- Answer *all* of the questions before you quit the exam, even if you're unsure about an answer. Because an unanswered item is scored as a wrong answer, it can't hurt to make an educated guess.

- Try to relax, and to not rush through the exam. People often make avoidable, careless mistakes when they rush.

- Pause every few minutes during the exam and take a couple of deep breaths — this will bring more oxygen into your body, and, hopefully, help you to think more clearly. More importantly, this should help you relax and relieve some of the tension of the testing environment.

After the exam

- o If you don't pass the exam the first time, use your score report to determine the areas where you need additional study, and take the exam again later (for an additional fee).

- o Don't get discouraged if you don't pass the exam your first time — or second time. Many intelligent, seasoned professionals fail an exam once, twice, or more times before eventually passing it. If at first you don't succeed, try, try again . . . perseverance pays.

Windows NT Planning Forms

Windows NT planning forms in this appendix include:

- Form 1: Preinstallation Checklist. This form is designed to be used for gathering the information required to install Windows NT Server.

- Form 2: Sharing and Securing Resources. This form is designed to help you plan how to apply share and/or NTFS permissions to shared resources on your network.

pt link **ResourcesRegarding Form 1:**

If you need a detailed explanation of any of the items in the Preinstallation Checklist, see the expanded version in the "Preinstallation Checklist" section in Chapter 2.

Regarding Form 2:

For more information on share and NTFS permissions, see Chapter 12.

RM 1: PREINSTALLATION CHECKLIST

Consider using this form to gather information about your computer and network environment prior to installing Windows NT Server. If you need a detailed explanation of any of the items in this form, see the expanded version in the "Preinstallation Checklist" section in Chapter 2.

Mass storage devices: SCSI, IDE, and CD-ROM adapter information

SCSI/IDE/CD-ROM Adapter	IRQ	I/O Port	DMA Channel
_____	_____	_____	_____
_____	_____	_____	_____
_____	_____	_____	_____
_____	_____	_____	_____

Hardware and software components

Computer type:

Display:

Keyboard:

Keyboard layout:

Pointing device:

Upgrade

Upgrade previous version of Windows?   Yes_____ No_____

Hard disk partition information

Disk Partition Number	Type of Partition	Available Disk Space
1	_____	_____
2	_____	_____
3	_____	_____

Partition # to be used for installation of Windows NT: _____

File system used for installation (choose one)

FAT _____   NTFS _____

Installation directory

Installation directory for new installation: _____

Registration

10 Digit CD Key #: _____-_____

Licensing mode

Choose one of the following licensing modes, and determine the number of client access licenses you have purchased.

Per server _____ Per seat _____

Number of client access licenses: _____

Computer name

Computer name: _____

Server type

Choose one of the following server types. Then fill in all information requested for that choice.

Primary domain controller

Domain name: _____

Backup domain controller

Domain name: _____

Administrator's account name: _____

Administrator's password: _____

Member server

Domain name: _____

Administrator's account name: _____

Administrator's password: _____

Stand-alone server

Workgroup name: _____

Administrator password

Although you may not want to write down the password on this worksheet, you need to enter an administrator password during the installation process.

Emergency Repair Disk

Will an Emergency Repair Disk be created during installation? Yes___ No___

Select components
Choose the components you want to install.

Accessibility options   Yes___ No___
Accessories

Calculator   ___

Character Map   ___

Clipboard Viewer   ___

Clock   ___

Desktop Wallpaper   ___

Document Templates   ___

Imaging   ___

Mouse Pointers   ___

Object Packager   ___

Paint   ___

Quick View   ___

Screen Savers   ___

WordPad   ___

Communications

Chat   ___

HyperTerminal   ___

Phone Dialer   ___

Games

Freecell   ___

Minesweeper   ___

Pinball   ___

Solitaire   ___

Multimedia

CD Player   ___

Jungle Sound Scheme   ___

Media Player   ___

Musica Sound Scheme   ___

Robotz Sound Scheme   ___

Sample Sounds   ___

Sound Recorder   ___

Utopia Sound Scheme   ___

Volume Control   ___

Windows Messaging

Internet Mail   ___

Microsoft Mail   ___

Windows Messaging   ___

Type of network access

Select one of the following:

Wired to the network: ___

Remote access to
the network: ___

Microsoft Internet Information Server

Install Microsoft Internet Information Server? Yes____ No____

Network adapter

Network adapter manufacturer (if applicable): _____

Network adapter name (if applicable): _____

Interrupt: _____   I/O Port: _____

Network protocols   Select the protocols you want to install:

TCP/IP: Yes ____ No ____
(If Yes, then Windows NT Setup offers you an opportunity to configure TCP/IP by using DHCP.)

DHCP: Yes ____   No ____
(If No, fill in information below.)

IP address: _____

Subnet mask: _____

Default gateway: _____

DNS server #1: _____

DNS server #2: _____

WINS server #1: _____

WINS server #2: _____

NWLink IPX/SPX Compatible Transport: Yes____ No____
(If Yes) Frame Type: _____

NetBEUI: Yes____ No____

Network services
Network services to add: _____

Network bindings
Network bindings to disable: _____

Make this computer a member of . . . You *must* choose to participate in either a workgroup or a domain.

Workgroup: Yes_____ No_____

(If Yes) Workgroup name: _____

Domain: Yes_____ No_____

(If Yes) Domain name: _____

Create a computer account in the domain? Yes ___ No ___

Administrator's account name: _____

Administrator's password: _____

Internet Information Server

Select the publishing directories you want to install:

World Wide Web publishing directory _____

FTP publishing directory _____

Gopher publishing directory _____

Time zone

Time zone: _____

Video adapter display settings

Video adapter type: _____

Display settings desired: _____

FORM 2: SHARING AND SECURING RESOURCES

Consider using this form to help you plan how to apply share and/or NTFS permissions to shared resources on your network. For more information on share and NTFS permissions, see Chapter 12.

Resource (Include path)	Share Name	Share Permissions Applied		NTFS Permissions Applied	
		User/Group	Permission	User/Group	Permission
(Example) D:\Data\Sales	Sales Data	Domain Users (Remove the Everyone group)	Full Control	Sales	Change

What's on the CD-ROM?

·-ROM CONTENTS

The CD-ROM included with this book contains the following materials:

- Adobe Acrobat Reader
- An electronic version of this book, Windows NT Server 4.0 MCSE Study Guide
- A bonus Mini-Lab Manual
- Microsoft Internet Explorer version 4.0
- Transcender Windows NT 4.0 practice exams (demo version)
- Micro House Technical Library (evaluation copy)
- Diskeeper Lite (evaluation copy)

STALLING AND USING THE CD-ROM

The following sections describe each product and include detailed instructions for installation and use.

Adobe Acrobat Reader and the Adobe Acrobat Version of Windows NT Server 4.0 MCSE Study Guide

The Adobe Acrobat Reader is a helpful program that will enable you to view the electronic version of this book in the same page format as the actual book, and also the Mini-Lab Manual.

TO INSTALL AND RUN ADOBE ACROBAT READER AND VIEW THE ELECTRONIC VERSION OF THIS BOOK, FOLLOW THESE STEPS:

1. Start Windows Explorer (if you're using Windows 95) or Windows NT Explorer (if you're using Windows NT), and then open the Acrobat folder on the CD-ROM.

2. In the `Acrobat` folder, double-click `Setup.exe` and follow the instructions presented onscreen for installing Adobe Acrobat Reader.

3. To view the electronic version of this book after you have installed Adobe Acrobat Reader, start Windows Explorer (if you're using Windows 95) or Windows NT Explorer (if you're using Windows NT), and then open the `Books\MCSE WINDOWS NT 4.0` folder on the CD-ROM.

4. In the MCSE `WINDOWS NT 4.0` folder, double-click the chapter or appendix file you want to view. All documents in this folder end with a `.pdf` extension.

Microsoft Internet Explorer Version 4.0

This is a complete copy of Microsoft Internet Explorer. With Internet Explorer you'll be able to browse the Internet if you have an Internet connection, and view the contents of the Microsoft Training and Certification Offline CD-ROM (included on this CD-ROM).

 caution

Installing Internet Explorer 4.0 on your computer will make it impossible for you to complete Lab 10.17 as written, because Internet Explorer 4.0 places security on the user's profile settings in the Registry, and thus prevents the Administrator from copying user profiles.

I recommend that, if you need a Web browser on your lab computer, you use Internet Explorer 3.02 instead of Internet Explorer 4.0.

TO INSTALL AND RUN MICROSOFT INTERNET EXPLORER, FOLLOW THESE STEPS:

1. Start Windows Explorer (if you're using Windows 95) or Windows NT Explorer (if you're using Windows NT), and then open the `Mscert\Ie` folder on the CD-ROM.

2. In the `Mscert\Ie folder`, double-click `ie.exe` and follow the instructions presented onscreen for installing Microsoft Internet Explorer.

3. To run Microsoft Internet Explorer, double-click the Internet Explorer icon on the desktop.

Transcender Exam Simulation Software (Demo Version)

Included on the CD-ROM are demo versions of Transcender's exam simulation for the Windows NT 4.0 exam. Timed, predictive simulations of the actual Microsoft certification exam, the Transcender simulations are times study tools that model the exam in the graphical user interface to the difficulty of the questions.

TO INSTALL AND RUN THE TRANSCENDER EXAM SIMULATION SOFTWARE, FOLLOW THESE STEPS:

1. Start Windows Explorer (if you're using Windows 95) or Windows NT Explorer (if you're using Windows NT).

2. Open the Transncender folder on the CD-ROM.

3. In the Transcender folder, double-click Setup.exe and follow the onscreen prompts.

Micro House Technical Library (Evaluation Copy)

Micro House Technical Library is a useful CD-ROM-based set of encyclopedias that contains hardware configuration information. This evaluation copy of *Micro House Technical Library* includes only the Encyclopedia of I/O cards. Use this evaluation copy to determine whether or not you want to purchase the full version of the *Micro House Technical Library*.

TO INSTALL AND ACCESS THE *MICRO HOUSE TECHNICAL LIBRARY*, FOLLOW THESE STEPS:

1. Start Windows Explorer (if you're using Windows 95) or Windows NT Explorer (if you're using Windows NT), and then open the `Micro House` folder on the CD-ROM.

2. In the `Micro House` folder, double-click `Install.exe` and follow the instructions presented onscreen for installing the *Micro House Technical Library.*

3. To run the *Micro House Technical Library*, select Start ⇒ Programs ⇒ MH Tech Library ⇒ MTL Demo Edition.

Diskeeper Lite (Evaluation Copy)

Diskeeper is the premier defragmentation utility for use on Windows NT NTFS partitions.

 note **Diskeeper Lite runs *only* on Windows NT. Don't attempt to install or run this program on a Windows 95 computer.**

TO INSTALL AND RUN DISKEEPER LITE, FOLLOW THESE STEPS:

1. Start Windows Explorer (if you're using Windows 95) or Windows NT Explorer (if you're using Windows NT), and then open the `Diskeeper` folder on the CD-ROM.

2. In the `Diskeeper` folder, double-click `Setup.exe` and follow the instructions presented onscreen for installing Diskeeper Lite.

3. To run Diskeeper Lite, select Start ⇒ Programs ⇒ Diskeeper Lite ⇒ Diskeeper Lite.

Glossary

access control list (ACL)   The ACL is a list that contains user and group security identifiers (SIDs), with the associated privileges of each user and group. Each object, such as a file or folder, has an access control list associated with it. *See also* security identifier (SID).

account policy   The account policy is the set of rules indicating how passwords and account lockout are managed in Windows NT. Account policy is managed by using the Account Policy dialog box in User Manager for Domains.

active partition   The active partition is a primary partition on the first hard disk in a computer that has been marked active by a partitioning program, such as `Fdisk` or Disk Manager. A computer loads its operating system from the active partition.

answer files (`Unattend.txt`)   Answer files are text files that contain stylized responses to the queries posed by the Windows NT setup program during installation. You can use an answer file, in conjunction with a network installation startup disk, to fully automate the installation of Windows NT on a single computer (in other words, perform an unattended installation). The default name for an answer file is `Unattend.txt`, but you can use any file name you want for your answer files.

AppleTalk   AppleTalk is a routable network protocol developed by Apple Computer, Inc. This protocol is associated with Macintosh computers.

application programming interface (API)   An API is a set of operating system functions that can be called by an application running on the computer. Windows NT supports the Win32, Win16, POSIX, MS-DOS, and OS/2 1.*x* APIs.

archive bit   The archive bit is a file attribute that indicates that the file or folder has been modified since the last backup. The archive bit is applied by the operating system when a file or folder is saved or created, and is commonly removed by backup programs after the file or folder has been backed up. This file attribute is not normally changed by the administrator.

auditing   Auditing is a Windows NT feature that enables you to collect and view security-related information concerning the success and failure of specified events, such as: file access, printer access, logon and logoff, and security policy changes. File auditing is only available on NTFS partitions. File and printer auditing require that auditing of File and Object Access be selected in the Audit Policy dialog box.

authentication   Authentication is the verification of a user account name and password by Windows NT. Authentication can be performed by the local Windows NT computer or by a Windows NT Server domain controller.

Backup   *See* Windows NT Backup.

backup browser   A backup browser is a computer that maintains a backup copy of the browse list. The backup browser receives the browse list from the master browser, and then makes the browse list available to any computer that requests it. All computers on the network, when they request a copy of the browse list, do so from a backup browser. A backup browser updates its browse list by requesting an update from the master browser every twelve minutes. There can be more than one backup browser on each subnet. Any Windows NT Server, Windows NT Workstation, Windows 95, or Windows for Workgroups computer can perform the role of the backup browser. *See also* Computer Browser service and master browser.

backup domain controller (BDC)   A BDC is a Windows NT Server computer that is configured to maintain a backup copy of the domain Directory Services database (SAM). The BDC receives updates to the Directory Services database from the primary domain controller (PDC) via a process called synchronization. *See also* primary domain controller and synchronization.

binary tree A binary tree is the type of search used by the NTFS file system to quickly locate files and folders on an NTFS partition. A binary tree search is much faster than a sequential read or search. *See also* sequential read.

bindings Bindings are associations between a network service and a protocol, or between a protocol and a network adapter.

BIOS BIOS stands for *Basic Input/Output System*. The BIOS is a program which is stored in ROM (read-only memory) on a computer's motherboard. The BIOS contains instructions for performing the Power On Self Test (POST).

blue screen A blue screen is displayed by Windows NT when it encounters a STOP error that it cannot recover from. A blue screen contains information about the type of error that occurred, a list of loaded drivers, and a processor stack dump.

boot loader Boot loader is a program that is used to load a computer's operating system. In Windows NT, the boot loader is a program called `ntldr`, and it creates a menu (the boot loader menu) by parsing the contents of the `Boot.ini` file. Once the user selects an operating system from this menu (or the default time period expires), `ntldr` begins the process of starting the selected (or default) operating system.

boot partition The boot partition is the partition that contains the Windows NT system files. The boot partition contains the folder that Windows NT is installed in.

boot sequence The Windows NT boot sequence consists of a series of steps, beginning with powering on the computer and ending with completion of the logon process. The boot sequence steps vary according to the hardware platform you are using.

bottleneck A bottleneck is the component in the system that is slowing system performance. In a networking environment, the bottleneck is the part of the system that is performing at peak capacity while other components in the system are not working at peak capacity. In other words, if it weren't for the limiting component, the rest of the system could go faster.

browsing Browsing is the process of viewing a list of computers and their available shared resources, or viewing a list of files and folders on a local or network-connected drive.

built-in groups   Built-in groups are the default groups created by the operating system during a Windows NT installation. Different groups are created on Windows NT domain controllers than are created on non-domain controllers.

C2 secure environment   C2 is a designation in a range of security levels identified in the computer security specifications developed by the National Computer Security Center. If installed and configured correctly, Windows NT meets the C2 level of security.

cache   Cache is a section of memory used to temporarily store files from the hard disk.

capacity planning   Capacity planning is the process of determining current usage of server and/or network resources, as well as tracking utilization over time, in order to predict future usage and the additional hardware that will be required to meet the projected levels of utilization.

CDFS   CDFS stands for *Compact Disc Filing System*. CDFS supports access to compact discs, and is only used on CD-ROM devices.

client   A client is a computer that is capable of accessing resources on other computers (servers) across a network. Some computers are configured with both client and server software. *See also* server.

Client-based Network Administration Tools   Client-based Network Administration Tools are a collection of Windows NT Server utilities that, when installed on a Windows NT Workstation client computer, make it possible for a user at the client computer to remotely manage an NT Server computer on the network. Client-based Network Administration Tools are sometimes called Windows NT Server Tools, particularly when referring to these tools as installed or run on a Windows 95 client computer. *See also* Windows NT Server Tools.

complete trust domain model   This is a decentralized domain model that consists of two or more domains that contain both user accounts and shared resources. In the complete trust domain model, a two-way trust relationship must be established between each and every domain. Because of the excessive number of trusts required for this model, the complete trust domain model is not often implemented. *See also* trust relationship and two-way trust.

Computer Browser service   This Windows NT service is responsible for the process of building a list of available network servers, called a browse list. The Computer Browser service is also responsible for determining the role a computer will play in the browser hierarchy: domain master browser, master browser, backup browser, or potential browser. *See also* backup browser, domain master browser, master browser, and potential browser.

computer name   A computer name is a unique name, up to fifteen characters in length, that is used to identify a particular computer on the network. No two computers on the same internetwork should have the same computer name.

computer policy   A computer policy is a collection of Registry settings created in System Policy Editor that specify a local computer's configuration. A computer policy enforces the specified configuration on all users of a particular Windows NT (or Windows 95) computer.

Control Panel   Control Panel is a group of mini applications that are used to configure a Windows NT computer.

Default Computer policy   The Default Computer policy is a computer policy that applies to all computers that don't have an individual computer policy. *See also* computer policy.

default gateway   A default gateway is a TCP/IP configuration setting that specifies the IP address of the router on the local network segment.

Default User policy   The Default User policy is a user policy that applies to all users that don't have an individual user policy. *See also* user policy.

Default User profile   The `Default User` profile is a user profile folder created during the Windows NT installation process. The settings in the `Default User` profile are applied, by default, to new user profiles as they are created. The `Default User` profile can be modified by using the Registry Editors or by using Windows NT Explorer. *See also* user profile.

demand paging   Demand paging is a process used by the Windows NT Virtual Memory Manager that involves reading pages of memory from the paging file into RAM, and writing pages of memory from RAM into the paging file as required by the operating system. *See also* paging file.

desktop   The desktop is the screen that is displayed after Windows NT 4.0 boots and you log on. The desktop replaces the Program Manager interface from earlier versions of Windows and Windows NT.

DHCP   DHCP stands for *Dynamic Host Configuration Protocol*. This protocol is used to dynamically assign IP addresses to client computers on a network.

DHCP Relay Agent   The DHCP Relay Agent is a Windows NT Server service that forwards client computers' DHCP requests to a DHCP server on another subnet. *See also* DHCP.

Dial-Up Networking   Dial-Up Networking is a Windows NT service that enables a computer to use its modem to make a network connection over a telephone line to another computer. Dial-Up Networking is installed during the installation of the Remote Access Service (RAS) on a Windows NT computer. *See also* Remote Access Service (RAS).

directory   A directory is a folder. In Windows NT terminology, the terms *directory* and *folder* are synonymous. The two terms are used interchangeably throughout Windows NT documentation and the Windows NT user interface.

directory replication   Directory replication was designed to copy logon scripts from a central location, usually the PDC, to all domain controllers, thus enabling all users to execute their own logon scripts no matter which domain controller validates their logon. Replication involves copying subfolders and their files from the source folder on the source server to the destination folder on all Windows NT computers on the network that are configured as replication destinations. *See also* Directory Replicator service.

Directory Replicator service   The Directory Replicator service is a Windows NT service that copies (replicates) files from a source Windows NT computer to a destination Windows NT computer. *See also* directory replication.

Directory Services   *See* Windows NT Directory Services.

Directory Services database   *See* Security Accounts Manager (SAM) database.

disk duplexing   Disk duplexing is a fault tolerance method that involves duplication of a partition from one hard disk onto a second hard disk. In disk duplexing, each hard disk must be on a different hard disk controller.

disk mirroring   Disk mirroring is a fault tolerance method that involves duplication of a partition from one hard disk onto a second hard disk. In disk mirroring, each hard disk can be on the same or a different hard disk controller.

DNS   *See* Microsoft DNS Server.

domain   A domain is a logical grouping of networked computers in which one or more of the computers has shared resources, such as a shared folder or a shared printer, and in which all of the computers share a common central domain Directory Services database that contains user account and security information.

domain controller   A domain controller is a Windows NT Server computer that maintains a copy of the domain Directory Services database (also called the SAM). *See also* backup domain controller, primary domain controller, and Security Accounts Manager (SAM) database.

domain master browser   The domain master browser is a computer that maintains a list of available network servers located on all subnets in the domain. Additionally, the domain master browser maintains a list of available workgroups and domains on the internetwork. The domain master browser is the primary domain controller. *See also* Computer Browser service.

domain name   A domain name is a unique name, up to fifteen characters in length, assigned to identify the domain on the network. A domain name must be different than all other domain names, workgroup names, and computer names on the network.

Dr. Watson for Windows NT   Dr. Watson is a Windows NT tool that is used to debug application errors.

dual boot   Dual boot refers to the capability of a computer to permit a user to select from more than one operating system during the boot process. (Only one operating system can be selected and run at a time.)

dynamic routing   In dynamic routing, a router automatically builds and updates its routing table. In a dynamic routing environment, administrators don't have to manually configure the routing table on each individual router. As changes are made to the network, dynamic routers automatically adjust their routing tables to reflect these changes. Periodically, each dynamic router on the network broadcasts packets containing the contents of its routing table. Dynamic routers that receive these packets add the routing table information received to their own routing tables. In this way, dynamic routers are able to recognize other routers as they are added to and removed from the network.

Emergency Repair Disk   The Emergency Repair Disk is a floppy disk created during (or after) the Windows NT installation process that is used to repair Windows NT when its configuration files have been damaged or corrupted.

enhanced metafile (EMF)   An enhanced metafile is an intermediate print job format that can be created very quickly by the graphic device driver interface. Using an EMF enables Windows NT to process the print job in the background while the foreground process continues.

Event Log service   The Event Log service is a Windows NT service that writes operating system, application, and security events to log files. These log files can be viewed by an administrator using Event Viewer. *See also* Event Viewer.

Event Viewer   Event Viewer is a Windows NT administrative tool that enables an administrator to view and/or archive the System, Application, and Security Logs.

exabyte   An exabyte is a billion gigabytes (1,152,921,504,606,846,976 bytes).

Executive Services (Windows NT Executive)   Executive Services is the entire set of services that make up the kernel mode of the Windows NT operating system.

extended partition   An extended partition is a disk partition that can be subdivided into one or more logical drives. An extended partition can't be the active partition. *See also* active partition.

fault tolerance   Fault tolerance refers to the ability of a computer or operating system to continue operations when a severe error or failure occurs, such as the loss of a hard disk or a power outage.

file allocation table (FAT) file system   FAT is a type of file system that is used by several operating systems, including Windows NT. Windows NT does not support security or auditing on FAT partitions. The maximum size of a FAT partition is 2GB.

file attributes   File attributes are markers assigned to files that describe properties of the file and limit access to the file. File attributes include: Archive, Compress, Hidden, Read-only, and System.

file system   A file system is an overall architecture for naming, storing, and retrieving files on a disk.

folder   A folder is a directory. In Windows NT terminology, the terms *directory* and *folder* are synonymous. The two terms are used interchangeably throughout Windows NT documentation and the Windows NT user interface.

frame type   A frame type (also called a *frame format*) is an accepted, standardized structure for transmitting data packets over a network.

fully qualified domain name (FQDN)   An FQDN is a fancy term for the way computers are named and referenced on the Internet. The format for an FQDN is: `server_name.domain_name.root_domain_name`. For example, a server named `wolf` in the `alancarter` domain in the `com` root domain has a fully qualified domain name of `wolf.alancarter.com`. Fully qualified domain names always use lowercase characters.

gateway   A gateway is a computer that performs protocol or data format translation between two computers that use different protocols or data formats.

Gateway Service for NetWare (GSNW)   Gateway Service for NetWare (GSNW) is a Windows NT Server service that, when installed and configured on a Windows NT Server computer, provides all of the functionality of Client Service for NetWare (CSNW). Additionally, GSNW enables the Windows NT Server computer to transparently share resources (files, folders, and printers) located on a NetWare server to client computers of the Windows NT Server computer. GSNW accomplishes this by converting the Server Message Blocks (SMBs) from the client computers of the Windows NT Server computer into NetWare Core Protocol (NCP) requests that are recognized by the NetWare server. *See also* Client Service for NetWare.

gigabyte (GB)   A gigabyte is 1,024 megabytes (MB), or 1,073,741,824 bytes.

global group   A global group is a Windows NT Server group that can only be created in the domain Directory Services database. Global groups are primarily used to organize users that perform similar tasks or have similar network access requirements. In a typical Windows NT configuration, user accounts are placed in a global group, then the global group is made a member of one or more local groups, and each local group is assigned permissions to a network resource. The advantage of using global groups is ease of administration—the network administrator can manage large numbers of users by placing them in global groups. Global groups are only available in Windows NT Server domains—they are not available in workgroups or on a stand-alone server. *See also* local group.

Graphics Device Interface (GDI)   The GDI is a specific Windows NT device driver that manages low-level display and print data. The GDI used to be part of user mode in Windows NT 3.51, but is now part of the kernel mode (Executive Services) in Windows NT 4.0.

group dependencies   Group dependencies are groups of services or drivers that must be running before a given service (or driver) can start.

group policy   A group policy is a policy that applies to a group of users. Group policies apply to all users that are members of a group (that has a group policy), and that do not have individual user policies.

Hardware Compatibility List (HCL)   The HCL is a list of hardware that is supported by Windows NT. The HCL is shipped with Windows NT. You can access the latest version of the HCL at `www.microsoft.com/ntserver`.

hertz (Hz)   Hz is a unit of frequency measurement equivalent to one cycle per second.

hive   A hive is a group of Windows NT Registry keys and values that are stored in a single file. *See also* key, Registry, and value.

host   A host is a computer that is connected to a TCP/IP network, such as the Internet.

HPFS   HPFS stands for *high performance file system*. This is the file system used by OS/2. Windows NT used to support HPFS, but HPFS support was dropped for NT version 4.0.

Internet Information Server (IIS)   Internet Information Server is a Microsoft Windows NT Server service that provides World Wide Web (WWW), File Transfer Protocol (FTP), and Gopher publishing services.

internetwork   An internetwork consists of multiple network segments connected by routers and/or WAN links.

interrupt (IRQ)   An interrupt (or interrupt request) is a unique number between two and fifteen that is assigned to a hardware peripheral in a computer. No two devices in the computer should have the same interrupt, unless the devices are capable of (and correctly configured to) share an interrupt.

intranetwork   An intranetwork is a TCP/IP internetwork that is not connected to the Internet. For example, a company's multi-city internetwork can be called an intranetwork as long as it is not connected to the Internet. *See also* internetwork.

kernel   A kernel is the core component of an operating system.

kernel mode   Kernel mode refers to a highly privileged mode of operation in Windows NT. "Highly privileged" means that all code that runs in kernel mode can access the hardware directly, and can access any memory address. A program that runs in kernel mode is always resident in memory — it can't be written to a paging file. *See also* user mode.

key   A key is a component of the Registry that is similar to a folder in a file system. A key can contain other keys and value entries. *See also* Registry and value.

kilobyte (KB)   A kilobyte is 1,024 bytes.

line printer daemon (LPD)   LPD is the print server software used in TCP/IP printing. LPD is supported by many operating systems, including Windows NT and UNIX.

local group   A local group is a Windows NT group that can be created in the domain Directory Services database on a domain controller or in the SAM on any non-domain controller. Local groups are primarily used to control access to resources. In a typical Windows NT configuration, a local group is assigned permissions to a specific resource, such as a shared folder or a shared printer. Individual user accounts and global groups are then made members of this local group. The result is that all members of the local group then have permissions to the resource. Using local groups simplifies the administration of network resources, because permissions can be assigned once, to a local group, instead of separately to each user account. *See also* global group.

local print provider   A local print provider is a Windows NT kernel mode driver that manages printing for all print devices managed by the local computer.

LocalTalk   LocalTalk is a specification for the type of network cabling, connectors, and adapters developed by Apple Computer, Inc. for use with Macintosh computers.

logging on   Logging on is the process of supplying a user name and password, and having that user name and password authenticated by a Windows NT computer. A user is said to "log on" to a Windows NT computer.

logical drive   A logical drive is a disk partition (or multiple partitions) that has been formatted with a file system and assigned a drive letter.

logon hours   Logon hours are the assigned hours that a user can log on to a Windows NT Server domain controller. The logon hours configuration only affects the user's ability to access the domain controller — it does not affect a user's ability to log on to a Windows NT Workstation computer or to a non-domain controller.

logon script   A logon script is a batch file that is run when a user logs on. All MS-DOS 5.0 (and earlier versions) batch commands can be used in logon scripts.

mandatory user profile   A mandatory user profile is a user profile that, when assigned to a user, can't be modified by the user. A user can make changes to desktop and work environment settings during a single logon session, but these changes are not saved to the mandatory profile when the user logs off. Each time the user logs on, the user's desktop and work environment settings revert to those contained in the mandatory user profile. A mandatory user profile is created by renaming the user's `ntuser.dat` file to `ntuser.man`. *See also* user profile.

master browser   A master browser is the computer on the subnet that builds and maintains the browse list for that subnet. The master browser distributes this browse list to backup browsers on the subnet and to the domain master browser. *See also* backup browser, Computer Browser service, and domain master browser.

Maximum Password Age   The Maximum Password Age is the maximum number of days a user may use the same password.

megabyte (MB)   A megabyte is 1,024 kilobytes, or 1,048,576 bytes.

member server   A member server is a Windows NT Server computer that is not installed as a domain controller, and that has joined a Windows NT Server domain.

memory dump   The term memory dump refers to the process of Windows NT copying the contents of RAM into a file (the `memory.dmp` file) when a STOP error or blue screen occurs.

Microsoft DNS Server   Microsoft DNS Server is a Windows NT Server service. This service is a TCP/IP-based name resolution service. It is used to resolve a host name or an FQDN to its associated IP address.

Migration Tool for NetWare   Migration Tool for NetWare is a Windows NT Server administrative tool that makes it possible for an administrator to migrate a NetWare server's user accounts and files to a Windows NT Server computer. Migration Tool for NetWare requires that Gateway Service for NetWare and NWLink IPX/SPX Compatible Transport be installed in the Windows NT Server computer. *See also* Gateway Service for NetWare and NWLink IPX/SPX Compatible Transport.

million bits per second (Mbps)   Mbps is a measurement of data transmission speed that is used to describe WAN links and other network connections.

Minimum Password Age   The Minimum Password Age is the minimum number of days a user must keep the same password.

Minimum Password Length   Minimum Password Length specifies the minimum number of characters required in a user's password.

MS-DOS MS-DOS is a computer operating system developed by Microsoft. MS-DOS stands for *Microsoft Disk Operating System*.

multihomed A computer is said to be multihomed when it has more than one network adapter installed in it.

multiple master domain model This domain model consists of two or more master domains that contain user accounts, and any number of resource domains that contain shared resources. In this model, a two-way trust is used between each of the master domains, and a one-way trust is used from each resource domain to each and every master domain. *See also* trust relationship, one-way trust, and two-way trust.

multiprocessing Multiprocessing refers to the capability of an operating system to use more than one processor in a single computer simultaneously.

NetBEUI NetBEUI is a nonroutable protocol designed for use on small networks. NetBEUI is included in Windows NT 4.0 primarily for backward compatibility with older Microsoft networking products.

network access order The network access order specifies which protocol or service Windows NT will use first when it attempts to access another computer on the network.

network adapter A network adapter is an adapter card in a computer that enables the computer to connect to a network.

Network Client Administrator Network Client Administrator is a Windows NT Server tool you can use to create an installation disk set to install network clients or services on client computers. You can also use Network Client Administrator to create a network installation startup disk. A network installation startup disk, when run on a computer that needs to be set up (the target computer), causes the target computer to automatically connect to the server and to start an interactive installation/setup routine.

network device driver A network device driver is a Windows NT kernel mode driver that is designed to enable Windows NT to use a network adapter to communicate on the network.

Network Monitor Network Monitor is a Windows NT Server administrative tool that allows you to capture, view, and analyze network traffic (packets).

network number Network numbers are 32-bit binary numbers that uniquely identify an NWLink IPX/SPX Compatible Transport network segment for routing purposes. Because network numbers uniquely identify a network segment, they are used by IPX routers to correctly forward data packets from one network segment to another.

non-browser   A non-browser is a computer that is not capable of maintaining a browse list either because it was configured not to do so, or because the operating system on this computer is incapable of maintaining a browse list. *See also* Computer Browser service.

NT Hardware Qualifier (NTHQ)   The NT Hardware Qualifier (NTHQ) is a utility that ships with Windows NT. NTHQ examines and identifies a computer's hardware configuration, including the hardware settings used by each adapter.

NTFS   *See* Windows NT file system.

NTFS permissions   NTFS permissions are permissions assigned to individual files and folders on an NTFS partition that are used to control access to these files and folders. NTFS permissions apply to local users as well as to users who connect to a shared folder over-the-network. If the NTFS permissions are more restrictive than share permissions, the NTFS permissions will be applied. *See also* share permissions.

NWLink IPX/SPX Compatible Transport   NWLink IPX/SPX Compatible Transport is a routable transport protocol typically used in a combined Windows NT and NetWare environment. NWLink IPX/SPX Compatible Transport is Microsoft's version of Novell's IPX/SPX protocol. (IPX/SPX is the protocol used on most Novell NetWare networks.) NWLink provides protocol compatibility between Windows NT and NetWare computers. In addition to its functionality in a NetWare environment, NWLink also fully supports Microsoft networking.

ODBC   ODBC stands for *Open Database Connectivity*. ODBC is a software specification that enables ODBC-enabled applications (such as Microsoft Excel) to connect to databases (such as Microsoft SQL Server and Microsoft Access).

The ODBC application in Control Panel is used to install and remove ODBC drivers for various types of databases. Additionally, this application is used to configure ODBC data sources.

OEM subfolder   The OEM subfolder is used to store source files that are used to install applications, components, or files that do not ship with Windows NT. This subfolder is used during an automated setup of Windows NT.

one-way trust   When a single trust relationship exists between two domains, it is called a one-way trust. Both domains must be configured by an administrator in order to establish a trust relationship. Trusts are configured in Windows NT by using User Manager for Domains. The trusted domain should be configured first, and then the trusting domain. *See also* trust relationship, trusted domain, and trusting domain.

packet   A packet is a group of bytes sent over the network as a block of data.

paging file   A paging file (sometimes called a page file or a swap file) is a file used as a computer's virtual memory. Pages of memory that are not currently in use can be written to a paging file to make room for data currently needed by the processor. *See also* virtual memory.

partition   A partition is a portion of a hard disk that can be formatted with a file system, or combined with other partitions to form a larger logical drive. *See also* logical drive.

pass-through authentication   Pass-through authentication is a process in which one Windows NT computer passes a user name and password on to another Windows NT computer for validation. Pass-through authentication makes it possible for a user to log on to a Windows NT computer by using a user account from a Windows NT Server domain.

Password Uniqueness   Password Uniqueness specifies how many different passwords a user must use before a previous password can be reused.

Performance Monitor   Performance Monitor is a Windows NT tool that is used to gather statistics on current performance of a Windows NT computer. Performance Monitor statistics can be displayed in a Chart, Alert, or Report view; or can be saved to a log file for later viewing.

permissions   Permissions control access to resources, such as shares, files, folders, and printers on a Windows NT computer.

Plug and Play   Plug and Play is a specification that makes it possible for hardware devices to be automatically recognized and configured by the operating system without user intervention.

Point-to-Point Multilink Protocol   Point-to-Point Multilink Protocol is an extension of the Point-to-Point Protocol. Point-to-Point Multilink Protocol combines the bandwidth from multiple physical connections into a single logical connection. This means that multiple modem, ISDN, or X.25 connections can be bundled together to form a single logical connection with a much higher bandwidth than a single connection can support. *See also* Point-to-Point Protocol.

Point-to-Point Protocol (PPP)   Point-to-Point Protocol (PPP) is a newer connection protocol that was designed to overcome the limitations of the Serial Line Internet Protocol (SLIP). PPP is currently the industry standard remote connection protocol, and is recommended for use by Microsoft. PPP connections support multiple transport protocols, including: TCP/IP, NWLink IPX/SPX Compatible Transport, and NetBEUI. Additionally, PPP supports dynamic server-based IP addressing (such as DHCP). PPP supports password encryption, and the PPP connection process does not usually require a script file. *See also* Serial Line Internet Protocol (SLIP).

Point-to-Point Tunneling Protocol (PPTP)   Point-to-Point Tunneling Protocol (PPTP) permits a virtual private encrypted connection between two computers over an existing TCP/IP network connection. The existing TCP/IP network connection can be over a local area network or over a Dial-Up Networking TCP/IP connection (including the Internet). All standard transport protocols are supported within the Point-to-Point Tunneling Protocol connection, including NWLink IPX/SPX Compatible Transport, NetBEUI, and TCP/IP. A primary reason for choosing to use PPTP is that it supports the RAS encryption feature over standard, unencrypted TCP/IP networks, such as the Internet.

POSIX   *Portable Operating System Interface for Computing Environments* (POSIX) was developed as a set of accepted standards for writing applications for use on various UNIX computers. POSIX environment applications consist of applications developed to meet the POSIX standards. These applications are sometimes referred to as POSIX-compliant applications. Windows NT provides support for POSIX-compliant applications via the POSIX subsystem. Windows NT supports the POSIX subsystem on all hardware platforms supported by Windows NT. To fully support POSIX-compliant applications, at least one NTFS partition is required on the Windows NT computer. POSIX applications are source compatible across all supported hardware platforms. This means that POSIX applications must be recompiled for each hardware platform in order to be run on that platform.

potential browser   A potential browser is a computer that does not currently maintain or distribute a browse list, but is capable of doing so. A potential browser can become a backup browser at the direction of the master browser. *See also* backup browser, Computer Browser service, and master browser.

preemptive multitasking   In preemptive multitasking, the operating system allocates processor time between applications. Because Windows NT, not the application, allocates processor time between multiple applications, one application can be preempted by the operating system, and another application enabled to run. When multiple applications are alternately paused and then allocated processor time, they appear to run simultaneously to the user.

primary domain controller (PDC)   A PDC is a Windows NT Server computer that is configured to maintain the primary copy of the domain Directory Services database (also called the SAM). The PDC sends Directory Services database updates to backup domain controllers (BDCs) via a process called synchronization. *See also* backup domain controller, Security Accounts Manager (SAM) database, and synchronization.

primary partition   A primary partition is a disk partition that can be configured as the active partition. A primary partition can only be formatted as a single logical drive. *See also* active partition.

print device   In Windows NT, the term print device refers to the physical device that produces printed output — this is what most people refer to as a printer.

print device driver   A print device driver is a Windows NT kernel mode driver that formats print jobs into a RAW format. (The RAW format is ready to print, and no further processing is required.) A print device driver can also convert EMF formatted print jobs into a RAW format. *See also* enhanced metafile (EMF).

print job   A print job is all of the data and commands needed to print a document.

print monitor   A print monitor is a software component that runs in kernel mode. A print monitor sends ready-to-print print jobs to a print device, either locally or across the network. Print monitors are also called port monitors.

print processor   A print processor is a kernel mode driver that manages printer device drivers and the process of converting print jobs from one format into another.

print queue   In Windows NT terminology, a print queue is a list of print jobs for a specific printer that are waiting to be sent to a print device. The print queue is maintained by the Windows NT Spooler service. *See also* Spooler service.

print server   A print server is a software program on a computer that manages print jobs and print devices. The Windows NT Spooler service functions as a print server. The term print server is also used to refer to a computer used primarily to manage multiple print devices and their print jobs. *See also* Spooler service.

printer   In Windows NT, the term printer does not represent a physical device that produces printed output. Rather, a printer is the software interface between the Windows NT operating system and the device that produces the printed output. In other operating systems, what Windows NT calls a printer is often referred to as a print queue.

printer pool   When a printer has multiple ports (and multiple print devices) assigned to it, this is called a printer pool. Users print to a single printer, and the printer load-balances its print jobs between the print devices assigned to it.

RAM   *Random access memory*, or RAM, is the physical memory installed in a computer.

Rdisk.exe   Rdisk.exe is a Windows NT utility that is used to update the Emergency Repair Disk. Using Rdisk /s causes this utility to back up the SAM and Security hives in the Registry. (If the /s switch is not used, the SAM and Security hives in the Registry are not backed up.) *See also* Emergency Repair Disk.

refresh   The term refresh means to update the display with current information.

Registry   The Windows NT Registry is a database that contains all of the information required to correctly configure an individual Windows NT computer, its user accounts, and applications. Registries are unique to each computer — you shouldn't use the Registry from one computer on another computer. The Registry is organized in a tree structure consisting of five subtrees, and their keys and value entries. *See also* key and value.

Registry editors   Registry editors are tools that enable you to search and modify the Windows NT Registry. There are two primary tools for editing the Windows NT Registry: the Windows NT Registry Editor (regedt32.exe), and the Windows 95 Registry Editor (regedit.exe). Additionally, you can use the

Windows NT System Policy Editor (`poledit.exe`) to modify a limited number of settings in the Registry. However, you can't use System Policy Editor to search the Registry.

Remote Access Admin   Remote Access Admin is a Windows NT administrative tool that is primarily used to start and stop the Remote Access Service (RAS), to assign the dialin permission to users, and to configure a call back security level for each user. Remote Access Admin can also be used to view COM port status and statistics, to disconnect users from individual ports, and to remotely manage RAS on other Windows NT computers.

Remote Access Service (RAS)   Remote Access Service (RAS) is a Windows NT service that enables dial-up network connections between a RAS server and a Dial-Up Networking client computer. RAS includes software components for both the RAS server and the Dial-Up Networking client in a single Windows NT service. RAS enables users of remote computers to use the network as though they were directly connected to it. Once the dial-up connection is established, there is no difference in network functionality, except that the speed of the link is often much slower than a direct connection to the LAN.

RIP   *Routing Information Protocol* (RIP) is the software that enables routers to dynamically update their routing tables. Windows NT ships with two versions of RIP: RIP for Internet Protocol, and RIP for NWLink IPX/SPX Compatible Transport. *See also* dynamic routing, RIP for Internet Protocol, and RIP for NWLink IPX/SPX Compatible Transport.

RIP for Internet Protocol   RIP for Internet Protocol is a Windows NT service that enables Windows NT to dynamically update its routing tables when it is configured as a TCP/IP router. *See also* dynamic routing and RIP.

RIP for NWLink IPX/SPX Compatible Transport   RIP for NWLink IPX/SPX Compatible Transport is a Windows NT service that enables Windows NT to dynamically update its routing tables when it is configured as an IPX router. *See also* dynamic routing and RIP.

roaming user profiles   Roaming user profiles are user profiles that are stored on a server. Because these profiles are stored on a server instead of a local computer, they are available to users regardless of which Windows NT computer on the network they log on to. The benefit of using roaming user profiles is that users retain their own customized desktop and work environment settings even though they may use several different Windows NT computers.

router   A router is a network device that uses protocol-specific addressing information to forward packets from a source computer on one network segment across one or more routers to a destination computer on another network segment.

routing   Routing is the process of forwarding packets from a source computer on one network segment across one or more routers to a destination computer on another network segment by using protocol-specific addressing information. Devices that perform routing are called routers.

SAP Agent   The *Service Advertising Protocol* (SAP) Agent is a Windows NT service that advertises a Windows NT computer's services (such as SQL Server and SNA Server) to NetWare client computers. The SAP Agent requires the use of NWLink IPX/SPX Compatible Transport. The SAP Agent should be installed when NetWare client computers will access services on a Windows NT computer.

SCSI   SCSI stands for *Small Computer System Interface*. SCSI is a hardware specification for cables, adapter cards, and the devices that they manage, such as hard disks, CD-ROMs, and scanners.

Security Accounts Manager (SAM) database   The SAM is a Windows NT Registry hive that is used to store all user account, group account, and security policy information for a Windows NT computer or a Windows NT domain. On a domain controller, the SAM is also referred to as the domain Directory Services database.

security identifier (SID)   A security identifier (SID) is a unique number assigned to a user account, group account, or computer account in the Security Accounts Manager (SAM) database. *See also* Security Accounts Manager (SAM) database.

Security Log   The Security Log is a file that is managed by the Windows NT Event Log service. All auditing of security events is written to the Security Log. An Administrator can view the Security Log by using Event Viewer.

segment   In network terminology, a segment refers to a network subnet that is not subdivided by a bridge or a router. The term segment can also be used as a verb, describing the process of dividing the network into multiple subnets by using a bridge or a router.

sequential read   A sequential read is a read performed (normally by the operating system) from the beginning of a file straight through to the end of the file. No random access to different parts of the file can occur during a sequential read.

Serial Line Internet Protocol (SLIP)   The Serial Line Internet Protocol (SLIP) is an older connection protocol, commonly associated with UNIX computers, that only supports one transport protocol — TCP/IP. SLIP connections don't support NWLink IPX/SPX Compatible Transport or NetBEUI. The version of SLIP supported by Windows NT 4.0 requires a static IP address configuration at the client computer — dynamic IP addressing is not supported. Additionally, password encryption is not supported by this version of SLIP. A script file is usually required to automate the connection process when SLIP is used.

server   A server is a computer on a network that is capable of sharing resources with other computers on the network. Many computers are configured as both clients and servers, meaning that they can both access resources located on other computers across-the-network, and they can share their resources with other computers on the network. *See also* client.

Server Manager   Server Manager is a Windows NT Server administrative tool that allows remote management of shared folders, remote starting and stopping of services, remote management of Directory Replication, remote viewing to determine which users are currently accessing shared resources, and remote disconnection of users from shared resources on a Windows NT Server computer.

Server service   The Server service is a Windows NT service that enables Windows NT computers to share their resources with other computers on the network.

service dependencies   Service dependencies are services and drivers that must be running before a particular service (or driver) can start.

Services for Macintosh   Services for Macintosh is a Windows NT Server service that enables Macintosh client computers to connect to Macintosh-accessible volumes on a Windows NT Server computer, enables Macintosh client computers to access shared printers on a Windows NT Server computer, enables a Windows NT Server computer to connect to network-connected print devices that support the AppleTalk protocol, and enables a Windows NT Server computer to function as an AppleTalk router.

Setup Manager   Setup Manager is a Windows NT tool that is used to create an answer file (Unattend.txt) for use in automating the installation of Windows NT. *See also* answer files.

share name   A share name is a name that uniquely identifies a shared resource on a Windows NT computer, such as a shared folder or printer.

share permissions   Share permissions control access to shared resources, such as shared folders and shared printers on a Windows NT computer. Share permissions only apply to users who access a shared resource over the network.

shared folder   A shared folder is a folder on a Windows NT computer that can be accessed by other computers on the network because the folder has been configured to be shared and has been assigned a share name.

single domain model   This domain model consists of one domain, and does not use trust relationships. All user accounts and shared resources are contained within one domain.

single master domain model   This domain model consists of one master domain that contains all user accounts, and one or more resource domains that contain shared resources. This domain model uses one-way trusts from each resource domain to the master domain. *See also* trust relationship and one-way trust.

SNMP   SNMP stands for *Simple Network Management Protocol*. The Windows NT SNMP service, once installed on a Windows NT computer, gathers TCP/IP statistics on the local computer and transmits those statistics to any SNMP management station on the network that is correctly configured to receive them. Additionally, installing the SNMP service enables various TCP/IP counters within Windows NT Performance Monitor.

special groups   Special groups are groups created by Windows NT during installation that are used for specific purposes by the operating system. These groups don't appear in User Manager for Domains. Special groups are only visible in Windows NT utilities that assign permissions to network resources, such as a printer's Properties dialog box, and Windows NT Explorer. You can assign permissions to and remove permissions from special groups. You can't assign users to special groups, and you can't rename or delete these groups. Special groups are sometimes called system groups. There are five special groups: Everyone, Interactive, Network, System, and Creator Owner.

Spooler service   The Windows NT Spooler service manages the entire printing process on a Windows NT computer. The Spooler service performs many of the tasks that are associated with a print server.

stand-alone server   A stand-alone server is a Windows NT Server computer that is not installed as a domain controller, and that has not joined a Windows NT Server domain.

static routing   Static routing is basic, no-frills IP routing. No additional software is necessary to implement static routing in multihomed Windows NT computers. Static routers are not capable of automatically building a routing table. In a static routing environment, administrators must manually configure the routing table on each individual router. If the network layout changes, the network administrator must manually update the routing tables to reflect the changes.

stripe set   A stripe set is a disk configuration consisting of two to thirty-two hard disks. In a stripe set, data is stored, a block at a time, evenly and sequentially among all of the disks in the set. Stripe sets are sometimes referred to as disk striping. Disk striping alludes to the process wherein a file is written, or striped, one block at a time, first to one disk, then to the next disk, and then to the next disk, and so on, until all of the data has been evenly distributed among all of the disks.

stripe set with parity   A stripe set with parity is similar to a stripe set, but a stripe set with parity provides a degree of fault tolerance that a stripe set cannot. In a stripe set with parity, data is not only distributed a block at a time, evenly and sequentially among all of the disks in the set, but parity information is also written across all of the disks in the set. A stripe set with parity is made up of three to thirty-two hard disks. Like stripe sets, stripe sets with parity are created from identical amounts of free space on each disk that belongs to the set. *See also* stripe set.

subfolder   A subfolder is a folder that is located within another folder. Subfolders can contain other subfolders, as well as files.

subnet mask   A subnet mask specifies which portion of an IP address represents the network ID and which portion represents the host ID. A subnet mask enables TCP/IP to correctly determine whether network traffic destined for a given IP address should be transmitted on the local subnet, or whether it should be routed to a remote subnet. A subnet mask should be the same for all computers and other network devices on a given network segment. A subnet mask is a 32-bit binary number, broken into four 8-bit sections (octets), that is normally represented in a dotted decimal format. Each 8-bit section is represented by a whole number between 0 and 255. A common subnet mask is 255.255.255.0. This particular subnet mask specifies that TCP/IP will use the first three octets of an IP address as the network ID, and use the last octet as the host ID.

synchronization   Synchronization is a process performed by the NetLogon Service. In this process, domain Directory Services database update information is periodically copied from the primary domain controller (PDC) to each backup domain controller (BDC) in the domain.

`Sysdiff.exe`   `Sysdiff.exe` is a Windows NT utility that is used to automate the installation of applications that don't support scripted installation and that would otherwise require user interaction during the installation process.

system partition   The system partition is the active primary partition on the first hard disk in the computer. (This is usually the C: drive.) The system partition contains several files that are required to boot Windows NT, including: `ntldr`, `Ntdetect.com`, `Boot.ini`, and sometimes `Bootsect.dos`, and `Ntbootdd.sys`, depending on the installation type and hardware configuration. *See also* boot partition.

system policy   The Windows NT system policy file is a collection of user, group, and computer policies. System policy restricts the user's ability to perform certain tasks on any Windows NT computer on the network that the user logs on to. System policy can also be used to enforce certain mandatory display settings, such as wallpaper and color scheme. You can also create a system policy file that applies to users of Windows 95 computers. System policy gives the administrator far more configurable options than a mandatory profile. Administrators can use system policy to provide a consistent environment for a large number of users, or to enforce a specified work environment for "problem users" who demand a significant amount of administrator time.

System Policy Editor   System Policy Editor is a Windows NT Server tool that is used to edit Windows NT and Windows 95 system policy files. *See also* system policy.

Task Manager   Windows NT Task Manager is a Windows NT administrative utility that can be used to start and stop applications; to view performance statistics, such as memory and CPU usage; and to change a process's base priority.

TCP/IP   The *Transmission Control Protocol/Internet Protocol* (TCP/IP) is a widely used transport protocol that provides robust capabilities for Windows NT networking. TCP/IP is a fast, routable enterprise protocol. TCP/IP is the protocol used on the Internet. TCP/IP is supported by many other operating systems, including: Windows 95, Macintosh, UNIX, MS-DOS, and IBM mainframes. TCP/IP is typically the recommended protocol for large, heterogeneous networks.

TechNet   *Microsoft TechNet* is an invaluable knowledge base and troubleshooting resource. *TechNet* is published monthly by Microsoft on multiple compact discs. *TechNet* includes a complete set of all Microsoft operating system Resource Kits (currently in a help file format), the entire Microsoft Knowledge Base, and supplemental compact discs full of patches, fixes, and drivers (so you don't have to spend time downloading them).

terabyte   A terabyte is 1,024 gigabytes, or 1,099,511,627,776 bytes.

terminate-and-stay-resident (TSR) program   A terminate-and-stay-resident program is an MS-DOS program that stays loaded in memory, even when it is not running.

thread   A thread is the smallest unit of processing that can be scheduled by the Windows NT Schedule service. All applications require at least one thread.

trust relationship   A trust relationship, or *trust*, is an agreement between two Windows NT Server domains that enables authenticated users in one domain to access resources in another domain. A trust relationship enables users from the trusted domain to access resources in the trusting domain. *See also* one-way trust, trusted domain, trusting domain, and two-way trust.

trusted domain   The trusted domain is the domain that contains the user accounts of users who want to access resources in the trusting domain. The trusted domain is said to be trusted by the trusting domain. When graphically displaying a trust relationship, an arrow is used to point from the trusting domain to the trusted domain. *See also* trust relationship and trusting domain.

trusting domain   The trusting domain is the domain that has resources to share with users from the trusted domain. The trusting domain is said to trust the trusted domain. When graphically displaying a trust relationship, an arrow is used to point from the trusting domain to the trusted domain. *See also* trust relationship and trusted domain.

two-way trust   A two-way trust consists of two one-way trusts between two domains. *See also* one-way trust and trust relationship.

`Unattend.txt`   *See* answer files.

UNC (universal naming convention)   UNC is an accepted method of identifying individual computers and their resources on the network. A UNC name consists of a server name and a shared resource name in the following format: `\\Server_name\Share_name`. `Server_name` represents the name of the server that the shared folder is located on. `Share_name` represents the name of the shared folder. A UNC name in this format can be used to connect to a network share. For example, a shared folder named `Public` located on a server named Server1 would have the following UNC name: `\\Server1\Public`.

Uniqueness Database Files (`*.UDF`)   Uniqueness Database Files (UDFs) are text files, similar to answer files, that make it possible for one answer file to be used for the installation of many computers that have different identifying characteristics. For example, each computer has a different computer name and user name. A UDF, used in conjunction with a network installation startup disk and an answer file, enables you to fully automate the installation of Windows NT on multiple computers on a network. The UDF is structured like an answer file, and uses the same types of entries that an answer file uses. The UDF has an additional section, named `UniqueIds`. When the appropriate command-line switch is used, selected entries in the UDF replace entries with the same name in the answer file. *See also* answer files.

UPS   UPS stands for *uninterruptible power supply*. A UPS is a fault-tolerance device that enables a computer to continue operations for a short period of time after a power outage.

user account   A user account is a record in the Security Accounts Manager (`SAM`) database that contains unique user information, such as user name, password, and logon restrictions.

user account database   *See* Security Accounts Manager (`SAM`) database.

User Manager for Domains   User Manager for Domains is a Windows NT Server administrative tool that is used to administer user accounts, group accounts, security policy, and trust relationships for the Windows NT Server domain or for an individual Windows NT Server computer.

user mode   Within the Windows NT architecture, user mode is referred to as a less privileged processor mode because it does not have direct access to hardware. Applications and their subsystems run in user mode. User mode applications are limited to assigned memory address spaces and can't directly access other memory address spaces. User mode uses specific application programming interfaces (API's) to request system services from a kernel mode component. *See also* application programming interface (API) and kernel mode.

user name   A user name is the name assigned to a user account in the Security Accounts Manager (SAM) database.

user policy   A user policy is a collection of Registry settings that restricts a user's program and network options, and/or enforces a specified configuration of the user's work environment.

user profile   A user profile is a series of Registry settings and folders in the user's profile folder that define a user's work environment. The contents of a user profile include user-specific settings for: Windows NT Explorer, Notepad, Paint, HyperTerminal, Clock, Calculator, and other built-in Windows NT applications; screen saver, background color, background pattern, wallpaper, and other display settings; applications written to run on Windows NT; network drive and printer connections; and the Start menu, including program groups, applications, and recently accessed documents.

user rights   User rights authorize users and/or groups to perform specific tasks on a Windows NT computer. User rights are not the same as permissions — user rights enable users to perform tasks; whereas permissions allow users to access objects, such as files, folders, and printers. *See also* permissions.

value   A value is an individual entry in the Windows NT Registry. A value cannot contain keys or other values. *See also* key and Registry.

verbose mode   Verbose mode refers to running an application in such a way that the application returns the maximum amount of information and detail to the user. The verbose mode is initiated on many applications by using the /v switch.

virtual device driver   A virtual device driver is a 32-bit protected mode device driver that is used in Windows 95 and Windows for Workgroups. Virtual device drivers are not supported by Windows NT.

virtual memory   Virtual memory is the physical space on a hard disk that Windows NT treats as though it were RAM. *See also* paging file.

Virtual Memory Manager   Virtual Memory Manager is a Windows NT kernel mode component that manages memory in a Windows NT environment by using demand paging. *See also* demand paging and virtual memory.

volume   A volume is a logical drive. *See also* logical drive.

volume set   A volume set is a combination of two to thirty-two partitions that are formatted as a single logical drive. A volume set does not use disk striping to store data on its partitions. *See also* logical drive and stripe set.

Windows NT Backup   Windows NT Backup (simply called Backup in the user interface) is a Windows NT administrative tool that is used to back up and restore files, folders, and the Registry on a Windows NT computer. Windows NT Backup requires the use of a tape drive device.

Windows NT Diagnostics   Windows NT Diagnostics is a Windows NT administrative tool that allows you to view detailed system configuration information and statistics. This tool can help you troubleshoot system configuration problems. Windows NT Diagnostics can also be very useful in determining service and device driver dependencies.

Windows NT Directory Services   Windows NT Directory Services is a Microsoft catchall phrase that refers to the architecture, features, functionality, and benefits of Windows NT domains and trust relationships. Windows NT Directory Services (often referred to as Directory Services), as implemented in Windows NT 4.0, is not X.500 compliant. However, Microsoft plans on releasing a new version of Windows NT Directory Services, called the Active Directory, that will be X.500 compliant in a future release of Windows NT.

Windows NT file system (NTFS)   NTFS is the most powerful file system supported by Windows NT. Only Windows NT supports NTFS — no other operating systems currently support this file system. Windows NT auditing and security are only supported on partitions that are formatted with NTFS.

Windows NT Server   Windows NT Server is a powerful 32-bit operating system that is optimized to run on a network file, print, or applications server. Additionally, Windows NT Server is the operating system of choice for the Microsoft BackOffice products, including SQL Server, Exchange Server, and SNA Server. An NT Server computer can support several processors to provide powerful multiprocessing capability.

Windows NT Server Tools   Windows NT Server Tools are a collection of Windows NT Server utilities that, when installed on a Windows 95 client computer, enable a user at the client computer to remotely manage an NT Server computer on the network. Windows NT Server Tools make remote administration of an NT Server computer practical and convenient for many administrators. Windows NT Server Tools are also referred to as Client-based Network Administration Tools. *See also* Client-based Network Administration Tools.

WINS   *Windows Internet Name Service* (WINS) is a Windows NT Server service that provides NetBIOS name resolution services to client computers. A Windows NT Server computer that has WINS installed on it is called a WINS server.

workgroup   A workgroup is a logical grouping of networked computers in which one or more of the computers has shared resources, such as a shared folder or a shared printer. In a workgroup environment, the security and user accounts are maintained individually on each separate computer.

Workstation service   The Workstation service is a Windows NT service that enables a Windows NT computer to access shared resources on other computers across the network.

Index

B

minimize button, 15–16

Minimize Memory Used option for Server service, 679, 680

Minimum Password Age in the Account Policy dialog box, 324–325

Minimum Password Length in the Account Policy dialog box, 325

mirror images, 159

mirror set
  creating, 159–160, 161
  reestablishing, 178

modem Internet connection type, 512

modem log file
  configuring, 616
  recording, 68

Modem.inf file
  adding an entry to, 582
  verifying settings in, 616

modems
  autodetecting, 582
  configuration or compatibility problem, 616
  configuring, 588–590, 606
  installing, 114–115
  supported by Windows NT, 582
  troubleshooting, 68

Modems application, 67–69

Modify firmware environment values user right, 331

modular architecture of Windows NT Server, 8–9

Mouse application, 69

Mouse Properties dialog box, 115

MS-DOS, selecting from the boot loader menu, 711

MS Loopback Adapter, 37

MS Win32 Forum on CompuServe, 700

MS WinNT Forum on CompuServe, 700

MSN (Microsoft Network), Windows NT Server Forum, 700

multi operating system entries, 163

Multilink connections
  call back security and, 607
  configuring, 606–607
  enabling RAS to support, 592

Multimedia application, 69

multimedia components, 36

Multiple Line Configuration dialog box, 607

Multiple Lines option, selecting in the New Phonebook Entry dialog box, 606

My Computer icon on the desktop, 14

N

naming conventions, 132–133, 138
  for creating user accounts, 283–284
  in FAT, 147
  in NTFS, 148–149

net view command, 134–135

NetBEUI, 39, 79
  accessing shared resources from client computers using, 586
  accessing shared resources on other servers from client computers, 618
  browsing on, 130, 138
  configuration options, 593
  configuring as a dial out protocol, 593–594
  support by RAS, 585

NetBIOS Broadcast propagation, 131

NetBIOS broadcasts, automatically forwarding from IPX clients, 598

NetBIOS Interface, 80

NetBIOS name, 33

NetBIOS name resolution methods, supported by RAS, 586, 618

Net.exe utility, browsing the network, 134–135

IDG BOOKS WORLDWIDE, INC.
END-USER LICENSE AGREEMENT

READ THIS. You should carefully read these terms and conditions before opening the software packet(s) included with this book ("Book"). This is a license
agreement ("Agreement") between you and IDG Books Worldwide, Inc. ("IDGB").
By opening the accompanying software packet(s), you acknowledge that you have
read and accept the following terms and conditions. If you do not agree and do not
want to be bound by such terms and conditions, promptly return the Book and
the unopened software packet(s) to the place you obtained them for a full refund.

1. **License Grant.** IDGB grants to you (either an individual or entity) a
   nonexclusive license to use one copy of the enclosed software program(s)
   (collectively, the "Software") solely for your own personal or business
   purposes on a single computer (whether a standard computer or a
   workstation component of a multiuser network). The Software is in use on
   a computer when it is loaded into temporary memory (RAM) or installed
   into permanent memory (hard disk, CD-ROM, or other storage device).
   IDGB reserves all rights not expressly granted herein.

2. **Ownership.** IDGB is the owner of all right, title, and interest, including
   copyright, in and to the compilation of the Software recorded on the disk(s)
   or CD-ROM ("Software Media"). Copyright to the individual programs
   recorded on the Software Media is owned by the author or other authorized
   copyright owner of each program. Ownership of the Software and all
   proprietary rights relating thereto remain with IDGB and its licensers.

3. **Restrictions on Use and Transfer.**

   (a) You may only (i) make one copy of the Software for backup or
   archival purposes, or (ii) transfer the Software to a single hard disk,
   provided that you keep the original for backup or archival purposes.
   You may not (i) rent or lease the Software, (ii) copy or reproduce the
   Software through a LAN or other network system or through any
   computer subscriber system or bulletin-board system, or (iii) modify,
   adapt, or create derivative works based on the Software.

   (b) You may not reverse engineer, decompile, or disassemble the
   Software. You may transfer the Software and user documentation on
   a permanent basis, provided that the transferee agrees to accept the

terms and conditions of this Agreement and you retain no copies. If the Software is an update or has been updated, any transfer must include the most recent update and all prior versions.

4. **Restrictions on Use of Individual Programs.** You must follow the individual requirements and restrictions detailed for each individual program in Appendix E, "What's on the CD-ROM," of this Book. These limitations are also contained in the individual license agreements recorded on the Software Media. These limitations may include a requirement that after using the program for a specified period of time, the user must pay a registration fee or discontinue use. By opening the Software packet(s), you will be agreeing to abide by the licenses and restrictions for these individual programs that are detailed in Appendix E, "What's on the CD-ROM," and on the Software Media. None of the material on this Software Media or listed in this Book may ever be redistributed, in original or modified form, for commercial purposes.

5. **Limited Warranty.**

(a) IDGB warrants that the Software and Software Media are free from defects in materials and workmanship under normal use for a period of sixty (60) days from the date of purchase of this Book. If IDGB receives notification within the warranty period of defects in materials or workmanship, IDGB will replace the defective Software Media.

(b) **IDGB AND THE AUTHOR OF THE BOOK DISCLAIM ALL OTHER WARRANTIES, EXPRESS OR IMPLIED, INCLUDING WITHOUT LIMITATION IMPLIED WARRANTIES OF MERCHANTABILITY AND FITNESS FOR A PARTICULAR PURPOSE, WITH RESPECT TO THE SOFTWARE, THE PROGRAMS, THE SOURCE CODE CONTAINED THEREIN, AND/OR THE TECHNIQUES DESCRIBED IN THIS BOOK. IDGB DOES NOT WARRANT THAT THE FUNCTIONS CONTAINED IN THE SOFTWARE WILL MEET YOUR REQUIREMENTS OR THAT THE OPERATION OF THE SOFTWARE WILL BE ERROR FREE.**

(c) This limited warranty gives you specific legal rights, and you may have other rights that vary from jurisdiction to jurisdiction.

6. **Remedies.**

(a) IDGB's entire liability and your exclusive remedy for defects in materials and workmanship shall be limited to replacement of the Software Media, which may be returned to IDGB with a copy of your receipt at the following address: Software Media Fulfillment Department, Attn.: *Windows NT Server 4.0 MCSE Study Guide*, IDG Books Worldwide, Inc., 7260 Shadeland Station, Ste. 100, Indianapolis, IN 46256, or call 1-800-762-2974. Please allow three to four weeks for delivery. This Limited Warranty is void if failure of the Software Media has resulted from accident, abuse, or misapplication. Any replacement Software Media will be warranted for the remainder of the original warranty period or thirty (30) days, whichever is longer.

(b) In no event shall IDGB or the author be liable for any damages whatsoever (including without limitation damages for loss of business profits, business interruption, loss of business information, or any other pecuniary loss) arising from the use of or inability to use the Book or the Software, even if IDGB has been advised of the possibility of such damages.

(c) Because some jurisdictions do not allow the exclusion or limitation of liability for consequential or incidental damages, the above limitation or exclusion may not apply to you.

7. **U.S. Government Restricted Rights.** Use, duplication, or disclosure of the Software by the U.S. Government is subject to restrictions stated in paragraph (c)(1)(ii) of the Rights in Technical Data and Computer Software clause of DFARS 252.227-7013, and in subparagraphs (a) through (d) of the Commercial Computer — Restricted Rights clause at FAR 52.227-19, and in similar clauses in the NASA FAR supplement, when applicable.

8. **General.** This Agreement constitutes the entire understanding of the parties and revokes and supersedes all prior agreements, oral or written, between them and may not be modified or amended except in a writing signed by both parties hereto that specifically refers to this Agreement. This Agreement shall take precedence over any other documents that may be in conflict herewith. If any one or more provisions contained in this Agreement are held by any court or tribunal to be invalid, illegal, or otherwise unenforceable, each and every other provision shall remain in full force and effect.

my2cents.idgbooks.com

Register This Book — And Win!

Visit **http://my2cents.idgbooks.com** to register this book and we'll automatically enter you in our fantastic monthly prize giveaway. It's also your opportunity to give us feedback: let us know what you thought of this book and how you would like to see other topics covered.

Discover IDG Books Online!

The IDG Books Online Web site is your online resource for tackling technology — at home and at the office. Frequently updated, the IDG Books Online Web site features exclusive software, insider information, online books, and live events!

10 Productive & Career-Enhancing Things You Can Do at www.idgbooks.com

- Nab source code for your own programming projects.

- Download software.

- Read Web exclusives: special articles and book excerpts by IDG Books Worldwide authors.

- Take advantage of resources to help you advance your career as a Novell or Microsoft professional.

- Buy IDG Books Worldwide titles or find a convenient bookstore that carries them.

- Register your book and win a prize.

- Chat live online with authors.

- Sign up for regular e-mail updates about our latest books.

- Suggest a book you'd like to read or write.

- Give us your 2¢ about our books and about our Web site.

You say you're not on the Web yet? It's easy to get started with IDG Books' *Discover the Internet,* available at local retailers everywhere.

CD-ROM Installation Instructions

Each software item on the *Windows NT Server 4.0 MCSE Study Guide* CD-ROM is located in its own folder. To install a particular piece of software, open its folder with My Computer or Internet Explorer. What you do next depends on what you find in the software's folder:

1. First, look for a `ReadMe.txt` file or a `.doc` or `.htm` document. If this is present, it should contain installation instructions and other useful information.

2. If the folder contains an executable (`.exe`) file, this is usually an installation program. Often it will be called `Setup.exe` or `Install.exe`, but in some cases the filename reflects an abbreviated version of the software's name and version number. Run the `.exe` file to start the installation process.

3. In the case of some simple software, the `.exe` file probably is the software — no real installation step is required. You can run the software from the CD to try it out. If you like it, copy it to your hard disk and create a Start menu shortcut for it.

The `ReadMe.txt` file in the CD-ROM's root directory may contain additional installation information, so be sure to check it.

For a listing of the software on the CD-ROM, see Appendix E.

caution **Installing Internet Explorer 4.0 on your computer will make it impossible for you to complete Lab 10.17 as written, because Internet Explorer 4.0 places security on the user's profile settings in the Registry, and thus prevents the Administrator from copying user profiles.**

I recommend that, if you need a Web browser on your lab computer, you use Internet Explorer 3.02 instead of Internet Explorer 4.0.